Use these handy Zagat bookmarks to mark your favorites and the places you'd like to try. Plus, we've included re-useable blank bookmarks for you to write on (and wipe off). Browsing through your Zagat guide has never been easier!

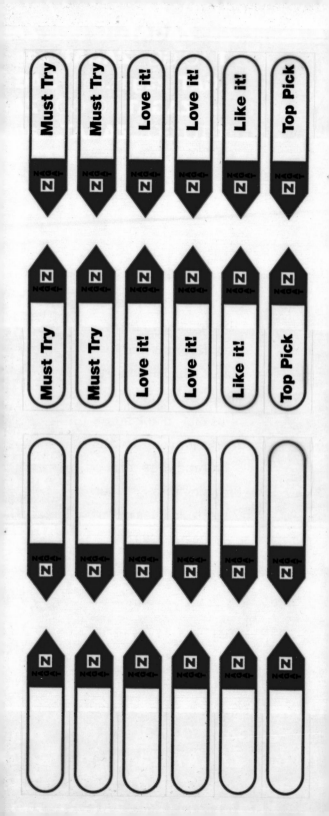

thomi

# ZAGAT®

## Los Angeles
## So. California
## Restaurants
## 2008

**LA EDITORS**
Lena Katz and Angela Pettera
**ORANGE COUNTY EDITOR**
Gretchen Kurz
**SENIOR CONSULTING EDITOR**
Merrill Shindler
**STAFF EDITORS**
Michelle Golden and Karen Hudes

Published and distributed by
Zagat Survey, LLC
4 Columbus Circle
New York, NY 10019
T: 212.977.6000
E: losangeles@zagat.com
www.zagat.com

## ACKNOWLEDGMENTS

We thank Kathy Aaronson, John Baer, Sterling Belefant, Karen Cole, Merri Howard, Bob and Marilyn Johnson, Naida and Joseph Katz, Alec Rubenstein, Sarah Shindler, Judy Stabile, and Jan and Hugh Stevenson, as well as the following members of our staff: Kelly Stewart (assistant editor), Caitlin Eichelberger (editorial assistant), Brian Albert, Sean Beachell, Maryanne Bertollo, Sandy Cheng, Reni Chin, Larry Cohn, Bill Corsello, Deirdre Donovan, Alison Flick, Jeff Freier, Caroline Hatchett, Roy Jacob, Natalie Lebert, Mike Liao, Christina Livadiotis, Allison Lynn, Dave Makulec, Andre Pilette, Becky Ruthenburg, Carla Spartos, Kilolo Strobert, Liz Borod Wright, Yoji Yamaguchi, Sharon Yates and Kyle Zolner.

# Contents

# About This Survey

Here are the results of our 2008 Los Angeles/So. California Restaurants Survey, covering 2,187 establishments in the greater Los Angeles area and in Orange County, Palm Springs and Santa Barbara as well. Like all our guides, it's based on the collective opinions of thousands of avid local consumers.

**WHO PARTICIPATED:** Input from 8,859 frequent diners forms the basis for the ratings and reviews in this guide (their comments are shown in quotation marks within the reviews). Of these surveyors, 47% are women, 53% men; the breakdown by age is 8% in their 20s; 25%, 30s; 22%, 40s; 22%, 50s; and 23%, 60s or above. Collectively they bring roughly 1.7 million annual meals worth of experience to this Survey. We sincerely thank each of these participants – this book is really "theirs."

**HELPFUL LISTS:** Whether you're looking for a celebratory meal, a hot scene or a bargain bite, our lists can help you find exactly the right place. See Most Popular (page 7), LA's Key Newcomers (page 9), Top Ratings (pages 10–16) and Best Buys (page 17) as well as Top Ratings for Orange County (page 308), Palm Springs (page 358) and Santa Barbara (page 367). We've also provided 38 handy indexes.

**OUR EDITORS:** Special thanks go to our local editors, Lena Katz, whose writing appears in many national consumer magazines; Gretchen Kurz, a Zagat editor for 13 years, who covers the OC dining scene for various publications and Cable Radio Network; Angela Pettera, a restaurant writer for Los Angeles publications including *The LA Times*; and Merrill Shindler, a CBS radio commentator and columnist, food writer, critic and Zagat editor for more than 20 years.

**ABOUT ZAGAT:** This marks our 28th year reporting on the shared experiences of consumers like you, over 20 of those years in LA. What started in 1979 as a hobby involving 200 of our friends has come a long way. Today we have over 300,000 surveyors and now cover dining, entertaining, golf, hotels, movies, music, nightlife, resorts, shopping, spas, theater and tourist attractions worldwide.

**SHARE YOUR OPINION:** We invite you to join any of our upcoming surveys – just register at **zagat.com,** where you can rate and review establishments year-round. Each participant will receive a free copy of the resulting guide when published.

**AVAILABILITY:** Zagat guides are available in all major bookstores, by subscription at **zagat.com** and for use on a wide range of mobile devices via **Zagat To Go** or **zagat.mobi.**

**FEEDBACK:** There is always room for improvement, thus we invite your comments and suggestions about any aspect of our performance. Just contact us at losangeles@zagat.com.

New York, NY
September 26, 2007

Nina and Tim Zagat

# What's New

From NYC star chefs to Tokyo tapas, this year LA is thinking globally, but sourcing ingredients close to home. Indeed, 61% of our surveyors say it's important that the food they eat be locally grown or raised, and 54% are willing to pay more for sustainably produced eats.

**IS LA THE NEW NY?** With the openings of Tom Colicchio's Craft in Century City and Mario Batali's Osteria Mozza (adjacent to Hollywood's piping-hot Pizzeria Mozza), New York is influencing LA in a big way. Coming up, Laurent Tourondel's BLT Steak is hitting the Sunset Strip, STK Steakhouse will land on La Cienega and Rosa Mexicano is rolling into Downtown's new LA Live complex.

**FROM SYRAH TO SAKE:** Given the trend toward wine bars serving small plates (Hollywood's Lou, Pasadena's Vertical, Rustic Canyon in Santa Monica) and the fact that Japanese ranks as LA's second favorite cuisine (after Italian), it's no wonder that Japanese pubs are on the rise. Newcomers such as Izaka-Ya by Katsu-Ya on Third Street, WeHo's Izakaya Kiichi, West LA's Bar Hayama and Little Tokyo's Honda-Ya (which opened at press time) all tempt after-work appetites with Nipponese nibbles and sakes.

**HOT SPOTS:** Among the areas emerging as dining destinations, Culver City is on fire thanks to Beacon, Ford's Filling Station, Fraiche, Tender Greens and Wilson; and Downtown is reviving with the arrivals of Blue Velvet, e3rd, Liliya and Takami Sushi – along with an army of late-night clubs. And with hip newcomers like Asia Los Feliz and Canele, could Atwater Village be next?

**DOWN IN ORANGE COUNTY:** It's been a banner year, as local stars Azmin Ghahreman and Florent Marneau seceded from corporate kitchens to spearhead Sapphire Laguna and Costa Mesa's Marché Moderne, and the Ghoukassian clan (Bayside, Bistango) launched trendy Kimera near John Wayne Airport. Costa Mesa further advanced its hot streak with the openings of Mesa, Old Vine Café and the Patina Group player Leatherby's Cafe Rouge in the glittering new Segerstrom Concert Hall. Izakaya Zero and Silvera's Steakhouse brought pub cachet and rock-star cred, respectively, to Surf City. Coming next from a cadre of Morton's alums is The Winery, a slick entry in Tustin.

**WALLET WATCH:** LA's average meal cost rose 4.3% from last year to $33.29, just shy of the national average ($33.39), but thankfully there are plenty of low-cost local favorites – from hot dog stands to taco shacks to pho houses – to help keep budgets in balance.

Los Angeles, CA

Orange County, CA
September 26, 2007

Merrill Shindler
Lena Katz
Angela Pettera
Gretchen Kurz

# Ratings & Symbols

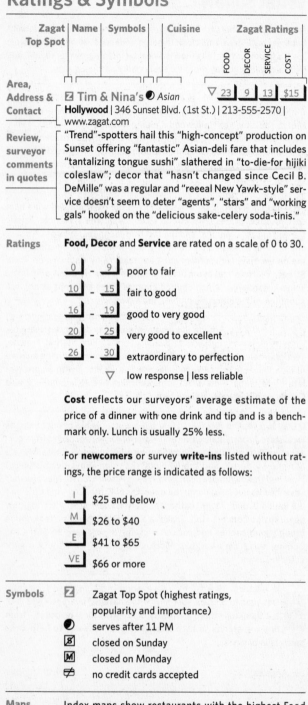

| Zagat Top Spot | Name | Symbols | | Cuisine | Zagat Ratings | | | |
|---|---|---|---|---|---|---|---|---|
| | | | | | FOOD | DECOR | SERVICE | COST |

**Area, Address & Contact**

☑ Tim & Nina's ◑ Asian    ▽ 23 | 9 | 13 | $15

Hollywood | 346 Sunset Blvd. (1st St.) | 213-555-2570 | www.zagat.com

**Review, surveyor comments in quotes**

"Trend"-spotters hail this "high-concept" production on Sunset offering "fantastic" Asian-deli fare that includes "tantalizing tongue sushi" slathered in "to-die-for hijiki coleslaw"; decor that "hasn't changed since Cecil B. DeMille" was a regular and "reeeal New Yawk-style" service doesn't seem to deter "agents", "stars" and "working gals" hooked on the "delicious sake-celery soda-tinis."

**Ratings**

**Food, Decor** and **Service** are rated on a scale of 0 to 30.

| 0 | – | 9 | poor to fair |
| 10 | – | 15 | fair to good |
| 16 | – | 19 | good to very good |
| 20 | – | 25 | very good to excellent |
| 26 | – | 30 | extraordinary to perfection |
| ▽ | | | low response | less reliable |

**Cost** reflects our surveyors' average estimate of the price of a dinner with one drink and tip and is a benchmark only. Lunch is usually 25% less.

For **newcomers** or survey **write-ins** listed without ratings, the price range is indicated as follows:

| I | $25 and below |
| M | $26 to $40 |
| E | $41 to $65 |
| VE | $66 or more |

**Symbols**

| ☑ | Zagat Top Spot (highest ratings, popularity and importance) |
| ◑ | serves after 11 PM |
| Ⓢ | closed on Sunday |
| Ⓜ | closed on Monday |
| ⊄ | no credit cards accepted |

**Maps**

Index maps show restaurants with the highest Food ratings in those areas.

# Most Popular

Each surveyor has been asked to name his or her five favorite places. This list reflects their choices (also see LA map in back of book).

## LOS ANGELES

1. Spago
2. A.O.C.
3. Café Bizou
4. Water Grill
5. Mélisse
6. Angelini Osteria
7. Lucques
8. Mastro's Steakhouse
9. Campanile
10. Hotel Bel-Air
11. Houston's
12. Matsuhisa
13. Joe's
14. Katsu-ya
15. Cheesecake Factory
16. Lawry's Prime Rib
17. Providence
18. Chinois on Main
19. Brent's Deli
20. JiRaffe
21. Crustacean
22. Ruth's Chris
23. Patina
24. Josie
25. Valentino
26. Arnie Morton's
27. Parkway Grill*
28. Lobster, The
29. Palm, The*
30. Pizzeria Mozza
31. P.F. Chang's
32. Il Fornaio
33. Roy's*
34. Sona
35. La Cachette
36. Bistro 45
37. Jar*
38. In-N-Out Burger
39. Grace
40. Ivy, The

If popularity were calibrated to price, many other restaurants would join the above ranks. Therefore, we have listed 80 Best Buys on page 17. These are restaurants that give real quality at extremely reasonable prices.

## ORANGE COUNTY

1. Napa Rose
2. French 75
3. Roy's
4. Sage
5. Fleming's Prime
6. Bayside
7. Opah
8. Mr. Stox
9. Zov's Bistro
10. Cedar Creek Inn

## PALM SPRINGS

1. LG's Prime Steakhouse
2. Cuistot
3. Le Vallauris
4. Jillian's
5. John Henry's

## SANTA BARBARA

1. La Super-Rica
2. Downey's
3. Ca' Dario
4. Wine Cask
5. Hitching Post

* Indicates a tie with restaurant above

# KEY NEWCOMERS

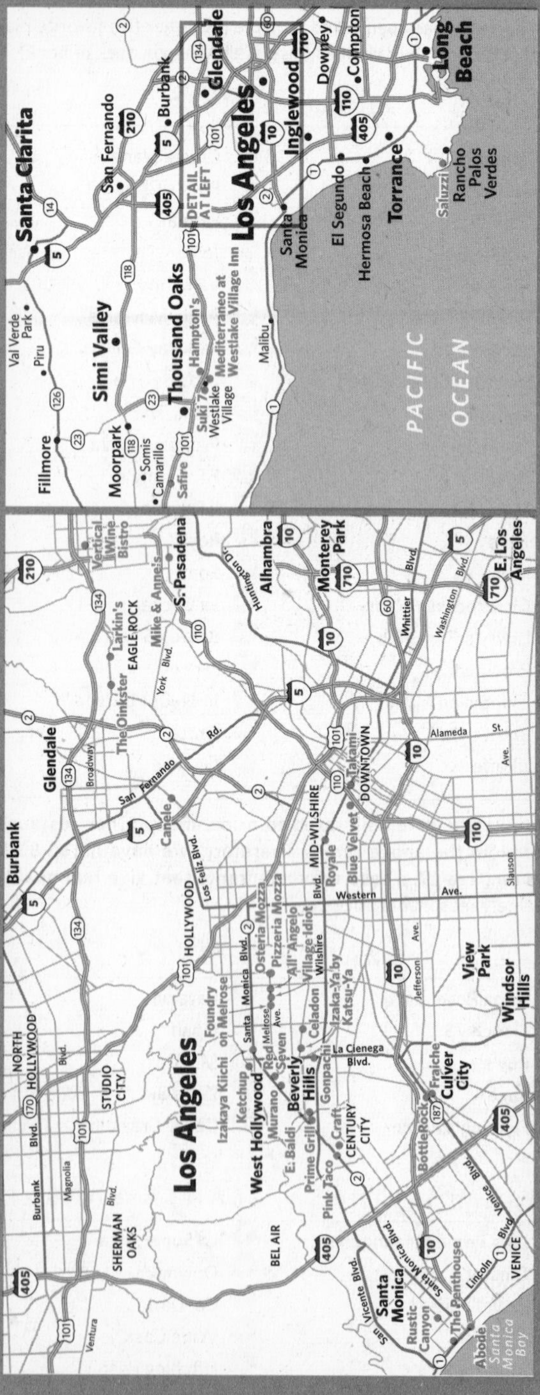

# Key Newcomers

Our take on the most notable new arrivals of the past year. For a full list, see the Noteworthy Newcomers index on page 288.

| | |
|---|---|
| Abode | Mike & Anne's |
| All' Angelo | Murano |
| Blue Velvet | Oinkster, The |
| BottleRock | Osteria Mozza |
| Canele | Penthouse, The |
| Celadon | Pink Taco |
| Craft | Pizzeria Mozza |
| E. Baldi | Prime Grill |
| Foundry on Melrose | Red Seven |
| Fraiche | Royale |
| Gonpachi | Rustic Canyon |
| Hampton's | Safire |
| Izaka-Ya by Katsu-Ya | Saluzzi |
| Izakaya Kiichi | Suki 7 |
| Ketchup | Takami |
| Larkin's | Vertical Wine Bistro |
| Mediterraneo/Westlake | Village Idiot |

2007 has already had its share of fireworks as both **Craft** and **Osteria Mozza** opened to great acclaim, and the coming months look to be filled with even more pyrotechnics. In the (hopefully) not-too-distant future, **Bastide** in West Hollywood will reopen with chef Walter Manzke at the helm, Alain Giraud will debut his yet-unnamed brasserie in Santa Monica's Clock Tower building and Todd English will unveil **Beso,** a Hollywood tapas place funded by Desperate Housewife Eva Longoria.

After gutting WeHo's L'Orangerie space, Nobu Matsuhisa will open his newest Japanese outpost while preserving his original after much outcry from longtime customers. John Sedlar is expected to return to the stove with the launch of his Downtown Pan-Latin restaurant, **Rivera,** and Brits are following New Yorkers staking their claim in the LA dining scene as Gordon Ramsay sets up shop in the London West Hollywood Hotel and SoHo House becomes a permanent fixture in the Morton's space.

Finally, in the OC, Charlie Palmer will be offering his food at a newcomer in South Coast Plaza's Bloomingdale's – haute cuisine and haute fashion, all under one roof.

# Top Food Ratings

Ratings are to the left of names. Lists exclude places with low votes, unless indicated by a ▽.

| | |
|---|---|
| **28** Mélisse | Hamasaku |
| Nobu Malibu | Frenchy's Bistro |
| Asanebo | Lucques |
| | Shiro |
| **27** Matsuhisa | |
| Brandywine | **26** Pizzeria Mozza |
| La Cachette | Mako |
| Angelini Osteria | Capo |
| Providence | A.O.C. |
| Katsu-ya | Chinois on Main |
| Piccolo | Hotel Bel-Air |
| Derek's | Saddle Peak |
| Tuscany | Café 14 |
| Sona | Valentino |
| Leila's | Via Veneto |
| Water Grill | Joe's |
| Hatfield's | Dal Rae |
| Spago | Cut |
| Josie | Mori Sushi |
| Sushi Nozawa | Ritz Huntington |
| Babita | Patina |

## BY CUISINE

### AMERICAN (NEW)

**27** Hatfield's
Josie
**26** Saddle Peak
Patina
**25** Belvedere, The

### AMERICAN (TRAD.)

**24** Grill on Alley
Lasher's
**23** Morton's
Marston's
**22** Vibrato

### ASIAN/ASIAN FUSION

**26** Mako
Chinois on Main
Gina Lee's Bistro
**24** 2117
Roy's

### BAKERIES

**25** Sweet Lady Jane
**24** Joan's on Third
Clementine
**23** Susina Bakery
**22** Doughboys

### BARBECUE

**24** Phillips BBQ
**23** Dr. Hogly Wogly's
Reddi Chick BBQ
**22** Baby Blues BBQ
Lucille's BBQ

### CALIFORNIAN

**27** Derek's
Leila's
Spago
**26** A.O.C.
Hotel Bel-Air

### CARIBBEAN/CUBAN

**21** Prado
Versailles
**20** Cha Cha Cha
Cha Cha Chicken
Cuban Bistro

### CHINESE

**26** Yujean Kang's
Din Tai Fung
**25** Sea Harbour
**24** Triumphal Palace
**23** Yang Chow

## COFFEE SHOPS/DINERS

23 Original Pancake
22 Uncle Bill's Pancake
21 Cora's Coffee
20 Pie 'N Burger
18 Fred 62

## CONTINENTAL

27 Brandywine
26 Dal Rae
23 Sir Winston's
   Mandevilla
22 Polo Lounge

## DELIS

26 Brent's Deli
25 Langer's Deli
21 Nate 'n Al
   Barney Greengrass
20 Johnnie's Pastrami

## DIM SUM

25 Sea Harbour
24 Triumphal Palace
22 Ocean Star
   Empress Harbor Seafood
   Mission 261

## ECLECTIC

26 Bistro K
25 Chez Melange
24 Nook Bistro
23 Chaya
   Depot

## FRENCH

28 Mélisse
27 La Cachette
   Sona
   Shiro
25 Maison Akira

## FRENCH (BISTRO)

27 Frenchy's Bistro
25 Julienne
   Mistral
23 La Crêperie Café
   Café Bizou

## GREEK

23 Petros
22 Papadakis Taverna
   Papa Cristo's
21 Taverna Tony
   Great Greek

## HAMBURGERS

24 Father's Office
   In-N-Out Burger
22 Apple Pan
   Tommy's
21 25 Degrees

## INDIAN

23 Bombay Cafe
   Addi's Tandoor
   All India Café
   Surya India
22 Nawab of India

## ITALIAN

27 Angelini Osteria
   Piccolo
   Tuscany
26 Pizzeria Mozza
   Capo

## JAPANESE

28 Nobu Malibu
   Asanebo
27 Matsuhisa
   Katsu-ya
   Sushi Nozawa

## KOREAN

24 Soot Bull
22 Seoul Jung∇
   Woo Lae Oak
20 BCD Tofu
19 O-Dae San

## MEDITERRANEAN

27 Lucques
26 Sam's by the Beach
   Campanile
25 Gardens
24 Canele

## MEXICAN

24 Lotería!
   Tlapazola Grill
   El Tepeyac
23 La Serenata
22 La Huasteca

## MIDDLE EASTERN

24 Carousel
   Sunnin
23 Carnival
22 Shaherzad
21 Javan

## PIZZA

- 26 Pizzeria Mozza
- 24 Village Pizzeria
- 23 Casa Bianca
  - Mulberry St. Pizzeria
  - Abbot's Pizza

## SEAFOOD

- 27 Water Grill
  - Providence
- 24 Hungry Cat
- 23 Lobster, The
  - Ocean Ave.

## SMALL PLATES

- 26 Mako
  - A.O.C.
  - Orris
- 25 Musha
- 23 Upstairs 2

## SOUL FOOD/ SOUTHERN

- 22 Roscoe's
  - Johnny Rebs'
- 20 Aunt Kizzy's
- 17 Memphis
- 15 House of Blues

## SOUTH AMERICAN

- 25 Mario's Peruvian
- 23 Carlitos Gardel

  Galletto B&G
  Fogo de Chão
  Green Field Churr.

## STEAKHOUSES

- 26 Cut
- 25 Fleming's Prime Steak
  - Mastro's Steak
  - Arnie Morton's Steak
  - Ruth's Chris

## THAI

- 24 Chadaka
  - Saladang
- 23 Palms Thai
- 22 Rambutan Thai
  - Talésai

## VEGETARIAN

- 23 M Café de Chaya
- 22 Native Foods
- 21 Real Food Daily
  - Urth Caffé
  - Inn of the Seventh Ray

## VIETNAMESE

- 23 Crustacean
  - Golden Deli
  - Michelia
- 22 Gingergrass
  - Pho Café

# BY SPECIAL FEATURE

## BREAKFAST

- 24 Lotería!
  - Square One▽
  - Asia de Cuba
- 22 Doughboys
  - Griddle Cafe

## BRUNCH

- 26 Hotel Bel-Air
  - Saddle Peak
  - Joe's
  - Campanile
- 25 Belvedere, The

## BUSINESS DINING

- 28 Mélisse
- 27 La Cachette
  - Providence
  - Derek's
  - Water Grill

## GARDEN DINING

- 26 Ritz Huntington
- 25 Belvedere, The
  - Gardens
- 24 Michael's
- 21 Il Cielo

## HOTEL DINING

- 26 Hotel Bel-Air
  - Cut (Beverly Wilshire)
  - Ritz Huntington
- 25 Chez Melange
  - (Palos Verdes Inn)
  - Belvedere, The
  - (Peninsula Hotel)

## LATE DINING

- 22 Pacific Din. Car
- 21 Bowery
  - Ruen Pair
- 19 Pink's
- 18 Canter's

subscribe to zagat.com

## LUNCH

- 28 Asanebo
- 27 Matsuhisa
- Brandywine
- La Cachette
- Angelini Osteria

## NEWCOMERS (RATED)

- 26 Pizzeria Mozza
- 24 Canele
- 22 Celadon
- Blue Velvet
- 21 Rustic Canyon
- E. Baldi
- Oinkster, The
- 20 Mike & Anne's

## PEOPLE-WATCHING

- 28 Nobu Malibu
- 27 Spago
- 26 Pizzeria Mozza
- A.O.C.
- Cut

## POWER SCENES

- 27 Matsuhisa
- La Cachette
- Providence

Water Grill
Spago

## TRENDY

- 28 Nobu Malibu
- 27 Sona
- 26 Pizzeria Mozza
- Cut
- 24 Katsuya

## WINNING WINE LIST

- 28 Mélisse
- 27 La Cachette
- Sona
- Water Grill
- Spago

## WORTH A TRIP

- 28 Nobu Malibu
  Malibu
- 27 Tuscany
  Westlake Village
- Leila's
  Oak Park
- Babita
  San Gabriel
- Frenchy's Bistro
  Long Beach

## BY LOCATION

### BEVERLY BOULEVARD

- 27 Angelini Osteria
- Hatfield's
- 25 Hirozen
- Jar
- Grace

### BEVERLY HILLS

- 27 Matsuhisa
- Spago
- 26 Mako
- Cut
- 25 Mastro's Steak

### BRENTWOOD

- 25 Takao
- Vincenti
- Osteria Latini
- 24 Palmeri
- Toscana

### CHINATOWN

- 23 Yang Chow
- 22 Ocean Seafood
- 21 Philippe the Original
- Empress Pavilion

- 20 Sam Woo

### DOWNTOWN

- 27 Water Grill
- 26 Patina
- 25 Noé
- Arnie Morton's Steak
- Langer's Deli

### FAIRFAX

- 24 Lotería!
- Chameau
- 22 French Crêpe Co.
- 21 Nyala Ethiopian
- Chao Krung

### HOLLYWOOD

- 27 Providence
- 26 Pizzeria Mozza
- 25 Mario's Peruvian
- 24 Hungry Cat
- In-N-Out Burger

### LA BREA

- 26 Campanile
- 23 Susina Bakery

| 22 | Ca'Brea |
| 21 | Sonora Cafe |
| 19 | Pink's Chili Dogs |

## LONG BEACH

| 27 | Frenchy's Bistro |
| 25 | 555 East |
| 24 | Christy's |
| | Lasher's |
| | Sunnin |

## LOS FELIZ/
## SILVER LAKE

| 23 | Blair's |
| | Chi Dynasty |
| 22 | Rambutan Thai |
| | Madame Matisse |
| | Farfalla Trattoria |

## MALIBU

| 28 | Nobu Malibu |
| 22 | Geoffrey's |
| | Tra Di Noi |
| 21 | Taverna Tony |
| | D'Amore's Pizza |

## MELROSE

| 25 | Sweet Lady Jane |
| 24 | Table 8 |
| 23 | Carlitos Gardel |
| | Angeli Caffe |
| | M Café de Chaya |

## PASADENA/
## SOUTH PASADENA

| 27 | Derek's |
| | Shiro |
| 26 | Ritz Huntington |
| | Bistro K |
| | Yujean Kang's |

## SAN FERNANDO
## VALLEY

| 28 | Asanebo |
| 27 | Brandywine |
| | Katsu-ya |
| | Sushi Nozawa |
| 26 | Saddle Peak |

## SAN GABRIEL VALLEY

| 27 | Babita |
| 26 | Dal Rae |
| 25 | Sea Harbour |
| 24 | Triumphal Palace |
| 23 | Golden Deli |

## SANTA MONICA

| 28 | Mélisse |
| 27 | Josie |
| 26 | Capo |
| | Chinois on Main |
| | Valentino |

## SOUTH BAY

| 27 | Frenchy's Bistro |
| 26 | Gina Lee's Bistro |
| 25 | Christine |
| | Fleming's Prime Steak |
| | Chez Melange |

## THIRD STREET

| 26 | A.O.C. |
| 25 | Locanda Veneta |
| | Ortolan |
| 24 | Joan's on Third |
| 23 | Michelia |

## VENICE

| 27 | Piccolo |
| 26 | Joe's |
| 23 | Chaya |
| | Abbot's Pizza |
| 22 | Wabi-Sabi |

## WEST HOLLYWOOD

| 27 | Sona |
| | Lucques |
| 26 | Madeo |
| 25 | Vivoli Café |
| 24 | Palm, The |

## WEST LA

| 27 | Hamasaku |
| 26 | Mori Sushi |
| | Orris |
| | Sushi Sasabune |
| 25 | Il Grano |

# Top Decor Ratings

Ratings are to the left of names.

| | |
|---|---|
| **29** Hotel Bel-Air | Koi |
| **27** Ritz Huntington | Trump's |
| Madison, The | Sky Room |
| Belvedere, The | Crustacean |
| Yamashiro | Madeleine's |
| Il Cielo | Wilshire |
| Sir Winston's | Vertical Wine Bistro |
| **26** Geoffrey's | Mélisse |
| One Pico | Geisha House |
| Saddle Peak* | Michael's |
| Inn of the Seventh Ray | Spago |
| Blue Velvet | Asia de Cuba |
| Republic | O-Bar |
| Cicada | Tantra |
| Bistro Gdn./Coldwater | Cliff's Edge |
| Polo Lounge | Getty Center |
| **25** Little Door | Jer-ne |
| La Cachette | Katana* |
| Whist | **24** Vibrato |
| Katsuya | Chateau Marmont |
| Gardens | Chakra |

## OUTDOORS

| | |
|---|---|
| Belvedere, The | Il Cielo |
| Chateau Marmont | Inn of the Seventh Ray |
| Cliff's Edge | Michael's |
| Gardens | Ritz Huntington |
| Hotel Bel-Air | Salt Creek Grille |

## ROMANCE

| | |
|---|---|
| Bistro de la Gare | Il Cielo |
| Capo | Josie |
| Getty Center | Little Door |
| Grace | Mélisse |
| Hampton's | Saddle Peak |

## STARGAZING

| | |
|---|---|
| Brentwood, The | Matsuhisa |
| Cut | Nobu Malibu |
| Koi | Pizzeria Mozza |
| Il Sole | Providence |
| Katsuya | Spago |

## VIEWS

| | |
|---|---|
| Asia de Cuba | Moonshadows |
| Blue Velvet | Noé |
| Geoffrey's | Penthouse, The |
| Getty Center | West |
| Lobster, The | Yamashiro |

# Top Service Ratings

Ratings are to the left of names.

<u>28</u> Hotel Bel-Air

<u>27</u> Sam's by the Beach

<u>26</u> La Cachette
Ritz Huntington
Gardens
Mélisse
Sona
Providence
Belvedere, The

<u>25</u> Brandywine
Water Grill
Dal Rae
Valentino
Spago
Patina
Mako
Josie
Derek's
Papadakis Taverna

<u>24</u> Polo Lounge

Raymond, The
Vivoli Café
Lawry's Prime Rib
Café 14
Sir Winston's
Hatfield's
Maison Akira
Tuscany
Mandevilla
Chez Melange
Leila's
Mistral
Lasher's
Bistro 45
Asanebo
Cut
Fogo de Chão
Marino
Nobu Malibu
Lucques

# Best Buys

In order of Bang for the Buck rating.

1. In-N-Out Burger
2. Tommy's
3. Noah's NY Bagels
4. Carney's Express
5. Lamonica's NY Pizza
6. Chipotle
7. Sandbag Sandwiches
8. Jody Maroni's
9. Poquito Más
10. Astro Burger
11. Philippe the Original
12. Susina Bakery
13. Asahi Ramen
14. Stand, The
15. Baja Fresh Mex.
16. Cha Cha Chicken
17. El Tepeyac
18. California Chicken
19. Apple Pan
20. Chili My Soul
21. Pink's Chili Dogs
22. Oinkster, The
23. Uncle Bill's Pancake
24. Abbot's Pizza
25. Le Saigon
26. Pho 79
27. Original Pancake
28. Chabuya Tokyo
29. Sharky's Mexican
30. Golden Deli
31. Reddi Chick BBQ
32. Village Pizzeria
33. Zankou Chicken
34. French Crêpe Co.
35. Falafel King
36. Martha's 22nd St.
37. Johnny Rockets
38. Hurry Curry
39. Feast from the East
40. Café 50s

## OTHER GOOD VALUES

Alcove
Alejo's
Back Home/Lahaina
BottleRock
Breadbar
Brent's Deli
Buca di Beppo
Café Bizou
Cali. Pizza Kitchen
Casa Bianca
Counter, The
Din Tai Fung
Doña Rosa
Duke's
George's Greek
Griddle Café
Gumbo Pot
Jinky's
Koo Koo Roo
La Serenata

Lemon Moon
Loft, The
Malibu Seafood
Mandarin Deli
Mishima
Palms Thai
Papa Cristo's
Pei Wei Diner
Porky's BBQ
Porto's Bakery
Ragin' Cajun
Reel Inn
Roscoe's
Shack, The
Soot Bull Jeep
Sunnin
Swinging Door
2117
Uncle Darrow's
Versailles

# LOS ANGELES
# RESTAURANT
# DIRECTORY

|  | FOOD | DECOR | SERVICE | COST |
|---|---|---|---|---|

### Abbey, The ◑ *American* — 16 | 22 | 15 | $27

**West Hollywood** | 692 N. Robertson Blvd. (Santa Monica Blvd.) |
310-289-8410 | www.abbeyfoodandbar.com

"The food ain't much, but oh Mary, the scene" quips one customer of
the "gayest restaurant in West Hollywood", whose recently revamped
American menu features burgers, chocolate fondue and "divine",
"pricey" martinis; be warned that the "fabulous" ("even for straights")
atmosphere is "standing room only on weekends" throughout the "artfully redecorated" space, so consider reserving one of the cabanas.

### Abbot's Pizza *Pizza* — 23 | 6 | 14 | $11

**Santa Monica** | 1811 Pico Blvd. (18th St.) | 310-314-2777
**Venice** | 1407 Abbot Kinney Blvd. (California Ave.) | 310-396-7334
www.abbotspizzacompany.com

"Love the bagel crust" praise "pizza aficionados" who line up for
"inventive combinations" of sauces, toppings and styles as well as
"unfussy classics" at these "must-go" Santa Monica and Venice pie
parlors; takeout is recommended for each, but burned customers pan
the delivery ("it may never come") and nearly "nonexistent" service by
a "grumpy" staff.

### ABC Seafood *Chinese/Seafood* — 19 | 10 | 14 | $21

**Chinatown** | 205 Ord St. (New High St.) | 213-680-2887

"Lots of carts" of "hot and fresh" dim sum draw daytime crowds to
this "inexpensive" "Hong Kong–style" Chinatown haunt, which plates
up "succulent" lobster and other saltwater fare in the evenings – just
"point to anything moving and flipping in the fish tanks"; while it's constantly "busy", the sometimes "variable" quality, "dumpy" decor and
"inattentive" service (which may result from the language barrier) can
detract from the experience.

### NEW Abode *American* — ▽ 23 | 26 | 20 | $93

**Santa Monica** | 1541 Ocean Ave. (Colorado Ave.) | 310-394-3463 |
www.aboderestaurant.com

"Gorgeous" "modern-retro" furnishings with "beautiful banquettes"
set a "promising" tone for this sustainability-touting Santa Monica
newcomer, which rewards early samplers with New American fare
they deem "avant-garde", "pleasurable" and even "gastrodynamic";
the coinage puts off others, however, who find it too "pretentious" and
"overpriced for the food quality and portions", given tasting menus
ranging from $85 to $145.

### Absolutely Phobulous 🖻 *Vietnamese* — ▽ 19 | 12 | 17 | $15

**West Hollywood** | 350 N. La Cienega Blvd. (Beverly Blvd.) | 310-360-3930 |
www.abpho.com

With its "savory" "steaming bowls" and "crunchy" spring rolls, noodlers
say this "budget pho shop" "fills a void for good Vietnamese in WeHo";
though the colorful setting falls short of fab, its "fast" turnaround – with
orders "ready in less than three minutes" – fulfills a craving "on the run".

### A Cow Jumped Over the Moon *French* — ▽ 22 | 16 | 21 | $22

**Beverly Hills** | Rodeo Collection | 421 N. Rodeo Dr. (Santa Monica Blvd.) |
310-274-4269

*Pan bagnat*, fondue, raclette and other French specialties, matched by
"great wines", stand out on the "impressive" kosher dairy menu at this

"enjoyable" daytime Beverly Hills gourmet shop tended by a "helpful" staff; on the downside, it's situated in an "underground garage", but you can "watch the Astons, Ferraris and Lambos drive by" while indulging in a "quiet bite"; N.B. closed Saturdays.

### Adagio Ⓜ Italian
23 | 16 | 22 | $36

**Woodland Hills** | 22841 Ventura Blvd. (Fallbrook Ave.) | 818-225-0533
"Congenial host" and owner Claudio Gontier wins kudos for his "civilized" Northern Italian in Woodland Hills, where he plates up "wonderful" pasta and "still makes the Caesar salads at your table"; while it's a "rather intimate place", most find the "uninspiring", "banquet-room" furnishings fail to match the "excellent service" and "home cooking."

### Addi's Tandoor Indian
23 | 16 | 22 | $26

**Redondo Beach** | 800 Torrance Blvd. (bet. PCH & Prospect Ave.) | 310-540-1616 | www.addistandoor.com
"Spicy Goan cuisine" ("just ask and they'll set your mouth on fire") and "fantastic" tandoori dishes bring Redondo Beach foodies to this "cozy" Indian "find" "slotted into a strip mall"; it's a bit "pricier" than the competition, but pays off with a staff that's "smooth, efficient" and "accommodating to novices."

### Admiral Risty Seafood
21 | 18 | 21 | $41

**Rancho Palos Verdes** | 31250 Palos Verdes Dr. W. (Hawthorne Blvd.) | 310-377-0050 | www.admiral-risty.com
A "favorite" in Rancho Palos Verdes, this seafooder presents "well-prepared", "old-fashioned" fish and steaks for a "faithful following"; its "wonderful sunset views", "homey" atmosphere and "swinging bar" keep it "crowded on the weekends", even though some think it's "overpriced", "long overdue for a rehab" and better left to "local seniors."

### Adobe Cantina BBQ/Mexican
19 | 16 | 17 | $22

**Agoura Hills** | 29100 Agoura Rd. (Kanan Rd.) | 818-991-3474
"Hot summer evenings" and "lazy Sunday brunches" filled with "fine" fish tacos and "magic" margaritas on the patio make you "feel like you're in Cabo" at this "casual", mostly outdoor Mexican and BBQ in Agoura Hills; since some call the food merely "standard" and the service not-so-speedy, it's wise to "order your drinks two at a time."

### Ago Italian
21 | 19 | 19 | $55

**West Hollywood** | 8478 Melrose Ave. (N. La Cienega Blvd.) | 323-655-6333 | www.agorestaurant.com
"You get the real California feel" from this "tasty" Tuscan in West Hollywood, whose wood-fired T-bone steaks "sizzle" as much as the "heavy-hitter industry crowd" populating the back tables and "lively" patio; it's "too pretentious", "rushed" and high-cost for some, though that doesn't keep away the "blond starlets at the bar looking for a meal ticket and a SAG card", or gawkers hoping for an appearance by backer "Bob De Niro himself."

### Agra Cafe Indian
▽ 22 | 12 | 16 | $19

**Silver Lake** | 4325 Sunset Blvd. (Fountain Ave.) | 323-665-7818 | www.agracafe.com
"Delicate and fragrant" Indian dishes, made extra enticing by the "crazy-huge" lunch special, win over visitors to this "strip-mall

oasis" that's gaining serious Silver Lake cred (though some still "wish it was busier"); the burgundy-toned room is "comfortable" if not captivating, and most don't mind the middling service in light of such "flavorful" fare.

### Ahi Sushi _Japanese_

▽ 22 | 15 | 20 | $38

**Studio City** | 12915 Ventura Blvd. (Coldwater Canyon Ave.) | 818-981-0277 | www.ahisushi.com

"If you can get in" to this sushi and sake-martini spot in Studio City, admirers assure you'll be treated to "top-grade sashimi" and "creative" rolls as well as "amazing" Asian fusion fare; the staff is generally "happy to answer questions", and although it gets "crowded", the bamboo-adorned patio offers a respite.

### Aioli _Mediterranean/Spanish_

17 | 19 | 18 | $33

**Torrance** | 1261 Cabrillo Ave. (Torrance Blvd.) | 310-320-9200 | www.aiolirestaurant.net

"Go with a large group and share" recommend value-conscious Torrance tapas hoppers of this "pleasant" Spanish-Med that attracts the "automotive crowd for business lunches"; the cooking is "solid" and the service on par, but it's the expansive, white-tablecloth interior and "convivial outdoor patio" that keep it "popular."

### Ajisen Ramen _Japanese_

17 | 13 | 13 | $14

**San Gabriel** | Hilton Plaza | 227 W. Valley Blvd. (S. Del Mar Ave.) | 626-281-8388

For "reliable ramen" in San Gabriel, slurpers arrive "early to avoid huge lines" at this Japanese noodle nook (part of a global chain) in the Hilton Plaza hotel; though some naysayers call it "not authentic" and complain of a "tight seating arrangement" and parking "hassles", it's still "inexpensive" and "cheerful" enough for a "decent" lunch that arrives "quickly" once you sit down.

### Akbar Cuisine of India _Indian_

20 | 15 | 18 | $26

**Marina del Rey** | 3115 Washington Blvd. (Yale Ave.) | 310-574-0666
**Santa Monica** | 2627 Wilshire Blvd. (26th St.) | 310-586-7469
**Hermosa Beach** | 1101 Aviation Blvd. (Prospect Ave.) | 310-937-3800
**Pasadena** | 44 N. Fair Oaks Ave. (Union St.) | 626-577-9916
www.akbarcuisineofindia.com

Offering a "surprising" dose of "panache", this Indian quintet pleases with mint chicken kebabs, "tender lamb" and other "flavorful" dishes that are "not dumbed down for Anglo taste buds"; while the ambiance varies by location, and some find the cooking can "fluctuate" too, its "reasonable prices" and "expert" "recommendations for wine-pairing to the level of spice" ease the way for initiates; N.B. the Third Street location has closed.

### Akwa 🅱 _Californian_

19 | 24 | 18 | $40

**Santa Monica** | 1413 Fifth St. (Santa Monica Blvd.) | 310-656-9688 | www.akwarestaurant.com

A "beautiful" two-story space with a sushi bar, "pretty patio" and "loungey beats" lures "trendy" tipplers and diners to this "eclectic" Asian-influenced Californian in Santa Monica; while the cocktails are "terrific", many deem the service "mediocre" and the food sometimes "delish" but otherwise "not up to the price or decor."

|  | FOOD | DECOR | SERVICE | COST |
|---|---|---|---|---|

### A La Tarte Bistrot 🅼 *Bakery/French* ▽ 18 | 19 | 11 | $24

**Pacific Palisades** | 1037 Swarthmore Ave. (bet. Monument St. & Sunset Blvd.) | 310-459-6635

"Sunday brunch on the street at the farmer's market" is the claim to fame of this "slice of Provence" in the Palisades, where patrons "splurge on slabs of French toast" and "wonderful pastries" among other baked goods and bistro fare (served till 4 PM); still, "attitude, attitude, attitude" from the staff can "ruin the experience" unless you "know what to expect"; N.B. no alcohol served and no BYO allowed.

### Albano's Brooklyn Pizzeria *Pizza* ▽ 23 | 11 | 16 | $12

**Melrose** | 7261 Melrose Ave. (Alta Vista Blvd.) | 323-934-2494

"New York expats" attest it's "great to stop by and just grab a slice" of "authentically East Coast" pizza sporting the "right weight, texture and flavor" with "simple but tasty" toppings from this Melrose destination; they also approve of the "red-sauce" pastas, so all in all, it's "as close to Brooklyn as you're going to get"; N.B. no alcohol and no BYO.

### Alcove *American* 22 | 21 | 16 | $18

**Los Feliz** | 1929 Hillhurst Ave. (Franklin Ave.) | 323-644-0100 | www.alcovecafe.com

"Always packed", this converted bungalow with an "oasis" of outdoor seating hosts "hip" Los Feliz lunchers digging into "pricey", "hearty" salads, "tasty" panini and desserts sliced "so large, they have their own zip code"; habitués say the "nonchalant ambiance is ideal for people-watching" as long as you "don't mind standing in line" and ordering from a counter staff that "manages to keep up" but is "often as fresh" as the food.

### Alegria *Nuevo Latino* 21 | 20 | 19 | $28

**Long Beach** | 115 Pine Ave. (bet. B'way & 1st St.) | 562-436-3388 | www.alegriacocinalatina.com

Flamenco dancing and other nightly entertainment sets the stage for "super sangria" and "delicious" tapas at this mosaic-tiled Nuevo Latino "retreat" in Long Beach; some say "you go for the drinks, not the food", but that's just fine by the "crowds of friends" and "singles of all ages" who keep it "loud" and "lively" on the weekends.

### Alegria on Sunset 🅱🔴 *Mexican* 22 | 12 | 17 | $21

**Silver Lake** | Sunset Plaza | 3510 W. Sunset Blvd. (Golden Gate Ave.) | 323-913-1422 | www.alegriaonsunset.com

"Zingy, authentic" "Mexican home cooking" is the soul of this Silver Lake "strip-mall sensation" where the carnitas are "some of the best you'll find in LA" and the *café de olla* is "can't miss"; though service is "slow" and it "looks like a dive", it's also "colorful" and congenial, so "bring your own alcohol and eat among friends."

### Alejandro's 🅼 *Filipino* – | – | – | I

**Eagle Rock** | 4126 Verdugo Rd. (York Blvd.) | 323-550-1063

"Happily stuffed" chowhounds hail this "homey", under-the-radar Filipino cafe in Eagle Rock, urging "get the fried pork knuckle", along with the goat stew and purple ice cream (made from ube, a type of yam); it's all delivered from the open kitchen by an "encouraging" staff; N.B. no lunch on Tuesdays.

|  | FOOD | DECOR | SERVICE | COST |
|---|---|---|---|---|

### Alejo's  *Italian*
**21 | 8 | 17 | $18**

**Marina del Rey** | 4002 Lincoln Blvd. (Washington Blvd.) | 310-822-0095
**Westchester** | 8343 Lincoln Blvd. (84th St.) | 310-670-6677
You "gotta love garlic" to appreciate the "terrific" pastas and other "comfort food" at these two "inexpensive" Italians that *mangiatori* say make you "miss the mamma you never had"; the larger Westchester location is particularly "family-friendly", but there's often a "wait" for a table at the Marina del Rey BYO, which is a go-to spot for takeout.

### Alessio Ristorante Italiano  *Italian*
**22 | 20 | 20 | $33**

**Northridge** | 9725 Reseda Blvd. (Superior St.) | 818-709-8393
**West Hills** | Platt Vill. | 6428 Platt Ave. (Victory Blvd.) | 818-710-0270
**Westlake Village** | 3731 E. Thousand Oaks Blvd. (Marmon Ave.) | 805-557-0565
www.alessiorestaurant.com
Valley dwellers delight over the "unmatched" meatballs and other "plentiful" portions of Italian fare complemented by an "admirable" wine list at this trio of "warmly decorated", "upscale neighborhood" trattorias that are "always busy"; despite some agita about "overpriced specials" and too much "noise", especially on live music nights, most guests are appeased by the "professional" staff.

### NEW All' Angelo  Ⓢ *Italian*
**▽ 26 | 20 | 24 | $58**

**Hollywood** | 7166 Melrose Ave. (bet. Formosa Ave. & N. Detroit St.) | 323-933-9540
A "surprisingly grown-up" addition to Melrose Avenue, this Hollywood Italian serves chef Stefano Ongaro's "personally prepared" dishes full of "earthy, rich flavors", such as risotto with saffron and bone marrow, and antipasto meats sliced on a vintage "hand-cranked" machine; the "charming" room, decorated in brown and cream tones with Murano glass lamps, complements the cuisine, while the "exemplary" staff impresses diners by "doing everything right."

### Allegria  *Italian*
**21 | 16 | 20 | $37**

**Malibu** | 22821 PCH (south of Malibu Pier) | 310-456-3132 | www.allegriamalibu.com
"Italian comfort food" wins over both Malibu "celebrities" and "families" at this "'in' place" for "tasty" pastas, thin-crust pizzas and roasted chicken on PCH; indeed, it's a kick to "eat where Dick Clark eats" while being tended to by the "unpretentious", "Old Country" staff, so although some deem the decor and menu a bit "tired", the "vibe is always upbeat"; P.S. "ask for a booth" and remember it's beer-and-wine only.

### All India Café  *Indian*
**23 | 14 | 17 | $23**

**West LA** | Santa Monica Plaza | 12113 Santa Monica Blvd. (Bundy Dr.) | 310-442-5250
**Pasadena** | 39 S. Fair Oaks Ave. (bet. Colorado Blvd. & Green St.) | 626-440-0309
www.allindiacafe.com
Masala mavens hail the "extraordinary flavors" of the "wholesome" Indian fare ("especially the vegetarian dishes") at these separately owned, "inexpensive" eateries in Pasadena and West LA; the "food well surpasses the decor" and "erratic" service, though the staff often pitches in with "good recommendations."

| | FOOD | DECOR | SERVICE | COST |
|---|---|---|---|---|

### Amalfi   *Italian* ▽ 18 | 18 | 16 | $35

**La Brea** | 143 N. La Brea Ave. (bet. Beverly Blvd. & 1st St.) | 323-938-2504 | www.room5lounge.com

Fusili fans "grab a table by the fireplace" and dig into "pasta paradise" at this "lovely" La Brea Italian co-owned by comic Adam Corolla; although much of the "reasonably priced" menu is "middle-of-the-road" and the quality of service "depends on the server", live music upstairs adds to an "elegant" atmosphere that feels "more expensive than the bill."

### Amici   *Italian* 21 | 17 | 19 | $39

**Beverly Hills** | Beverly Terrace Hotel | 469 N. Doheny Dr. (Santa Monica Blvd.) | 310-858-0271
**Brentwood** | 2538 San Vicente Blvd. (26th St.) | 310-260-4900
www.tamici.com

"*Fantastico!*" exclaim fans of this Brentwood Italian designed with "high ceilings and twinkling candles", as well as its more casual cousin "hidden" in the Beverly Terrace Hotel, which pleases with its "delightful" patio (rather than the "close quarters" inside); though opinions of the cuisine range from "top-notch" to "Americanized" ("more Brentwood than Bologna"), and both "noise" and "spotty" service sometimes mar the experience, "lots of regulars" just "love" it.

### Ammo   *Californian* 22 | 19 | 20 | $39

**Hollywood** | 1155 N. Highland Ave. (bet. Fountain Ave. & Santa Monica Blvd.) | 323-871-2666 | www.ammocafe.com

"Nouveau Californian comfort" dishes, featuring "organic, innovative" renditions of grilled leg of lamb, wild bass and other seasonal specialties, meet a "Hollywood casual" vibe at this "film-industry" hang for "fabulous lunches" and "relaxing dinners"; its "sleek architecture" and "intelligent" service also impress, though some knock that it's "a bit into itself" and perhaps "too expensive for what you get."

### Amori   Ⓜ *Californian/French* ▽ 22 | 16 | 15 | $39

**Monrovia** | 110 E. Lemon Ave. (Myrtle Ave.) | 626-358-1908

"Monrovians don't know what they're missing" assert champions of chef-owner Pedro Simental's "sensual" Cal-French cuisine at this "secluded" spot where "you can always find a seat"; still, some critics decry the often "snail's pace" kitchen, "Keystone Cops" service and "unavailable" wines, wishing the treatment could be as "lively" as the dishes.

### Angelena's Southern Cuisine   *Southern* ▽ 15 | 14 | 15 | $20

**Alhambra** | 33 W. Main St. (Garfield Ave.) | 626-284-7685 | www.angelenas.com

Catfish connoisseurs find a "pretty decent evocation of Southern" dishes at this Alhambra outpost for "down-home cooking in the SGV"; while a few also appreciate its simple, "cool" decor touches, with portraits of Aretha Franklin and Ray Charles on the walls, the "super-friendly but super-slow" servers "have too many tables to cover" and the offerings are too "ordinary" for some.

### Angeli Caffe   Ⓜ *Italian* 23 | 15 | 21 | $31

**Melrose** | 7274 Melrose Ave. (Poinsettia Pl.) | 323-936-9086 | www.angelicaffe.com

Chef-owner Evan Kleiman's "stupendous" Italian cuisine, notably the "fresh pastas", "exotic pizzas" and bread that's a "revelation" ("you'll think you died and went to carb heaven"), has been "going the distance" at this Melrose *cucina* since 1984; despite its "dated" digs, most appreciate the "unpretentious", "kid-friendly" service and agree that "given the quality of the cooking, it's a bargain."

## ☑ Angelini Osteria ☒ *Italian*  27 | 17 | 23 | $49

**Beverly Boulevard** | 7313 Beverly Blvd. (Poinsettia Pl.) | 323-297-0070 | www.angeliniosteria.com

"Incomparable feasts" crafted by "masterful" chef Gino Angelini "transport" guests at this "intimate" Beverly Boulevard Italian whose "rustic" dishes like pork chop *alla Milanese* "put you in pig heaven"; "tight seating" is part of the "bargain", but both "in-the-know locals and celebs" sit "cheek-by-jowl" as they savor "personal" service and "exquisite" wines to accompany the "superb" fare; P.S. "reserve early."

## Angelique Cafe *French*  22 | 13 | 17 | $18

**Downtown** | 840 S. Spring St. (bet. 8th & 9th Sts.) | 213-623-8698 | www.angeliquecafe.com

"Fabulous" French food shines a "beacon of light in LA's Downtown smog storm" at this "hidden treasure" for daytime dining on "elegant omelets", "homemade pâtés" and "delicious charcuterie"; the menu has been slightly tweaked by new ownership (no more foie gras) – so regulars hope the often "lackluster" service and "funky" looks ("a cross between a diner and a bistro") will follow suit.

## Angolo DiVino ☒ *Italian*  ▽ 23 | 18 | 24 | $50

**West LA** | Santa Monica Plaza | 11047 Santa Monica Blvd. (Sepulveda Blvd.) | 310-477-7080

"Amazing service" with a "family vibe" makes this "unexpectedly good" West LA trattoria a "comfortable" choice for "enjoyable" Italian meals; although it's a touch "pricey", that hardly ruffles the regulars relaxing on the "cozy outdoor patio."

## Anna's *Italian*  14 | 12 | 17 | $25

**West LA** | 10929 W. Pico Blvd. (bet. Veteran Ave. & Westwood Blvd.) | 310-474-0102 | www.annaitalian.com

"An old family favorite" in West LA, this "red-sauce" Roman has provided "huge portions" of "heavy" staples like chicken cacciatore since 1969; it's "hardly outstanding" and the "time-capsule" decor "needs a refurbish" even more than the menu, but it caters to "regulars who know the staff", among other "nostalgic" types "in the mood to pig out."

## Antica Pizzeria *Pizza*  20 | 14 | 17 | $22

**Marina del Rey** | Villa Marina Mktpl. | 13455 Maxella Ave. (Lincoln Blvd.) | 310-577-8182 | www.anticapizzeria.net

"Authentic", "thin, crispy" wood-fired pies – made by the U.S. President of the prestigious Vera Pizza Napolitana – distinguish this "certified" Marina del Rey Italian from competing *paesani*; on the downside, the strip-mall location is "odd", the room is "spare" and other entrees arouse little comment, but regulars get a kick out of the "chummy service."

## Antonio's ☒ *Mexican*  ▽ 22 | 15 | 21 | $25

**Melrose** | 7470 Melrose Ave. (bet. Fairfax & La Brea Aves.) | 323-658-9060 | www.antoniosonmelrose.com

The "warm, welcoming host – Antonio himself", sets the tone for dining on "delicious" Mexican "regional specialties" and "killer margaritas" at this Melrose "oldie" but "goodie"; though its muralled interior "may need an update" and some wish the mariachi players (Thursday–Sunday) didn't "drown out your conversation", few can complain about the 70-strong "tasty tequila list."

## ☒ A.O.C. *Californian/French* 26 | 22 | 23 | $53

**Third Street** | 8022 W. Third St. (bet. Crescent Heights Blvd. & Edinburgh Ave.) | 323-653-6359 | www.aocwinebar.com

Suzanne Goin's "small-plates heaven" (and sib to Lucques) presents "marvelous" Cal-French dishes complemented by "spectacular wines and cheeses", which are all ideal for "sharing with a group" and "perfect for dates" (whether romantic or "bacon-wrapped"); the "lovely, understated" interior hosts "enough of a scene to entertain but not intimidate", and the "informed", "attentive" staff can convince you to "nosh all night", even if tabs do "add up quickly"; P.S. arrive early to "get a seat at the bar" if you don't have a reservation.

## Aphrodisiac ☒Ⓜ *Continental* 18 | 23 | 19 | $45

**Century City** | 10351 Santa Monica Blvd. (Beverly Glen Blvd.) | 310-282-8870 | www.aphrodisiacrestaurant.com

Despite the "horrible name", diners find this red-accented Century City Continental "attractive" and "elegant" – "a good place for eating with someone special"; still, others arrive "expecting sexier food" and service more "in sync" with the theme, saying it packs "more style than substance" with a "dinner-in-bed" option that's something of a "gimmick."

## Apple Pan ●Ⓜ⇄ *American* 22 | 10 | 19 | $13

**West LA** | 10801 W. Pico Blvd. (Glendon Ave.) | 310-475-3585

A West LA "institution", this "pan-tastic" family-run American diner boasts "famous" hickory burgers, "just-right" fries and "unreal" pies (apple, banana cream, boysenberry and more); sure, service at the "old-school" wraparound counter can be "curmudgeonly", particularly if you "go in acting posh", but "elbow-to-elbow" crowds and "regulars who don't even need a menu" swear "my father brought me here, and I'll bring my kids one day."

## ☒ Arnie Morton's The Steakhouse *Steak* 25 | 22 | 24 | $61

**Downtown** | 735 S. Figueroa St. (bet. 7th & 8th Sts.) | 213-553-4566
**Beverly Hills** | Le Méridien Hotel | 435 S. La Cienega Blvd. (bet. San Vicente & Wilshire Blvds.) | 310-246-1501
**Burbank** | The Pinnacle | 3400 W. Olive Ave. (Lima St.) | 818-238-0424
www.mortons.com

All branches of this "steakhouse classic", part of the national Morton's chain, are touted for their "top-notch", "simply" prepared 24-ounce porterhouse, double-cut filet and other "huge" prime cuts, as well as for a wine list that "reads like a novel"; while a few find the pre-dinner "raw meat parade" "unnerving" and the atmosphere "stuffy", many are amused by the "kitschy introductory spiel" as well as the "dark", "old-school" environs where "expense accounts" reign.

## Aroma Ⓜ *Italian* - | - | - | M

**Silver Lake** | 2903 W. Sunset Blvd. (bet. Silver Lake Blvd. & Reno St.) | 323-644-2833 | www.aromaatsunset.com

Chef-owner Edin Marroquin (ex Valentino) helms the open kitchen at this "cozy", "crowded" Silver Lake Italian, bringing his expertise (and "especially good" way with sauces) to bear on traditional steak, pasta and veal dishes; in marked contrast to his former venue, the tiny, white-tablecloth room thrives on a sunny ambiance, casual service and moderate prices.

### Arroyo Chop House  Steak

| 25 | 23 | 23 | $55 |

**Pasadena** | 536 S. Arroyo Pkwy. (bet. California & Del Mar Blvds.) | 626-577-7463 | www.arroyochophouse.com

Meat mavens adore the "perfectly done prime beef" (including a "cowboy rib-eye sure to satisfy"), "awesome sides", "fabulous soufflés for dessert" and expansive wine selection at this "boisterous boys' club" of a steakhouse that competes as "the best place in Pasadena to close a business deal"; its "professional, nonintrusive" service, cultivated by owners Bob and Gregg Smith (Parkway Grill), and decor of "dark woods and mood lighting" enhance the "classic vibe", but "brace yourself for modern-day prices."

### Artisan Cheese Gallery  Cheese/Sandwiches

| 24 | 14 | 20 | $18 |

**Studio City** | 12023 Ventura Blvd. (Laurel Canyon Blvd.) | 818-505-0207 | www.artisancheesegallery.com

"Screw Disneyland – this may be the happiest place on earth" exclaim indulgers dazzled by the "magnificent", 400-strong selection of "unusual" imported and domestic cheeses and "fantastic" panini with fillings ranging from grilled cheddar to "duck confit – my candidate for sandwich of the year"; the mainly take-out Studio City storefront also sells "exotic peanut butters" and "spicy pickles", and the "helpful" staff will "jump at the chance to feed you samples until you cry 'uncle'" but wallet-watchers warn "you pay for it in the end."

### Art's Deli  Deli

| 19 | 12 | 17 | $20 |

**Studio City** | 12224 Ventura Blvd. (bet. Laurelgrove & Vantage Aves.) | 818-762-1221 | www.artsdeli.com

For "wonderful corned beef", "quality bakery goods" and the "freshest lox", "where else would you take the whole *mishpucha*?" wonder supporters of this 50-year-old Jewish deli, whose "no-nonsense" looks get a lift from Studio City "celebs meeting for breakfast"; still, some critics call the sandwiches "giant but not great" and the servers "brusque" ("they throw the food at you a bit when it's busy") – "go figya!"

### Asahi Ramen  ⊅ Japanese

| 21 | 8 | 19 | $11 |

**West LA** | 2027 Sawtelle Blvd. (bet. La Grange & Mississippi Aves.) | 310-479-2231

"Huge, steaming bowls" of "consistently good" Japanese noodles keep "lines out the door" at this "beyond-cheap", "unassuming" West LA storefront staffed by "fast, friendly" servers; though detractors deem the quality "only fair", many contend it's "the perfect cure for a cold (or a cold night)."

### Asaka  Japanese

| ▽ 20 | 16 | 18 | $29 |

**Rancho Palos Verdes** | Golden Cove Shopping Ctr. | 31208 Palos Verdes Dr. W. (Hawthorne Blvd.) | 310-377-5999 | www.asakausa.com

Locals call the "fresh" sushi and Japanese cooking at this Rancho Palos Verdes "neighborhood spot" "some of the best on the Peninsula", even if it falls a bit short of "more sophisticated" competition in the city;

still, it's a "great place for the little ones" and "you can't beat" the "fantastic" view of the Pacific, which is the highlight of the decor and helps make up for somewhat "inconsistent" service.

**Asakuma** *Japanese*                     21 | 16 | 19 | $33

**Beverly Hills** | 141 S. Robertson Blvd. (bet. Charleville & Wilshire Blvds.) | 310-659-1092
**Marina del Rey** | Hoyt Plaza | 2805 Abbot Kinney Blvd. (Washington Blvd.) | 310-577-7999
**West LA** | Brentwood Shopping Ctr. | 11701 Wilshire Blvd. (Barrington Ave.) | 310-826-0013
**West LA** | 11769 Santa Monica Blvd. (bet. Granville & Stoner Aves.) | 310-473-8990
www.asakuma.com

With three take-out locations and one sit-down flagship, this "dependable" sushi chain has made its name on "excellent" marinated black cod ("the classic dish") and "creative" rolls among other "solid Japanese food"; while delivery is generally "fast", "bargain"-hunters seek out the "early-bird dinner" at the Wilshire Boulevard hub.

**Z Asanebo M** *Japanese*                 28 | 15 | 24 | $61

**Studio City** | 11941 Ventura Blvd. (bet. Carpenter & Radford Aves.) | 818-760-3348

At this "superb find" on Studio City's "sushi row", Tetsuya Nakao slices up "incredible" sashimi in a "traditional Japanese" style that's "beautifully presented", though "sometimes not for the faint of heart" and never "for the faint of budget"; both insiders and initiates appreciate the "excellent" servers who "explain each dish", adding there's "no ambiance, but who cares?"

**Asia de Cuba** ● *Asian/Cuban*           24 | 25 | 20 | $59

**West Hollywood** | Mondrian Hotel | 8440 Sunset Blvd.
(bet. La Cienega Blvd. & Olive Dr.) | 323-848-6000 |
www.chinagrillmanagement.com

"Delightful" Asian-Cuban fusion cuisine served "family-style" is the "multiculti order of the day" at Jeffrey Chodorow's "swank boîte" crowning the Mondrian in West Hollywood; its "clean white" interior and terrace afford a "spectacular view of the city and the beautiful people", and although the service receives mixed reviews, most are pleased to bask in an ambiance that's both "bustling" and "relaxing."

**NEW Asia Los Feliz** ⑤ *Asian/Californian*    ▽ 20 | 22 | 19 | $39

**Atwater Village** | 3179 Los Feliz Blvd. (Glenfeliz Blvd.) | 323-906-9498 |
www.asialosfeliz.com

A "happening" newcomer on a "modest stretch of Los Feliz" in Atwater Village, this "worldly" Cal-Asian dishes up "artfully arranged" "twists on classics" – such as spicy mango lamb chops and lobster mac 'n' cheese – among earthy and "lush urban decor"; some find it "too pricey" and "pretentious", however, concluding that "you can get the same quality fish and ambiance elsewhere for less."

**NEW Asian-Ya Soy Boy** *Korean*          - | - | - | I

**West LA** | 11660 Gateway Blvd. (Barrington Ave.) | 877-518-5151
This plain-Jane newcomer in a strip mall just south of Pico joins the growing number of small Korean tofu and BBQ shops that have ap-

peared on the Westside; its cheap prices and spicy, filling fare make up for its functional setting.

### Astro Burger  *Hamburgers*                    20 | 9 | 15 | $10

**Hollywood** | 5601 Melrose Ave. (Gower St.) | 323-469-1924 🌙
**West Hollywood** | 7475 Santa Monica Blvd. (bet. Fairfax & La Brea Aves.) |
323-874-8041 🌙
**Montebello** | 3421 W. Beverly Blvd. (Bradshawe St.) | 323-724-3995
www.astroburger.com

"Cheap, greasy" burgers, "sensational" onion rings, omelets and Mexican nibbles cater to all walks of Angeleno ("even vegetarians") at this "dependable" counter-service fallback for "quick lunches", "middle-of-finals junk-food runs" and "post-Oscar win" meals; considering the late hours (till 4 AM on the weekends in WeHo) and "fast-food prices" with "better-quality ingredients", "who doesn't love" it?

### Asuka  *Japanese*                    20 | 12 | 19 | $31

**Westwood** | 1266 Westwood Blvd. (Wilshire Blvd.) | 310-474-7412 |
www.asukasushi.com

"Tasty morsels are barbecued right before your eyes" at the charcoal grill of this "family-friendly" Westwood eatery that's served as a "trusted" Japanese "standby" since 1974; although it's not quite "fabulous" and "isn't a place to see and be seen", it's a "decently priced" sushi "favorite" for many, and the staff is "so nice the food seems even better."

### NEW Ate-1-8  *Eclectic*                    ▽ 15 | 15 | 16 | $30

**Encino** | 17620 Ventura Blvd. (Texhoma Ave.) | 818-728-1212 |
www.ate18.com

Though it's still "new and just finding its place", this Eclectic sidewalk cafe in the 818 often pleases the early Encino crowd with its "surprisingly good lunches" of American, Israeli, French and Moroccan fare served in "casual", loungey environs with live bossa nova on the weekends; some dinner guests, though, report being "disappointed" by the "minuscule" plates and long cooking times; N.B. beer and wine are now available.

### Auld Dubliner, The  *Pub Food*                    ▽ 21 | 21 | 19 | $22

**Long Beach** | Pike at Rainbow Harbor | 71 S. Pine Ave. (Ocean Blvd.) |
562-437-8300 | www.aulddubliner.com

Stop by this Long Beach pub "if you're in the mood for a Guinness" advise locals, but "don't miss the great Irish menu selections", including "traditional" salmon boxty, "winning" fish 'n' chips and shepherd's pie; with a "friendly staff", live music nightly and a bar "built and then shipped from Ireland", it's truly "transplanted from the old sod."

### Auntie Em's Kitchen  *American*                    - | - | - | I

**Eagle Rock** | 4616 Eagle Rock Blvd. (Corliss St.) | 323-259-6432 |
www.auntieemskitchen.com

It's the pies, cupcakes and brownies that keep folks lining up at the counter of this colorful Eagle Rock breakfast and lunch cafe, which also satisfies with scrambled eggs, sandwiches and salads made with seasonal produce, as well as cheeses from the attached marketplace; a prix fixe Farmers Market dinner (reservation-only) takes place once a month.

| | FOOD | DECOR | SERVICE | COST |
|---|---|---|---|---|

## Aunt Kizzy's Back Porch *Southern*  20 | 13 | 16 | $22

**Marina del Rey** | Villa Marina Mktpl. | 4325 Glencoe Ave. (Mindanao Way) | 310-578-1005 | www.auntkizzys.com

You can "replenish your carbs" and "cholesterol" at Marina del Rey's home of Southern "down-home soul food", where the "awesome" fried chicken and catfish "capture the spirit" of Dixie and the mac 'n' cheese "counts as a vegetable"; Sunday brunchers say the buffet "will be your one meal of the day", and advise dressing as neatly as the "church crowd" and heading early to the "rustic", "country" dining room to get first dibs on the "feast."

## Avenue *American*  23 | 20 | 20 | $51

**Manhattan Beach** | 1141 Manhattan Ave. (Manhattan Beach Blvd.) | 310-802-1973 | www.avenuemb.com

Some of the "most sophisticated food in the South Bay" brings Manhattan Beach gourmets to this New American where chef/co-owner Christian Shaffer (Auberge at Ojai) "surprises" with a "creative menu that changes monthly" – so it's best to "bring people who like to try new things"; both the "excellent" wines (half-price on Monday) and "lovely", understated dining room enhance the "romance", though some reviewers would like to see "better service for the price."

## A Votre Sante *Vegetarian*  20 | 13 | 18 | $23

**Brentwood** | 13016 San Vicente Blvd. (26th St.) | 310-451-1813 | www.avotresantela.com

"Delicious and healthy are not oxymorons" at this Brentwood "veggie standby" serving "hearty" salads and sandwiches as well as a handful of chicken dishes to a "groovy crowd"; although a few fret the furniture is "only functional" and the staff is middling, most agree it delivers a "different dining experience for natural foods" at a "reasonable" price.

## Axe Ⓜ *Californian*  22 | 18 | 19 | $38

**Venice** | 1009 Abbot Kinney Blvd. (bet. Brooks Ave. & B'way) | 310-664-9787 | www.axerestaurant.com

"Healthy hipsters hang out" at this Venice Californian for its "farm-fresh" dinners and "unique breakfasts" – starring a nine-grain pancake that's "worth the trek"; while some favor the "minimalist", backless furnishings, others aren't as keen on "sitting like a monk" while waiting out often "slow" service, and find the menu choices as "slim" as the surrounding "trendy Westsiders."

## Azami Ⓩ Ⓜ *Japanese*  – | – | – | E

**Hollywood** | 7160 Melrose Ave. (bet. Detroit St. & Formosa Ave.) | 323-939-3816 | www.azamisushi.net

This Hollywood sushi bar is notable not only for its omakase options (four- and seven-course available) but also for its female chef-owner, Niki Nakayama – a rarity in the local Japanese restaurant game – who prepares coveted catches such as satiny yellowtail carpaccio and special lobster rolls; the upscale yet low-key setting, decorated with woods and soft yellow walls, plays host to a clientele of dialed-in connoisseurs.

## Babalu *Californian*  20 | 17 | 18 | $26

**Santa Monica** | 1002 Montana Ave. (10th St.) | 310-395-2500

Dishing up "inventive, well-presented" Californian cuisine with a Caribbean twist, this "neighborhood place" "spices up" Santa Monica and sweetens it too with "outrageous homemade desserts" like the banana brownie cream pie; its "caring" (if somewhat "erratic") service and "tropical" decor contribute to a "hopping social scene", though "noisy" surroundings and "long wait times" are part of the package.

### ⊠ Babita Mexicuisine Ⓜ Mexican  `27` `14` `21` `$35`

**San Gabriel** | 1823 S. San Gabriel Blvd. (Norwood Pl.) | 626-288-7265
"No burritos or taquitos here", this mecca for "haute Mexican cuisine" by chef Roberto Berrelleza delivers a "superior", "sensual" dining experience that converts call "the best reason to go to San Gabriel"; true, its 10-table space in a "humble building" is "far from ideal", but combined with the "warm family service", it provides an "extremely unpretentious" backdrop for the "awesome" food.

### Baby Blues BBQ  *BBQ*  `22` `9` `18` `$20`

**Venice** | 444 Lincoln Blvd. (Rose Ave.) | 310-396-7675 |
www.babybluesbarbq.com
"Belly-busting" helpings of "first-class Carolina ribs", Memphis baby-backs and "succulent" shrimp in "tantalizing" sauces make for what good ol' boys and girls call the "ultimate Southern" vittles at this Venice BBQ joint; "get there late and you're waiting on the sidewalk with a lot of hungry folk", but appetites are appeased when the "hip" staff sets down the "reasonably priced" plates; P.S. it's currently "dry", pending a liquor license.

### Back Home in Lahaina  *Hawaiian*  `17` `14` `17` `$17`

**Carson** | 519 E. Carson St. (Grace Ave.) | 310-835-4014
**Manhattan Beach** | 916 N. Sepulveda Blvd. (10th St.) | 310-374-0111
www.backhomeinlahaina.com
"Casual enough for a drop-in, but exotic enough to be out of the ordinary", this South Bay Hawaiian duo serving fried chicken and slow-cooked pork that "broke da mouth" (to quote a Pidgin-speaking fan) offers "a little piece of the islands with the Spam to prove it!"; the "bang for the buck" impresses mainlanders and ex-islanders alike, though some chide that it's fairly "mediocre" and "cheesy as Waikiki."

### Back on the Beach  *American*  `14` `20` `15` `$21`

**Santa Monica** | 445 PCH (California Ave.) | 310-393-8282
"Sand, waves and volleyball" views are the main draw at this Santa Monica oceanfront American eatery, which is "best in the summer" when the "low-key" "brunch on the beach" showcases "all that is right in Southern California" – and inspires people to forgive "slow service", "aggressive" birds and "hit-or-miss" food while they eat with their "toes in the sand."

### Baja Fresh Mexican Grill  *Mexican*  `18` `10` `14` `$10`

**Third Street** | 8495 W. Third St. (La Cienega Blvd.) | 310-659-9500
**Beverly Hills** | 475 N. Beverly Dr. (Little Santa Monica Blvd.) | 310-858-6690
**Brentwood** | 11690 San Vicente Blvd. (Barrington Ave.) | 310-826-9166
**Marina del Rey** | Villa Marina Mktpl. | 13424 Maxella Ave. (Del Rey Ave.) |
310-578-2252
**Westwood** | Westwood Vill. | 10916 Lindbrook Ave. (Westwood Blvd.) |
310-208-3317
**Long Beach** | Los Altos Shopping Ctr. | 2090 Bellflower Blvd.
(bet. Abbeyfield St. & Britton Dr.) | 562-596-9080
**Pasadena** | 899 E. Del Mar Blvd. (Lake Ave.) | 626-792-0446

*(continued)*

**Baja Fresh Mexican Grill**

**Burbank** | Virgin Megastore Complex | 877 N. San Fernando Blvd. (Burbank Blvd.) | 818-841-4649

**Studio City** | Bistro Ctr. | 12930 Ventura Blvd. (Coldwater Canyon Ave.) | 818-995-4242

**Woodland Hills** | Winnetka Sq. | 19960 Ventura Blvd. (bet. Lubao & Penfield Aves.) | 818-888-3976

www.bajafresh.com

Additional locations throughout Southern California

"Always reliable at all locations" assert amigos of this "cheap and cheerful" chain, a "top-notch purveyor of not-quite-fast-food Mexican", including "favorite" fish tacos and "baj-eautiful" burritos; while the "surroundings are sterile" and some "can't understand the big following", it's often "healthier and tastier than other joints in the vicinity" (even if most choices are "definitely not low-fat").

**NEW Baleen Los Angeles** *American*  ▽ 22 | 24 | 17 | $39

**Redondo Beach** | Portofino Hotel & Yacht Club | 260 Portofino Way (Harbor Dr.) | 310-372-1202 | www.hotelportofino.com

Those who've sampled this Redondo Beach respite are "charmed" by its "beautiful" dining room with a "great view of the harbor", as well as indoor and outdoor fireplaces, following the multimillion-dollar remodel of the Portofino Hotel & Yacht Club; its "fine menu" of New American and seafood dishes is also up to snuff, though some say the service is "unacceptable for such prices."

**Bamboo** *Caribbean*  19 | 13 | 18 | $26

**Culver City** | 10835 Venice Blvd. (bet. Overland Ave. & Sepulveda Blvd.) | 310-287-0668 | www.bamboorestaurant.net

A taste of "the tropics" arrives via this "funky" Culver City Caribbean "find" where "fresh", "unpretentious" island fare (like jerk chicken and plantains) pleases even those with "picky palates"; there may be "no atmosphere to speak of" – although a new bar area might change that – but "accommodating" servers and "fair prices" still satisfy, especially in warm weather when you can "sit outside on the little patio."

**Bamboo Cuisine** *Chinese*  22 | 17 | 19 | $23

**Sherman Oaks** | 14010 Ventura Blvd. (bet. Hazeltine & Woodman Aves.) | 818-788-0202 | www.bamboocuisine.com

Locals lusting after "gourmet" Chinese declare this "popular" Sherman Oaks Mandarin a "winner" for its "thoughtfully prepared" renditions of "authentic" dishes – including a particularly "fabulous" black pepper chicken – "served up in hearty portions" on "large, round tables"; "efficient" servers work the understated room which remains "soothing" in spite of being "mobbed" with a "soccer mom" clientele, especially on "weekends."

**Bamboom** Ⓜ *Californian*  – | – | – | M

**Agoura Hills** | Whizin's Shopping Arcade | 28914 Roadside Dr. (Cornell St.) | 818-707-6226 | www.bamboombar.com

This glammed up, industrial-accented newcomer presents an "eclectic" menu including "not-traditional" sushi rolls (like the shrimp tempura Royale with Cheese) and such Cal cuisine as tobiko-topped seared salmon and "good Kobe beef burgers" with avocado; DJ sets, cushiony chairs and a patio with semiprivate, screened nooks keep the room "busy" and customers comfy, and the sushi bar stays open till 1 AM.

**Bandera** *American/Southwestern* | 22 | 20 | 20 | $35 |

**West LA** | 11700 Wilshire Blvd. (Barrington Ave.) | 310-477-3524 | www.hillstone.com

"Killer ribs" and "tender, tasty chicken" head up the Southwestern-American menu at these Corona del Mar and West LA "upscale brothers to Houston's", run by a "courteous" if sometimes "rushed" staff; at both, the "expensive" mojitos and other mixed drinks fuel the "singles scene" at the bar, while the "dark, clubby" dining room lends itself to dates (with the bonus of "no corkage" fee for BYO wine) once diners get through the "long waits" on the weekends.

**Banzai Sushi** *Japanese* | 22 | 16 | 19 | $35 |

**Calabasas** | 23508 Calabasas Rd. (Valley Circle Blvd.) | 818-222-5800 | www.banzaisushi.com

"Excellent sashimi" among a "diverse" menu of sushi, tempura and teppanyaki keeps Calabasas customers contented, especially since the dishes "don't come with Nobu-spheric prices"; the wooden, Japanese-style room and covered patio suit "weekday" dining, though it's also popular for "good takeout."

**NEW** **Baran** *Persian* | ∇ 20 | 22 | 16 | $23 |

**Westwood** | 1916 Westwood Blvd. (Missouri Ave.) | 310-475-4500

"There are cheaper places nearby" in Westwood's Little Persia, but this "relative newcomer to the skewer battle" grills up "mounds" of "just right" beef, chicken and baran (lamb chops) over a "heap of steaming rice", capping off the meal with exotic ice creams; its polished decor, soft lighting and nightly live organ music contribute to the "wonderful ambiance", though the service could use a boost to match the "pleasant" vibe.

**Barbara's at the Brewery** Ⓩ *Eclectic* | ∇ 15 | 13 | 14 | $19 |

**Downtown** | Brewery Art Complex | 620 Moulton Ave. (Main St.) | 323-221-9204 | www.bwestcatering.com

At Downtown's "hidden" haven for the "super-hip" in an artists' residential colony, the Eclectic, daily changing cuisine is "secondary" to the "beyond-cool" factor of "just knowing about it"; meanwhile, the semi-industrial space, staffed by "friendly" servers and decorated with rotating gallery displays, inspires less awestruck visitors to dub it "kinda like *Cheers* for artists."

**Bar Celona** *Spanish* | 16 | 19 | 16 | $30 |

**Pasadena** | 46 E. Colorado Blvd. (bet. Fair Oaks & Raymond Aves.) | 626-405-1000 | www.barcelonapasadena.com

A "beautiful bar", two outdoor patios and nightly DJs add up to an "awesome atmosphere" at this "energetic" Spanish tapas bar that habitués call "a real addition to the Pasadena scene"; still, while the sangria, "interesting selection of wines by the glass" and live flamenco guitar on Tuesdays all add flavor, many diners describe the service as "uninspired" and the dishes as "decent but not fantastic", with a resulting "out-of-sync" tab.

| | FOOD | DECOR | SERVICE | COST |
|---|---|---|---|---|

**Barefoot Bar & Grill** *Californian/Eclectic* | 18 | 20 | 19 | $32 |

**Third Street** | 8722 W. Third St. (bet. George Burns Rd. & Robertson Blvd.) | 310-276-6223 | www.barefootrestaurant.com

"Meet a doctor or nurse" from nearby Cedars-Sinai at this Cal-Eclectic Third Street "haunt" known for its "pretty patio" and "unpretentious" dining room with an upstairs that plays host to "special parties"; apart from the atmosphere, however, customers say the quality of the service varies, and the salads, pastas and "bar bites" on the menu tend to make for "average" meals.

**NEW Bar Hayama** 🗷 *Japanese* | - | - | - | M |

**West LA** | 1803 Sawtelle Blvd. (Nebraska Ave.) | 310-235-2000 | www.bar-hayama.com

In the Westside equivalent of Little Tokyo, California Sushi Academy head Frank Toshi Sugiura has opened a trendy Japanese in Sushi Sasabune's former home, which has been remodeled into an elegant multisection space with a sake bar, sushi bar, *kozara* (small plate) bar and an outdoor fire pit; though much of the cooking is traditional, many of the dishes are built around macrobiotic principles.

**Barney Greengrass** *Deli* | 21 | 17 | 16 | $32 |

**Beverly Hills** | Barneys New York | 9570 Wilshire Blvd., 5th fl. (bet. Camden & Peck Drs.) | 310-777-5877

It's "like NYC with palm trees" attest noshers about this "bustling" Beverly Hills deli above Barneys department store, serving "first-rate food" like smoked sturgeon and "terrific sable" topping "real" bagels (flown in from Manhattan's H&H) for an "expensive" "fab breakfast", lunch or Sunday brunch; the terrace allows a peek at the Hollywood sign ("what a view!") and often the latest "'it' girl or boy", though critics cite "tired" decor (it "gets a higher score if you count the patrons") and service with a schmear of "attitude."

**Barney's Gourmet Hamburgers** *Hamburgers* | 21 | 11 | 16 | $15 |

**Brentwood** | 11660 San Vicente Blvd. (bet. Darlington & Mayfield Aves.) | 310-447-6000

**Brentwood** | Brentwood Country Mart | 225 26th St. (San Vicente Blvd.) | 310-899-0133

**NEW Sherman Oaks** | Westfield Fashion Sq. | 14006 Riverside Dr. (Woodman Ave.) | 818-808-0680
www.barneyshamburgers.com

"Thick, juicy burgers that could make a vegetarian have second thoughts" (though many of them already "love the veggie" patties) matched with a range of "fresh toppings", "spicy", "addictive" curly fries and "delicious old-style" milkshakes draw devotees to this "casual" chain out of San Francisco with two Brentwood locations (the one in the Country Mart has no indoor seating, the other "can be a zoo") and a Fashion Square mall storefront in Sherman Oaks; though the servers are "upbeat", "when they're busy, it can take a while."

**Barsac Brasserie** 🗷 *Californian/French* | ▽ 23 | 19 | 23 | $41 |

**North Hollywood** | 4212 Lankershim Blvd. (bet. Moorpark St. & Ventura Blvd.) | 818-760-7081 | www.barsac.com

"Charming" owners Lisa Long – "she's the bomb" – and James Saliba "make you feel at home" at their "sophisticated", longstanding Cal-French in NoHo serving "satisfying" fare (frequently prepared by one of their European visiting chefs); between the open kitchen and the martini bar, it's "buzzing at lunch" with entertainment execs and lively later on for "grown-up drinks."

**Basix Cafe** *Californian/Italian*                18 | 14 | 18 | $24

**West Hollywood** | 8333 Santa Monica Blvd. (N. Flores St.) | 323-848-2460 | www.basixcafe.com

"Skinny" mesquite-grilled pizzas, soups and salads head up the "healthy", "easy-listening" Cal-Italian menu at this "inexpensive" "local hang" (in the Marix family) with a Sunday-brunch following; its "fantastic blood orange martinis" are also a draw with the after-work crowd, many of whom enjoy WeHo's "beautiful boy" passersby and the patio's "celebrity sightings" more than the "solid" fare and "competent" but "just a little slow" staff.

**BBC by the Sea** *Mediterranean*              ▽ 20 | 14 | 17 | $20

**NEW** **Malibu** | 22935 PCH (by Malibu Pier) | 310-456-9411

**BBC Cafe** *Mediterranean*

**(aka Bistro Baguette Cafe)**

**Beverly Hills** | 8620 Wilshire Blvd. (Stanley Dr.) | 310-855-0055 | www.bbccafe.com

Serving kosher cuisine with a Mediterranean focus, this duo provides "delicious" eats that even those on unrestricted diets "crave"; they're "family-friendly" with outdoor seating, plus the "convenient" Beverly Hills location offers beer and wine, while the BYO Malibu branch (kosher bottles only) has no corkage fee; N.B. closes at 8 PM in the winter on PCH, and both are closed weekly for Shabbat (beginning 3 PM Friday).

**BCD Tofu House** *Korean*                    20 | 10 | 12 | $15

**Downtown** | 1201 S. Los Angeles St. (12th St.) | 213-746-2525 🅢
**Koreatown** | 3575 Wilshire Blvd. (Kingsley Ave.) |
213-382-6677 ◑
**Koreatown** | 869 S. Western Ave. (9th St.) | 213-380-3807 ◑
**Cerritos** | 11818 South St. (Pioneer Blvd.) | 562-809-8098
**Torrance** | 1607 Sepulveda Blvd. (Western Ave.) | 310-534-3480
**Reseda** | 18044 Saticoy St. (Lindley Ave.) | 818-342-3535 ◑
**Rowland Heights** | 1731 Fullerton Rd. (Colima Rd.) | 626-964-7073 ◑
www.bcdtofu.com

The "spicy" "hot pots" "actually make tofu taste good" assure champions of this Korean chain whose specialty soup, along with selections like BBQ ribs and bibimbop, provide the "perfect hangover cure" or "late-night fix" (especially at the 24/7 Koreatown and Garden Grove locations); since it's so "cheap", few complain about the "cafeteria" setting and a staff that "speaks little English" and may "rush you around" during peak times.

**Beacon** *Pan-Asian*                         22 | 17 | 20 | $37

**Culver City** | Helms Bldg. | 3280 Helms Ave. (Washington Blvd.) | 310-838-7500 | www.beacon-la.com

An "innovator" in Culver City's increasingly "hot" culinary scene, this "stylish" Pan-Asian offers a "fantastic collection of little tastes" and larger plates ("love the miso cod") from "brilliant" chefs/co-owners Kazuto Matsusaka and Vicki Fan; while the high-ceilinged, "modern" room strikes some as too "spartan" and "noisy", many are soothed by the two outdoor patios, "reasonable prices" and "unpretentious" service.

| | FOOD | DECOR | SERVICE | COST |
|---|---|---|---|---|

### Beau Rivage  *Mediterranean*

| 20 | 23 | 20 | $49 |

**Malibu** | 26025 PCH (Corral Canyon Rd.) | 310-456-5733 |
www.beaurivagerestaurant.com

"Lovely views of the Malibu surf" ("if you're in the right seats") and a
"romantic" albeit "damp-smelling" wine cellar enhance the "old-world
charm" of this "gorgeous" Mediterranean "getaway"; the food is
largely "well-prepared", though some "wish" that it could better
match the scenery and "expense", and that the staff could smooth out
the sometimes "uneven" service.

### Beckham Grill  *American*

| 18 | 18 | 18 | $35 |

**Pasadena** | 77 W. Walnut St. (Fair Oaks Ave.) | 626-796-3399 |
www.beckhamgrill.com

While it has a "U.K." feel, this Pasadena pub specializes in American
"Sunday-dinner comfort food", including the "classic prime rib" for
steak seekers on a "middle-class" budget; sure, it's accommodating as
your "favorite old chair", though seeing as it opened in 1978 (well before David Beckham knew how to bend it), some beef eaters "would
appreciate a little updating" to "ye olde" decor.

### Beechwood  *American*

| 20 | 23 | 18 | $38 |

**Venice** | 822 Washington Blvd. (Abbot Kinney Blvd.) | 310-448-8884 |
www.beechwoodrestaurant.com

"More than just a trendy place for beautiful slackers", this "mod-
ernist lodge" in Venice, complete with a "swanky" lounge and a fire
pit outside on the patio, delivers simple but "flavorful" New American
dishes (including "can't-miss" sweet potato fries) both at the bar
and in the "quieter" back room; on the downside, servers can be
"too cool for school", and most agree the "food is secondary" to
the scene.

### Bel-Air Bar & Grill  *Californian*

| 19 | 19 | 20 | $45 |

**Bel-Air** | 662 N. Sepulveda Blvd. (bet. Moraga Dr. & Ovada Pl.) |
310-440-5544 | www.belairbarandgrill.com

"Convenient" for "Bel-Air folks", "Westside/Valley" lunch dates and
"post-Getty retreats", this "upscale" "neighborhood" eatery offers
"pleasant" environs – notably the "lovely heated patio" – to dig into
sirloin chili and chopped vegetable salad among other "dependable"
Californian dishes; the "attention of the owners" and bartenders who
"know their drinks" appeals to the "Hollywood royalty" in attendance,
though doubters dis the "uninviting" entrance ("advice: put lots of
potted trees in front") and "wish the average age" of the diners were
"lower than 70."

### Bella Cucina Italiana  *Italian*

| 19 | 19 | 18 | $36 |

**Hollywood** | 1708 N. Las Palmas Ave. (Hollywood Blvd.) | 323-468-8815 |
www.dolcegroup.com

"Part of the booming Hollywood scene", this Southern Italian by the
Dolce Group dishes up "tasty" fare, along with robust helpings of
"celeb sightings" and "strong drinks", in an easy location to "start off
the night"; despite its warm touches of exposed brick and dark woods,
critics say you'll still "feel like you're trying to have dinner in the
middle of a disco" due to the "jammed" room and "cute" but "cooler-
than-thou" staff.

|  | FOOD | DECOR | SERVICE | COST |
|---|---|---|---|---|

### NEW Bella Roma SPQR 🗷 Ⓜ *Italian*  — | — | — | M

**Pico-Robertson** | 1513 S. Robertson Blvd. (Horner St.) | 310-277-7662
Situated on an odd strip of Robertson just south of Pico, chef-owner Roberto Amico's understated Roman with simple but comfortable wood-and-fabric decor has found a quick following among locals hungry for a reasonably authentic Italian cafe-bar experience; its well-priced menu offers freshly rolled and cut pasta and a wide selection of salumi and tramezzini, as well as a strong espresso.

### Bellavino Wine Bar 🗷 *Eclectic*  ▽ 21 | 19 | 21 | $43

**Westlake Village** | 3709 E. Thousand Oaks Blvd. (2 blocks west of Westlake Blvd.) | 805-557-0202 | www.bellavinowinebar.com
"Eclectic" dishes – ranging from Tasmanian barramundi to Kobe beef burgers – join up with a "first-class wine selection" at this Westlake "hideaway"; though most agree it's "pricey", the "heavenly" cheese board, "pleasant" staff and "sophisticated but not pretentious" ambiance make it an "area favorite."

### Belmont Brewing Co. *American*  18 | 19 | 18 | $24

**Long Beach** | 25 39th Pl. (1 block south of Ocean Blvd.) | 562-433-3891 | www.belmontbrewing.com
"Terrific" ocean views distinguish this Long Beach American brewpub from other SoCal competitors; the menu focuses on simple seafood – "enjoy beer-battered fish 'n' chips with a snakebite" (half-cider, half-lager) – as well as martinis and "wonderful" small-batch beers, and while service can be "so-so", the bar is a "friendly" place to hang.

### 🅩 Belvedere, The *American*  25 | 27 | 26 | $72

**Beverly Hills** | Peninsula Hotel of Beverly Hills | 9882 S. Santa Monica Blvd. (Wilshire Blvd.) | 310-788-2306 | www.peninsula.com
It's the *grand cru classé* of LA hotel restaurants" praise posh visitors to this "exceptional" Beverly Hills "power place" where the breakfasts are "oh-so-cool", the people-watching is "intense" ("don't be surprised to be seated next to Nancy Reagan") and the "punctilious" servers treat guests "like royalty"; chef Sean Hardy prepares an "exquisite" New American menu with "favorites like truffle mac 'n' cheese" that make surveyors sing "o to be on an expense account"; N.B. high tea is served at 2:30 and 5 PM in the Living Room.

### Benihana *Japanese*  18 | 16 | 19 | $36

**Beverly Hills** | 38 N. La Cienega Blvd. (Wilshire Blvd.) | 323-655-7311
**Santa Monica** | 1447 Fourth St. (Santa Monica Blvd.) | 310-260-1423
**Ontario** | 3760 E. Inland Empire Blvd. (N. Haven Ave.) | 909-483-0937
**Encino** | 16226 Ventura Blvd. (bet. Libbet & Woodley Aves.) | 818-788-7121
**City of Industry** | Plaza at Puente Hills | 17877 Gale Ave. (Fullerton Rd.) | 626-912-8784
www.benihana.com
"Kitsch"-hounds and their kids "still enjoy the tableside theatrics" performed by "knife-tossing", steak-sizzling teppanyaki chefs who roll out all their "shrimp tricks and high jinks" for "office lunches, birthdays" and "tourist" outings at these Japanese chain links (some of which also serve sushi); while the jaded jeer "1974 called and wants its restaurant back", the general limit for tolerant types is "once a year", since it "feels repetitive", the food is "decent" but "not sensational" and "you leave smelling like a barbecue."

| | FOOD | DECOR | SERVICE | COST |
|---|---|---|---|---|

### Benley Vietnamese Kitchen 🖪 *Vietnamese*  ▽ 26 | 16 | 24 | $22

**Long Beach** | 8191 E. Wardlow Rd. (Los Alamitos Blvd.) | 562-596-8130
"Lively, beautifully balanced" flavors earn raves for this "outstanding" Vietnamese BYO in Long Beach, which offers "best-in-the-area" pho, specialty shaken beef and "exceptional desserts"; despite the "minor setback" of what critics call a "cramped, zero-decor" space, it still "sparkles" in the eyes of admirers who appreciate its "reasonable prices" and an "A+" staff that "makes you feel like the owner's best friend."

### Berri's Pizza Cafe *Pizza*  17 | 17 | 15 | $25

**Third Street** | 8412 W. Third St. (S. Orlando Ave.) | 323-852-0642 ◗
**Playa del Rey** | 8415 Pershing Dr. (Manchester Ave.) | 310-823-6658
While "neither truly traditional, nor cheap", this pizza pair satisfies with "good", "gooey" pies anchoring what samplers say is a largely "mediocre" Italian menu; the Playa del Rey location provides a "coastal comfort zone", and the Third Street original offers "after-the-club" eats till 4 AM nightly, though at both "indifferent" service is the norm.

### Big Mama's Rib Shack 🅜 *BBQ/Soul Food*  ▽ 20 | 13 | 17 | $22

**Pasadena** | 1453 N. Lake Ave. (Rio Grande St.) | 626-797-1792 | www.bigmamas-ribshack.com
"If the ribs don't get you, the many sides will" at this "authentic" soul food and BBQ "joint" in Pasadena, serving "huge portions" of smoked beef and "amazing" fried chicken inside a colorful if "strange" interior; faultfinders cluck, however, "when the restaurant's busy, the service suffers."

### Billingsley's *Steak*  14 | 10 | 19 | $24

**West LA** | 11326 W. Pico Blvd. (Sawtelle Blvd.) | 310-477-1426 | www.billingsleysrestaurant.com
A "blast from the past" opened by Barbara Billingsley's husband in 1946, this West LA "place for regular Joes to get a steak" is known for its "veteran waitresses" and "terrific value", particularly during the daily "early-bird dinners"; even though the red-booth decor "hasn't changed one bit in 50 years" according to fans, it's "somehow appropriate", so bring "a few of your best booze-addled blue-haired-friends" and fulfill your "meat-and-potatoes" "cravings."

### BIN 8945 ◗🅜 *European*  21 | 16 | 20 | $51

**West Hollywood** | 8945 Santa Monica Blvd. (N. Robertson Blvd.) | 310-550-8945 | www.bin8945.com
WeHo wine lovers call this contemporary European bistro a "hidden treasure", with its "incredible" 1200-bottle cellar, "grazey apps" and an "outgoing" owner-sommelier who "knows his stuff" when it comes to pairings; a new chef "has made large improvements" to the "pricey" menu, but unfortunately can't remedy the sometimes "noisy" street-side patio seating or overly "snug" quarters.

### Bistro de la Gare 🅜 *French*  20 | 18 | 19 | $39

**South Pasadena** | 921 Meridian Ave. (bet. El Centro & Mission Sts.) | 626-799-8828 | www.bistrodelagare.com
For "Parisian dining without the smoke and attitude" hungry souls hop the metro Gold Line to South Pasadena for "satisfying" bistro fare (like sautéed halibut and filet mignon with Roquefort sauce) at "reasonable prices"; its "deep, soothing colors" and "cute exterior" with patio

seating blend well with the "idyllic" neighborhood and "those French waiters make any dish sound delish", so although some tut that it's "too loud to have a conversation", the new liquor license may help take the edge off.

**Z Bistro 45** M *Californian*  26 | 23 | 24 | $55

**Pasadena** | 45 S. Mentor Ave. (bet. Colorado Blvd. & Green St.) | 626-795-2478 | www.bistro45.com

"Simple and superb" French-accented Californian cuisine pairs up with a "spectacular" wine list for a "top-of-the-line" taste of "Napa in Pasadena" at this "hidden jewel" set in a "warm", renovated 1939 building that offers "alfresco dining" on the terrace; "consummate host" and owner Robert Simon and his "gracious" staff "remember the regulars", so although some suggest it's "coasting" on reputation, many return to indulge in a "worthwhile and satisfying splurge."

**Z Bistro Garden at Coldwater, The** *Continental*  20 | 26 | 23 | $52

**Studio City** | 12950 Ventura Blvd. (Coldwater Canyon Ave.) | 818-501-0202 | www.bistrogarden.com

Inside "one of the prettiest dining rooms in the San Fernando Valley" – "bright and airy during the day and lovely at night" – the piano player "always sets a romantic mood" and the staff "treats you well" purr patrons of this "costly but impressive" Continental; while it provides "reliably good, if not the most inventive" cooking, even those who find the menu "stale" (and "as old as most of the diners") agree that the "amazing" "chocolate soufflé is the topper."

**Z Bistro K** S M *Eclectic*  26 | 16 | 20 | $45

**South Pasadena** | 1000 Fremont Ave. (El Centro St.) | 626-799-5052

Fans assure that "foodies will love" the "culinary extravaganza" of "vibrant" Eclectic dishes, including sweetbread egg rolls and bubble gum ice cream, at this South Pasadena "surprise"; despite its "understaffed", "tight quarters" and "experimental" eats that aren't for everyone, most are "excited" to encounter such "big-city dining in the 'burbs" with tremendous "bang for the buck" and the bonus of "free corkage."

**Bistro Provence** S *French*  22 | 18 | 20 | $37

**Burbank** | Lakeside Ctr. | 345 N. Pass Ave. (Rte. 134) | 818-840-9050 | www.bistroprovence.net

"A nice bit of France" comes to "plain ol' Burbank" at this "true find" where chef-owner Miki Zivkovic prepares "delightful" dishes for a "bargain" and an "engaging staff" enhances the "warm" if "incongruous" setting ("yes, they put a high-end bistro in a Vons strip mall – deal with it"); while the "loud and crowded" dining room cramps some folks' style, "that's the price of popularity" for guests who attest it's "well worth the trouble to get a reservation."

**Bistro 767** S M *Californian*  ▽ 22 | 20 | 21 | $44

**Rolling Hills** | 767 Deep Valley Dr. (bet. Drybank & Roxcove Drs.) | 310-265-0914 | www.bistro767.com

"Innovative" cooking and a "thoughtful wine list" create a "better-than-average" Californian culinary experience in Rolling Hills, where regulars congregate for cocktails like the Zebratini and signatures

| | FOOD | DECOR | SERVICE | COST |
|---|---|---|---|---|

including grilled halibut with slow-cooked pork belly; though both the menu and banquette seating are "limited", its "inviting" looks and "attentive" service make it a "real find" on the Peninsula.

### Bistro 31 🛣 *Californian* ▽ 23 17 21 $28

**Santa Monica** | Art Institute of Los Angeles | 2900 31st St. (Ocean Park Blvd.) | 310-314-6057

"The students are the masters" at this Santa Monica training ground for culinary up-and-comers at the Art Institute, where the seasonal Californian menu is "always interesting" and mostly "well prepared", especially given the "bargain" prices; the servers are "never perfect, but always try hard" (after all, they're "being graded") and there's no corkage for BYO, which leaves only one lingering complaint: "too bad they're only open limited hours" – Monday–Wednesday, with a varied seasonal schedule.

### Bite ● *Pan-Asian* ▽ 16 16 16 $28

**Marina del Rey** | 30 Washington Blvd. (Pacific Ave.) | 310-305-4010 | www.bitestreetfood.com

An array of Pan-Asian plates, such as "solid" sushi, skewers and Saigon BBQ ribs, makes up the "street food"–oriented menu that's paired with a variety of martinis at this clubby, Buddha-decorated restaurant in Marina del Rey, which seduces some with a "romantic" patio and fire pit; unfortunately, a number of nibblers say the "exotic" concept sounds "terrific on paper" but goes "downhill" from there.

### BJ's *Pub Food* 17 16 16 $19

**Cerritos** | 11101 183rd St. (I-605) | 562-467-0850
**Westwood** | 939 Broxton Ave. (bet. Le Conte & Weyburn Aves.) | 310-209-7475 ●
**Long Beach** | 5258 E. Second St. (bet. Covina & La Verne Aves.) | 562-439-8181
**Moreno Valley** | 22920 Centerpoint Dr. (Frederick St.) | 951-571-9370
**Arcadia** | 400 E. Huntington Dr. (Gateway Dr.) | 626-462-1494 ●
**Burbank** | 107 S. First St. (Olive Ave.) | 818-557-0881 ●
**Woodland Hills** | 6424 Canoga Ave. (bet. Erwin St. & Victory Blvd.) | 818-340-1748 ●
**West Covina** | Eastland Shopping Ctr. | 2917 E. Eastland Center Dr. (Barranca St.) | 626-858-0054
**Westlake Village** | 3955 E. Thousand Oaks Blvd. (Westlake Blvd.) | 805-497-9393
**Valencia** | Valencia Town Ctr. | 24320 Town Center Dr. (McBean Pkwy.) | 661-288-1299 ●
www.bjsbrewhouse.com
Additional locations throughout Southern California

"If you can stand the noise" you'll score "microbrews with macro taste" (even at locations without an attached brewery) and "satisfying munchies" like "gourmet" deep-dish pizzas and the "giant", "life-changing" 'pizookie' (a warm cookie topped with ice cream) that will "make you obese instantly" at these "high-energy" American pubs with outposts all over Southern California; they frequently get "jammed with students" (both drinking and serving), so customers say "long waits" and "lacking service" often go with the suds.

|  | FOOD | DECOR | SERVICE | COST |
|---|---|---|---|---|

### Blair's *American* — 23 | 18 | 21 | $42

**Silver Lake** | 2903 Rowena Ave. (bet. Glendale & Hyperion Blvds.) |
323-660-1882 | www.blairsrestaurant.com

"Wonderfully creative" New American fare, such as "superior" truffled
mac 'n' cheese, distinguishes this "fine" Silver Laker "masquerading as
a neighborhood restaurant"; its "warm" staff and a "stylish", recently
expanded space enhance the allure for its "cool" clientele, who now go
for breakfast and brunch in addition to "simple" yet "sophisticated"
dinners – though a few still long for "full liquor service" at the bar.

### bld *American* — 21 | 18 | 19 | $33

**Beverly Boulevard** | 7450 Beverly Blvd. (N. Vista St.) | 323-930-9744 |
www.bldrestaurant.com

Beverly Boulevard habitués "love the breakfast" (with "superb" pancakes) at chef/co-owner Neal Fraser's "chicer, cheaper" New
American cousin to Grace; although some find the service "needs improvement" and call the "diner-inspired gourmet food" a little "less exciting at dinner", the "modern" dining room is "bright with lots of
windows", adding to its "refreshing" appeal.

### NEW Bloom Cafe *American/Californian* — ▽ 23 | 20 | 17 | $18

**Mid-City** | 5544 W. Pico Blvd. (S. Sierra Bonita Ave.) | 323-934-6900 |
www.go2bloom.com

This Californian–New American is a "welcome addition" to the Mid-
City neighborhood with its "cheery, modern" decor and "contemporary vibe" say granola groupies geared up for the "health-friendly" fare
of organic eggs, "refreshingly light and fluffy" lemon pancakes, "terrific salads" and organically produced meats; since it still needs to
"work on service", some caution "don't be in a hurry."

### Blossom 🗷 *Vietnamese* — ▽ 22 | 15 | 16 | $15

**Downtown** | 426 S. Main St. (Winston St.) | 213-623-1973 |
www.blossomrestaurant.com

"Delectable" Vietnamese food that's "not dumbed down for the main-
stream" is matched with a variety of house teas at this liquor-free
Downtowner; the "prices can't be beat", though the "shoebox"
dining room and "dodgy" (but "gentrifying") area mean takeout
often "works best."

### Blowfish Sushi To Die For *Japanese* — 20 | 23 | 18 | $45

**West Hollywood** | 9229 W. Sunset Blvd. (bet. Doheny Rd. & Sierra Dr.) |
310-887-3848 | www.blowfishsushi.com

"Sleek" contemporary Tokyo decor, complete with plasma TVs playing
Japanimation, lends this West Hollywood sushi spot (co-owned by
Julian Lennon) an "electric", "clublike" energy that often outshines the
food itself; diners call the rolls "above average" but "not revolution-
ary", commenting that the management caters to "hipsters" rather
than "foodies", but agree the sake cocktails and location "give it an
edge for a pre-bar-hopping dinner."

### Blue Hen *Vietnamese* — ▽ 16 | 13 | 15 | $18

**Eagle Rock** | 1743 Colorado Blvd. (Argus Dr.) | 323-982-9900 |
www.eatatbluehen.com

"Affordable", "light" Vietnamese dishes "prepared with organic" and
local ingredients draw the "digerati, the literati" and other "laid-back"

Eagle Rockers to this "tiny" eatery "in the middle of an ugly strip mall"; although some find the food "bland", others tout that it's as "tasty as the seats are uncomfortable (yummy, but ouch!)."

### blue on blue *American*                              | 18 | 23 | 19 | $43 |

**Beverly Hills** | Avalon Hotel | 9400 W. Olympic Blvd. (Cañon Dr.) | 310-407-7791 | www.avalonbeverlyhills.com

"The pool just adds that special something" and the curtained cabanas lend extra "intimacy" (plus a "Lucy-and-Ricky old-Hollywood" feel) to dining and downing mojitos at this "chic" restaurant on the ground floor of Beverly Hills' Avalon Hotel, where "glam patrons" nibble on seasonal New American dishes that bring "loads of flavor without being too complicated"; a seven-course tasting at the chef's table is also an option, but although the "free valet parking helps", a few fret that it's "too expensive" and best for "apps and drinks."

### ☑ NEW Blue Velvet *American*                         | 22 | 26 | 21 | $56 |

**Downtown** | The Flat | 750 S. Garland Ave. (bet. 8th & 7th Sts.) | 213-239-0061 | www.bluevelvetrestaurant.com

This "techno-glam" Downtown New American promises to "give the Standard a run for its money" as it "blows away" the crowd with a "stunning", environmentally savvy design boasting skyline views (and "must-see" restrooms); encouragingly, the kitchen succeeds as well with "innovative" cuisine that's a "sensory indulgence", elevated by a "knowledgeable" sommelier and "attentive" staff.

### Bluewater Grill *American/Seafood*                   | 20 | 18 | 19 | $33 |

**Redondo Beach** | King Harbor Marina | 665 N. Harbor Dr. (Beryl St.) | 310-318-3474 | www.bluewatergrill.com

These "unfussified" waterside fish houses in Newport and Redondo turn out "fresh", "respectable" seafood accompanied by "typical starch sides and coleslaw"; fans give them "a high fin for value", "good cheer" and "beautiful views" ("eye the yachts of the rich and not famous"), so they're "great for families" or "come-as-you-are" "first dates"; N.B. the Santa Ana location has closed, and a new branch is set to open in Tustin.

### Blvd, The *Californian*                               | 21 | 24 | 22 | $57 |

**Beverly Hills** | Beverly Wilshire, A Four Seasons Hotel | 9500 Wilshire Blvd. (Rodeo Dr.) | 310-385-3901 | www.fourseasons.com

"Tables looking out onto Rodeo Drive" afford a fine view of the "Tiffany & Co. crowd" at this "civilized", "modern" deco-style stop in the Beverly Wilshire, which offers "spot-on" service and "high-end" Cal cuisine; beyond its "business breakfasts" and "fab alfresco" lunches, the lustrous onyx bar and live jazz on Friday and Saturday set the mood for "quite a scene on the weekends."

### Boa *Steak*                                           | 23 | 24 | 21 | $58 |

**West Hollywood** | Grafton Hotel | 8462 W. Sunset Blvd. (La Cienega Blvd.) | 323-650-8383
**Santa Monica** | 101 Santa Monica Blvd. (Ocean Blvd.) | 310-899-4466
www.innovativedining.com

"Swanky" wood-and-leather decor and "pretty people" define both the West Hollywood and Santa Monica locations of this "über-California" steakhouse where "excellent" dry-aged cuts are prepared with an "extensive choice of rubs and sauces", paired with "amazing" wines and complemented by numerous veggie choices; "intelligent" servers help the "noisy" dining rooms run smoothly, even though the "extremely high prices" are a snag for some; P.S. you can shake the markup at "Sunday's half-price bottle night."

### boé  *American*   ▽ 14 | 19 | 15 | $40

**Beverly Hills** | The Crescent | 403 N. Crescent Dr. (Brighton Way) | 310-247-0505 | www.crescentbh.com

This "Euro-style" hotel hang in Beverly Hills opens up to a mostly outdoor, "sleek" dining venue with a "loungey" atmosphere and New American plates like garlic fries and "baby hamburgers at grown-up prices"; despite the "fabulous drinks", however, critics call the fare "uninspired" and advise "a few more seats and heat lamps could help."

### Boiling Pot  *Japanese*   ▽ 16 | 16 | 15 | $28

**Pasadena** | 345 S. Lake Ave. (E. Del Mar Blvd.) | 626-796-8870

Providing "simple", "cook-it-yourself" "hot-pot" meals that "fog the windows on a cold day", this casual Japanese is convenient if you're a shabu-shabu buff "living in Pasadena"; while some find it "romantic", however, authenticity-seekers assert that "better and cheaper" can be found elsewhere, and still others ask "why work so hard when you're paying this much for dinner?"

### Bombay Bite  *Indian*   21 | 17 | 18 | $21

**Westwood** | 1051 Gayley Ave. (bet. Le Conte & Weyburn Aves.) | 310-824-1046 | www.bombaybite.com

Naan noshers call this "small", "inviting" Indian a "powerhouse" for "wonderful", "well-priced" dishes and ambiance that's a "cut above" other Westwood restaurants; service can be a little "slow" and the food could use "more pizzazz", but most conclude that the overall "quality meets your expectations."

### ☒ Bombay Cafe  *Indian*   23 | 15 | 19 | $29

**West LA** | 12021 W. Pico Blvd. (Bundy Dr.) | 310-473-3388 | www.bombaycafe-la.com

"Sensational" Indian fare exhibiting a "fine use of spices" and a staff that "helps first-timers" make this "affordable" West LA "favorite" "the place to go for curry with friends", its "colonial-outpost" looks notwithstanding; while a few worry that new owners "won't keep up the high standards", regulars say they "seem to have worked out the tension."

### Bombay Palace  *Indian*   21 | 20 | 19 | $35

**Beverly Hills** | 8690 Wilshire Blvd. (bet. Hamel & Willaman Drs.) | 310-659-9944

"Now that's Indian" declare enthusiasts of this "attractive", "low-key place" in Beverly Hills, serving "upscale", "flavorful" dinners as well as a lunch buffet that's "a must"; the service prompts a mixed response, though, as some rate it "reliable" and others feel "snubbed."

### NEW  Bondi BBQ   - | - | - | I
### Australian Style  *Australian/BBQ*

**Venice** | 46 Windward Ave. (Pacific Ave.) | 310-392-3809

There's nothing that passes for decor at this Venice beach-adjacent Australian-style BBQ joint, with its handful of tables and a counter that does a lot of takeout; its babybacks, beef ribs, chicken and shrimp on the barbie – meaning they're charcoal-grilled rather than smoked – are served with a characteristically sweet-and-vinegar-tart sauce.

### Boneyard Bistro *BBQ*

20 | 15 | 20 | $33

**Sherman Oaks** | 13539 Ventura Blvd. (2 blocks east of Woodman Ave.) | 818-906-7427 | www.boneyardbistro.com

"Solid BBQ" meets "nouveau bistro" at this Sherman Oaks grill where the ribs are "tasty" and the "fried mac 'n' cheese can't be beat", especially when paired with an ale from the "outrageous" beer list; the "down-to-earth" staff largely keeps the "loud" crowd happy, though dissenters brand it "expensive for what it is" and snort "trendy and 'cue don't always work."

### Bono's *Californian*

21 | 21 | 18 | $38

**Long Beach** | 4901 E. Second St. (St. Joseph Ave.) | 562-434-9501 | www.bonoslongbeach.com

This "classy joint" owned by Christy Bono serves "creative", "seasonal" Californian cuisine and "killer" cocktails to "Long Beach's finest"; though many comment the cuisine is "not what the hype suggests" and the service is "spotty", its "open-air" "Miami"–style setting in "the heart of Belmont Shore" offers a "prime location" for "people-watching" and a "stroll after dinner."

### Bora Bora Ⓜ *Californian/Polynesian*

▽ 23 | 20 | 22 | $35

**Manhattan Beach** | 3505 Highland Ave. (35th St.) | 310-545-6464

"Island-spicy ribs" and "artery-clogging sides" are the hallmarks of the Cal-Polynesian menu at this "reasonably priced" Manhattan Beach "gem" presided over by "personable owners"; its "hard-to-find" locale, large booths and low lighting (what some call "trip-over-something dark") create an "intimate" feel for "dates."

### Border Grill *Mexican*

22 | 18 | 19 | $33

**Santa Monica** | 1445 Fourth St. (bet. B'way & Santa Monica Blvd.) | 310-451-1655 | www.bordergrill.com

The "colorful", "high-end" Mexican dishes and "mean margaritas" are "still killer" "after all these years" at Santa Monica's "loud" and "lively" longtimer, although some say both the "modern" menu and "whimsical decor" "could use an update" to stay "innovative"; fortunately when celeb owners Susan Feniger and Mary Sue Milliken "hold court" on-site and oversee the ops, it maintains the "vibrant" energy that made it "famous" in the first place.

### Bossa Nova *Brazilian*

21 | 13 | 17 | $22

**Hollywood** | 7181 W. Sunset Blvd. (Formosa Ave.) | 323-436-7999 ◑
**Pico-Robertson** | 10982 W. Pico Blvd. (bet. Greenfield & Veteran Aves.) | 310-441-0404
**West Hollywood** | 685 N. Robertson Blvd. (bet. Melrose Ave. & Santa Monica Blvd.) | 310-657-5070 ◑
**Beverly Hills** | 212 S. Beverly Dr. (Charleville Blvd.) | 310-550-7900
www.bossafood.com

"A lot of variety" characterizes the menu of this mini-chain that dishes up "large" plates of "affordable" and "surprisingly" "above-average" "Brazilian comfort food" like "crave-able" steak and chicken and rice (plus pizza at two locations) at a "not-rushed, just-right" beat; many "prefer takeout" and going "late-night" in WeHo, but for naysayers it's "nothing special."

**Boss Sushi** *Japanese*  ▽ 24 | 14 | 19 | $38

**Beverly Hills** | 270A S. La Cienega Blvd. (Gregory Way) | 310-659-5612 | www.bosssushi.com

A passionate following praises chef-owner Tom Sagara's "imaginative" combos of "first-rate fish" at this Beverly Hills Japanese where the staff "remembers everything you like" and will put together a moderately priced five-course omakase menu or nine-course tasting menu upon request; a few protesters pout about decor (both "nondescript" and "oh-so-black"), adding "I liked it better before the attitude" rolled in.

**NEW BottleRock** *European*  16 | 15 | 17 | $27

**Culver City** | 3847 Main St. (bet. Culver & Venice Blvds.) | 310-836-9463 | www.bottlerock.net

Oenophiles appreciate this European wine bar and patio in Culver City, whose "well-curated" selection of cheeses, charcuterie and panini is accompanied by more wines (by the glass or bottle) "than you know what to do with"; the staff's recommendations are usually "on-target", creating an "unintimidating" atmosphere, though the interior is "a little too clattery and metallic" for some, and many wish it were more geared toward "eating a meal than snacking on fatty tidbits."

**Bourbon Street Shrimp Company** *Cajun*  16 | 15 | 17 | $19

**West LA** | 10928 W. Pico Blvd. (½ block west of Westwood Blvd.) | 310-474-0007

Although some call this West LA Cajun "more gimmicky than good", it's "not bad for a place outside of New Orleans", turning out shrimp dishes and grilled chicken "without a lot of fuss"; its "roadhouse"-meets–"frat house" setting suits "slackers and early birds alike", especially since the half-price entrees on Tuesdays are a "terrific value."

**Bowery** ● *American/French*  21 | 22 | 21 | $26

**Hollywood** | 6268 W. Sunset Blvd. (bet. Argyle Ave. & Vine St.) | 323-465-3400 | www.theboweryhollywood.com

"Excellent burgers" among other American-French fare make up the "belly-warming bar food (with some higher-end specials)" at this Hollywood "taste of New York style and attitude" resembling an "East Village boîte"; some find the menu "limited", but most appreciate the strong "waiter-to-customer ratio", "extensive" selection of cognacs, single-malts and small-production wines, and an atmosphere so "cool" that "if you're too hip for this place, you need a hip-ectomy"; nearby spin-off Delancey is set to open soon.

**Z Brandywine Z** *Continental*  27 | 20 | 25 | $58

**Woodland Hills** | 22757 Ventura Blvd. (Fallbrook Ave.) | 818-225-9114

For "amazing" albeit "rich" Continental cuisine encompassing foie gras, sweetbreads and flourless chocolate cake, Valleyites flock to this "teeny", "expensive" but "worth-every-penny" Woodland Hills "favorite" that's hard to find – "we drove by it three times" – but rewards diehards with "charming" live music and "top-notch" service; since the "special" lace-curtained booths are in high-demand, reviewers recommend "reserving well in advance."

|  | FOOD | DECOR | SERVICE | COST |
|---|---|---|---|---|

### Brass.-Cap. ● *French* | 19 | 22 | 19 | $52

**Santa Monica** | 100 W. Channel Rd. (PCH) | 310-454-4544 |
www.brasseriecapo.com

Santa Monica's moneyed set go for cassoulet, escargots and other
"tasty", "upscale" French bistro specialties at Bruce Marder's "comfortable" offshoot of Capo, furnished with a zinc bar and heated patio;
the service is generally "attentive", helping create an "unexpected treat"
in a "wonderful location" across from the ocean on the Palisades border.

### Bravo Cucina *Italian/Pizza* | 18 | 11 | 14 | $20

**Santa Monica** | 1319 Third St. Promenade (bet. Arizona Ave. &
Santa Monica Blvd.) | 310-394-0374

### Bravo Pizzeria *Italian/Pizza*

**Santa Monica** | 2400D Main St. (bet. Hollister Ave. & Ocean Park Blvd.) |
310-392-7466
www.bravosantamonica.com

With a pizzeria on Main Street (open till 3 AM on weekends) and a full
dining room on the Promenade, this Santa Monica Italian pair is a
"solid" go-to for "comforting" pastas, "enormous slices" and cannoli
flown in from NYC cousin Ferrara Cafe; both "could use a face-lift" and
the service tends to "fall short", but "reasonable" prices are a draw.

### Breadbar *American/Bakery* | 19 | 14 | 15 | $18

**West Hollywood** | 8718 W. Third St. (1 block east of Robertson Blvd.) |
310-205-0124

**NEW** **Century City** | Westfield Shopping Ctr. | 10250 Santa Monica Blvd.
(Ave. of the Stars) | 310-277-3770
www.breadbar.net

"The finest carbs on the West Side" are now offered in two locations,
Century City and West Hollywood, for patrons of this New American
bakery serving "delicious salads" and "fine" breakfast items in addition to breads in a variety of flavors (the white chocolate is a "must-
eat"); if the "shopping-mall-rest-stop" decor and "almost comically
slow" service deter you, in-the-know folks say "order to go."

### Breeze *Californian/Seafood* | 19 | 19 | 18 | $40

**Century City** | Hyatt Regency Century Plaza Hotel | 2025 Ave. of the Stars
(Constellation Ave.) | 310-551-3334 | www.centuryplaza.hyatt.com

Acting as the "commissary of the Century City power brokers", this
Californian serving "solid" dishes, focusing on seafood and "quite
good" sushi, draws patrons from the nearby towers who find it "pleasing" to "sit on the back patio"; some, however, cite "slow" service and say
it smacks of "mediocre hotel dining."

### ☑ Brent's Deli *Deli* | 26 | 14 | 21 | $20

**Northridge** | 19565 Parthenia St. (bet. Corbin & Shirley Aves.) | 818-886-5679
**Westlake Village** | 2799 Townsgate Rd. (Westlake Blvd.) | 805-557-1882
www.brentsdeli.com

"Finally, a deli we can brag about in the Conejo Valley" effuse fans of
the "fancier and more spacious" new Westlake Village outpost of the
"super-popular" 40-year-old Northridge original, both of which "richly
reward" guests with "world-class pastrami", "righteous Reubens" and
"shout-out"-worthy soups, as well as desserts that "require a derrick"
to get from case to plate; "snappy" waitresses set down everything
"with a smile", causing many to declare this "the daddy of all delis."

| | FOOD | DECOR | SERVICE | COST |
|---|---|---|---|---|

### Brentwood, The  *American*
21 | 18 | 19 | $47

**Brentwood** | 148 S. Barrington Ave. (1 block south of Sunset Blvd.) | 310-476-3511

"Well-heeled Brentwood comes to dine" at this "deliberately dark", "clubby", "always lively" scene on Barrington Avenue, where Bruce Marder creates "delicious" New American "homestyle favorites" (like Kansas City steak and fries) accompanied by a lengthy wine list; less comforted customers call the service "uneven" and the bill "one step too expensive", and while the dimness can be "seductive", some shout "who turned the lights out?"

### NEW Briganti  *Italian*
▽ 22 | 17 | 21 | $36

**Pasadena** | 1423 Mission St. (bet. Fair Oaks & Fremont Aves.) | 626-441-4663

At this "welcome addition" to South Pasadena's Mission Street, customers find "authentic" Italian fare of "superior quality", including homemade stuffed pasta and branzino; the "well-run", "unpretentious" dining room is "lovely" both as a "date place and one to take your mom", though pickier patrons say it's "not a weekend" destination and would like to see a stronger wine selection.

### Brighton Coffee Shop  *Diner*
16 | 9 | 16 | $16

**Beverly Hills** | 9600 Brighton Way (Camden Dr.) | 310-276-7732

Hash hounds characterize this "classic" daytime diner (opened in 1930) as an "old standby" that despite its Beverly Hills address "doesn't pretend to be any more than it is", with a "pleasant" staff dishing up an "expansive" menu of "reliable" American eats; all in all, it's the kind of "no-frills" coffee shop that "could be in Manhattan - except you wouldn't see Warren Beatty having a meatloaf sandwich."

### Broadway Deli  ◖ *Deli*
14 | 13 | 14 | $23

**Santa Monica** | 1457 Third St. Promenade (B'way) | 310-451-0616

Regulars recommend tasting vintages and "having little bites" "before taking the Third Street walk" or "after a movie" at this Eclectic Santa Monica combo of a wine bar and "New York"–style deli; though numerous naysayers call the food "nothing special", the service often "forgetful" ("should be called the Broadway Delay") and the prices fit for "tourists", its "cavernous" dining room still appeals for "star sightings" and a "late-night" "nosh and slosh."

### Buca di Beppo  *Italian*
15 | 17 | 17 | $24

**Santa Monica** | 1442 Second St. (bet. B'way & Santa Monica Blvd.) | 310-587-2782
**Redondo Beach** | 1670 S. PCH (Palos Verdes Blvd.) | 310-540-3246
**Pasadena** | 80 W. Green St. (De Lacey Ave.) | 626-792-7272
**Encino** | 17500 Ventura Blvd. (Encino Ave.) | 818-995-3288
**Universal City** | Universal CityWalk | 1000 Universal Studios Blvd. (off Rte. 101) | 818-509-9463
**Claremont** | 505 W. Foothill Blvd. (Indian Hill Blvd.) | 909-399-3287
**Thousand Oaks** | Janss Mall | 205 N. Moorpark Rd. (Hillcrest Dr.) | 805-449-3688
**Valencia** | 26940 Theater Dr. (Magic Mountain Pkwy.) | 661-253-1900
www.bucadibeppo.com

"The food is an afterthought" at this "campy" chain that's like an "Italian-American theme park" with "kitschy" decor honoring popular

|  | FOOD | DECOR | SERVICE | COST |

paesani "from Sinatra to the Pope" and an "upbeat" staff (some feel they should "chill out a little") that brings out "ginormous", "shareable" platters of "hearty" but "undistinguished" red-sauce fare; cynics suggest "the kid-less get it to go" and shudder "the number of times 'Happy Birthday' is sung is unbearable."

## Buddha's Belly *Pan-Asian*

| 20 | 18 | 19 | $26 |

**Beverly Boulevard** | 7475 Beverly Blvd. (Gardner St.) | 323-931-8588 | www.bbfood.com

"Fabulous Pan-Asian" fare and Eclectic small plates, including "butter-like" black cod, make this Beverly Boulevard "hipster hangout" the "favorite drop-in neighborhood restaurant" of "aspiring actors" and local professionals, whether in groups or on a "first date"; it's "a step up" from your typical takeaway spot, thanks to its impressive "variety", "casual" "Zen design" and "warm" service ("one night our waitress helped us talk out boy issues"), all at the "right price."

## Buffalo Club Ⓢ *American*

| 19 | 20 | 17 | $53 |

**Santa Monica** | 1520 Olympic Blvd. (bet. 14th & 16th Sts.) | 310-450-8600 | www.thebuffaloclub.com

The "romantic", "Chinese lantern"–lit outdoor patio has a touch more allure than the American "comfort food" dished up at this Santa Monica "anomaly"; while the cuisine "has its moments", most "don't understand the appeal" of the intentionally "snobby" service, saying "they fancy themselves as so exclusive they don't need a sign" and it's so loud "you can't hear yourself pay."

## Buffet City *Eclectic*

| ▽ 13 | 8 | 12 | $16 |

**West LA** | 11819 Wilshire Blvd. (Granville Ave.) | 310-312-0880 | www.buffetcity.net

"Hungry" customers "load up" on Chinese dishes (including "lots of seafood"), sushi and other Eclectic fare at this West LA "bang-for-the-buck" buffet, which is particularly "great for the kids", because pricing is determined by their age; veterans advise "don't expect culinary bliss", just fill your plate "three times over" and "get out as quickly as possible."

## Buggy Whip *Seafood/Steak*

| 19 | 15 | 19 | $36 |

**Westchester** | 7420 La Tijera Blvd. (74th St.) | 310-645-7131 | www.thebuggywhip.com

"Mostly locals" frequent this "old-style" steakhouse in Westchester, where prime rib, Florida stone crab claws and "signature Green Goddess" salad are the standouts on an "always reliable" menu; while its "throwback" decor gets mixed reviews, the "kitschy" ambiance tickles fans of the "big booths, strong booze" and waitresses who ask "what'll you have, honey?"

## NEW Bulan Thai
## Vegetarian Kitchen Ⓜ *Thai*

| - | - | - | l |

(fka Busaba Thai)

**Melrose** | 7168 Melrose Ave. (La Brea Ave.) | 323-857-1882 | www.bulanthai.com

Formerly known as Busaba, this inexpensive vegetarian Thai on Melrose has had fans "hooked since it opened", as "even carnivores can appreciate" the "delicious, creative" dishes, some of which are bolstered by mock meats; lending it extra character, "sweet ladies" oversee the kitchen as well as the small, contemporary dining room decorated in orange, burgundy and avocado tones.

### Buona Sera  *Italian*
▽ 22 | 19 | 18 | $40

**Redondo Beach** | 247 Avenida del Norte (off S. Catalina Ave.) | 310-543-2277
Homemade pastas are the highlight on the menu of "very Italian" eats at this "dependable dinner stop" in Redondo Beach; while it's a bit "pricey", the "inviting" if "cacophonous" setting is otherwise "family-friendly."

### Burger Continental  *Mideastern*
16 | 10 | 15 | $18

**Pasadena** | 535 S. Lake Ave. (California Blvd.) | 626-792-6634
The name is a bit "strange" for this "quirky", largely outdoors Pasadena "institution", considering its menu of "decent" and "cheap" Middle Eastern specialties like schwarma and kebabs served alongside eclectic American eats, including only "ok burgers"; live music and belly dancers Thursday–Sunday plus "strong drinks" draw a motley mix of "Cal-Techies and upscale business types" who've claimed this "loud" but "rather enjoyable" "dive" as their "neighborhood haunt."

### NEW Burger 90210  *Hamburgers*
- | - | - | I

**Beverly Hills** | 242 S. Beverly Dr. (Olympic Blvd.) | 310-271-7900
Adding to the culinary circus along South Beverly Drive, this industrial-looking burger joint is built of metal and glass, all the better to watch gourmet patties being made; there are nearly 50 toppings (goat cheese? sun-dried tomatoes?), along with fries, wings and rings, plus beer and wine too – this is Beverly Hills, after all.

### Cabo Cantina ● *Mexican*
12 | 13 | 14 | $17

**West Hollywood** | 8301 W. Sunset Blvd. (Sweetzer Ave.) | 323-822-7820
**West LA** | 11829 Wilshire Blvd. (bet. Barrington & Bundy Aves.) | 310-312-5840
"Eye candy" and "flowing" margaritas distract from the "average gringo Mexi-chow" at this "body-to-body" "crowded" twosome that's "like being on spring break", what with the "frat-house" feel ("you'll undoubtedly step on a sticky floor"), piñata decor (West LA) and all-you-can-eat tacos on Tuesdays (West Hollywood) – it's "a party every day" for those who like the "crazy" scene.

### Ca'Brea  *Italian*
22 | 20 | 21 | $41

**La Brea** | 346 S. La Brea Ave. (bet. 3rd & 4th Sts.) | 323-938-2863 | www.cabrearestaurant.com
Following a kitchen fire, this multilevel Italian trattoria on La Brea reopened post-Survey with a rebuilt back-of-house and a freshened-up dining room; chef-owner Antonio Tommasi plans to augment the "delicious pastas" and other "affordable" "homestyle" dishes with a tasting menu, and most of the "friendly" staff has returned, so overall quality should be as "consistent" as ever; P.S. low-key eaters advise that "lunch is agent hell, but the Hollywood types disperse during the dinner hours."

### Ca' del Sole  *Italian*
22 | 21 | 21 | $37

**North Hollywood** | 4100 Cahuenga Blvd. (Lankershim Blvd.) | 818-985-4669 | www.cadelsole.com
"Professional at lunch" when filled with "showbizzy" execs and "romantic at dinner" ("especially on the patio with twinkling lights in the

trees"), this "delightful" North Hollywood Venetian option "does not disappoint" with "strong Italian flavors" and a "wonderful" wine list "with some good buys if you're willing to search" the 700-label list; "responsive" service adds to the "charming" atmosphere that's "an oasis" in an area otherwise filled with "car dealerships."

### Café Beaujolais 🗷 Ⓜ *French*
- | - | - | M

**Eagle Rock** | 1712 Colorado Blvd. (bet. La Roda Ave. & Mt. Royal Dr.) | 323-255-5111

Those with a "hankering for old-fashioned French fare" that's "reasonably priced" head to this Eagle Rock cafe for fresh baguettes and "fantastic" dishes like escargots, onion soup and rack of lamb served by "delightful" waiters; with live music and a funky crowd, it's a "popular place that hits the spot."

### ☑ Café Bizou *Californian/French*
23 | 19 | 21 | $32

**Pasadena** | 91 N. Raymond Ave. (Holly St.) | 626-792-9923
**Sherman Oaks** | 14016 Ventura Blvd. (bet. Costello & Murietta Aves.) | 818-788-3536
www.cafebizou.com

These "dependable", "all-occasion" Cal-French bistros in Pasadena and Sherman Oaks win kisses from the crowd for their "well-prepared" fare that's a "wonderful value" (especially with an "unbelievably low" $2 corkage fee); though the "no-attitude" staff is primarily "attentive", a few turn a cold shoulder after "long waits", "even with reservations."

### Café Brasil *Brazilian*
19 | 13 | 14 | $17

**Palms** | 10831 Venice Blvd. (Westwood Blvd.) | 310-837-8957
**West LA** | 11736 W. Washington Blvd. (McLaughlin Ave.) | 310-391-1216
www.cafe-brasil.com

A "tropical" "beach-shack atmosphere" and "pleasant courtyard" "make you feel a world away from Venice Boulevard" at this Palms Brazilian with a "kicky", "colorful" new branch in West LA; both feature "fresh", "fairly authentic" fare (including "killer" rice and beans and "tasty marinated meats") and order-at-the-counter service at "reasonable" prices.

### Cafe Del Rey *Californian/French*
23 | 22 | 21 | $45

**Marina del Rey** | 4451 Admiralty Way (bet. Bali Way & Via Marina) | 310-823-6395 | www.cafedelreymarina.com

"Superb" French-Californian cuisine surprises first-time visitors to this Marina del Rey "favorite", who chuckle "don't assume you're paying for the view" – even if the "elegant" setting's waterfront vista is "unsurpassed"; "gracious" service tops off what many consider the most "romantic" "gastronomic experience" in the area.

### Cafe des Artistes *French*
19 | 22 | 18 | $41

**Hollywood** | 1534 N. McCadden Pl. (Sunset Blvd.) | 323-469-7300 | www.cafedesartistes.info

"From the outside" it may not "look like much", but within, this Hollywood French sib to Mimosa is "enchanting" in a "shabby-chic" way; while the food is "enjoyable" if "not exciting", the management knows how to "supply the romance" with a fireplace, "lovely" enclosed patio and "casual" service that appeals to an "expat" crowd.

|  | FOOD | DECOR | SERVICE | COST |
|---|---|---|---|---|

### Cafe 50's  *Diner*  | 15 | 18 | 17 | $15 |

**Venice** | 838 Lincoln Blvd. (Lake St.) | 310-399-1955 ⊞
**West LA** | 11623 Santa Monica Blvd. (bet. Barry & Federal Aves.) |
310-479-1955 | www.cafe50s.com ●
**Sherman Oaks** | 4609 Van Nuys Blvd. (Hortense St.) |
818-906-1955 ●

"You half-expect Fonzie and Richie to walk through the door" at this
"kitschy" trio of "retro" diners with '50s memorabilia on the walls,
"real rock 'n' roll" on the jukebox and "poodle skirts" on the staff; it's
all "fun", if a little "forced", while the "all-American" food is "fair" and
"varied" enough to make it a "cheap and easy" place for "families";
N.B. each location is separately owned.

### ☒ Café 14  Ⓜ *Californian*  | 26 | 18 | 24 | $44 |

**Agoura Hills** | 30315 Canwood St. (Reyes Adobe Rd.) |
818-991-9560

In spite of its "unassuming" location in an Agoura Hills strip mall,
devotees declare this "casual" bistro a "special place" serving "sublime"
Californian dishes with French and Asian twists from chef Neil Kramer's
"frequently changing" "seasonal" menu (the "superb" desserts come
courtesy of his pastry-chef wife, Claudine); the "cozy" dining room
"exhibits incredible charm" while a "hospitable" staff takes the sting
off "high" prices and "makes you feel like a truly valued guest";
N.B. they now have a full liquor license.

### Cafe Med  *Italian*  | 17 | 16 | 18 | $31 |

**West Hollywood** | 8615 Sunset Blvd. (Sunset Plaza Dr.) | 310-652-0445 |
www.cafemedsunsetplaza.com

This Italian "standard" in West Hollywood's Sunset Plaza serves up
"casual" lunches and "reliable" dinners of "consistent pastas and pizzas"; though the cuisine "doesn't impress" as much as at NYC sister
restaurant Bice, service is "personal" and the location is "ideal" for
"meeting a friend" or just "people-watching" as "amazingly beautiful
women wander by every minute."

### Cafe Montana  *Californian*  | 20 | 16 | 18 | $32 |

**Santa Monica** | 1534 Montana Ave. (16th St.) | 310-829-3990

An "institution" on Santa Monica's trendy Montana Avenue, this "upbeat" Californian "makes you feel healthy and attractive" with
"thoughtfully prepared" dishes like chicken Toscana and lamb chops –
or, alternatively, "sinful" with its "huge", "excellent" homemade pies;
the "fishbowl-style windows are a voyeur's delight", offering "ritzy"
regulars the chance to seriously "see and be seen", especially during
"brunch on the weekends", and service is "prompt despite the back-
to-back, elbow-to-elbow seating."

### Café Mundial  Ⓜ *Californian/Mediterranean*  | ▽ 20 | 18 | 20 | $34 |

**Monrovia** | 514 S. Myrtle Ave. (Colorado Blvd.) | 626-303-2233 |
www.cafemundial.net

The "attentive staff seems to know all the regulars" at this Monrovia
Californian-Mediterranean that stirs up a "Hollywood vibe in the
San Gabriel Valley"; while its seafood-strong menu ranges from
"excellent" to "average", and the crowd can be a "trifle loud", it's a
"nice local" choice for those nearby.

| | FOOD | DECOR | SERVICE | COST |
|---|---|---|---|---|

### Café Pacific *American*                      ▽ 24 | 24 | 21 | $48

**Rancho Palos Verdes** | Trump National Golf Club | 1 Ocean Trails Dr.
(Palos Verdes Dr. S.) | 310-303-3260 | www.trumpgolf.com

New American cuisine "continues to shine" at this cafe in the Trump
National Golf Club, whose devotees advise "don't miss the brunch if
you can afford it"; while the "panoramic ocean views" and "luxurious"
(if "pretentious") ambiance still hit "spectacular" notes, some lament
it "lost the serenity" in its move to a different space, and the ordinarily
"attentive" staff seems "overwhelmed" during peak times

### Café Pierre *French*                          22 | 18 | 21 | $42

**Manhattan Beach** | 317 Manhattan Beach Blvd. (bet. Highland Ave. &
Morningside Dr.) | 310-545-5252 | www.cafepierre.com

"A South Bay favorite" in Downtown Manhattan Beach, this "intimate"
French eatery (a sib to Zazou) features "delicious" standards such as
steak au poivre and mussels supplemented by "interesting" specials;
although the service quality is a bit "mixed", both "business meetings
and romantic dinners" at the "close tables" conclude with an "unexpectedly reasonable" bill; N.B. a recent remodeling may not be reflected in the Decor score.

### Cafe Pinot *Californian/French*               22 | 23 | 21 | $47

**Downtown** | 700 W. Fifth St. (Flower St.) | 213-239-6500 |
www.patinagroup.com

Customers like to "wine and dine clients" at this "more relaxed"
Downtowner (in the Patina Group), distinguished by its "beautiful patio" that's like an "enchanted forest with twinkly lights"; the Cal-
French fare is "superior" as well (particularly the "tasting menus"),
the service "decent" and the "surprise location" is "perfect before the
theater" or a "program at the public library."

### Cafe Rodeo *Californian*                      ▽ 16 | 17 | 16 | $35

**Beverly Hills** | Luxe Hotel Rodeo Dr. | 360 N. Rodeo Dr. (bet. Santa Monica &
Wilshire Blvds.) | 310-273-0300 | www.luxehotelrodeodrive.com

In the Luxe Hotel Rodeo Drive, this "very small" and some would add
"very snooty" Californian is "always packed with tourists" and others
"grabbing a bite on a sunny afternoon" or "having a drink" come cocktail hour; the sidewalk seating offers a prime view of boutique shoppers, but eyefuls aside, some say it's "good for coffee only."

### Café Santorini *Mediterranean*               20 | 20 | 20 | $33

**Pasadena** | 64 W. Union St. (bet. De Lacey & Fair Oaks Aves.) |
626-564-4200 | www.cafesantorini.com

"Eating on the balcony is always special" at this Pasadena
Mediterranean "right in the middle of Old Town", which plays host to
both "business lunches" and "romantic" dinners served by a largely
"accommodating" staff; while most approve of the "wonderfully
hearty" meze, lamb and other specialties, some sniff that the cooking
is simply "typical" and "you're paying" for the "prime location."

### Cafe Stella *French*                          21 | 21 | 16 | $40

**Silver Lake** | 3932 W. Sunset Blvd. (bet. Hyperion & Sanborn Aves.) |
323-666-0265

"Lots of European atmosphere" meets the "East Village in the '60s" at
this "elegant yet bohemian" bistro and wine bar in Silver Lake offering

"simply delicious" French food along with "charming" outdoor seating; although some find it "too expensive" and cite service with "attitude", many maintain it's "perfect for a date or something special."

### Cafe Surfas *American*

20 | 11 | 13 | $14

**Culver City** | 8777 W. Washington Blvd. (National Blvd.) | 310-558-1458 | www.cafesurfas.com

An extension of the "major gourmet supplier" next door, this Culver City "order-at-the-counter" spot goes to the source for "top-quality ingredients" that make up its salads, baked goods and "unusual sandwiches", including "super panini" and the aptly billed "ultimate" grilled cheese; although "comfort is not part of the equation" and some consider the "indifferently served" items "a little pricey for lunch", most agree that the "eat-and-shop" combo is a "foodie's dream."

### Cafe Sushi ● *Japanese*

▽ 19 | 13 | 18 | $33

**Beverly Boulevard** | 8459 Beverly Blvd. (N. La Cienega Blvd.) | 323-651-4020

"Healthy-sized" portions of "consistently good", "value"-priced sushi keep this Beverly Boulevard "neighborhood" Japanese on the map; though some say it's slipped over the years from "excellent" to "decent", and the patio gets the space's only "love", many appreciate that it's "unpretentious", "quick" and "open late" (till 1 AM on the weekends).

### Café Tu Tu Tango *Eclectic*

20 | 21 | 17 | $26

**Universal City** | Universal CityWalk | 1000 Universal Studios Blvd. (Cahuenga Blvd.) | 818-769-2222 | www.cafetututango.com

"Bright and cheerful" "bohemian" loft decor combines with "dancing, live music" and other spontaneous "artwork in progress" (on the weekends) at this Orange and Universal City Eclectic pair where a shopper-heavy crowd shares "creative" "tapas galore" (e.g. Cajun chicken egg rolls) that "can be uneven but still enjoyable"; critics caution, however, that service tends to be "a bit slow" and you'll "spend and spend to finally get full."

### Caffé Delfini *Italian*

23 | 19 | 22 | $41

**Santa Monica** | 147 W. Channel Rd. (PCH) | 310-459-8823

"Tiny but tasty", this "accommodating" Italian cafe is "still one of the best-kept secrets in Santa Monica", serving "top-notch" penne arrabbiata, branzino and other "daily catches" at a "fraction of the price" of other area restaurants; as it's "quaint", "intimate" and quite "dark", romantics recommend "taking a date" (just "don't skimp" and opt for valet parking).

### Caffe Latte *American*

▽ 16 | 11 | 17 | $17

**Mid-Wilshire** | 6254 Wilshire Blvd. (Crescent Heights Blvd.) | 323-936-5213 | www.caffelattela.com

This "unassuming but popular" American stop for a "light lunch or breakfast" is "dependable" when it comes to "roasting its own" java ("not a bad drop in the place") and "convenient if you work in Mid-Wilshire"; despite "cramped seating arrangements", the operation is still "holding its own" after a change of management – though some continue to "pine for the iced coffee" of yesteryear.

| | FOOD | DECOR | SERVICE | COST |
|---|---|---|---|---|

**NEW Caffe Luxxe** *Coffeehouse* — | — | — | I

**Santa Monica** | 925 Montana Ave. (bet. 9th & 10th Sts.) | 310-394-2222 |
www.caffeluxxe.com

Light-roasted Northern Italian espresso made from handcrafted
Syneffo machines is the focus of this Santa Monica coffeehouse,
which supplements its cups with organic granola, panini and pastries;
a growing clientele of double-ristretto devotees, including a fair share
of celebs, lends a lively air to the Euro-chic space.

**Caffe Pinguini** Ⓜ *Italian* — 22 | 19 | 19 | $35

**Playa del Rey** | 6935 Pacific Ave. (Culver Blvd.) | 310-306-0117 |
www.caffepinguini.com

"Delectable Italian plates" come from a "kitchen that obviously cares"
at this "Playa hideaway"; though some find it "expensive for a neighborhood place", regulars say it offers a "warm welcome" and "romantic" patio dining, plus you can "visit the beach afterwards."

**NEW Caffe Primo** *Italian* — ▽ 17 | 19 | 13 | $19

**West Hollywood** | Sunset Millennium Plaza | 8590 Sunset Blvd. (2 blocks west
of La Cienega Blvd.) | 310-289-8895 | www.iloveprimo.com

"A real up-and-comer" approve early visitors to this loungey Italian
(open till midnight on the weekends) in the Sunset Millennium Plaza,
which offers panini, pizza and salads, as well as "great coffee" and
"homemade gelato" to chase "a shopping day on the Strip" or begin a
WeHo night out in "European-cafe" style.

**Caffe Roma** *Italian* — 16 | 14 | 17 | $36

**Beverly Hills** | 350 N. Cañon Dr. (bet. Brighton & Dayton Ways) |
310-274-7834

Customers commend a "change for the better" at this Beverly Hills
Italian "old-schooler" since new owner Ago Sciandri (Ago and Sor
Tino) has "spiffed it up and expanded the menu"; live piano music enhances the "bar action" and the "food goes with fine cigars" at the
sidewalk tables, so no wonder "frequent Governor Arnold sightings"
are part of the "people-watching" that tends to trump the "tasty"
pasta, pizza and calzones.

**Caioti Pizza Cafe** *Pizza* — 22 | 11 | 17 | $19

**Studio City** | 4346 Tujunga Ave. (Moorpark St.) | 818-761-3588 |
www.caiotipizzacafe.com

"When you can't get into Mozza", thin-crust connoisseurs recommend this "eternally popular" Californian in Studio City, serving
"delicious", "ingenious" pizza (both new- and "old-world" style)
along with unconventional pastas, salads and garlic knots to
"dream about"; there's "slooow" service and "no booze", but "no
corkage" keeps the tab low; N.B. a post-Survey renovation is not
reflected in the Decor score.

**California Chicken Cafe** Ⓢ *American* — 21 | 9 | 16 | $12

**Hollywood** | 6805 Melrose Ave. (Mansfield Ave.) | 323-935-5877
**Santa Monica** | 2401 Wilshire Blvd. (24th St.) | 310-453-0477
**NEW Venice** | 424 Lincoln Blvd. (Sunset Ave.) | 310-392-3500
**West LA** | 2005 Westwood Blvd. (bet. Olympic & Santa Monica Blvds.) |
310-446-1933

*(continued)*

*(continued)*

### California Chicken Cafe

**Encino** | 15601 Ventura Blvd. (bet. Haskell Ave. & Sepulveda Blvd.) | 818-789-8056

**Northridge** | University Plaza | 18445 Nordhoff St. (Reseda Blvd.) | 818-700-9977

**NEW** **Woodland Hills** | 22333 Ventura Blvd. (Shoup Ave.) | 818-716-6170
www.californiachickencafe.com

"We call it Chinese Chicken Cafe" after its signature salad – "tangy" with "tender" and "crispy" rotisserie-cooked meat – crow customers of this "bargain" American chain that also serves up "fresh", "fantastic wraps" for a "packed" crowd of "fit people" ordering from the "efficient" counter; though a few are ruffled by the "bland", "way-too-loud" environs and advise it's "better to take out" (and "call ahead" too), most maintain it's "fast-food heaven"; N.B. closed Sunday.

### California Pizza Kitchen  *Pizza*    18 | 14 | 16 | $20

**Downtown** | Wells Fargo Ctr. | 330 S. Hope St. (bet. 3rd & 4th Sts.) | 213-626-2616

**Hollywood** | Hollywood & Highland Complex | 6801 Hollywood Blvd., upstairs (Highland Blvd.) | 323-460-2080

**Beverly Hills** | Beverly Ctr. | 121 N. La Cienega Blvd. (bet. Beverly Blvd. & 3rd St.) | 310-854-6555

**Beverly Hills** | 207 S. Beverly Dr. (bet. Olympic & Wilshire Blvds.) | 310-275-1101

**Santa Monica** | 210 Wilshire Blvd. (bet. 2nd & 3rd Sts.) | 310-393-9335

**Westwood** | Westwood Vill. | 1001 Broxton Ave. (Weyburn Ave.) | 310-209-9197

**Manhattan Beach** | Manhattan Village Mall | 3280 N. Sepulveda Blvd. (Rosecrans Ave.) | 310-796-1233

**Pasadena** | Plaza Las Fuentes | 99 N. Los Robles Ave. (Union St.) | 626-585-9020

**Burbank** | 601 N. San Fernando Blvd. (Cypress Ave.) | 818-972-2589

**Studio City** | 12265 Ventura Blvd. (Laurel Grove Ave.) | 818-505-6437
www.cpk.com

Additional locations throughout Southern California

Customers "count on" this "steady" chain that "pretty much invented California pizza as it is today", offering "classic" BBQ chicken pies and toppings with "ethnic twists", along with "complex", "appealing" salads; though by now it feels a bit "formulaic" to those who "grew up on it", it's still popular among "post-soccer practice families" and tweens "gabbing on cell phones" in surroundings that are "like eating at the Gap, but louder"; service can be "slapdash", so be sure to "allow time."

### California Wok  *Chinese*    18 | 8 | 16 | $16

**Third Street** | Cienega Plaza | 8520 W. Third St. (La Cienega Blvd.) | 310-360-9218

**Brentwood** | 12004 Wilshire Blvd. (Bundy Dr.) | 310-479-0552

**Encino** | Encino Vlg. | 16656 Ventura Blvd. (Petit Ave.) | 818-386-0561

"Flavorful", "healthy" and "inexpensive" Chinese with "light sauces" draws stir-fry fans to this LA mini-chain; due to its "dreary" dining rooms, however, office-lunchers and others dial up for "quick" delivery."

|  | FOOD | DECOR | SERVICE | COST |
|---|---|---|---|---|

### Camden House ⌧ *Californian/French*   ▽ 15 | 16 | 15 | $51

**Beverly Hills** | 430 N. Camden Dr. (Little Santa Monica Blvd.) | 310-285-9848
This "big", "beautiful" space (formerly the Mandarin) on Camden
Drive in the 90210 hosts a "noisy" "disco" crowd late at night but during dinner observers claim "no one is ever there" ("can't find a waiter
either"); while some find the Cal-French menu "overblown", others
call the cooking "good" and "creative."

### Camilo's Ⓜ *Californian*   20 | 18 | 19 | $29

**Eagle Rock** | 2128 W. Colorado Blvd. (Caspar Ave.) | 323-478-2644
Patrons are largely "pleased" with the "tasty" Californian cuisine and
"carefully selected" wines at this "midpriced" Eagle Rock bistro;
despite some "inconsistency" in the kitchen and on the floor, its
"homey" environs, enhanced by brick walls, local artwork and sidewalk tables, and "change-from-the-ordinary" breakfasts have helped
earn it a place as a "neighborhood mainstay."

### ⛋ Campanile *Californian/Mediterranean*   26 | 24 | 23 | $56

**La Brea** | 624 S. La Brea Ave. (bet. 6th St. & Wilshire Blvd.) | 323-938-1447 |
www.campanilerestaurant.com
At this La Brea "must for LA dining", chef-owner Mark Peel delivers
Cal-Med cuisine that's "sumptuous", "elegant" and "impervious to
fashion"; enamored eaters call the weekend brunch the "discovery of
the year", Thursday night's grilled cheese the "best you'll ever taste"
and Monday's three-course family-style meal a "real steal", also noting the "properly attentive" service and lofty space built by Charlie
Chaplin – a "timeless" "part of Hollywood history."

### Canal Club *Californian/Eclectic*   18 | 18 | 18 | $33

**Venice** | 2025 Pacific Ave. (N. Venice Blvd.) | 310-823-3878 |
www.canalclubvenice.com
Venice bon vivants "nosh and crack wise" over the Californian-Eclectic
eats ranging from carne asada to sushi ("a little something for everyone") that are especially sought out during the "hopping" happy hour
at this James' Beach bro; a "well-trained" staff and oceanfront-
inspired look are bonuses, though a few who wash ashore dub it a
"weird mix of food and people."

### C & O Cucina *Italian*   19 | 17 | 19 | $22

**Marina del Rey** | 3016 Washington Blvd. (Thatcher Ave.) | 310-301-7278 |
www.cocucina.com

### C & O Trattoria *Italian*

**Marina del Rey** | 31 Washington Blvd. (Pacific Ave.) | 310-823-9491 |
www.cotrattoria.com
Both of these Marina del Rey Italians provide "big bang for the buck"
with their "killer complimentary garlic rolls" and pasta dishes that are
"gigantic" enough to share and served by a "singing staff"; despite
complaints of "uninspired" cooking, many agree the "kitschy", "over-
the-top" atmosphere fueled by "jugs of house Chianti" is "great
for large groups."

### NEW Canele Ⓜ *Mediterranean*   24 | 18 | 21 | $35

**Atwater Village** | 3219 Glendale Blvd. (Edenhurst Ave.) | 323-666-7133
"Lucky Atwater Village" (the "next Culver City"?) houses this "hip"
"hangout" graced by the "splendid" Mediterranean cooking of "imag-

FOOD | DECOR | SERVICE | COST

inative" chef Corina Weibel; although the "no-reservations policy sometimes makes for a wait", its "joyful" atmosphere – energized by a "fabulous" family-style table – rewards the intrepid, along with "caring" (if sometimes "sporadic") service and "reasonable" prices.

### Canter's ❶ Deli

18 | 10 | 15 | $19

**Fairfax** | 419 N. Fairfax Ave. (bet. Oakwood & Rosewood Aves.) | 323-651-2030 | www.cantersdeli.com

"Celebrities and construction workers sit side by side and pound down pastrami", "tender corned beef" and pickles that "taste like they were made in the barrel" at this kosher-style "dowager" of Fairfax, where the sandwiches are "piled high" and served by "old-time" waitresses whose "sassy" shtick seems "straight out of Central Casting"; sure, the room "hasn't changed since the '50s", but that makes it just "like a Woody Allen film."

### ▣ Capo 🅢🅜 Italian

26 | 24 | 24 | $77

**Santa Monica** | 1810 Ocean Ave. (Pico Blvd.) | 310-394-5550

"Bring the Gold Card" to this Santa Monica Italian where chef/co-owner Bruce Marder oversees a dining experience "fit for a king" ("yes, that's Tom Hanks in the corner"), encompassing "amazing" wood-grilled New York steaks, "excellent" homemade pastas and an "impressive wine list" inside a "charming" interior dominated by a raised fireplace; even if some call it "too cool for school", "they never rush you" and you can reserve ahead to dine at the bar – "the best seat in town."

### Carlitos Gardel Argentinean/Steak

23 | 20 | 24 | $45

**Melrose** | 7963 Melrose Ave. (bet. Edinburgh & Hayworth Aves.) | 323-655-0891 | www.carlitosgardel.com

The steak has "pizzazz" at this "family-run", "upscale" Argentinean on Melrose, whose rib-eye is "cooked to perfection", sided with "irresistible" garlic french fries, and served by a "kind" staff; while the retro room could use a little extra "style", live music on the weekends entices a nighttime "Evita Peron–looking crowd."

### Carmine's Italian Italian

18 | 13 | 18 | $23

**Arcadia** | 311 E. Live Oak Ave. (bet. 2nd & Tyler Aves.) | 626-445-4726
**South Pasadena** | 424 Fair Oaks Ave. (bet. Columbia & State Sts.) | 626-799-2266

"Old standards" and "tasty" "house specials" are served in "huge portions" ("bring your biggest appetite") at this pair of "relaxing", plant-filled trattorias in Arcadia and South Pasadena; for carbonara connoisseurs it's "just ok", but the "bargain prices", "easy menu" and "friendly" staff continue to attract families for "midweek dinners."

### Carney's Express Hot Dogs

19 | 15 | 16 | $11

**West Hollywood** | 8351 W. Sunset Blvd. (Sweetzer Ave.) | 323-654-8300 ❶
**Studio City** | 12601 Ventura Blvd. (Whitsett Ave.) | 818-761-8300
www.carneytrain.com

They're "on the right track" at this Studio City and West Hollywood twosome serving "addictive" chili-cheeseburgers, "fantastic" fries and "not fancy, not fussy" but "top-notch" hot dogs to "rival Pink's" inside "cool-looking" vintage train cars that the "kids will love"; the line moves "fast", all the better to "fill that craving" with a "cheap and satisfying meal."

| | FOOD | DECOR | SERVICE | COST |
|---|---|---|---|---|

### Carnival  *Lebanese*
23 | 8 | 15 | $20

**Sherman Oaks** | 4356 Woodman Ave. (bet. Moorpark St. & Ventura Blvd.) | 818-784-3469 | www.carnivalrest.com

"Smooth" hummus, "delicious" kebabs and other "authentic", "generous" eats draw Sherman Oaks schwarma hounds to this longstanding Lebanese; sure, the strip-mall space is "not much to look at", the service is "matter-of-fact" and you'll probably "wait on line", but most agree it's worth heading "over the hill" for, seeing as the clientele proves "it's possible for Jews and Arabs to agree on something."

### ☑ Carousel ⓜ *Mideastern*
24 | 15 | 20 | $27

**East Hollywood** | High Plaza | 5112 Hollywood Blvd. (Normandie Ave.) | 323-660-8060

**Glendale** | 304 N. Brand Blvd. (California Ave.) | 818-246-7775
www.carouselrestaurant.com

"Superb" "feasts" of Middle Eastern cuisine, particularly the "excellent" meze, attract aficionados of Armenian and Lebanese flavors to this duo staffed by "accommodating" servers; while the "tiny", humble Hollywood original has "little ambiance", its "lavish" (some say "gaudy") Glendale cousin "transports" the "energetic" weekend crowd with "live music" and "fabulous belly dancing."

### Casa Bianca ●☒ⓜ⊅ *Pizza*
23 | 12 | 17 | $18

**Eagle Rock** | 1650 Colorado Blvd. (Vincent Ave.) | 323-256-9617 | www.casabiancapizza.com

"Once you get past" the "legendary wait" at this Eagle Rock "institution" – with an atmosphere out of "New Jersey circa 1954" – you'll encounter "awesome" pizza as well as pesto potent enough to smell "from the kitchen"; still, the disappointed contend it "doesn't live up to its vaunted reputation" due to "ordinary" entrees, "canned"-tasting mushrooms and an "unapologetic use of iceberg lettuce"; N.B. no credit cards accepted, closed Sundays and Mondays.

### Casablanca *Mexican*
18 | 18 | 18 | $24

**Venice** | 220 Lincoln Blvd. (Rose Ave.) | 310-392-5751 | www.casablancacatering.com

Its "Moroccan" look with "Bogey and Bacall"-heavy memorabilia provides the incongruous backdrop for "crêpe"-like, "handmade tortillas" and calamari "made more ways than you can count" at this "funky" Venice Mexican where Latin guitar provides entertainment and a "voluminous" tequila selection fuels the "strong margaritas"; sober assessors shrug "what a gimmick" – the "cheesy" theme "truly lives up to LA weirdness."

### Casa Vega ● *Mexican*
18 | 16 | 17 | $23

**Sherman Oaks** | 13301 Ventura Blvd. (Fulton Ave.) | 818-788-4868 | www.casavega.com

A "nostalgic vibe" is part of the "allure" at this "cavelike" haunt in Sherman Oaks that draws "B-level celebrities" and "lots of pretty peeps" to its "hot" bar and red booths for "rich", "old-style" Mexican food with "kick-ass" margaritas; despite middling reviews for the service and knocks for "greasy" grub, it gets "extra props for the late-night hours" (until 1 AM).

### Cassell's ☒ *Hamburgers*  | 21 | 7 | 13 | $12 |

**Koreatown** | 3266 W. Sixth St. (bet. S. Berendo St. & S. New Hampshire Ave.) | 213-480-5000

"Classic-style" burgers with "build-your-own trimmings" and "standout potato salad" continue to draw plenty of fans to this "'70s timewarp" Koreatown "cafeteria"; critics sigh that the "prices have gone up" and "it's not what it used to be", but many gush the "greasy" patties are still their "favorite."

### Castaway *Californian*  | 17 | 22 | 18 | $33 |

**Burbank** | 1250 E. Harvard Rd. (Sunset Canyon Dr.) | 818-848-6691 | www.castawayrestaurant.com

A "perennial prom-night favorite", this 500-seater in the Burbank hills is "popular for weddings and quinceañeras" due to its "outstanding" views of the Valley, especially at sunset; the Sunday buffet brunch is also "quite an affair", though many prefer evening drinks and apps "at the fire pit" to a full meal of the "nothing-special" Californian food.

### NEW Catch *Seafood*  | – | – | – | E |
### (fka Oceanfront)

**Santa Monica** | Hotel Casa Del Mar | 1910 Ocean Way (Pico Blvd.) | 310-581-7714 | www.catchsantamonica.com

At the latest restaurant to occupy Santa Monica's elegant Casa Del Mar, Le Bernardin vet Michael Reardon shows off his piscatorial prowess with pricey dishes like Chatham cod with cauliflower couscous, along with sushi and crudo; dominated by floor-to-ceiling windows that open onto the beach, the handsome setting mixes dark woods and white woven-leather chairs.

### NEW Celadon M *Eurasian*  | 22 | 24 | 20 | $47 |

**Third Street** | 7910 W. Third St. (bet. Edinburgh & Fairfax Aves.) | 323-658-8028 | www.celadongalerie.com

Offering a "unique riff on fusion cuisine", this "swank" Third Street arrival presents "surprising", "big flavors" in Eurasian dishes like "tasty" tuna lollipops and hamachi citrus salsa served in a "Zen-like" dining room and "comfy bar"; though a few feel the service needs polishing and the "tad-expensive" food "takes a back seat" to the decor, most are "impressed" with the whole package.

### Celestino ☒ *Italian*  | 23 | 18 | 21 | $43 |

**Pasadena** | 141 S. Lake Ave. (bet. Cordova & Green Sts.) | 626-795-4006 | www.celestinopasadena.com

"Definitely not a red-sauce-and-pasta joint", this Drago brothers' Pasadena outpost offers "terrific" Tuscan cuisine like spaghetti bottarga and steak fiorentina out of the open kitchen; although critics complain that it's "noisy" and "overpriced", the "beautiful outside patio" and waiters who "ham up the Italian accents" but "do a fine job" help justify the "splurge."

### NEW Central Park *American/Californian*  | ▽ 18 | 15 | 16 | $25 |

**Pasadena** | Old Pasadena | 219 S. Fair Oaks Ave. (bet. Orange Pl. & Valley St.) | 626-449-4499

"Hearty breakfasts" and "affordable", "comforting" Cal-American dinners define this new Pasadena "treat" across from the park; although neither the menu nor the decor of black-and-white "old Hollywood" photos are "outstanding", it's an "upgrade" from the location's previous resident, and the service is "agreeable" enough for a "quick bite."

### Cézanne  *Californian/French*  21 | 20 | 20 | $55

**Santa Monica** | Le Merigot Hotel | 1740 Ocean Ave. (bet. Colorado Ave. & Pico Blvd.) | 310-899-6122 | www.lemerigothotel.com
"Reliable", "attractively presented" Cal-French cuisine serves Le Merigot Hotel guests and a few Santa Monica locals in a "pretty" dining room decorated with Cézanne reproductions; though it's "ordinary" to some, others recommend "sitting outside during the day" for a pleasant lunch or weekend brunch.

### Chaba  *Thai*  20 | 19 | 18 | $27

**Redondo Beach** | 525 S. PCH (Ruby St.) | 310-540-8441 | www.chabarestaurant.com
Diners find a "fresh take" on Thai cuisine at this "reasonably priced" Redondo Beach "standout" offering salmon Mango Tango and other "unusual" choices among its "elegantly" plated dishes; at happy hour, the "nice-looking" bamboo-furnished room plays host to a bit of a "singles scene", as the "pleasant" staff "keeps the drinks coming."

### Chabuya Tokyo Noodle Bar ● *Japanese*  21 | 17 | 16 | $15

**West LA** | 2002 Sawtelle Blvd. (La Grange Ave.) | 310-473-1013
The ramen "rocks the house and then some" at this West LA offshoot of an "authentic Tokyo chain" known for its "fine bowls of noodles" and *Blade Runner* atmosphere; though "portions are a bit small" according to some, they're still "more than enough" to suffice when you want a "quick, cheap" meal.

### Cha Cha Cha  *Caribbean*  20 | 18 | 19 | $26

**Silver Lake** | 656 N. Virgil Ave. (bet. Clinton St. & Melrose Ave.) | 323-664-7723
**West Hollywood** | 7953 Santa Monica Blvd. (Hayworth Ave.) | 323-848-7700
www.theoriginalchachacha.com
"Latin flavor" fires up the Caribbean dining experience at this LA two-fer where regulars go for "fruity" sangria, "tasty small plates priced right" and "signature" Jamaican jerk chicken; both the "ultimate happy hour" (three courses plus a drink for $15, 5-7 PM) at the "chic" WeHo locale and "hangover breakfasts" in Silver Lake have their fans, so while the "funky", "festive" atmosphere strikes some as "overwhelming", others encourage "bring a large group of people - the louder, the better."

### Cha Cha Chicken  *Caribbean*  20 | 15 | 16 | $13

**Santa Monica** | 1906 Ocean Ave. (Pico Blvd.) | 310-581-1684 | www.chachachicken.com
"Spicy", "filling" and "inexpensive" Caribbean fare makes this Santa Monica "secret" an "excellent local choice" for "Negril-meets-the-Southwest" dishes like jerk chicken enchiladas; both the "casual" order-at-the-counter setup and "tacky" yet "tropical" patio fit the bill for those seeking an "urban escape" by the beach.

### ☑ Chadaka  *Thai*  24 | 23 | 20 | $24

**Burbank** | 310 N. San Fernando Blvd. (Palm Ave.) | 818-848-8520 | www.chadaka.com
It's "hard to do better in Burbank" than this "elegant" yet "affordable" "nouvelle" Thai whose customers coo that the "crying tiger beef is not

to be missed"; while it's "more chichi than authentic", the service is acceptably "understated" and the setting well-suited to "first dates."

### Chakra Indian
| 21 | 24 | 19 | $37 |

**NEW** **Beverly Hills** | 151 S. Doheny Dr. (Wilshire Blvd.) | 310-246-3999 | www.chakracuisine.com

"Modern" takes on Indian cuisine are served in "stunning", "romantically lit" surroundings at this "chic" Beverly Hills and Irvine pair; though a few foes fault "Americanized" fare and "unresponsive" service, the "colorful martinis", "reasonable pricing" and a "hip" "loungey feel" lure locals back nonetheless.

### Chameau 🖂 Ⓜ French/Moroccan
| 24 | 22 | 21 | $41 |

**Fairfax** | 339 N. Fairfax Ave. (bet. Beverly Blvd. & Oakwood Ave.) | 323-951-0039 | www.chameaurestaurant.com

The "welcoming" staff delivers "fantastic" French-Moroccan dishes at this Fairfax "tagine heaven" whose signature b'steeya pie is "one of the wonders of the modern world" according to fans; amid its "groovy", "softly lit" interior, the service is "friendly" and the "focus is appropriately on the dining experience, not on some Disney-esque floor show" – another reason connoisseurs would gladly "walk a mile for this camel."

### Chan Dara Thai
| 19 | 16 | 18 | $27 |

**Hancock Park** | 310 N. Larchmont Blvd. (Beverly Blvd.) | 323-467-1052 | www.chandaralarchmont.com
**West LA** | 11940 W. Pico Blvd. (Bundy Dr.) | 310-479-4461 | www.chandarawestla.com

### Chan Darae Thai

**Hollywood** | 1511 N. Cahuenga Blvd. (Sunset Blvd.) | 323-464-8585 | www.chan-darae.com

While the "versatile", "upscale" menu is "consistent" at these three Thais, the "babe waitresses" in "hot pants" and "high heels" arouse the most commentary, ranging from positive ("hired on looks but still competent") to annoyed ("appealing to Western fantasies does not a good server make"); whether or not they appreciate "the view", many find it "comfortable" for a "casual meal" – but "ladies, don't ever go here on a date!"

### Chao Krung Thai
| 21 | 17 | 19 | $21 |

**Fairfax** | 111 N. Fairfax Ave. (bet. Beverly Blvd. & W. 1st St.) | 323-932-9482 | www.chaokrung.com

This "inexpensive" family-run Fairfax "stalwart" "ranks up there" among LA Thai options for its "trusty" dinners and "excellent lunch buffet"; to "seal the deal", its "inviting" teak-accented room with "exotic glow-in-the-dark" paintings "hasn't changed a bit, and that's ok with me" according to longtimers.

### Chapter 8
### Steakhouse & Dance Lounge 🖂 Ⓜ Steak
| 18 | 22 | 20 | $47 |

**Agoura Hills** | 29020 Agoura Rd. (Kanan Rd.) | 818-889-2088 | www.chapter8lounge.com

"A little bit of Vegas in Agoura Hills", this "trendy" offshoot of P6 is better known for its "clublike" red-and-black decor and "singles bar" than its steakhouse fare, though the aged cuts are largely "done well" and complemented by "ample" sides; still, some sniff that it's "overpriced" and the management is "trying to do the big city" rather than "attempting any sort of dining ambiance"; N.B. look out for those unisex bathrooms.

**NEW Charcoal** ● *American* — | — | — | M

**Hollywood** | 6372 W. Sunset Blvd. (Ivar St.) | 323-465-8500
The latest creation of ubiquitous restaurateur Adolfo Suaya (Gaucho Grill, Dolce, Geisha House) and his partner Michael Sutton (The Lodge Steakhouse, Memphis), this ultramodern New American boasts eye-catching decor (complete with elk-horn chandelier) and a heart-of-Hollywood location; Yuri Samano, who gave The Lodge its sizzle, is preparing the midpriced fare, much of which is cooked over mesquite.

**Chart House** *Seafood/Steak* 19 | 22 | 19 | $41

**Malibu** | 18412 PCH (Topanga Canyon Rd.) | 310-454-9321
**Marina del Rey** | 13950 Panay Way (Via Marina) | 310-822-4144
**Redondo Beach** | 231 Yacht Club Way (Harbor Dr.) | 310-372-3464
www.chart-house.com
"Stupendous" water vistas ("get a window seat at sunset") are the cachet of this "always-crowded" national chain of surf 'n' turfers offering "consistent" service along with "prime rib the way you like it", "well-prepared fish" and an "extensive salad bar" (except in Malibu); despite complaints that it's "too expensive and uninspired", few diners are disappointed by the "million-dollar view."

**Chateau Marmont** *Californian/French* 21 | 24 | 20 | $53

**West Hollywood** | Chateau Marmont | 8221 W. Sunset Blvd. (bet. Havenhurst Dr. & Marmont Ln.) | 323-656-1010 | www.chateaumarmont.com
"Don't gawk when you see the über-stars sipping Pellegrino next to you" at this Cal-French "classic" in West Hollywood's "legendary" Hotel Marmont – the "real LA" rather than a "hot spot that flashes and burns"; fortunately the kitchen turns out "fab food to match" the "superb atmosphere", so even if "they always claim to be 'booked'" and it's "not cheap (and doesn't need to be)", "lunch in the garden is a thrill."

**Chaya Brasserie** *Asian/Eclectic* 23 | 22 | 21 | $49

**West Hollywood** | 8741 Alden Dr. (bet. Beverly Blvd. & W. 3rd St., off Robertson Blvd.) | 310-859-8833 | www.thechaya.com
The "innovative" Asian-Eclectic menu at this West Hollywood "favorite" changes seasonally, but its "amazing" steaks, "out-of-this-world desserts" and "unique drinks" anchor the dining experience; with "unstuffy" servers and a "gorgeous" room uplifted by a bamboo garden centerpiece, it hosts a "lively", "noisy" "scene" (especially at "happy hour") that "never goes out of style."

**Chaya Venice** *Japanese/Mediterranean* 23 | 22 | 20 | $47

**Venice** | 110 Navy St. (Main St.) | 310-396-1179 | www.thechaya.com
"It doesn't hurt to be good-looking" at the "hopping happy hour" of this "tasteful", "romantic but also hip" Venice cousin to Chaya Brasserie, which provides a "wonderful mix" of Japanese-Mediterranean flavors along with "terrific sushi" served by a staff that "wants you to enjoy yourself"; doubters cite the "din", the "crush" and "some attitude", however, knocking it's "starting to feel a bit like a scene from an '80s movie."

| | FOOD | DECOR | SERVICE | COST |
|---|---|---|---|---|

### Checkers Downtown  *Californian*   22 | 22 | 21 | $49

**Downtown** | Hilton Checkers | 535 S. Grand Ave. (bet. 5th & 6th Sts.) | 213-624-0000 | www.checkershotel.com

"Breakfast is especially transportive" at this Downtown "bit of old-fashioned LA" inside the Hilton Checkers, which cooks up "well-executed" Californian cuisine; admirers appreciate that "you can actually talk" during "business lunches" and "pre-theater" dinners, enhanced by the "elegant", "clubby" surroundings and "excellent service."

### Cheebo  *Italian*   19 | 15 | 15 | $25

**Hollywood** | 7533 W. Sunset Blvd. (bet. Gardner St. & Sierra Bonita Ave.) | 323-850-7070 | www.cheebo.com

"If you're craving a chopped salad" and "flavorful" "pizza by the slab", regulars recommend this Italian "Hollywood hangout" that's big on "organic" eats; "quiet at breakfast, mellow at lunch and lit up at night", the "funky orange" room maintains a "local vibe", though some wish they would "lower the prices" and upgrade the "distant" service – so consider "ordering takeout."

### ☒ Cheesecake Factory  *American*   20 | 18 | 18 | $26

**Beverly Hills** | 364 N. Beverly Dr. (Brighton Way) | 310-278-7270
**Brentwood** | 11647 San Vicente Blvd. (bet. Barrington Ave. & Wilshire Blvd.) | 310-826-7111
**Marina del Rey** | 4142 Via Marina (Admiralty Way) | 310-306-3344
**Redondo Beach** | 605 N. Harbor Dr. (190th St.) | 310-376-0466
**Pasadena** | 2 W. Colorado Blvd. (Fair Oaks Ave.) | 626-584-6000
**Sherman Oaks** | Sherman Oaks Galleria | 15301 Ventura Blvd. (Sepulveda Blvd.) | 818-906-0700
**Woodland Hills** | Warner Center Trillium | 6324 Canoga Ave. (Victory Blvd.) | 818-883-9900
**Thousand Oaks** | Thousand Oaks Mall | 442 W. Hillcrest Dr. (Lynn Rd.) | 805-371-9705
www.thecheesecakefactory.com
Additional locations throughout Southern California

"Mass-produced happiness" is the promise of this "constantly buzzing" ("if you like it loud with a crowd") national chain dishing up "dependable" American fare in such "ridiculously large" portions there's "barely enough room" for their "amazing" signature dessert; the service is generally "decent", though "a long wait for a table is a virtual certainty" since they don't take reservations, leaving some to sigh "so many cheesecakes, so little time."

### Chef Melba's Bistro  Ⓜ *Californian*   ▽ 23 | 14 | 19 | $33

**Hermosa Beach** | 1501 Hermosa Ave. (15th St.) | 310-376-2084 | www.chefmelbasbistro.com

Chef Melba Rodriguez "cares about her food" at this "refreshing" Hermosa Californian that's gaining fame for its "unique stews, fresh fish" and a "winning" Sunday brunch; among its "older, more subdued" crowd (compared to the neighboring college bars), many find the open-kitchen space "lackluster" but are "charmed" by the "chitchatting" owner and her cuisine nonetheless; P.S. it's "tiny", so make "reservations on the weekends" and for the monthly wine dinners.

### Chez Allez *Eclectic/Sandwiches*  ▽ 21 | 13 | 18 | $22

**Palos Verdes Estates** | 36 Malaga Cove Plaza (Palos Verdes Dr.) | 310-378-5664 | www.chezmelange.com

The team behind Chez Melange attracts Palos Verdes patrons with its Eclectic small plates and "consistently good" sandwiches at this "inexpensive little" daytime cafe; though some say "it doesn't hold a candle to its big sister", others feel it's a "much-needed" addition that will "probably only get better" with age.

### Chez Jay *Steak*  16 | 15 | 17 | $33

**Santa Monica** | 1657 Ocean Ave. (Colorado Ave.) | 310-395-1741 | www.chezjays.com

"Delightfully frozen in time", Santa Monica's 48-year-old "steak-and-martini" "shack" is "the best of the beachfront dives", with a "top-notch" bar staff and "dark" feel that "Raymond Chandler would have loved"; although some recommend "go for a drink, but fill your belly elsewhere", many leave sated since Jay himself will often "come to your table" and "spin yarns about Marilyn, JFK and the Rat Pack."

### Chez Melange *Eclectic*  25 | 15 | 24 | $44

**Redondo Beach** | Palos Verdes Inn | 1716 S. PCH (bet. Palos Verdes Blvd. & Prospect Ave.) | 310-540-1222 | www.chezmelange.com

What many call the "most original" cooking in the area lures residents of Redondo Beach and beyond to this "superb" Eclectic "fixture" owned by "gracious" manager Michael Franks and chef Robert Bell, whose menu ranging from Cajun meatloaf to "excellent sushi" changes daily according to "what's fresh and in season"; while most agree the service is "tops" and prices are "fair", they gripe that the "diner look just doesn't do it justice"; N.B. no corkage fee on Tuesdays.

### Chez Mimi Ⓜ *French*  21 | 24 | 21 | $46

**Santa Monica** | 246 26th St. (San Vicente Blvd.) | 310-393-0558 | www.chezmimirestaurant.com

Santa Monica *amis* find a "touch of paradise" at this French restaurant evoking a "quaint Provençal home", which serves "traditional country" dishes like *gigot d'agneau* (leg of lamb) and bouillabaisse; the staff provides a "relaxing" experience, but it's the "marvelous patio" and "cozy" interior (in winter, "dine by the fireplace") that really distinguish it as a "perfect date spot."

### Chichen Itza *Mexican*  ▽ 24 | 14 | 21 | $20

NEW **Downtown** | 2501 W. Sixth St. (Carondelet St.) | 213-380-0051
**Downtown** | 3655 S. Grand Ave. (Hope St.) | 213-741-1075
www.chichenitzarestaurant.com

Surveyors "swoon" over the signature roasted pork among other "sublime" offerings "prepared with intelligence and style" at these "unassuming" Downtown "temples of Yucatán cuisine"; the "fancier" West Sixth Street locale elicits raves as a "real bright newcomer", with the added advantage of beer and wine on the menu.

### Chi Dynasty *Chinese*  23 | 15 | 20 | $23

**Los Feliz** | 2112 Hillhurst Ave. (bet. Ambrose Ave. & Avocado St.) | 323-667-3388

"Sophisticated Chinese cuisine" for "everyday prices" makes this longtimer a "first choice" for Los Feliz patrons who pronounce themselves "addicted" to its "aromatic shrimp", chicken in lettuce cups and other dishes off the "expansive" menu, served by waiters who "remember you, make jokes and are on the ball"; though the "dated" decor "feels out of place" in the "trendy" neighborhood, a move in the works may change it up.

### Chili John's ☒ American  ▽ 23 | 11 | 21 | $11

**Burbank** | 2018 W. Burbank Blvd. (Keystone St.) | 818-846-3611
"The last of the old-fashioned chili joints" (since 1946), this Burbank "greasy spoon" sits its customers down around the horseshoe-shaped counter for "serious" bowls of the "spicy" specialty, with "several types" to choose from; loyalists "love the crazy, old decor" and call it "a keeper for understanding the virtue of doing one thing and doing it very, very well"; N.B. closed from July through Labor Day.

### Chili My Soul  Southwestern/Tex-Mex  22 | 8 | 18 | $12

**Encino** | 4928 Balboa Blvd. (Ventura Blvd.) | 818-981-7685 | www.chilimysoul.com
It's a "chili lover's dream" that "pushes the boundaries" hail hotheads of this Encino "strip-mall joint" that stirs up at least a dozen "tempting" varieties daily (two of them vegetarian) on a heat scale from 1 ("to please weak palates") to 10 ("scorching"); assisted by servers "encouraging free samples", it's easy for most to ignore the "somewhat inflated prices", because "this place hits the spot."

### China Beach Bistro  Vietnamese  ▽ 18 | 10 | 14 | $13

**Venice** | 2024 Pacific Ave. (Venice Blvd.) | 310-823-4646 | www.chinabeachbistro.com
"Fabulous pho" among other "fresh and flavorful" dishes draw oceanside eaters to this "teeny tiny" Venice joint with "just a few tables" inside and on the "comfortable" patio; there's "virtually no parking", but the "cheap Vietnamese sandwiches" are convenient on the go.

### China Grill  Californian/Chinese  20 | 15 | 17 | $26

**Manhattan Beach** | Manhattan Village Mall | 3282 Sepulveda Blvd. (Rosecrans Ave.) | 310-546-7284 | www.chinagrillbistro.com
A "modern", "light" and "interesting blend of cuisines" – "not your typical Chinese" – comes from the California-Cantonese kitchen at this Manhattan Beach "surprise in a shopping strip"; even if the service and furnishings could use a boost, reviewers rely on it as a "sure bet", especially for "lunch specials."

### Chin Chin  Chinese  17 | 13 | 16 | $22

**West Hollywood** | Sunset Plaza | 8618 W. Sunset Blvd. (Sunset Plaza Dr.) | 310-652-1818 | www.chinchin.com
**Beverly Hills** | 206 S. Beverly Dr. (Charleville Blvd.) | 310-248-5252 | www.chinchin.com
**Brentwood** | San Vincente Plaza | 11740 San Vicente Blvd. (bet. Barrington & Montana Aves.) | 310-826-2525 | www.chinchin.com
**Marina del Rey** | Villa Marina Mktpl. | 13455 Maxella Ave. (Lincoln Blvd.) | 310-823-9999 | www.chinchin.com
**Studio City** | 12215 Ventura Blvd. (Laurel Canyon Blvd.) | 818-985-9090
"Can't beat it for a quick Chinese chicken salad fix" chirp champions of this "easy", "reasonably priced" LA chain whose 'dim sum and then sum' combo also wins kudos; still, what some call "the old-school of the new-school Cal-Chinese" others regard as "reliable but not re-

|  | FOOD | DECOR | SERVICE | COST |

markable", noting that "barely adequate" service takes it down a notch; N.B. the Studio City location is now separately owned.

### ☑ Chinois on Main  *Asian/French*    | 26 | 20 | 23 | $59 |

**Santa Monica** | 2709 Main St. (Hill St.) | 310-392-9025 | www.wolfgangpuck.com

An "adventure" awaits at Wolfgang Puck's Santa Monica "temple" of Asian-French fusion, whose "inventive appetizers", whole catfish and other "superlatively" designed dishes still "impress", as does the "terrific" staff; although it loses points for a "cramped, noisy" dining room with a "late-'80s" look, insiders suggest "sitting at the bar and watching the show . . . it's better than the cooking channel."

### Chipotle  *Mexican*    | 19 | 11 | 15 | $10 |

**Fairfax** | 110 S. Fairfax Ave. (1st St.) | 323-857-0608
**Third Street** | 121 N. La Cienega Blvd. (3rd St.) | 310-855-0371
**Beverly Hills** | 244 S. Beverly Dr. (bet. Charles Blvd. & Gregory Way) | 310-273-8265
**Marina del Rey** | 4718 Admiralty Way (Mindanao Way) | 310-821-0059
**Torrance** | 24631 Crenshaw Blvd. (Skypark Dr.) | 310-530-0690
**Pasadena** | 3409 E. Foothill Blvd. (Madre St.) | 626-351-6017
**Burbank** | 135 E. Palm Ave. (1st St.) | 818-842-0622
www.chipotle.com

"Plentiful", "build-as-you-go" burritos please patrons of this "consistent" Mexican chain owned by McDonald's, which some call "your wallet's best friend and your diet's arch nemesis" – although "healthy" options (such as "sans-tortilla" style) are available; the "efficient assembly-line" service is a "simple concept that works", and the "clean", "minimal" dining rooms at most of the LA locations are "always packed."

### Chocolat  *Californian/French*    | 16 | 18 | 16 | $36 |

**Melrose** | 8155 Melrose Ave. (bet. Kilkea Dr. & La Jolla Ave.) | 323-651-2111 | www.chocolatrestaurant.com

"Beautiful atmosphere", both in the candlelit dining room and on the "pleasant" patio, outshines the Cal-French cuisine at this Melrose "neighborhood" place; many recommend "eat dinner elsewhere and come by for a chocolate martini and the soufflé", adding that "service can be random if you're not dressed to the nines."

### Cholada  *Thai*    | ▽ 26 | 9 | 22 | $20 |

**Malibu** | 18763 PCH (Topanga Beach Dr.) | 310-317-0025 | www.choladathaicuisine.com

This "Topanga-funky", "unpretentious" "beach cottage" sitting "across from the ocean" in Malibu serves up "Thai-rific" dishes with "clean, crisp flavors" in a building that's in "urgent need of a remodel"; while the beleaguered call it "too crowded and noisy", the outdoor patio is "perfect when it gets busy", and the Ventura outpost offers an additional option.

### Chop Suey Cafe  *Asian Fusion*    | ▽ 11 | 14 | 14 | $21 |

**Little Tokyo** | Far East Cafe Bldg. | 347 E. First St. (Los Angeles St.) | 213-617-9990 | www.chopsueycafe.com

"Maintaining the original atmosphere" of the Far East Cafe once housed here, this Asian fusion eatery in Little Tokyo attempts to put a "new twist on old ways", but samplers say "poor execution" mars a "good idea", as the food is "fair at best", service "leaves a lot to be desired" and the scene at the bar is "too trendy" for its "history-imbued" surroundings.

### ChoSun Galbee *Korean*

| - | - | - | M |

**Koreatown** | 3330 W. Olympic Blvd. (bet. S. Manhattan Pl. & S. Western Ave.) | 323-734-3330 | www.chosungalbee.com

A design-conscious contender for Korean BBQ, this K-towner serves cook-it-yourself meats, hot pots and other prepared dishes in an airy, modern indoor-outdoor setting; though not as authentic-feeling as some of its competitors, the staff speaks more English and the ventilation system works double-time to clear the noxious, cling-to-your-clothes grill smoke out of the air.

### Christine *Mediterranean/Pacific Rim*

| 25 | 19 | 23 | $42 |

**Torrance** | Hillside Vill. | 24530 Hawthorne Blvd. (Via Valmonte) | 310-373-1952 | www.restaurantchristine.com

It's the "Spago of the South Bay" according to admirers of this "foodies' delight" where chef Christine Brown crafts an "ambitious" Mediterranean–Pacific Rim menu that's "unmatched" and best showcased in her "superb" weekly tasting menu; while the staff is "spot-on", "there's not a lot of room between tables", which "slightly diminishes" the "gourmet experience" for some.

### Christy's *Italian*

| 24 | 22 | 22 | $41 |

**Long Beach** | 3937 E. Broadway (bet. Mira Mar & Termino Aves.) | 562-433-7133 | www.christysristorante.com

"Superior Northern Italian cuisine" with a Tuscan emphasis meets a "huge", "high-caliber" wine list at this Long Beach "class act" whose "quiet", "low-lit" rooms offer an "inviting" ambiance for "leisurely" dinners; its "attentive" servers also come through in delivering "fine dining at a reasonable price."

### Chung King ☞ *Chinese*

| - | - | - | I |

**Monterey Park** | 206 S. Garfield Ave. (bet. Garvey & Newmark Aves.) | 626-280-7430

Young Chinese folks and other chowhounds come to this inexpensive Monterey Park Szechuan for "fantastic" spareribs and chile-laced fried chicken cubes and wash down the fiery dishes with "plenty of water (or Tsing Tao beer)"; despite "dumpy" surroundings and a frequent language barrier, the "enthusiastic" staff is appreciated; N.B. cash only.

### Ciao Trattoria Ⓩ *Italian*

| 19 | 19 | 19 | $36 |

**Downtown** | 815 W. Seventh St. (bet. Figueroa & Flower Sts.) | 213-624-2244 | www.ciaotrattoria.com

This "traditional" Downtown Italian offers "well-prepared" cuisine that's "surprisingly affordable", but the 1928 "art deco" building it's housed in draws the most attention, as admirers deem the "elegant", "white-tablecloth" room with "high-ceilings" a natural for "business lunches" and "pre-theater dinners"

### Ⓩ Cicada Ⓩ *Californian/Italian*

| 23 | 26 | 24 | $52 |

**Downtown** | 617 S. Olive St. (bet. 6th & 7th Sts.) | 213-488-9488 | www.cicadarestaurant.com

"Stunning" "art deco" decor, complete with "the most gorgeous chandeliers ever to light your dinner", wows Downtown crowds even more than the "wonderful" Cal-Italian fare at this "theatrical" destination for "special occasions" and other rendezvous; a few critics complain it's "pricey", but most agree that the "opulent" surroundings and "relaxed, professional" staff set the stage when you're playing "princess" for a day; N.B. closed weekends for private parties.

**NEW Circa 55** *American/Californian*  ▽ 21 | 22 | 21 | $48

**Beverly Hills** | Beverly Hilton | 9876 Wilshire Blvd. (Santa Monica Blvd.) | 310-887-6055 | www.circa55beverlyhills.com

"Retro" digs house this New American–Californian at the remodeled Beverly Hilton, whose location "next to the swimming pool" is a draw for sightseers; a "well-mannered" staff and "tasty" bites add substance, though some recommend it for lunch or a "drink before dinner", noting that the kitchen still seems to be "getting the kinks out."

**Citizen Smith** ☻ *American*  18 | 24 | 17 | $39

**Hollywood** | 1600 N. Cahuenga Blvd. (bet. Hollywood & Sunset Blvds.) | 323-461-5001 | www.citizensmith.com

Scenesters populate this "swanky space" whose "magic" wooden doors lead to a "beautiful" heated patio; its New American noshes like jalapeño mac 'n' cheese (served till 1:30 AM) often take second place to the Hollywood "party", which runs on "strong" drinks, "full-blast" DJ music and "marginal service" – making unenthused eaters remark it's merely "one of those places of the moment."

**City Bakery** *Bakery*  18 | 13 | 13 | $19

**Brentwood** | Brentwood Country Mart | 225 26th St. (San Vicente Blvd.) | 310-656-3040 | www.thecitybakery.com

"Their sweets are legendary and well worth the extravagant price" extol Brentwood breadheads who eat up the "mind-blowing" cookies and "dessertlike" French toast, as well as an "organic and diverse" salad bar with "farmer's market ingredients" (charged by the ounce) at this NYC American import; still, critics complain of a "disjointed" experience, considering the "cold, cavernous" space, "dippy service" and pastries that cost "no more than lobster at The Palm"; N.B. the kitchen closes at 3 PM, but prepared items are available till evening.

**Ciudad** *Nuevo Latino*  21 | 19 | 19 | $38

**Downtown** | Union Bank Plaza | 445 S. Figueroa St. (5th St.) | 213-486-5171 | www.ciudad-la.com

"Creative, zippy" Nuevo Latino cuisine and "slammin' mojitos" define this "still-hot" and "colorful" "Downtown mainstay" by owners Susan Feniger and Mary Sue Milliken; while some find the food "fails to meet the hype", service can slide to the "slow side" and during peak hours "there's no possibility of conversation without a megaphone", especially at the "festive" bar, partisans call the patio "heavenly" on "warm summer nights"; P.S. "they have a Music Center shuttle too."

**Clafoutis** ☻ *French/Italian*  18 | 16 | 18 | $32

**West Hollywood** | Sunset Plaza | 8630 W. Sunset Blvd. (Sunset Plaza Dr.) | 310-659-5233

"One of the better Sunset Plaza joints", this sidewalk bistro offers "consistent" French-Italian fare and some of West Hollywood's "best people-watching" according to admirers, while the "showy", smoking "expat" crowd and "leased Ferraris driving by" evoke the

"Champs" district of Paris – except that the staff "cheerfully" serves even "late-nighters."

### Claim Jumper *American*  | 19 | 17 | 18 | $25 |

**Long Beach** | Marketplace Shopping Ctr. | 6501 E. PCH (2nd St.) | 562-431-1321

**Torrance** | Torrance Crossroads | 24301 Crenshaw Blvd. (Lomita Blvd.) | 310-517-1874

**Monrovia** | 820 W. Huntington Dr. (bet. 5th & Monterey Aves.) | 626-359-0463

**Northridge** | Northridge Mall | 9429 Tampa Ave. (Plummer St.) | 818-718-2882

**City of Industry** | 18061 Gale Ave. (Fullerton Rd.) | 626-964-1157

**Valencia** | 25740 N. The Old Rd. (McBean Pkwy.) | 661-254-2628

www.claimjumper.com

Additional locations throughout Southern California

"Stake your claim to the next pant size up" if you indulge in the "decadent" American offerings – the steaks are "pretty good" but "who can beat the 'motherlode' chocolate cake with six layers?" – in portions "big enough to feed a hungry miner" at this Cali-based chain complete with woodsy trappings, a "family-friendly" staff and "long waits on the weekends"; reluctant regulars admit "I'm ashamed to say I love this place", but its "cheesiness" sometimes does the trick.

### Clay Pit *Indian*  | 22 | 15 | 19 | $30 |

**Brentwood** | 145 S. Barrington Ave. (Sunset Blvd.) | 310-476-4700

This "understated" Indian offers "tasty" tandoori and "delicious" curries in a "pleasant" environment that's suited to both "bargain lunch buffets" and evening "dates", especially if you want to "take a vegetarian"; still, a few say the service could be smoother, and dinner is "a little spendy" thanks to its "prime Brentwood location."

### Clementine 🛇 *Bakery*  | 24 | 12 | 16 | $18 |

**Century City** | 1751 Ensley Ave. (Santa Monica Blvd.) | 310-552-1080 | www.clementineonline.com

"Oh, my darling" utter Century City aficionados of this breakfast and lunch nook whose chef-owner, Annie Miller, prepares "artisanal home cooking" such as "wonderful sandwiches", "unreal" soups and "sublime baked goods"; the "calamitous parking situation", "scramble for tables" and staff that "needs a little more help", however, "discourage anything but off-peak visits", so practical patrons advise "taking it home."

### Cliff's Edge ☻ *Californian/Italian*  | 20 | 25 | 18 | $41 |

**Silver Lake** | 3626 Sunset Blvd. (Edgecliffe Dr.) | 323-666-6116

"Paradise awaits" at this unmarked Cal-Italian ("look for the 99-cent store") whose "tranquil" "treehouse" setting makes Silver Lakers feel "a million miles away from LA"; the seasonal cuisine, and Sunday brunch in particular, can also be "delicious", though some comment that the kitchen is "trying too hard" and the staff could try a little harder.

### Club 41 *Steak*  | 19 | 21 | 21 | $35 |

**Pasadena** | 41 S. De Lacey St. (bet. Colorado Blvd. & Green St.) | 626-795-4141

"A Pasadena throwback" that "remains current enough to draw a trendy crowd", this "neat" mahogany- and leather-decked American

| | FOOD | DECOR | SERVICE | COST |

steakhouse still offers a "clubby" environment to match "old-style" chops and a "Caesar salad made right at your table"; it's tough for the "new management" to win over everyone, however, since some tut that the food is "tired", and others "miss the vibe" it had previously.

### NEW Coast 🅱 🅼 *Californian*
— — — I

**Santa Monica** | Shutters on the Beach | 1 Pico Blvd. (Ocean Ave.) | 310-458-0030

This well-priced Californian with chef Ray Luna (ex Patina Group and Spago) at the helm has settled into the space that was last home to Pedals, on the lower level of Santa Monica's Shutters on the Beach; with its cozy fabrics, floor-to-ceiling windows and trellises heavy with flowers, it feels just like a beach house.

### Cobras & Matadors *Spanish*
21 16 17 $33

**Beverly Boulevard** | 7615 W. Beverly Blvd. (bet. Curson & Stanley Aves.) | West Hollywood | 323-932-6178

**Los Feliz** | 4655 Hollywood Blvd. (Vermont Ave.) | 323-669-3922

Those who savor anything "stuffed with Cabrales" commend Steven Arroyo's "loud and fantastic" Beverly Boulevard and Los Feliz Spanish duo for its "tasty" tapas that are "great for groups" and couples, even if some really go for the "tattooed waiters"; just be warned that you may need to "keep ordering" to feel full, and the BYO WeHo original (with a wine shop next door) is "so small" and dimly lit, you'll "think you're playing footsie with your date, but it's actually your neighbor."

### NEW Coccole
▽ 21 15 13 $38

### Laboratorio Del Gusto 🅼 *Italian*

**Redondo Beach** | 320 S. Catalina Ave. (Torrance Blvd.) | 310-374-6929 | www.coccoledelgusto.com

"If this is a laboratory, I'm glad to be a guinea pig" assert early samplers of this Redondo Beach regional Italian, owned by the married team of chef Collette and Guido Fratesi, where the "quality ingredients and preparation" are largely "top-notch"; still, a bit of "unevenness" is evident in both the food and the "minimal" staff, and since the restaurant adheres (rather literally) to the Slow Food movement, it's "not a place to go when you want to get in and out quickly."

### NEW Coco D'Amour 🅼 *Eclectic*
— — — M

**Simi Valley** | 2321 Tapo St. (Cochran St.) | 805-578-2622 | www.cocodamourcuisine.com

With its tikis and indoor grass huts, this colorful Simi Valley newcomer dishing up affordable Eclectic-Polynesian fare is out to prove that the South Seas are alive and well in SoCal; its bar serves plenty of tropical cocktails, which guests can sip while enjoying karaoke, comedy or live music depending on the night.

### NEW Coco Noche *Dessert/Eclectic*
▽ 22 18 22 $29

**Manhattan Beach** | 1140 Highland Ave. (Manhattan Beach Blvd.) | 310-545-4925 | www.coconoche.com

"Small plates and desserts" draws nibblers to this Manhattan Beach Eclectic where you "can't go wrong" with the Korean dishes or "delightful" pairings of chocolate and vino; while some would like to see "more pizzazz" and "coziness" in the furnishings, and stronger definition in the menu, most agree it has potential as a "wine lovers' hangout."

### Colony Cafe & Papa's Porch  *American*    ▽ 18 | 16 | 14 | $13

**West LA** | 10939 W. Pico Blvd. (Kelton Ave.) | 310-470-8909 |
www.thecolonycafe.com

A "welcome addition" to West LA, this "adorable" American opened
by Lilly Tartikoff conjures up the feel of a "New England beach town"
for daytime diners feasting on "great burgers", hot dogs and "addictive" garlic fries; on the downside, what critics call "erratic" service
and a "weird setup" of adjoining cafes can detract from the comfort
cuisine; N.B. open till 9 PM in the summer.

### Cooks Double Dutch  *American*    22 | 15 | 21 | $26

**Culver City** | 9806 Washington Blvd. (Delmas Terr.) | 310-280-0991 |
www.cooksdoubledutch.com

Vegans, vegetarians and carnivores hop, skip and jump over to Culver
City for "superb" New American dishes ranging from "super-healthy
to super-decadent", out of a kitchen that's "attentive to food allergies
and sensitivities"; its "personable" staff and "quirky" decor have their
charms, and though fans are sometimes thrown by the "strange"
hours ("check before going"), every last Tuesday of the month the
"family-style vegan night is like a fabulous dinner party."

### Coral Tree Café  *Californian/Italian*    19 | 15 | 13 | $17

**Brentwood** | 11645 San Vicente Blvd. (Darlington Ave.) | 310-979-8733
**NEW** **Encino** | 17499 Ventura Blvd. (Encino Ave.) | 818-789-8733
### Coral Tree Express  *Californian/Italian*
**Century City** | Century City Westfield Mall | 10250 Santa Monica Blvd.
(bet. Ave. of the Stars & S. Beverly Glen Blvd.) | 310-553-8733
www.coraltreecafe.net

"Refreshing", organic Cal-Italian fare, with a focus on "beautiful" salads and "filling" panini, attracts "actors and agents" among others to
the original Brentwood locale that's "cozy" with an outdoor fire pit; the
younger Century City and Encino outposts draw their share of
businesspeople and "laptop toters", respectively, though despite the
trio's "popularity", many take issue with its "prices fit for celebrities"
considering the "inexplicably slow" cafeteria-style service.

### Cora's Coffee Shoppe  *Diner*    21 | 13 | 17 | $21

**Santa Monica** | 1802 Ocean Ave. (Pico Blvd.) | 310-451-9562
"Scrumptious" gourmet diner fare made with "first-class ingredients"
attracts Santa Monica brunch crowds to Capo's "sleeper" sis, whose
signatures include a burrata caprese omelet and "awesome" orange
blueberry pancakes; its outdoor tables provide an alternative to the
"lunch counter" inside, so even if some find it a little "yuppified" and
"avant-garde for the AM", most advise "pretend you don't hear the
traffic outside the patio, read the paper and enjoy"; N.B. open till 9 PM
in the early summer.

### **NEW** Corkscrew Cafe  *Eclectic*    – | – | – | M

**Manhattan Beach** | 2201 Highland Ave. (Marine Ave.) | 310-546-7160 |
www.corkscrewcafemb.com

Located a block from Manhattan Beach, this wine-and-small-plates
cafe offers a midpriced Eclectic menu served in a handful of dining
areas, each about the size of a walk-in closet; the cozy quarters don't
faze locals who like to sit at high tables and look out onto the ocean.

|  | FOOD | DECOR | SERVICE | COST |
|---|---|---|---|---|

### Counter, The  *Hamburgers*                    21 | 14 | 16 | $16

**Santa Monica** | 2901 Ocean Park Blvd. (29th St.) | 310-399-8383
"An endless combination of toppings" makes this "build-your-own" hamburger joint popular with the Santa Monica set, who appreciate the "unusual" "possibilities", "fresh" ingredients" and "pre-existing choices" for those "too lazy to choose"; a "helpful", "attractive" staff imposes order on the "über-crowded" dining room, which is a "great place for kids" as long as they can deal with the "long waits for a table."

### NEW  Coupa Cafe  *Eclectic*              ▽ 14 | 16 | 16 | $22

**Beverly Hills** | 419 N. Canon Dr. (bet. Brighton Way & Santa Monica Blvd.) | 310-385-0420 | www.coupacafe.com
"Strong Venezuelan coffee" is the "standout" at this Beverly Hills new-comer where the other Eclectic fare – like arepas, panini, pizza and salads – "needs to improve" to please critics; still, "reasonable" tabs, "accommodating" service and an "attractive" high-ceilinged room mean it works for a cuppa joe either out in the garden or by the fire-place "on a rare cold, rainy day."

### Courtyard, The ● *Spanish*                 17 | 18 | 17 | $30

**West Hollywood** | 8543 Santa Monica Blvd. (La Cienega Blvd.) | 310-358-0301 | www.dinecourtyard.com
Opinions are split on this West Hollywood tapas spot that admirers "adore", but others find "just so-so", adding that the portions are "tiny" and yet still command "full-plate prices"; meanwhile, the "wide selection of sangrias" wins high marks from all, as does the "lovely", "romantic courtyard" and "even lovelier" "actors, uh, I mean waiters."

### Coyote Cantina  *Southwestern*            20 | 16 | 19 | $25

**Redondo Beach** | King Harbor Ctr. | 531 N. PCH (190th St.) | 310-376-1066 | www.coyotecantina.net
The Southwestern menu "goes beyond" "standard" Mexican fare at this "unassuming" Redondo Beach strip-mall "standby" that "satisfies" with "innovative" dishes and "potent margaritas" that make good use of the bar's 75-label tequila selection; in all, allies attest it's "a howling good time" with a "dark and crowded" atmosphere and "friendly" servers who add to the "upbeat" vibe.

### Cozymel's  *Mexican*                        14 | 15 | 14 | $21

**El Segundo** | 2171 Rosecrans Ave. (Continental Way) | 310-606-5464 | www.cozymels.com
Straddling the El Segundo/Manhattan Beach border, this "ersatz" Mexican watering hole (a link in a national chain) is most memorable as "a pleasant place to get soused" on "big, tasty margaritas"; the service can be "slow" and the food quality "so-so", but if you "sit at the bar and have free chips and salsa", you'll get your money's worth.

### NEW  Craft  *American*                      – | – | – | E

**Century City** | 10100 Constellation Blvd. (Bet. Ave. of the Stars & Century Park E) | 310-279-4180 | www.craftrestaurant.com
Top chef (and *Top Chef* judge) Tom Colicchio plants the first Los Angeles outpost of his popular NYC-bred New American right next to Century City's new Creative Artists HQ; featuring a glass-enclosed dining room, shiny glass-and-chrome bar and sprawling outdoor patio with cabanalike lounges, it's already being referred to as the 'CAA

Commissary', so expect much moving and shaking over the plates of seasonal fare.

### Crazy Fish  *Japanese*

| 17 | 7 | 13 | $27 |

**Beverly Hills** | 9105 W. Olympic Blvd. (Doheny Dr.) | 310-550-8547

It's "not very glamorous" but this Beverly Hills Japanese is "clearly doing something right" given that it's "jammed every night" with a "cool alt crowd"; "big pieces" of "fresh" fish and an "infamous" spicy tuna roll all at "bargain" prices may account for the "hype" – it's certainly not the service, which is "mediocre" at best.

### Creole Chef, The  *Creole*

| – | – | – | I |

**Baldwin Hills** | Baldwin Hills Plaza | 3715 Santa Rosalia Dr. (Stocker St.) | 323-294-2433

"The po' boys and gumbo are no joke" at this "quaint" (read: "small") Baldwin Hills strip-mall Creole with "authentic" fare like fried catfish, crawfish étouffée and bread pudding prepared by chef-owner Norm Theard; the cafeteria-style service is "fast" while jazz on the speakers, French Quarter photos on the walls and patio dining bring "a little bit of New Orleans right here" to LA.

### CrêpeVine, The  *French*

| 21 | 18 | 20 | $29 |

**Pasadena** | 36 W. Colorado Blvd. (bet. De Lacey & Fair Oaks Aves.) | 626-796-7250 | www.thecrepevine.com

"Tucked away on an alley off busy Colorado Boulevard", this "endearing" Pasadena bistro is "worth seeking out" for "wonderful" sweet and savory namesake crêpes as well as other "quintessential" French dishes and "a wine selection that changes on a regular basis"; with a "pleasant" staff and prices that "won't deplete your wallet", the only downside is "tight seating"; P.S. there's "lively" jazz Tuesday–Thursday nights.

### Crescendo at Fred Segal  *Italian*

| ▽ 17 | 12 | 17 | $22 |

**Santa Monica** | Fred Segal | 500 Broadway (5th St.) | 310-395-5699

"Meet the girls for a late lunch" at this "busy" red-tablecloth Italian cafe within Santa Monica's tony Fred Segal store where the "satisfying" salads and pastas are bested only by the stellar "people-watching"; the staff is generally "warm and welcoming" while moderate menu prices take the sting off the cost of those True Religion jeans inside.

### Crocodile Cafe  *Californian*

| 16 | 15 | 16 | $24 |

**Pasadena** | 140 S. Lake Ave. (bet. Cordova & Green Sts.) | 626-449-9900
**Glendale** | 626 N. Central Ave. (Doran St.) | 818-241-1114
www.crocodilecafe.com

For a "quick bite" in a "family-friendly" habitat surveyors select this Smith brothers (Arroyo Chop House, Parkway Grill) duo where the "decent" if "uninspiring" Californian fare comes in "huge portions" while prices are "reasonable" too; patio seating at both Glendale and Pasadena locations provides a "comfortable" environment, but otherwise, claim critics, they're really "nothing special."

### ☒ Crustacean  *Asian Fusion/Vietnamese*

| 23 | 25 | 21 | $60 |

**Beverly Hills** | 9646 Little Santa Monica Blvd. (Bedford Dr.) | 310-205-8990 | www.anfamily.com

"A koi stream underfoot" is only part of the "dazzling" French colonial decor at this Beverly Hills "destination" where a "showbiz" crowd

| | FOOD | DECOR | SERVICE | COST |
|---|---|---|---|---|

("B-listers", "pro athletes") and "tourists" crack open "big messy crabs" and slurp up "addictive" noodles from a "pricey" menu of Vietnamese and Asian fusion dishes; though critics carp it's "lost its luster" even they concede this LA "institution" "has to be experienced at least once."

### Cuban Bistro Ⓜ Cuban
| 20 | 20 | 18 | $25 |

**Alhambra** | 28 W. Main St. (Garfield Ave.) | 626-308-3350 | www.cubanbistro.com

At this "lively" Alhambra spot there's "lots of sizzle" both on the "filling" plates of Cuban fare ("go for the plantains") and on the dance floor on Fridays and Saturdays when both live salsa music and "delicious" mojitos provide plenty of "kicks"; during the week, insiders insist the "lunch deals are a real bargain."

### CUBE Ⓢ Italian
| ▽ 25 | 14 | 20 | $30 |

**La Brea** | 615 N. La Brea Ave. (Clinton St.) | 323-939-1148 | www.divinepasta.com

"Wonderful" artisanal cheese and charcuterie lure La Brea foodies to this "authentic" Italian cafe/retail shop where the "knowledgeable" staff will guide you through the menu of pizzas, pastas and small plates that's perfect for "exploration"; moderate prices and "tiny" quarters mean you may need a "strategy" to snag a seat; N.B. a wine license is pending, and until then, corkage is free.

### Cucina Paradiso Italian
| 21 | 17 | 20 | $35 |

**Palms** | 3387 Motor Ave. (bet. National Blvd. & Woodbine St.) | 310-839-2500 | www.cucinaparadiso.net

An "unassuming hideaway" in "the heart of Palms", this Northern Italian "neighborhood restaurant" pleases with "mouthwatering" pastas, meats and fish served in a "cozy" room with white tablecloths and rustic details; "considerate" servers soften prices that critics call "expensive"; N.B. the adjacent lounge (The Palmer room) plays host to a mix of live music and comedy acts on weekends.

### Ⓩ Cut Ⓢ Steak
| 26 | 24 | 24 | $94 |

**Beverly Hills** | Beverly Wilshire | 9500 Wilshire Blvd. (Beverly Dr.) | 310-276-8500 | www.wolfgangpuck.com

"The new king" of Kobe, Wolfgang Puck has a "winner" with this "quintessential" steakhouse in the Beverly Wilshire hotel that "sets the bar" with "amazing" cuts of beef ("Wagyu as rich and tender as foie gras") and "inventive" sides served in a "professional", if "sometimes over-the-top", manner befitting the "outlandish" prices (you may as well "just hand your wallet to the hostess when you walk in"); the "magnificent" Richard Meier-designed room is a "total scene" where "celeb-spotting is highly probable", but reservations are a "pain" "unless you've been nominated for an Academy Award"; N.B. a limited menu is available at the adjacent Sidebar.

### Daily Grill American
| 18 | 17 | 18 | $30 |

**Brentwood** | Brentwood Gdns. | 11677 San Vicente Blvd. (Barrington Ave.) | 310-442-0044

**El Segundo** | 2121 Rosecrans Ave. (bet. Apollo & Nash Sts.) | 310-524-0700

**LAX** | LA Int'l Airport | 280 World Way (Tom Bradley Terminal) | 310-215-5180

*(continued)*

| | FOOD | DECOR | SERVICE | COST |

(continued)

## Daily Grill

**Burbank** | Burbank Marriott | 2500 Hollywood Way (bet. Empire & Thornton Aves.) | 818-840-6464
**Studio City** | Laurel Promenade | 12050 Ventura Blvd. (Laurel Canyon Blvd.) | 818-769-6336
**Universal City** | Universal CityWalk | 1000 Universal Studios Blvd. (off Rte. 101) | 818-760-4448
www.dailygrill.com

"Consistency" rules at this "tried-and-true" Traditional American chain spun off from The Grill on the Alley that "pleases the pickiest eaters" with "comforting" classics like "hearty chicken pot pie" and other "wholesome" eats served by a "prompt" and "polite" staff; yet in spite of "fair" prices, adventurous eaters attest the "uninspired" menu's "boring" and beg them to "expand" their offerings.

## Dakota *Steak*  22 | 24 | 20 | $57

**Hollywood** | Roosevelt Hotel | 7000 Hollywood Blvd. (N. Orange Dr.) | 323-769-8888 | www.dakota-restaurant.com

An "oasis" in Hollywood's "tragically hip" Roosevelt Hotel, Tim and Liza Goodell's steakhouse has a "romantic feel" thanks to "huge, comfy" leather and suede booths and dim lighting; "pricey" meat and seafood dishes "live up to the hype" with "five-star flavors", though some are put off by the occasional "heaping side of attitude" from usually "accommodating" servers.

## ☑ Dal Rae *Continental*  26 | 20 | 25 | $49

**Pico Rivera** | 9023 E. Washington Blvd. (Rosemead Blvd.) | 562-949-2444 | www.dalrae.com

Sentimentalists swoon over this Pico-Rivera "throwback" where the "absolutely amazing" "1950s" decor befits the "superb" Continental menu featuring "old-fashioned" dishes like lobster Thermidor, steak Diane and bananas flambé; "stiff drinks", "tableside preparations" and servers with "grace and charm" are other "real-deal" touches that make it "a favorite" in spite of its out-of-the-way location.

## Damon's Steakhouse *Steak*  16 | 17 | 19 | $26

**Glendale** | 317 N. Brand Blvd. (bet. California Ave. & Lexington Dr.) | 818-507-1510 | www.damonsglendale.com

"Sip your mai tai amid fish tanks and palm fronds" at this "tacky" "tiki paradise" in Glendale searing "decent" steaks "that come in huge portions" and are served by tropically attired staff that's "been around forever"; a handful of detractors dub the decor "old" (applying the same adjective to the customers), but they're outvoted by those who think it still makes for a "fun and frolicking night out."

## D'Amore's Pizza Connection *Pizza*  21 | 7 | 17 | $14

**Malibu** | 22601 PCH (Cross Creek Rd.) | 310-317-4500
**Westwood** | 1077 Broxton Ave. (Kinross Ave.) | 310-209-1212
**Canoga Park** | 7137 Winnetka Ave. (Sherman Way) | 818-348-5900
**Encino** | 15928 Ventura Blvd. (bet. Gavlota & Gloria Aves.) | 818-907-9100
**Sherman Oaks** | 12910 Magnolia Blvd. (Coldwater Canyon Ave.) | 818-505-1111
**Sherman Oaks** | Sherman Oaks Collection | 14519 Ventura Blvd. (Van Nuys Blvd.) | 818-905-3377

*(continued)*

## D'Amore's Pizza Connection

**Thousand Oaks** | Skyline Shopping Ctr. | 2869 Thousand Oaks Blvd. (Skyline Dr.) | 805-496-0030

"Pretty darn close to East Coast pizza", the "impossibly thin-crust" pies at this LA chain owe their "incredible" flavor and "high" prices to "imported water and ingredients" from Boston; though the staff has "lots of personality", the "drab" decor has most relegating these "small, casual spots" to meals "on the go" or "delivery."

## NEW Danny's Venice Deli *Deli*

∇ 18 | 18 | 17 | $23

**Venice** | 23 Windward Ave. (bet. Pacific Ave. & Spdwy.) | 310-566-5610 | www.dannysvenicedeli.com

"California cool meets NY deli" at this "arty" Venice newcomer with an "eclectic" menu of "fresh-tasting" dishes (some made from organic ingredients) focusing on Jewish "comfort" fare like pastrami, chicken liver and matzo ball soup; breakfast served until 3 PM and "reasonable prices" have already made it "popular with locals", though some regulars are "rooting for it to get the kinks out" of sometimes "slow" service.

## Dan Tana's ◗ *Italian*

21 | 17 | 20 | $53

**West Hollywood** | 9071 Santa Monica Blvd. (Doheny Dr.) | 310-275-9444 | www.dantanasrestaurant.com

"Tony Soprano might roll in and order a martini and a steak" at West Hollywood's "old-school" "fixture" where an "always entertaining" cast of "characters" ("A-list stars", "has-beens", "starlets", "James Woods") chows down on "red-sauce" classics from a menu of Italian fare that – just like the "dark", "clubby" decor – never changes; while some gripe about "gruff" service, "outrageous prices" and long waits ("even with a reservation"), loyalists contend it's "well worth it", even if it's just for "a drink or three", especially "late-night."

## Danube Bulgarian *Bulgarian*

∇ 15 | 7 | 15 | $23

**Westwood** | 1303 Westwood Blvd. (Wellworth Ave.) | 310-473-2414

"Bulgarian home cooking" comes to Westwood via this relative newcomer boasting a "vast" menu that also offers an "odd mishmash" of cuisines from neighboring countries like Greece; though adventurous eaters rate the fare "disappointing", the saving graces are the "fabulous" "multilayered" Garash cake and "friendly", if "distracted" servers.

## Da Pasquale ⓩ *Italian*

21 | 15 | 20 | $34

**Beverly Hills** | 9749 Little Santa Monica Blvd. (bet. Linden & Roxbury Drs.) | 310-859-3884 | www.dapasqualecaffe.com

"Only locals know about this" "reasonably priced" family-run Beverly Hills Italian that's been a "haven" since 1989 for chef-owner Anna Morra's "fabulous homemade pastas" that really "hit the spot"; "everyone works hard to serve you well" in the "lovely" "small" dining room where stuccoed walls and rustic wrought-iron accents give it a feel so "authentic", "it's like being in Italy."

## Dar Maghreb *Moroccan*

18 | 23 | 20 | $48

**Hollywood** | 7651 Sunset Blvd. (bet. Fairfax & La Brea Aves.) | 323-876-7651 | www.darmaghrebrestaurant.com

"Dazzle a date" or a "group of out-of-towners" at this "glitzy" "little slice of Morocco" smack-dab in Hollywood where diners recline on pillows while ogling "belly dancers" and picking at "tasty" fare from a seven-course prix fixe feast (eating "with your fingers is encouraged here"); critics complain the food and service "have gone down considerably" since the loss of the original owner, but the majority still finds this "exotic" spot "a hoot."

### Delmonico's Lobster House  Seafood

| 21 | 19 | 21 | $43 |

**Encino** | 16358 Ventura Blvd. (Hayvenhurst Ave.) | 818-986-0777 | www.delmonicoslobsterhouse.com

"Cushy private booths" add a "comforting" air to this "old-school" Encino seafooder done up in "dark mahogany wood" that "packs them in" for "reliable", if "unimaginative", takes on "traditional" dishes like stuffed lobster, steaks and chops; servers are "well-versed" on the offerings, and if some say tabs are "pretty pricey", they also admit "it's a good place to impress the folks when they're visiting."

### Delphi Greek Cuisine ☒ Greek

| 17 | 11 | 17 | $21 |

**Westwood** | 1383 Westwood Blvd. (Wilshire Blvd.) | 310-478-2900

This "small", "casual" Westwood Greek is presided over by a "genial host who never forgets a customer", but diners divide on the fare ("authentic" vs. "lacks character"); still, moderate tabs mean it works for a "basic" "lunch" while sidewalk seating is an additional draw.

### Depot, The ☒ Eclectic

| 23 | 21 | 23 | $39 |

**Torrance** | 1250 Cabrillo Ave. (Torrance Blvd.) | 310-787-7501 | www.depotrestaurant.com

"Creative" Eclectic cuisine from chef-owner Michael Shafer really "wakes up your taste buds" at this Torrance "standout" set in a "quaint" converted train station where the "wonderful" food and "warm, inviting atmosphere" make it a "popular" "neighborhood" spot; even with "crowded" quarters during "business lunches", say fans, it's still "pleasant."

### Derby, The  Steak

| ▽ 24 | 23 | 24 | $42 |

**Arcadia** | 233 E. Huntington Dr. (bet. Gateway Dr. & 2nd Ave.) | 626-447-2430 | www.thederbyarcadia.com

"A must-visit among the track crowd", this "racing-themed" Arcadia steakhouse near Santa Anita Park is a "longtime favorite" (it dates back to 1938) for "carnivores" craving prime rib and bacon-wrapped filet mignon; the decor oozes "old-world style and charm" with "red leather booths, dimmed lights" and Seabiscuit memorabilia courtesy of former owner George Woolf, while the "cordial" service is another "timeless" touch.

### ☑ Derek's ☒☒ Californian/French

| 27 | 23 | 25 | $62 |

**Pasadena** | 181 E. Glenarm St. (bet. Arroyo Pkwy. & Marengo Ave.) | 626-799-5252 | www.dereks.com

It's "a real find!" exclaim enthusiasts of Derek Dickenson's "exceptional" bistro "hidden" away in a Pasadena strip mall where the "inspired" menu of "adventurous and creative" Cal-French dishes "consistently delivers" as does the "fabulous wine list"; an "extremely knowledgeable" staff works the various dining rooms, which have a "high-end, but not stuffy" vibe; it may be "wildly expensive", but cognoscenti coo it's "worth every penny."

| | FOOD | DECOR | SERVICE | COST |
|---|---|---|---|---|

### Devon, Restaurant Ⓜ *Californian/French* ▽ 25 | 21 | 24 | $46

**Monrovia** | 109 E. Lemon Ave. (Myrtle Ave.) | 626-305-0013

Monrovia's "suburban gem" attracts those game for game (like caribou and quail) from the "wonderfully creative" Cal-French menu with "amazing" specials that "change daily" and a wine list with 350 bottles; though the "classy" room done up in "lovely" warm tones earns raves from reviewers, some are put off by prices they perceive as "expensive."

### Din Tai Fung *Chinese* 26 | 12 | 15 | $20

**Arcadia** | 1108 S. Baldwin Ave. (bet. Arcadia Ave. & Duarte Rd.) | 626-574-7068

The "succulent" soup dumplings are like "handmade pieces of art" muse those mesmerized by this "simply decorated" Arcadia outpost of a Taipei-based chain, which has become the LA "benchmark" for Shanghai fare; "don't expect a leisurely meal" as the "friendly", if overly "efficient", staff "is all about increasing turnover", and if "an hour's drive" or "an hour's wait" deter some, others insist they'd "crawl through broken glass" for what they say is "the best Chinese food around."

### Dish *American* 18 | 16 | 17 | $22

**La Cañada Flintridge** | 734 Foothill Blvd. (Commonwealth Ave.) | 818-790-5355 | www.dishbreakfastlunchanddinner.com

"Tasty twists" on Traditional American comfort food and "great prices" make this "down-home" La Cañada Flintridge "staple" "reliably satisfying" for a "casual" meal (locals laud the "wonderful breakfasts"); the "cheerful" whitewashed interior has a "small-town" feel that fans find "charming", so the "slow" service is the only drawback.

### NEW Dive, The ☉ *Californian/Eclectic* - | - | - | I

**Hollywood** | 742 N. Highland Ave. (Melrose Ave.) | 323-466-1507 | www.thedivela.com

From the owners of Hugo's comes this well-priced Cal-Eclectic just off busy Melrose, featuring an outdoor patio and lively bar; its main room is done in dark colors and heavy fabrics – it's a bit like dining in a velvet-lined box; N.B. it opens early for breakfast and closes late.

### Divino *Italian* 23 | 17 | 21 | $42

**Brentwood** | 11714 Barrington Ct. (Sunset Blvd.) | 310-472-0886

"Divine" describes the "top-notch" fare at this "upscale" Brentwood "neighborhood trattoria" with "terrific" seasonal dishes from the Adriatic coast and a "friendly host" (chef-owner Goran Milic) "who always treats you well"; those who hate the "noise" and "crowds" downstairs (where "love thy neighbor must be the theme" of the "cozy" room) head to a "quieter" space upstairs.

### Dolce Enoteca e Ristorante *Italian* 16 | 20 | 16 | $51

**Melrose** | 8284 Melrose Ave. (Sweetzer Ave.) | 323-852-7174 | www.dolcegroup.com

A "hopping bar" "is the biggest draw" for "young wannabes" at this Dolce Group-backed Melrose Italiano where the "overpriced" cuisine "pales in comparison" to the "flashy" room (made even brighter with a "wall of flame" illuminating the bar area); the staff is "a bit arrogant", while a "DJ who starts spinning too early" underscores the notion that it's "more about the scene" here than anything else.

| | FOOD | DECOR | SERVICE | COST |
|---|---|---|---|---|

## Dominick's ● *Italian*    20 | 22 | 19 | $41

**Beverly Boulevard** | 8715 Beverly Blvd. (San Vicente Blvd.) | West Hollywood | 310-652-2335 | www.dominicksrestaurant.com

Whether on the "lovely patio" or in a "dimly lit booth" by the working fireplace, this "sceney" West Hollywood spot caters to a "hipster" crowd with Italian cuisine that's an "excellent value", particularly during Sunday suppers ("a bargain" at $15 for three courses); in spite of occasional "attitude" from servers, it remains a "great place to meet for a drink" or even a "first date."

## Doña Rosa *Bakery/Mexican*    16 | 12 | 14 | $13

**Arcadia** | Westfield Shoppingtown | 400 S. Baldwin Ave. (Huntington Dr.) | 626-821-3556

**Pasadena** | 577 S. Arroyo Pkwy. (California Blvd.) | 626-449-2999 ●
www.dona-rosa.com

Surveyors say the breakfasts and baked goods are most "satisfying" (though much of the rest of the menu is fairly "mediocre") at these Mexican cafe offshoots of El Cholo in Arcadia and Pasadena; "rustic taco-stand decor and order-at-the-counter-style service are "nothing fancy" so consider them "convenient" and "not-too-pricey" picks for a "quick" meal.

## NEW Dong Ting Spring *Chinese*    - | - | - | I

**San Gabriel** | San Gabriel Sq. | 140 W. Valley Blvd. (Del Mar Ave.) | 626-288-5918

On the second floor of the sprawling San Gabriel Square (aka "The Great Mall of China"), this bustling Hunanese offers a touch of unexpected elegance (understated lighting, framed Chinese scrolls on the walls), along with big-screen TVs showing martial arts movies, and a menu that sizzles with the flavors of Northern China; do be warned – when there's a pepper icon next to an item on the menu, it's because it's seriously hot.

## Doug Arango's ⊠ *Californian/Italian*    22 | 20 | 22 | $50

**West Hollywood** | 8826 Melrose Ave. (N. Robertson Blvd.) | 310-278-3684 | www.dougarangos.com

"Finally, a restaurant for adults" exclaim enthusiasts of this "upscale" West Hollywood "sleeper" where California-Italian specialties of the "highest quality" are paired with wines from an "extensive and eclectic" list; adding to the appeal for the "older" crowd are an "attractive", "comfortable" room with "tables set far apart" and "personal attention" from servers; "stay as long as you like – they'll never rush you out."

## Doughboys ● *Bakery*    22 | 12 | 16 | $18

**NEW Hollywood** | 1156 N. Highland Ave. (bet. Lexington Ave. & Santa Monica Blvd.) | 323-467-9117

**Third Street** | 8136 W. Third St. (Crescent Heights Blvd.) | 323-651-4202
www.doughboys.net

"Bountiful" breakfasts, "inventive" sandwiches on "the warmest, softest bread ever", plus an "Oprah-endorsed" red-velvet cake make this Third Street bakery (with a newer Hollywood outpost) a "staple" in spite of "lackluster" service and "waits that can last an eternity" ("especially during peak hours"); still, "reasonable" prices and an "unpretentious" atmosphere keep it "fun", though cynics still cite it as "overhyped."

|  | FOOD | DECOR | SERVICE | COST |
|---|---|---|---|---|

### Drago *Italian*
24 | 21 | 23 | $55

**Santa Monica** | 2628 Wilshire Blvd. (26th St.) | 310-828-1585 | www.celestinodrago.com

Celestino Drago's Santa Monica "flagship" "does the family proud" with "superb" Italian cuisine (like a "pumpkin tortellini" that's "out of this world") and an "incredible wine list" served with "a touch of class" to "media moguls" and "celebs" alike; "serene", "elegant" surroundings make this "favorite" "one of the most consistent high-end" experiences in town.

### Dr. Hogly Wogly's BBQ *BBQ*
23 | 6 | 17 | $21

**Van Nuys** | 8136 Sepulveda Blvd. (Roscoe Blvd.) | 818-780-6701 | www.hoglywogly.com

"Perfectly smoked meats" come in "heapin' helpings" at this "funky as hell" Van Nuys BBQ where "the line forms early" and "waitresses who have seen it all" work the "dumpy" room with vinyl booths and "bargain-basement wood paneling"; though "connoisseurs" claim "it's the best this side of Texas", a handful of holdouts insist it "can't compare" to joints "in South Central."

### Duke's *Pacific Rim*
17 | 21 | 18 | $32

**Malibu** | 21150 PCH (Las Flores Canyon Rd.) | 310-317-0777 | www.hulapie.com

"Breathtaking ocean views" are the "stars" at these "crowded" coastal twins in Huntington Beach and Malibu that "feel like Hawaii" right down to the "out-of-this-world sunsets" and "mai tais" at the "terrific barefoot bars" at both locations; "not much can be said" for the "ok" Pacific Rim eats or the slightly "ADD" service, but they're still "ideal for out-of-town guests" who hanker for a "cold beer", "fresh sea breeze" and a peek at "the surfer crowd."

### Duke's Coffee Shop *Diner*
18 | 11 | 18 | $17

**West Hollywood** | 8909 Sunset Blvd. (San Vicente Blvd.) | 310-652-3100 | www.dukescoffeeshop.com

A "weird mix" of "celebs", "bikers, musicians and a few working girls" fill up this "truck-stop"-style coffee shop in West Hollywood, where "rocking breakfasts" and other "hangover"-worthy meals are served at "long communal tables"; it's a "dive", for sure, but fans still flock to this "cheap", "cool little spot" that's a "Sunset Strip staple."

### Du-par's *Diner*
16 | 11 | 15 | $16

**Fairfax** | Farmers Mkt. | 6333 W. Third St. (Fairfax Ave.) | 323-933-8446 ◐

**Studio City** | Studio City Plaza | 12036 Ventura Blvd. (Laurel Canyon Blvd.) | 818-766-4437 ◐

**Thousand Oaks** | Best Western Thousand Oaks Inn | 75 W. Thousand Oaks Blvd. (bet. Moorpark Rd. & Rte. 101) | 805-373-8785

www.dupars.com

"Welcome back!" scream fans of the Farmers Market locale of this LA coffee shop trio that reopened with a "sparkling new interior" after a recent redo; in terms of the grub, "it's all about the pancakes" "oozing with melted butter and syrup" and "famous pies" say supporters who dub the other eats "uninspired" – more "memorable" are the "hundred-year-old" waitresses "squeezed into old-time uniforms."

### Dusty's  *American/French*

| 21 | 20 | 19 | $32 |

**Silver Lake** | 3200 W. Sunset Blvd. (Descanso Dr.) | 323-906-1018 | www.dustysbistro.com

An "upscale surprise" in "edgy" Silver Lake, this "charming" French-American bistro is "great on a lazy Sunday afternoon" when a "cool clientele" "crowds" into "comfy booths" and sups on "unbelievable crêpes" and soju Bloody Marys; service is "friendly" if "slow", while tabs can "add up quickly" during dinner.

### eat. on sunset  🗷 *American*

| 19 | 21 | 19 | $42 |

**Hollywood** | 1448 N. Gower St. (Sunset Blvd.) | 323-461-8800 | www.patinagroup.com

New American nibbles are washed down with "inventive cocktails" at this Hollywood "hipster" hang in the former Pinot Hollywood space where the disappointed deem the "unremarkable" fare "overpriced" and "not quite up to the standards" of its Patina Group "pedigree"; still, it's a "safe" bet if you're "in the neighborhood", and the "contemporary" room done up in "nautical" blues makes it "pleasant", especially on the roomy front patio or during "happy hour."

### Eat Well Cafe  *American*

| 15 | 13 | 15 | $17 |

**NEW** **Beverly Boulevard** | 7385 Beverly Blvd. (Martel Ave.) | 323-938-1300
**Silver Lake** | 3916 Sunset Blvd. (Santa Monica Blvd.) | 323-664-1624
www.eatwellcoffeeshop.com

"Inexpensive, all-purpose" Traditional American "diner" fare sustains both the Beverly Boulevard and Silver Lake locations of this "casual", "hippie-styled" cafe with plenty of "healthy options"; the food's only "ok", but service is "friendly", making it a "decent" "trendy" option without "the massive crowds" of its neighborhood competitors.

### NEW E. Baldi  🗷 *Italian*

| 21 | 15 | 14 | $57 |

**Beverly Hills** | 375 N. Canon Dr. (bet. Brighton & Dayton Ways) | 310-248-2633

There's a "gifted" kitchen staff turning out "sophisticated" Northern Italian specialties at this "expensive" Beverly Hills boîte, but some feel it has a ways to go before catching up with "older sibling" Giorgio Baldi: the majority says it's marred by "cramped" conditions, prices that "make your eyes pop" and "arrogant" service, so while "regulars" are rooting for it "to turn around", until then, critics conclude "it's not worth the hassle."

### Ebizo's Skewer  *Japanese*

| ▽ 16 | 11 | 18 | $23 |

**Manhattan Beach** | 229 Manhattan Beach Blvd. (Highland Ave.) | 310-802-0765

Sukiyaki and shabu-shabu head up an otherwise "limited" menu at this Manhattan Beach Japanese that's "different", if not exactly "authentic" (one particularly "Anglo" touch is the shabu-shabu burger); still, even with a "claustrophobic" interior, it's a "friendly" spot where skewer-happy sorts say a "seat at the counter" in front of the open kitchen affords the "coolest" "experience."

### Echigo  🗷 *Japanese*

| – | – | – | M |

**West LA** | 12217 Santa Monica Blvd. (Amherst Ave.) | 310-820-9787

Sushi only – and strictly the freshest fish in the simplest presentations – is on chef-owner Hitoshi Kataoka's (ex Sushi Sasabune) menu at this

West LA strip-mall eatery distinguished for its use of warm, vinegary rice and relatively inexpensive omakase ($38 at dinner); a well-informed staff services the basic, bare-bones setting.

### Edendale Grill *American*

| | | | |
|15|22|18|$36|

**Silver Lake** | 2838 Rowena Ave. (bet. Auburn & Rokeby Sts.) | 323-666-2000 | www.edendalegrill.com

The "converted firehouse" setting of this Silver Lake "nightspot" wins high marks for its expansive "'20s-era" bar "crowded" with "cool kids" and the "beautifully tended patio" that's "charming" "on a balmy summer night"; however, "inconsistent" service and "pricey", "hit-or-miss" Traditional American "comfort" fare lead insiders to insist you "steer clear of almost anything that comes out of the kitchen" and focus on the "generously sized drinks."

### NEW Eight-18 Ⓢ *Mediterranean*

| | | | |
|-|-|-| |

**Toluca Lake** | 10151 Riverside Dr. (bet. Forman & Talofa Aves.) | 818-761-4243

The latest in a firestorm of wine bars, this newcomer sits adjacent to the sprawling Burbank and Disney Studios in a room filled with racks of bottles and many small tables at which to consider the encyclopedic vino list; its wallet-friendly Med menu offers cheeses and charcuterie, along with more substantial chow like filet mignon with Roquefort butter.

### El Cholo Cafe *Mexican*

| | | | |
|18|18|18|$23|

**Mid-City** | 1121 S. Western Ave. (bet. 11th & 12th Sts.) | 323-734-2773
**Santa Monica** | 1025 Wilshire Blvd. (bet. 10th & 11th Sts.) | 310-899-1106
**Pasadena** | 958 S. Fair Oaks Ave. (bet. Arlington Dr. & Hurlbut St.) | 626-441-4353

### El Cholo Cantina *Mexican*

**LAX** | LA Int'l Airport | 209 World Way (Terminal 5) | 310-417-1910 www.elcholo.com

"A real icon" for "potent margaritas" and "huge platters" of "old-school Mexican", this "historic", family-owned chain opened more than 80 years ago but still "appeals to all ages, groups and cultures" for "festive", "dependable" meals; although the service is a "mixed bag" and some call the cooking "Anglo-cized", specialties like the "made-to-order" guacamole and "first-rate" "green corn tamales in season" are "difficult to pass up."

### El Coyote Cafe *Mexican*

| | | | |
|13|14|17|$20|

**Beverly Boulevard** | 7312 Beverly Blvd. (bet. Fuller Ave. & Poinsetta Pl.) | 323-939-2255 | www.elcoyotecafe.com

"Tasty margaritas" as "strong" as "jet fuel" kick-start the "mediocre" Mexican menu at this "popular" Beverly Boulevard "landmark" (open 75 years) with "cheap" tabs and "fast" service; the "delightfully tacky" atmosphere with "vinyl tablecloths", "plastic flowers" and "year-round Christmas lighting" adds to the "fun", and even if detractors deem it "the most overhyped" Mexperience in LA, people "pile in" nonetheless.

### Electric Lotus ☽ *Indian*

| | | | |
|19|20|17|$27|

**Los Feliz** | 4656 Franklin Ave. (Vermont Ave.) | 323-953-0040 | www.electriclotus.com

"Flowing saris, ambient lighting" and "cozy curtained private booths" conjure up a "den of iniquity" at this "dark", "hip" Los Feliz Indian where "ultraloud" music spun by an in-house DJ enhances "flavorful" curries and vindaloos that are "just spicy enough"; service is "relaxed" even by neighborhood standards, but is made more tolerable with "reasonable" prices and "generous" pours on drinks.

**NEW Eleven** *American*  ▽ 21 | 24 | 18 | $48

**West Hollywood** | 8811 Santa Monica Blvd. (Larrabee St.) | 310-855-0800
*H.R. Pufnstuf* co-creator Sid Krofft is behind this "beautifully decorated" WeHo newcomer housed in a "historic bank building" in Boystown with a "surprisingly delicious" New American menu from veteran chef Vincent Manna; at 11 PM the venue becomes a nightclub, and "servers who look as if they jumped out of a fashion magazine" are overshadowed by the "novel acrobatics show" and other "stage acts."

**NEW Elf Café** Ⓜ⊘ *Mediterranean/Vegetarian*  - | - | - | I

**Echo Park** | 2135 W. Sunset Blvd. (N. Alvarado St.) | 213-484-6829
Word-of-mouth has much to do with the success of this relatively inexpensive new Echo Park cafe where Mediterranean vegetarian dishes have an enthusiastic fan base (as does the band, Viva K, who own the place); the staff is friendly but the space is small and hours are sporadic (open Wednesday–Sunday for dinner); N.B. cash only.

**El Pollo Inka** *Peruvian*  19 | 12 | 15 | $16

**Lawndale** | Lawndale Plaza | 15400 Hawthorne Blvd. (154th St.) | 310-676-6665
**Gardena** | Gateway Plaza | 1425 W. Artesia Blvd. (Normandie Ave.) | 310-516-7378
**Hermosa Beach** | 1100 PCH (Aviation Blvd.) | 310-372-1433
**Torrance** | 23705 Hawthorne Blvd. (bet. Lomita Blvd. & PCH) | 310-373-0062
www.elpolloinka.com
"Juicy rotisserie chicken", "amazingly fresh ceviche" and other "craveable" Peruvian specialties are served in "huge portions" and "washed down with Inka cola" at this "no-frills" chain "locals" "count on" for a "quick", "quality" meal; though the "colorful" decor "won't wow you" and service can be "slow", "low prices" and a "family-friendly" vibe mean it's a "great value" and ensure it's "always packed"; N.B. there's live music on weekends at some locations.

**El Tepeyac** ⊘ *Mexican*  24 | 9 | 17 | $12

**East LA** | 812 N. Evergreen Ave. (Winter St.) | 323-267-8668
"You could feed a family of four" on the "monster" burritos ("as large as an adult thigh") at this East LA Mexican "institution" where those in-the-know go for "Manual's Special", named after the "legendary" owner who charms customers with his "friendly" demeanor (and occasionally "a shot of tequila"); if the decor's a bit "bare-bones", it's enlivened by the "mix of locals", "tourists", "firemen" and USC fans who bring "mucho gusto" to the party; P.S. beware of "long lines on weekends."

**El Torito** *Mexican*  15 | 15 | 16 | $21

**Hawthorne** | 11855 Hawthorne Blvd. (bet. 118th & 119th Sts.) | 310-679-0233
**Marina del Rey** | 13715 Fiji Way (Lincoln Blvd.) | 310-823-8941
**Long Beach** | 6605 PCH (bet. 2nd St. & Westminster Ave.) | 562-594-6917
**Redondo Beach** | Fisherman's Wharf | 100G Fisherman's Wharf (S. Catalina Ave.) | 310-376-0547
**Pasadena** | 3333 E. Foothill Blvd. (Sierra Villa Madre Ave.) | 626-351-8995

(continued)
## El Torito
**Burbank** | 4012 W. Riverside Dr. (Pass Ave.) | 818-848-4501
**Northridge** | 8855 Tampa Ave. (bet. Nordhoff & Parthenia Sts.) | 818-349-1607
**Sherman Oaks** | 14433½ Ventura Blvd. (Van Nuys Blvd.) | 818-990-5860
**Woodland Hills** | Warner Ctr. | 6040 Canoga Ave. (Oxnard St.) | 818-348-1767
**Thousand Oaks** | 449 N. Moorpark Rd. (bet. Brazil St. & Wilbur Rd.) | 805-497-3952
www.eltorito.com
Additional locations throughout Southern California

"You won't be thrilled, but you won't be disappointed either" with the "gringo-friendly" fare served "slowly" (at least "they never rush you") at this Mexican chain that's "a safe choice" for "families" and "the corporate lunch crowd"; adventurous eaters attest "you can do much better" in SoCal and suggest a stop at "the local taco stand" instead.

## El Torito Grill *Mexican*
18 | 17 | 17 | $25

**Beverly Hills** | 9595 Wilshire Blvd. (Camden Dr.) | 310-550-1599
**Torrance** | 21321 Hawthorne Blvd. (Torrance Blvd.) | 310-543-1896
**Sherman Oaks** | Sherman Oaks Galleria | 15301 Ventura Blvd. (Sepulveda Blvd.) | 818-907-7172
www.eltorito.com

El Torito's "trendy little sister", this "upscale" chain dishes out "perfectly decent" Mexican with "interesting twists" in locales that are "comfortably gringo-esque"; amigos praise "addictive housemade tortillas", "tableside guacamole" and "killer margaritas" but cynics call the *comida* "lackluster" and the service "nondescript", but hey – at least it's a "good value."

## Emle's *Californian/Mediterranean*
▽ 19 | 11 | 19 | $18

**Northridge** | 9250 Reseda Blvd. (Prairie St.) | 818-772-2203

"A perfectly sweet venue" (despite its Northridge "strip-mall" setting), this Cal-Med "cafe" charms "locals" with "great breakfasts", "early-bird" specials and other "well-prepared" fare "for a pittance"; considering "first-class" service, the only downsides are "cramped and noisy" seating and parking that can be "difficult depending on the time of day."

## Empress Harbor
## Seafood Restaurant *Chinese*
22 | 15 | 15 | $20

**Monterey Park** | Atlantic Plaza | 111 N. Atlantic Blvd., Ste. 350 (Garvey Ave.) | 626-300-8833 | www.empressharbor.com

Those who "don't mind paying a little more" for their turnip cakes and shark's fin dumplings sail into this Monterey Park Chinese that's a "reliable" pick for "tasty" dim sum and other "authentic" (if a little "cookie-cutter") Cantonese fare; the "banquet-style" room is typically "chaotic", especially on "weekends" when "it can be hard to get the attention" of the otherwise "friendly cart ladies."

## Empress Pavilion *Chinese*
21 | 14 | 14 | $21

**Chinatown** | Bamboo Plaza | 988 N. Hill St. (Bernard St.) | 213-617-9898 | www.empresspavilion.com

"The default destination" for "classic dim sum", this "cavernous" low-cost Chinatown Cantonese specializes in "steaming carts" of "authentic" fare appealing to adventurous and "timid" diners alike; service is "predictably unfriendly" but most say that's no matter "as long as they keep the food coming" (watch out for "traffic jams!"); considering the "huge lines on weekends", some "skip the fuss and go straight to the take-out window."

**Engine Co. No. 28** *American*  | 19 | 21 | 20 | $38 |

**Downtown** | 644 S. Figueroa St. (bet. 7th St. & Wilshire Blvd.) | 213-624-6996 | www.engineco.com

"Classic" American "comfort food" "done right" describes this Downtown "standby" set in a restored 1912 Los Angeles firehouse where pressed-tin ceilings and mahogany booths give it a "wonderfully nostalgic" feel; "warm" service, "decent prices" and bartenders with a "heavy pour" are other "old-school" touches – no wonder it's a perennial "pre-theater" pick; N.B. they also have free shuttle service to the Music and Staples Centers.

**Enoteca Drago** *Italian*  | 21 | 19 | 19 | $46 |

**Beverly Hills** | 410 N. Canon Dr. (Brighton Way) | 310-786-8236 | www.celestinodrago.com

It's "the closest thing to a European sports bar" you'll find in Beverly Hills, this Celestino Drago Italian marries "unique wines" (75 available by the glass) with "pricey" "plates of pastas, salads and salumi" served in a "comfortable" setting that some say is made "distracting" by the presence of a "blaring" plasma TV; though it's "less crowded" than its Westside cousins, some say this "relative" is "less wonderful than the other family creations" as well.

**Enoteca Toscana**  | ▽ 18 | 16 | 18 | $32 |
**Wine Bistro** Ⓜ *Italian/Spanish*

**Camarillo** | 2088 E. Ventura Blvd. (Fir St.) | 805-445-1433 | www.enotecatoscanawinebistro.com

Tagged a "home away from home" for Camarillo locals, this "intimate" spot offers a "unique" but "limited" menu of Tuscan and Spanish dishes to pair with a variety of vintages (45 by the glass) and housemade sangrias; though a few respondents report some issues with "service", most concur it's "worth a try" "especially for lunch."

**Enterprise Fish Co.** *Seafood*  | 18 | 17 | 18 | $33 |

**Santa Monica** | 174 Kinney St. (Main St.) | 310-392-8366 | www.enterprisefishco.com

The hook is "fresh fish" at "reasonable prices" say supporters of this "lively" Santa Monica seafooder (and its Santa Barbara twin) with a "hopping" bar scene where Monday and Tuesday's $29.95 lobster deal "can't be beat"; service is "friendly", though the less-faithful fault "harrowing" wait times and a "noisy" "chain"-like atmosphere.

**Enzo & Angela** Ⓢ *Italian*  | 21 | 16 | 22 | $36 |

**West LA** | 11701 Wilshire Blvd. (Barrington Ave.) | 310-477-3880 | www.enzoandangela.com

A "gracious" husband-and-wife team operate this eponymous West LA "diamond in the rough" serving from a "thoughtful menu" of "authentic" Italian specialties; "attentive" waiters and moderate prices keep the experience "pleasant" in spite of its "nondescript mini-mall setting.

| | FOOD | DECOR | SERVICE | COST |
|---|---|---|---|---|

## NEW e3rd
### Steakhouse & Lounge ● Steak

| ▽ 20 | 22 | 17 | $38 |

**Downtown** | 734 E. Third St. (bet. S. Alameda St. & Santa Fe Ave.) | 213-680-3003 | www.eastthird.com

The steakhouse formula gets a "unique Korean twist" at this Downtown newcomer from the owners of Zip Fusion, where kimchi mashed potatoes and soy-marinated beef share menu space alongside more classic meat-and-spuds fare; early reports say the food's "terrific", but the space is "too dark" and the in-house DJ "too loud" – "it's still finding its legs."

## Fabiolus Café, The  *Italian*

| 19 | 14 | 18 | $26 |

**Hollywood** | 5255 Melrose Ave. (Van Ness Ave.) | 323-464-5857 | www.fabiolus.net 🅂

**Hollywood** | 6270 W. Sunset Blvd. (bet. Argyle Ave. & Vine St.) | 323-467-2882 | www.fabiolus.com

They're "nothing fancy", but locals laud these "no-attitude" Northern Italians in Hollywood where the combination of "simple fresh food" ("solid" pastas, "healthy salads") and locations "close to the Arclight" (Sunset) and Paramount Studios (Melrose) make them "perennial" "pre-theater" and lunch "mainstays"; "reasonable prices" and "attentive" service add to the "good value"; N.B. the Sunset locale has outdoor seating and a more extensive wine list.

## Factor's Famous Deli  *Deli*

| 16 | 11 | 17 | $21 |

**Pico-Robertson** | 9420 W. Pico Blvd. (Beverly Dr.) | 310-278-9175 | www.factorsdeli.com

A "longtime supplier" of "artery-clogging" "New York–style" deli fare, this family-run Pico-Robertson standby "satisfies" with "generously sized" corned beef and pastrami sandwiches, lox and eggs, soups, salads and other "cheap nosh" from an "expansive" menu (quesadillas, anyone?); though some say the "old-fashioned" interior has "seen better days", those in-the-know "head right to the back patio on sunny afternoons."

## Falafel King  *Mideastern*

| 18 | 6 | 13 | $10 |

**Santa Monica** | The Promenade | 1315 Third St. Promenade (bet. Arizona Ave. & Santa Monica Blvd.) | 310-587-2551

**Westwood** | 1059 Broxton Ave. (bet. Kinross & Weyburn Aves.) | 310-208-4444

There are "not a lot of bells and whistles" at this Middle Eastern duo in Santa Monica's Third Street Promenade and Westwood, just "tasty" falafel, "side salads" and chips at prices that are a "fantastic bargain"; though a few nostalgics note they're "not as good as they used to be", most find them "reliable" for a meal "on the run."

## Farfalla Trattoria  *Italian*

| 22 | 17 | 19 | $30 |

**Los Feliz** | 1978 Hillhurst Ave. (Finley Ave.) | 323-661-7365 | www.farfallatrattoria.com

"A hit with locals", this "longtime" Los Feliz Italian coddles customers with "wholesome" pastas and "tasty" pizzas "prepared with care" and served by a staff "that treats you like family"; though the "cozy" brick-walled space is "tight" enough you'll be "sitting on your neighbor's lap", it still works for a "comfortable" "midweek dinner" or even a "second date."

| | FOOD | DECOR | SERVICE | COST |
|---|---|---|---|---|

### Farm of Beverly Hills  *American*

19 | 16 | 17 | $29

**Fairfax** | The Grove at Farmers Mkt. | 189 The Grove Dr. (bet. Fairfax Ave. & 3rd St.) | 323-525-1699
**Beverly Hills** | 439 N. Beverly Dr. (bet. Brighton Way & Santa Monica Blvd.) | 310-273-5578
**NEW Woodland Hills** | Topanga Mall | 6600 Topanga Canyon Blvd. (Randi Ave.) | 818-888-6738
www.thefarmofbeverlyhills.com

"This is one upscale farm" crow country-folk who choose this "cute" New American chainlet (with a new Woodland Hills outpost) for "hearty breakfasts", "semi-healthful" lunches and dinners and "killer" brownies ("they're the reason people eat the salads here") in a "casual", "barnlike" setting where the staff is "welcoming to families"; a few skeptics squawk it's "overpriced" and "underwhelming", concluding "no veggie burger on the planet is worth $15."

### Farm Stand  ☒ *Eclectic*

22 | 19 | 21 | $25

**El Segundo** | 422 Main St. (Holly Ave.) | 310-640-3276 | www.farmstand.us
"A breath of fresh air" in "Mayberry" (aka El Segundo) praise proponents digging into "wholesome" Eclectic cuisine served in "robust" portions at this "popular" relative newcomer in South Bay; add in reasonable tabs and a staff that's "well-informed about the menu" and supporters say this "cute" (though "noisy") spot "puts a little snap" in an otherwise routine day.

### Far Niente  *Italian*

25 | 20 | 23 | $37

**Glendale** | 204½ N. Brand Blvd. (Wilson Ave.) | 818-242-3835
"Excellent" Northern Italian cuisine (including "divine" flatbread "drizzled with olive oil") and "wonderful wines" await at this Glendale "secret" that supporters say is "serious about food"; considering the "experienced" staff and "warm" terra-cotta decor, it's a "neighborhood restaurant" that "never disappoints."

### Fat Fish  *Asian Fusion/Japanese*

20 | 16 | 17 | $37

**NEW Koreatown** | 3300 W. Sixth St. (Berendo St.) | 213-384-1304
**West Hollywood** | 616 N. Robertson Blvd. (bet. Melrose Ave. & Santa Monica Blvd.) | 310-659-3882
www.fatfishla.com

"Graze on appetizers" and "innovative maki" at this West Hollywood Japanese–Asian fusion "hang-out" (and its Koreatown cousin) where the "festive" "scene", "frou frou drinks" and "happy-hour specials" draw "crowds" in spite of what critics call "average" fare and "distracted service"; the "trendy" room with red banquettes switches over to "Boystown" adrenaline with "loud, loud music" as the night wears on.

### ☒ Father's Office  *Hamburgers*

24 | 13 | 11 | $21

**Santa Monica** | 1018 Montana Ave. (bet. 10th & 11th Sts.) | 310-393-2337 | www.fathersoffice.com

"Believe the hype" swear supporters of this Santa Monica "staple" where the "juicy" signature burger is "pure bliss on a bun", but served with a heaping side of "trauma" thanks to a "surly" staff that "reinforces the strict no-substitutions policy" (translation: "don't ask for ketchup"); nonetheless, "college students", "tourists" and other "masochists" "crowd" in to sample bar nibbles and brews from a "spectacular" selection that's the best antidote to the "frustrating" "every-man-for-himself" seating situation; N.B. a Culver City branch is in the works.

### Fatty's & Co. Ⓜ *Vegetarian*                  ▽ 20 | 16 | 15 | $26

**Eagle Rock** | 1627 Colorado Blvd. (Vincent Ave.) | 323-254-8804 | www.fattyscafe.com

While the new dinner-only hours are a "tragic loss for the brunch set", this "funky" Eagle Rock vegetarian (which recently "morphed into a wine bar") is still "popular" thanks to a "creative menu" that even has "total carnivores" touting the "satisfying" fare; some critics, however, cite "not cheap" tabs and "nonexistent service", concluding "it was so much better before it got fancy"; N.B. closed Monday and Tuesday.

### Feast from the East Ⓢ *Asian*                  21 | 9 | 14 | $13

**West LA** | 1949 Westwood Blvd. (bet. Olympic & Santa Monica Blvds.) | 310-475-0400 | www.feasteast.com

Devotees "dream about" the now-"legendary" Chinese chicken salad at this West LA Asian eatery that's both "cheap" and "convenient"; considering the somewhat "sterile" digs, some opt for "takeout", while those "hooked" on the "addictive" sesame salad dressing can "buy a bottle" and "replicate" their own concoctions at home.

### Figaro Bistrot *French*                  18 | 22 | 15 | $35

**Los Feliz** | 1802 N. Vermont Ave. (bet. Franklin Ave. & Hollywood Blvd.) | 323-662-1587

"Authentically French, right down to the servers' accents", this "quaint" Los Feliz "cafe" "draws a boho crowd" for "enjoyable" (if "uneven") bistro cuisine that gets a boost from "organic" ingredients and "guaranteed star-spotting" ("Keanu", "Katherine Heigl") from the sidewalk seating area; "snooty" servers add to the "Parisian" feel while "expensive" tabs have a few patrons pondering "are the prices in dollars or francs? *sacré Dieu!*"

### Fins *Continental/Seafood*                  22 | 19 | 21 | $41

**Calabasas** | 23504 Calabasas Rd. (Mulholland Dr.) | 818-223-3467
**Westlake Village** | Westlake Plaza | 982 S. Westlake Blvd., Ste. 8 (bet. Agoura & Townsgate Rds.) | 805-494-8163
www.finsinc.com

"Creatively prepared" fin fare (the macadamia encrusted halibut is a "favorite") is the centerpiece of a "consistent", "casual" meal at these Continental seafooders in Calabasas (with "beautiful" outdoor dining by the creek) and Westlake Village (a "class act" since the remodel); "pleasant" service and live jazz are additional niceties, but a few crab it's "not worth the price" – "we only eat here because we are too lazy to drive over the hill."

### Firefly ●Ⓢ *American*                  20 | 24 | 18 | $42

**Studio City** | 11720 Ventura Blvd. (Colfax Ave.) | 818-762-1833

Only the valet parking sign identifies this "chic" Studio City spot where all the action is "hidden" away on the "Moroccan-themed covered patio" out back studded with "hundreds of candles" where "trendy" locals nosh on "carefully crafted" New American dishes; while loyalists laud the "happening" vibe, cynics say the "loungelike" "singles" scene "upstages" the "pricey" fare while the "smoky environment" ruins the otherwise "stunning" outdoor area.

| | FOOD | DECOR | SERVICE | COST |
|---|---|---|---|---|

### Firefly Bistro  🅼 *American* — 19 | 20 | 19 | $33

**South Pasadena** | 1009 El Centro St. (Meridian Ave.) | 626-441-2443 | www.eatatfirefly.com

"Eating in a tent with fairy lights" is one of the main appeals of this "utterly charming" South Pas "neighborhood bistro" where the "satisfying" seasonal New American menu is enhanced by the "magical" outdoor setting; less shining is slightly "amateur service" (though they "mean well") and tabs that can tally "a bit on the pricey side."

### Fish Grill  *Seafood* — 19 | 8 | 15 | $15

**Beverly Boulevard** | 7226 Beverly Blvd. (Alta Vista Blvd.) | 323-937-7162

**Pico-Robertson** | 9618 W. Pico Blvd. (bet. Beverwil & Whitworth Drs.) | 310-860-1182

**NEW Brentwood** | 12013 Wilshire Blvd. (Bundy Dr.) | 310-479-1800 www.fishgrill.com

"Fresh", "tasty" kosher seafood lures "locals", "studio denizens" and "yeshiva students" to this "informal" mini-chain for "healthy" plates of mesquite-grilled fish at "reasonable" prices; "pressed for time" and confronting "packed" conditions, a few fin-ophiles opt for "takeout"; N.B. closed Friday evenings and Saturday.

### 555 East  *Steak* — 25 | 22 | 23 | $49

**Long Beach** | 555 E. Ocean Blvd. (Linden Ave.) | 562-437-0626 | www.555east.com

This "old-time steakhouse" in the heart of Long Beach meets "New York standards" with an "elegant", "jazzy" atmosphere, "first-rate" wine list and prime beef so "phenomenal" it might just "make you cry"; add in "unhurried" service and it's an "excellent", if "pricey", choice for "business dinners" and "romantic" escapades alike; P.S. "top-notch" piano players perform on weekends (Thursday–Saturday).

### Five Sixty-One  Ⓔ *Californian/French* — ∇ 19 | 19 | 21 | $45

**Pasadena** | Southern CA School of Culinary Arts | 561 E. Green St. (Madison Ave.) | 626-405-1561 | www.561restaurant.com

Budding chefs "apply their skills" in the open kitchen of the Southern CA School of Culinary Arts in Pasadena where the nine-course prix fixe meals are "quite a bargain" ($35 at lunch, $65 at dinner) considering the "fine" quality of the Cal-French cuisine; as for service, they "try hard", but foes fault occasional "mistakes" saying the experience can be "hit-or-miss" for patrons who are "essentially guinea pigs"; N.B. open weekdays only.

### Flavor of India  *Indian* — 21 | 15 | 18 | $26

**West Hollywood** | 9045 Santa Monica Blvd. (Doheny Dr.) | 310-274-1715 | www.theflavorofindia.com

"Nothing lacks for spice" at this "gourmet" West Hollywood Indian that's "high on the list" for their "tasty" "house specialties" (like chicken tikka masala) and "varied" lunch buffet; an enclosed patio with "little white holiday lights" enhances the "cozy atmosphere", though critics complain the "service doesn't match the quality of the food."

### Fleming's Prime Steakhouse & Wine Bar  *Steak* — 25 | 23 | 23 | $55

**El Segundo** | 2301 Rosecrans Ave. (Douglas St.) | 310-643-6911

*(continued)*

## Fleming's Prime Steakhouse & Wine Bar

**Woodland Hills** | 6373 Topanga Canyon Blvd. (Victory Blvd.) |
818-346-1005
www.flemingssteakhouse.com

"Get your red meat groove on" at this "impressive" chain trio of "posh"
steakhouses that "get everything right" from the "perfectly cooked"
beef down to the "huge variety of wines by the glass" and "wonderful
martinis" all served by a staff that "treats you like a king"; considering
these "high-energy" spots get "noisy" ("what did the waiter say?")
and the "bill can add up fast", you might consider "earplugs" an essen-
tial addition along with a fat wallet.

## Fogo de Chão  *Brazilian*

23 | 21 | 24 | $62

**Beverly Hills** | 133 N. La Cienega Blvd. (Clifton Way) | 310-289-7755 |
www.fogodechao.com

"Skewers of grilled meats" come out "fast and furious" at this "festive", "all-you-can-eat" Brazilian chain churrascaria in Beverly Hills
where "each passing waiter has a new experience to offer" in the form
of "luscious" cuts of beef, lamb and chicken carved "off swords" (the
salad bar provides the perfect "palate cleanser"); if the whole thing
strikes some cynics as "an overpriced buffet", they're outnumbered by
those who who'd gladly "starve for a week" for what they say is a "glut-
ton's paradise" and a "definite crowd-pleaser."

## Fonz's  *Seafood/Steak*

22 | 18 | 22 | $43

**Manhattan Beach** | 1017 Manhattan Ave. (bet. 10th Pl. & 11th St.) |
310-376-1536 | www.fonzs.com

"Solid" steaks and seafood plus "great martinis" earn a thumbs-up for
this Manhattan Beach "hangout" that's "packed with locals", particularly
on weekends, when "the bar scene starts early and goes late"; though
some call it too "crowded" and "noisy", it retains a "neighborhood"
feel thanks to the "friendly staff" and a "personable" owner who
"makes everyone feel like a regular."

## Ford's Filling Station  ⓩ *Gastropub*

19 | 16 | 16 | $39

**Culver City** | 9531 Culver Blvd. (Irving Pl.) | 310-202-1470 |
www.fordsfillingstation.net

"Throngs of lively local foodies" and those hoping to catch a glimpse
of "Harrison" (chef-owner Ben Ford's dad) contribute to the "deafening scene" at this "hip" Culver City gastropub turning out "high-end"
New American fare that's "creative and fresh", though a chorus of critics say it's "not amazing enough" to suffer "painful waits", "extravagant" tabs and an "overwhelmed" staff; more forgiving types insist
they're "still ironing out wrinkles", adding it's the kind of "place you
want to love" even if as of yet, it "doesn't live up to the hype."

## Formosa Cafe  *Asian Fusion*

15 | 20 | 17 | $26

**West Hollywood** | 7156 Santa Monica Blvd. (La Brea Ave.) | 323-850-9050 |
www.formosacafe.com

"One of the last of the historic Hollywood restaurants", this circa-1939
"throwback" is "good for snacks", but the "average" Asian fusion fare
generally "plays second fiddle" to the "old-school" atmosphere; nonetheless, "hipsters" and "nostalgic" types say it's "still fun" to sip a
"Singapore sling" and soak up the "tarnished glamour" of "Tinseltown's

days gone by", even if jaded critics conclude "it'll never be as cool" as it used to be; N.B. the Food score may not reflect a 2007 chef change.

### NEW Forte *Italian*
— | — | — | M

**Beverly Hills** | 362 N. Camden Dr. (bet. Brighton Way & Wilshire Blvd.) | 310-277-4171

Beverly Hill's former branch of the once-ubiquitous Prego chain (which still has an Irvine location) has changed its name under new ownership, though not much else so far, with the same menu offering a reasonably authentic taste of Italian cooking in a warm trattoria setting with a private room upstairs; a bar and lounge is in the works.

### NEW Foundry on Melrose, The Ⓜ *American*
— | — | — | M

**Melrose** | 7465 Melrose Ave. (N. Gardner St.) | 323-651-0915 | www.thefoundryonmelrose.com

Chef-owner Eric Greenspan (ex Meson G) has transformed what used to be a neighborhood pizza parlor on Melrose into an impressive art deco-style cafe with a handsome hand-carved bar; the midpriced New American menu features innovative dishes of the moment like short ribs with sunchoke purée and pork belly with corn velouté and wild mushroom agnolotti.

### 410 Boyd Ⓩ *Californian*
20 | 15 | 17 | $27

**Downtown** | 410 Boyd St. (San Pedro St.) | 213-617-2491

An "urban pioneer" in "gritty" Downtown, this "funky" affordable spot "attracts a good lunch crowd" with its Californian cuisine that rates from "exceptional" to "decent", depending on who you ask; local artist exhibits "change regularly" and give this "little hideaway" a "cool vibe."

### NEW Fraiche *Mediterranean*
— | — | — | M

**Culver City** | 9411 Culver Blvd. (Main St.) | 310-839-6800 | www.fraicherestaurantla.com

Built to resemble a Tuscan villa, this midpriced Mediterranean with a busy bar boasts one of the best-looking room in newly gentrified Culver City; its culinary team of Jason and Miho Travi, along with Providence veteran Thierry Perez in the front of the house, is bringing a touch of elegance to the neighborhood.

### Fred 62 ☻ *Diner*
18 | 17 | 16 | $18

**Los Feliz** | 1850 N. Vermont Ave. (Russell Ave.) | 323-667-0062 | www.fred62.com

"Late-night cravings" are well-served at Los Feliz's "über-cool" 24-hour "neon-green corner diner" where a "varied" menu of "quirky" American dishes and "plenty of vegan options" draws a "painfully hip" crowd, particularly "after hours"; sure, the servers "give a little 'tude", but "the prices are right-on", the "retro" ambiance is "comfy" and there's "always great people-watching, indoors or out."

### French Crêpe Co. *French*
22 | 9 | 14 | $13

**Fairfax** | Farmers Mkt. | 6333 W. Third St. (Fairfax Ave.) | 323-934-3113
NEW **Hollywood** | Hollywood Highland Mall | 6801 Hollywood Blvd., Ste. 403 (N. Highland Ave.) | 323-960-0933
www.frenchcrepe.com

The "*magnifique*" crêpes are "made fresh in front of you" pleasing Francophiles who fawn over the "fabulous varieties" of savory and sweet fillings at these "inexpensive" French stands inside the Farmers

| | FOOD | DECOR | SERVICE | COST |
|---|---|---|---|---|

Market and the Hollywood Highland Mall; both have cafeteria-style service that makes ordering "quick and easy", save for the occasional "lines", especially on "weekends."

### French 75 *French* | 21 | 23 | 20 | $45 |

**Century City** | Westfield Century City | 10250 Santa Monica Blvd., Ste. 480 (Ave. of the Stars) | 310-788-0700
**Burbank** | The Pinnacle | 3400 W. Olive Ave. (Lima St.) | 818-955-5100
www.culinaryadventures.com

David Wilhelm's expanding "empire" of "non-intimidating" "Parisian" bistros offers "excellent", "consistent" fare served by a "warmly professional" staff in settings that might "impress your date", even if some deem them "baroque" and "French at its fauxest"; perhaps it's "a bit ersatz, but that's part of the charm" say voters willing to pay "pricey" tabs for "live jazz", "champagne cocktails" and the "best onion soup this side of the Eiffel Tower."

### ☑ Frenchy's Bistro Ⓜ *French* | 27 | 17 | 24 | $48 |

**Long Beach** | 4137 E. Anaheim St. (bet. Termino & Ximeno Aves.) | 562-494-8787 | www.frenchysbistro.com

"Dedicated" "chef-owner Andre Angles is amazing" coo those captivated by this "extraordinary" Long Beach bistro that's a "destination" for a "sophisticated" menu of "scrumptious" Provençal dishes (including "to-die-for" lamb shank and "must-try" soufflés); "attentive" servers "are always willing to make recommendations" while the "pleasant-enough" decor "transports you to Paris", once you get past the "not-so-superb" location and exterior.

### Fresco Ristorante Ⓢ *Italian* | ▽ 22 | 18 | 22 | $47 |

**Glendale** | 514 S. Brand Blvd. (Colorado St.) | 818-247-5541 | www.fresco-ristorante.com

"Still one of the best restaurants in Glendale" laud loyalists who seek out this "consistent" Italian where lamb risotto, osso buco and other dishes are served in "huge portions" in a contemporary dining room with Venetian plaster walls; some surveyors say it's "slipped a bit", though most maintain it's "still adequate."

### Fritto Misto *Italian* | 21 | 13 | 19 | $21 |

**Santa Monica** | 601 Colorado Ave. (6th St.) | 310-458-2829
**Hermosa Beach** | 316 Pier Ave. (Monterey Blvd.) | 310-318-6098

"Mix-and-match pastas" in "abundant" portions pair with "well-chosen" wines at these "thriving" "no-fuss" (and "no atmosphere") Italians in Hermosa Beach and Santa Monica, which have "energetic" servers and "oh-so-reasonable" prices; the "ever popular" status of these "neighborhood joints" means "waits", "especially on weekends", so be prepared to "get there early" or opt for "takeout."

### Fromin's Deli *Deli* | 15 | 9 | 16 | $17 |

**Santa Monica** | 1832 Wilshire Blvd. (19th St.) | 310-829-5443
**Encino** | 17615 Ventura Blvd. (bet. Encino & White Oak Aves.) | 818-990-6346

"Ordinary" but "dependable" sums up these separately owned "old-time" delis in Encino and Santa Monica where "irreverent waitresses" deliver "generous portions" of pastrami, pickles, matzo ball soup and other "decently priced" "basics" that "fill you up"; if a few find the "at-

| | FOOD | DECOR | SERVICE | COST |
|---|---|---|---|---|

mosphere a little depressing" ("at least for anyone under 65"), most shrug off the "no-frills" setting – "it is what it is."

### Fu-Shing  Chinese
▽ 21 | 11 | 18 | $22

**Pasadena** | 2960 E. Colorado Blvd. (El Nido Ave.) | 626-792-8898 | www.fu-shing.com

"A local find" attest enthusiasts of this two-story Pasadena mainstay where some "fantastic" Szechuan dishes round out the "large menu" of "tasty" Chinese offerings; "gracious service" and "cheap" tabs make it a "wonderful hangout" for "families" in spite of decor that some say needs an "update."

### Fusion Sushi  Japanese
16 | 12 | 15 | $25

**Hermosa Beach** | 1200 PCH (11th Pl.) | 310-318-2781
**Long Beach** | 6415 E. Spring St. (Palo Verde Ave.) | 562-429-8818
**Manhattan Beach** | 1150 Morningside Dr. (bet. Center Pl. & 12th St.) | 310-802-1160
**Torrance** | 3963 PCH (bet. Ladeene & Ocean Aves.) | 310-378-2990
www.fusionsushi.com

The sushi is "serviceable" but "not stellar" at this South Bay mini-chain where a "family-friendly" crowd munches on "mass consumption" fare that's "good enough" for a "quick, cheap" "crazy roll" fix; service ranges from "efficient" to "nonexistent", while less-optimistic sorts opine "it needs upgrades in all areas"; N.B. the Costa Mesa branch is separately owned.

### Gaby's
### Mediterranean  ◑ Lebanese/Mediterranean
- | - | - | I

**Marina del Rey** | 20 Washington Blvd. (Speedway) | 310-821-9721
**West LA** | 10445 Venice Blvd. (Motor Ave.) | 310-559-1808

This crowd-pleasing Marina del Ray and West LA duo dishes out inexpensive Lebanese-Mediterranean dishes like chicken kaffa and warm pita bread served with za'atar (an herb-oil mixture); the MDR branch does a big take-out business with locals, while the Venice Boulevard location offers late-night meals in an atmospheric tented setting.

### Gale's  Ⓜ Italian
21 | 17 | 21 | $33

**Pasadena** | 452 S. Fair Oaks Ave. (Bellevue Dr.) | 626-432-6705 | www.galesrestaurant.com

"A neighborhood vibe" prevails at this "somewhat undiscovered", "informal" Pasadena Northern Italian where "robust" dishes are served with "style and grace" to a "friendly" crowd that includes "lots of regulars"; supporters say that "gracious host" Gale Kohl makes the somewhat "cramped" brick-walled dining room feel "homey", instructing: "go just once and you'll feel like family."

### Galletto Bar and Grill  Brazilian/Italian
23 | 16 | 20 | $34

**Westlake Village** | Westlake Plaza | 982 S. Westlake Blvd. (Townsgate Rd.) | 805-449-4300 | www.gallettobarandgrill.com

"Something different in the 'burbs" say "big-city" adventurers who choose this "jumping and jiving" Westlake Village "haunt" with "live music" nightly and dinner served till midnight on weekends; the "diverse" menu features a "fine selection" of Brazilian and Italian specialties sent over by servers "who are accommodating to your needs."

| | FOOD | DECOR | SERVICE | COST |
|---|---|---|---|---|

### Galley, The  *Seafood/Steak*

| | 18 | 18 | 19 | $35 |

**Santa Monica** | 2442 Main St. (bet. Ocean Park & Pico Blvds.) | 310-452-1934 | www.thegalleyrestaurant.net

Swashbucklers sup on "surprisingly good" steamers and steaks at this "funky", "old" Santa Monica surf 'n' turfer that's done up in a "kitschy" nautical style ("rustic wood booths", porthole windows, year-round Christmas lights); though it's "not cheap", it's a "fun, neighborhood joint" where owner Captain Ron holds court at the bar over "potent cocktails" and a rotating cast of "truly unique individuals."

### NEW Garden Cafe  *Asian/Californian*

| | - | - | - | I |

**Little Tokyo** | 100 N. Central Ave. (First St.) | 213-621-2022

Akira Hirose, who built a fine reputation at his Maison Akira in Pasadena, has opened this casual Cal-Asian spin-off on the southern edge of Little Tokyo, convenient to the tidal wave of upscale condos rising in the neighborhood; its clean, bright space is the setting for breakfast and lunch (with an inexpensive menu full of soups and salads) Tuesdays through Sundays, and an early dinner on Thursdays.

### ☑ Gardens  *Californian/Mediterranean*

| | 25 | 25 | 26 | $68 |

**Beverly Hills** | Four Seasons Hotel | 300 S. Doheny Dr. (Burton Way) | 310-273-2222 | www.fourseasons.com

"An oasis of fine dining and quiet", this "impeccable" Cal-Med "hideaway" set in the Beverly Hills Four Seasons Hotel is "lovely for brunch", either outside on the garden patio or in the "beautiful" chandeliered dining room; in spite of excessive "cell-phone chatter" and "cigar smoke", allies attest it's the picture of "elegance" where an "incredibly attentive" staff dotes on the "dealmaker" and "movie star" clientele.

### Gardens on Glendon  *Californian*

| | 19 | 21 | 19 | $37 |

**Westwood** | 1139 Glendon Ave. (Lindbrook Dr.) | 310-824-1818 | www.gardensonglendon.com

A "safe" choice, this Westwood "classic" with a "pretty indoor atrium" draws a "mix of UCLA students, glitterati and neighborhood folks" for "solid" Californian fare including especially "fabulous" guacamole made tableside; detractors declare that service is "uneven" and say prices can feel "too expensive", though they still rely on it for "pretheater" dining (it's near UCLA's Royce Hall and The Geffen Playhouse).

### Gate of India  *Indian*

| | ▽ 20 | 16 | 14 | $26 |

**Santa Monica** | 115 Santa Monica Blvd. (Ocean Ave.) | 310-656-1664

"When the kitchen is on", this moderately priced Santa Monica Indian is "one of the best on the Westside" attest local enthusiasts, particularly for the "satisfying" signature chicken tikka masala; otherwise, wags warn that vittles and service can be "unpredictable" in spite of a staff that tries its best to be "accommodating."

### Gaucho Grill  *Argentinean/Steak*

| | 18 | 14 | 17 | $25 |

**West Hollywood** | 7980 Sunset Blvd. (Laurel Ave.) | 323-656-4152
**Brentwood** | 11754 San Vicente Blvd. (Gorham Ave.) | 310-447-7898
**Santa Monica** | 1251 Third St. Promenade (3rd St.) | 310-394-4966
**Pasadena** | 121 W. Colorado Blvd. (bet. De Lacey & Pasadena Aves.) | 626-683-3580
**Studio City** | 12050 Ventura Blvd. (Laurel Canyon Blvd.) | 818-508-1030

*(continued)*

*(continued)*

## Gaucho Grill

**Woodland Hills** | 6435 Canoga Ave. (Victory Blvd.) | 818-992-6416
www.gauchogrillrestaurant.com

"Decent" steaks are made more "memorable" by the "flavorful" chimichurri dipping sauce at this "casual" Argentinean steakhouse chain stuffed with "tourists" and twentysomethings on "dates"; they're "reliable", and while grouchos grouse about "siesta-inducing service" and "uninspiring" decor, many maintain they're "a good value."

## Geisha House ● *Japanese*

| 19 | 25 | 18 | $51 |

**Hollywood** | 6633 Hollywood Blvd. (Cherokee Ave.) | 323-460-6300 | www.geishahousehollywood.com

"Think of it as a club that serves food" and you may be "impressed" with the "surprisingly good" sushi, specialty rolls and rock shrimp tempura at this "comically hip" bi-level Japanese smack-dab in Hollywood, where "a high concentration of beautiful people" (including the servers) complements the "fabulous" "futuristic" atmosphere; even with tabs deemed "overpriced", *"Entourage"* types and *US Weekly* readers" continue to "crowd" in, though some scenesters insist they're "over it", sniffing "the party moved on years ago."

## Genghis Cohen  *Chinese*

| 20 | 14 | 17 | $27 |

**Fairfax** | Fairfax Plaza | 740 N. Fairfax Ave. (Melrose Ave.) | 323-653-0640 | www.genghiscohen.com

"Everyone needs a hook", and this Fairfax Szechuan joint plays up the "New York Chinese" angle with "irresistible" "fat egg rolls", crispy duck and other "comfort" cuisine at "surprisingly reasonable" prices; the "old-school supper club" look is enhanced by a full bar and live music nightly in the adjacent performance area.

## Gennaro's Ristorante ⊠ *Italian*

| ▽ 24 | 21 | 24 | $50 |

**Glendale** | 1109 N. Brand Blvd. (Dryden St.) | 818-243-6231 | www.gennarosristorante.com

A "special-occasion" Italian that "lives up to its reputation" gush groupies of this "old-world" Glendale "gem" where "solid", "traditional" fare is served in "quiet", "elegant" surroundings; "attentive" service proceeds at a "relaxed" (some say "glacial") pace, and despite a slightly "stodgy" feel, most brand this "hidden" spot "a real find."

## ⊠ Geoffrey's  *Californian*

| 22 | 26 | 22 | $55 |

**Malibu** | 27400 PCH (¼ mi. west of Latigo Canyon Rd.) | 310-457-1519 | www.geoffreysmalibu.com

"Moneyed Malibu locals" and a smattering of "tourists" tout this "stunning" Californian "overlooking the ocean" where the "breathtaking" vistas and "spectacular sunsets" are best appreciated from the "perfect patio" perch; non-neighbors note the "romantic" setting is "worth the drive" ("take a date here and they're yours") while adding that the fare can be "disappointing" considering the "pricey" tabs; P.S. the "enjoyable brunch" is a less expensive option.

## George's Greek Café  *Greek*

| 20 | 14 | 20 | $19 |

**Downtown** | Seventh Street Market Pl. | 735 S. Figueroa St., Ste. 131 (bet. 7th & 8th Sts.) | 213-624-6542 ⊠
**Long Beach** | 318 Pine Ave. (bet. 3rd & 4th Sts.) | 562-437-1184

*(continued)*

### George's Greek Café

**Long Beach** | 5316 E. Second St. (Pomona Ave.) | 562-433-1755
www.georgesgreekcafe.com

"Hearty", "unpretentious" Greek fare is served in "generous" portions at this "inexpensive" mini-chain where "hugs-and-smiles" service creates a "hospitable" vibe; "alfresco" seating is available at all branches if you "don't mind street traffic" (Long Beach) or a "mall food-court" setting (Downtown).

### Getty Center, Restaurant at the ⓜ *Californian*

22 | 25 | 21 | $45

**Brentwood** | The Getty Ctr. | 1200 Getty Center Dr. (N. Sepulveda Blvd.) | 310-440-6810 | www.getty.edu

"Worlds away" from the "LA mobs", this "picturesque" spot inside the Getty museum complex sits atop the hills of Brentwood affording "spectacular" panoramic views of the "ocean and the city below" (just beware of prices as "steep" as the setting); the "underrated" kitchen turns out "fresh"-flavored Californian plates delivered by a "courteous" staff, which makes for a "pleasant break", "after strolling the grounds" or even as a "destination" on its own; N.B. open for lunch Tuesday-Sunday and dinner Friday–Saturday.

### Gina Lee's Bistro ⓜ *Asian/Californian*

26 | 15 | 23 | $37

**Redondo Beach** | Riviera Plaza | 211 Palos Verdes Blvd. (bet. Catalina Ave. & PCH) | 310-375-4462

"Eclectic" and "beautifully presented", Scott and Gina Lee's Cal-Asian cuisine makes this South Bay spot a "strip-mall" "surprise" where the "renowned" crispy catfish ("call ahead and reserve one – they do run out!") and "wonderful" bento box specials are served by a staff that "always greets you with a smile"; regulars regret the "noisy" acoustics and "crowded" room, adding that this "convivial crowd-pleaser" deserves "better decor."

### Gingergrass *Vietnamese*

22 | 14 | 16 | $22

**Silver Lake** | 2396 Glendale Blvd. (Brier Ave.) | 323-644-1600 | www.gingergrass.com

"Bringing Southeast Asian fare to the hipster crowd for several years now", this Silver Lake "neighborhood haunt" specializes in "clean-flavored" "nouvelle" Vietnamese cuisine that may be "less than authentic", but is still "tasty" enough "to please the most jaded Angeleno palate"; decor is of the "minimalist", "industrial" variety making for a rather "noisy" atmosphere."

### Giorgio Baldi ⓜ *Italian*

24 | 15 | 17 | $69

**Santa Monica** | 114 W. Channel Rd. (PCH) | 310-573-1660 | www.giorgiobaldi.com

A "pricey" Italian "extravaganza" for Santa Monica's "elite" diners, this "slice of heaven" off PCH sets "the gold standard" for "indescribably excellent" pastas in a "crowded", "star-studded" setting ("would you like your lobster with a side of Spielberg?"); the service, however, is far too "pretentious" for some – yes, it's "one of the best" in its class, but does the staff "really have to have such an attitude?"

### Girasole Cucina Italiana ⬛Ⓜ *Italian*

| 24 | 15 | 22 | $33 |

**Hancock Park** | 225½ N. Larchmont Blvd. (bet. Beverly Blvd. & 3rd St.) | 323-464-6978

"Mama's in the kitchen" at this "family-run" Hancock Park "gem", where "delicious homemade pastas" and other "amazing", "inexpensive" Italian dishes are "worth the fight" for one of the few tables ("get there early" or "make a reservation"); it's BYO with no corkage fee, so "raid your wine cellar" or pop into the store next door before settling into the "cozy" quarters of this "delightful" "little secret."

### Gladstone's Malibu *Seafood*

| 15 | 19 | 15 | $36 |

**Pacific Palisades** | 17300 PCH (Sunset Blvd.) | 310-573-0212 | www.gladstones.com

"Huge crowds" pack this Pacific Palisades beachfront seafooder where "so-so" fare is merely a "supporting player" to the "dramatic" ocean views best experienced from the "breezy" patio; "questionable" service and "pricey for what you get" tabs mean that even the "cute", animal-shaped "foil doggy bags" and "free peanuts" can't convince those who insist this "past-its-heyday" place is best "left to the tourists."

### Golden Deli ⇩ *Vietnamese*

| 23 | 8 | 13 | $12 |

**San Gabriel** | Las Tunas Plaza | 815 W. Las Tunas Dr. (Mission Dr.) | 626-308-0803

"Delicious" deem devotees who ignore the decor and concentrate on "top-notch" pho, noodles and other "authentic" specialties at this "bargain-basement-priced" San Gabriel Vietnamese; with "weekend crowds" packing the room "to the rafters", waiters try to "rush you out of there", but on the bright side: "food comes out in about 10 minutes."

### 🆕 Gonpachi *Japanese*

| - | - | - | M |

**Beverly Hills** | 134 N. La Cienega Blvd. (Wilshire Blvd.) | 310-659-8887

After years of construction, this shogun's palace finally takes its place on La Cienega's resurgent Restaurant Row to serve a midpriced Japanese menu featuring fresh fish flown in daily and handmade soba noodles; expect to be dazzled by its complex of three buildings situated around a formal Japanese garden with a stone bridge and a koi-filled pond, as well as by the sumiyaki bar (specializing in skewers cooked over charcoal) and sake cellar.

### Gordon Biersch *Pub Food*

| 17 | 17 | 17 | $24 |

**Pasadena** | 41 Hugus Alley (Colorado Blvd.) | 626-449-0052
**Burbank** | 145 S. San Fernando Blvd. (Angeleno Ave.) | 818-569-5240
www.gordonbiersch.com

The "fresh" suds made on-site are the highlight of these otherwise "predictable" chain microbreweries in Burbank and Pasadena with "standard-issue" American pub eats ("go for the garlic fries"), "TVs" and "nice patio seating" at both locations; they're basically "bars", but they're a "good value" and "pleasant" enough for "after-work drinks" or to add as a "staple" to your "lunchtime rotation."

### Gorikee Ⓜ *Californian*

| 21 | 11 | 18 | $28 |

**Woodland Hills** | Warner Plaza Shopping Ctr. | 21799 Ventura Blvd. (Canoga Ave.) | 818-932-9149

"Quirky" defines this "fantastic little find" in Woodland Hills where "ambitious" chef-owner Atsuhiro Tsuji dispenses "delicious" dishes from a garlic-centric menu of Californian cuisine; though a recent makeover has "made it more homey", some patrons are still put off by the "name and strip-mall location", while wallet-watchers are willing to "overlook" both for what they call "a super value."

### ☑ Grace Ⓜ American    25 | 24 | 24 | $62

**Beverly Boulevard** | 7360 Beverly Blvd. (Fuller Ave.) | 323-934-4400 | www.gracerestaurant.com

"East Coast sophistication" comes to Beverly Boulevard via chef-owner Neil Fraser's "ambitious" "neighborhood jewel" that marries "chic, modern" surroundings with "big-flavored" American fare, an "unbelievable wine list" and "delectable" desserts (Wednesday's Doughnut Night "rules"); "effortless" service exudes "class", and if the less-captivated claim they're "underwhelmed" by what they deem "overpriced" and "overhyped" fare, they're overruled by the majority that maintains this "grown-up" "culinary adventure" is "one of LA's top tables."

### Grand Lux Cafe Eclectic    19 | 20 | 19 | $28

**Beverly Hills** | Beverly Ctr. | 121 N. La Cienega Blvd. (3rd St.) | 310-855-1122 | www.grandluxcafe.com

"The Cheesecake Factory with a kick", this "amped-up", "higher-priced" spin-off at the Beverly Center serves "a vast selection" of Eclectic cuisine with "Vegas-style" flair and, not surprisingly, in the "same huge portions", with the "same long waits" as the original; the "grander" scale carries over into the "faux-elegant" decor where the high ceilings, "cavernous" size and "carnival-esque" color scheme strike some as "over the top."

### Great Greek Greek    21 | 16 | 20 | $28

**Sherman Oaks** | 13362 Ventura Blvd. (bet. Dixie Canyon & Nagle Aves.) | 818-905-5250 | www.greatgreek.com

"Surprisingly good" Hellenic fare is served in "huge portions" with "rollicking, corny pizzazz" by "singing and dancing servers" at this Sherman Oaks Greek that's a "great value" as well; memorabilia-heavy decor "hasn't changed in years", but it's full of "atmosphere" nonetheless – "just be careful line-dancing on a full stomach."

### Greenblatt's Deli & Fine Wines ◑ Deli    19 | 10 | 16 | $20

**Hollywood** | 8017 Sunset Blvd. (Laurel Ave.) | 323-656-0606

"Where else can you get matzo ball soup and chase it down with a '61 Bordeaux" but this "classic" Hollywood Jewish deli with the somewhat "incongruous" pairing of "dependable" "Lower East Side"–style fare (like "pastrami piled sky-high") and "an impressive wine shop" on premises; it's a "little expensive", and NYC expats miss the "kvetching waitresses" back east, but it works for "a fix", "especially late at night" since they're open till 1:30 AM.

### Green Field Churrascaria Brazilian    23 | 17 | 20 | $35

**Long Beach** | 5305 E. PCH (Anaheim St.) | 562-597-0906 | www.greenfieldchurrascaria.com
**West Covina** | 381 N. Azusa Ave. (Workman Ave.) | 626-966-2300 | www.greenfieldbbq.com

"It's all about the meat" at these Long Beach and West Covina churrascaria chain links where "wandering waiters" wield "swords" of "succulent" Brazilian BBQ in a "never-ending parade" of food that lasts "until you cry 'uncle'"; a buffet with "plentiful sides" means you "won't leave hungry", so bring a "big appetite" along with your "wallet."

### Griddle Cafe, The  *American*

22 | 11 | 16 | $16

**Hollywood** | 7916 Sunset Blvd. (bet. N. Fairfax & N. Hayworth Aves.) | 323-874-0377 | www.thegriddlecafe.com

The "*Flintstones*-scale" pancakes outsize "manhole covers" and are offered in countless variations at this "satisfying" breakfast and lunch-only Hollywood American that's "always packed" with "slackers" and "out-of-work actors" with "ripped jeans and great hair"; "be prepared to wait", "especially on weekends" when the "reality TV" servers are "trying to get discovered" instead of tending to the "interminable" lines.

### Grill on Hollywood, The  *American*

19 | 19 | 20 | $42

**Hollywood** | Hollywood & Highland Complex | 6801 Hollywood Blvd. (Highland Ave.) | 323-856-5530 | www.thegrill.com

"A classy joint" in the "touristy" Hollywood & Highland complex, this American option "doesn't have the mega-powered people-watching" of its Beverly Hills sibling (Grill on the Alley), but it still "pleases" for a "solid", albeit "outrageously priced", meal; the atmosphere is "warm and comfortable" while service is appropriately "courteous", so "if you have to eat near the Kodak Theatre", it's a "dependable" choice.

### ⧆ Grill on the Alley, The  *American*

24 | 20 | 24 | $56

**Beverly Hills** | 9560 Dayton Way (Wilshire Blvd.) | 310-276-0615 | www.thegrill.com

Beverly Hills' "dealmaking HQ", this "expensive" American plays host to "one of the best power-lunch scenes in the city" with "actors", "agents" and other "industry types" angling for a "coveted green-leather booth", all the better from which to enjoy "top-notch" filet mignon and Cobb salads ferried by a "polished" staff; non-celebs realize snagging a seat at this "old-line" "staple" "is a tough ticket" since "VIPs get priority."

### Grub  *American*

21 | 16 | 17 | $17

**Hollywood** | 911 N. Seward St. (bet. Melrose Ave. & Santa Monica Blvd.) | 323-461-3663 | www.grub-la.com

"Comfort food with extra *oomph*" is how devotees describe this "perfectly charming" Hollywood "find" helmed by *Top Chef*'s Betty Fraser with "amazingly fresh" American breakfasts and lunches served in a "converted bungalow" with a "homey vibe"; "service could be a bit more attentive" and the "crowded" dining room isn't always "conducive to conversation", but "it's all so cute and cozy" that most customers don't seem to care; N.B. dinner service is reportedly in the works.

### Guelaguetza  *Mexican*

21 | 9 | 15 | $18

**Huntington Park** | 2560 E. Gage Ave. (bet. Pacific Blvd. & Rugby Ave.) | 323-277-9899
**Koreatown** | 3014 W. Olympic Blvd. (S. Normandie Ave.) | 213-427-0608
**Koreatown** | 3337½ W. Eighth St. (Irolo St.) | 213-427-0601
**Lynwood** | 11215 Long Beach Blvd., Ste. 1010 (Beechwood Ave.) | 310-884-9224
**Palms** | 11127 Palms Blvd. (Sepulveda Blvd.) | 310-837-1153
www.guelaguetzarestaurante.com

"Tremendous mole" (in "lots of varieties") is only part of the enchilada at these separately owned chain outposts known for "down-home"

|  | FOOD | DECOR | SERVICE | COST |
|--|------|-------|---------|------|

Oaxacan dishes that are an "incredible value"; the "no-frills" "cantina" settings may not be "much to look at" (service "isn't great" either), but supporters swear they fulfill the promise of "what Mexican food is supposed to be."

### Guido's  *Italian*                    20 | 18 | 22 | $40

**Malibu** | 3874 Cross Creek Rd. (PCH) | 310-456-1979 | www.guidosmalibu.com
**West LA** | 11980 Santa Monica Blvd. (Bundy Dr.) | 310-820-6649
This pair of "nostalgic" Northern Italians in Malibu and West LA are "better than the name or red-velvet booths" would suggest with "above-average" *cibo* "served with class" to a crowd of "regulars", "rat-packers" and other assorted "weird characters"; boosters at both branches say "decor could use a face-lift", though even they admit the "dated" rooms "somehow still work" with the "old-fashioned" vibe.

### Gulfstream  *American/Seafood*        21 | 20 | 21 | $38

**Century City** | Westfield Century City Shopping Ctr. | 10250 Santa Monica Blvd. (Century Park W.) | 310-553-3636 | www.hillstone.com
"First-class fish" and other "well-prepared" American fare keep this "upscale" Houston's-affiliated duo "packed" with "power-lunchers" by day and "singles" at night; the Century City spot boasts an "open kitchen" while Newport Beach has "pleasant outdoor fire pits"; both employ a "team-based staff" that provides an oasis of "efficiency" in the otherwise "noisy" and "chaotic" environments.

### Gumbo Pot  *Cajun*                     21 | 7 | 15 | $13

**Fairfax** | Farmers Mkt. | 6333 W. Third St. (Fairfax Ave.) | 323-933-0358 | www.thegumbopotla.com
"Get your eat on" at this "quick-bite" Cajun food stall in the Farmers Market on Fairfax that "magically transports you to New Orleans" with fresh-shucked oysters, jambalaya and "fantastic gumbo" that "warms you up on a cold day"; "don't expect much decor" (or "genuine Southern hospitality" either), just "fill up" on "inexpensive" grub that's "authentic" enough to leave some locals "wish[ing] there was one on every corner."

### Gyu-Kaku  *Japanese*                   20 | 18 | 18 | $31

**Beverly Hills** | 163 N. La Cienega Blvd. (Clifton Way) | 310-659-5760
**West LA** | 10925 W. Pico Blvd. (bet. Kelton & Midvale Aves.) | 310-234-8641
**Torrance** | Cross Road Plaza | 24631 Crenshaw Blvd. (Sky Park Dr.) | 310-325-1437
**Pasadena** | 70 W. Green St. (De Lacey Ave.) | 626-405-4842
**NEW** **Canoga Park** | 6600 Topanga Canyon Blvd. (Victory Blvd.) | 310-415-7555 🅢 🅜
**Sherman Oaks** | 14457 Ventura Blvd. (Van Nuys Blvd.) | 818-501-5400 | www.gyu-kaku.com
"Heavenly" "morsels" of marinated meats and veggies get the "DIY" treatment at this cook-your-own Japanese Yakiniku chain that some find a "refined alternative" to "Korean BBQ" with "much better atmosphere" and a more "modern" vibe ("s'mores for dessert" is a "nice touch" too); a few are befuddled over "expensive" prices, especially considering you "work hard for your meal", but others look at the bright side – "at least you don't have to do the dishes."

### NEW Hadaka Sushi ☽ *Japanese*

| - | - | - | M |

**West Hollywood** | 8226 W. Sunset Blvd. (N. Harper Ave.) | 323-822-2601 | www.hadakasushi.com

It's name means 'Naughty Sushi', but naughty may be an understatement at this midpriced West Hollywood Japanese where a neon sign advises 'Adults Only' and the menu features special rolls bearing porn-caliber names; paintings worthy of a Nevada bordello dress up the room while come-hither outfits dress the statuesque young servers.

### Hal's Bar & Grill ☽ *American*

| 20 | 19 | 19 | $36 |

**Venice** | 1349 Abbot Kinney Blvd. (bet. Main St. & Venice Blvd.) | 310-396-3105 | www.halsbarandgrill.com

This "lively" Venice "hangout" "has it all" from live jazz Sundays and Mondays to "awesome drinks" and "solid" New American fare, plus a "boho scene" full of "beautiful people in their 30s and 40s" who pack into the "modern" space with "local art on the walls"; in spite of its tendency to get "loud", it keeps things "relaxed" with a "friendly staff" and a "low-key" "New York vibe."

### ☑ Hamasaku ☒ *Japanese*

| 27 | 17 | 21 | $59 |

**West LA** | 11043 Santa Monica Blvd. (Sepulveda Blvd.) | 310-479-7636 | www.hamasakula.com

A sushi "scene" in West LA, this "expensive, but worth it" "celeb"-heavy hot zone is well-nigh "unparalleled" claim cognoscenti praising the "creative", "beautifully presented" rolls and "standout" signature dishes; "strip-mall" digs are mostly "nondescript" though the "hip crowd" gives it "a touch of Hollywood" that appeases the "power" clientele; N.B. a branch on Melrose is in the works.

### Hama Sushi *Japanese*

| 21 | 14 | 18 | $38 |

**Venice** | 213 Windward Ave. (Main St.) | 310-396-8783 | www.hamasushi.com

"An always entertaining crowd" fills up this "rowdy" Venice Japanese that's a neighborhood "staple" for "damned good" sushi, "people-watching" and "lots of drinking" (by both "staff" and customers); "ample outdoor space" augments the otherwise "cramped", "no-frills" setting that's also made more bearable by "friendly chefs and servers."

### Hamburger Mary's ☽ *Diner*

| 15 | 14 | 17 | $20 |

**West Hollywood** | 8288 Santa Monica Blvd. (Sweetzer Ave.) | 323-654-3800 | www.hamburgermarysweho.com

"The portions are big and the drag queens are plentiful" (especially on Wednesday's "legendary" Bingo Night) at this "campy" West Hollywood American that's definitely "more about the atmosphere than the food", although "massive burgers" and "strong drinks" don't go amiss; the "boisterous" atmosphere draws comparisons to a "gay Hooters", with "cute waiters" and low prices keeping the "target audience" coming back.

### Hamlet Restaurant *American*
### (fka Hamburger Hamlet)

| 16 | 14 | 16 | $21 |

**West Hollywood** | 9201 Sunset Blvd. (N. Doheny Dr.) | 310-278-4924
**Brentwood** | Topa Old Country Shopping Ctr. | 11648 San Vicente Blvd. (bet. Darlington & Mayfield Aves.) | 310-826-3558
**West LA** | 2927 Sepulveda Blvd. (National Blvd.) | 310-478-1546

*(continued)*

**Hamlet Restaurant**

**Pasadena** | 214 S. Lake Ave. (bet. E. Colorado & E. Del Mar Blvds.) | 626-449-8520

**Sherman Oaks** | 4419 Van Nuys Blvd. (Ventura Blvd.) | 818-784-1183
www.hamletrestaurants.com

"They can take 'Hamburger' out of the name, but it's still the same" declare denizens visiting this "classic" chain where, despite a "revamped menu" and "spruced up" decor, folks can still find the same "mouthwatering" "trademark" patties along with more "healthy", "upscale" "diner" options; skeptics say that service is still "hit-or-miss" (from "prompt" to "unbearably slow") while loyalists lament that in spite of the "upgrade", "its glory days are gone and aren't coming back soon."

**NEW** **Hampton's** *Californian* ▽ 24 | 26 | 23 | $46

**Westlake Village** | Four Seasons Westlake Vill. | 2 Dole Dr. (Lindero Canyon Rd.) | 818-575-3000 | www.fourseasons.com

It's "a class act all the way" beam boosters of this new "destination" inside the Four Seasons Westlake Village that draws a "mostly older crowd" of "haute suburban" locals for chef Sandro Gamba's "wonderful", "light" Californian cuisine served in "small portions" perfect for "health-oriented diners" (others, however, complain they "left hungry"); despite a few "kinks", service is "everything you would expect" given the swanky setting, and if a few find the decor "institutional", others gaze outwards at the exterior "gardens" that include a "serene" man-made waterfall.

**NEW** **Happi Songs** - | - | - | I
**Asian Tavern** ◑ *Pan-Asian*

**La Brea** | 460 S. La Brea Ave. (6th St.) | 323-936-7622

Set in the La Brea space that housed Flora Kitchen for many years, this latest entry from the increasingly ubiquitous Steven Arroyo (Malo, Cobras & Matadors, 750 ml) serves a budget-friendly menu of Pan-Asian small plates complemented by a wide selection of beer and sake; decor oozes cool with vintage film posters covering the walls and oversized paper lanterns hanging from the beams; N.B. a plan for a DJ on weekends is in the works.

**Hard Rock Cafe** *American* 14 | 21 | 15 | $23

**Universal City** | Universal CityWalk | 1000 Universal Studios Blvd. (off Rte. 101) | 818-622-7625 | www.hardrock.com

"A rock 'n' roll museum" that's "loaded with musical artifacts", this CityWalk outpost of the international chain attracts a "mostly tourist" clientele for "generic" American eats that can be "ok" as long as you "don't expect too much"; service is "not the best", while those without children say the "screaming loud" atmosphere makes it "unsuitable for anyone over 21."

**Harold & Belle's** *Creole* ▽ 24 | 18 | 19 | $33

**Mid-City** | 2920 W. Jefferson Blvd. (bet. Arlington Ave. & Crenshaw Blvd.) | 323-735-3376

For an "excellent example" of "authentic" Creole cuisine, proponents point to this Mid-City eatery where "fabulous" renditions of crawfish étouffée and other "comfort-food" staples are served in "insane" portions (if prices seem "exorbitant", fans say it's "well worth it"); the "friendly" dining room has a "feeling of community" while "valet parking" is a perk in view of the somewhat "sketchy neighborhood."

### Harper's  Continental/Italian
| 16 | 16 | 18 | $34 |

**Century City** | Westfield Plaza | 10250 Santa Monica Blvd. (Ave. of the Stars) | 310-553-1855 | www.harperscenturycity.com

"Weary shoppers" at the Westfield mall welcome the "variety" of Italian-Continental dishes (like pizzas and pastas) at this Century City eatery with "unpretentious" service and a quiet atmosphere "conducive to conversation"; critics call it "overpriced" and "uninspiring", concluding there are "other better choices" nearby.

### ⊠ Hatfield's ⑤ American
| 27 | 19 | 24 | $63 |

**Beverly Boulevard** | 7458 Beverly Blvd. (Gardner St.) | 323-935-2977 | www.hatfieldsrestaurant.com

"No feuds here" quip proponents of this "real McCoy" run by "gracious" married team Quinn and Karen Hatfield and set in a "sliver" of a space with "elegant", "modern" decor and a "beautiful" front patio; the "pitch-perfect" New American cuisine prepared from "impeccable" "farmer's market" ingredients "deserves all of its recent accolades" (and its high price), and if a few deem the "small portions" "a little precious", most "rave" this "darling" spot is shaping up to be "a real highlight" of the "burgeoning Beverly Boulevard" dining scene.

### Hayakawa Ⓜ Japanese
| ▽ 26 | 18 | 23 | $40 |

**Covina** | 750 Terrado Plaza (bet. Citrus & Workman Aves.) | 626-332-8288

"An absolute treat" cheer champions of this "reasonably priced", "family-friendly" Covina Japanese helmed by Kazuhiko Hayakawa (ex Matsuhisa) who "does it right" with "spectacular" sushi and other "imaginative" dishes; locals feel "lucky to have" this "sophisticated" "favorite" amongst the other "lean", "suburban" pickings in the area.

### Heroes Bar & Grill  Pub Food
| 16 | 16 | 16 | $20 |

**Claremont** | 131 N. Yale Ave. (bet. 1st & 2nd Sts.) | 909-621-6712 | www.heroesrestaurant.net

The "amazing selection of suds on tap" and "friendly sports bar atmosphere" draws "lots of college students" to these inexpensive "pub"-like American twins in Claremont and Fullerton; "typical tavern fare" comes in "huge portions" while "peanut shells on the floor" and "TVs" make up most of the decor.

### Hide Sushi Ⓜ⇗ Japanese
| 24 | 10 | 17 | $27 |

**West LA** | 2040 Sawtelle Blvd. (bet. La Grange & Mississippi Aves.) | 310-477-7242

Informally acknowledged as LA's "best-bang-for-your-sushi-buck", this "old reliable" on the Westside is "packed all the time" with a motley crew of "chefs", "poor college students" and "steady Japanese customers who know what they want"; "fresh, well-presented" nigiri and hand rolls are served up "fast" once you get past the "excruciating waits" and, not surprisingly, the servers "rush you out the door" after that last bite.

### Hirosuke  Japanese
| 24 | 13 | 20 | $33 |

**Encino** | Plaza de Oro | 17237 Ventura Blvd. (Louise Ave.) | 818-788-7548

"Thumbs-up!" declare denizens of this "casual" Encino Japanese that scores for "freshness" and "consistency" making it stand out "amongst the glut of other sushi joints" on Ventura Boulevard; chef-owner Hirosuke Nagahata "runs a tight ship" ensuring "prompt" (if sometimes "frantic") service in spite of the "crowds" that "pack" this "noisy" place; N.B. closed Wednesdays.

### Hirozen ☒ *Japanese* | 25 | 10 | 20 | $37

**Beverly Boulevard** | 8385 Beverly Blvd. (Orlando Ave.) | West Hollywood | 323-653-0470 | www.hirozen.com

Beverly Boulevard's "go-to for fresh, quality sushi", this "neighborhood treasure" also "mixes it up" with "fabulous and unusual" daily specials; digs are "shoebox"-sized so insiders advise those who dislike being "muzzle-loaded" into the "tiny" dining room to "settle" at the bar instead and "let the chef feed you like a king."

### Hoboken *American/Italian* | 18 | 14 | 19 | $26

**West LA** | 2323 Westwood Blvd. (bet. Olympic & Pico Blvds.) | 310-474-1109 | www.matteosla.com

A more casual version of big brother Matteo's next door, this West LA Italian-American joint is "like a trip back East", though a few sticklers suggest it's actually "too polite and quiet" to be mistaken for its namesake; the "old-fashioned" red-sauce fare (like lasagna and eggplant Parmesan) is served in a low-key "storefront" setting that some say is just right for a "comfortable" meal; N.B. after a December 2006 chef change, a menu update is in the works.

### NEW Hokusai *French/Japanese* | - | - | - | M

**Beverly Hills** | 8400 Wilshire Blvd. (S. Gale Dr.) | 323-782-9717 | www.hokusairestaurant.com

Situated in an art deco building on Wilshire halfway between the busy intersections at La Cienega and San Vicente, this sleek new French-Japanese eatery offers a midpriced menu of inventive dishes like Kobe beef-cheek stew and red-bean cheesecake; a weekday 5-7 PM happy hour draws customers to the backlit bar.

### NEW Holdren's Steaks & Seafood *Steak* | - | - | - | E

**Thousand Oaks** | 1714 Newbury Rd. (N. Ventu Park Rd.) | 805-498-1314 | www.holdrens.com

This old-fashioned Middle American steakhouse with spacious booths has moved into Thousand Oaks; its selection of steaks can be combined with shrimp or lobster, which raises the cost to surprising levels, but at least all entrees come with a choice of soup or salad, and a vegetable on the side.

### Holly Street Bar & Grill *Californian* | 21 | 19 | 20 | $34

**Pasadena** | 175 E. Holly St. (bet. Marengo & Raymond Aves.) | 626-440-1421 | www.hollystreetbarandgrill.com

"Great specials", "reasonable" Cal cuisine and "Sunday brunch on the patio" have kept this Old Pasadena "hideaway" "around for 20 years"; fans still praise the "welcoming service", "relaxing atmosphere" and live music nightly that includes everything from jazz to Latin to R&B.

### NEW Holy Cow Indian Express *Indian* | - | - | - | I

**Third Street** | 8474 W. Third St. (La Cienega Blvd.) | 323-852-8900

"Bare-bones" decor does nothing to distract diners from the "fresh and tasty" curries that are a "real bang for your buck" at this "charming" new Indian storefront on Third Street (sister Surya is down the block); with "fast" service, "plentiful parking" and only 20 seats available, most opt for takeout.

### Hop Li  *Chinese*
| 18 | 11 | 15 | $20 |

**Chinatown** | 526 Alpine St. (N. Hill St.) | 213-680-3939
**West LA** | 10974 W. Pico Blvd. (Westwood Blvd.) | 310-441-3708
**NEW** **West LA** | 11901 Santa Monica Blvd. (Armacost Ave.) | 310-268-2463
**Arcadia** | 855 S. Baldwin Ave. (Huntington Dr.) | 626-445-3188 ●
www.hoplirestaurant.com

With four locations dotted around LA, this "old-fashioned" Chinese mini-chain is a go-to for "fresh and tasty" Cantonese and Hong Kong-style seafood dishes; "cheap" and "fast", it's also "great for groups", overly "funky" decor and "brusque" service notwithstanding.

### Hop Woo  *Chinese*
| 19 | 10 | 14 | $17 |

**Chinatown** | 845 N. Broadway (bet. Alpine & College Sts.) | 213-617-3038 ●🚫
**West LA** | 11110 W. Olympic Blvd. (S. Sepulveda Blvd.) | 310-575-3668
**Alhambra** | 1 W. Main St. (Garfield Ave.) | 626-289-7938
www.hopwoo.com

Fans of Cantonese BBQ find that these "mainstays" spread throughout LA mean you "no longer need to drive" too far for "solid" takes on Peking duck, "greasy", "family-style" staples and lunchtime "bargains"; service is "lackluster", but they'll "keep an eye out for any requests", including no MSG; N.B. the Chinatown branch is open till 1 AM.

### ☒ Hotel Bel-Air Restaurant  *Californian/French*
| 26 | 29 | 28 | $75 |

**Bel-Air** | Hotel Bel-Air | 701 Stone Canyon Rd. (Sunset Blvd.) | 310-472-1211 | www.hotelbelair.com

"A little slice of heaven" "nestled in the hills", this "opulent", "idyllic" Bel-Air "landmark" is once again voted No. 1 for Decor and Service thanks to its "enchanting" flower-filled garden, "elegant dining room" and "top-flight" staff that treats diners like "royalty"; "superb" Cal-French fare also makes it a "place to impress", and though tabs are "expensive", insiders insist it's "very much worth the cost" since "dining here is a vacation in itself"; N.B. jacket suggested.

### House of Blues  *Southern*
| 15 | 20 | 16 | $33 |

**West Hollywood** | 8430 Sunset Blvd. (Olive Dr.) | 323-848-5100 | www.hob.com

"Grab a bite before the show" and you'll "get priority admission" to see some of the "best musicians and performers around" at these WeHo and Anaheim chain venues that some dismiss as a "tourist trap" but others appreciate for their roadhouse looks and "outsider art"; while the "filling" Southern vittles range from "decent" to "disappointing", and the "unorganized" service feels "subpar", Sunday's "heavenly" gospel brunch "remains a hit."

### ☒ Houston's  *American*
| 21 | 19 | 20 | $33 |

**Century City** | Westfield Century City Shopping Ctr. | 10250 Santa Monica Blvd. (bet. Ave. of the Stars & Century Park W.) | 310-557-1285
**Santa Monica** | 202 Wilshire Blvd. (2nd St.) | 310-576-7558

*(continued)*

**Houston's**

**Manhattan Beach** | Bristol Farms | 1550A Rosecrans Ave.
(bet. Aviation & Sepulveda Blvds.) | 310-643-7211
**Pasadena** | 320 S. Arroyo Pkwy. (Del Mar Blvd.) | 626-577-6001
www.hillstone.com

Like "a well-oiled machine" these chain outposts pump out "predict-able" (yet still "enjoyable") renditions of "classic" American dishes – the "well-seasoned" French dip sandwich and "knife-and-fork ribs" are "favorites – while service is equally "efficient" too; in spite of "comfy booths", the "glossy" decor "loses a point", however, "due to horrible acoustics", and many hate "the constant wait to be seated" thanks to a no-reservations policy.

**Hugo's** *Californian*  | 21 | 13 | 19 | $23 |

**West Hollywood** | 8401 Santa Monica Blvd. (bet. Kings Rd. & Orlando Ave.) |
323-654-3993
**Studio City** | 12851 Riverside Dr. (Coldwater Canyon Ave.) | 818-761-8985
www.hugosrestaurant.com

"Healthful" Cal–New American fare with "amazing veggie options" makes "granola" types and "movie industry" folk feel "virtuous" at this pair of "relaxed" but "cluttered" cafes in Studio City and WeHo; "breakfast and lunch" draw the biggest "scene" (and often a "celeb" or two), though a handful of reviewers report that "simple" food plus moderate tabs and an organic wine list make it "nice for dinner" as well.

**NEW Hummus Bar** ⬛Ⓜ *Mideastern*  | - | - | - | I |

**Tarzana** | 18743 Ventura Blvd. (Reseda Blvd.) | 818-344-6606
This functionally designed, mini-mall Middle Easterner is the latest destination-of-choice for Tarzana's sizable Israeli émigré population; it serves hummus in just about every way but dessert, and, of course, there's falafel too.

**Hump, The** *Japanese*  | 25 | 22 | 22 | $61 |

**Santa Monica** | Santa Monica Airport | 3221 Donald Douglas Loop S.
(Airport Ave.) | 310-313-0977 | www.thehump.biz

"Spectacular sunsets" are bested only by the "first-class fish" at this "hidden gem" perched "above the runway" at the Santa Monica Airport with "heavenly sushi so "fresh", it might just "wriggle in your mouth" (indeed, the "live dishes" on the menu are "not for the squea-mish"); though it's "staggeringly expensive", the "expertly trained" staff creates an experience "high on the list of last meals", and one well-deserving of its "rave reviews."

**Hungry Cat, The** ☀ *Seafood*  | 24 | 15 | 20 | $41 |

**Hollywood** | 1535 N. Vine St. (Sunset Blvd.) | 323-462-2155 |
www.thehungrycat.com

"Imaginative" cocktails kick off an "idiosyncratic" yet "superb" sea-food experience at David Lentz's Hollywood "hot spot" (and its newer Santa Barbara spin-off) with "terrific" raw-bar selections and a "killer lobster roll" delivered by "knowledgeable" servers; though the "semi-industrial" decor isn't helped much by "uncomfortable" seating or "brash lighting emanating" from the open kitchen, it's all part of the "Maryland crab house meets LA hip" motif, which certainly "has its charms"; N.B. a planned expansion is expected to be completed this fall.

FOOD | DECOR | SERVICE | COST

### Hurry Curry  *Indian*
19 | 12 | 16 | $13

**West LA** | 12825 Venice Blvd. (Beethoven St.) | 310-398-2948 |
www.hurrycurryla.com

This Westside Indian is "easy to pass by" but still sought out by locals for its "dinner deals" and "staples ready all day long"; "cheap and "friendly", it's a "good fast-food option when In-N-Out won't cut it", particularly since a recent redecoration adds "colorful charm" to the formerly drab dining room.

### Hurry Curry of Tokyo  *Japanese*
17 | 12 | 16 | $15

**West LA** | 2131 Sawtelle Blvd. (bet. Mississippi Ave. & Olympic Blvd.) |
310-473-1640
**Pasadena** | 37 S. Fair Oaks Ave. (Colorado Blvd.) | 626-792-8474
www.hurrycurryoftokyo.com

"Hearty Japanese curry" is served over various cutlets and croquettes as well as beef, tofu and shrimp at these Pasadena and West LA "joints" serving "solid", "workmanlike" eats in settings that rate "a notch above a fast-food restaurant"; the staff is more "inexperienced" than some would like, but "reasonable" prices and "voluminous" portions make it a "good value."

### Hu's Szechwan  *Chinese*
20 | 6 | 16 | $17

**Palms** | 10450 National Blvd. (bet. Motor & Overland Aves.) | 310-837-0252 |
www.husrestaurant.com

"Tucked in the backroads of Palms", this "old-time favorite" may be "in desperate need of an interior designer", but fans are willing to overlook the "divey" atmosphere and "waiters who don't smile" for the "flavorful" Szechuan dishes that make it "one of the better Chinese joints on the Westside"; in spite of "sparse parking" and "busy weekends", locals are "glad to have it nearby."

### i Cugini  *Italian/Seafood*
21 | 22 | 20 | $42

**Santa Monica** | 1501 Ocean Ave. (B'way) | 310-451-4595 | www.icugini.com
Regulars report the seafood "never lets you down" at this Santa Monica Italiano where the Sunday jazz brunch "can't be beat" for "all-you-can-eat" shellfish and "free-flowing champagne"; "fabulous" "ocean views" plus "attentive service" means it fits the bill for "any occasion", often beating out "ritzier" "competition in the neighborhood."

### Il Boccaccio  *Italian*
▽ 22 | 14 | 19 | $39

**Hermosa Beach** | 39 Pier Ave. (bet. Hermosa Ave. & The Strand) |
310-376-0211 | www.ilboccaccio.com

A respite from the "throngs of drunken USC frat boys" crowding the Hermosa Beach pier, this "romantic" "sliver" of a restaurant "delights" with "authentic" Northern Italian fare like "mouthwatering lasagna" and "terrific seafood"; while some are less-than-enthusiastic about the service ("put quarters in the meter . . . it can be slow"), most agree that it "feels like home", "dreary" decor notwithstanding.

### Il Buco  *Italian*
22 | 16 | 22 | $35

**Beverly Hills** | 107 N. Robertson Blvd. (Wilshire Blvd.) | 310-657-1345 |
www.giacominodrago.com

Fans of this "charming" Beverly Hills Italian have even more about this "neighborhood" "gem" to love, thanks to a recent renovation that imparted a "hipper" vibe; meanwhile, the "delectable" fare remains the same with especially "notable" pasta and thin-crust pizzas from chef-owner Giacomino Drago at prices that "aren't cheap but won't break the bank" either.

### Il Capriccio on Vermont  *Italian/Pizza*

| | | | |
|---|---|---|---|
| 22 | 14 | 20 | $24 |

**Los Feliz** | 1757 N. Vermont Ave. (bet. Kingswell & Melbourne Aves.) | 323-662-5900

### Il Capriccio Wood Fire Pizzeria ● *Italian/Pizza*

**NEW** **Los Feliz** | 4518 Hollywood Blvd. (Sunset Blvd.) | 323-644-9760
www.ilcapriccioonvermont.com

"Excellent value" for "very fine", if "workmanlike", Italian fare lures Los Feliz locals to this "dependable" "neighborhood" trattoria and its newer pizzeria spin-off; the "upbeat" staff gives it a "friendly, family" feel, while the somewhat "crowded" dining room is equally "homey."

### Il Chianti Ⓜ *Italian*

| | | | |
|---|---|---|---|
| ▽ 25 | 19 | 21 | $31 |

**Lomita** | 24503 Narbonne Ave. (Lomita Blvd.) | 310-325-5000

"Weird but tasty" Japanese-accented Italian cuisine like "wonderful", "al dente" pastas are on offer at this "true find" in an out-of-the-way Lomita locale; "reasonable" prices help keep the dining room "crowded", and regulars warn its "popularity" means that "reservations" are usually needed.

### ☒ Il Cielo ☒ *Italian*

| | | | |
|---|---|---|---|
| 21 | 27 | 22 | $53 |

**Beverly Hills** | 9018 Burton Way (bet. Almont & Wetherly Drs.) | 310-276-9990 | www.ilcielo.com

"Romance incarnate" murmur lovebirds enchanted with this Beverly Hills special-occasion spot boasting a "fairy tale", "tree-lined" patio "with a thousand twinkling lights" and a "charming" dining room with a fireplace; "gracious" servers add to the "elegant" ambiance that's "perfect for proposals", though a few quibble the "expensive" Northern Italian cuisine "doesn't live up to" the "lovely setting."

### ☒ Il Fornaio *Italian*

| | | | |
|---|---|---|---|
| 20 | 19 | 19 | $34 |

**Beverly Hills** | 301 N. Beverly Dr. (Dayton Way) | 310-550-8330
**Santa Monica** | 1551 Ocean Ave. (Colorado Ave.) | 310-451-7800
**Manhattan Beach** | Manhattan Gateway Shopping Ctr. | 1800 Rosecrans Ave. (bet. S. Sepulveda Blvd. & Village Dr.) | 310-725-9555
**Pasadena** | One Colorado | 24 W. Union St. (Fair Oaks Ave.) | 626-683-9797
www.ilfornaio.com

"*Molto buono cibo*" like "solid" pastas and "interesting" dishes from monthly regional menus please patrons at this "convivial" chain of Italian eateries with on-site bakeries churning out "fresh-baked" loaves of bread; service tends toward "harried during the peak times" (breakfast and lunch), but they're "friendly" (and "welcoming" to kids too) while "decent prices" make it "one of the best values around."

### Il Forno *Italian*

| | | | |
|---|---|---|---|
| 20 | 17 | 21 | $33 |

**Santa Monica** | Water Gdn. | 2450 Colorado Ave. (bet. Cloverfield Blvd. & 26th St.) | 310-449-9244 ☒
**Santa Monica** | 2901 Ocean Park Blvd. (bet. 29th & 30th Sts.) | 310-450-1241
www.ilfornocaffe.com

With two Santa Monica locations, this "neighborhood" Northern Italian is a "home away from home" for Westsiders craving "reliable", "reasonably priced" fare and "friendly" service; the Ocean Park branch does a brisker dinner business, while Water Garden is busier at lunch and the room can be "so loud you'll get an earache", but the staff "hustles to please."

## Il Forno Caldo ⑤ Italian                                    ▽ 20 | 16 | 19 | $29

**Beverly Hills** | 9705 Santa Monica Blvd. (Roxbury Dr.) | 310-777-0040
Few surveyors have found this "cozy" (read: "tiny") Beverly Hills trattoria dishing out well-priced "authentic" Italian fare from a menu with "lots of choices"; in spite of a "warm" staff and live music on the weekends, the less-enthused label it "boring"

## Il Grano ⑤ Italian                                         25 | 20 | 22 | $58

**West LA** | 11359 Santa Monica Blvd. (Purdue Ave.) | 310-477-7886
"They're serious about the food" at this West LA "treasure" where chef-owner Sal Marino prepares "fantabulous" Italian dishes with "passion and creativity", turning out "exemplary" fresh seafood (including especially noteworthy crudo platters) and "top-notch" pastas in an "elegant", "high-style" dining room; add in "gracious, unhurried" service, and it's a "stellar experience every time."

## Il Moro Italian                                            22 | 21 | 21 | $41

**West LA** | 11400 W. Olympic Blvd. (Purdue Ave.) | 310-575-3530 | www.ilmoro.com
"It's a keeper" assert enthusiasts of this West LA "oasis" "hidden away in an office building" with a "charming" landscaped patio and an "elegant" dining room done up in chocolate tones; "truly authentic" Italian cuisine is "executed beautifully" while the "very professional" servers are "consistently working to improve" on an already "solid operation."

## Il Pastaio Italian                                         25 | 16 | 20 | $41

**Beverly Hills** | 400 N. Cañon Dr. (Brighton Way) | 310-205-5444 | www.giacominodrago.com
The "name means 'the pasta maker' and the kitchen does it more than justice" gush groupies of Giacomino Drago and his "superb" Italian dishes like "heavenly", "homemade" ravioli and "terrific" branzino at this Beverly Hills eatery "jam-packed with celebs and neighborhood families"; those who find the "small" dining room "as crowded and noisy as Rome in June" retire to the sidewalk patio where sitting outside "on a sunny Friday afternoon" is an "immensely pleasurable" experience.

## Il Sole Italian                                            23 | 18 | 21 | $57

**West Hollywood** | 8741 Sunset Blvd. (Sherbourne Dr.) | 310-657-1182
This "sceney" West Hollywood "neighborhood trattoria" draws quite the "hip", "well-heeled' crowd (including plenty of "celebs" with "paparazzi" in tow) who munch on mostly organic "traditional" Italian cuisine served in "quaint" quarters with additional patio seating; supporters sigh it used to be "better" before it "got too popular", adding it's "overpriced" and a bit "snooty" now as well.

## Il Tiramisù Ristorante & Bar Ⓜ Italian                     22 | 18 | 23 | $34

**Sherman Oaks** | 13705 Ventura Blvd. (Woodman Ave.) | 818-986-2640 | www.il-tiramisu.com
"Huggy kissy treatment" from "attentive" owners Peter Kastelan and his father, Ivo, warms up this "inviting" Sherman Oaks Northern Italian with "solid" cuisine (including "heavenly desserts") served in an "at-

tractive" candlelit room; "reasonable prices" keep it "busy" while "monthly wine dinners" are "a special treat."

### Il Tramezzino  *Italian*

21 | 12 | 17 | $20

**Beverly Hills** | 454 N. Cañon Dr. (Santa Monica Blvd.) | 310-273-0501
**Studio City** | 13031 Ventura Blvd. (Coldwater Canyon Ave.) | 818-784-2244
www.iltram.net

"Fab" panini are what this Italian duo in Beverly Hills and Studio City do best say surveyors sitting next to "young actors and private-school kids" sipping "killer" coffee on the patios of these reasonably priced "sidewalk cafes"; they're "reliable" stops for a "quick" "snack or meal", though insiders insist you opt for "takeout" on Saturdays to avoid the late-night "crowds."

### India's Oven  *Indian*

20 | 10 | 17 | $22

**Beverly Boulevard** | 7233 Beverly Blvd. (bet. Alta Vista Blvd. & Formosa Ave.) | 323-936-1000 | www.indiasovenla.com

Serving "consistent", "toothsome" Indian food, this "no-frills" Beverly Boulevard "standby" wins points for its mixed grill and "rich, creamy" chicken tikka masala, but not so much for its "presentation"; though service is "friendly, the decor is "nothing mind-blowing", leading locals to relegate it to "takeout" or delivery.

### India's Tandoori  *Indian*

19 | 12 | 17 | $19

**Mid-City** | 5947 W. Pico Blvd. (S. Point View St.) | 323-936-2050
**Hawthorne** | 4850 W. Rosecrans Ave. (bet. Inglewood & Shoup Aves.) | 310-675-5533
**West LA** | 11819 Wilshire Blvd., Ste. 206 (bet. Granville & S. Westgate Aves.) | 310-268-9100
**Burbank** | Burbank Vlg. | 142 N. San Fernando Blvd. (E. Olive Ave.) | 818-846-7500
**Tarzana** | Windsor Ctr. | 19006 Ventura Blvd. (Donna Ave.) | 818-342-9100

Opinions are split on this chain of separately owned Indian eateries: proponents look past the "homely" decor and "hit-or-miss" service for what they say is "authentic" fare with "abundant amounts of flavor and spice"; detractors declare the food "bland and boring" and say "disappearing" waiters contribute to an overall "disappointing" experience.

### Indo Cafe  *Indonesian*

▽ 19 | 12 | 17 | $21

**Palms** | 10428½ National Blvd. (Motor Ave.) | 310-815-1290

"We need more of these east of Jakarta" attest enthusiasts of this "little" BYO Indonesian that "really livens up" its corner of Palms with "wonderful" fare like beef rending and gado gado at "very nice prices"; "hole-in-the-wall" decor may soon be alleviated by a forthcoming expansion.

### Indochine Vien  Ⓜ  *Vietnamese*

18 | 15 | 18 | $18

**Atwater Village** | 3110 Glendale Blvd. (Glenhurst Ave.) | 323-667-9591 | www.indochinevien.com

"Delicious" phos at a "bargain" are the standout at this "hip" "minimall" Vietnamese in Atwater Village where diners deem the rest of the menu a bit "skimpy" on the portions, but "healthy" and "reasonably priced" otherwise; while the "simple", modern decor strikes some as a bit "cold", "excellent", "super-speedy" service adds a "friendly" touch.

| | FOOD | DECOR | SERVICE | COST |
|---|---|---|---|---|

### ☑ Inn of the Seventh Ray *Californian* | 21 | 26 | 20 | $43 |

**Topanga** | 128 Old Topanga Canyon Rd. (4 mi. north of PCH) |
310-455-1311 | www.innoftheseventhray.com

"It doesn't get any more romantic than this" swoon those enchanted
with this "magical" Topanga "haven" that exudes "tranquility" with its
"natural" "outdoor" setting surrounded by "beautiful trees" and fountains; Californian fare with vegan and raw-food options (and organic
and biodynamic wines) strikes some as "a little too healthy", but in
spite of that and "spacey" service, aging "baby boomers" suggest you
"go at least once", for the "truly unique experience"; N.B. the Food
score may not reflect a 2007 chef change.

### ☑ In-N-Out Burger ● *Hamburgers* | 24 | 10 | 18 | $8 |

**Hollywood** | 7009 Sunset Blvd. (N. Orange Dr.)
**Culver City** | 13425 Washington Blvd. (bet. Glencoe & Walnut Aves.)
**West LA** | 9245 W. Venice Blvd. (Exposition Dr.)
**Westwood** | 922 Gayley Ave. (Levering Ave.)
**Westchester** | 9149 S. Sepulveda Blvd. (bet. Westchester Pkwy &
W. 92nd St.)
**North Hollywood** | 5864 Lankershim Blvd. (bet. Califa & Emelita Sts.)
**Sherman Oaks** | 4444 Van Nuys Blvd. (bet. Milbank & Moorpark Sts.)
**Studio City** | 3640 Cahuenga Blvd. (bet. Fredonia Dr. & Regal Pl.)
**Van Nuys** | 7930 Van Nuys Blvd. (bet. Blythe & Michaels Sts.)
**Woodland Hills** | 19920 Ventura Blvd. (bet. Lubao & Oakdale Aves.)
800-786-1000
www.in-n-out.com
Additional locations throughout Southern California

"Fanatical" followers "plan their road trips around" this "family-
owned" chain, voted top Bang for the Buck in LA, that's "famous" for
"fantastic", "messy" burgers made with "high-quality ingredients" and
matched with "real" "thick, tasty shakes" (though the "cut-fresh" fries
get mixed reviews); a "clean-cut young staff" keeps the "long lines"
moving at these "sparkling", "'50s-style" "joints" where just "a few
bucks" still buys the "ultimate SoCal experience"; P.S. the "double-
double animal-style" off the "secret menu" "rocks."

### Iroha ● *Japanese* | 24 | 17 | 20 | $35 |

**Studio City** | 12953 Ventura Blvd. (Coldwater Canyon Ave.) |
818-990-9559

Though "it might be in a shack", this Studio City Japanese delivers
"delicious and perfectly presented" sushi and other dishes, including
"fresh" fin fare and "lots of unusual salads", that have "stood the test of
time"; while the staff "can be a tad impatient", service is "fast" and locals
"lucky enough to know where it is" "love the intimacy of the place."

### Islands *American* | 16 | 16 | 17 | $16 |

**Beverly Hills** | 350 S. Beverly Dr. (Olympic Blvd.) | 310-556-1624
**Marina del Rey** | 404 Washington Blvd. (Via Dolce) | 310-822-3939
**West LA** | 10948 W. Pico Blvd. (Veteran Ave.) | 310-474-1144
**Manhattan Beach** | 3200 Sepulveda Blvd. (bet. 30th & 33rd Sts.) |
310-546-4456
**Torrance** | 2647 PCH (Crenshaw Blvd.) | 310-530-5383
**Pasadena** | 3533 E. Foothill Blvd. (Rosemead Blvd.) | 626-351-6543
**Burbank** | 101 E. Orange Grove Ave. (N. 1st St.) | 818-566-7744
**Encino** | 15927 Ventura Blvd. (Gloria Ave.) | 818-385-1200
**Glendale** | 117 W. Broadway (Orange St.) | 818-545-3555

*(continued)*

## Islands

**Woodland Hills** | 23397 Mulholland Dr. (Calabasas Rd.) |
818-225-9839
www.islandsrestaurants.com
Additional locations throughout Southern California

"Leave your diet at the door" but "bring your earplugs" to guard against "screaming kids" at these "entertaining" chain "mainstays" with a "Hawaiian-surfer theme", serving up "big, fat juicy burgers" and "heaps" of "crunchy" fries and onion rings; families find them a "mecca for the après-soccer crowd" (even if a few gripe it's "getting too pricey"), while for others the "greasy" fare and "coldest beers in town" evoke "Hooters without the girls."

## Ita-Cho 🗷 🕅 *Japanese* 24 | 11 | 20 | $37

**Beverly Boulevard** | 7311 Beverly Blvd. (bet. Fuller Ave. & Poinsettia Pl.) |
323-938-9009

"Inventive" "Japanese tapas" "come out fast and furious" at this Beverly Boulevard izakaya that's a "favorite" with the "young Hollywood" set; service is "efficient" and prices a mere "pittance", so if "not much energy went into" the "minimally decorated" room, most are so "pleased" with the "experience" that they hardly care.

## 🗷 Ivy, The *Californian* 22 | 22 | 20 | $61

**West Hollywood** | 113 N. Robertson Blvd. (bet. Beverly Blvd. & 3rd St.) |
310-274-8303

"All the LA clichés come to vivid life" at West Hollywood's "celeb-sighting" epicenter whose Californian menu (best when it comes to the "scrumptious" crab cakes) plays a supporting role to the "power scene" on the patio, lit up with "stars, exotic cars" and "popping flash-bulbs"; veterans advise "prepare to be seated in Siberia" amid the "quaint", "cottage-inspired" setting "if you're not Harrison Ford" (or "Keanu Reeves" or "Helen Mirren"), and "consider the sticker shock from the final tab to be the price of admission."

## Ivy at the Shore *Californian* 21 | 20 | 21 | $57

**Santa Monica** | 1535 Ocean Ave. (bet. B'way & Colorado Ave.) |
310-393-3113

"Though its not as atmospheric" or "star-studded" as the WeHo original, this Santa Monica outpost of an "all-time Los Angeles favorite" delivers the same "tasty" Californian cuisine (like "famous salads" and "exceptional crab cakes") as the original that fans find "worth it" for a "three-hour lunch" on the "cheery patio"; critics claim it's "living off its reputation" with "dreadfully forgettable fare", "snobbish service" and "laugh-out-loud prices" as well.

## NEW Izaka-Ya by Katsu-Ya 🗷 *Japanese* ▽ 25 | 17 | 21 | $43

**Third Street** | 8420 W. Third St. (Orlando Ave.) | 323-782-9536

"Another quality creation" by Katsuya Uechi, this Third Street off-shoot serves Japanese small plates of "innovative" cooked combinations and "divine" sushi "with all the flourish" of the other locales; the "crowded, hip" atmosphere is "much more casual" than that of its sibs (if a bit "randomly" decorated), but be forewarned that "whoever said that it's Katsu-ya at a fraction of the price must have had 3/4 in mind as a fraction."

| | FOOD | DECOR | SERVICE | COST |
|---|---|---|---|---|

**NEW Izakaya Kiichi** 🔣 *Japanese* | – | – | – | M

**West Hollywood** | 8351 Santa Monica Blvd. (N. Kings Rd.) | 323-654-4404
With a sushi bar in virtually every neighborhood in LA, it was inevitable that Nipponophiles would discover the colorful world of izakaya, essentially Japanese tapas, a wide assortment of dishes meant to be consumed with sake (though beer works just as well); among the latest purveyors, this wood-and-glass newcomer with high ceilings sits in the heart of WeHo and was opened by the same Japanese company that gave Los Angeles the fabled (and long-defunct) Tokyo Kaikan – the restaurant universally credited as the birthplace of the California Roll.

**Izayoi** 🔣 *Japanese* | 23 | 14 | 19 | $36

**Little Tokyo** | 132 S. Central Ave. (bet. 1st & 2nd Sts.) | 213-613-9554
The "cult following" of this Little Tokyo izakaya waxes lyrical about its "crunchy, deep golden seafood croquettes", "silken" homemade tofu and "delicate" sushi, complemented by "generous pours of sake"; though dinner can "add up", insiders recommend the "bargain" bento boxes at lunch, and say the staffers are "personable" once they "know you" – so sit at the bar, let the chef "tell you what and how to eat" and you'll experience "the closest thing to a restaurant in Japan."

**Jack n' Jill's** *American* | 19 | 14 | 16 | $20

**Beverly Hills** | 342 N. Beverly Dr. (bet. Brighton & Dayton Ways) | 310-247-4500
**Santa Monica** | 510 Santa Monica Blvd. (5th St.) | 310-656-1501
www.eatatjacknjills.com
"Lunchtime perfection" comes in the form of "large plates" of American "down-home cookin'" at these Beverly Hills and Santa Monica bakery/cafes, where the "huge selection" includes "fantastic muffins" and "delightful" cupcakes; critics carp that they "run hot and cold, like their coffee", and while the staff is "refreshingly nice", "be prepared to wait."

**Jackson's Village Bistro** Ⓜ *American* | ▽ 23 | 18 | 22 | $33

**Hermosa Beach** | 517 Pier Ave. (bet. Bard St. & Cypress Ave.) | 310-376-6714
"Delightful", "eclectic" New American fare and a mere $3 corkage fee (along with a California-focused wine list) attract Hermosa Beach foodies to this "reliable neighborhood bistro", which is "one of the few on Pier Avenue" to offer "sophisticated" food, a "comfortable" atmosphere and a "fine" staff that "remembers your name" if you're a regular.

**Jack Sprat's Grille** *Californian* | 19 | 12 | 18 | $22

**West LA** | 10668 W. Pico Blvd. (Overland Ave.) | 310-837-6662 | www.jackspratsgrille.com
"Awesome" air-baked fries and "soft pretzels instead of bread" win the most affection at this "semi-healthy" West LA Californian with an emphasis on vegetarian and vegan choices; while it's a "quaint hole-in-the-wall" that some diners deem merely "serviceable", the "helpful", "kid-friendly" staff helps makes it an "easy experience" overall.

**Jacopo's** *Pizza* | 17 | 9 | 14 | $19

**Beverly Hills** | 490 N. Beverly Dr. (Little Santa Monica Blvd.) | 310-858-6446
**Pacific Palisades** | 15415 Sunset Blvd. (Via de la Paz) | 310-454-8494
www.jacopos.com
This "time-tested" pizzeria pair in Beverly Hills and Pacific Palisades does a "brisk take-out business" while offering a "basic" "go-to" op-

| | FOOD | DECOR | SERVICE | COST |

tion for "family fare"; on Tuesday nights, when children eat free at both, what's "kid-friendly" to some can become a "nightmare" for those who chafe at the "Chuck E. Cheese" crowd.

### James' Beach American

| | 18 | 18 | 20 | $40 |

**Venice** | 60 N. Venice Blvd. (Pacific Ave.) | 310-823-5396 | www.jamesbeach.com

"Dude, check out the ambiance" at this Venice American with a "rockin' bar scene late at night" and "mellow good beachy times" during the day when the "swim trunks–flip-flops–and-sunglasses" set shows up for "straightforward" eats such as fried chicken and fruit cobblers; it's "steps from the beach", but "parking is a beast", and while most agree it's a "happening" hang, some feel the fare "needs to improve."

### Jan's ● Diner

| | ▽ 14 | 8 | 22 | $16 |

**West Hollywood** | 8424 Beverly Blvd. (Croft Ave.) | 323-651-2866

"Standard-issue coffee-shop food" comes in "huge portions" at this "open-late" West Hollywood "reliable" that's been treating its "cops" and "old-folks" clientele well for 50 years; among the perks – prices are "reasonable", "they have a parking lot" and "where else can you get a decent bite to eat" starting at 6 AM?

### Japon Bistro Japanese

| | ▽ 23 | 17 | 19 | $35 |

**Pasadena** | 927 E. Colorado Blvd. (bet. Lake & Mentor Aves.) | 626-744-1751 | www.japonbistro-pasadena.com

This Pasadena Japanese "feels like a Tokyo neighborhood gastropub" with "incredibly imaginative" sushi, including *uni to die for*", "interesting" *omakase* courses that feature some "innovative dishes most have never tried" and "fabulous sake choices"; "service is steady" and the humble digs are "cozy."

### ☑ Jar American/Steak

| | 25 | 22 | 22 | $56 |

**Beverly Boulevard** | 8225 Beverly Blvd. (Harper Ave.) | West Hollywood | 323-655-6566 | www.thejar.com

"Comfort food with a modern twist" "shines" at this "buzzy" Beverly Boulevard New American chophouse where chef/co-owner Suzanne Tracht turns out "sublime" steaks and a "famous" pot roast that "makes you forget about mom's"; a "courteous" staff also helps justify the "premium price", and the wood-paneled, "retro-style" "but not overdone" look adds extra "warmth"; N.B. its new offshoot, Tracht's, has opened in the Renaissance Long Beach Hotel.

### Javan Persian

| | 21 | 15 | 19 | $24 |

**West LA** | 11500 Santa Monica Blvd. (Butler Ave.) | 310-207-5555 | www.javanrestaurant.com

"Aromatic", "ample" Persian dishes, including "juicy" kebabs, draw a global crowd (including lunchers "on jury duty") to this "cost-effective" West LA "staple"; although critics say the "upscale" bar and dining room "could use some warming up", the "attentive" staff tends to please.

### Jer-ne Californian

| | 22 | 25 | 22 | $58 |

**Marina del Rey** | Ritz-Carlton Marina Del Rey | 4375 Admiralty Way (off Lincoln Blvd.) | 310-574-4333 | www.ritzcarlton.com

A "stupendous" view meets "well-done" Californian dinners and "breezy" brunches at this "upscale alternative for the Marina" inside the Ritz-Carlton; while some appreciate "DJs spinning loungey music on the weekends", others sniff it's "still a hotel restaurant" – so "expect to pay accordingly."

### Jinky's Southwestern
20 | 10 | 16 | $16

**West Hollywood** | 8539 W. Sunset Blvd. (Alta Loma Rd.) | 310-659-9670
**Santa Monica** | 1447 Second St. (bet. B'way & Santa Monica Blvd.) | 310-917-3311
**Sherman Oaks** | 14120 Ventura Blvd. (Stansbury Ave.) | 818-981-2250
www.jinkys.com

The "wait at the DMV is shorter" than the weekend "throngs" that gather at this Southwestern breakfast-and-lunch trio that serves "free coffee" to those queuing up for "healthy portions" of "amazing" pancakes and other "hearty" fare; there are "enough choices to please meatlovers and vegetarians", and while the "overworked" servers are "hard to pin down" and the digs are "basic" "coffee shop", for most it's still a "terrific value."

### ☒ JiRaffe Californian
26 | 21 | 24 | $56

**Santa Monica** | 502 Santa Monica Blvd. (5th St.) | 310-917-6671 | www.jirafferestaurant.com

"Bravo to Raphael [Lunetta]" effuse fans of the chef-owner who "knows how to cook and create" "delicious surprises" at this "phenomenal" Santa Monica Californian; even though the chandelier-accented space has "tight seating" downstairs (with a "quieter" upper level), the "smashing martinis", "impeccable service" and Monday 'Bistro Night' "deal" elicit lots of "love" – indeed, as one admirer attests, "I went into labor and stayed to finish my meal."

### Jitlada ☒ Thai
∇ 21 | 11 | 16 | $22

**East Hollywood** | 5233½ W. Sunset Blvd. (bet. Harvard Blvd. & Kingsley Dr.) | 323-667-9809

"Fiery" fare awaits at this inexpensive East Hollywood "strip-mall" "treasure" that adventurous eaters "rank as one of the best" for "authentic", "rightly spiced" Thai dishes, including many "rare" Southern-style specialties; "parking is tough" and "there's not much in the way of atmosphere" but fans find the trouble is "worth it."

### JJ Steak House ☒ Steak
20 | 21 | 20 | $55

**Pasadena** | 88 W. Colorado Blvd., 3rd fl. (De Lacey Ave.) | 626-844-8889

"Your guests will be impressed" by the "intimate" environs at this "upscale" Pasadena chophouse where a harpist plays on weekends and the patio is "wonderful in the summer"; service is "upstanding", but some chafe at the "snooty" vibe, and while carnivores rave about steaks "like buttah", skeptics feel they "could be better for the price tag."

### Joan's on Third American
24 | 14 | 17 | $21

**Third Street** | 8350 W. Third St. (bet. Fairfax Ave. & La Cienega Blvd.) | 323-655-2285 | www.joansonthird.com

The "art of lunch is perfected" at this "upscale", "gourmet" American cafe and market on Third, where "awesome" sandwiches, "terrific" salads, "sinful" cupcakes and more are served by an "earnest but overworked" staff; "parking's a nightmare" and the "small" space gets "bottlenecked" at peak hours, but a "long-overdue" expansion (due to be completed in fall 2007) should help "minimize the wait-times."

| | FOOD | DECOR | SERVICE | COST |
|---|---|---|---|---|

### Jody Maroni's Sausage Kingdom  *Hot Dogs*  | 19 | 7 | 14 | $10 |

**Culver City** | Howard Hughes Ctr. | 6081 Center Dr. (Sepulveda Blvd.) |
310-348-0007
**Venice** | 2011 Ocean Front Walk (20th Ave.) | 310-822-5639
**LAX** | LA Int'l Airport | 201 World Way (Terminals 3 & 6) | 310-646-8056
**Torrance** | South Bay Galleria | 1815 Hawthorne Blvd. (Redondo Beach Blvd.) |
310-370-6921
**Universal City** | Universal CityWalk | 1000 Universal Studios Blvd.
(off Rte. 101) | 818-622-5639
**NEW  Camarillo** | Camarillo Premium Outlet Mall | 740 E. Ventura Blvd.
(Camarillo Outlet) | 805-384-9300
www.jodymaroni.com

"Gourmet" franks that "make you sit up and beg" and "zesty",
"unique" sausages made with "fresh" "quality ingredients" and "nice,
snappy casings" attract frankophiles to this chain of hot dog stands
that started on Muscle Beach; although the staff may "need some
training", fans "love the free samples" from the "great selection."

### ☑ Joe's Ⓜ  *Californian/French*  | 26 | 20 | 24 | $51 |

**Venice** | 1023 Abbot Kinney Blvd. (B'way) | 310-399-5811 |
www.joesrestaurant.com

This "gem" is the "closest thing to elegance Venice has to offer" show-
casing "perfectly balanced combinations of flavors and textures" in
the Cal-French cuisine, which is served by a "professional" staff in a
"stylish", if somewhat "cramped" space; the "personable", "hands-
on" chef-owner, Joe Miller, is a "mensch" who "adds to the enjoyable
atmosphere", and one more reason pros promise "you'll always want
to eat at Joe's."

### Joe's Crab Shack  *Seafood*  | 13 | 15 | 15 | $26 |

**Long Beach** | 6550 E. Marina Dr. (Studebaker Rd.) | 562-594-6551
**Redondo Beach** | 230 Portofino Way (Harbor Dr.) | 310-406-1999
**City of Industry** | 1420 S. Azusa Ave. (Colima Rd.) | 626-839-4116
www.joescrabshack.com

"Tacky", "festive" and "chain-y", these "seafood versions of Chuck E.
Cheese" with a "dancing staff" play host to "picnic-bench" "celebrations" that are "very kid-friendly" and "not for shy" birthday boys or
girls of any age; crabby voters dismiss the "so-so" "fried and salted"
fare, but the "sweet and boozy" drinks "take the edge off" a "schlocky"
vibe that has adults asking "where's SpongeBob?"

### NEW  Joey's Smokin' BBQ  *BBQ*  | - | - | - | I |

**Manhattan Beach** | Manhattan Vill. | 3564 N. Sepulveda Blvd.
(Rosecrans Ave.) | 310-563-9072 | www.joeyssmokinbbq.com

Joey is Joey Maggiore, an affable guy from da Bronx who has part-
nered with the Lakers' Luke Walton to open this new eat-in/take-out
'cue chainlet with lots of big-screen TVs on the northern edge of the
Manhattan Beach Village mall; its easy-on-the-wallet menu offers
smoked brisket, pulled pork and a wide selection of ribs.

### Johnnie's New York Pizzeria  *Pizza*  | 18 | 10 | 14 | $16 |

**Mid-Wilshire** | Museum Park Sq. | 5757 Wilshire Blvd. (Courtyard Pl.) |
323-904-4880
**Century City** | Fox Apts. | 10251 Santa Monica Blvd. (bet. Ave. of the Stars &
Beverly Glen Blvd.) | 310-553-1188

*(continued)*

*(continued)*

**Johnnie's New York Pizzeria**

**Malibu** | 22333 PCH (bet. Carbon Canyon Rd. & Malibu Pier) | 310-456-1717
**Marina del Rey** | Hoyt Plaza | 2805 Abbot Kinney Blvd. (Washington Blvd.) |
310-821-1224
www.johnniesnypizza.com
It's "better than most that claim the NY moniker" assess samplers of
the "legit" pizza, garlic knots and salads at this "not-too-expensive"
quartet whose kids' menu lends it extra family appeal; true, the
checkered-tablecloth decor has a "cheesy-chain" look while the
"cramped quarters do make it seem a bit like Gotham", so many
advocate ordering in.

**Johnnie's Pastrami** ●⇄ *Deli*     20 | 8 | 15 | $13

**Culver City** | 4017 Sepulveda Blvd. (bet. Washington Blvd. &
Washington Pl.) | 310-397-6654
The "biggest, greasiest" pastrami sandwiches provide "heaven on rye"
at this "classic" Culver City deli counter staffed by "gruff waitresses"
who nevertheless "remember your favorite songs on the tabletop
jukebox"; "late-night" diners love "sitting by the fire pit and ordering
beer by the pitcher", though skittish types say "the take-out crowd always makes it a fire marshal's nightmare" and request a "defibrillator
on the menu too."

**Johnny Rebs'** *BBQ*     22 | 16 | 20 | $21

**Bellflower** | 16639 Bellflower Blvd. (bet. Alondra & Flower Sts.) |
562-866-6455
**Long Beach** | 4663 Long Beach Blvd. (bet. 46th & 47th Sts.) | 562-423-7327
www.johnnyrebs.com
This BBQ chain delivers "finger-lickin'", "diet-busting" cooking in
"generous portions" with "cheap beer" and "free peanuts"; add in
"down-home" service and appropriately "funky" "roadhouse" decor,
and "Southern friends say" it's "the real thing" that "will not disappoint"; N.B. following a fire, the Long Beach location is closed
until further notice.

**Johnny Rockets** *Hamburgers*     15 | 15 | 16 | $13

**Fairfax** | Farmers Mkt. | 6333 W. Third St. (Fairfax Ave.) | 323-937-2093
**Hollywood** | Hollywood & Highland Complex | 6801 Hollywood Blvd.
(Highland Ave.) | 323-465-4456
**Melrose** | 7507 Melrose Ave. (Gardner St.) | 323-651-3361
**Culver City** | Howard Hughes Ctr. | 6081 Center Dr. (Sepulveda Blvd.) |
310-670-7555
**Long Beach** | Pine Ct. | 245 Pine Ave. (bet. B'way & 3rd St.) | 562-983-1332
**Manhattan Beach** | Manhattan Mktpl. | 1550-C Rosecrans Ave.
(Sepulveda Blvd.) | 310-536-9464
**Arcadia** | Westfield Santa Anita Mall | 400 S. Baldwin Ave.
(Huntington Dr.) | 626-462-1800
**Burbank** | Media City Ctr. | 201 E. Magnolia Blvd. (3rd St.) |
818-845-7055
**Encino** | 16901 Ventura Blvd. (Balboa Blvd.) | 818-981-5900
**Alhambra** | 19 E. Main St. (Garfield Ave.) | 626-281-8831
www.johnnyrockets.com
Additional locations throughout Southern California
Hamburger hounds tag it "*American Graffiti* revisited" at this "sparkling" red and chrome "rendition of a '50s diner" chain that children

"love", with "classic burgers and fries" plus "thick and generous" milk-shakes; though most agree that "serious diners should look elsewhere", "fans of the era" who dig the "fun" staff and "retro" music agree it's "really about the experience."

### John O'Groats American — 20 | 11 | 19 | $17

**Rancho Park** | 10516 W. Pico Blvd. (½ block west of Beverly Glen Blvd.) | 310-204-0692 | www.ogroatsrestaurant.com

Rancho Park's "shrine" to coffee-shop fare (and West LA's unofficial "social center") "hasn't changed in 1000 years", but regulars report that the "habit-forming biscuits" and other breakfast and lunch "classics" keep them "coming back"; the "homey", "kid-friendly" setting and "chivalrous" chef-owner offset downsides like "decor past its prime" and "guaranteed waits" on weekends.

### NEW Jollibee Filipino — ∇ 12 | 8 | 12 | $8

**Koreatown** | 3821 Beverly Blvd. (Vermont Ave.) | 323-906-8617 | www.jollibee.com.ph

Even though it's the "McDonald's of the Philippines", American palates may need time to adjust to the often "fried" and "sweetened" fare, which includes 'aloha burgers' and chicken and spaghetti, at this "bright" fast-food joint in Koreatown; still, families longing for a "taste of the Old Country" find it "hits the spot."

### Jones Hollywood ● American/Italian — 18 | 19 | 17 | $30

**West Hollywood** | 7205 Santa Monica Blvd. (Formosa Ave.) | 323-850-1727 | www.committedinc.com

An "old-school", "late-night" WeHo "hangout", this Italian-American eatery is known more for "the scene" than the food, but the "hearty" fare still pleases the "heavy-drinking hipster crowd"; "sexy, but aloof bartenders" and "low-lit room with red leather booths" contribute to the "sultry" atmosphere, which is further enhanced by the occasional "celeb sighting."

### Joseph's Cafe ⑧ Greek — 18 | 16 | 17 | $28

**Hollywood** | 1775 N. Ivar Ave. (Yucca St.) | 323-462-8697 | www.josephscafe.com

Quite a few customers of this Hollywood Hellenic "taverna" "come for the drinks" and "surprisingly good" nibbles and stay for the "hopping party" on the patio and in the bar; maybe the DJ "doesn't spin the newest" tunes, but the vibe is "relaxed", the ambiance "cozy" and equally suited to "an early evening glass of wine and meze platter" or a night out on the town; N.B. no food served Sundays.

### ⓩ Josie American — 27 | 23 | 25 | $60

**Santa Monica** | 2424 Pico Blvd. (25th St.) | 310-581-9888 | www.josierestaurant.com

"Entirely pleasurable on all levels", this Santa Monica "favorite" "isn't trendy", but it's "pretty much perfect" say those praising chef Josie Le Balch's "sumptuous" New American fare that spotlights "fresh, local" ingredients and "excellent game"; "attentive service" and a "gorgeous" room with "romantic" fireside tables make it a "favorite haunt" for well-heeled locals, and if the "pricey" final tab intimidates some, insiders say "no-corkage Mondays" and Wednesday night's Farmers Market prix fixe are less expensive options.

|  | FOOD | DECOR | SERVICE | COST |
|---|---|---|---|---|

**NEW** J Restaurant & Lounge ⊠ *American/Mediterranean* — ▽ 13 | 20 | 15 | $37

**Downtown** | 1119 S. Olive St. (bet. W. 11th & 12th Sts.) | 213-746-7746 | www.jloungela.com

This "trendy" two-story New American–Med eatery and club inside Downtown's former Little J's boasts a "cool lounge", patio and smoking area, along with a location suited to "pre-event dinners"; while early reviewers report it can get "loud", the bigger complaint is "they need to get a grip" on the "disappointing" food, which comes with service that "needs improvement."

**JR's BBQ** ⊠ *BBQ* — 20 | 10 | 19 | $16

**Culver City** | 3055 S. La Cienega Blvd. (Blackwelder St.) | 310-837-6838 | www.jrs-bbq.com

Brisket buffs hit this Culver City "joint" for "legitimate BBQ" with "serious Memphis-style" meat tasting of "real smoke" (but "wowee, watch out for the spicy sauce") served by "friendly" people, including "terrific" owner Bobby Johnson and his "salty" mom, Jeannie Jackson; the "large portions make it a bargain", though for some the dinerlike setting means "these meals are better enjoyed at home."

**Juliano's Raw** *Vegan* — ▽ 21 | 15 | 16 | $35

**Santa Monica** | 609 Broadway (6th St.) | 310-587-1552 | www.planetraw.com

"Much improved" (it's up six Food points from last year), this "pricey" Santa Monica haven of "living cuisine" is "proof that raw food can be exciting" claim converts who are left "feeling rejuvenated" by chef-owner Juliano Brotman's "beautifully prepared" creations; unfortunately bare-bones decor is still "lacking", while critics say the staff could use some work in the "customer service" department.

**Julienne** ⊠ *French* — 25 | 21 | 20 | $26

**San Marino** | 2651 Mission St. (bet. El Molino & Los Robles Aves.) | 626-441-2299 | www.juliennetogo.com

"Elegant ladies of leisure" breakfast and lunch at this "French sidewalk cafe" and "gourmet take-out" shop in San Marino, where the servers "won't rush you" through a "scrumptious", "well-herbed" repast of "fresh, tasty salads" and sandwiches; though "you'll wait horrendously long for a table", you can always pick up "script ideas for *Desperate Housewives*" as you do.

**Junior's** *Deli* — 16 | 10 | 16 | $20

**West LA** | 2379 Westwood Blvd. (W. Pico Blvd.) | 310-475-5771

The "traditional deli fare" at this West LA "standby" may be "ordinary", but it still "satisfies" for "basics" like matzo ball soup, pastrami sandwiches and other fare that harken back to the old days in "Brooklyn" or "Miami"; some noshers note a 2007 remodel gives a "fresh feel" to the "bustling" dining room and "large take-out counter" area, while service remains "indifferent" at best.

**Kanpai Japanese Sushi Bar & Grill** *Japanese* — ▽ 22 | 15 | 17 | $34

**Westchester** | 8325 Lincoln Blvd. (83rd St.) | 310-338-7223

An "easygoing", "neighborhood" spot, this Westchester Japanese wins kudos for its "superb" sushi and "creative" specials, though regulars warn "it doesn't come cheap"; as for the "tiny" dining room, comfort-hounds call it "crowded", and suggest you choose the bar to avoid "slow" table service and get the best views of the "flat-screen TVs."

**NEW Kansas City BBQ Company** *BBQ* | _ | _ | _ | I |

**Studio City** | 4141 Lankershim Blvd. (Aqua Vista St.) | 818-754-0030
Real Kansas City–style BBQ has arrived in SoCal with this storefront located just north of Universal Studios; it's devoid of decor, which doesn't bother the true believers who flock here for slow-smoked meats, babyback ribs and other standards slathered with sauce flown in from KC.

**Katana** ● *Japanese* | 23 | 25 | 20 | $55 |

**West Hollywood** | 8439 W. Sunset Blvd. (bet. La Cienega Blvd. & Sweetzer Ave.) | 323-650-8585 | www.katanarobata.com
A "super scene for the super hip", this "high-end" WeHo sushi spot (and sib of Boa and Sushi Roku) attracts a "hot blond" crowd for drinks and "crazy rolls" on their "beautiful" sunset-facing patio; unfortunately, apart from "amazing" robata, many customers report the food "didn't offer the religious experience" they'd been hoping for, while service is "a little rushed" at times.

**Kate Mantilini** *Diner* | 18 | 18 | 18 | $34 |

**Beverly Hills** | 9101 Wilshire Blvd. (Doheny Dr.) | 310-278-3699 ●
**Woodland Hills** | 5921 Owensmouth Ave. (bet. Califa St. & Oxnard Ave.) | 818-348-1095
"Movie people of all stripes" "wine, dine" and engage in "a ritual of au-tomated head-turning" at this "upscale" Beverly Hills "coffee shop" set in "stylish", "industrial" digs; the American "comfort-food" menu is "dependable" and "convenient", especially "after a film screening" (it's a "short walk" from the Academy) or "late-night", though jaded sorts sigh "only in LA can you get a mediocre $14 hamburger"; N.B. the newer spin-off in Woodland Hills keeps earlier hours than the original.

**Z Katsu-ya** *Japanese* | 27 | 15 | 19 | $40 |

**Encino** | 16542 Ventura Blvd. (Hayvenhurst Ave.) | 818-788-2396
**Studio City** | 11680 Ventura Blvd. (Colfax Ave.) | 818-985-6976
"Sublime sushi" and "phenomenal", "nontraditional" "handrolls that are a work of art" as well as the signature spicy tuna on crispy rice keep these Japanese twins in Encino and Studio City "mobbed" with a "hip crowd" of "locals" and "stars" in spite of somewhat "sterile", "claustrophobic" surroundings; "prices can add up fast" and service is "rushed", but supporters swear the "flat-out terrific" fare "makes you forget" any shortcomings.

**Katsuya** *Japanese* | 24 | 25 | 20 | $56 |

**Brentwood** | 11777 San Vicente Blvd. (Montana Ave.) | 310-207-8744 | www.sbeent.com/katsuya
Though it's the kind of place where you might "actually hear someone say 'do you know who I am?'", this Brentwood Japanese "palace" is more than a "white-hot" "celebrity-sighting" "scene" thanks to the "inventive", "out-of-this-world" sushi of Katsuya Uechi, coupled with "wonderfully delicious specialty cocktails"; the "buzzing" dining room – featuring a "theatrical" "black, white" and "cool" design by Philippe

Starck – is overseen by managers whose "full-time job" seems to be "apologizing" for the often "indifferent service"; N.B. a Hollywood branch is coming soon.

### Kay 'n Dave's  Mexican

18 | 14 | 19 | $20

**Pacific Palisades** | 15246 W. Sunset Blvd. (bet. Monument St. & Swarthmore Ave.) | 310-459-8118
**Rancho Park** | 10543 W. Pico Blvd. (bet. Patricia & Prosser Aves.) | 310-446-8808
**Santa Monica** | 262 26th St. (San Vicente Blvd.) | 310-260-1355
www.kayndaves.com

This "family-oriented" Westside trio puts a "fresh spin" on Mexican fare with an emphasis on "healthy" preparations; they're "noisy" spots where the "pleasant staff" and "crayon-drawn pictures from young patrons" decorating the walls provide "unpretentious" "neighborhood" appeal.

### Kendall's Brasserie  French

17 | 20 | 16 | $43

**Downtown** | Dorothy Chandler Pavilion | 135 N. Grand Ave. (bet. Temple St. & Tom Bradley Blvd.) | 213-972-7322 | www.patinagroup.com

"Convenience" is king at this Downtown French brasserie (from the Patina Group) whose biggest asset is its location "so close to the Music center and Disney Hall" that you "couldn't possibly miss your show" even if you tried; in spite of food that's "not memorable" and "hit-or-miss service", it's still your "best bet" in the area.

### NEW Ketchup  American

∇ 16 | 19 | 22 | $41

**West Hollywood** | Millennium Ctr. | 8590 W. Sunset Blvd. (La Cienega Blvd.) | 310-289-8590 | www.dolcegroup.com

With a ceiling covered by orangey-red globe lights, this latest entry from the Dolce Group (Dolce, Geisha House) picks up the slack at the so-far-unlucky Millennium Center in WeHo with a menu of glammed-up retro American favorites – a $19 sloppy joe, Kobe beef hot dogs and sliders – to be washed down with cocktails made with Kool-Aid and Yoo-hoo; yes, it serves housemade ketchup with just about everything.

### Killer Shrimp  Seafood

21 | 10 | 16 | $22

**Marina del Rey** | The Marina Connection | 523 Washington Blvd. (Via Marina) | 310-578-2293
**Studio City** | 4000 Colfax Ave. (Ventura Blvd.) | 818-508-1570

"They make one thing and they do it well" at these Marina del Rey and Studio City twins where those who aren't afraid to "get their hands dirty" dig into "buckets of shrimp" served in a "Cajun-style broth" that's best "mopped up with French bread" and washed down with a "cold beer"; enthusiasts endure "ugly" digs and "spotty service", but cons complain the "limited menu" means this "one-trick wonder" "gets old fast."

### Kincaid's  Seafood/Steak

21 | 23 | 20 | $40

**Redondo Beach** | Redondo Beach Pier | 500 Fisherman's Wharf (Torrance Blvd.) | 310-318-6080 | www.kincaids.com

Redondo Beach's "dependable" surf 'n' turf chain outpost gets a "thumbs-up" for its "beautiful setting" on the pier and "excellent views of the harbor", particularly at sunset; the "menu doesn't change much", but it's "solid", and the service "nice, if lacking a little etiquette", so all in all, it's "popular with tourists" but "unremarkable" as far as local foodies are concerned.

| | FOOD | DECOR | SERVICE | COST |
|---|---|---|---|---|

### King's Fish House  *Seafood*  | 21 | 18 | 18 | $32 |

**Long Beach** | 100 W. Broadway (Pine Ave.) | 562-432-7463
**Calabasas** | The Commons | 4798 Commons Way (Calabasas Rd.) | 818-225-1979
www.kingsfishhouse.com

Seafood-seekers report this school of "busy", "unpretentious" eateries is a "good catch any day" for "always consistent", "simply" prepared fish with "comfort-food sides", along with the "best fresh oysters" and sushi too; while blasé types deem it "very acceptable but not extraordinary", and somewhat uneven in the service department, it's a "solid choice" for "after-work" nibbles or "family dinners" that "won't empty your wallet."

### Kings Road Cafe  *American*  | 19 | 14 | 17 | $18 |

**Beverly Boulevard** | 8361 Beverly Blvd. (Kings Rd.) | West Hollywood | 323-655-9044 | www.kingsroadcafe.com

"Everybody's got a script in hand" at this "hip" WeHo American "hangout" favored for "fresh breakfasts" and "free-flowing" "nitro coffee" that some swear "puts hair on your chest"; "expect to fight for a scarce table" on weekends, but otherwise it's a "happy-go-lucky" place with an equally "accommodating" staff.

### Kitchen, The ● *American*  | 19 | 12 | 17 | $24 |

**Silver Lake** | 4348 Fountain Ave. (Sunset Blvd.) | 323-664-3663 | www.thekitchen-silverlake.com

"Comfort food in a not-so-comfortable setting" sums up this "reasonably priced" Silver Lake BYO serving "starchy", "tasty" American "home cooking" in an "edgy", "urban" interior that still feels like a "work in progress"; the staff is "friendly" and it's "open late", making it an ideal spot to "sober up" after hitting the bars nearby.

### Koi  *Japanese*  | 24 | 25 | 19 | $62 |

**West Hollywood** | 730 N. La Cienega Blvd. (bet. Melrose & Willoughby Aves.) | 310-659-9449 | www.koirestaurant.com

With "sleek" decor, a prime West Hollywood address, a retractable bamboo roof and "paparazzi outside" lending *Entourage* appeal, this "swanky" Japanese still holds its place in the pantheon, thanks to "expertly prepared" sushi boosted by "imaginative" drinks and an "A-lister" crowd; still, many surveyors walk away feeling "mistreated" after enduring a "rude" staff, "long waits (even with a reservation)" and "the whole velvet rope/bouncer thing" that's "kind of a joke."

### Kokomo Cafe  *Southern*  | ▽ 20 | 12 | 16 | $16 |

**Fairfax** | Farmers Mkt. | 6333 W. Third St. (Fairfax Ave.) | 323-933-0773 | www.kokomocafe.com

The Southern vittles at this Fairfax "meeting place" in the Farmers Market "always satisfy" say fans who also cheer the "great breakfasts" and other "diner"-like fare; despite "crowds" at peak times it's "a pleasant place to eat and chat", and the staff will "accommodate special requests."

### Koo Koo Roo  *American*  | 16 | 9 | 13 | $12 |

**Downtown** | 255 S. Grand Ave. (3rd St.) | 213-620-1800 Ⓢ
**Downtown** | 445 S. Figueroa St. (5th St.) | 213-629-1246 Ⓢ

*(continued)*

*(continued)*

## Koo Koo Roo

**Hancock Park** | 301 N. Larchmont Blvd. (Beverly Blvd.) | 323-962-1500
**Mid-City** | 5779 Wilshire Blvd. (bet. Courtyard Pl. & Curson Ave.) | 323-954-7200
**West Hollywood** | 8520 Santa Monica Blvd. (La Cienega Blvd.) | 310-657-3300
**Beverly Hills** | 262 S. Beverly Dr. (bet. Charleville Blvd. & Gregory Way) | 310-274-3121
**Marina del Rey** | Villa Marina Mktpl. | 4325 Glencoe Ave. (bet. Maxella Ave. & Mindanao Way) | 310-305-8100
**West LA** | 11066 Santa Monica Blvd. (Sepulveda Blvd.) | 310-473-5858
**Manhattan Beach** | Manhattan Village Mall | 3294 N. Sepulveda Blvd. (Rosecrans Ave.) | 310-546-4500
**Pasadena** | 238 S. Lake Ave. (bet. Cordova St. & E. Del Mar Blvd.) | 626-683-9600
www.kookooroo.com
Additional locations throughout Southern California

Angelenos laud this rotisserie chicken chain for its "cheap" and "healthy" skinless birds and "multitude of sides" that "prove that fast food need not be dull"; service is "nonexistent", but the "cafeteria-style" setup is "quick" for "takeout", which surveyors suggest is the best option considering the "unspectacular" surroundings.

## Koutoubia M *Moroccan*

20 | 18 | 19 | $38

**Westwood** | 2116 Westwood Blvd. (bet. Mississippi Ave. & Olympic Blvd.) | 310-475-0729 | www.koutoubiarestaurant.com

It "feels like you're eating inside a Bedouin tent" at this Westwood Moroccan where "ornate" North African details and "pillows everywhere" make the "authentic" atmosphere both "comfortable" and "perfect for a date"; "gourmet" cuisine and "warm" service win accolades although a few find it "a bit pricey" and say that while they "enjoy" the "belly dancing on weekends", they could "do without" the "audience participation."

## Kung Pao Bistro *Chinese*

19 | 12 | 17 | $20

**West Hollywood** | San Fair | 7853 Santa Monica Blvd. (Fairfax Ave.) | 323-848-9888 | www.kpbistro.com
**Sherman Oaks** | 15025 Ventura Blvd. (bet. Kester & Noble Aves.) | 818-788-1689 | www.kpchinabistro.com
**Studio City** | 11838 Ventura Blvd. (bet. Colfax Ave. & Laurel Canyon Blvd.) | 818-766-8686 | www.kpbistro.com

"Healthy takes" on "traditional" Chinese recipes and plenty of "veg-friendly" options (like "five-star" "fake-meat dishes") make this mini-chain a local "take-out" "staple" and "a bargain" to boot; "speedy delivery" and "half-portion" options are additional appeasements, though a few thrill-seekers find these "extremely average" spots are a bit on the "boring" side; N.B. the Sherman Oaks location is separately owned.

## K-Zo Z *Japanese*

- | - | - | M

**Culver City** | 9240 Culver Blvd. (Canfield Ave.) | 310-202-8890 | www.k-zo.com

At his Culver City eatery, "genius" chef-owner Keizo Ishiba fuses European and Japanese techniques turning out "delicious" sushi and raw dishes as well as "outstanding" small plates, which can be ordered à la carte or in a five-course tasting menu; reservations are recom-

|  | FOOD | DECOR | SERVICE | COST |
|---|---|---|---|---|

mended since the "stylish" industrial setting fills up fast, and while a few find it a bit expensive, most concede it's "well worth the price."

### La Botte  *Italian*
**24** | **21** | **22** | **$62**

**Santa Monica** | 620 Santa Monica Blvd. (7th St.) | 310-576-3072 | www.labottesantamonica.com

In suburban Santa Monica, this "still undiscovered" sister of Piccolo in Venice attracts an "older crowd" for "delicious", "inventive" seasonal Italian dishes and "amazing wines" served by a "fawning" staff; a few are irked by "hefty prices" and the no-corkage policy, but otherwise, it "feels like Tuscany."

### La Bottega Marino  *Italian*
**20** | **12** | **16** | **$21**

**Hancock Park** | Larchmont Vill. | 203 N. Larchmont Blvd. (bet. Beverly Blvd. & 1st St.) | 323-962-1325

**West LA** | 11363 Santa Monica Blvd. (Purdue Ave.) | 310-477-7777 www.Labottegausa.com

This "cute" self-styled "typical Italian deli" duo in Hancock Park and West LA draws "regulars" who "relax" over "delicious" homemade pastas with "light and flavorful" sauces, "classic sandwiches", pizzas and other inexpensive fare; front-of-house management "treats everyone like family" creating a "charming" experience in spite of occasionally "slow" kitchen turnaround.

### La Bruschetta Ristorante  *Italian*
**21** | **18** | **22** | **$39**

**Westwood** | 1621 Westwood Blvd. (bet. Massachusetts & Ohio Aves.) | 310-477-1052 | www.labruschettaristorante.com

"Utterly dependable", this "low-key" Italian woos Westwooders with its "simple", seasonal fare, "warm" staff and "earnest" chef/co-owner, Angelo Peloni, who fosters a "family feel"; "adults" appreciate the "appealingly quiet" atmosphere with "well-spaced" tables, and even if some say "it could use a little sprucing up", they find it "relaxing" nevertheless.

### ◪ La Cachette  *French*
**27** | **25** | **26** | **$66**

**Century City** | 10506 Little Santa Monica Blvd. (Thayer Ave.) | 310-470-4992 | www.lacachetterestaurant.com

A "dignified", "gorgeous" light-filled "retreat in the middle of Century City" is how admirers view this "real treasure" and its "very talented" chef-owner Jean François Meteigner, who "removes most of the butter and cream", but none of the "flavor", from his "exquisite" seasonal New French creations; "spot-on" service sometimes veers toward "stuffy", but that's no matter to the "posh" deep-pocket crowds who continue to celebrate it as "one of LA's finest" tickets – "it's outstanding in every way."

### La Crêperie Café  *French*
**23** | **22** | **19** | **$22**

**Long Beach** | 4911 E. Second St. (bet. Argonne & St. Joseph Aves.) | 562-434-8499 | www.lacreperiecafe.net

"Could it get any more French?" ask admirers of this Long Beach boîte with "huge gold mirrors", a "Moulin Rouge mural" and "velvet curtains" draped around a peep-through window on the chefs preparing "scrumptious" crêpes and other bistro fare; "cozy" environs and "friendly" staff are conducive to "lounging" especially in the sidewalk seating area where "people-watching" is an additional perk.

| | FOOD | DECOR | SERVICE | COST |
|---|---|---|---|---|

## La Dijonaise Café et Boulangerie  *French*    18 | 15 | 16 | $24

**Culver City** | Helms Bldg. | 8703 Washington Blvd. (Helms Ave.) |
310-287-2770 | www.ladijonaise.com

An "early entrant" in "newly trendy" Culver City, this "bright and airy"
"très français" bistro is "justifiably crowded" thanks to "buttery croissants", "decent salads" and other "simple", "solid" fare in addition to
"a nice pastry selection" available to go; wallet-watchers overlook
servers with "lots of attitude" for what they call "a bargain" that
"never lets you down."

## La Dolce Vita  ●🗷  *Italian*    20 | 19 | 23 | $57

**Beverly Hills** | 9785 Santa Monica Blvd. (Wilshire Blvd.) | 310-278-1845 |
www.ladolcevitabeverlyhills.com

"A Dean Martin, Frank Sinatra-type of place" that's worthy of a "sport
coat", this "expensive" Beverly Hills relic of the "swinging '60s" specializes in "Italian standards" boosted by "formal" service offering za-
baglione prepared tableside and "quiet" candlelit digs; it "caters to an
older crowd", but "has a bit of new life" as well.

## L.A. Farm  🗷  *Californian*    20 | 20 | 19 | $40

**Santa Monica** | 3000 W. Olympic Blvd. (Stewart St.) | 310-449-4000 |
www.lafarm.com

"Nestled in" amongst "high-powered media companies", this Santa
Monica "industry hangout" pleases for "solid and consistent" Californian
cuisine; service is "welcoming" and the "serene" garden patio "feels
like you're in *A Midsummer Night's Dream*", except at peak times, when
it more closely resembles "a scene out of *LA Story*"; N.B. dinner service has been suspended till 2008 due to construction next door.

## La Fondue  *Fondue*    ▽ 14 | 13 | 15 | $35

**Sherman Oaks** | 13359 Ventura Blvd. (bet. Dixie Canyon & Fulton Aves.) |
818-788-8680

"They've got the gimmick", but it's getting "a bit old" claim critics of this
"longtime" Sherman Oaks fondue spot that's "cheesy" both in terms
of the "ho-hum" food and "Bavarian"-style decor; though some pros
proclaim it "fun with a large group", most say it's "seriously disappointing" and "way overpriced" for what basically amounts to "some
cheese, meat and bread."

## LA Food Show  *American*    19 | 18 | 18 | $26

**Manhattan Beach** | Manhattan Village Mall | 3212 N. Sepulveda Blvd.
(Rosecrans Ave.) | 310-546-5575 | www.cpk.com

Situated in the Manhattan Village Mall, this "mod" American eatery
(from the folks behind California Pizza Kitchen) offers "a little bit of
everything – from crab cakes to chicken and waffles – in a "family-
friendly" "upscale-chain" setting; it's "nothing to write home about",
but it's a "decent" option for a "quick meal" after "shopping" or a
"movie" nearby; N.B. a Beverly Hills branch is expected to open by the
end of the year.

## La Frite  *French*    20 | 15 | 18 | $27

**Sherman Oaks** | 15013 Ventura Blvd. (Lemona Ave.) | 818-990-1791
**Woodland Hills** | 22616 Ventura Blvd. (Sale Ave.) | 818-225-1331

"Charming relics" from the 1970s, these "inexpensive"
"neighborhood favorites" in Sherman Oaks and Woodland Hills

|  | FOOD | DECOR | SERVICE | COST |
|---|---|---|---|---|

turn out "simple", "home-cooked" French fare like poached salmon, filet mignon and their signature fries (which are best "extra-crispy"); "accommodating" servers work the "casual", "understated" quarters that have a tendency to get "crowded" and "loud", but "no one seems to mind."

## La Huasteca *Mexican*                22 | 21 | 20 | $28

**Lynwood** | Plaza Mexico | 3150 E. Imperial Hwy., Ste. 100 (bet. Peach & State Sts.) | 310-537-8800 | www.Lahuasteca.com

A "sure bet" in Lynwood, this "snazzy" "haute" Mexican "delights" "those who yearn beyond the usual" with "sophisticated preparations" of "authentic" Southern-style "delicacies"; the "warehouse"-sized digs are livened up by mariachi players while the staff "knows the menu, listens, and is eager to please"; N.B. the Pasadena location closed in 2007.

## Lake Spring Shanghai *Chinese*        ▽ 21 | 11 | 13 | $21

**Monterey Park** | 219 E. Garvey Ave. (Lincoln Ave.) | 626-280-3571

What this moderately priced Monterey Park Shanghai stalwart lacks in decor, it makes up for in dishes that have long attracted foodies like the Shanghai-style ham hocks, referred to on the menu as a "pork pump" – a towering pile of rump meat encased in fat that goes best with a Lipitor chaser; like many dishes that are less than healthy, it makes up for its salt and cholesterol with a lot of flavor.

## NEW Lal Mirch *Indian*                - | - | - | I

**Studio City** | 11138 Ventura Blvd (Vineland Ave.) | 818-980-2273 | www.lmdining.com

This budget-friendly Indian has landed in the Studio City space that for years was home to a Hungarian restaurant; it's kept the same dark-wood interior, but the smell of goulash has been replaced with garam masala, well-charred tandoori dishes and creamy concoctions like chicken coconut curry.

## La Loggia *Italian*                    20 | 19 | 21 | $42

**Studio City** | 11814 Ventura Blvd. (bet. Colfax Ave. & Laurel Canyon Blvd.) | 818-985-9222

"Spot the stars" at this Studio City "mainstay" across the street from the "CBS sound stages", where "a dedicated staff" (lead by "class-act" owner Frank Leon) "keeps customers coming" with a somewhat "limited" menu of "consistently good" Italian cuisine; though the "pleasant" surroundings include a "nice covered patio", a few complain the "noise level" can be "overwhelming" when the room is "packed"; N.B. there's an affiliated tapas lounge next door.

## La Luna *Italian*                      22 | 20 | 22 | $35

**Hancock Park** | 113 N. Larchmont Blvd. (bet. Beverly Blvd. & 1st St.) | 323-962-2130

Folks transplanted "from New York" to Hancock Park get their pizza fix at this "quaint Italian food joint", which also whips up "amazing", "fresh-made" "pastas with luxurious ingredients" and "desserts too yummy to resist", all "well-priced" and paired with an "extensive wine list"; a staff that "really knows its clientele" "makes them feel special" whether in the "casual" dining room or "wonderful" "sidewalk dining" area.

| | FOOD | DECOR | SERVICE | COST |
|---|---|---|---|---|

### La Maschera Ristorante *Italian* ▽ 22 | 16 | 22 | $36

**Pasadena** | 82 N. Fair Oaks Ave. (Holly St.) | 626-304-0004 |
www.lamascheraristorante.com

"An interesting mix of Tuscan and Northern African" dishes as well as
some "tapas-esque" cheese and salami plates distinguish this "friendly"
Pasadena eatery that's "well worth a try" for "a nice change from the
usual" neighborhood choices; "dark" Moroccan decor is deemed
"funky", though a few take issue with the "uncomfortable" chairs.

### Lamonica's NY Pizza ●∅ *Pizza* 22 | 10 | 14 | $10

**Westwood** | 1066 Gayley Ave. (Kinross Ave.) | 310-208-8671

Pieheads profess this Westwood "joint" "really gets it right" with
"classic", "crisp-crust" pizza that's "as close to NY-style as you can get
in LA" and "cheap too"; considering the "no-frills" space has the
"grungy" feel of a "subway station", most opt for "takeout" or "delivery."

### Langer's Deli ⊠ *Deli* 25 | 9 | 18 | $17

**Downtown** | 704 S. Alvarado St. (7th St.) | 213-483-8050 |
www.langersdeli.com

The "unforgettable pastrami" is the "crown jewel" of this Downtown
"landmark" with "heavenly" meats handcut by "Al Langer's son and
staff" and served up on "wonderful rye bread" by "crusty waitresses"
in an appropriately "no-frills" setting; "iffy" neighborhood aside, it
"beats the pants off" any other deli in LA, and even has a few supporters swearing "NYC can't compete!"; N.B. legendary founder Al Langer
passed away in June 2007.

### La Paella ⊠ *Spanish* 22 | 19 | 22 | $38

**West Hollywood** | 476 S. San Vicente Blvd. (bet. La Cienega &
Wilshire Blvds.) | 323-951-0745 | www.usalapaella.com

"Darn good paella" and "authentic tapas" are washed down with
"incredible sangria" at this "charming" West Hollywood Spanish;
"helpful servers" plus a congenial host and decor that "feels like you're
in the owner's grandmother's house" add up to a "sweet, soulful" ambiance that's "not the hippest", but still "great for dates."

### La Parisienne ⊠ *French* ▽ 23 | 21 | 23 | $42

**Monrovia** | 1101 E. Huntington Dr. (bet. Buena Vista & Mountain Aves.) |
626-357-3359

"Old-fashioned" French fare meets "old-world charm" at this
Monrovia mainstay where "professional" servers dole out "delish
pàtés", "heavenly" flambéed desserts and other "traditional" dishes
from the "forget-about-your-cholesterol" menu; while it still earns
fans among the "gray-haired" crowd that favors it as a "special-
occasion" spot, modern millies deem it "dated and stuffy" and wonder
if it's "past its prime."

### La Pergola *Italian* 23 | 20 | 22 | $37

**Sherman Oaks** | 15005 Ventura Blvd. (Lemona Ave.) |
818-905-8402

"Eat fresh from the garden" at this Sherman Oaks Italian that's been "a
favorite for years" thanks to a "creative" menu that makes extensive
use of "organic vegetables and herbs" grown on the premises; "romantic" Tuscan-style digs plus an "inviting" staff makes it "a treat"
that's "worth every penny" of its somewhat high price.

| | FOOD | DECOR | SERVICE | COST |
|---|---|---|---|---|

### La Piazza  *Italian* ▽ 18 | 19 | 18 | $32

**Fairfax** | The Grove at Farmers Mkt. | 189 The Grove Dr. (bet. Fairfax Ave. & 3rd St.) | 323-933-5050

Snag an "outdoor table" and enjoy the "great location" with views of the fountains and the quick-stepping Fairfax crowds at this "busy" Italian eatery at the Grove; apart from the "crispy pizzas", diners remain mostly unmoved by the "too expensive" fare concluding "they should pay more attention to their food."

### NEW  Larchmont Grill 🅢 *American* ▽ 21 | 20 | 22 | $34

**Hollywood** | 5750 Melrose Ave. (Lucerne Ave.) | 323-464-4277 | www.larchmontgrill.com

"Doting servers" create a "comfy" environment for customers to enjoy pan roasted chicken, mac 'n' cheese and other examples of New American "home cooking" at this Hollywood newcomer; the "homey" setting in a converted Craftsman house reminds some of "mom's", adding one more reason locals say it's "worth getting to know" this "welcome addition to the 'hood."

### La Rive Gauche  *French* 22 | 18 | 22 | $44

**Palos Verdes Estates** | 320 Tejon Pl. (Palos Verdes Dr.) | 310-378-0267

Fans of "old-style" Gallic cuisine applaud the "buttery sauces" and "tasty" signatures like rack of lamb at this Palos Verdes "throwback" where the "classic" fare is complemented by the "quietly elegant" setting and service; critics fear "the food and service have fallen off", and add that the French country decor "could use some sprucing up" as well.

### NEW  Larkin's 🅜 *Southern* - | - | - | I

**Eagle Rock** | 1496 Colorado Blvd. (Loleta Ave.) | 323-254-0934 | www.larkinsjoint.com

After months of delays, chef-owner Larkin Mackey has finally opened the modern soul fooder of his dreams in a Craftsman cottage on the eastern edge of Eagle Rock; in this warm space gleaming with polished wood, traditional Southern cooking meets Californian ingredients (think warm okra and heirloom tomato salad), but the prices remain decidedly down-home.

### L'Artiste Patisserie  *Bakery* ▽ 20 | 11 | 16 | $14

**Encino** | 17312A Ventura Blvd. (Louise Ave.) | 818-386-0061 | www.lartistepatisserie.com

"Straightforward" soups, salads and sandwiches augment a "tempting" selection of "fresh-baked" goodies (brioche, croissants, macaroons) at this Encino patisserie; the "cafe-type" setting is "not terribly comfortable", but "pleasant" enough, as is the staff, as long as "you're not in a hurry."

### La Scala 🅢 *Italian* 20 | 16 | 19 | $34

**Beverly Hills** | 434 N. Cañon Dr. (bet. Brighton Way & Santa Monica Blvd.) | 310-275-0579

### La Scala Presto 🅢 *Italian*

**Brentwood** | 11740 San Vicente Blvd. (bet. Barrington & Montana Aves.) | 310-826-6100

"It's all about the chopped salad" at this "popular" Beverly Hills "lunchtime fave" (with a full bar and "cozy" booths) and its more casual Brentwood cousin where a "loyal, older" crew munches on the "signature" mixed greens as well as other "reasonably priced", "light" Italian specials; while the "old-school" feel strikes some as "dull", supporters swear it's a "classic' and "rightly so."

### La Serenata de Garibaldi  *Mexican/Seafood*  | 23 | 16 | 18 | $29

**Boyle Heights** | 1842 E. First St. (bet. Boyle Ave. & State St.) | 323-265-2887

**Santa Monica** | 1416 Fourth St. (Santa Monica Blvd.) | 310-656-7017

### La Serenata Gourmet  *Mexican/Seafood*

**West LA** | 10924 W. Pico Blvd. (Westwood Blvd.) | 310-441-9667
www.laserenataonline.com

The "sophisticated" Mexican-style seafood "never fails" attest amigos of this "outstanding", "authentic" trio in Boyle Heights (the flagship, and some say "the best"), Santa Monica and West LA; they're "class acts" all the way from the "accommodating" service to the "intimate", haciendalike decor and "reasonable prices."

### Lasher's  Ⓜ *American*  | 24 | 22 | 24 | $43

**Long Beach** | 3441 E. Broadway (bet. Newport & Redondo Aves.) | 562-433-0153

### Lasher's American Steakhouse  *American*

**NEW Burbank** | 250 E. Olive Ave. (bet. S. San Fernando Blvd. & 3rd St.) | 818-843-8800
www.lashersrestaurant.com

"Charming" "husband-and-wife"-team Ray and Lynn Lasher run this "unpretentious" American eatery "tucked away" in a "reclaimed craftsman bungalow" in Long Beach with "first-rate" fare and service and prices falling on the "steep" side; the newer Burbank branch puts the focus on prime steaks and a more "upscale" environment, but the "friendly" service remains the same.

### La Sosta Enoteca  Ⓜ *Italian*  | ▽ 27 | 21 | 23 | $48

**Hermosa Beach** | 2700 Manhattan Ave. (27th St.) | 310-318-1556

*Amici* who "miss Italy" flock to this "quaint", "down-to-earth" restaurant and wine bar in Hermosa Beach where "authentic" dishes are paired with imported vintages (some "virtually unknown") from owner Luca Manderino's list; by most accounts he's a "delightful" host who creates an "unmatched" experience that's worth the "pricey" final bill.

### La Terza  *Italian*  | 22 | 19 | 20 | $53

**Third Street** | Orlando Hotel | 8384 W. Third St. (Orlando Ave.) | 323-782-8384

"Elegant yet earthy", this Third Street sister to Angelini Osteria specializes in "wood-fired meats" among its "slightly rustic" Italian fare; critics complain, however, that experiences of "inconsistent food and service" at a "high cost" turn them off from what, despite its bright palette, "still feels like a hotel restaurant."

### La Vecchia Cucina  *Italian*  | 21 | 17 | 21 | $36

**Santa Monica** | 2654 Main St. (bet. Hill St. & Ocean Park Blvd.) | 310-399-7979 | www.lavecchiacucina.com

"Surprisingly good" pasta and other simple Italian dishes come with a "reasonable" price tag at this Santa Monica "local joint", which is "reliable", "cozy" (if a bit "crowded" during peak times) and a welcome "respite" from the normal LA scene – especially since the staff

| | FOOD | DECOR | SERVICE | COST |
|---|---|---|---|---|

"quickly recognizes regulars and treats them well", and the weekday happy hour (5–7 PM) offers food and drink deals at the bar.

## ☑ Lawry's The Prime Rib  *Steak*  | 25 | 21 | 24 | $50 |

**Beverly Hills** | 100 N. La Cienega Blvd. (Wilshire Blvd.) | 310-652-2827 | www.lawrysonline.com

"Succulent meat is carved tableside from huge, elegant silver carts" at this "cornerstone of LA history" in Beverly Hills – the "original and still the best" for roast prime rib au jus and the "famous spinning salad"; sure, its "British hunt club" decor "hasn't changed in decades", but even though it's "overrun with tourists", loyalists laud the "impeccable" service ("we always feel as though we're family") and a meal that's "worth every cent."

## Lazy Dog Cafe, The  *Eclectic*  | 19 | 17 | 21 | $21 |

**Torrance** | Del Amo Fashion Ctr. | 3525 Carson St. (Madrona Ave.) | 310-921-6080 | www.thelazydogcafe.com

"Attentive service" and a "family-friendly" atmosphere are the hallmarks of this "comfortable" Eclectic chainlet boasting a "very diverse" menu from a kitchen with "high standards"; "cavernous" digs "accommodate large parties without fuss" (just beware of "unruly children running rabid") while "the only complaint" is that these "casual" spots get "plenty crowded."

## Leaf Cuisine  *Vegan*  | - | - | - | I |

**NEW** **West Hollywood** | 8365 Santa Monica Blvd. (Kings Rd.) | 323-301-4982

**Culver City** | 11938 W. Washington Blvd. (Sawtelle Blvd.) | 310-390-6005

**Sherman Oaks** | 14318 Ventura Blvd. (Beverly Glen Blvd.) | 818-907-8779
www.leafcuisine.com

There's hardly a stove to be found in these raw vegan cafes from Rod Rotundi (a disciple of Juliano of Juliano's Raw) who transforms organic fruits, veggies and nuts into "innovative" dishes like "rawsagna" and pad Thai all "at reasonable prices"; service is cafeteria-style and decor bright, spare and clean, making them ideal for a "quick" healthy meal.

## Le Chêne  *French*  | ▽ 25 | 21 | 22 | $43 |

**Saugus** | 12625 Sierra Hwy. (Sierra Vallejo Rd.) | 661-251-4315 | www.lechene.com

"Overdressed Valencians and the nouveau riche wearing cowboy hats" meet at this "romantic", castlelike Saugus "treasure" "two miles past the edge of nowhere", named after the "beautiful" 100-year-old oak trees surrounding it; day-trippers deem the French menu "outstanding" (particularly the more "adventurous" choices of game) and the wines "wonderful" for an "old-fashioned" "country" experience.

## ☑ Leila's  🅂 🅼 *Californian*  | 27 | 20 | 24 | $47 |

**Oak Park** | RE/MAX Plaza | 706 Lindero Canyon Rd., Ste. 752 (Kanan Rd.) | 818-707-6939 | www.leilasrestaurant.com

Supporters call this Oak Park Californian the "Spago of the suburbs" for chef Richie De Mane's "exquisite", "cleverly crafted" cuisine that's finished with "fantastic wine pairings"; though its "shop-front setting" and "minimalist" decor are a "major drawback" for some, the "quality service" makes for a "mellow", "intimate" meal, leading locals to cry "Leila's is ours! – stay away."

### Le Marmiton  *French*

18 | 15 | 17 | $30

**Santa Monica** | 1327 Montana Ave. (14th St.) | 310-393-7716

### Le Marmiton Marina  *French*

**Marina del Rey** | 4724 Admiralty Way (Mindanao Way) | 310-773-3560

Now that the Santa Monica original has "shrunk in size" to become a largely take-out purveyor of "gourmet" pastries, crêpes and other bistro eats (served till 8 PM), its Marina del Rey sib is the new dinner destination for "people-watching" over "best-in-town" moules frites; on the downside, some surveyors call the cooking "inconsistent", adding that the "service needs help" and the atmosphere, while "cute", "doesn't make the grade."

### Lemon Moon  ⑤ *Californian/Mediterranean*

20 | 14 | 14 | $17

**West LA** | Westside Media Ctr. | 12200 W. Olympic Blvd. (S. Bundy Dr.) | 310-442-9191 | www.lemonmoon.com

Inside a West LA office building, this "cafeteria-style" Cal-Med surprise by chefs Josiah Citrin (Mélisse) and Rafael Lunetta (JiRaffe) offers "lucky" nearby workers "unusual", "fabulous salads" among other "delish" dishes for weekday breakfast and lunch ("too bad it's not open at night"); although it strikes some as a "tad expensive" and too "corporate", the "open, airy" space, particularly on the patio, lends a "serene" note to the midday meal.

### Le Pain Quotidien  *Bakery/Belgian*

21 | 17 | 16 | $19

**West Hollywood** | 8607 Melrose Ave. (Westbourne Dr.) | 310-854-3700

**Beverly Hills** | 9630 Little Santa Monica Blvd. (bet. Bedford & Camden Drs.) | 310-859-1100

**Brentwood** | Barrington Ct. | 11702 Barrington Ct. (bet. Barrington Ave. & Sunset Blvd.) | 310-476-0969

**Santa Monica** | 316 Santa Monica Blvd. (bet. 3rd St. Promenade & 4th St.) | 310-393-6800

**Westwood** | 1055 Broxton Ave. (bet. Kinross & Weyburn Aves.) | 310-824-7900

**Manhattan Beach** | Metlox Ctr. | 451 Manhattan Beach Blvd. (bet. Morningside & Valley Drs.) | 310-546-6411

**Studio City** | 13045 Ventura Blvd. (bet. Coldwater Canyon & Ethel Aves.) | 818-986-1929

www.lepainquotidien.com

Carb conquerors who are "willing to spend some dough" congregate at "big wooden communal tables" for "fab bread" (with "delicious" spreads), "delectable" pastries and "terrific" tartines ("fancy" open-faced sandwiches) from these largely organic Belgian bakeries whose quality "makes it easy to forget" they're part of an international chain; despite sometimes "snobby" service, they maintain a "simple farmhouse" feel; N.B. most locations close around 6 PM while WeHo stays open until 9:30 PM.

### Le Petit Bistro  *French*

21 | 19 | 19 | $40

**West Hollywood** | 631 N. La Cienega Blvd. (Melrose Ave.) | 310-289-9797

"A real Frenchies' hangout", this WeHo bistro delivers the "best pommes frites" and other "honest" fare that tastes all the more "authentic" amid the "traditional cramped quarters" and patio where the "older, well-mannered side of LA sits alongside younger generations"; although some customers quip "the staff is usually more fresh than the fish", others find the attitude "adds to the allure."

| | FOOD | DECOR | SERVICE | COST |
|---|---|---|---|---|

### Le Petit Cafe ⊠ *French*

21 | 15 | 20 | $33

**Santa Monica** | 2842 Colorado Ave. (bet. Stewart & Yale Sts.) | 310-829-6792

"Refreshingly" "real", this "little" Santa Monica bistro wins kudos for its "simple" "home-cooked" French dishes listed on the "bargain" "chalkboard menu"; although it can get "hectic", francophiles find the ambiance evokes a "roadside restaurant in Provence", meaning "you can really relax."

### Le Petit Four *French*

19 | 17 | 18 | $35

**West Hollywood** | Sunset Plaza | 8654 W. Sunset Blvd. (Sunset Plaza Dr.) | 310-652-3863 | www.lepetitfour.net

Known for its Euro crowds, this West Hollywood bistro "really feels like Paris", what with French staples like pork cheeks in red wine sauce, "incessant smoking on the patio" and a prime view of Sunset Plaza's passersby (until 1 AM on weekends); grazers get that "it's not about the service" or even the "decent" food, but more of a place to "chat up your neighbor" and "gawk" at the view.

### Le Petit Greek *Greek*

21 | 16 | 20 | $31

**Hancock Park** | 127 N. Larchmont Blvd. (bet. Beverly Blvd. & 1st St.) | 323-464-5160

"Delectable rack of lamb" and "flaming cheese" are the standouts on a "solid" Greek menu in this Hancock Park taverna offering "reliable" quality "without all the macho kissing and dancing"; the servers are always "warm" (and a few are "hot" too), plus the "simple but pleasant" environs make it a fine place to "linger", particularly for a "sidewalk lunch on a sunny day."

### Le Petit Restaurant *French*

21 | 19 | 19 | $34

**Sherman Oaks** | 13360 Ventura Blvd. (Dixie Canyon Ave.) | 818-501-7999 | www.lepetitrestaurant.net

"When I need a fix of Paris, it's a reasonable facsimile" approve visitors to this Sherman Oaks bistro that steams mussels "right" and simmers "outstanding" onion soup; it's "comfortable" and "affordable", and although the service can be "hit-or-miss", for the most part "these folks really try and it shows."

### Le Saigon 🅜≠ *Vietnamese*

21 | 10 | 19 | $13

**West LA** | 11611 Santa Monica Blvd. (bet. Barry & Federal Aves.) | 310-312-2929

This "tiny" West LA Vietnamese delivers "fresh", "brightly flavored" fare from pho to pork skewers for a "fast", "cheap" meal; while service is mainly "attentive", "it's no longer a secret", so regulars advise "plan on waiting for a table" or getting takeout; N.B. cash only.

### Le Sanglier French Restaurant 🅜 *French*

▽ 22 | 20 | 20 | $51

**Tarzana** | 5522 Crebs Ave. (Ventura Blvd.) | 818-345-0470 | www.Lesanglierrestaurant.com

A "broad-ranging, classical French menu" and "elegant", "relaxed" interior suit "special occasions" at this "Tarzana side-street" "country restaurant", known for its wild boar and "unusual" game; despite an "out-of-the-way" location, after 37 years it's "popular" as ever (though "you may feel like the youngest person in the room"); N.B. reservations recommended.

| | FOOD | DECOR | SERVICE | COST |
|---|---|---|---|---|

## Les Sisters Southern Kitchen 🅜 *Southern*

▽ 25 | 7 | 21 | $19

**Chatsworth** | 21818 Devonshire St. (Jordan Ave.) | 818-998-0755

The Southern food "takes you back home" declare devotees of this Chatsworth longtimer with "owners who aim to please" serving up "excellent jambalaya", "wow"-worthy buttermilk pie and other Gulf Coast dishes that "don't disappoint"; sure, it's little more than "a kitchen" with "funky" Mardi Gras beads on the walls – and decidedly "not for dieters" – but "what a wonderful treat."

## NEW Liberty Grill 🅢 *American*

- | - | - | M

**Downtown** | 1037 S. Flower St. (11th St.) | 213-746-3400 | www.liberty-grill.com

This down-home American is housed in a historic Spanish-style building adjacent to the Staples Center; the menu is built around solid comfort food (spinach artichoke dip or deep fried mac 'n' cheese bites, anyone?), and there's an open-air patio bordered by an exhibition kitchen and herb garden, along with a full-sized replica of the Liberty Bell, hence the name.

## Library Alehouse *Eclectic*

19 | 18 | 19 | $22

**Santa Monica** | 2911 Main St. (bet. Ashland Ave. & Marine St.) | 310-314-4855 | www.libraryalehouse.com

Eclectic "high-end" bar bites complement an "incredible" selection of craft beers at this Santa Monica "pit stop" where you can "bring visitors" or "catch up with a friend" in a "casual, inviting" space ("sit outside for the best experience") where the staff helps "keep pretense low."

## Lido di Manhattan *Italian/Mediterranean*

▽ 21 | 18 | 20 | $34

**Manhattan Beach** | 1550 Rosecrans Ave. (bet. Market Pl. & Parkway Dr.) | 310-536-0730 | www.lidodimanhattan.com

Manhattan Beachers seeking "delicious" Italian-Med fare head to this "quiet", "cheerful" spot offering "consistent" cooking and service at "moderate prices"; though a bit of "strip-mall ambiance" is part of the package, the location makes it "perfect after shopping" and a "favorite for business lunches."

## NEW Liliya China Bistro 🅢🅜 *Pan-Asian*

- | - | - | I

**Downtown** | 108 W. Second St. (S. Main St.) | 213-620-1717 | www.liliyachinabistro.com

On the ground floor of Downtown's historic Higgins Building, this sleek Pan-Asian offers an inexpensive menu of dishes largely from China and Korea; with its modern glass-and-metal decor, it's a fine stop-off before or after visiting the nearby galleries.

## Lilly's French Cafe & Wine Bar *French*

20 | 19 | 18 | $36

**Venice** | 1031 Abbot Kinney Blvd. (bet. Main St. & Westminster Ave.) | 310-314-0004 | www.lillysfrenchcafe.com

While the French fare is "delectable" at this "casual, yet fancy" Venice bistro, insiders insist its "secret weapon" is the "tranquil", "romantic" back patio, "one of the most charming open-air dining areas on Abbot Kinney"; the lunch menu is "a deal", and though the service varies between "friendly" and "abrupt", it's nonetheless a "popular local haunt" that "appeals to all ages."

|  | FOOD | DECOR | SERVICE | COST |
|--|------|-------|---------|------|

### NEW Limon Latin Grill  *Pan-Latin*
| | - | - | - | M |

**Simi Valley** | 1555 Simi Town Center Way (Erringer St.) | 805-955-9277 | www.limongrill.com

A reasonably priced menu of gazpacho, ceviche, Argentinean steak and Cuban pork celebrates all things Hispanic at this new Pan-Latin eatery in what used to be the culinary wasteland of Simi Valley; its brightly colored setting – decorated with original Latino artwork – frequently showcases live music.

### Literati Café  *Californian/Eclectic*
| | 20 | 17 | 17 | $33 |

**West LA** | 12081 Wilshire Blvd. (S. Bundy Dr.) | 310-231-7484 | www.literaticafe.com

### Literati II  *Californian/Eclectic*

**West LA** | 12081 Wilshire Blvd. (S. Bundy Dr.) | 310-479-3400 | www.literati2.com

This West LA "coffee hangout" serving soups and salads and its adjacent upscale restaurant offer a choice between a place to "park your laptop" replete with "college students camping out", or an "attractive", more refined environment with "imaginative" Cal-Eclectic cuisine; a few knock them, however, for "slow" service and "overpriced" eats.

### ☒ Little Door, The  *Mediterranean*
| | 23 | 25 | 21 | $55 |

**Third Street** | 8164 W. Third St. (bet. Crescent Heights Blvd. & La Jolla Ave.) | 323-951-1210 | www.thelittledoor.com

"Sultry" dining is the draw of this "stunning little garden hideaway" on Third Street, suited to "first dates" and "pre-adulterous meals" of "exceptional" Mediterranean cuisine complemented by a "killer" cellar; the servers are "knowledgeable about the menu and wine" (and their "French accents" "don't hurt the ambiance either"), so all in all, if your beau brings you here "he really likes you."

### NEW Little Tokyo Shabu Shabu  *Japanese*
| | - | - | - | I |

**Rowland Heights** | Diamond Plaza | 1330 S. Fullerton Rd. (Hwy. 60, ext. 19) | 626-810-6037 | www.littletokyoshabushabu.com

In a city of many shabu-shabu bars, this budget-friendly shopping mall eatery on the eastern edge of the San Gabriel Valley may be the busiest of them all; its brightly lit space with floor-to-ceiling windows is dominated by a rectangular bar in the center of the main room that's the place to sit for those who love to dip and swirl.

### ☒ Lobster, The  *Seafood*
| | 23 | 24 | 20 | $53 |

**Santa Monica** | 1602 Ocean Ave. (Santa Monica Pier) | 310-458-9294 | www.thelobster.com

You "feel like you're floating above the ocean" at this Santa Monica seafooder distinguished by "breathtaking" sunset views and the "impressive", "expensive" namesake specialty served by an "accommodating" staff; surveyors surmise "it's a lifesaver when picky tourists are in town", and one local sighs "I can't wait to meet that 'special someone' who will take me here whenever I want."

### Local Place, The  *American/Hawaiian*
| | ▽ 17 | 11 | 15 | $11 |

**Torrance** | 18605 S. Western Ave. (W. 186th St.) | 310-523-3233

"Cheap, fast" and "simple" Hawaiian–Traditional American plates draw South Bay denizens to this Torrance take-out place whose "local faves" like lau lau, kalua pork and "paradise cake" are the "way to go";

from the cooking to the island-themed look, many call the quality "average", but the "location is convenient for pickup."

### Locanda del Lago *Italian* | 20 | 19 | 21 | $37 |

**Santa Monica** | 231 Arizona Ave. (3rd St. Promenade) | 310-451-3525 | www.lagosantamonica.com

"The low-key menu does not disappoint" at this "tempting" Northern Italian in Santa Monica, and while the view of the "tourist" crowds is "not up to Piazza San Marco" standards, its "gracious, accommodating" owner and "lovely", "upscale" ambiance create an "unexpected pleasure" "right in the midst" of the Promenade bustle.

### Locanda Veneta *Italian* | 25 | 17 | 20 | $49 |

**Third Street** | 8638 W. Third St. (bet. Robertson & San Vicente Blvds.) | 310-274-1893

"Fantastic" homemade pastas stand out on the "authentic", "high-end" Venetian menu at this Third Street "jewel" whose fans advise "be friendly to your neighbors" as "sometimes you'll have to sit on their lap"; most appreciate its "family feeling", although some longtimers lament that "what used to be truly magnificent" is lately "losing its luster."

### Lodge Steakhouse, The *Steak* | 20 | 22 | 19 | $66 |

**Beverly Hills** | 14 N. La Cienega Blvd. (Wilshire Blvd.) | 310-854-0024 | www.thelodgesteakhouse.com

Boosters boast the "food stands up to the scene" at this "super-trendy" Beverly Hills "twist on a steakhouse" where a "classic" menu (including "terrific, but limited" sides) and a "well-planned wine list" are served in a "mountain-lodge" setting, and the "bar gets hopping at night" thanks to "A+ bartenders" and "excellent eye candy"; cynics, though, find it fairly "touristy" and the steaks merely "eh", not to mention "overpriced."

### Loft, The *Hawaiian* | 17 | 12 | 16 | $18 |

**Cerritos** | 20157 Pioneer Blvd. (bet. Del Amo Blvd. & 195th St.) | 562-402-3538 Ⓜ

**Torrance** | 23305 Hawthorne Blvd. (Lomita Blvd.) | 310-375-4051 | www.thelofthawaii.com

"One of the originals" in LA's "burgeoning Hawaiian-style plate-lunch scene", this mini-chain provides "gargantuan" portions of "comforting" (some say "heavy") fare, like "island fried chicken" and Korean BBQ beef; the "reasonable prices and friendly staff" make it a "family favorite", even though many customers see it as "more for takeout."

### Lola's ☽ *American* | 18 | 17 | 17 | $31 |

**West Hollywood** | 945 N. Fairfax Ave. (bet. Romaine St. & Willoughby Ave.) | 213-736-5652 | www.lolasla.com

"Whip-you-off-your-chair" martinis (more than 50 kinds) and "heavenly" mac 'n' cheese satisfy the eclectic crowd at this moderately priced WeHo New American; while both the cooking and the leopard-accented decor are a bit "lacking" according to some, tipplers tout that it has all the ingredients for a "casual night out with friends."

### L'Opera *Italian* | 24 | 24 | 23 | $51 |

**Long Beach** | 101 Pine Ave. (bet. Broadway & Ocean Blvd.) | 562-491-0066 | www.lopera.com

"Well-prepared", "innovative appetizers and pastas" earn praise at Long Beach's bastion of Northern Italian cuisine, as does the "spectac-

| | FOOD | DECOR | SERVICE | COST |
|---|---|---|---|---|

ular wine list"; its "helpful" staff "handles large groups easily", and though some call it "overpriced", the "elegant" setting "hits the mark" for Roman-tics, especially on weekends when "the fat lady sings."

### NEW Los Angeles Pizza Co. ⓼ *Pizza*

| | – | – | – | I |
|---|---|---|---|---|

**Downtown** | 712 N. Figueroa St. (Sunset Blvd.) | 213-626-5272 | www.losangelespizzacompany.com

It looks like a typical New York pizzeria, but the twist is that this little eatery is not only in LA, but on the edge of Chinatown; thanks to the co-ownership of Jean-Louis De Mori (Locanda Veneta), locals are flocking here for a taste of NYC-style pies and tasty empanadas.

### Los Balcones del Peru Ⓜ *Peruvian*

| | ▽ 21 | 7 | 18 | $24 |
|---|---|---|---|---|

**Hollywood** | 1360 N. Vine St. (Leland Way) | 323-871-9600

"Authentic Peruvian cuisine" featuring "top-notch ceviche" pleases those who find "tremendous value" at this Hollywood stop near the Arclight; the "staff is obviously family" and "extremely friendly", which makes up for the "sparse" setting.

### ⓩ Lotería! Grill *Mexican*

| | 24 | 9 | 14 | $14 |
|---|---|---|---|---|

**Fairfax** | Farmers Mkt. | 6333 W. Third St. (Fairfax Ave.) | 323-930-2211

"Dark, sweet, spicy" mole sauce, "killer chilaquiles" and shredded beef tacos ("the stuff of legend") "burst with flavor" at this counter-service Mexican "gem" in the Fairfax Farmers Market; diehards say "don't let the long lines daunt you", since "unique", "fresh-as-can-be" food for "reasonable, if not bargain-basement, prices" awaits.

### Lou ❶ⓩ *Eclectic/Mediterranean*

| | 22 | 17 | 20 | $35 |
|---|---|---|---|---|

**Hollywood** | 724 Vine St. (Melrose Ave.) | 323-962-6369 | www.louonvine.com

"Creative small tastes" – such as "addictive 'pig candy'" (the house bacon), farmstead cheeses and salumi by Armandino Batali (father of Mario) – make up the "intelligent" Med-Eclectic menu paired with "unique", "thoughtfully chosen" wines at this "darling little" strip-mall "surprise" in Hollywood; while it hosts a "hip scene", guests appreciate that it's "unpretentious" with an "intimate ambiance" and "accessible", "no-attitude" staff.

### Louise's Trattoria *Californian/Italian*

| | 16 | 15 | 18 | $25 |
|---|---|---|---|---|

**Hancock Park** | 232 N. Larchmont Blvd. (Beverly Blvd.) | 323-962-9510
**Los Feliz** | 4500 Los Feliz Blvd. (Hillhurst Ave.) | 323-667-0777
**Melrose** | 7505 Melrose Ave. (Gardner St.) | 323-651-3880
**Brentwood** | 264 26th St. (Minerva St.) | 310-451-5001
**Santa Monica** | 1008 Montana Ave. (10th St.) | 310-394-8888
**West LA** | 10645 W. Pico Blvd. (bet. Manning & Overland Aves.) | 310-475-6084
**Pasadena** | 2-8 E. Colorado Blvd. (Fair Oaks Ave.) | 626-568-3030
**Studio City** | 12050 Ventura Blvd. (Laurel Canyon Blvd.) | 818-762-2662
**Westlake Village** | North Ranch Mall | 3825 E. Thousand Oaks Blvd. (Westlake Blvd.) | 805-373-6060
www.louises.com

For "those spur-of-the-moment nights out", a "quick dinner with friends" or takeout on a "lazy weeknight", fans find this Cal-Italian chain a "dependable" option for "comforting", if somewhat "formulaic", fare at "affordable prices"; service is "competent" and the "low-key", "family-friendly" surroundings are "pleasant", and while it's "nothing to rock your world", "you could do worse."

### Lucia's 🅼 *Italian*

▽ 18 | 18 | 19 | $30

**Pacific Palisades** | 538 Palisades Dr. (Sunset Blvd.) | 310-573-1411 | www.luciasitaliankitchen.com

While this often "right-on" Pacific Palisades Italian occasionally "misses" when it comes to cuisine, the candlelit setting is "inviting", the service "pleasant" and it's "dependable" for "dinner on the way home from work", especially given the "dearth of choices in the highlands."

### Lucille's Smokehouse Bar-B-Que *BBQ*

22 | 19 | 19 | $25

**Long Beach** | 4828 E. Second St. (St. Joseph Ave.) | 562-434-7427
**Long Beach** | 7411 Carson St. (Nectar Ave.) | 562-938-7427
**Torrance** | Del Amo Fashion Ctr. | 21420 Hawthorne Blvd. (Del Amo Circle Blvd.) | 310-370-7427
www.lucillesbbq.com

"Delicious" house-smoked ribs and chicken come in "humongous" portions ("it seems like everyone walks out with a doggy bag") at this "crazy busy" Cali-based barbecue chain; the "enthusiastic" staff and "kitschy" rooms decorated with folk art cater to "family feasts" – even if critics complain in "North Carolina, or even Compton, you can get better soul food for much cheaper"; P.S. order some "nicely packed" takeout to beat the "long waits on the weekends."

### Lucky Devils *American*

21 | 16 | 17 | $22

**Hollywood** | 6613 Hollywood Blvd. (Whitley Ave.) | 323-465-8259

At this "gourmet diner on Hollywood Boulevard", barbecue and burgers "fit for a Rockefeller", not to mention "other-worldly" desserts and the "thickest" milkshakes, will "make your taste buds tango"; insiders say the "upbeat" ambiance overcomes the rather "dubious location", while "cute servers" add to the "polished" but "not pretentious" appeal.

### 🅿 Lucques *French/Mediterranean*

27 | 24 | 24 | $58

**West Hollywood** | 8474 Melrose Ave. (La Cienega Blvd.) | 323-655-6277 | www.lucques.com

Suzanne Goin's "sublime" organic French-Mediterranean cuisine "lives up to its promise" at this West Hollywood "landmark of LA eating" whose "winning" tree-planted patio fills up quickly; in addition to a "cordial", "knowledgeable" staff, steered by sommelier and part-owner Caroline Styne, it boasts a "bargain" prix fixe Sunday dinner that continues to provide an "unbelievable gastronomic evening", making reservations "difficult to come by."

### Luna Park *American*

19 | 18 | 18 | $30

**La Brea** | 672 S. La Brea Ave. (Wilshire Blvd.) | 323-934-2110 | www.lunaparkla.com

This La Brea bistro serving "stylish" American "comfort food" pulls in a "boisterous, youthful" crowd of "attractive professionals" who can't get enough of the "dazzling drinks", "make-your-own s'mores" and "hard-to-beat" mac 'n' cheese; it's "not too expensive", and though it gets "packed and loud", seductive souls "reserve a curtained booth" to clinch a "third date."

| | FOOD | DECOR | SERVICE | COST |
|---|---|---|---|---|

### Macau Street ● *Chinese* | ▽ 20 | 14 | 15 | $20 |

**Monterey Park** | 429 W. Garvey Ave. (bet. Atlantic & Garfield Blvds.) | 626-288-3568

"Definitely one of the more interesting restaurants in the San Gabriel Valley", this Monterey Park Chinese specializes in regional dishes from Macau (think "Hong Kong with a twist"); the room is often "filled to capacity" with locals craving garlicky fried crab, "Portuguese egg custard" and more adventurous Far Eastern fare for a "deal."

### Madame Matisse *American* | 22 | 12 | 18 | $20 |

**Silver Lake** | 3536 W. Sunset Blvd. (Golden Gate Ave.) | 323-662-4862 | www.madamematisse.net

"Omelets with a wealth of toppings" among other American "farmer's-market" dishes satisfy the daytime crowd at this "funky" "hole-in-the-wall" where "you'll most likely sit outside" following the "weekend wait"; orders generally turn around "fast for such a small kitchen", but since it closes at 3 PM, supper-seeking Silver Lakers are left "broken-hearted."

### Madeleine Bistro Ⓜ *French/Vegan* | ▽ 22 | 19 | 19 | $30 |

**Tarzana** | 18621 Ventura Blvd. (Amigo Ave.) | 818-758-6971 | www.madeleinebistro.com

The "high-end vegan restaurant we've been waiting for" is how fans tout David Anderson's Tarzana French offering "amazing presentations" of "creative" animal-free fare that "even carnivores will enjoy"; a "knowledgeable" staff enhances the "lovely, warm" atmosphere in the earthy space sporting lots of dark wood; N.B. closed Monday and Tuesday.

### Madeleine's Ⓜ *Californian* | 23 | 25 | 21 | $46 |

**Pasadena** | 1030 E. Green St. (Catalina Ave.) | 626-440-7087 | www.madeleinesrestaurant.com

Chef Claud Beltran (ex Cayo and Restaurant Halie, formerly in this space) "has done it again" according to Pasadena diners who say his "spot-on" Californian cooking (chock-full of "seasonal ingredients and real pride") paired with a "unique and affordable" wine selection makes it a "definite hit"; the staff is "knowledgeable", but the highest ratings go to the "absolutely romantic" decor of the "historic building", warmed by "cozy" fireplaces.

### Madeo *Italian* | 26 | 20 | 24 | $58 |

**West Hollywood** | 8897 Beverly Blvd. (bet. Doheny Dr. & Robertson Blvd.) | 310-859-4903

"Lots of action" accompanies the "stunningly rich" Northern Italian cuisine at this WeHo "favorite" whose "fresh-cut" roasted veal and "excellent pasta dishes" earn raves; while an "industry" crowd "jams the room", it maintains a "nostalgic" feel courtesy of "back-in-time" "New York" decor, a "superb", "old-time" staff and "charming" proprietors who greet friends with "hugs and kisses", all of which could make you "want to become a regular" if you don't mind the "pricey" tab.

### ☒ Madison, The ●☒ *Seafood/Steak* | 21 | 27 | 22 | $52 |

**Long Beach** | 102 Pine Ave. (1st St.) | 562-628-8866 | www.themadisonrestaurant.com

Guests go gaga for the "most gorgeous ceilings and bar in Long Beach" at this "beautiful" converted bank with an "old-school posh" ambiance beefed up by traditional steak and seafood dishes; though some "wish the food were as good as the decor", others report that the "flavorful" fare and "professional" service round out a "near-perfect experience."

### Madre's Ⓜ *Puerto Rican*                    14 | 20 | 16 | $41
**Pasadena** | 897 Granite Dr. (Lake Ave.) | 626-744-0900 |
www.madresrestaurant.com
"Gorgeous" Havana-style surroundings and a "vibrant crowd" fulfill some of the "high expectations" guests bring to J. Lo's *bebé*, a Puerto Rican dinner spot in Pasadena serving "large portions" of ropa vieja and arroz con pollo; still, many deem the fare "mediocre" and "over-priced" and the service only slightly sharper, and despite the owner's assets "pretentious with nothing to back it up."

### Maggiano's Little Italy *Italian*            19 | 19 | 18 | $28
**Fairfax** | The Grove at Farmers Mkt. | 189 The Grove Dr. (bet. Fairfax Ave. & 3rd St.) | 323-965-9665
**Woodland Hills** | Westfield Promenade | 6100 Topanga Canyon Blvd. (bet. Erwin & Oxnard Sts.) | 818-887-3777
www.maggianos.com
"*Fabuloso!*" cry fans of this "chain that has its act together", where a "pleasant" staff conveys "prodigious" family-style portions of pasta "sure to induce food coma" while "Frank Sinatra and Tony Bennett" croon in the background; although "crowded seating", "big waits" and some say "ordinary" eats are the downsides of its popularity, few can argue with "major bang for the buck."

### Magic Carpet *Mideastern*              ▽ 22 | 12 | 18 | $23
**Pico-Robertson** | 8566 W. Pico Blvd. (La Cienega Blvd.) | 310-652-8507
The "well-seasoned" kosher Middle Eastern cuisine at this Pico-Robertson "secret" truly "sweeps you away" according to fans who call the Yemenite "delicacies" like jachnun (a pan bread served Sundays only) and "flaky" mellawach the "finest" around; while some comment the room is "short on decor", the "warm service" lends plenty of "at-mosphere"; N.B. it's BYO (kosher bottles only) and closed on Shabbat.

### Magnolia ◗ *American*                    20 | 20 | 17 | $37
**Hollywood** | 6266½ Sunset Blvd. (bet. Argyle & Vine Sts.) | 323-467-0660 |
www.magnoliahollywood.com
"Young Hollywood" "launches into a night out", dines on ahi "after the movie" or indulges in "mac 'n' cheese midnight decadence" at this "cool and convenient late-night" New American, whose "exciting" en-virons are energized by a deco-accented "modern" design, "loud rock in the background" and a staff that generally gives "no attitude."

### NEW Magnolia Lounge *Contemp. Louisiana*   ▽ 16 | 23 | 14 | $29
**Pasadena** | 492 S. Lake Ave. (California Blvd.) | 626-584-1126 |
www.magnoliaonlake.com
Offering a "step out of sleepy Pasadena", this "hip" newcomer plays host to plenty of "see-and-be-seen" preening amid "chic" decor "evoking a bordello from days gone by"; although many call its Contemporary Louisiana bites (like bayou pizza) simply "ok" and the "hot" staff in need of help, most "keep going back" for the martinis, the "outdoorsy feel" on the patio and the "NYC" atmosphere – so "does the food matter?"

|  | FOOD | DECOR | SERVICE | COST |
|---|---|---|---|---|

### Maison Akira ⓜ French/Japanese — 25 | 20 | 24 | $55

**Pasadena** | 713 E. Green St. (bet. El Molino & Oak Knoll Aves.) |
626-796-9501 | www.maisonakira.com

"Superb" French-inflected Japanese cuisine ("best miso seabass I
have ever had") pleases Pasadenans at this "innovative" "capital of
the foodies club"; though its "austere" atmosphere is a bit too "sedate" for some, the "warm" servers have "excellent tableside manners" and the price points are softened with prix fixe dinners and
"exotic" bento box lunches.

### ② Mako ⑤ Asian Fusion — 26 | 19 | 25 | $49

**Beverly Hills** | 225 S. Beverly Dr. (Charleville Blvd.) | 310-288-8338 |
www.makorestaurant.com

Keen customers "get a seat at the counter" of this Asian fusion bistro
in Beverly Hills to "enjoy the preparation" as chef-owner Makoto
Tanaka composes "deceptively simple" small plates "with the most intense flavors"; some feel the "vibrant" room is "too noisy to have a
conversation", but still the service is "truly helpful" and the food "not
extraordinarily pricey" for the quality.

### Malibu Seafood Seafood — 21 | 10 | 13 | $20

**Malibu** | 25653 PCH (1½ mi. north of Malibu Canyon Rd.) | 310-456-6298 |
www.malibufishandseafood.com

It's "just a shack on the highway" in Malibu, but it fries up or grills
"fresh, straightforward seafood" for eating on the "ramshackle patio
areas" with "spectacular views" of the Pacific; though some find the
PCH "road noise" "objectionable", most "surfers" and others who
"line up" agree the "ocean air seems to make everything taste better."

### Malo Mexican — 17 | 17 | 13 | $27

**Silver Lake** | 4326 W. Sunset Blvd. (Fountain Ave.) | 323-664-1011 |
www.malorestaurant.com

"Decent tacos" ("don't miss the ground beef and pickle" version), "addictive" salsas and other "tapas-style" Mexican eats "prep the tum-
mies" of "partying" guests at this stylish Silver Lake "staple" owned by
Steven Arroyo (Cobras & Matadors) that flatters with "subdued lighting"; though some bemoan "mediocre" service and "high prices for
skimpy" portions, most agree the "strong" drinks, fueled by more than
170 tequilas, add to the "fun", "sceney" atmosphere inside and out.

### Mama D's Italian — 22 | 12 | 21 | $22

**Manhattan Beach** | 1125 Manhattan Ave. (Manhattan Beach Blvd.) |
310-546-1492

"A huge selection of pastas" and other "old-fashioned" dishes draw
Manhattan Beach locals to this Italian "family favorite" where "fantastic, never-ending garlic bread" "helps make the wait worthwhile" (and
there "almost always" is one); the "decor is simple", but the "friendli-
est crew ever" runs the room, ensuring that while "there are many fancier" places nearby, this actually "feels like home."

### Mandarette Chinese — 18 | 13 | 17 | $29

**West Hollywood** | 8386 Beverly Blvd. (bet. N. Kings Rd. & N. Orlando Ave.) |
323-655-6115

"Satisfying Chinese with an American flag in its lapel" caters to West
Hollywood denizens who recommend the "strawberry shrimp" and

other "pleasing" "nouvelle" specialties over the "standard" main menu at this Szechuan stalwart; the room is "presentable" enough, and though some say it's a touch "pricey" and sliding "downhill", many find the "reliable" formula still works.

### Mandarin Deli   *Chinese*

| 21 | 8 | 15 | $13 |

**Northridge** | 9305 Reseda Blvd. (Prairie St.) | 818-993-0122
**Monterey Park** | 701 W. Garvey Ave. (Atlantic Blvd.) | 626-570-9795 ⊄
"Oodles of good noodles" plus "distinctive dumpling dishes" keep this "low-priced" Chinese pair in Monterey Park and Northridge "crowded" (oddly, the Chinatown location closed); while a few mind the "limited" menu, "strictly business" service and "old chairs and decor", others simply "wish they served those scallion pancakes in stacks."

### Mandevilla   *Continental*

| 23 | 20 | 24 | $37 |

**Westlake Village** | 951 S. Westlake Blvd. (bet. Hampshire & Townsgate Rds.) | 805-497-8482 | www.mandevillarestaurant.com
A "light touch" in the kitchen makes for seasonal cuisine that's "enjoyable" if "not cutting-edge" at this "consistent" Continental in Westlake Village; patrons say the "pleasant service", "generously sized" tables and a "pretty" enclosed patio with heated floors add to the "accommodating" feel.

### Mäni's Bakery Café   *Bakery/Vegan*

| 18 | 11 | 16 | $15 |

**Santa Monica** | 2507 Main St. (Ocean Park Blvd.) | 310-396-7700
### Mäni's on Fairfax ● *Bakery/Vegan*
**Fairfax** | 519 S. Fairfax Ave. (bet. 3rd St. & Wilshire Blvd.) | 323-938-8800 | www.manisbakery.com
"Creative yet comforting" vegan cooking and "delicious sugar- and dairy-free desserts" are a "healthy" hit at these Fairfax and Santa Monica cafes; even if some find the staff a bit "too laid-back", the "ultracasual" vibe lends itself to "lunching, gossiping, networking" or a quick stop-in before "heading to the beach."

### Manna   *Korean*

| 18 | 8 | 12 | $22 |

**Koreatown** | 3377 W. Olympic Blvd. (bet. Gramercy Dr. & St. Andrews Pl.) | 323-733-8516 | www.mannakoreanrestaurant.com
"Festive" groups and "club-headed K-towners" head to this "cheap", "cafeteria-style" Korean barbecue for "all-you-can-eat", "grill-your-own" meats; it's "kicking on weekends" with the soju flowing, "house music blasting" and "long lines" proving a challenge for the staff, so a "massive sensory overload" often awaits the unsuspecting diner.

### Maria's Italian Kitchen   *Italian*

| 17 | 13 | 16 | $21 |

**Brentwood** | 11723 Barrington Ct. (Sunset Blvd.) | 310-476-6112
**West LA** | 10761 Pico Blvd. (bet. Oberland Ave. & Westwood Blvd.) | 310-441-3663
**Pasadena** | Hastings Ranch Shopping Ctr. | 3537 E. Foothill Blvd. (bet. N. Rosemead Blvd. & Sierra Madre Villa Ave.) | 626-351-2080
**Encino** | 16608 Ventura Blvd. (Rubio Ave.) | 818-783-2920
**Northridge** | 9161 Reseda Blvd. (Nordhoff St.) | 818-341-5114
**Sherman Oaks** | 13353 Ventura Blvd. (bet. Dixie Canyon & Fulton Aves.) | 818-906-0783
**Woodland Hills** | El Camino Shopping Ctr. | 23331 Mulholland Dr. (Calabasas Rd.) | 818-225-0586

*(continued)*
### Maria's Italian Kitchen

**Agoura Hills** | Ralph's Shopping Ctr. | 29035 Thousand Oaks Blvd.
(Kanan Rd.) | 818-865-8999
www.mariasitaliankitchen.com

Red-sauce regulars find "you can always count on a decent meal" at
this "modest" "family" chain; still, their "tried-and-true" Italian dishes
"aren't gourmet by any stretch", and critics complain that the "cheery"
but "spotty" service, "tacky" decor and "lots of kids, lots of noise" fail
to elevate the "generic" offerings.

### Marino ⑧ *Italian*    `24` `16` `24` `$41`

**Hollywood** | 6001 Melrose Ave. (Wilcox Ave.) | 323-466-8812
"A solid old choice", this Hollywood Italian serving "sophisticated"
pastas and regional fare maintains such a "traditional" feel that some
eaters "expect Al Pacino to be holding court" in a corner booth; indeed, the "welcoming" Marino family and their "courteous, professional" staff remind reviewers of "the days when dining was about
relationships with the restaurateur."

### ☑ Mario's Peruvian & Seafood *Peruvian*   `25` `7` `15` `$16`

**Hollywood** | 5786 Melrose Ave. (Wilcox Ave.) | 323-466-4181
"Magic" sauces and "crave"-worthy signatures explain the "popularity" of this Peruvian Hollywood "dive", an "unlikely" but "faboo eatery"
whose "generous helpings of seafood" help make up for "depressing"
digs, so-so service and sometimes a "30-minute wait during dinner."

### Marix Tex Mex Café *Tex-Mex*    `17` `15` `18` `$23`

**West Hollywood** | 1108 N. Flores St. (Santa Monica Blvd.) | 323-656-8800
### Marix Tex Mex Playa *Tex-Mex*

**Santa Monica** | 118 Entrada Dr. (PCH) | 310-459-8596
www.marixtexmex.com

"The boys may outrank the food, but the margaritas outrank the boys"
at this "tasty, basic" Tex-Mex duo's West Hollywood branch (sib to
Basix), whose retractable roof allows "the few stars you can actually
see in LA" to shine on down; the Santa Monica locale lures more of a
"laid-back surfer" crowd, but both are conducive to "connecting with
your friends" or scoping out "pretty" neighbors in an "upbeat" setting.

### Market City Caffe *Californian/Italian*   `18` `17` `17` `$23`

**Burbank** | 164 E. Palm Ave. (N. San Fernando Blvd.) | 818-840-7036 |
www.marketcitycaffe.com

Hungry guests say "the antipasto buffet is usually a hit" at this Brea
and Burbank duo, which serves "better-than-average" Cal-Italian fare
like wood-fired pizzas and seafood pasta in a "casual, country setting"; though the service could use work, all in all it's a "suburban alternative" that won't "break the bank."

### Mark's Restaurant *Californian*    `16` `16` `16` `$36`

**West Hollywood** | 861 N. La Cienega Blvd. (Waring Ave.) | 310-652-5252 |
www.marksrestaurant.com

Dubbed the WeHo *Cheers* by habitués, this Californian cafe "caters
to the gay community" more than the foodie crowds, as most reviewers find the fare "nothing special" and assess that the "hot waiters
keep it going" (even if they keep their customers "waiting"); on the up-

side, it offers a "backup plan" for a "casual night out", especially on "half-price Mondays" when the menu's "a steal."

## Marmalade Café *American/Californian*   18 | 17 | 18 | $25
**Rolling Hills** | Avenue of the Peninsula Mall | 550 Deep Valley Dr. (Crossfield Dr.) | 310-544-6700
**Malibu** | 3894 Cross Creek Rd. (PCH) | 310-317-4242
**Santa Monica** | 710 Montana Ave. (7th St.) | 310-395-9196
**NEW El Segundo** | Plaza El Segundo | 2014 E. Park Pl. (Rosecrans Ave.) | 310-648-7200
**Calabasas** | The Commons | 4783 Commons Way (Calabasas Rd.) | 818-225-9092
**Sherman Oaks** | 14910 Ventura Blvd. (Kester Ave.) | 818-905-8872
**Westlake Village** | Promenade at Westlake | 140 Promenade Way (Thousand Oaks Blvd.) | 805-370-1331
www.marmaladecafe.com
"Don't let the twee Victoriana put you off" reassure less froufrou diners who find this chain a "pleasant place to meet and greet" despite decor that's "drowning in chintz"; among its "pages and pages" of "eclectic", "moderately priced" Cal-American options, the "terrific breakfasts" and "out-of-this-world" mushroom soup – which arouse more enthusiasm than the "fair" dinners – attract their share of "stroller moms" as well as "stars hiding in sunglasses and sweats."

## Marouch Ⓜ *Lebanese*   ▽ 24 | 14 | 16 | $26
**East Hollywood** | 4905 Santa Monica Blvd. (N. Edgemont St.) | 323-662-9325 | www.marouchrestaurant.com
"Awesome", "fresh" Lebanese fare attracts devotees to this "pleasant" Middle Eastern eatery, even if they don't relish the "funky" East Hollywood neighborhood or the "slow" service quite as much as the kebabs, "family-style" meze and "nice prices"; occasional belly dancing on the weekends "adds extra spice" for those "having a party."

## Marrakesh *Moroccan*   ▽ 19 | 21 | 19 | $42
**Studio City** | 13003 Ventura Blvd. (Coldwater Canyon Ave.) | 818-788-6354 | www.marrakeshrestaurant.com
"Save room for belly dancing" at this Studio City Moroccan whose "standout entrees" like roasted lamb and b'steeya are designed to "share with a group" or a "date"; the "cultural experience" is enriched by "low upholstered stools" and "beautiful service complete with handwashing at the table" (for eating without utensils), not to mention the nightly entertainment, which may pull you "out of your seat."

## Marston's Ⓜ *American*   23 | 16 | 19 | $20
**Pasadena** | 151 E. Walnut St. (bet. N. Marengo & N. Raymond Aves.) | 626-796-2459 | www.marstonsrestaurant.com
"This old house serves a mean breakfast" praise Pasadenans who roll out of bed and brave the "long lines" for the "best blueberry pancakes" among other "hearty" American eats; both the "adorable cottage" digs and "charming" staff make it "inviting" from morning to night, though some find the whole package a bit "quaint" and "uninspiring."

## Martha's 22nd St. Grill *American*   22 | 14 | 20 | $16
**Hermosa Beach** | 25 22nd St. (Hermosa Ave.) | 310-376-7786
Serving "the quintessential beach breakfast", this American cafe draws Hermosa locals who declare "you'll never think about scram-

bled eggs the same way" after trying their white corn or sun-dried tomato varieties; despite a "sub-utilitarian" interior, the outdoor patio is "perfect" for "soaking in the surf and sand", and the service, while "sparse" during busy times, is "always pleasant."

**NEW Marty's** 🖾 🅼 *Californian*          — | — | — | M

**Highland Park** | 5137 York Blvd. (Ave. 51) | 323-256-2400

Named by Mia Sushi owner Rudy Martinez for his son, this ultracool lounge and Californian eatery is the latest newcomer that's turning Highland Park into the next Eagle Rock (which is, in turn, the next Silver Lake); its windowless space with low lights and casual conversation areas is an arty destination for those with more cool than cash, though it's not necessarily priced for those on a starving artist's budget.

**Mason Jar Cafe** *Californian*          ▽ 17 | 10 | 15 | $14

**West Hollywood** | 8928 Santa Monica Blvd. (San Vicente Blvd.) | 310-659-9111

"Special", "generously sized sandwiches" (including a pressed Cuban variety) appeal to the fan base of this breakfast-and-lunch West Hollywood "find" whose Californian menu – including 'guiltless fried chicken' – offers a "healthy angle" on American standards; its "small" dining room is "convenient" for "a quick bite on the go", and the homespun presentation of (all non-alcoholic) beverages "lives up to its name."

**Massimo** *Italian*          22 | 19 | 20 | $50

**Beverly Hills** | 9513 Little Santa Monica Blvd. (bet. Camden & Rodeo Drs.) | 310-273-7588 | www.massimobh.com

"*Bellissimo!*" praise pasta lovers of this Beverly Hills Tuscan whose "contemporary" cooking boasts "outstanding flavors" orchestrated by chef-owner Massimo Ormani, who "might visit your table if you're lucky"; an "attentive" staff warms up the "casually elegant" room, decorated with red brick walls and white linens, though detractors are daunted by the "giant graphic of the chef on the ceiling", not to mention the "expensive" tab.

**Z Mastro's Steakhouse** *Steak*          25 | 22 | 23 | $70

**Beverly Hills** | 246 N. Cañon Dr. (bet. Clifton & Dayton Ways) | 310-888-8782

**NEW Thousand Oaks** | 2087 E. Thousand Oaks Blvd.
(bet. Conejo School Rd. & Los Feliz Dr.) | 805-418-1811

www.mastrosoceanclub.com

"Welcome to the high rollers' steakhouse" where "overdoing it is a must", as the "first-rate" "bone-in filet" is "T. rex" size, the "seafood tower is extraordinary" and the "drinks are colossal"; its "glam" locations are staffed by "courteous" servers, though some surveyors balk at the "steep prices" and all the "businessmen with blonds" at the bar.

**Z Matsuhisa** *Japanese*          27 | 16 | 23 | $74

**Beverly Hills** | 129 N. La Cienega Blvd. (bet. Clifton Way & Wilshire Blvd.) | 310-659-9639 | www.nobumatsuhisa.com

"Place yourself in their hands and order omakase" advise those who've found sushi "nirvana" at Nobu Matsuhisa's "phenomenal" Beverly Hills original, which also excels with "exquisite" Peruvian-influenced Japanese cooking; space is so tight that "you might end up sitting in some famous person's lap", but the staff "makes everyone feel like a celebrity" according to grateful guests who find the "sublime" experience worth the "mighty" tab; N.B. his next restaurant in the former L'Orangerie is slated to open soon.

### Matteo's ⓜ *Italian*

19 | 19 | 20 | $45

**West LA** | 2321 Westwood Blvd. (bet. Olympic & Pico Blvds.) | 310-475-4521 | www.matteosla.com

West LA diners welcome a "revitalized" Italian "classic" back to the scene, commending chef Don Dickman (formerly of the defunct Rocca) for "reinventing this old Sinatra-worshiping haunt from the ground up"; its "imaginative" menu, which shines during "special" Sunday dinners, still offers longtime "taste-of-Hoboken" favorites, while the "solicitous staff" enhances the room's "old-school elegance."

### Max *Asian Fusion*

24 | 18 | 21 | $44

**Sherman Oaks** | 13355 Ventura Blvd. (bet. Dixie Canyon & Fulton Aves.) | 818-784-2915 | www.maxrestaurant.com

Sherman Oaks explorers hail this "sleeper in the Valley" for its "delicate", "modern" Asian fusion dishes by chef-owner André Guerrero (The Oinkster) and "desserts almost too pretty to eat" by pastry chef Jan Purdy; its "simple dining room" is staffed by servers who "take the edge off" the "noisy" surroundings, and though some complain about "close tables", most attest "the food is worth the invasion of your personal space."

### Maxwell's Cafe *American*

19 | 12 | 17 | $15

**Venice** | 13329 W. Washington Blvd. (Walgrove Ave.) | 310-306-7829

"All the locals" head to this diner-style Venice "fixture" "after a long night out" for "ample", "well-made" American breakfast and lunch plates ("it's all about the garbage omelet") in a room "still decorated from way back when"; though some call it "a little pricey" for what's offered, the "lines keep getting longer" (but they "move faster than you'd think").

### ☑ M Café de Chaya *Vegetarian*

23 | 13 | 16 | $20

**Melrose** | 7119 Melrose Ave. (La Brea Ave.) | 323-525-0588 | www.mcafedechaya.com

Vegans, macrobiotics and the like laud the "clean" cuisine at this Melrose health-food hub (which supplements its veggies with a few fish dishes) as "innovative", "flavorful" and "pleasing" enough to sway "any carnivore" while fulfilling "your tree-hugging fix"; though "aggressive lunch crowds" snap up the limited indoor and sidewalk tables, the "quick if informal" counter service generally keeps apace.

### McCormick & Schmick's *Seafood*

19 | 20 | 19 | $40

**Downtown** | US Bank Tower | 633 W. Fifth St. (Grand Ave.) | 213-629-1929
**Beverly Hills** | Two Rodeo | 206 N. Rodeo Dr. (Wilshire Blvd.) | 310-859-0434
**El Segundo** | 2101 Rosecrans Ave. (Parkway Dr.) | 310-416-1123
**Pasadena** | 111 N. Los Robles Ave. (Union St.) | 626-405-0064
**NEW** **Burbank** | The Pinnacle | 3500 W. Olive Ave. (W. Riverside Dr.) | 818-260-0505
www.mccormickandschmicks.com

"Widest range of seafood I've found in LA" purrs one hungry cat over this fish-house chain with a "daily changing menu that ensures the freshest catch of the day" plus "the best $2 burger in town at happy hour"; it caters to a clientele of "bankers, lawyers" and "accounting types" (especially Downtown) with "clubby" furnishings and "efficient" service, though some guests gripe about "plain" preparations of food (it "doesn't have any pizzazz") and calculate "somehow it just doesn't all add up"; N.B. the Beverly Hills branch, called Pacific Seafood Grill, offers a shorter, more upscale menu.

### McKenna's on the Bay  *Seafood/Steak*    20 | 23 | 19 | $39

**Long Beach** | 190 Marina Dr. (PCH) | 562-342-9411 | www.mckennasonthebay.com

The "divine" view of Alamitos Bay puts this Long Beach steak and seafood house on the "dining short list", particularly for entertaining "out-of-towners" with "sunsets", "cocktails" and "wonderful" wood-fired beef; while there's a "noisy happy hour", the nautical room's "warm and casual" atmosphere is also "suitable for kids."

### Mediterraneo  *Mediterranean*    20 | 21 | 18 | $29

**Hermosa Beach** | 73 Pier Ave. (Hermosa Ave.) | 310-318-2666 | www.mediterraneohb.com

"Tapas and wine are a winning combination" at this Hermosa Beach Mediterranean "hang" whose fans declare it a "pretty place" to "gather with friends" away from the "throngs of college students" that overwhelm the other pier establishments; sure, "service could sharpen up", but "when weather cooperates" it offers a "pleasant night out" "right by the beach."

### NEW Mediterraneo    ▽ 21 | 25 | 21 | $39
### at Westlake Village Inn  *Mediterranean*

**Westlake Village** | Westlake Village Inn | 32037 Agoura Rd. (bet. Lakeview Canyon & Lindero Canyon Rds.) | 818-889-9105 | www.med-rest.com

"A first-class redo" cry admirers of this Westlake Village Inn dining room that was formerly Le Cafe but now boasts an "absolutely fabulous" new look with lots of white leather and marble, wrought iron and candles, plus "beautiful" views of the surrounding gardens and lake; the "top-notch" Med menu mostly pleases the "country-club crowd", and the ambiance "makes up for any mistakes" in the "fast, friendly" service.

### Ⓩ Mélisse Ⓢ Ⓜ *American/French*    28 | 25 | 26 | $90

**Santa Monica** | 1104 Wilshire Blvd. (11th St.) | 310-395-0881 | www.melisse.com

"Incredible talent" Josiah Citrin earns this Santa Monica "temple" of French–New American dining the No. 1 Food score in LA for his "outstanding", "cutting-edge" dishes that strike a "balance between traditional and imaginative", matched with "always right-on" recommendations by sommelier Brian Kalliel; the "pristine" service and "sophisticated", "romantic" room ("love the purse stools") lend themselves to "three-hour" dinners that are "stratospherically" expensive but "stay in your memory as a beautiful experience."

### Mel's Drive-In ⓵ *American*    16 | 17 | 16 | $16

**Hollywood** | 1650 N. Highland Ave. (Hollywood Blvd.) | 323-465-2111
**West Hollywood** | 8585 Sunset Blvd. (La Cienega Blvd.) | 310-854-7200
**Sherman Oaks** | 14846 Ventura Blvd. (Kester Ave.) | 818-990-6357
www.melsdrive-in.com

"Resplendent in '50s kitsch" ("I kept looking for Richie Cunningham"), this neon-adorned American diner trio with "classic LA status" offers "breakfast for dinner", "thick burgers" and "icy-cold milkshakes" to satisfy "late-night hunger attacks"; fortunately the WeHo location is open 24/7, and the staff is "very understanding of hangovers."

### NEW Meltdown Etc. ☒ American — | — | — | I

**Culver City** | 9739 Culver Blvd. (bet. Duquesne & Lincoln Aves.) | 310-838-6358 | www.meltdownetc.com

Just around the corner from the sprawling Sony Studios in Culver City, this casual indoor/outdoor cafe is a tribute to cheese melted on bread in every imaginable permutation – its 'basic' is a triple threat of cheddar, Muenster and fontina melted on sourdough; to simplify the ordering process, there are combos of sandwiches with soups or salads, along with housemade pickles and fennel-and-red-onion slaw; N.B. those disinclined to dairy will be glad for the peanut butter options.

### Melting Pot, The Fondue 19 | 19 | 20 | $45

**Pasadena** | 88 W. Colorado Blvd., 2nd fl. (De Lacey Ave.) | 626-792-1941
**Westlake Village** | 3685 E. Thousand Oaks Blvd. (bet. Auburn & Marmon Aves.) | 805-370-8802
www.meltingpot.com

"Be adventurous" and "dunk everything, and then some" into "gooey" fondues at these DIY outposts of a national chain that "can be fun with the right people" if you "don't set the bar too high"; cynics label it a "gimmick", and say this "real time commitment", though "mildly entertaining", can feel "way too expensive", especially "for a place that expects you to cook your own food"; N.B. reservations recommended.

### Memphis ◐ Ⓜ Southern 17 | 23 | 18 | $45

**Hollywood** | 6541 Hollywood Blvd. (Hudson St.) | 323-465-8600 | www.memphishollywood.com

It's "a cross between an old bordello and the Haunted Mansion" quip visitors to this Hollywood kitsch-en set inside a "great old Victorian house", whose Southern cooking is more "down-home" but "not as distinctive" as its furnishings; while the quality of the service is a bit "spotty" too, "beautiful people" and a "tourist crowd" keep stopping in, whether for a "comfort-food pick-me-up" or simply to "check out the ambiance."

### Mexicali ◐ Mexican 16 | 15 | 15 | $24

**Studio City** | 12161 Ventura Blvd. (Laurel Canyon Blvd.) | 818-985-1744

"The 'cali' means you can eat Mexican with less lard" (like seared ahi tuna tacos) at this veritable Studio City "onslaught", complete with a "roaring singles scene", "dark lighting and stylish decor" to go with the "kick-ass" cocktails and "average", "inexpensive" fare; many diners are "deaf and hoarse" by the time they leave, and most of the disgruntled understand that the "great-looking" servers weren't "hired for their smarts."

### Mexico City Mexican 17 | 14 | 16 | $22

**Los Feliz** | 2121 Hillhurst Ave. (Avocado St.) | 323-661-7227

Both the "obligatory burritos" and "interesting specials" with "a little flair" satisfy Los Feliz appetites at this "high-energy" Mexican "standby" in the Hillhurst "'hood"; while the "hipster service" provides "variable" experiences, "after a few of their excellent margaritas, you won't care."

|  | FOOD | DECOR | SERVICE | COST |
|---|---|---|---|---|

### Mia Sushi *Japanese*
▽ 20 | 20 | 19 | $36

**Eagle Rock** | 4741 Eagle Rock Blvd. (Las Colinas Ave.) | 323-256-2562 | www.mia-sushi.com

The "sushi chefs are accommodating" to nori nibblers who adore the "novel" albeit "Americanized" rolls, finished with "ridiculously good tempura strawberries and bananas", at this Eagle Rock Japanese; "far-out" for the "up and coming" neighborhood, it flaunts a softly lit, "hyper-sleek" interior with a "funky vibe", but it's "not insanely priced."

### Miceli's *Italian*
17 | 19 | 19 | $26

**Hollywood** | 1646 N. Las Palmas Ave. (Hollywood Blvd.) | 323-466-3438
**Universal City** | 3655 Cahuenga Blvd. W. (Regal Pl.) | 323-851-3345
www.micelis1949.com

"Chummy" waiters "break into song" nightly at this "entertaining" "old-school" pair in Hollywood and Universal City, which serves up Southern Italian fare that's "pretty decent" if "not up-to-date"; Chianti tipplers call it a "fun evening with the right group", though "a little too hectic for a romantic dinner."

### Michael's ◙ *Californian*
24 | 25 | 24 | $66

**Santa Monica** | 1147 Third St. (bet. California Ave. & Wilshire Blvd.) | 310-451-0843 | www.michaelssantamonica.com

Cognoscenti hail "visionary" owner Michael McCarty as the "father" of Californian cuisine, and his Santa Monica "institution" as "still the classic LA dining experience", from the "superior" dishes to the "gorgeous garden" ("the place to be", as it trumps the interior); though some critics tut that's it's "too expensive vs. the competition", the staff is a "class act" (plus Michael is often there), catering to a crowd comprised of "gentry and A-listers."

### Michelia ◙ *Vietnamese*
23 | 16 | 20 | $37

**Third Street** | 8738 W. Third St. (Robertson St.) | 310-276-8288 | www.micheliabistro.com

Chef/co-owner Kimmy Tang is a "wizard in the kitchen" (and a "delight" to boot) at this Third Street Vietnamese, preparing "fresh", "enticing", fusion-accented dishes (many of them vegetarian) that are "even better" than fans have found across the Pacific; opinions of the decor range from "understated" to "uninviting" to "Florida"-like, but to some it's "ideal for a date", plus the lunch specials are the "best deal."

### Michel Richard *Bakery/French*
20 | 12 | 16 | $27

**Beverly Hills** | 310 S. Robertson Blvd. (bet. Burton Way & 3rd St.) | 310-275-5707 | www.maisonrichard.com

"Amazing pastries and cakes" ("similar to my favorites in Paris"), "wonderful" breads and "high-quality" roasted chicken still distinguish this '70s-era Beverly Hills bistro and bakery; though many find the decor "tired" and the staff middling, it remains a "great value" for "guilty pleasures."

### NEW Mike & Anne's Ⓜ *American*
20 | 18 | 20 | $34

**South Pasadena** | 1040 Mission St. (bet. Fairview & Meridian Aves.) | 626-799-7199 | www.mikeandannes.com

This "nifty" New American arrival "shines the most with simpler fare" and "seasonal specials" among its "fusion"-accented cooking; although the staff appears "overwhelmed" at times, the atmosphere is "energetic", "comfy" and especially "lovely" outside, providing what some South Pasadenans call the "perfect neighborhood place."

**Milky Way** *Californian* ▽ 18 | 13 | 22 | $26

**Pico-Robertson** | 9108 W. Pico Blvd. (Doheny Dr.) | 310-859-0004

Fans vow "I will always love Leah" Adler, the owner and "nice Jewish mother" ("Steven Spielberg's" to be exact) of this Californian kosher dairy kitchen on Pico-Robertson, who famously dishes "funny stories" and words of wisdom in addition to "comforting" blintzes, latkes and other staples in a laid-back room in the heart of the Orthodox district.

**Mimi's Cafe** *Diner* 17 | 17 | 16 | $19

**Atwater Village** | 2925 Los Feliz Blvd. (bet. Revere & Seneca Aves.) | 323-668-1715

**Cerritos** | 12727 Towne Center Dr. (Bloomfield Ave.) | 562-809-0510

**Downey** | 8455 Firestone Blvd. (Brookshire Ave.) | 562-862-2828

**Long Beach** | 6670 E. PCH (N. Studebaker Rd.) | 562-596-0831

**Torrance** | 25343 S. Crenshaw Blvd. (PCH) | 310-326-4477

**Monrovia** | 500 W. Huntington Dr. (S. Mayflower Ave.) | 626-359-9191

**Chatsworth** | 19710 Nordhoff Pl. (Corbin Ave.) | 818-717-8334

**City of Industry** | 17919 Gale Ave. (S. Azusa Ave.) | 626-912-3350

**Whittier** | 15436 E. Whittier Blvd. (Santa Gertrudes Ave.) | 562-947-0339

**Santa Clarita** | 24201 W. Magic Mountain Pkwy. (Valencia Blvd.) | 661-255-5520

www.mimiscafe.com

Additional locations throughout Southern California

"Dependable homestyle lunches and dinners" as well as "muffins larger than your head" are the draw at this "bang-for-the-buck" American coffee-shop chain (owned by the Bob Evans group) that's decorated with "cute N'Awlins" knickknacks; generally it works as a "place to take the kids and grandparents after church", although the service can be "erratic" and more demanding diners say "they need an electric jolt to update everything."

**Mimosa** Ⓢ *French* 22 | 18 | 20 | $47

**Beverly Boulevard** | 8009 Beverly Blvd. (bet. N. Edinburgh & N. Laurel Aves.) | 323-655-8895 | www.mimosarestaurant.com

After more than 10 years, this Beverly Boulevard bistro continues to serve, "as the French would say, 'correct'" Gallic "comfort food" prepared with "traditional" techniques by chef Jean Pierre Bosc; the recently renovated indoor/outdoor seating area and "warm service" bring "a touch of Lyon", even though the disenchanted "just don't get" the "nostalgic" approach.

**Minibar** ◗ *Eclectic* ▽ 23 | 21 | 20 | $40

**Universal City** | 3413 Cahuenga Blvd. W. (bet. Barham & Universal Studios Blvds.) | 323-882-6965 | www.minibarlounge.com

"They aren't kidding about the 'mini'" at this "intimate" Universal City hang serving Eclectic small plates that are "bite-sized" (you may need a "real dinner after") but nonetheless "provocative" and "prepared with just the right amount of spice and detail"; while it packs a "bit of 'tude" considering its location, both "fortysomethings" and "black-attired twentysomethings" approve of its "ultramod", loungey looks and late-night hours (till 2 AM).

| | FOOD | DECOR | SERVICE | COST |
|---|---|---|---|---|

**NEW Minotaure** ◐ *Spanish* ▽ 19 | 17 | 20 | $35
**Playa del Rey** | 333 Culver Blvd. (Vista del Mar) | 310-306-6050
Live flamenco guitar on the weekends "adds to the Spanish flavor" of this "little" newcomer that customers call a "fabulous addition" to Playa del Rey; while "not a bargain", the "tasty" tapas are enhanced by a "very nice wine selection" and a "friendly" staff that caters to "you and your date."

**Minx** *Eclectic* ▽ 19 | 24 | 16 | $41
**Glendale** | 300 Harvey Dr. (bet. Hwys. 2 & 134) | 818-242-9191 | www.minx-la.com
"Spectacular" views from a "stunning" wood, stone and glass interior beguile Glendale guests at this Eclectic yearling serving "imaginative", if at times "over-the-top" and "costly", dishes by Joseph Antonishek (ex Fenix at the Argyle and O-Bar); sober surveyors say the "service needs to improve", and warn it can get "way too loud and sceney at dinner", as a "real young" crowd takes over on weekend DJ nights.

**Mio Babbo's** *Italian* ▽ 21 | 16 | 23 | $23
**Westwood** | 1076 Gayley Ave. (bet. Kinross & Weyburn Aves.) | 310-208-5117 | www.miobabbos.com
"Two thumbs-up!" trumpet lasagna lovers who frequent this family-run Westwood "find" with "aromatic" Italian eats served by a "sweet and wonderful" staff; although the space is just a "joint", it's a "good value" and convenient "before a concert or play."

**Mi Piace** *Californian/Italian* 19 | 18 | 16 | $33
**Pasadena** | 25 E. Colorado Blvd. (bet. Fair Oaks & Raymond Aves.) | 626-795-3131 ◐
**Calabasas** | The Commons | 4799 Commons Way (Calabasas Rd.) | 818-591-8822 | www.mipiace.com
"The atmosphere is jolly" at this "busy, busy, busy" pair of clean-lined Cal-Italians in Calabasas and Pasadena, which provide "delicate pastas" and "beautiful desserts" for moderate prices; still, they strike some as "kind of commercial" and get knocks for a "plain" menu, "long waits" and a "less-than-stellar" staff.

**Mirabelle** ◐ *Californian/Eclectic* 20 | 18 | 20 | $39
**West Hollywood** | 8768 W. Sunset Blvd. (bet. Horn Ave. & N. Sherbourne Dr.) | 310-659-6022 | www.mirabellehollywood.com
Seafood and "fall-off-the-bone" Angus short ribs anchor the "tasty" Cal-Eclectic menu at this West Hollywood "staple" decorated with plush fabrics and opening to a "comfortable yet elegant patio" (for smoking and drinking only); happy hour regulars report the "helpful, cheery" staff makes it a "nice place to hang" while nibbling and "sipping the housemade sangria."

**Mi Ranchito Family Mexican** *Mexican* 16 | 14 | 17 | $18
**Culver City** | 12223 W. Washington Blvd. (Centinela Ave.) | 310-398-8611
Culver City compadres find "Vera Cruz in LA" at this "family Mexican" serving "solid" eats like marinated shrimp, chicken mole and home-made flan; with the "myriad tchotchkes on the walls" it's a bit like "eating in the *It's a Small World* ride", but that makes it easy to "keep the kids occupied by playing 'I Spy'" while you wait.

| | FOOD | DECOR | SERVICE | COST |
|---|---|---|---|---|

### Mirü8691  *Pan-Asian*
▽ 24 | 21 | 27 | $32

**Beverly Hills** | Beverly Palm Plaza | 9162 W. Olympic Blvd. (S. Palm Dr.) | 310-777-8378 | www.miru8691.com

The faux "Louis Vuitton"–patterned seating "is a hoot" and so are the equally cheeky "Gucci and Ferragamo rolls (without the high prices of Rodeo)" according to early admirers of this "different", "inventive" Pan-Asian newcomer serving "wild sushi" and "beef at its best" in Beverly Hills; its "eager" staff earns high marks, and the room's "new wave" touches, such as colorful, changing lighting, "please young and old alike."

### Mishima  *Japanese*
21 | 13 | 20 | $19

**Third Street** | 8474 W. Third St. (La Cienega Blvd.) | 323-782-0181 | www.mishima.com

"Healthful and delicious" udon, tofu salad, ten don and other "value" Japanese specialties make this Third Street noodle house a "cold-day" favorite; it's "quick" and "informal" all around, catering to families with a menu of "kids' dishes."

### Mission 261  *Chinese*
22 | 20 | 17 | $26

**San Gabriel** | 261 S. Mission Dr. (W. B'way) | 626-588-1666 | www.mission261.com

"It must be the best-looking dim sum restaurant in SoCal" what with the onetime rancho's "mission-style" architecture, "bright, spacious" interior and a courtyard where San Gabriel groups choose dumplings "bigger and meatier than most" off a "colorful picture menu" instead of from "clanging" carts; the "diligent" servers also bring such "sensational" Chinese dishes as Peking duck and BBQ pig, but critics contend that "you can get the same thing for much less in Monterey Park."

### Misto Caffé & Bakery  *Californian*
21 | 15 | 19 | $24

**Torrance** | Hillside Vill. | 24558 Hawthorne Blvd. (bet. Newton St. & Via Valmonte) | 310-375-3608 | www.mistocaffe.com

"A gathering place" for plenty of "returning patrons", this "dependable" Torrance cafe provides a Cal-Eclectic menu of salads, pastas and "homestyle cooking", plus an "excellent selection of desserts" baked in-house; its "relaxing" feel and "fast service" are a boon considering the shopping-center locale.

### Mistral  🗷 *French*
25 | 21 | 24 | $47

**Sherman Oaks** | 13422 Ventura Blvd. (bet. Dixie Canyon & Greenbush Aves.) | 818-981-6650

Not only is this Sherman Oaks bistro "a joy" for its "fantastic" French cuisine, but the "energetic", "cozy dining room" and bar dating back to the 1920s "make you feel elegant" to boot; enthusiasts agree the "stellar" staff pulls together an experience that's sometimes "expensive" but "worth it."

### Modo Mio Cucina Rustica  *Italian*
22 | 19 | 20 | $37

**Pacific Palisades** | 15200 W. Sunset Blvd. (La Cruz Dr.) | 310-459-0979 | www.modomiocucinarustica.com

"Definitely not a spaghetti joint" assess allies of these "underrated" Italian sibs in Newport Beach and Pacific Palisades praised for a "solid" menu with "creative" choices and a vibe that straddles the line between "casual and upscale"; the staff is "gracious", though a few nitpickers note that "too-high prices" make these "neighborhood" spots "more expensive than they should be."

### Moishe's ⊅ Mideastern
▽ 21 | 5 | 12 | $13

**Fairfax** | Farmers Mkt. | 6333 W. Third St. (Fairfax Ave.) | 323-936-4998

"Fill your belly at the Farmers Market" advise Fairfax foodies in the mood for Middle Eastern nosh with "Israeli flair", since the schwarma, kebabs and falafel "rival those of any other place"; walk-up counter service and "problematic" seating make it "better for takeout" according to some; N.B. cash only.

### Momoyama  Japanese
▽ 21 | 23 | 19 | $34

**Redondo Beach** | 1810 S. PCH (bet. Prospect Ave. & Vista Del Parque) | 310-540-8211

"Fresh", "beautifully presented" sushi in Redondo Beach is enhanced by a "lovely" design capped off with a ceiling "lit to resemble a starry night sky"; still, some wonder if the "New York" prices and "long waits" for service are why the dining room appears "relatively empty" at times.

### Monsieur Marcel  French
19 | 14 | 15 | $24

**Fairfax** | Farmers Mkt. | 6333 W. Third St. (Fairfax Ave.) | 323-939-7792 | www.breadwineandcheese.com

A "Farmers Market gem" on Fairfax, this "no-frills", open-air French bistro is where locals in-the-know go for "a glass of wine" with "killer fondue" or a "wonderful cheese plate" (drawing from a 200-strong selection) "on a summer evening"; it offers "unhurried" service and a "cozy" respite from the Grove "chaos" – though surveyors warn it's "not for the health-conscious"; N.B. a second location on Santa Monica's Third Street Promenade is in the works.

### Monsoon Cafe  Pan-Asian
17 | 23 | 16 | $30

**Santa Monica** | 1212 Third St. Promenade (bet. Arizona Ave. & Wilshire Blvd.) | 310-576-9996 | www.monsoon-cafe.com

Most distinguided by its "dramatic", "funky" interior adorned with carved masks and bamboo, this Santa Monica Pan-Asian provides a "decent" menu for moviegoers and Third Street shoppers; insiders "would recommend hot dishes over sushi", and say that despite "inconsistent" service and a fairly "touristy", "hokey" atmosphere, the frequent live salsa, jazz and reggae bands (often with a cover charge) keep it "entertaining."

### Monte Alban ◑ Mexican
22 | 12 | 18 | $18

**West LA** | 11927 Santa Monica Blvd. (bet. Armacost & Brockton Aves.) | 310-444-7736

It "puts the 'A' in authentic" declare reviewers of this "serious" West LA Mexican whose "fabulous moles" distinguish its Oaxacan cuisine; a "nice staff" and bang for the buck balance out its "mini-mall" setting.

### Monty's Steakhouse  Steak
21 | 16 | 21 | $46

**Woodland Hills** | 5371 Topanga Canyon Blvd. (Ventura Blvd.) | 818-716-9736

The Pasadena original has closed, but at the Woodland Hills spin-off, they still "know how to grill a piece of cow", mix a "potent martini" and "serve them well"; trendier types are taken aback, however, by the "shopworn" decor and the "midlife-crisis pickup scene at the bar."

| | FOOD | DECOR | SERVICE | COST |
|---|---|---|---|---|

### Moonshadows  *American*
| | 17 | 21 | 17 | $43 |

**Malibu** | 20356 PCH (Big Rock Dr.) | 310-456-3010 | www.moonshadowsmalibu.com

"The deck can become quite the party spot" with "beautiful people" and "dressed-down celebs" milling about "right over the water" in "dreamy" Malibu; while the New American food ranges from "innovative" to "disappointing", the service is "not consistent" and the "Euro beat in the background" can get "loud", most agree it's a "unique experience."

### Morels First Floor Bistro  *French*
| | 17 | 18 | 17 | $31 |

**Fairfax** | The Grove at Farmers Mkt. | 189 The Grove Dr. (bet. Fairfax Ave. & 3rd St.) | 323-965-9595

Patio spectators take to the "sport of people-watching" at Fairfax's "ersatz Paris" bistro by the "Bellagio-lite fountain" in the Grove; its "wonderful baguettes and cheeses" (from the house 'cave') make it right "for a snack" after a "hard day of shopping", though many call both the cooking and service merely "passable."

### Morels French Steakhouse  **M** *French/Steak*
| | 19 | 19 | 17 | $48 |

**Fairfax** | The Grove at Farmers Mkt. | 189 The Grove Dr. (bet. Fairfax Ave. & 3rd St.) | 323-965-9595

The saucy fare largely "fits the standards" of francophiles at this "decent" Fairfax steakhouse whose view from "high above the fray at the Grove" and "sophisticated" jazz on the weekends keep it "crowded" with shoppers and wandering twosomes; still, some are "disappointed" by "slow" service ("try the bar to get served more quickly") and what they deem a "Disneyland interpretation" of a French bistro.

### **Z** Mori Sushi  **Z** *Japanese*
| | 26 | 17 | 21 | $64 |

**West LA** | 11500 W. Pico Blvd. (Gateway Blvd.) | 310-479-3939 | www.morisushi.org

"Serious nigiri sushi" by Morihiro Onodera arrives in "elegant presentations" at this West LA haven whose "hipster" clientele advocates omakase as the best way to sample the "extraordinary", "sumptuous" cuisine; it's served on unique plates (many of them handmade by the chef-owner) in a "simple" space and suited to those with "deep pockets", but "worth it" for special occasions.

### Moroccan Room at Social Hollywood  *Eclectic*
| | ▽ 18 | 27 | 20 | $60 |

**Hollywood** | 6525 W. Sunset Blvd. (Schrader Blvd.) | 323-462-5222 | www.socialhollywood.com

Jeffrey Chodorow's "terrific redo of the old Athletic Club" hits the heights of "fabulousness" with restored 1920s vaulted ceilings, Moroccan furnishings and a fireplace; considering its appeal to the "youth of Hollywood", surveyors are often "pleasantly surprised" by the "unique" if "pricey" Eclectic menu and "knowledgeable" staff, praising it as a place for "guests to remember."

### Morton's  **Z** *American/Californian*
| | 23 | 21 | 23 | $62 |

**West Hollywood** | 8764 Melrose Ave. (N. Robertson Blvd.) | 310-276-5205

This "expensive" West Hollywood "classic" is set to close by the end of 2007 to transform into SoHo House; in the meantime, diehards can linger over a last taste of lime grilled chicken, tuna sashimi and other "fine Cal-American" dishes served in the "airy, light" dining room.

| | FOOD | DECOR | SERVICE | COST |
|---|---|---|---|---|

## Mo's  *American*
**17 | 14 | 17 | $22**

**Burbank** | 4301 W. Riverside Dr. (bet. N. Rose & N. Valley Sts.) | 818-845-3009 | www.eatatmos.com

You can "build your own best hamburger" and take it to the condiment bar for more dressing up at this "no-frills" Burbank American joint stocked with "funky old wood tables" ("like stepping into the '70s") and filled with "local studio staffers"; the staff is "competent" but many find the menu "lacking" and the space too "damn loud."

## Moun of Tunis  *Tunisian*
**▽ 20 | 21 | 19 | $38**

**Hollywood** | 7445½ W. Sunset Blvd. (bet. Fairfax & La Brea Aves.) | 323-874-3333 | www.mounoftunisrestaurant.com

"Atmospheric" with "tables low to the ground and pillows to sit on", this "intimate" Tunisian in Hollywood encourages guests to "eat with their hands" while savoring "delicious" couscous and other North African specialties; navel gazers say nightly belly dancing is the "icing on the cake", whether for "groups" out celebrating (for a "lower cost" than at similar venues) or "Aunt Maude from Iowa."

## MOZ Buddha Lounge  *Asian Fusion*
**20 | 22 | 18 | $39**

**Agoura Hills** | 30105 W. Agoura Rd. (Reyes Adobe Rd.) | 818-735-0091 | www.mozbar.com

Loungers "love the atmosphere on weekend nights" at this "gorgeous" Agoura Hills "mecca in the middle of nowhere" turning out "tasty", "creative" Asian fusion cuisine and live music nightly to keep the "singles scene" "hoppin'"; still, naysayers can't abide the "high noise level" or lack of fresh air on the "smoking patio", and knock that "big boobs get better service."

## Mr. Cecil's California Ribs  *BBQ*
**18 | 10 | 14 | $24**

**West LA** | 12244 W. Pico Blvd. (Bundy Blvd.) | 310-442-1550
**Sherman Oaks** | 13625 Ventura Blvd. (Woodman Ave.) | 818-905-8400

"Rubbed with seasoning", "slow-cooked and tender", the ribs at these "smoke shacks" are "so flavorful" they "don't need to be drenched in sauce" according to 'cue connoisseurs; while the '40s-era "chili bowl-shaped" West LA location gets rather "cramped", the Sherman Oaks offshoot is "larger and more comfortable" (serving liquor in addition to beer and wine), though doubters call them "overpriced and underwhelming", with "school kid"–caliber service.

## Mr. Chow  ❶ *Chinese*
**23 | 19 | 21 | $66**

**Beverly Hills** | 344 N. Camden Dr. (bet. Brighton Way & Wilshire Blvd.) | 310-278-9911 | www.mrchow.com

"Be ready to meet the paparazzi at the door" of this "always crazy" Beverly Hills "celeb-sighting haven" displaying art by Andy Warhol and Helmut Newton, and serving "polished versions of standard Chinese" ("the most expensive on the planet") in "Nicole Richie" portions; more practical peeps "don't recommend allowing the waiter to bring you his favorites" but do admit "the maitre d's are classy dudes."

## NEW Mubee  🅂 🄼 *Japanese*
**– | – | – | M**

**West Hollywood** | 359 N. La Cienega Blvd. (Beverly Blvd.) | 310-854-0356

More than a few restaurants have come and gone in this plain-Jane storefront space just north of the Beverly Center, though this may be the first sushi bar to give it a try; the room is as cleanly designed as a bento box – a spare but cozy setting to sample traditional rolls plus exotic versions with saucy names like the Sexy Roll.

### Mulberry Street Pizzeria  *Pizza*

| 23 | 9 | 16 | $14 |

**Beverly Hills** | 240 S. Beverly Dr. (bet. Charleville Blvd. & Gregory Way) | 310-247-8100
**Beverly Hills** | 347 N. Canon Dr. (bet. Brighton & Dayton Ways) | 310-247-8998
**Encino** | 17040 Ventura Blvd. (Oak Park Ave.) | 818-906-8881
www.mulberrypizza.com

"By the slice or by the pie, you're in for a treat" attest Big Apple expats gaga over the "crispy, thin" pizza tossed in "authentic NYC storefronts" with celeb headshots on the walls; given their locations in Beverly Hills and Encino, the "Brooklyn attitude" from the staff is a bonus.

### NEW Murano  M  *Mediterranean*

| – | – | – | M |

**West Hollywood** | 9010 Melrose Ave. (N. Almont Dr.) | 310-246-9118 | www.murano9010.com

Seasonal Mediterranean fare with an Italian emphasis is served in a modern black-and-white setting at this upscale WeHo newcomer, which offers brunch all day on Sunday; the interior is dominated by several brightly colored chandeliers made from its namesake glass, and opens to an outdoor patio for smoking and sipping.

### Musha  *Japanese*

| 25 | 16 | 19 | $30 |

**Santa Monica** | 424 Wilshire Blvd. (bet. 4th & 5th Sts.) | 310-576-6330 ●
**Torrance** | 1725 W. Carson St. (S. Western Ave.) | 310-787-7344

"Innovative" yet "sublimely simple" izakaya plates delight Santa Monica and Torrance sake tipplers at these "Tokyo-like" "little joints" dishing up omelets, BBQ and sashimi (no sushi); a "celebratory" atmosphere and "congenial staff" ensure that "friends", "clients" and others "will thank you" for bringing them – "especially when the blowtorch comes out."

### Musso & Frank Grill  S M  *American*

| 19 | 20 | 20 | $40 |

**Hollywood** | 6667 Hollywood Blvd. (bet. Cherokee & Las Palmas Aves.) | 323-467-7788

"Old Hollywood still lives" at this third-generation American chophouse with "iconic" appeal – "anyone who's read some Bukowski should enjoy the experience" – and "justly famous martinis" that tend to trump its "traditional" meat-and-potatoes fare; regulars appreciate the "period" waiters, who are "properly dressed and never say 'no problem'", but critics find them "as crusty as the bread" and the place rather "touristy these days" – "like a trip to the museum of ordinary food."

### Nak Won Korean  ●  *Korean*

| ▽ 14 | 8 | 12 | $16 |

**Koreatown** | 3879 Wilshire Blvd. (Western Ave.) | 213-388-8889

"This is where you go for 2 AM Korean food" advise K-town insiders who find their "after-drinks hangover cure" in the spicy pork and BBQ served 24/7; it's "cheap" and "easy to order", so although the room is nothing to look at, it's prime for pigging out with a "big party."

### Napa Valley Grille  *Californian*

| 20 | 22 | 20 | $43 |

**Westwood** | 1100 Glendon Ave. (Lindbrook Dr.) | 310-824-3322 | www.napavalleygrille.com

The "inviting atmosphere" at this "stylish" homage to Napa in Westwood is enhanced by fireplaces and grapevines greening the patio in which oenophiles dine on "rustic" New American–Cal cuisine with wine flights available; those who find it "sort of vanilla", being part of a chain, still appreciate that it "will accommodate a large group."

### Naraya Thai  *Thai*
▽ 19 | 20 | 21 | $27

**Pico-Robertson** | 1128 S. Robertson Blvd. (Olympic Blvd.) | 310-858-7738
"Nouveau Thai (with nouveau prices)" can be found at this Pico-Robertson arrival offering "refreshing" cuisine; though a few find it "a little highbrow for the location", fans appreciate the "personalized service" and "sleek decor" with "serene" water features.

### Natalee Thai  *Thai*
19 | 15 | 16 | $21

**Beverly Hills** | 998 S. Robertson Blvd. (Olympic Blvd.) | 310-855-9380
**Palms** | 10101 Venice Blvd. (Clarington Ave.) | 310-202-7003
www.nataleethai.com
This "techno-Thai" pair "packs a punch" with both traditional "favorites", "tasty originals" and sushi, as well as with "modern", plant-filled surroundings (though some cite "terrible lighting"); while scouts call it one of the "cheapest secrets" in Beverly Hills and Palms, its "packed" following keeps it at a "chainsaw" volume that's just somewhat ameliorated by "pleasant" if "lackluster" service.

### Nate 'n Al  *Deli*
21 | 10 | 17 | $23

**Beverly Hills** | 414 N. Beverly Dr. (bet. Brighton Way & Little Santa Monica Blvd.) | 310-274-0101 | www.natenal.com
"Ancient waitresses take your order" with "a mixture of boredom and disdain" (which is "part of the charm") at this non-kosher "LA equivalent of New York's Stage Deli" in Beverly Hills serving "fantastic", "jaw-stretching" hot pastrami sandwiches and other "old-school faves" like lox and eggs; some think the "Formica" furnishings "need some sprucing up", but that doesn't deter the "rich, famous and not always Jewish" from lining up for breakfast on the weekends.

### Native Foods  *Californian/Eclectic*
22 | 12 | 17 | $16

**Westwood** | 1110½ Gayley Ave. (Wilshire Blvd.) | 310-209-1055 | www.nativefoods.com
"Farm animals can rejoice" because surveyors adore these "healthy" Cal-Eclectic "alternatives" offering "sophisticated", "affordable" organic vegan fare that that makes "what George Washington Carver did with peanuts look like child's play"; a "hard-working" staff provides counter service, but dining can be a squeeze since "space is limited."

### Nawab of India  *Indian*
22 | 14 | 19 | $29

**Santa Monica** | 1621 Wilshire Blvd. (bet. 16th & 17th Sts.) | 310-829-1106 | www.nawabindia.com
"Subtle and complex" dishes, including specialties from the "real tandoori oven", distinguish this Santa Monica Indian eatery whose guests choose among a "comprehensive" menu with the assistance of a "helpful" staff; its lunch buffet remains "unbeatable", and thanks to a recent redo, the dining room "looks much better" of late.

### NBC Seafood  *Chinese/Seafood*
22 | 13 | 14 | $21

**Monterey Park** | 404 S. Atlantic Blvd. (bet. Harding & Newmark Aves.) | 626-282-2323
"Famous" for "killer dim sum" to "rival Hong Kong", this "large, gaudy" Monterey Park palace also offers "choice selections of live seafood

|  | FOOD | DECOR | SERVICE | COST |
|---|---|---|---|---|

from their tanks" for Cantonese dinners; it's "busy and noisy", as it should be, though sensitive souls wish they would "stop banging the dishes."

### NEW Neomeze ● *Eclectic*

| | - | - | - | M |
|---|---|---|---|---|

Pasadena | 20 E. Colorado Blvd. (Fair Oaks Ave.) | 626-793-3010 | www.neomeze.com

This relentlessly modern space – all sharp angles and hard surfaces – in Old Pasadena offers cocktails like 'Fig and the City' (made with fig-flavored vodka) and a midpriced Eclectic-Mediterranean menu of bright dishes like the 'Watermelon Neo' – stacked watermelon and feta with herbs; despite its concealed location down an alleyway, local trendies have already discovered the place.

### Neptune's Net *Seafood*

| | 17 | 10 | 11 | $18 |
|---|---|---|---|---|

Malibu | 42505 PCH (2 mi. north of Leo Carillo Bch.) | 310-457-3095 | www.neptunesnet.com

"Bikers and surfers and seafood – oh my!" fill this "earthy" "fresh-fish dive" in Malibu where an "entertaining crowd to say the least" chows down on "lots of fried food" and "good chowder" at communal tables with an "awesome view" of the Pacific; P.S. "go on a Sunday for the whole experience."

### New Flavors *Chinese/Hawaiian*

| | ▽ 19 | 8 | 16 | $15 |
|---|---|---|---|---|

Culver City | 4135 S. Centinela Ave. (Washington Blvd.) | 310-390-7849

It's a "crazy mix of Chinese and Hawaiian food", such as honey-walnut shrimp and tangerine-flavored spicy chicken, plated in "large portions" at this Culver City spot; "quick" service is a bonus, especially for delivery.

### New Moon *Chinese*

| | 22 | 19 | 20 | $25 |
|---|---|---|---|---|

Montrose | 2138 Verdugo Blvd. (Clifton Pl.) | 818-249-4868 | www.newmoonrestaurants.com

"Saucy appetizers" and other Chinese "delectables" with an "upscale touch" stand out at this "trendy", "gently modern" Montrose "crowd-pleaser"; it's "a bit pricey" for the genre, though the full bar and smoking patio are perks, and "seating is normally fast"; N.B. a Valencia branch is in the works.

### Newsroom Café *Vegetarian*

| | 19 | 14 | 17 | $21 |
|---|---|---|---|---|

West Hollywood | 120 N. Robertson Blvd. (bet. Alden Dr. & W. Beverly Blvd.) | 310-652-4444

"Tasty" veggie burgers, "attractive" artichokes and "awesome smoothies" among other "healthy" fare are served in a "casual", "filmmaker-friendly" setting with "accommodating" service and a fine view of the "action at The Ivy" at this West Hollywood herbivore hang; though the offerings are fairly "basic", most agree it's a "fairly priced", "easy, breezy" choice for a "quick lunch."

### Next Door at La Loggia ● *Spanish*

| | ▽ 20 | 23 | 19 | $36 |
|---|---|---|---|---|

Studio City | 11814 Ventura Blvd. (Laurel Canyon Blvd.) | 818-985-9222

"Excellent" small plates, from Spanish tapas to "sliders", complemented by "amazing wines and cocktails" sate modest appetites at this La Loggia neighbor on the "hip Studio City bar and club circuit"; sippers say that both its "sleek" decor and suitable staff create an easy setting "to lounge and get to know someone."

| | FOOD | DECOR | SERVICE | COST |
|---|---|---|---|---|

### Nick & Stef's Steakhouse  *Steak*
22 | 21 | 22 | $54

**Downtown** | Wells Fargo Ctr. | 330 S. Hope St. (bet. 3rd & 4th Sts.) | 213-680-0330 | www.patinagroup.com

The Patina group caters to the "cholesterol circuit" with this "serious" Downtown steakhouse, known for its "flavorful" dry-aged rib-eyes and New York strips proffered from a "meat locker in plain view" to please "hard-core carnivores"; its blond wood–decked dining room and patio lounge are "elegant" with "sparkling skyscraper views", the service is "professional" and the bar plays host to "throbbing crowds" digging into the "terrific happy-hour menu."

### Nicola's Kitchen  *Californian/Italian*
18 | 11 | 19 | $21

**Woodland Hills** | French Quarter | 20969 Ventura Blvd. (bet. Canoga & De Soto Aves.) | 818-883-9477 | www.nicolaskitchen.com

"Novel and light" Cal-Italian fare, including the "ultimate chopped salad" and sandwiches on "wonderful bread", appeals to Woodland Hills diners in search of a "simple, inexpensive" meal; although some customers call the food "only ok", its "friendly neighborhood vibe puts it on the short list" for most.

### Nic's  🗷 *American*
21 | 21 | 19 | $44

**Beverly Hills** | 453 N. Canon Dr. (Little Santa Monica Blvd.) | 310-550-5707 | www.nicsbeverlyhills.com

Habitués "love the martinis", "the gnocchi" and the "fabulous oysters" at this New American "place to hear music and be seen", which hosts what many call "the best happy hour in Beverly Hills" (complete with $5 bar bites); while the mood is "surprisingly warm", it brings on the chill in the walk-in 'Vodbox' for tasting spirits, "an experience in and of itself."

### Nine Thirty  *American*
▽ 23 | 24 | 22 | $49

**Westwood** | W Los Angeles Westwood | 930 Hilgard Ave. (bet. La Conte & Weyburn Aves.) | 310-443-8211 | www.ninethirtyw.com

"A people-watcher's paradise" label the onlookers at the "hot" scene inside this W hotel New American where the woodsy, Asian-inflected design "impresses", as does the service and the "surprising" cuisine driven by local produce; while the "chic" environs help justify "pricey" tabs, some wallet-watchers set their clocks for lunch "on a sunny day" instead of dinner.

### Nirvana  ● *Indian*
▽ 20 | 22 | 17 | $41

**Beverly Hills** | 8689 Wilshire Blvd. (bet. N. Hamel & N. Willaman Drs.) | 310-657-5040

"Canopy beds are hard to come by" due to their popularity at this "sexy" Beverly Hills "oasis" (open until 1 AM) whose "welcoming" staff provides a "provocative" Indian menu with "gourmet" offerings like tandoori lobster; even if the "food tastes better than it actually is" given the "romantic" atmosphere – made extra vivacious with Bollywood films showing on big screens – fans assure "you'll leave full and happy."

### Nishimura  🗷 *Japanese*
▽ 28 | 20 | 21 | $85

**West Hollywood** | 8684 Melrose Ave. (N. San Vicente Blvd.) | 310-659-4770

The West Hollywood cognoscenti who have discovered this unmarked "private world of sublime sushi" rave about its "true craftsman" chef-owner Hiro Nishimura and his "exquisite" sashimi; most agree the spare "Zen" setting with a bamboo garden makes it feel "closer to Japan than LA", though the more extravagant final tab "could challenge even the most generous interpretation of an expense account."

### Nizam *Indian*  ▽ 21 | 15 | 21 | $23

**West LA** | 10871 W. Pico Blvd. (Westwood Blvd.) | 310-470-1441
"Flavorful" if "predictable" Indian fare draws fans to this West LA Indian eatery whose "reasonably priced" lunch and brunch buffets appeal to even those who are "not usually" all-you-can-eat types; still, some would like to see "refurbishing" of the statue-adorned space, commenting "there's no magic in the presentation or the ambiance."

### Noah's New York Bagels *Sandwiches*  18 | 11 | 14 | $9

**Hancock Park** | 250 N. Larchmont Blvd. (Beverly Blvd.) | 323-466-2924
**Palos Verdes Estates** | 895 Silver Spur Rd. (Crenshaw Blvd.) | 310-541-7824
**Brentwood** | 11911 San Vicente Blvd. (Montana Ave.) | 310-472-5651
**Marina del Rey** | Marina del Rey Shopping Ctr. | 546-548 Washington Blvd. (Via Marina) | 310-574-1155
**Westwood** | 10910 Lindbrook Dr. (Westwood Blvd.) | 310-209-8177
**Manhattan Beach** | 330 Manhattan Beach Blvd. (Highland Ave.) | 310-937-2206
**Pasadena** | Hastings Ranch Shopping Ctr. | 3711 E. Foothill Blvd. (Rosemead Blvd.) | 626-351-0352
**Pasadena** | 605 S. Lake Ave. (E. California Blvd.) | 626-449-6415
**Sherman Oaks** | 14622 Ventura Blvd. (Cedros Ave.) | 818-907-9570
www.noahs.com
"All kinds" of "big and fluffy" bagels plus a "nice schmear selection" come out of this national sandwich chain "packed with the working masses", "lots of students" and the "farmer's market crowd" on weekends; skeptics find the "bagel-shaped objects" to be "too soft" – about "as Jewish as Wonder bread" – while optimists are happy that "10 percent of the time they get your order right."

### ⊠ Nobu Malibu *Japanese*  28 | 21 | 24 | $71

**Malibu** | 3835 Cross Creek Rd. (PCH) | 310-317-9140 | www.nobumatsuhisa.com
"The food is off the charts" at Nobu Matsuhisa's "phenomenal" locale off PCH, presenting "superb" "sushi as art" as well as other "unbelievable" Japanese cuisine; "celebrities" and "Malibu mogul sightings" add a spark to the "traditional room" – "who cares if it's in a strip-mall?" – while the staff "ensures every need is fulfilled", leaving just the "samurai"-strength bill to give one pause.

### Noé *American*  25 | 23 | 24 | $60

**Downtown** | Omni Los Angeles Hotel | 251 S. Olive St. (2nd St.) | 213-356-4100 | www.noerestaurant.com
"Marvelous" New American cooking at this Downtown "gem" in the Omni Hotel beguiles guests with "artistic", "exotic" combinations, particularly those showcased on the tasting menus; meanwhile, the "gracious staff" and "beautiful environment" inspire many to make it a "pre-theater" staple, though one visitor admits "my expense account got flagged on this one"; N.B. the recent departure of chef Robert Gadsby is not reflected by the Food score.

|  | FOOD | DECOR | SERVICE | COST |
|---|---|---|---|---|

### Nook Bistro ☒ American/Eclectic
| 24 | 18 | 21 | $31 |

**West LA** | Plaza West | 11628 Santa Monica Blvd. (Barry Ave.) | 310-207-5160 | www.nookbistro.com

"Nouvelle" American-Eclectic "comfort food" changes with the seasons at this "unpretentious" West LA cranny "hidden" in a shopping center, with a "warm staff" and a menu priced "just right"; the only drawback is it's nearly "impossible to get a reservation" at the few private tables, while the "thriving" communal one fills up fast.

### Nyala Ethiopian  Ethiopian
| 21 | 15 | 17 | $21 |

**Fairfax** | 1076 S. Fairfax Ave. (bet. Whitworth Dr. & W. Olympic Blvd.) | 323-936-5918 | www.nyala-la.com

The "boldly flavored" Ethiopian fare is a "bargain" at this Fairfax stew specialist, which benefits from "welcoming" service and "cheerful" decor; when it comes to "group dining", both vegetarians and carnivores find "it's quite fun to eat with your hands and not get in trouble for it", but a few first-timers find the "sour" injera bread and potentially "messy" dining style to be an "acquired taste."

### O-Bar ● American
| 20 | 25 | 19 | $39 |

**West Hollywood** | 8279 Santa Monica Blvd. (N. Sweetzer Ave.) | 323-822-3300 | www.obarrestaurant.com

"Super-chic" Miami-inspired looks and a "hot", "pan-sexual" WeHo crowd often overshadow the "highbrow comfort food" at this "appealing" New American, though signature dishes like 'Grandma's fried chicken' and lobster macaroni and cheese are "worth going for" according to devotees; despite the "flashiness", "sincere, friendly" management fortunately ensures "competent" service.

### Ocean & Vine  American
| 22 | 23 | 22 | $51 |

**Santa Monica** | Loews Santa Monica Beach Hotel | 1700 Ocean Ave. (Pico Blvd.) | 310-576-3180 | www.oceanandvine.com

Guests of this New American beachsider in the Loews Santa Monica say it's "perfect for viewing the sea by day, the pier by night" (especially under a "full moon"); the food generally "exceeds expectations" – "both the cheese and chocolate fondues are amazing" – and the improved service is "excellent", plus the fire pit is a "wonderful" touch.

### Ocean Ave. Seafood  Seafood
| 23 | 20 | 21 | $47 |

**Santa Monica** | 1401 Ocean Ave. (Santa Monica Blvd.) | 310-394-5669 | www.oceanave.com

"Consistently fine" seafood keeps fin-o-files swimming up to this Santa Monica "favorite" (Water Grill's "cheaper cousin") where "families, couples and singles" bond over oysters, Maine lobster and "well-prepared" fish, as well as martinis at happy hour; both the service and the "classy" room with "excellent" Pacific Ocean views still "shine."

### Ocean Seafood  Chinese/Seafood
| 22 | 14 | 17 | $24 |

**Chinatown** | 750 N. Hill St. (bet. Alpine & Ord Sts.) | 213-687-3088 | www.oceansf.com

Specializing in fresh lobster and crab, plus "unbeatable dim sum", this "big" Chinatown "seafood emporium" wins high marks for "selection and variety", though "long waits" can be a drawback; still, fans find it "affordable" and steeped in "genuine Hong Kong style."

| | FOOD | DECOR | SERVICE | COST |
|---|---|---|---|---|

### Ocean Star  *Chinese* — 22 | 15 | 16 | $22

**Monterey Park** | 145 N. Atlantic Blvd. (bet. Emerson & Garvey Aves.) |
626-308-2128

It's "a perfect way to spend a lazy Saturday morning" sigh fans of the
"killer dim sum" (served until 3 PM daily), including "heavenly" custard buns, carted around this "enormous" Monterey Park emporium
filled with "hundreds of guests" and the sound of "clanking teacups";
although the dinners are "average" and the room "a bit worn", the staff
is "generally helpful" – but "speaking Chinese" is a bonus.

### O-Dae San  *Seafood* — ▽ 19 | 15 | 18 | $39

**Koreatown** | 2889 W. Olympic Blvd. (Fedora St.) | 213-383-9800

"Not cheap but fresh" fish receives the most praise from early visitors
to this marble-decked K-towner specializing in Asian BBQ, sushi and
other seafood, including some "weird and wonderful" delicacies; despite mixed reviews on the cuisine, most agree it's "better to get group
dishes" and surmise "the mostly Korean clientele" lends it cred.

### Odyssey  *Continental/Seafood* — ▽ 14 | 21 | 18 | $31

**Granada Hills** | 15600 Odyssey Dr. (Rinaldi St.) | 818-366-6444 |
www.theodysseyrestaurant.com

"Breathtaking Valley views" are the prime draw of this Granada Hills
perch serving buffet-style Continental fare and seafood; though some
find the multiple "upscale" rooms "romantic", many are "not overly
impressed", calling it "mostly a corporate banquet facility" with "mediocre" food to match.

### Off Vine  *American/Californian* — 22 | 23 | 23 | $38

**Hollywood** | 6263 Leland Way (Vine St.) | 323-962-1900 |
www.offvine.com

The "lovely" ambiance (enhanced by a fireplace) inside this converted
Arts and Crafts house "in the middle of Hollywood" makes you "forget
the hustle and bustle just on the other side of the hedges" assure visitors who savor the "simple", "enticing" Cal-American "comfort food
with a gourmet twist"; topping it off, the "graceful" staff has the "unbelievable ability to get you served and out the door" in time for a
show at the neighboring Pantages.

### O4U  *Mideastern* — - | - | - | M

**Beverly Hills** | 214 S. Beverly Dr. (Charleville Blvd.) |
310-550-8655

Elias and Liora Amkie turn out kosher Middle Eastern cuisine like
chicken shishleek and homemade baklava to Beverly Hills visitors
ready to grab a sidewalk seat at this small cafe; Friday hours vary seasonally, and it's closed Saturday.

### Ohana BBQ  🗷 *Korean* — ▽ 19 | 3 | 16 | $13

**Studio City** | 11269 Ventura Blvd. (Eureka Dr.) | 818-508-3192 |
www.ohanabbq.com

"A small taste of Hawaii in the San Fernando Valley", along
with some of the "best" Korean BBQ ribs "outside K-town", attract
Studio City denizens to this "fine alternative to everyday fast
food"; while the digs are tiny, the "big portions" come "cheap",
making takeout so popular that the wise advise "ordering ahead" to
avoid a "bit of a wait."

| | FOOD | DECOR | SERVICE | COST |
|---|---|---|---|---|

**NEW Oinkster, The** *BBQ* | 21 | 13 | 17 | $13

**Eagle Rock** | 2005 Colorado Blvd. (Shearin Ave.) | 323-255-6465 |
www.oinkster.com

"Try the homemade pastrami", "awesome pulled pork" and "crispy fries with chipotle ketchup" advise enthusiasts of this "promising" American BBQ joint owned by chef André Guerrero (Max) in Eagle Rock, which aims to "elevate 'lowbrow'" eats with "high-quality" ingredients; still, it "doesn't live up to the hype" for those who say the items "could use improvement", or assert that "slow-cooked food is great, but slooow service isn't."

**Olé! Tapas Bar** *Spanish* | 17 | 19 | 16 | $33

**Studio City** | 13251 Ventura Blvd. (bet. Coldwater Canyon & Woodman Aves.) | 818-986-3190 | www.oletapasbar.com

Some bullfighters say *"bueno"* to this Spanish tapas bar in Studio City where the "sangria rocks", the warmly toned decor is done "to a T" and the atmosphere is "lively", especially with flamenco on Tuesday nights; still, critics call the dishes "inconsistent" and "costly", citing service with "attitude."

**Oliva** *Italian* | 22 | 19 | 22 | $28

**Sherman Oaks** | 4449 Van Nuys Blvd. (Moorpark St.) | 818-789-4490 | www.olivarestaurant.com

This "not-so-secret" Northern Italian in Sherman Oaks is "highly recommended" for "generous portions" of "fresh, beautiful" fare; a "charming" host oversees "top-notch" servers in a room that's "warm and inviting", especially during the "bargain martini night" every Thursday.

**Omelette Parlor** *American* | 18 | 15 | 17 | $16

**Santa Monica** | 2732 Main St. (Ocean Park Blvd.) | 310-399-7892

An "old reliable" in Santa Monica, this American eatery whips up "loads of signature egg dishes", including the 'sexy' omelet (with mushrooms, chicken and Swiss cheese); however, some say "execution isn't always 100 percent" and the "long lines for weekend brunches" aren't necessarily justified unless you can get a seat on the "vine-enclosed back patio."

**Omino Sushi** *Japanese* | ∇ 23 | 10 | 19 | $35

**Chatsworth** | 20957 Devonshire St. (De Soto Ave.) | 818-709-8822 | www.ominosushi.com

Omakase connoisseurs recommend "sit at the bar" for an "amazing" experience of "superb" sushi and "premium" sakes at this Chatsworth Japanese that's "like a secret club" for those in-the-know; though it's just a small "neighborhood joint", the quality of service well surpasses the decor, making it all in all an "oasis in the North Valley."

**O-Nami** *Japanese* | 16 | 10 | 11 | $26

**Torrance** | 1925 W. Carson St. (Cabrillo Ave.) | 310-787-1632
**West Covina** | West Covina Plaza | 1526 Plaza Dr. (Vincent Ave.) | 626-962-8110
www.o-nami.com

"If you want a seafood buffet, this is the place" say advocates of the all-you-can-eat sushi and other Japanese dishes offered at this "self-serve" trio; though the concept is "frightening" to some, its target market says it provides "better quality than you would expect" at a "great value."

| | FOOD | DECOR | SERVICE | COST |
|---|---|---|---|---|

**Z One Pico** *Californian/Mediterranean* — 23 | 26 | 23 | $55

**Santa Monica** | Shutters on the Bch. | 1 Pico Blvd. (Ocean Ave.) |
310-587-1717 | www.shuttersonthebeach.com
This "refined dining room" with "smashing" views of Santa Monica's
busy pier is "a playground for beautiful people" day and night at
Shutters on the Beach; most rate the "expensive" Cal-Med cuisine
"delicious", proffered by "excellent yet unpretentious" servers.

**NEW One Sunset ●** *American* — - | - | - | E

**West Hollywood** | 8730 W. Sunset Blvd. (N. Sherbourne Dr.) |
310-657-0111 | www.theonerestaurants.com
An offshoot of NYC's trendy One, this multiroom space in WeHo (raw
bar, champagne lounge, candle lounge, etc.) feels like a high-design
Moroccan oasis, albeit one that serves pricey New American fare by
Christopher Ennis (ex Asia de Cuba and Vibrato); in case this all
sounds too serious, there are cocktails with names like The Naughty
Schoolgirl to remind patrons that they're still on the Strip.

**NEW On Sunset �ⓈⓂ** *Californian* — - | - | - | M

**Brentwood** | Luxe Hotel | 11461 Sunset Blvd. (Church Ln.) |
310-476-6571
The creation of this new midpriced Californian was part of the update
of the Luxe Hotel; its glass-walled dining room surrounded by greenery
caters to Westside movers and shakers as well as Brentwood sho-
paholics; N.B. check out the Sunday jazz buffet brunch.

**Opus Ⓢ** *Eclectic* — 22 | 22 | 20 | $48

**Mid-Wilshire** | Wiltern Theatre Bldg. | 3760 Wilshire Blvd. (Western Ave.) |
213-738-1600 | www.opusrestaurant.net
"Daring" dishes and "memorable" tasting menus give Eclectic cuisine
"a good name" according to devotees of this "fascinating work-in-
progress" inside Mid-Wilshire's Wiltern Theatre; the "sleek", "comfortable" space, with an open kitchen and leather booths, overcomes
the "strange locale", while service is "gloriously attitude-free" if occasionally "slow as a snail."

**Z Original Pancake House** *Diner* — 23 | 10 | 17 | $14

**Redondo Beach** | 1756 S. PCH (bet. Palos Verdes Blvd. &
Paseo De Las Delicias) | 310-543-9875 | www.originalpancakehouse.com
Early-risers "salivate" for "fabulous", "fluffy" flapjacks in all varieties
and "amazing" "omelets as big as your head" at this "crowded", "family breakfast" chainlet with an "old-style" "diner feel"; "waits on weekends" are par for the course so insiders suggest you cool your heels
with a "newspaper" and remember that servers here "have turning tables down to an art form."

**Original Pantry Cafe ●⊟** *Diner* — 16 | 10 | 18 | $17

**Downtown** | 877 S. Figueroa St. (9th St.) | 213-972-9279 |
www.pantrycafe.com
Customers glimpse "what dining in the '40s might have been like" at
this all-night Downtown American "hash house" that's been serving
"meat and potatoes" and "breakfasts fit for a lumberjack" since 1924;
its "no-nonsense waiters" are "newbies if they've only been there 15
years", and in spite of decor that's "totally without charm", it's a
"cheap" and "classic LA diner."

|  | FOOD | DECOR | SERVICE | COST |
|---|---|---|---|---|

### Original Texas BBQ King, The ⊅ BBQ (aka BBQ King)

| 20 | 5 | 12 | $15 |

**Downtown** | 867 W. Cesar E. Chavez Ave. (Figueroa St.) | 213-437-0881 | www.texasbbqking.com

"Sweet", "messy" and "damn fine" barbecue stars at this Downtown "joint" that makes a "great detour on the way to Dodger Stadium"; though it's "not pretty", civic-minded critics assert the "gas-station-chic" space defies neighborhood "gentrification", and table service is "better than most" when it comes to "true dives" of its ilk.

### Orris M French/Japanese

| 26 | 15 | 21 | $40 |

**West LA** | 2006 Sawtelle Blvd. (La Grange Ave.) | 310-268-2212 | www.orrisrestaurant.com

"Small-plate brilliance" attracts "knowledgeable locals" to this French-Japanese in West LA, where chef-owner Hideo Yamashiro (Shiro) crafts "delectable", "unexpected flavor combinations"; while the no-rez policy leads to "agonizing" waits, a "well-functioning support staff" at work in the open kitchen buoys the rest of the meal, and the bill is "reasonable."

### Orso Italian

| 21 | 21 | 21 | $46 |

**Third Street** | 8706 W. Third St. (S. Hamel Rd.) | 310-274-7144 | www.orsorestaurant.com

Third Street denizens dub this Italian "industry hangout" (with NYC and London locations) "a 'no big deal' place where some big deals actually get done"; staples like veal scaloppine and pan-fried calf's liver are "masterfully made", the "romantic" patio "puts you in Tuscany" and the "sweet" staff adds to the "relaxed pleasure" of it all.

### Ortolan ⑤M French

| 25 | 24 | 23 | $84 |

**Third Street** | 8338 W. Third St. (bet. Orlando & Sweetzer Aves.) | 323-653-3300 | www.ortolanrestaurant.com

"Clever", "true gourmet" creations distinguish this "exceptional" New French on Third Street by the married team of chef Christophe Émé and actress Jeri Ryan, which is furnished with creamy "high leather booths" up front, as well as a fragrant "herb wall" in the darker back room; still, some experimenters are irked by "fussy" presentations ("foie gras does not need to be put into a mascarpone cookie") for "inflated prices", and say the service wavers between "wonderful" and "pretentious."

### Osteria Latini Italian

| 25 | 17 | 22 | $42 |

**Brentwood** | 11712 San Vicente Blvd. (Barrington Ave.) | 310-826-9222 | www.osterialatini.com

Don't let the "modest storefront" fool you: this "cozy nook" serves "impressive" Italian fare by chef-owner Paulo Pasio that's "upscale" enough "for gourmands" and features a nightly "list of specials a mile long" ("try any of them, they're all amazing"); what's more, the "spectacular menu" is "recited by savants" who "somehow remember it all" – and "they don't play favorites with the rich and famous that visit" either, making for an "unusually egalitarian" experience for Brentwood.

### NEW Osteria Mozza ●⑤ Italian

| - | - | - | M |

**Hollywood** | 6602 Melrose Ave. (Highland Ave.) | 323-297-0100 | www.mozza-la.com

Mario Batali follows up his and partner/über-baker Nancy Silverton's Hollywood hit, Pizzeria Mozza, with this adjoining, understated and

Milanese-looking Italian in Hollywood with high ceilings, dark walls, exotic hanging lights and a mozzarella bar in the middle; it's without a doubt the hottest rez in town, with locals hungry for a taste of Batali's cuisine (or maybe a glimpse of his orange Crocs) snapping up every table the moment the phone lines open.

### Outback Steakhouse  *Steak*
17 | 14 | 18 | $28

**Lakewood** | 5305 Clark Ave. (Candlewood St.) | 562-634-0353
**Torrance** | Del Amo Fashion Ctr. | 21880 Hawthorne Blvd. (bet. Carson St. & Sepulveda Blvd.) | 310-793-5555
**Arcadia** | 166 E. Huntington Dr. (bet. 1st & 2nd Aves.) | 626-447-6435
**Burbank** | Empire Ctr. | 1761 N. Victory Pl. (W. Empire Ave.) | 818-567-2717
**Northridge** | 18711 Devonshire St. (Reseda Blvd.) | 818-366-2341
**City of Industry** | Puente Hills Mall | 1418 S. Azusa Ave. (Rte. 60) | 626-810-6765
**Covina** | 1476 N. Azusa Ave. (Arrow Hwy.) | 626-812-0488
**Thousand Oaks** | 137 E. Thousand Oaks Blvd. (Moorpark Rd.) | 805-381-1590
**Valencia** | 25261 N. The Old Rd. (I-5) | 661-287-9630
www.outback.com
Additional locations throughout Southern California

"Come in with low expectations" and you just may leave "pleasantly surprised", because these "middle-market steak places" "aren't that bad" "for a chain"; yes, the meat, fish and "shrimp on the barbie" are "consistently ok" ("plus, everyone loves the blooming onion", though it "can't be too healthy") – just know that you'll have to tolerate "significant waits", "corny pseudo-Aussie decor", "noise that might kill you" and a "'flag-'em-down' staff."

### Outlaws Bar & Grill  *American*
15 | 10 | 14 | $19

**Playa del Rey** | 230 Culver Blvd. (Vista del Mar) | 310-822-4040 | www.outlawsbar-grill.com

"Straight-shooting" burgers "hit the spot" for Playa del Rey sun-worshipers at this American pub-grubber "within walking distance from the beach", and though the "rest of the menu is just ok", at least there's a "great selection of beers" to wash it all down; the "cowboy-themed" interior "revolves around a dark, dingy bar area", so it's often preferable to sit on the "nice patio" and "enjoy the sea breezes."

### Pace  *Italian*
22 | 21 | 19 | $40

**Laurel Canyon** | 2100 Laurel Canyon Blvd. (Kirkwood Dr.) | 323-654-8583 | www.peaceinthecanyon.com

"A little hippie-trippy" "yet serious when it comes to food", this "creative" Italian dishes up "Cali-style" pizza and other "solid, organic" eats to "Laurel Canyon locals who flood it every night of the week"; the "LA-cool, country-provincial" decor is complemented by a "low-key celebrity vibe", and despite a few gripes that it's "too expensive", most find it a "lovely little" "hideaway" in the hills.

### Pacific Dining Car  ◐ *Steak*
22 | 20 | 22 | $56

**Downtown** | 1310 W. Sixth St. (bet. Valencia & Witmer Sts.) | 213-483-6000
**Santa Monica** | 2700 Wilshire Blvd. (Princeton St.) | 310-453-4000
www.pacificdiningcar.com

Both the 1921 Downtown steakhouse and its Santa Monica branch carry on a "tradition of excellence" as they "stick to the basics and do 'em just right" for customers dining on "well-aged" cuts and "power breakfasts" 24/7; despite quips that it's "yesterday's food at tomorrow's prices", most are satisfied by the "historic" "private rail-car" setting with "large booths" and servers who act as "your personal butler for the evening."

### Pacifico's  *Mexican/Seafood*

16 | 14 | 16 | $22

**Culver City** | 9341 Culver Blvd. (Washington Blvd.) | 310-559-3474

"A neat trick" is pulled off by this Culver City "Mexican seafood shack", as it manages to be "good for drinkers", "families" and lunchers alike – the "strong margaritas" (best enjoyed "outside next to the fire pit") get you "totally hammered" while the fajitas, grilled whole fish and sushi (yes, sushi) are "fresh" and "served with no pretensions"; many feel, however, that they're "overpriced" for their "just plain plain" preparations.

### Paco's Tacos  *Mexican*

18 | 14 | 17 | $18

**Mar Vista** | 4141 S. Centinela Ave. (bet. Culver & Washington Blvds.) | 310-391-9616

**Westchester** | 6212 W. Manchester Blvd. (bet. La Tijera & Sepulveda Blvds.) | 310-645-8692

www.pacoscantina.com

"Always fresh" Mexican *comida* appeals to Mar Vista and Westchester residents at these "unsung" "neighborhood joints" serving "handmade tortillas" and a Supermex burrito that's "enough for two meals"; the "margaritas are a definite hit" too, so despite so-so "ranch-style" looks and service that ranges from "speedy" to "spotty", no wonder it's "crowded from 5:30 PM on."

### Padri  *Italian*

21 | 21 | 20 | $39

**Agoura Hills** | 29008 Agoura Rd. (bet. Cornell & Kanan Rds.) | 818-865-3700 | www.padrirestaurant.net

"Tucked away" in Agoura Hills, this "cozy cottage" proffers an "appealing menu" of "original and authentic" Italian eats to "chic, affluent crowds" ensconced in "overstuffed furniture" while enjoying "romantic" evenings; but there's "even better action" in the "incredibly loud and bustling martini lounge with which it shares its space", a veritable "pickup joint" catering to "an abundance of over-intoxicated singles" "on the dance floor" and "pretty patio."

### Palermo  *Italian*

17 | 16 | 22 | $19

**Los Feliz** | 1858 N. Vermont Ave. (bet. Franklin Ave. & Hollywood Blvd.) | 323-663-1178

You "gotta love a cheap-eats pasta pit" like this Los Feliz Italian "warhorse" – just "don't stray from the pizza", made with "fresh ingredients and generous toppings that make every bite a treat", and "you'll be safe"; the "cheesy decor" is "so retro", it "feels like a movie set", and owner Tony Fanara (who "makes you feel like you're his best customer") is the star.

### ◪ Palm, The  *Seafood/Steak*

24 | 20 | 22 | $60

**Downtown** | 1100 S. Flower St. (11th St.) | 213-763-4600

**West Hollywood** | 9001 Santa Monica Blvd. (bet. Doheny Dr. & Robertson Blvd.) | 310-550-8811

www.thepalm.com

When visiting these branches of the "evergreen chain" of steak and seafood "stalwarts", "think hunks: hunks of meat, hunks of bread, hunks of tomatoes in the salad", always "superbly" prepared and "satisfying"; the Downtown locale, a go-to spot "before an event at Staples", sports "breathtaking" high ceilings, the WeHo incarnation (slated for a short-distance move in the near future) boasts "celebrity sightings" (in the booths and "on the walls") and both guarantee "killer martinis" and "heart-attack prices."

**Palmeri** *Italian*                          24 | 21 | 21 | $45

**Brentwood** | 11650 San Vicente Blvd. (bet. Darlington & Mayfield Aves.) | 310-442-8446

In Brentwood's "cluttered" Italian-restaurant market, chef-owner Ottavio Palmeri's entry is a "rising star", as his "creative" Sicilian cooking not only "adds a unique angle" to the genre, but delivers a "fantastic" "depth of flavor" to the "well-presented" dishes; the environment is "warm" enough to make it "a place to run into old friends", while sufficiently "upscale" to draw "celebrities" who "know a good restaurant" when they see one.

**Palms Thai** ● *Thai*                       23 | 14 | 16 | $19

**East Hollywood** | 5900 Hollywood Blvd. (Bronson St.) | 323-462-5073 | www.palmsthai.com

From plain pad to "wild things" like a "delicious deer in peppercorn sauce", the "authentic", "adventurous" eats at this "cheap" East Hollywood Thai make "loyalists out of connoisseurs" (it certainly isn't the "cafeteria-style seating" or "fluorescent lighting"); "service seems to be focused on getting everyone in and out as fast as possible", but that's to be expected given the "overflow" of folks for live entertainment Wednesday–Sunday, often featuring a "spectacular Thai Elvis."

**Palomino** *American/European*              18 | 20 | 19 | $36

**Westwood** | 10877 Wilshire Blvd. (Glendon Ave.) | 310-208-1960 | www.palomino.com

"It's all about" the "bargains" at this Westwood chain link where "young professionals" congregate for "hopping" happy hours featuring "half-priced appetizers", while "budget"-minded "undergrads" afford "classy nights out" thanks to the "great early-bird dinners" (three courses for $19.95 before 6 PM); although they're "not really gourmet", the European New American dishes are mostly "fine" and "flavorful", and the "slick" surroundings decorated with lots of artwork feel "a little upscale."

**Panda Inn** *Chinese*                       20 | 17 | 19 | $25

**Ontario** | Centrelake Plaza | 3223 Centre Lake Dr. (Guasti Rd.) | 909-390-2888
**Pasadena** | 3488 E. Foothill Blvd. (Rosemead Blvd.) | 626-793-7300
**Glendale** | 111 E. Wilson Ave. (bet. Brand Blvd. & Maryland Ave.) | 818-502-1234
www.pandainn.com

"Miles apart" from the Panda Express chain it spawned, this "very popular" Chinese threesome serves an "extensive menu" of "consistently good" fare at "reasonable prices" – "who cares if it's Americanized?"; though the "simple" spaces "need updating", they're "nicely set up" for "large groups", whether they come for a "quick meal" or a "special occasion."

|  | FOOD | DECOR | SERVICE | COST |
|--|------|-------|---------|------|

### Pane e Vino  *Italian*  | 21 | 20 | 19 | $38 |

**Beverly Boulevard** | 8265 Beverly Blvd. (Sweetzer Ave.) | 323-651-4600 | www.panevinola.com

Though separately owned, these Tuscan trattorias on Beverly Boulevard and in Brea and Santa Barbara all share the same "warm" feel and "relaxed" vibe and serve similarly "simple", "affordable" Italian cuisine that's "dependable", if "nothing mind-blowing"; "modest" digs at all three locations include "lovely patio" seating that's the "highlight" of the overall "relaxing" experience that fans favor for an "easy" meal in the "neighborhood."

### NEW Panini Cafe  *Italian/Mediterranean*  | ▽ 16 | 13 | 16 | $29 |

**Beverly Hills** | 9601 Santa Monica Blvd. (Camden Dr.) | 310-247-8300 | www.mypaninicafe.com

"A welcome addition" to Beverly Hills assert locals who appreciate the "healthy" Italian pressed sandwiches and Mediterranean salads that make for "fast lunches" or dinners at this new cafe; still, some assert the "mediocre" fare is "not a good value for the cost", asking why "can't they find a good restaurant for this" troubled, "prime location."

### Panzanella  *Italian*  | 23 | 22 | 21 | $47 |

**Sherman Oaks** | 14928 Ventura Blvd. (bet. Sepulveda & Van Nuys Blvds.) | 818-784-4400 | www.giacominodrago.com

"For a seriously wonderful night out", Sherman Oaks folks head to the "Drago empire's" "upper-class" Valley entry for "delightful" Sicilian cooking that's "wonderfully presented", "flavorful" and "not too heavy"; although some bean-counters feel it's "pricey for what it is", the "impressive" decor ("chic" furnishings juxtaposed with rustic colors) and largely "warm service" make it "worth it" for most.

### Papa Cristo's  Ⓜ *Greek*  | 22 | 10 | 16 | $19 |

**Mid-City** | 2771 W. Pico Blvd. (Normandie Ave.) | 323-737-2970 | www.papacristo.com

At this Mid-City "surprise", you "order at the counter", grab a "funky table" and scarf down "sublime" Greek specialties like "sizzling plates of feta and tomato", gyros and moussaka, all "served on paper plates"; yes, the "setting is camp", but the "not-to-be-missed" Thursday night prix fixe "party/feast" and "rock-bottom prices" are no joke; P.S. "get some olives to take home" from the on-site grocery.

### Papadakis Taverna  *Greek*  | 22 | 18 | 25 | $41 |

**San Pedro** | 301 W. Sixth St. (Centre St.) | 310-548-1186 | www.papadakistaverna.com

"Always a riot", this Greek taverna in San Pedro offers a "total" "dinner-and-a-show" "experience" that begins with "warm" "owners John and Tom" "greeting patrons with a handshake or a kiss" before plying them with "fantastic" "traditional" fare; when not providing "impeccable service", "the entire staff breaks into song", "belly dancing", "plate breaking" – "the whole shebang."

### Paradise Cove  *American/Seafood*  | 16 | 18 | 16 | $31 |

**Malibu** | 28128 PCH (Paradise Cove Rd.) | 310-457-2503 | www.paradisecovemalibu.com

You "can't beat" this Malibu beach "diner" for "toes-in-the-sand" seating and "perfect" Pacific views – that's why you'll see "huge" "dressed-down" "crowds" of "tourists" and "noisy" children "tripping over each other's feet" on "warm summer days"; they're certainly "not here for the food", which includes an "overabundance of fried", "mediocre" American sea fare, nor the "off-and-on" service, "absurd waits" and "outrageous parking charge if you don't have validation."

**NEW Parc** ◐ *Asian/French*                    – | – | – | M

**Hollywood** | 6683 Hollywood Blvd. (N. Las Palmas Ave.) | 323-465-6200 | www.parchollywood.com

The trendification of Hollywood continues with this stylish French-Asian in the space last home to BlackSteel; it features mirror-covered columns, a patio dominated by a two-story-tall tree surrounded by glowing lamps and a bar at which all the drinks-of-the-moment are being served.

**Parker's Lighthouse** *Seafood*          18 | 21 | 17 | $34

**Long Beach** | 435 Shoreline Village Dr. (E. Shoreline Dr.) | 562-432-6500 | www.parkerslighthouse.com

"Sunlit tables by the water" and "beautiful" "views of the Queen Mary" and Long Beach harbor are why folks "go for" this "small" seafooder in a "mostly glass building"; the "surf 'n' turf" may be solely "standard" stuff (conveyed by "friendly" if "not altogether professional" servers), and it might be "noisy" with "tourists", "but it's enjoyable nonetheless."

**Z Parkway Grill** *Californian*          25 | 24 | 24 | $49

**Pasadena** | 510 S. Arroyo Pkwy. (bet. California & Del Mar Blvds.) | 626-795-1001 | www.theparkwaygrill.com

"Highly regarded and deservedly so", this "suave, sophisticated" Pasadena "event destination" from the Smith brothers (Arroyo Chop House, Smitty's Grill) turns out "trendy" yet "consistently scrumptious" (and "predictably expensive") Californian cuisine "year after year"; the "clubby" decor remains "beautiful", just as the "knowledgeable" staff is as "congenial" as ever – no wonder it's an "all-time favorite for anniversaries", "impressing" "out-of-town guests", even "a place to propose"; P.S. it's "lots of fun" to have "wine and apps" in the piano bar.

**Pastina** Ⓩ *Italian*                    21 | 16 | 19 | $34

**West LA** | 2260 Westwood Blvd. (bet. Olympic & Pico Blvds.) | 310-441-4655

Italian food fans consider themselves "fortunate to live" in West LA when they have a "charming" trattoria like this to dig into; the "traditional" "red-sauce" pasta dishes, augmented by more "upscale beef, veal and seafood entrees", are "dependable" and "fairly priced", and "owner 'Franco' is always there" to make sure his "funny", "warm" staff "takes care of" his clientele.

**Pastis** *French*                        22 | 19 | 22 | $45

**Beverly Boulevard** | 8114 Beverly Blvd. (Crescent Heights Blvd.) | 323-655-8822 | www.lapastis.com

"When restaurants grow up", they become like this "cozy" Beverly Boulevard bistro, a "delightful hideaway" where "deceptively simple" French "comfort" classics are "fresh, lovely" and "reasonably priced", and servers who "chat back and forth in their native tongue" "couldn't be nicer"; to top it all off, the "wine list really sparkles", especially during the "rockin'" monthly *vin*-paired prix fixe dinners.

|  | FOOD | DECOR | SERVICE | COST |
|---|---|---|---|---|

### ☑ Patina  *American/Californian*  | 26 | 24 | 25 | $75 |

**Downtown** | Walt Disney Concert Hall | 141 S. Grand Ave. (2nd St.) |
213-972-3331 | www.patinagroup.com

Even if you "fall asleep at the symphony", you can at least start the
evening "on a high note" by making reservations ("well in advance") at
Joachim Splichal's "swellegant" flagship adjacent to the Walt Disney
Concert Hall Downtown; "flawlessly prepared" Cal–New American cuisine is presented as "edible art" by "professional, knowledgeable waiters" in a "formal, minimalist" space, creating an "extraordinary dining
experience" that's "mind-blowing in every way – including the check."

### Patinette Cafe at MOCA  *Continental/French*  | 16 | 14 | 13 | $20 |

**Downtown** | Museum of Contemporary Art | 250 S. Grand Ave.
(bet. 2nd & 3rd Sts.) | 213-626-1178 | www.patinagroup.com

"Relax during your day" at the Museum of Contemporary Art Downtown
by having a "bite" on the "delightful patio" of this "self-serve" French-
Continental cafe; though some feel the "selection of sandwiches and salads" is not only "too expensive for the area", but "basically recooked
fast food", "somehow it seems to taste better" amid all that "great" art.

### Patrick's Roadhouse  *Diner*  | ▽ 16 | 16 | 18 | $21 |

**Santa Monica** | 106 Entrada Dr. (PCH) | 310-459-4544

Santa Monica's "see-and-be-seen" beachside "dive" for breakfast and
lunch does an eclectic take on "greasy" diner food, from burgers to
Austrian omelets (reportedly the Governator's mom's recipe), all "excellent hangover fighters"; service strikes some as "lazy", but at least
there's lots of "colorful" bric-a-brac to entertain – in fact, it "feels like
you're eating in an eccentric's living room."

### Pat's  *Californian/Italian*  | ▽ 22 | 16 | 21 | $41 |

**Pico-Robertson** | 9233 W. Pico Blvd. (Glenville Dr.) | 310-205-8705

Regarded by many as the "reigning" queen of kosher, this "upscale"
Pico-Robertson Cal-Ital kitchen makes everything from pasta to rib-
eye steak "so deliciously, you would never know" there were cooking re-
strictions; if you find the interior "nothing special", you can always have
Pat come to you – there's a separate catering division.

### Paul's Cafe  *Californian/French*  | 18 | 15 | 18 | $32 |

**Tarzana** | 18588 Ventura Blvd. (Mecca Ave.) | 818-343-8588

A "nice li'l charm of a spot you wouldn't expect to see in Tarzana", this
Cal-French cafe serves "quality" cuisine at "reasonable prices"; still,
some customers conclude "you get what you pay for", lamenting it's
"nowhere as good as it used to be."

### Pearl Dragon  *Pan-Asian*  | 19 | 19 | 15 | $35 |

**Pacific Palisades** | 15229 Sunset Blvd. (bet. Monument St. &
Swarthmore Ave.) | 310-459-9790 | www.thepearldragon.com

"The only game" for "strong drinks" in otherwise nearly "dry" Pacific
Palisades, this "dark, cool" Pan-Asian entertains a "captive martini audience", but it's "surprisingly good for families" too, which all together
create an atmosphere that can "border on chaotic"; many feel the "diverse" offerings, featuring "unique sushi rolls", are of only "marginal"
quality, but their perceptions may be skewed by service that "could be
more patron-friendly."

### Pecorino *Italian*    20 | 19 | 21 | $48

**Brentwood** | 11604 San Vicente Blvd. (Mayfield Ave.) | 310-571-3800 | www.pecorinorestaurant.com

"It's named after a cheese" so it should come as no surprise that the "*molto* Italiano" dishes are "strong" and "tasty" at this ristorante on what is fast becoming Brentwood's "Little Italy" (aka "Via Vicente"); sure, the setting is "loud" and the chairs are "slightly uncomfortable", but most pasta-philes overlook those quibbles because owners Raffaele (also the chef) and Mario Sabatini "always make you feel welcome."

### Pei Wei Asian Diner *Pan-Asian*    16 | 13 | 14 | $16

**Torrance** | 2777 PCH (bet. Crenshaw Blvd. & Rolling Hills Way) | 310-517-9366

**Pasadena** | 3455 E. Foothill Blvd. (bet. N. Rosemead Blvd. & Sierra Madre Villa Ave.) | 626-325-9020

**Santa Clarita** | Valencia Crossroads | 24250 Valencia Blvd. (McBean Pkwy.) | 661-600-0132

www.peiwei.com

You'll "pei wei less than you'd think" at this "express version of P.F. Chang's", and while its Pan-Asian platters "won't blow you away", they are "freshly cooked" when you "place your order at the counter" and brought to your table "quickly" (usually, everything "comes at once", so don't expect "to pace" your meal); while there are "plentiful brown-rice-and-vegetable"-filled options for the "health-conscious", some other items are "too salty and greasy."

### NEW Penthouse, The *American*    ∇ 20 | 28 | 19 | $55

**Santa Monica** | Huntley Santa Monica Beach Hotel | 1111 Second St. (Wilshire Blvd.) | 310-394-5454 | www.thehuntleyhotel.com

"Chic and modern" with a "fabulous" "view from the top", this "exciting" New American arrival designed by Thomas Schoos (Koi) in the revamped Huntley Hotel is the "hippest place on the Westside", complete with "individual cabana dinner tables" for groups; the cooking garners mixed reviews – from "delicious" to "needs to iron itself out" – and the bar scene tended by "cocktail waitresses out of a Robert Palmer video" can be "overbearing" (with "intrusive" noise), but most find the "expense" a "fair trade" for the ocean vista.

### Pentimento *Californian/Mediterranean*    ∇ 17 | 16 | 16 | $25

**Mid-Wilshire** | LA County Museum of Art | 5905 Wilshire Blvd. (Fairfax Ave.) | 323-857-4761 | www.patinagroup.com

"If you're touring LACMA, or if you work in the area", this "tiny" Mid-Wilshire Cal-Med offers a "convenient" "place to relax" while "patio dining"; it's "nothing to write home about", though, harrumph critics who cite "ennui"-inducing choices "sloppily executed", "total service chaos" and "(literally) cold metal chairs" as proof this "money-making automaton" is "not the Patina Group's finest hour."

### Peppone *Italian*    21 | 17 | 20 | $58

**Brentwood** | 11628 Barrington Ct. (Sunset Blvd.) | 310-476-7379 | www.peppone.com

"This place hasn't changed since Nixon was president", and that's the way Brentwood's "elderly" "rich folks" like it, as the "large portions" of "fancy" "red-sauce" Italian always have them "leaving fat and happy"; while the "old-fashioned" interior ("red-leather booths", "stained glass") may be "too dark", at least "nobody will see you" if you get snippy with the servers (they can be "arrogant" "if they don't know you") or if you "faint when you get the bill."

### Pete's Cafe & Bar ● *American*

| 18 | 18 | 17 | $27 |

**Downtown** | 400 S. Main St. (W. 4th St.) | 213-617-1000 | www.petescafe.com

"Filled at lunch" with "Downtown professionals" and "at night with loft dwellers", this New American with "New York atmosphere" works to "convince [out-of-towners] that LA is a real city, not a collection of strip malls"; the "service can vary, but not the late hours" – in fact, the only real "drawback is constantly having to look out the window to make sure your car isn't being vandalized", given its "proximity to skid row."

### Petrelli's Steakhouse *Italian/Steak*

| 17 | 14 | 18 | $31 |

**Culver City** | 5615 Sepulveda Blvd. (Jefferson Blvd.) | 310-397-1438 | www.georgepetrellisteaks.com

There are "no bells and whistles" at this Culver City "old-time" Italian steakhouse (except for the "toy train at the bar"), just red meat "at reasonable prices" – accompanied, alas, by what many suspect are "canned veggies"; it's "drab inside", but the "nice" servers (many of whom seem to "have been here since its inception") help lighten it up.

### ⧫ Petros *Greek*

| 23 | 21 | 19 | $44 |

**Manhattan Beach** | 451 Manhattan Beach Blvd. (Valley Dr.) | 310-545-4100 | www.petrosrestaurant.com

"They don't throw plates" at this "upscale" Greek eatery in Manhattan Beach – rather, the "focus" is on the "authentic" food, prepared with "a Southern California twist" and "without cutting corners" (which may explain why some perceive the service as "slow"); the "clean, modern" interior and "beachy" yet "elegant" patio has folks dreaming of "Mykonos", until a "pain in the wallet" brings them back to reality.

### Petrossian Paris ⧫ *French*

| – | – | – | M |

**West Hollywood** | 321 N. Robertson Blvd. (W. Beverly Blvd.) | 310-271-0576 | www.petrossian.com

"Caviar heaven" is found at this tiny French cafe and smoked fish-specialist, a WeHo spin-off of New York's restaurant and gourmet shop, that's open for daytime meals including "delectable but rather pricey" brunches; while it's a "pretty setting", patrons would like to see better service as it "could be a fabulous place."

### ⧫ P.F. Chang's China Bistro *Chinese*

| 19 | 19 | 18 | $28 |

**Beverly Hills** | Beverly Ctr. | 121 N. La Cienega Blvd. (bet. Beverly Blvd. & 3rd St.) | 310-854-6467
**Santa Monica** | 326 Wilshire Blvd. (4th St.) | 310-395-1912
**El Segundo** | 2041 E. Rosecrans Ave. (Nash St.) | 310-607-9062
**Pasadena** | Paseo Colorado | 260 E. Colorado Blvd. (Garfield Ave.) | 626-356-9760
**Sherman Oaks** | Sherman Oaks Galleria | 15301 Ventura Blvd. (Sepulveda Blvd.) | 818-784-1694
**Woodland Hills** | The Promenade at Woodland Hills | 21821 Oxnard St. (Topanga Canyon Blvd.) | 818-340-0491
www.pfchangs.com

Though 'P.F.' could stand for "Pretty Far" (from authentic, that is), the "corporate Chinese" eats at this "clean, attractive" national chain are

FOOD · DECOR · SERVICE · COST

"tasty", a "good value" and as "reliable as your dog, Rover" – and "shareable servings" make it "fun for group outings" ("everyone's favorite" is the "famous lettuce wrap"); the food "comes out pretty quick once you order", but "even with reservations" ("yeah, they finally take them"), "you will wait" for a table.

**Philippe the Original** ⊈ *Sandwiches*    21 | 13 | 16 | $12

**Chinatown** | 1001 N. Alameda St. (Ord St.) | 213-628-3781 | www.philippes.com
Folks "flip for the French dip" today just as they have for the past 99 years at this "cash-only" Chinatown "landmark" where the "mouthwatering", "sloppy" sandwich was "supposedly originated" (there's "much debate on this point"); while the "crusty" servers at the counter do their "carving in front of you", you can select a "$15 glass of Cabernet" to "wash down your $5" main course, making this truly a "one-of-a-kind LA experience."

**Z Phillips Bar-B-Que** *BBQ*    24 | 6 | 14 | $16

**Leimert Park** | 4307 Leimert Blvd. (43rd St.) | 323-292-7613 ⑤
**Mid-City** | 2619 Crenshaw Blvd. (W. Adams Blvd.) | 323-731-4772 Ⓜ
**Inglewood** | 1517 Centinela Ave. (Beach Ave.) | 310-412-7135 ⑤
"Flinstonian-sized" ribs, "superb" tips, "excellent" brisket, hot links and chicken, all "slathered in an unbeatable sauce", are what make these barbecue triplets "well worth the pilgrimage" from anywhere (just follow "the smell of smoke"); at the mostly take-out-only "joints" (Mid-City has a few seats outside), you'll find "no glamour" and often "lousy parking", but "once you get the food, you forget what you had to go through."

**Pho Café** ◑⊈ *Vietnamese*    22 | 12 | 17 | $15

**Silver Lake** | 2841 W. Sunset Blvd. (Silver Lake Blvd.) | 213-413-0888
This "down-to-earth Vietnamese" is "always crowded for a reason": despite "lackluster decor" and "way-too-bright" lighting, "hip" Silver Lakers know they can get "simple" pho and noodle bowls that are "consistently delicious" at prices that "won't break the bank"; just "bring cash" and plan on "being out of there in a half hour or less" – "the staff will certainly not encourage you to linger."

**NEW Phoenicia** *Lebanese*    - | - | - | M

**Glendale** | 343 N. Central Ave. (bet. Myrtle St. & W. Lexington Dr.) | 818-956-7800
One of the most stylish Middle Eastern restaurant/nightclubs in a city with stiff competition, this Glendale party place features live music, belly dancers and a wide selection of prix fixe group platters, along with numerous dishes not often found on Lebanese menus; the best strategy is to go hungry, with lots of friends, and be ready to hit the dance floor after dinner to work it all off.

**Pho 79** *Vietnamese*    21 | 8 | 13 | $11

**Alhambra** | 29 S. Garfield Ave. (Main St.) | 626-289-0239
"Waiting crowds" attest to the "devotion" of slurping supporters of this Vietnamese chain serving "huge bowls" of "truly superior noodle soup" topped with a "garden of fresh herbs"; "don't expect great service" or "ambiance" insist insiders who focus on the "ridiculously low prices" and always leave "satisfied."

| | FOOD | DECOR | SERVICE | COST |
|---|---|---|---|---|

### Piatti *Italian* | 20 | 20 | 20 | $34 |

**Thousand Oaks** | 101 S. Westlake Blvd. (Thousand Oaks Blvd.) |
805-371-5600 | www.piatti.com

"It's easy to forget" these "underappreciated" Italian siblings are
"chain restaurants", as they "boast innovative dishes" that "look as
good as they taste"; at the Montecito location, "the kitchen is so close
to the seating" that it feels "cozy", while the Thousand Oaks incarnation, now called Piatti Locali because of its "special emphasis on local
fresh produce", boasts an "enjoyable" wraparound patio.

### Picanha Churrascaria *Brazilian* | 19 | 15 | 19 | $39 |

**Burbank** | 269 E. Palm Ave. (bet. San Fernando Blvd. & 3rd St.) |
818-972-2100 | www.picanharestaurant.com

"Prior to joining Weight Watchers", have your 'last hurrah' at one of
these "Brazilian beef houses" where "hot waiters" carve "endless
quantities" of "steak on a stick" "at your table until you tell them to
stop with a nifty red-and-green doodad"; "even though it's great, skip
the salad bar", because if they don't "have to roll you out the door"
with "meat coming through your pores", you've missed the point.

### Z Piccolo *Italian* | 27 | 17 | 24 | $51 |

**Venice** | 5 Dudley Ave. (Spdwy.) | 310-314-3222 | www.piccolovenice.com
"Just off the beach" in Venice, in what may be the "weirdest location
for a fine-dining restaurant in LA", resides this "aptly named" "hole-in-
the-wall" that "deserves its grand reputation" for fashioning "heavenly, inventive" Italian cuisine bursting with "big, authentic flavors"
and coupled with an "impressive" (although "exceedingly expensive")
wine list; "they don't take reservations", but "warm, helpful service"
helps to allay the "hassle" of "waiting for a table."

### Piccolo Paradiso *Italian* | 24 | 18 | 23 | $45 |

**Beverly Hills** | 150 S. Beverly Dr. (Wilshire Blvd.) | 310-271-0030 |
www.giacominodrago.com

"Another Drago masterpiece" from brother Giacomino, this "expensive" Beverly Hills ristorante entices "lovers of fine Italian food" with
"great pasta" and "excellent fish and truffle dishes" in a "cute" *Cinema
Paradiso*-themed room; it may be "noisy", but that's to be expected in a
place whose staff "treats everyone like a very missed long-lost relative."

### Pie 'N Burger ⊉ *Diner* | 20 | 8 | 15 | $14 |

**Pasadena** | 913 E. California Blvd. (bet. S. Lake & S. Mentor Aves.) |
626-795-1123 | www.pienburger.com

"Everything is from another era" at this "popular" 1963 Pasadena
"institution" that dishes up "home-cooked" diner fare, from "scrumptious breakfasts" to "thoroughly satisfying" hamburgers to "mouthwatering pies" (try the "the superb olallieberry" "with a scoop of
vanilla ice cream"); "old-coffee-shop" decor and an "over-stretched
staff" further add to the days-of-yore feel – however, many feel "the
prices are anything but nostalgic."

### Pig, The *BBQ* | 15 | 9 | 14 | $17 |

**La Brea** | 612 N. La Brea Ave. (Melrose Ave.) | 323-935-1116
"Without many other barbecue joints" in the La Brea area, this one
"suffices" for a "fix", as it serves all the basics with an "assortment of
sides and sauces" – although 'cue connoisseurs carp the Memphis-

style grub "fails to live up to its promise"; a staff whose "attitude" "can be as tough as the ribs" and decor that looks like a "franchise" (it's not) mean it's altogether too "arid" for some.

### Pig 'n Whistle  *Continental*

| 15 | 18 | 16 | $24 |

**Hollywood** | 6714 Hollywood Blvd. (bet. Highland & Las Palmas Aves.) | 323-463-0000 | www.pignwhistle.com

"There's always something different going on" at this "restored" "old-school Hollywood restaurant", be it DJs, karaoke or "sporting events" on the "huge screen" – no wonder many feel it "can't decide whether it's a pub or an eatery"; indeed, it's "better for drinks and people-watching from the sidewalk patio" than for it's "outdated" Continental "grub", but if nothing else, it's "convenient" for "a bite before a movie" at the nearby theaters.

### Pike Restaurant & Bar ● *American*

| – | – | – | I |

**Long Beach** | 1836 E. Fourth St. (Hermosa Ave.) | 562-437-4453 | www.pikelongbeach.com

"Rock 'n' roll" and "fish 'n' chips" are the headliners at this "cool" Long Beacher from former Social Distortion drummer Christopher Reece; a jukebox, DJs and live bands create a "punk atmosphere", while "decent" American "pub grub" keeps the "funky" crowd in check.

### Pink's Famous Chili Dogs ●♥ *Hot Dogs*

| 19 | 6 | 13 | $9 |

**La Brea** | 709 N. La Brea Ave. (Melrose Ave.) | 323-931-4223 | www.pinkshollywood.com

"You know what, it is just hot dogs, but something about" this "historical dump" on La Brea tempts all stripes to endure "torturous waits" "any hour" of the "day or night" (until 3 AM on weekends); "maybe it's all the choices" of "meals in a bun" – overflowing with "innovative toppings" and branded with names like the Harry Potter and the Martha Stewart ("among the messiest") – or perhaps it's just that this is a "rite of passage" for people with "steel guts"; P.S. surveyors also award it "style points" for being the "only hot dog stand I know that has a valet."

### NEW Pink Taco  *Mexican*

| – | – | – | I |

**Century City** | Westfield Century City | 10250 Santa Monica Blvd. (Century Park West) | 310-789-1000 | www.pinktaco.com

The latest branch of this high-concept Mexican from Harry Morton (son of Peter, grandson of Arnie) lands in the renovated Westfield Century City Mall with a design that's pure Ensenada fever dream, ranging from sacred icons to Day of the Dead tchotchkes; its affordable menu actually does feature pink tacos filled with grilled chicken and topped with pickled onions, in case you're wondering.

### Pinot Bistro  *French*

| 23 | 22 | 22 | $46 |

**Studio City** | 12969 Ventura Blvd. (Coldwater Canyon Ave.) | 818-990-0500 | www.patinagroup.com

"Paris in the Valley" "without the attitude" is what this Studio City "haven" for "terrific" French bistro food with "updated touches" offers in an "utterly charming" environment of rich wood and checkered floors; "they don't charge a corkage fee", so a "romantic dinner" can actually be a "great value", and children 10 and under eat free, making it easy to treat your "big, crazy family" to a "special night out."

| | FOOD | DECOR | SERVICE | COST |
|---|---|---|---|---|

### Pistachio Grill *Persian*

▽ 23 | 10 | 22 | $19

**Beverly Hills** | 8560 Wilshire Blvd. (bet. Le Doux & Stanley Rds.) | 310-854-1020

"The pistachio hummus is a must" at this tiny BYO Persian in Beverly Hills plating up "large portions" of "wonderful" kebabs among other Mid-East cuisine; most "cannot say much for the decor", other than the "lovely" patio, but it "isn't expensive" and the servers "go way above and beyond" for their guests.

### Pizza Rustica *Pizza*

▽ 17 | 11 | 14 | $16

**NEW** **Downtown** | 231 E. Ninth St. (bet. Santee & S. Los Angeles Sts.) | 213-627-7798
**West Hollywood** | 8410 W. Sunset Blvd. (Kings Rd.) | 323-656-6800 ☽
**Beverly Hills** | 231 N. Beverly Dr. (Wilshire Blvd.) | 310-550-7499
**Sherman Oaks** | 15030 Ventura Blvd., Ste. 2 (bet. Lemona & Noble Aves.) | 818-788-7667 ⬛
www.pizzarusticacalifornia.com

"When it's good, it really is" assert regulars about this pizza chain that originated in Miami's South Beach district and therefore uses relatively "healthy" main ingredients in addition to unusual toppings like artichoke hearts, steak and potatoes; less generous guests call the pies "terribly inconsistent", though "better when eaten on premises"; amenities vary by location – Beverly Hills has table service and sidewalk seating, and the BYO WeHo branch is open past midnight every night.

### ⚡NEW Pizzeria Mozza ☽ *Pizza*

26 | 19 | 22 | $37

**Hollywood** | 641 N. Highland Ave. (Melrose Ave.) | 323-297-0101 | www.mozza-la.com

Mario Batali "has taken LA by storm" in partnership with Nancy Silverton, turning out "regional Italian" pies that "actually live up to the hype" with their "extravagantly bubbly" crust supporting an "amazing synthesis of ingredients" ("the fennel sausage is a definite favorite"); it's "so trendy it's almost silly", the "noise level is over the top" and seating's "tight", but the "buoyant" staff and "terrific", "affordable wine list" keep Hollywood customers "rejoicing"; P.S. "book a month" in advance, or arrive early and "eat at the bar to avoid a hellacious wait."

### Pizzicotto *Italian*

23 | 15 | 19 | $32

**Brentwood** | 11758 San Vicente Blvd. (bet. Gorham & Montana Aves.) | 310-442-7188

"You have to squeeze yourself into the narrow space with a shoehorn", but once you do the reward is "soul-warming" Italian dishes, an "accommodating" staff and the "occasional Brentwood notable" at this "true trattoria"; it's a "fine value" according to most, plus the upstairs area allows for slightly "roomier" and "quieter" dining.

### ⚡ Polo Lounge ☽ *Californian/Continental*

22 | 26 | 24 | $60

**Beverly Hills** | Beverly Hills Hotel | 9641 Sunset Blvd. (bet. Beverly & Crescent Drs.) | 310-887-2777 | www.beverlyhillshotel.com

"Dine with the rich and famous" in the Beverly Hills Hotel's "impeccable icon" boasting "well-manicured surroundings with old Hollywood sophistication" that set the stage for a "power breakfast" or a "heavenly" lunch among other "delicious" Cal-Continental meals, best

| | FOOD | DECOR | SERVICE | COST |
|---|---|---|---|---|

taken on the "gorgeous patio"; as the staff "treats you with respect" ("no matter how unimportant you are"), mavens call it a "must" to "take that special senior citizen in your life, especially if they're picking up the tab"; N.B. a late-night menu is served till 2 AM.

## Pomodoro Cucina Italiana *Italian* | 17 | 14 | 17 | $22 |

**West Hollywood** | 7100 Santa Monica Blvd. (La Brea Ave.) | 323-969-8000
**Manhattan Beach** | 401 Manhattan Beach Blvd. (Morningside Dr.) | 310-545-5401
**Burbank** | 201 E. Magnolia Blvd. (San Fernando Blvd.) | 818-559-1300
**Sherman Oaks** | 14622 Ventura Blvd. (Vesper Ave.) | 818-501-7400
**Woodland Hills** | 21600 Victory Blvd. (bet. Canoga & Owensmouth Aves.) | 818-340-2400
www.pastapomodoro.com
Additional locations throughout Southern California

"Good-quality" recipes "for a mini-chain" ("who would have thought you'd be craving Brussels sprouts?") keep these "midrange" Italians "one notch above Olive Garden" according to arbiters; though "servers can be a little lax sometimes", for the most part they "happily make substitutions" and kids don't mind the "cheap flatware."

## Poquito Más *Mexican* | 22 | 10 | 16 | $11 |

**West Hollywood** | 8555 Sunset Blvd. (Londonderry Pl.) | 310-652-7008
**West LA** | 2215 Westwood Blvd. (Olympic Blvd.) | 310-474-1998
**Torrance** | Rolling Hills Plaza | 2625 PCH (Crenshaw Blvd.) | 310-325-1001
**Burbank** | 2635 W. Olive Ave. (Buena Vista St.) | 818-563-2252
**North Hollywood** | 10651 Magnolia Blvd. (Cartwright Ave.) | 818-994-8226
**Studio City** | 3701 Cahuenga Blvd. W. (bet. Barham & Lankershim Blvds.) | 818-760-8226 ◗
**Woodland Hills** | 21049 Ventura Blvd. (Alhama Dr.) | 818-887-2007
**Valencia** | Valencia Town Ctr. | 24405 Town Center Dr. (McBean Pkwy.) | 661-255-7555
www.poquitomas.com

"You can watch the tortillas being made while you wait" for "perfect little tacos" and the "best shrimp burritos" among other "superior" fare at this "original fresh Mex" chain; a "courteous" counter staff and "reasonable" prices add to the appeal.

## Porky's BBQ *BBQ* | - | - | - | ⌐ |

**Inglewood** | 801 E. Manchester Blvd. (Osage Ave.) | 310-671-2900 | www.ribs123.com

Ample amounts of ribs and brisket are slow-cooked over hickory wood for about 16 hours at this unassuming Inglewood joint, which also offers Golden Bird fried chicken and sides like mac 'n' cheese and greens of the day; picnic tables and cafeteria-style service are available, though many customers opt for takeout and delivery;

## Porta Via *Californian* | 22 | 16 | 21 | $32 |

**Beverly Hills** | 424 N. Cañon Dr. (Santa Monica Blvd.) | 310-274-6534

Beverly Hills habitués head to this "comfortable" Californian "where everyone knows everyone" for "fab", "fresh" meals ("always check the specials board"); both the "terrific brunches" and "friendly folks" staffing the room are "popular", and while many say it's "best if you sit outside", a post-Survey remodel is expanding the formerly tight quarters.

| | FOOD | DECOR | SERVICE | COST |
|---|---|---|---|---|

### Porterhouse Bistro *Steak*

| | 20 | 18 | 20 | $45 |

**Beverly Hills** | 8635 Wilshire Blvd. (Carson Rd.) | 310-659-1099 | www.porterhousebistro.com

Now "reopened after having a fire", this Beverly Hills chophouse (and sib of Aphrodisiac) has refurbished, replacing its diner-style booths with party-friendly tables in the clean-lined space; it still offers "one of the best steak deals in LA" with its "bargain" prix fixe menu – four courses and two drinks for $39.50; while most agree the cooking is "solid", snobbier types sniff at "slow" service and say dinner here feels like "the early-bird special at the retirement community."

### Porto Alegre *Brazilian/Steak*

| | – | – | – | M |

**Pasadena** | Paseo Colorado | 260 E. Colorado Blvd. (Arroyo Pkwy.) | 626-744-0555

Pasadena patrons "love the endless" and "delicious" selection of meats "cut in front of you" at this new Brazilian churrascaria where it's best to arrive "hungry"; set inside a high-end shopping center, the large and somewhat "loud" dining room welcomes kids, as those between four and 10 years old eat for half-price.

### Porto's Bakery *Bakery*

| | – | – | – | I |

**Burbank** | 3614 W. Magnolia Blvd. (Cordova St.) | 818-846-9100
**Glendale** | 315 N. Brand Blvd. (California Ave.) | 818-956-5996
www.portosbakery.com

Plenty of people stop into these "Cuban delights" with "lots of hustle and bustle" for "flaky" pastries and impressively decorated cakes from the cafe/bakery's display case, but others wait in the "ever-present line" for a pressed *media noche* sandwich that's an "unbelievable deal"; trolling for a table is easier at the larger, newer Burbank cafe, but the Glendale "staple" is the beloved original of the pair.

### ☑ Prado *Caribbean*

| | 21 | 18 | 22 | $32 |

**Hancock Park** | 244 N. Larchmont Blvd. (bet. Beverly Blvd. & 1st St.) | 323-467-3871 | www.pradola.com

Caribbean "zing" intrigues palates at this Hancock Park "neighborhood" place providing "eclectic", "pleasurable" eats; "personal service", "cozy", "rustic" decor and good "value" also appeal to most customers, though a few "wish the menu had more going on."

### NEW Prana Cafe *Pan-Asian*

| | ▽ 22 | 17 | 16 | $17 |

**West Hollywood** | 650 N. La Cienega Blvd. (Melrose Pl.) | 310-360-0551

Opened by the adjacent Republic Restaurant in West Hollywood, this healthy, daytime-only Pan-Asian serves breakfast and lunch tinged with buzzwords like 'bee pollen' and 'egg white', along with items like the blackened chicken wrap; in a nod to its name, a Sanskrit word meaning 'vital energy', the casual, earth-toned setting strives to be both soothing and energizing.

### NEW Prime Grill *Steak*

| | ▽ 21 | 24 | 19 | $65 |

**Beverly Hills** | Rodeo Collection | 421 N. Rodeo Dr. (bet. Brighton Way & Little Santa Monica Blvd.) | 310-860-1233 | www.theprimegrill.com

A "chic" kosher steakhouse on Rodeo Drive, this multiroom newcomer (spun off from the New York original) impresses with "amazing" looks, amped up by luxe purple booths and outdoor cabanas, while satisfying appetites with sushi and "delicious" beef that's dry-aged in-house; though it strikes some as "expensive and pompous", others call it the kind of "cool" contender that "LA has been missing"; N.B. closed for Shabbat.

### Primitivo Wine Bistro *Mediterranean*    21 | 20 | 19 | $38

**Venice** | 1025 Abbot Kinney Blvd. (bet. Brooks Ave. & Westminster Ave.) | 310-396-5353 | www.primitivowinebistro.com
"People in-the-know ask for the back patio seating" unless they're game for a "shockingly loud happy hour" at this "dark" Venice Mediterranean "buzzing with energy" where samplers say you "must keep trying" the "flavorful small plates" and "wonderful" wines; although some caution it's "pretentious" and the bill "adds up", most agree the staff ably handles "small groups", "keeping everyone happy."

### Prizzi's Piazza *Italian*    22 | 18 | 19 | $29

**Hollywood** | 5923 Franklin Ave. (bet. Bronson Ave. & Gower St.) | 323-467-0168 | www.prizzispiazza.com
The "wholesome Italian food", including "great" Sicilian deep-dish pizza, features organic produce at this stone-floored Hollywood "haunt" whose regulars rave that the "garlic-soaked breadsticks" alone "are reason enough" to visit; despite complaints about the "actor" staff, service ratings have improved since last year.

### Prosecco *Italian*    ▽ 25 | 22 | 24 | $33

**Toluca Lake** | 10144 Riverside Dr. (Forman Ave.) | 818-505-0930
Toluca Lakers "highly recommend" this "charming neighborhood destination" for its "cut-above" Northern Italian fare like chicken lasagna and charred veal chop; the staff "takes care of you", the atmosphere is "pleasant" and the "cappuccinos are like dessert", making for a moderately priced "favorite."

### ☑ Providence *American*    27 | 24 | 26 | $84

**Hollywood** | 5955 Melrose Ave. (Cole Ave.) | 323-460-4170 | www.providencela.com
"Unstoppable" chef/co-owner Michael Cimarusti creates "absolutely sublime" New American seafood dishes ("of all stripes, colors and textures") at this "sensational" Hollywood "treasure chest" boasting a "memorable" tasting menu; the "seamless" staff "goes out its way to serve you" amid a room that's "elegant", "subdued" and enlivened by aquatic touches, so while it demands a bit of "bling", gastronomes deem it "the Holy Grail" of LA dining experiences.

### P6 Restaurant & Lounge *American*    20 | 24 | 20 | $43

**Westlake Village** | 2809 Agoura Rd. (Westlake Blvd.) | 805-778-0123 | www.p6lounge.com
"Young, rich" Westlake Villagers feel like they're "actually on the Westside" at this "ultrahip" New American that provides "visual interest" with midcentury modern touches and an outdoor fire pit; the addition of "excellent new chef" Robert Lia has epicureans applauding the "stylish" food – however, when they spy "cougars" and "swingers" swigging "fun cocktails" at the bar, some suspect "pickup joint" is its raison d'être.

| | FOOD | DECOR | SERVICE | COST |
|---|---|---|---|---|

**NEW Punch Grill** *American* | 18 | 18 | 20 | $37

**Santa Monica** | 3001 Wilshire Blvd. (Stanford St.) | 310-828-8812 | www.punchgrill.com

This "posh" New American addition to Santa Monica "fills the gap between trendy restaurants and family ones" according to fans who appreciate its "high-quality" cooking and "commendable wine selection", along with "happy-hour specials" in the lounge; its warm-toned, "elegant" space is staffed by "terrific" servers who "adeptly" cater to the sometimes "high-volume" "baby-boomer" crowd.

**Quincy's BBQ** *BBQ* | 15 | 12 | 16 | $21

**Encino** | 17201 Ventura Blvd. (Louise Ave.) | 818-784-6292

A "large, pet-friendly patio" is, for many people, the chief attraction at this Encino barbecue joint where "decent" ribs and "kids' plates called 'puppy chow'" are served at a "low price" in a "honky-tonk" setting that showcases photos of regulars with their dogs; it comes complete with free peanuts, so "you crunch your way across the floor."

**NEW Qusqo** ⑤Ⓜ *Peruvian* | – | – | – | I

**West LA** | 11633 Santa Monica Blvd. (Barry Ave.) | 310-312-3800 | www.qusqo.com

With a name that's worth lots of points on a Scrabble board, this stylish new Peruvian in West LA serves a menu of classic dishes that won't tax the wallet; it looks more like an art gallery than a restaurant, thanks to its unique works of art that line the darkly painted walls.

**NEW Raaga** *Indian* | – | – | – | M

**Chatsworth** | 10110 Topanga Canyon Blvd. (Devonshire St.) | 818-407-8898

Diners in the restaurant-challenged North Valley are singing the praises of this exceedingly authentic storefront Indian, decorated in handsome tones of green and yellow, with a menu featuring classic preparations of breads and tandoori dishes, along with house specialties like chicken hariyali (prepared with yogurt, green chiles and mint); there's pickled goat as well, for those seeking a culinary adventure.

**NEW Rack, The** ● *Californian* | ▽ 15 | 14 | 17 | $23

**Woodland Hills** | Westfield Promenade | 6100 Topanga Canyon Blvd. (bet. Erwin & Oxnard Sts.) | 818-716-0123 | www.therack.us

"Pool takes center stage" at this Woodland Hills establishment boasting 17 carved billiards tables as well as a cigar bar and smoking patio; although the Cal-cuisine concepts are often "not matched by the execution", its burgers, pizza and other standards can be "surprisingly good" and the "bosses are always coming around to say hi", so while some assess it "lacks atmosphere", others ask "where else can you have dinner" and shoot stick too?

**Radhika's** *Indian* | ▽ 18 | 16 | 19 | $25

**Pasadena** | 140 Shoppers Ln. (Cordova St.) | 626-744-0994 | www.radhikas.com

"The buffet is top drawer" for lunch and brunch at this Pasadena "performer for slightly upscale" Indian with "sauces that set it apart"; an "extremely attentive" staff brings a somewhat "formal" touch to the "cozy", "accommodating" atmosphere.

| | FOOD | DECOR | SERVICE | COST |
|---|---|---|---|---|

### Rae's ⊄ *Diner*
▽ 16 | 12 | 17 | $12

**Santa Monica** | 2901 Pico Blvd. (29th St.) | 310-828-7937

"It sure does the trick on a hungover Sunday morning" report reviewers of this restorative (but "unrestored") 1950s diner on the outer streets of Santa Monica, which delivers the "breakfast of anti-champions" headlined by the "best biscuits and gravy"; it's "greasy" and "cheap", and to cap it off the "waitresses really call you 'honey.'"

### ☑ Ragin' Cajun Cafe Ⓜ *Cajun*
21 | 16 | 19 | $20

**Hermosa Beach** | 422 Pier Ave. (PCH) | 310-376-7878 | www.ragincajun.com

"Crawfish cravings" meet their match with grub "as good as Cajun can be in LA" according to bayou buffs who "cram" inside this "quirky" Hermosa hang just blocks from the beach; a few dishes are "so spicy you'll be guzzlin' Dixie", but that means you'll fit right in amid the "kitschy" environs and "somewhat rowdy" atmosphere.

### Rainforest Cafe *American*
13 | 23 | 15 | $22

**Ontario** | Ontario Mills | 1 S. Mills Circle (4th St.) | 909-941-7979 | www.rainforestcafe.com

"Monkey screeches", "thunderstorms" and "gimmicky" "animated animals" supply the "sensory overload" "kids just love" at these American eateries with a "jungle atmosphere" ; veterans warn the "hectic" environs are "too noisy for talking", the "chain food" is "average" "at best", but it's a "party" geared toward parents, "toddlers and tourists" who can "go for the show, not the food."

### Rambutan Thai *Thai*
22 | 21 | 17 | $26

**Silver Lake** | 2835 W. Sunset Blvd. (Silver Lake Blvd.) | 213-273-8424 | www.rambutanthai.com

"Gourmet", "creative" Thai dishes and "fabulous" soju cocktails are served by a "decent" staff for "reasonable prices" at this "oasis in a run-down Silver Lake strip mall"; its "sleek", orange-accented dining room and bar suit the "cool" clientele who make it "practically a club scene" on weekend nights; P.S. prepare for "tight parking."

### NEW RA Sushi *Japanese*
▽ 18 | 18 | 18 | $29

**Torrance** | Del Amo Fashion Ctr. | 3525 W. Carson St. (Torrance Blvd.) | 310-370-6700 | www.rasushi.com

It's "trying hard to be trendy, and might get there" according to surveyors who've sampled this Torrance branch of an "amped-up" Asian fusion and sushi chain by Benihana; although the food and service get mixed reviews, many agree it's "rocking" with "music played at nightclub volume."

### Raymond, The Ⓜ *Californian*
24 | 23 | 24 | $45

**Pasadena** | 1250 S. Fair Oaks Ave. (Columbia St.) | 626-441-3136 | www.theraymond.com

"Go when you can settle in for a long, leisurely evening" advise lovers of this "charming converted bungalow" with "a series of intimate dining rooms" in which to savor "boutique Cabs with your steak or duck" among other "excellent" Californian fare, which may be sampled on a seven-course tasting menu; with "graceful" service and a "pretty patio" (just watch out when it's "chilly"), it channels "old-school Pasadena at its best."

| | FOOD | DECOR | SERVICE | COST |
|---|---|---|---|---|

### Real Food Daily  *Vegan*

| | 21 | 15 | 19 | $23 |

**West Hollywood** | 414 N. La Cienega Blvd. (bet. Beverly Blvd. & Melrose Ave.) | 310-289-9910
**Santa Monica** | 514 Santa Monica Blvd. (bet. 5th & 6th Sts.) | 310-451-7544
www.realfood.com

"Dynamite" vegan dishes earn this Westside duo a "stable roster of regulars" savoring "healthy", "guilt-free" riffs on meaty fare (club sandwiches, Salisbury seitan) that are kosher too at the "light, airy" WeHo branch; though the tab is "a little high" for some, the "competent" service and "classic cafeteria-style" setting allows you to "eat alone with a book and not feel weird."

### Red Corner Asia  *Thai*

| | ▽ 22 | 16 | 17 | $17 |

**East Hollywood** | 5267 Hollywood Blvd. (Normandie Ave.) | 323-466-6722 |
www.redcornerasia.com

"Good, clean Thai food at affordable prices" entices appetites at this East Hollywood shopping-center eatery; though "parking can get a little hairy" and a language barrier can impede service, the dining room wins points for its "upscale" vibe.

### Reddi Chick BBQ  ☒⊅ *BBQ*

| | 23 | 5 | 18 | $13 |

**Brentwood** | Brentwood Country Mart | 225 26th St. (San Vicente Blvd.) | 310-393-5238

"Finger-licking" BBQ, "rotisserie chicken" and "oh-so-tasty" fries are "worth every calorie" at this local "institution" – "a nostalgic kick" dating back to 1948 – in the Brentwood Country Mart; "cheap" tabs draw loyalists (and a few "celebs") who settle in on the patio by the "outdoor fireplace", while others simply opt for "takeout."

### Red Pearl Kitchen  *Pan-Asian*

| | 19 | 22 | 17 | $39 |

**NEW** **Hollywood** | 6703 Melrose Ave. (Citrus Ave.) | 323-525-1415 |
www.domainerestaurants.com

"Chinese kitschy cool" is the "hip" motif at Hollywood's "dark, sexy" Pan-Asian den by the Goodells (Dakota, 25 Degrees), proffering "spicy" "small plates" that are "good for groups", along with "innovative" cocktails; critics "see red", however, over "lackluster" service and sniff that the fare "doesn't measure up" to the "stunning", silk-adorned interior, but for the "moneyed" "young" "drink-and-party crowd", it "isn't really about the food, is it?"

### NEW Red Seven  ☒Ⓜ *Pan-Asian*

| | - | - | - | M |

**West Hollywood** | Pacific Design Ctr. | 700 N. San Vicente Blvd. (Melrose Ave.) | 310-289-1587

It might seem that Wolfgang Puck chose an odd name for this mid-priced eatery set in PDC's Blue Building, but the moniker is actually an homage to the soon-to-be-built Red Building; with lots of chrome and glass, the minimalist space is perfect for designistas, as is the Pan-Asian lunch and happy-hour menu (no dinner yet) complete with the popular Chinois chicken salad.

### NEW redwhite+bluezz  *American*

| | ▽ 21 | 22 | 22 | $46 |

**Pasadena** | 70 S. Raymond Ave. (Green St.) | 626-792-4441 |
www.redwhitebluezz.com

Locals "come for the entertainment and stay for the food" at this new Pasadena "joint" that's "jumpin'" with live blues and jazz every night and

| | FOOD | DECOR | SERVICE | COST |
|---|---|---|---|---|

during weekend brunch; meanwhile "memorable" (if "pricey") New American nibbles are paired with vintages from a "fantastic" list (30 by the glass) that's made more accessible by a "very knowledgeable" staff.

### Reed's M *Californian/French*

| | 21 | 17 | 21 | $36 |
|---|---|---|---|---|

**Manhattan Beach** | Manhattan Village Mall | 2640 N. Sepulveda Blvd. (bet. Marine & Rosecrans Aves.) | 310-546-3299 | www.reedsrestaurant.com

Despite its "unlikely location" in a Manhattan Beach mall, this "tiny" Cal-French "hideaway" packs a "surprising amount of atmosphere" with "personal" service and patio seating adding to the pleasantries; though diners divide on food ("consistently flavorful" vs. "declined"), "reasonable" prices still make it an "enjoyable" shopping "retreat."

### Reel Inn *Seafood*

| | 20 | 14 | 13 | $24 |
|---|---|---|---|---|

**Malibu** | 18661 PCH (Topanga Canyon Rd.) | 310-456-8221

"Truly the reel deal" exclaim afishionados of this "laid-back" Malibu "beach shack" that's "always jammed" for "cooked-to-order" seafood served "quickly" from a take-out window; those in-the-know grab a "cold beer" and a seat at one of the "communal picnic tables" and settle in for a "relaxing" end to "a perfect day at the beach."

### Z Republic *American*

| | 20 | 26 | 20 | $59 |
|---|---|---|---|---|

**West Hollywood** | 650 N. La Cienega Blvd. (Melrose Ave.) | 310-360-7070 | www.therepublicla.com

This "swanky" West Hollywood scenester spot marks a "triumph of style over substance" with its "over-the-top" decor that includes a waterfall, fire pit and 20-ft.-tall wine wall from which "leotard-clad female acrobats" retrieve pricey picks for patrons ("be sure to order from the top of the rack"); "imaginative" New American comfort fare may seem "gimmicky, but they pull it off", though some suggest you "skip dinner" and concentrate on the "great cocktails" and "people-watching."

### Ribs USA *BBQ*

| | 20 | 8 | 16 | $21 |
|---|---|---|---|---|

**Burbank** | 2711 W. Olive Ave. (bet. Buena Vista & Florence Sts.) | 818-841-8872 | www.ribsusa.com

"Sawdust" and "peanut shells on the floor" add "ambiance" to this "total dive" in Burbank serving up "tasty", "meaty" BBQ babyback ribs and the "hottest wings on the planet" all at "super" prices; cons call it "inconsistent", but it's still a local "favorite" for "families."

### NEW Riordan's Tavern S M *Steakhouse*

| | - | - | - | M |
|---|---|---|---|---|

**Downtown** | 875 S. Figueroa St. (9th St.) | 213-627-6879

Former Mayor Richard Riordan opened the Original Pantry Cafe and the adjacent Original Pantry Bakery more than a decade ago, but it's taken him this long to change the latter from a burger joint into this steakhouse that's rich with polished wood and a stamped tin ceiling; the walls offer a tribute to his years as Hizzoner, while the kitchen pays homage to his favorite food at decidedly democratic prices for Downtown.

### Z Ritz-Carlton Huntington Dining Room S M *Californian*

| | 26 | 27 | 26 | $69 |
|---|---|---|---|---|

**Pasadena** | Ritz-Carlton Huntington Hotel & Spa | 1401 S. Oak Knoll Ave. (Huntington Dr.) | 626-568-3900 | www.ritzcarlton.com

It's "first-class all the way" at this "wonderful retreat" in the Ritz-Carlton Huntington Hotel in Pasadena where "amazingly creative" chef Craig Strong prepares "sophisticated" seasonal Californian fare that's served in a "luxurious" chandeliered room where diners are "well taken care of"; in all, it's a "destination" that's "well worth" the "splurge" for any "special occasion" or even a "superb" Sunday brunch; N.B. jacket suggested.

### Rive Gauche Cafe Ⓜ French  | 20 | 22 | 20 | $35 |

**Sherman Oaks** | 14106 Ventura Blvd. (Hazeltine Ave.) | 818-990-3573
"Very romantic" say surveyors sweet on this Sherman Oaks "respite" serving "consistent", "old-style" French fare in "classy" quarters that include an especially "lovely patio area"; the less-enthused call it "stuffy" and say both the "outdated menu" and decor could "use a makeover."

### Riviera Restaurant & Lounge Italian  | 24 | 22 | 22 | $47 |

**Calabasas** | 23683 Calabasas Rd. (Park Granada) | 818-224-2163
"Creative spins on traditional Italian" bring the Calabasas crews to this "pricey" "neighborhood" "favorite" where "classically prepared" dishes are served up with "a few surprises"; "attentive" servers make all "feel welcome" though a few quibble that the "crowds" can make the "elegant" room decorated with Venetian glass light fixtures a little "noisy."

### Robin's Woodfire BBQ & Grill Ⓜ BBQ  | 17 | 13 | 17 | $22 |

**Pasadena** | 395 N. Rosemead Blvd. (Foothill Blvd.) | 626-351-8885 | www.robinsbbq.com
"Massive plates" of "down-home" BBQ await at this "casual", "family-friendly" Pasadena "joint" that's done up with small-town memorabilia like neon beer signs and "lots of old license plates" on the walls; service is spotty and critics claim it's "not memorable", but concede it "does the job" when you don't want to "drive down to Slauson."

### Rock 'N Fish Seafood/Steak  | 21 | 17 | 18 | $34 |

**Manhattan Beach** | 120 Manhattan Beach Blvd. (bet. Manhattan Ave. & Manhattan Bch.) | 310-379-9900 | www.rocknfishmb.com
"Always packed and deservedly so", this "raucous" Manhattan Beach steak 'n' seafooder is a "fun" spot where "stellar" dishes are always "fresh and well prepared", the wine list is "fabulous", service is "solid" and thanks to a "cool bar scene" "the eye candy isn't bad either"; its location "only steps from the pier" means "a stroll down the beach" is a post-dinner "must"; P.S. "reservations recommended."

### Rocky Cola Café Diner  | - | - | - | I |

**Hermosa Beach** | 1025 PCH (Aviation Blvd.) | 310-798-3111 ◖
**Montrose** | 2201 Honolulu Ave. (Verdugo Rd.) | 818-249-2233
**Whittier** | 6757 Greenleaf Ave. (Philadelphia St.) | 562-907-3377
Though the burgers and fries at this diner mini-chain are nothing out of the ordinary, the extensive "health-food" menu, featuring ostrich burgers, egg-white omelets and the like, is worth a try if you're craving guilt-free fast food; service is friendly and usually efficient, while the bright, '50s retro settings attract a family-friendly crowd.

### Roll 'n Rye Deli Deli  | 18 | 11 | 19 | $20 |

**Culver City** | Studio Village Shopping Ctr. | 10990 W. Jefferson Blvd. (Machado Rd.) | 310-390-3497
"New York–style" nosh (like "standout soups" and "tasty pastrami") is served in "very generous portions" and "without the attitude" at this

"dependable, if not exciting" Culver City deli; a few locals find it "vastly overpriced", and also suggest that those put off by "outdated" decor "order it to go."

**Romano's Macaroni Grill**  *Italian*          17 | 16 | 17 | $23

**Cerritos** | 12875 Towne Center Dr. (bet. Bloomfield Ave. & 183rd St.) | 562-916-7722
**El Segundo** | 2321 Rosecrans Ave. (Aviation Blvd.) | 310-643-0812
**Torrance** | Rolling Hills Plaza | 25352 S. Crenshaw Blvd. (Airport Dr.) | 310-534-1001
**Monrovia** | 945 W. Huntington Dr. (5th Ave.) | 626-256-7969
**Northridge** | Northridge Fashion Ctr. | 19400 Plummer St. (Tampa Ave.) | 818-725-2620
**Thousand Oaks** | Promenade Shopping Ctr. | 4000 E. Thousand Oaks Blvd. (Westlake Blvd.) | 805-370-1133
**Santa Clarita** | 25720 N. The Old Rd. (McBean Pkwy.) | 661-284-1850
www.macaronigrill.com

These "noisy" outposts of a national chain are "family favorites" for both the "comfortable" surroundings with "crayons" for the kiddies and "inexpensive", "mass-market" Italian fare that's "certainly good enough for when you don't feel like cooking"; in addition to "pleasant service" some locations have opera singers "roaming the restaurant", though not everyone appreciates the sometimes "off-key serenades."

**NEW Romanov**  *Russian/Steak*          - | - | - | E

**Studio City** | 12229 Ventura Blvd. (Laurel Canyon Blvd.) | 818-760-3177 | www.romanovla.com

In a space that looks like a modern vision of a czar's palace (complete with an eye-popping onion-dome chandelier), this upscale Russian in the middle of Studio City's busy shopping district is a trendy destination for those hungry for a taste of the old world as well as steaks and chops; it also offers an encyclopedic selection of Ruski vodka, including one that goes for $2,800 a bottle; N.B. open for dinner Friday and Saturday only.

**Z Roscoe's House of**          22 | 9 | 16 | $16
**Chicken 'n Waffles**  *Soul Food*

**Hollywood** | 1514 N. Gower St. (bet. Hollywood & Sunset Blvds.) | 323-466-7453 ●
**Mid-City** | 106 W. Manchester Ave. (S. Main St.) | 323-752-6211
**Mid-City** | 5006 W. Pico Blvd. (La Brea Ave.) | 323-934-4405 ●
**Long Beach** | 730 E. Broadway (bet. Alamitos & Atlantic Aves.) | 562-437-8355
**Pasadena** | 830 N. Lake Ave. (bet. Mountain St. & Orange Grove Blvd.) | 626-791-4890
www.roscoeschickenandwaffles.com

Fried chicken paired with "syrup-and-butter-soaked waffles" proves a "Nobel prize"-worthy combination at this LA chain "phenomenon" where "all races and ages" join "ever-present lines" for "quality soul food" with "mouthwatering sides"; sure, it's "a heart attack on a plate", "but who cares?" - risk it "at least once" and experience firsthand the wood-paneled decor with "'70s charm" and sometimes "short-tempered servers" ("pretty entertaining as long as you don't take them too seriously").

|  | FOOD | DECOR | SERVICE | COST |
|---|---|---|---|---|

### Rose Cafe *Californian* | 18 | 16 | 17 | $22

**Venice** | 220 Rose Ave. (Main St.) | 310-399-0711 |
www.rosecafe.com

A "favorite among the arty crowd", this "sunny" Venice spot is "sure
to satisfy" with its "fresh", "healthy" Californian menu that some say
"can't be beat for breakfast" or a "relaxing" lunch; patrons "order at
the counter" or sit on the "delightful" patio (with table service), often
checking out the rotating art displays and "wonderful gift shop"
before they leave.

### Rosti *Italian* | 17 | 13 | 17 | $22

**Beverly Hills** | 233 S. Beverly Dr. (bet. Olympic & Wilshire Blvds.) |
310-275-3285
**Santa Monica** | 931 Montana Ave. (10th St.) | 310-393-3236
**Encino** | Encino Mktpl. | 16403 Ventura Blvd. (Hayvenhurst Ave.) |
818-995-7179
**Westlake Village** | Promenade at Westlake | 160 Promenade Way
(Thousand Oaks Blvd.) | 805-370-1939
www.rostituscankitchen.com

Time-pressed types find this Tuscan chain – and its "tasty" rose-
mary roast chicken – a "dependable" option "for weekday takeout"
or an "easy" lunch or dinner; service "varies, a lot" but it's "inexpensive" and the surroundings are "pleasant" enough with patios
at all locations.

### NEW Royale *American* | ▽ 18 | 22 | 18 | $45

**Mid-Wilshire** | Wilshire Royale Hotel | 2619 Wilshire Blvd. (Rampart Blvd.) |
213-388-8488 | www.royaleonwilshire.com

Few have found this New American eatery housed in the historic
Wilshire Royale Hotel, but those who have laud the "upscale comfort-
food" menu with its emphasis on "quality ingredients" and "affordable
wines"; the "fashionable" 1920s throwback decor includes soaring
ceilings, subway tiles and an indoor patio with a pool.

### Z Roy's *Hawaiian* | 24 | 22 | 22 | $47

**Downtown** | 800 S. Figueroa St. (8th St.) | 213-488-4994
**Woodland Hills** | 6363 Topanga Canyon Blvd. (Victory Blvd.) |
818-888-4801
www.roysrestaurant.com

"The best Hawaiian export since Don Ho" claim those "wowed" by the
"imaginative" and "beautifully presented" Asian fusion dishes at Roy
Yamaguchi's "pricey" SoCal spin-offs of his Honolulu original; though
the "well-trained staff" strike many as "exceptional", a rising minority
complains it's left "disappointed" by "unfulfilled expectations" and
"too-sweet" fare, leading some to wonder if this chain is "just
getting too big."

### R23 Z *Japanese* | 26 | 22 | 21 | $49

**Little Tokyo** | 923 E. Second St. (bet. Alameda St. & Santa Fe Ave.) |
213-687-7178 | www.r23.com

Devotees who "dream about the crab salad", "fabulous sushi" and
"stellar" dishes like the lobster tempura prize this Little Tokyo "secret"
on "skid row"; the "thoughtful" staff is "always happy to answer questions", while the "minimalist", "arty" interior enhances the "first-
class" meals in an "unlikely" locale.

| | FOOD | DECOR | SERVICE | COST |
|---|---|---|---|---|

**Ruby's** *Diner* | 16 | 16 | 17 | $16

**Rolling Hills** | Avenue of the Peninsula Mall | 550 Deep Valley Dr. (Crossfield Dr.) | 310-544-7829
**LAX** | LA Int'l Airport | 209 World Way (Terminal 6) | 310-646-2480
**Redondo Beach** | 245 N. Harbor Dr. (Beryl St.) | 310-376-7829
**Woodland Hills** | Westfield Promenade | 6100 Topanga Canyon Blvd. (bet. Erwin & Oxnard Sts.) | 818-340-7829
**Whittier** | Whittwood Mall | 10109 Whittwood Ln. (Cullen St.) | 562-947-7829
www.rubys.com
Additional locations throughout Southern California

OC's "classic" chain of "upbeat", "retro-hamburger" joints offers "tasty" "soda-fountain fare" including "crispy fries" and "shakes enough for two"; branches vary according to "local flavor", so sites with an "ocean view" are "particularly fun", especially for kids who are treated with "infinite patience" by the "cute" staff.

**NEW Ruen Pair** ● *Thai* | ∇ 21 | 12 | 17 | $15

**East Hollywood** | 5257 Hollywood Blvd. (Western Ave.) | 323-466-0153

"You'd think you were in Bangkok" declare devotees of this East Hollywood "gem" who visit "as often as [they] can" for "authentic" Thai dishes that don't skimp on "spiciness"; though some grumble that the "portions have shrunk" after a recent revamp, it's still a "relaxing", low-key spot with "cheap" tabs, "prompt" service and an eclectic "late-night" crowd (till 4 AM).

**Russell's Burgers** *Diner* | ∇ 17 | 12 | 15 | $15

**Pasadena** | 30 N. Fair Oaks Ave. (bet. Colorado Blvd. & Union St.) | 626-578-1404

Pasadena's "better-than-average" coffee shop is under new ownership but it still turns out the same "juicy burgers", "thick shakes" and "mile-high meringue pies" of its past in "no pretensions" surroundings; "weekend mornings" are especially "popular" when "repeat customers" line up for "solid" breakfasts.

**NEW Rustic Canyon** *Californian/Mediterranean* | 21 | 19 | 21 | $46

**Santa Monica** | 1119 Wilshire Blvd. (bet. 11th & 12th Sts.) | 310-393-7050 | www.rusticcanyonwinebar.com

"Perfectly fresh ingredients" sourced from the Santa Monica farmer's market take the spotlight at this "unpretentious" newcomer where "imaginative" Cal-Med dishes (including several small-plates options) are paired with wines from a "smart" list; "informed and enthusiastic" servers and a "happening" vibe mean it's off to a "great start", though a few find it "hampered" by "too-tight seating" and "deafening" noise levels.

**Rustico** *Italian* | 23 | 19 | 23 | $37

**Westlake Village** | 1125 Lindero Canyon Rd. (off Kanan Rd.) | 818-889-0191 | www.rustico-restaurant.com

This "bustling" Westlake Village "neighborhood" eatery is "worth seeking out" say surveyors smitten with its "wonderful", "modern" Italian cuisine served in "generous" portions; the "warm" atmosphere is made all the more "inviting" by "friendly" servers and "reasonable" prices too; N.B. they no longer serve lunch.

| | FOOD | DECOR | SERVICE | COST |
|---|---|---|---|---|

**Z Ruth's Chris Steak House** *Steak* | 25 | 21 | 23 | $59 |

**Beverly Hills** | 224 S. Beverly Dr. (bet. Olympic & Wilshire Blvds.) | 310-859-8744

**Pasadena** | 369 E. Colorado Blvd. (bet. Euclid & Los Robles Aves.) | 626-583-8122

**Woodland Hills** | Westfield Promenade | 6100 Topanga Canyon Blvd., Ste. 1360 (bet. Erwin & Oxnard Sts.) | 818-227-9505
www.ruthschris.com

"Sizzling steaks" are "slathered in butter" and "served on hot plates" by "professional waiters" at these "old-fashioned"-feeling branches of the national chain; a few bemoan "bare-minimum presentation" ("at least place an attractive, colorful garnish somewhere on there") and "outlandish prices", but say they're "satisfying" nonetheless.

**Z Saddle Peak Lodge M** *American* | 26 | 26 | 24 | $63 |

**Calabasas** | 419 Cold Canyon Rd. (Piuma Rd.) | 818-222-3888 | www.saddlepeaklodge.com

"Wealthy cowboys" "eat like real men" at this "secluded", "romantic" and "expensive" Calabasas spot set in "rustic" "hunting lodge"-like quarters with an "extraordinary" menu of "exquisite" game dishes (like elk tenderloin and "terrific" wild boar sausages) and a "very good wine selection"; it's a "unique" "adventure", one that's suited to a myriad of "special occasions", just not to "vegans."

**Saddle Ranch Chop House ●** *Steak* | 16 | 18 | 16 | $27 |

**West Hollywood** | 8371 Sunset Blvd. (bet. Crescent Heights & La Cienega Blvds.) | 323-656-2007

**Universal City** | 666 Universal Hollywood Dr. (off Rte. 101) | 818-760-9680
www.srrestaurants.com

"There's never a dull moment" at these "cheesy", "Old West"–styled eateries on the Sunset Strip and Universal City's CityWalk where "wannabes" and "tourists" "crowd" in for *Flintstone*-sized portions" of "chain-quality" steaks, "huge drinks" and a mechanical bull (word to the wise: "ride before you eat") when it "gets crazy later on" when this meatery turns into a "meat market" and even the "ridiculously good-looking waiters" "aren't opposed to flirting with your date."

**NEW Safire** *American* | – | – | – | M |

**Camarillo** | 4850 Santa Rosa Rd. (Verdugo Way) | 805-389-1227

Manning the impressive display kitchen at this West Valley New American is Michael Muirhead, former sous-chef under Lee Hefter at Spago Beverly Hills; the midpriced innovative fare includes Californian-style pizzas prepared in a wood-burning oven and served in a Tuscan-like setting of brown and deep yellow hues.

**Sagebrush Cantina** *Southwestern* | 14 | 15 | 14 | $24 |

**Calabasas** | 23527 Calabasas Rd. (El Canon Ave.) | 818-222-6062 | www.sagebrushcantina.com

"The human scenery can't be beat" at this "hugely popular" "laid-back" "saloon" in Calabasas where "yuppies", "bikers" and "the Valley's porn community" down "icy long-neck beers" and Southwestern fare on the "sunny patio" that plays host to "a hot party scene" on "Sundays"; those who complain about "indifferent" service and "so-so" menu miss the point – "it's all about the ambiance."

| | FOOD | DECOR | SERVICE | COST |
|---|---|---|---|---|

### Sai Sai ⚅ *Japanese* — 17 | 17 | 17 | $43

**Downtown** | Millennium Biltmore Hotel | 501 S. Olive St. (5th St.) |
213-624-1100 | www.milleniumhotels.com

At this Japanese in the "beautiful" Millennium Biltmore Downtown,
"technically" prepared "high-end" sushi makes it an "elegant" choice,
especially for "lunch"; otherwise critics contend the "fare falls short"
while tabs don't, and say service "needs to improve."

### Saito's Sushi ⚅⊘ *Japanese* — ▽ 25 | 9 | 21 | $37

**Silver Lake** | 4339 W. Sunset Blvd. (Fountain Ave.) | 323-663-8890

"A mostly undiscovered Silver Lake treasure", this "reasonably priced"
sushi joint lures locals for "master" chef Saito Taka's "personal interpretations" of usually "ordinary" dishes utilizing "extremely fresh"
fish; despite "hole-in-the-wall" decor and the "strip-mall" setting, it
gets "slammed on weekends" by those seeking his "expertise."

### Saketini *Asian Fusion* — ▽ 20 | 14 | 20 | $31

**Brentwood** | 150 S. Barrington Ave. (Sunset Blvd.) | 310-440-5553

"Personalized attention from a creative chef" keeps locals "going
back" for "fresh takes" on Asian dishes at this "tiny" Brentwood fusion
spot featuring 12 different flavors of its signature cocktails; "lunch
specials" and "friendly service" are additional niceties, though some
say the "tiny" minimalist digs "need updating."

### Saladang *Thai* — 24 | 19 | 20 | $24

**Pasadena** | 363 S. Fair Oaks Ave. (bet. California & Del Mar Blvds.) |
626-793-8123

### Saladang Song *Thai*

**Pasadena** | 383 S. Fair Oaks Ave. (bet. California & Del Mar Blvds.) |
626-793-5200

"Inventive", "perfectly seasoned" dishes await at these "sensational",
"side-by-side" Thais in Pasadena set in "modern" digs where the
"pretty waitresses" will adjust orders to "accommodate the most mas-
ochistic of taste buds"; fans find them "tough to get into" sighing "if
only they took reservations, they would be perfect"; P.S. Saladang is
the "older", more "traditional" of the two.

### NEW Salades de Provence ⚅Ⓜ *French* — - | - | - | I

**West Hollywood** | 1040 N. La Cienega Blvd. (Santa Monica Blvd.) |
310-666-8367 | www.saladesdeprovence.com

This cheerful French newcomer with sunny yellow walls offers
Boystown a menu of casual dishes that mirror the food served by the
owner's relatives at their restaurant in – where else? – Provence; those
with a sweet tooth may want to make note of the many dessert crêpes
as well as the gelato bar adjacent to the counter.

### Salt Creek Grille *Steak* — 18 | 19 | 17 | $34

**NEW El Segundo** | Plaza El Segundo | 2015 E. Park Pl. (Sepulveda Blvd.) |
310-335-9288
**Valencia** | Valencia Town Ctr. | 24415 Town Center Dr. (McBean Pkwy.) |
661-222-9999
www.saltcreekgrille.com

"Consistent, but unspectacular" is the consensus about this "casual
and comfy" chophouse chain where a "fairly standard" (though
"somewhat overpriced") menu of steaks and seafood is proffered by a

|  | FOOD | DECOR | SERVICE | COST |
|---|---|---|---|---|

"well-trained" staff; live music at all locations "is a definite plus", as is patio dining and a "lively" bar scene.

**NEW Saluzzi** ⓜ *Italian*                            — | — | — | E

**Rancho Palos Verdes** | Golden Cove Ctr. | 31206 Palos Verdes Dr. W. (Hawthorne Blvd.) | 310-377-7200 | www.saluzziristorante.com

This newcomer with a portion of the Sistine Chapel replicated on its coved ceiling brings a touch of Italy to Rancho Palos Verdes; its pricey, daily changing menu offers elegant preparations of old-school dishes, and the view of the Pacific from the outdoor patio is beyond dazzling.

**Z Sam's by**                            26 | 21 | 27 | $48
**the Beach** ⓜ *Californian/Mediterranean*

**Santa Monica** | 108 W. Channel Rd. (PCH) | 310-230-9100

"Charming owner" Sam "knows how to treat his customers" at this "unpretentious" Santa Monica "treasure" where a "flavorful" Cal-Mediterranean menu balances traditional "Middle-Eastern–inspired" dishes with more "eclectic" selections (all are paired with wines from "a gem" of a list); prices are "fair" for the "quality" while the "cozy" bistro-style interior has a "homey" feel enhanced by "gracious" service.

**Sam Woo** *Chinese*                            20 | 10 | 12 | $20

**Chinatown** | 727 N. Broadway (bet. Alpine & Ord Sts.) | 213-687-7236 ⓢ ⓜ
**Chinatown** | 803 N. Broadway (Alpine St.) | 213-687-7238 ●⊄
**Cerritos** | 19008 Pioneer Blvd. (South St.) | 562-865-7278
**Van Nuys** | 6450 Sepulveda Blvd. (Victory Blvd.) | 818-988-6813
**Alhambra** | 514 W. Valley Blvd. (bet. 5th & 6th Sts.) | 626-281-0038 ●⊄
**Montebello** | 2809 Via Campo (bet. N. Garfield & N. Wilcox Aves.) | 323-888-1700 ⓢ ⓜ
**Monterey Park** | 634 W. Garvey Ave. (bet. N. Chandler & N. Moore Aves.) | 626-289-4858 ●⊄
**San Gabriel** | 140 W. Valley Blvd. (Manley Dr.) | 626-572-8418
**San Gabriel** | 425 S. California St. (Agostino Rd.) | 626-287-6528 ⓢ ⓜ

"The setting may be average but the food isn't" at this "always busy" chain offering dim sum and BBQ among other Chinese specialties; followers wooed by "authentic" dishes like "can't-miss" Peking duck or "writhing"-fresh whole fish ("be prepared to meet your entree") deem them "the cheapest trip to Hong Kong ever", so they accept "no-frills" decor and endure "spotty" service with an often "dismal attitude."

**Sandbag's Gourmet**                            18 | 9 | 17 | $10
**Sandwiches** *Sandwiches*

**Downtown** | 818 Wilshire Blvd. (bet. Figueroa & Flower Sts.) | 213-228-1920 ⓢ
**Mid-Wilshire** | 6404 Wilshire Blvd. (bet. San Vicente Blvd. & S. Fairfax Ave.) | 323-655-4250 ⓢ
**West Hollywood** | 9255 Sunset Blvd. (W. Sunset Blvd.) | 310-888-0112 ⓢ
**Beverly Hills** | 9497 Santa Monica Blvd. (Rodeo Dr.) | 310-786-7878
**Brentwood** | 11640 San Vicente Blvd. (Bringham Ave.) | 310-207-4888
**Westwood** | 1134 Westwood Blvd. (Wilshire Blvd.) | 310-208-1133 ⓢ
**Long Beach** | 425 E. PCH (Long Beach Blvd.) | 562-591-7699
**Glendale** | 138 S. Brand Blvd. (bet. B'way & Colorado St.) | 818-241-0740

"Unique sandwiches" in countless "varieties" get a boost from a "free cookie in every bag" at this franchised chain that pros proclaim a "great value" for a "quick" lunch; critics feel sandbagged by "underwhelming" eats they find "overpriced" as well.

### San Gennaro Cafe *Italian* | 16 | 12 | 19 | $26 |

**Brentwood** | 140 S. Barrington Pl. (Sunset Blvd.) | 310-476-9696 | www.sangennarocafe.com

An "exhaustive menu" of "New York–style" Italian dishes (including "decent" pizzas and pastas) and "cheap by-the-glass wines" appeal to "neighborhood" "families" at this "comfortable", "no-frills" Brentwood "trattoria"; some say "you can do a lot better" elsewhere, but it remains a "standby" nonetheless.

### Sapori *Italian* | ▽ 24 | 21 | 23 | $33 |

**Marina del Rey** | Fishermans Vill. | 13723 Fiji Way (Lincoln Blvd.) | 310-821-1740 | www.sapori-mdr.com

"Small but mighty", this "relatively undiscovered" Italiano in Marina del Rey is a "solid option" for "waterside" dining, offering "superb" signatures ("try the branzino"), "personal service", "pretty views" and an outdoor patio, all at moderate prices; it's a good place to "take a babe and enjoy the night."

### Sassi Mediterranean *Mediterranean* | ▽ 19 | 10 | 16 | $26 |

**Encino** | 15622 Ventura Blvd. (Haskell Ave.) | 818-986-5345 | www.sassirestaurant.com

"Tasty" kosher fare is served in "huge portions" at this Encino Mediterranean "find" where patio seating augments otherwise barebones decor; if a few quibble it's "unreasonably expensive", it stays "crowded" nonetheless; N.B. closed Friday nights and Saturdays.

### Sea Empress *Chinese* | 19 | 13 | 16 | $23 |

**Gardena** | Pacific Sq. | 1636 W. Redondo Beach Blvd. (bet. Normandie & Western Aves.) | 310-538-6868

"A blessing" for South Bay denizens, this Gardena Chinese offers an almost "Monterey Park–caliber" dim sum experience "without the drive" and at nice prices as well; just "stick with the seafood dishes" brought out by the "relatively attentive" staff and ignore the "crowded" room that "could use a face-lift."

### ☑ Sea Harbour *Chinese/Seafood* | 25 | 16 | 17 | $29 |

**Rosemead** | 3939 N. Rosemead Blvd. (Valley Blvd.) | 626-288-3939

Diners are delighted to be "freed from the point-and-get approach to dim sum" at this "attractive" Rosemead Cantonese that eschews the "rolling carts" and ferries "outstanding", "freshly steamed" creations "from the kitchen to your table directly"; service is "brusque", though "efficient", but regulars urge "go early" or "prepare to starve as you wait in line."

### Second City Bistro *American* | 22 | 21 | 20 | $35 |

**El Segundo** | 223 Richmond St. (Grand Ave.) | 310-322-6085 | www.secondcitybistro.com

"Tucked away" in El Segundo, this "low-key" New American serves up "imaginative" "bistro food" and "excellent wines" in a "warm" "warehouse"-style interior with exposed brick and an open kitchen (there's also an outdoor patio with "moon views"); "accommodating" servers could probably use "better training", but fans still find it a "shining light" in the local dining scene and a "great value" as well.

|  | FOOD | DECOR | SERVICE | COST |
|--|------|-------|---------|------|

### Señor Fred ⬤ *Mexican*

17 | 19 | 16 | $29

**Sherman Oaks** | 13730 Ventura Blvd. (Woodman Ave.) | 818-789-3200 | www.senorfred.com

"Perfect for a night on the town with your Goth amigos", this "dark", "velvet curtained" Sherman Oaks Mexican draws a "hip" Valley crowd for a "happening bar scene" fueled by "strong margaritas"; "innovative" Mexican eats can be "hit-or-miss" and "overpriced" as well, but diners dig the "sexy" vibe nonetheless.

### Seoul Jung *Korean*

▽ 22 | 22 | 21 | $44

**Downtown** | Wilshire Grand | 930 Wilshire Blvd. (Figueroa St.) | 213-688-7880 | www.wilshiregrand.com

"It's not as funky" as its "more obscure" K-town neighbors, but this Downtown Korean in the Wilshire Grand still delivers "authentic" fare that makes for a "fine" meal; if the cost-conscious call it "a tad expensive", remember it's one of the more "elegant" of the cook-it-yourself meateries, catering to "a corporate crowd" and "flight attendants" on stopover.

### NEW 750 ml *French*

- | - | - | M

**South Pasadena** | 966 Mission St. (Prospect Ave.) | 626-799-0711

Steven Arroyo's (Cobras & Matadors) new South Pasadena bistro – named for the volume of a typical bottle of wine – serves small portions of French fare from a short seasonal menu designed to pair well with the many vintages served by the glass; while convenient to the Gold Line train station, it's higher-end than the typical eateries nearby.

### 17th Street Cafe *Californian*

19 | 15 | 19 | $26

**Santa Monica** | 1610 Montana Ave. (bet. 16th & 17th Sts.) | 310-453-2771

An "attitude-free oasis" on Santa Monica's Montana Avenue, this "comfortable" Californian satisfies "stroller moms" and "ladies who lunch" with a "huge" selection of salads, sandwiches, "seasonal" specials and baked goods (like "yummy muffins"); "accommodating" servers work the "bright, open" room at this "neighborhood" "staple" that draws "a line out the door" on Sundays for its "outstanding brunch."

### Shabu Shabu House Ⓜ *Japanese*

23 | 10 | 16 | $21

**Little Tokyo** | 127 Japanese Village Plaza Mall (bet. E. 1st & 2nd Sts.) | 213-680-3890

"So tender, so phenomenal" sigh surveyors of the "nicely marbled" beef at this "always crowded" Little Tokyo Japanese "joint" where the boil-your-own meats and veggies are accompanied by dipping sauces "so good you could drink them straight from the dish"; add in "affordable" tabs and it's "worth the excruciating waits", even with "rushed" service and "bare-bones" decor.

### NEW Shabu Shabu Ya *Japanese*

▽ 15 | 15 | 21 | $30

**La Brea** | 801 S. La Brea Ave. (8th St.) | 323-933-3229

"Decent, but not stellar" is the consensus on this new shabu-shabu on La Brea, where the Japanese hot pot meals come in "small portions" and "outrageous" prices leave some diners declaring "you could do better" elsewhere; "helpful" service is one bright spot while others appreciate the lack of "long lines."

|  | FOOD | DECOR | SERVICE | COST |
|---|---|---|---|---|

### Shack, The  *American*  | 18 | 11 | 14 | $14 |

**Playa del Rey** | 185 Culver Blvd. (Vista del Mar) | 310-823-6222
**Santa Monica** | 2518 Wilshire Blvd. (26th St.) | 310-449-1171
www.the-shacks.com

"The incredible Shackburger", topped with "spicy" Louisiana hotlinks, is the highlight of the inexpensive American menu at this "sawdust"-style "sports bar" mini-chain popular with "college students" and "locals"; on Sundays during football season, "prepare to be over-whelmed" by Philly Eagles fans who've claimed the Santa Monica location as their own.

### Shaherzad  *Persian*  | 22 | 13 | 16 | $25 |

**Westwood** | 1422 Westwood Blvd. (bet. Santa Monica & Wilshire Blvds.) | 310-470-9131

"Heaping plates" of "tasty" grilled meats and veggies "atop mountains of beautifully seasoned rice" are paired with "fresh-baked bread" from the in-house tandoor at this casual Westwood Persian that pros pro-claim a "transporting" "cultural experience" and a "bargain" too; digs are "family-friendly", though many opt for "takeout."

### Sharky's Mexican Grill  *Mexican*  | 17 | 12 | 15 | $12 |

**Hollywood** | 1716 N. Cahuenga Blvd. (Hollywood Blvd.) | 323-461-7881
**Beverly Hills** | 435 N. Beverly Dr. (bet. Brighton Way & Santa Monica Blvd.) | 310-858-0202
**Long Beach** | 51 The Paseo (Pine Ave.) | 562-435-2700
**Pasadena** | 841 Cordova St. (Lake Ave.) | 626-568-3500
**Burbank** | Burbank Empire Ctr. | 1791 N. Victory Pl. (Empire Ave.) | 818-840-9080
**Calabasas** | Creekside Village Shopping Ctr. | 26527 Agoura Rd. (Las Virgenes Rd.) | 818-880-0885
**Sherman Oaks** | 13238 Burbank Blvd. (Fulton Ave.) | 818-785-2533
**Tarzana** | 5511 Reseda Blvd. (1 block north of Ventura Blvd.) | 818-881-8760
**Simi Valley** | 2410 Sycamore Dr. (Cochran St.) | 805-522-2270
**Westlake Village** | 111 S. Westlake Blvd. (Thousand Oaks Blvd.) | 805-370-3701
www.sharkys.com
Additional locations throughout Southern California

The food is "not exactly authentic", but these "above-average" Mexican outposts are still praised for their "fresh", "healthy" ap-proach that utilizes mostly "organic" ingredients and "certainly tastes better than the processed junk at most chains"; the less-impressed call them "overrated" with "slow" counter service, but even critics ad-mit they work "in a pinch" and prices are "decent" too.

### Shima  🈐🅼  *Japanese*  ▽ | 25 | 24 | 22 | $50 |

**Venice** | 1432 Abbot Kinney Blvd. (bet. California Ave. & Palm St.) | 310-314-0882

"Simply amazing" say neighborhood denizens in awe of chef Yoshi Shigenobu's "healthy" Venice Japanese where he turns out "delicate" pieces of brown-rice sushi, "homemade tofu" and other "satisfying" (and "expensive") dishes that pair well with a selection of organic wines and vegan desserts; the "stylish, modern" light-filled space cre-ates a "Zen atmosphere" that diners deem "relaxing" and "never rushed" despite sentiments that "service could pick up a step or two."

|  | FOOD | DECOR | SERVICE | COST |
|--|------|-------|---------|------|

**Z Shiro M** *French/Japanese* | 27 | 17 | 24 | $49 |

**South Pasadena** | 1505 Mission St. (bet. Fair Oaks & Fremont Aves.) | 626-799-4774 | www.restaurantshiro.com

"Serious eaters" seek out this South Pasadena "landmark" that still "wows them every time" with "master" chef-owner Hideo Yamashiro's "memorable" Franco-Japanese creations, including the "must-have" deep-fried ginger catfish (served "head and all") that's the "definition of sublime"; "superb" service from the "friendly" staff overcomes minimal decor and somewhat high prices, though insiders insist the "Wednesday Night Bistro Dinner" ($30.50 for three courses) is a "great deal."

**SHU** *Italian/Japanese* | ▽ 20 | 17 | 17 | $45 |

**Bel-Air** | The Glen | 2932½ Beverly Glen Circle (Mulholland Dr.) | 310-474-2740 | www.shusushi.com

Sushi gets an "Italian twist" at this stylish Bel-Air Japanese backed by Giacomino Drago (Il Pastaio, Piccolo Paradiso) with Kenny Yamada's (Katsu-Ya) "interesting interpretations" deemed "creative", if "hit-or-miss"; despite "expensive" tabs and a "noisy" setting, it's a "fun" spot for "star sightings", particularly if you're "already in the neighborhood."

**Simon LA** *American* | 21 | 24 | 20 | $56 |

**West Hollywood** | Sofitel Los Angeles | 8555 Beverly Blvd. (La Cienega Blvd.) | 310-278-5444 | www.sofitel.com

"Skinny model types" and other "under-35" West Hollywood dwellers "nibble" on "celebrity chef" Kerry Simon's "playful" renditions of American "classics" in this "so hip it hurts" destination in the Sofitel LA, where the dining experience is bookended by a "fabulous" bread basket and "infamous" junk-food dessert sampler; no surprise, prices are "high" and service can be "snooty" "as is to be expected in this type" of "swanky" spot, leaving a disappointed few to muse that "like the cotton candy they serve, it's more fluff than substance."

**NEW Simpang Asia** *Indonesian* | - | - | - | I |

**West LA** | 10433 National Blvd. (Motor Ave.) | 310-815-9075 | www.simpangasia.com

This new Indonesian cafe/market in West LA looks like a neighborhood joint in Jakarta, with its handful of Formica-topped tables; its friendly staff will explain the difference between *soto betawi* (beef soup with tripe and tendons) and *soto ayam* (chicken soup with lime), while the retail area carries everything you need to make the food yourself at home.

**Z Sir Winston's** *Continental* | 23 | 27 | 24 | $60 |

**Long Beach** | Queen Mary | 1126 Queen's Hwy. (south of I-710) | 562-499-1657 | www.queenmary.com

"Close your eyes and imagine you're sailing across the ocean" at this "old-world" "destination" set inside the Queen Mary cruise ship docked in Long Beach with "impressive" Cal-Continental cuisine; service evokes the "grand style" of "days gone by" while "excellent views of the water" make it a "splurge" worthy of a "romantic" dinner or another "special occasion."

### Sisley Italian Kitchen  *Italian*

| 18 | 16 | 17 | $27 |

**West LA** | Westside Pavilion | 10800 W. Pico Blvd. (bet. Overland Ave. & Westwood Blvd.) | 310-446-3030
**Sherman Oaks** | 15300 Ventura Blvd. (Sepulveda Blvd.) | 818-905-8444
**Thousand Oaks** | Oaks Mall | 446 W. Hillcrest Dr. (bet. Lynn Rd. & McCloud Ave.) | 805-777-7511
**Valencia** | Valencia Town Ctr. | 24201 Valencia Blvd. (McBean Pkwy.) | 661-287-4444

"They're nothing spectacular", but these Italian outposts are "solid" bets for "plentiful portions" of a "wide variety" of "salads, pastas and entrees" as well as the "warm bread sticks" that "may be their best feature"; service comes "without a lot of hassle", and "reasonable prices" mean they're often favored by "families" for a "quick bite" after a "movie" or "shopping."

### Sky Room  🅢 *American*

| 21 | 25 | 23 | $60 |

**Long Beach** | The Historic Breakers Bldg. | 40 S. Locust Ave. (Ocean Blvd.) | 562-983-2703 | www.theskyroom.com

"Long Beach's version of NYC's Rainbow Room", this "blast from the past" set atop the Historic Breakers Building is a "perfect place" for "romance or celebration" with "stunning views", "sophisticated" New American cuisine, "live bands" and "divine" dancing; "formal" service (including "top-hatted" hosts) is somewhat "doting" and befitting of the high prices.

### Smitty's Grill  *American*

| 21 | 20 | 21 | $38 |

**Pasadena** | 110 S. Lake Ave. (bet. Cordova & Green Sts.) | 626-792-9999 | www.smittysgrill.com

"Always hustling and bustling at night", this Pasadena American "crowd-pleaser" from Bob and Gregg Smith (Arroyo Chop House, Parkway Grill) might "be the perfect Friday-night hangout" for the "over-40" set thanks to its "winning combination" of "satisfying", "upscale" "comfort fare" and "clubby" "good looks"; service is "solid" too, so some say the only "negative" is the "too noisy" room.

### Smoke House  *Steak*

| 19 | 17 | 19 | $35 |

**Burbank** | 4420 Lakeside Dr. (Barham Blvd.) | 818-845-3731 | www.smokehouse1946.com

"One of the last of the originals", this circa-1946 Burbank "holdout" is famed for its "heavy-duty cocktails", "no-surprises" steakhouse menu and "infamous" garlic cheese bread served by a staff that's straight "out of central casting"; cushy "red banquettes" and lounge singers Tuesday–Saturday give it an appropriately "retro" feel; meanwhile, cynics say it "doesn't have much to offer" beyond "nostalgia."

### Sofi  *Greek*

| 19 | 20 | 19 | $34 |

**Third Street** | 8030¾ W. Third St. (bet. Crescent Heights Blvd. & Fairfax Ave.) | 323-651-0346 | www.sofigreekrestaurant.com

A "hidden gem" on Third Street, this "reliable" Hellenic "taverna" "sets the scene for a romantic evening" with its "enchanting" outdoor patio "decorated with candles and overgrown vines"; "warm" service adds to the "countryside" feel, and though few feel it's "overpriced", it's still cheaper than "a trip to Greece."

### Soleil Westwood Ⓜ *Canadian/French* | 20 | 16 | 21 | $31

**Westwood** | 1386 Westwood Blvd. (Rochester Ave.) | 310-441-5384 |
www.soleilwestwood.com

"Welcoming" chef-owner Luc Alarie creates a "hearth of hospitality"
at his "cozy" Westwood bistro where he delivers an "interesting
menu" of French-Canadian dishes that bring a "little touch of Quebec"
to the area "near UCLA"; converts are particularly "charmed" by the
"incredible value" and "neighborhood vibe", though a few critics "wish
the food was just a little bit better."

### ❷ Sona Ⓢ Ⓜ *French* | 27 | 24 | 26 | $87

**West Hollywood** | 401 N. La Cienega Blvd. (bet. Beverly Blvd. &
Melrose Ave.) | 310-659-7708 | www.sonarestaurant.com

"Outstanding in every way" swoon smitten surveyors of David Myers'
West Hollywood boîte that "pushes the culinary envelope" with "exquisite" New French fare "prepared with imagination and care" and
best appreciated via the "brilliant" tasting menu (either with wine
pairings or "let the sommelier guide you" through the "biblical" list);
the "beautifully appointed" room is "elegant and warm" while service
is "top-notch" (if sometimes "overbearing"); all in all, it's "a strong
contender for one of LA's best restaurants" – just be prepared for
some "major sticker shock."

### Sona's *Californian/Eclectic* | 17 | 13 | 16 | $21

**Encino** | 16240 Ventura Blvd. (bet. Libbet & Woodley Aves.) | 818-528-7755 |
www.sonasrestaurant.com

"They try hard" attest allies of this Encino Cal-Eclectic with "homey",
"healthy" fare that offers "something for everyone" as well as "lots of
food for the buck"; critics call it "uneven" with sometimes "mediocre"
eats and service that "takes too long" in the "cafeterialike" space.

### Sonora Cafe Ⓜ *Southwestern* | 21 | 21 | 20 | $41

**La Brea** | 180 S. La Brea Ave. (bet. Beverly Blvd. & 3rd St.) | 323-857-1800 |
www.sonoracafe.com

"Santa Fe" meets La Brea at this "upscale" Southwestern "standby"
(and sibling of El Cholo) where "creative" dishes – including especially
"tasty" appetizers – are the draw for "rich cowboys" and cowgirls; the
"rustic" "'80s"-style setting is "romantic by the fireplace" or "hectic"
at the bar, with "friendly" servers delivering "generous, strong" drinks
no matter where you are.

### Soot Bull Jeep *Korean* | 24 | 7 | 12 | $26

**Koreatown** | 3136 Eighth St. (Catalina St.) | 213-387-3865

Meat lovers scale "the peak" of Korean barbecue at "K-town's perennial hole-in-the-wall" where "it's all about the charcoal" and the
"huge" portions of "wildly flavorful" "self-grill" beef, chicken and pork
("the kimchi rocks too"); the "shabby" "sweat lodge" setting and "un-
smiling" service are all "part of the charm" say "real foodies" who
gladly suffer "singed knuckles" and "smelling like a smokehouse" for
what they say is "possibly the best BBQ around."

### Sor Tino ● *Italian* | 19 | 16 | 18 | $38

**Brentwood** | 908 S. Barrington Ave. (San Vicente Blvd.) | 310-442-8466

"Less trendy" than its WeHo sib (Ago), this "likable" Brentwood Italian
from chef-owner Agostino Sciandri offers a "changing" menu of

Tuscan fare that's best appreciated from "a table in the sun" out on the patio; "knowledgeable service" and a "low-key" vibe are additional "positives", though cons contend it's "overpriced" and simply "doesn't stand out."

### Souplantation  *American*  | 16 | 10 | 12 | $12 |

**Third Street** | Beverly Connection | 8491 W. Third St. (La Cienega Blvd.) | 323-655-0381

**Lakewood** | 4720 Candlewood St. (Faculty Ave.) | 562-531-6778

**Brentwood** | 11911 San Vicente Blvd. (Montana Ave.) | 310-476-7080

**Marina del Rey** | Villa Marina Mktpl. | 13455 Maxella Ave. (Lincoln Blvd.) | 310-305-7669

**Arcadia** | 301 E. Huntington Dr. (bet. Gateway Dr. & 2nd Ave.) | 626-446-4248

**Pasadena** | 201 S. Lake Ave. (bet. Cordova St. & E. Del Mar Blvd.) | 626-577-4798

**Northridge** | 19801 Rinaldi St. (Corbin Ave.) | 818-363-3027

**Alhambra** | 2131 W. Commonwealth Ave. (bet. Date & Palm Aves.) | 626-458-1173

**City of Industry** | Puente Hills Mall | 17411 Colima Rd. (Asuza Ave.) | 626-810-5756

**Camarillo** | 375 W. Ventura Blvd. (S. Las Posas Rd.) | 805-389-3500
www.souplantation.com
Additional locations throughout Southern California

The "mega-sized" "salad bars" are the focal points of these "inexpensive", "family-friendly" American chain buffets where diners can either "eat healthy" or "pig out" on "unlimited servings" of "veggies, soups, breads and pastas" served in "no-frills" digs that some liken to a "hospital cafeteria"; cynics find them "cheerless", "impersonal" and say they value "quantity" over "quality" – "what good is all you can eat if you don't want to eat anything?"

### South Street  *Cheese Steaks*  | ▽ 18 | 9 | 12 | $11 |

**Westwood** | 1010 Broxton Ave. (Weyburn Ave.) | 310-443-9895

**Burbank** | 117 N. Victory Blvd. (Olive St.) | 818-563-2211
www.southstreetcheesesteak.com

It's all about the "Philadelphia cheese steak with whiz" at these "cute, little" joints in Burbank and Westwood turning out "tasty sandwiches" "on delicious bread" as well as hoagies, wings, fries and other "greasy" goodies (the Burbank outpost also offers East Coast–style pizza and beer); service and decor are "not great", while the budget-conscious complain the food is "overpriced for what it is."

### ⨀ Spago  *Californian*  | 27 | 25 | 25 | $73 |

**Beverly Hills** | 176 N. Cañon Dr. (Wilshire Blvd.) | 310-385-0880 |
www.wolfgangpuck.com

"Forget Gibraltar, this place is the rock of Los Angeles" sum up surveyors who award the Most Popular title to this "flashy", "irresistible" "legend" that's "well worth" the "big-ticket prices" for its "flawless" Californian cuisine from Lee Hefter and "cutting-edge" desserts from pastry chef Sherry Yard; owner Wolfgang Puck "can often be seen table hopping" in the "flamboyant" room that opens onto a "tree-filled patio" dotted with celebrities, while his "hard-to-fault" servers have been "trained by Beverly Hills' most high-maintenance clientele."

### Spanish Kitchen, The  *Mexican*

17 | 20 | 16 | $38

**West Hollywood** | 826 N. La Cienega Blvd. (bet. Melrose Pl. & Santa Monica Blvd.) | 310-659-4794 | www.thespanishkitchen.com

A "boisterous atmosphere" and "a high girl-to-guy ratio" are the hallmarks of this "trendy" WeHo watering hole where the "encyclopedic tequila selection" earns higher marks than the "Americanized" Mexican menu; hacienda-style decor is "pleasant enough", but the "attentive" staff can turn "surly" if you "won't splurge for primo" brands.

### Spark Woodfire Grill  *American*

17 | 17 | 17 | $34

**Pico-Robertson** | 9575 W. Pico Blvd. (Beverly Dr.) | 310-277-0133
**Studio City** | 11801 Ventura Blvd. (bet. Carpenter & Colfax Aves.) | 818-623-8883
www.sparkwoodfiregrill.com

"The basic concept is attractive" report reviewers of this mini-chain where pizzas, steaks and other American fare is cooked up on a "wood-fire grill"; most find it "satisfying", but a vocal minority knocks "mediocre" food as well as "sporadic" service and suggests it's "overpriced" as well.

### Spazio ● *Californian/Mediterranean*

▽ 19 | 20 | 19 | $43

**Sherman Oaks** | 14755 Ventura Blvd. (bet. Cedros & Willis Aves.) | 818-728-8400 | www.spazio.la

"High-caliber music" plus "interesting", "well-prepared" Cal-Med dishes make this "upscale" Sherman Oaks jazz supper club an "ideal" destination "for an evening out on the town" say fans who also favor it for "Sunday brunch"; critics call it "overpoweringly loud" and say the "outdoor seating" can be a welcome respite.

### NEW Spice Basil 🖼 Ⓜ *Thai*

- | - | - | I

**Alhambra** | 25 W. Valley Blvd. (Garfield Ave.) | 626-282-3200

This budget-friendly Thai newcomer may be set in a historic structure in the heart of the SG Valley's new Hong Kong neighborhood, but it features a modern interior with lots of vibrant orange and green tones; its extensive menu boasts more than 130 dishes, including an array of those with Laotian influences.

### Spin Rotisserie Chicken  *American*

▽ 17 | 7 | 11 | $12

**Marina del Rey** | 3216 Washington Blvd. (bet. Carter & Stanford Aves.) | 310-823-7299 | www.spinchicken.com

"Surprisingly tasty" rotisserie birds and "fresh" salads and sides draw diners to this "fast", "convenient", if not exactly "fancy", take-out staple in Marina del Ray; occasional "long waits" are overcome by low prices and a drive-thru option.

### Spumoni  *Italian*

▽ 23 | 15 | 22 | $22

**Santa Monica** | 713 Montana Ave. (7th St.) | 310-393-2944
**Calabasas** | 26500 Agoura Rd. (Las Virgenes Rd.) | 818-871-9848
**Sherman Oaks** | 14533 Ventura Blvd. (bet. Van Nuys Blvd. & Vesper Ave.) | 818-981-7218
**Camarillo** | 300 N. Lantana St. (E. Daily Dr.) | 805-445-6534
**Stevenson Ranch** | 24917 Pico Canyon Rd. (The Old Rd.) | 661-799-0360
www.spumonirestaurants.com

"Solid Italian" say surveyors of this SoCal mini-chain where "absolutely delicious" "red-sauce" specialties are served in "generous portions" in

| | FOOD | DECOR | SERVICE | COST |
|---|---|---|---|---|

"informal" surroundings; "warm" service gives it "the feel of a family place" while "cheap" prices mean it's a "very good value" as well.

### Square One Dining Ⓜ American
▽ 24 | 14 | 19 | $20

**East Hollywood** | 4854 Fountain Ave. (bet. N. Berendo & N. Catalina Sts.) | 323-661-1109 | www.squareonedining.com

"Killer breakfasts" and "inventive" lunches that make use of "the freshest" "local" ingredients attract a "cool crowd" to this "laid-back" East Hollywood American eatery where a seat at the window affords a prime view of the Scientology campus nearby; with a "pleasant" patio, "super-friendly" staff and fair prices, the only complaint is that fans "wish it were open later" (it closes at 4 PM).

### Stand, The Hot Dogs
18 | 14 | 16 | $12

**NEW** **Century City** | 2000 Ave. of the Stars (Olympic Blvd.) | 310-785-0400
**Encino** | 17000 Ventura Blvd. (bet. Genesta & Paso Robles Aves.) | 818-788-2700
www.thestandlink.com

Dog lovers devour "wieners of all shapes and sizes" "customized" with "unexpected condiments" at this "child-friendly" American duo in Century City (which opened post-Survey) and Encino; outdoor seating at both locations, "beer on tap" and prices that are "a real bargain" make them "popular" for a "pleasant", "picnic"-like meal.

### Standard, The ❶ Eclectic
16 | 21 | 15 | $34

**Downtown** | The Standard | 550 S. Flower St. (6th St.) | 213-892-8080
**West Hollywood** | The Standard | 8300 Sunset Blvd. (Sweetzer Ave.) | 323-650-9090
www.standardhotel.com

The "glorified coffee shop" concept goes "chic" and "ultramod" at the Standard hotel's "decent but overpriced" Downtown and West Hollywood outposts with the menu styled as French–Traditional American in the former and Eclectic in the latter; both are 24/7 with lots of "eye candy" and "sexy" servers who often err on the side of "attitude"; in sum, they're more about the "scene" and "drinks", "unless you're hungry after midnight, in which case they're a godsend."

### Stanley's Californian
19 | 15 | 18 | $24

**Sherman Oaks** | 13817 Ventura Blvd. (bet. Mammoth & Matillja Aves.) | 818-986-4623 | www.stanleys83.com

"Comfortable and casual", this Sherman Oaks "oldie but goodie" has "morphed from a hipster hangout to a dependable destination" with a Californian menu that "covers it all" from the "wonderful" Chinese chicken salad to "homestyle" dishes like meatloaf and sandwiches; service is "pleasant", as is the "charming", "tree-filled back patio" that some call "an oasis on the boulevard."

### Stevie's Creole Cafe Cajun
▽ 17 | 14 | 14 | $33

**Encino** | 16911 Ventura Blvd. (Balboa Blvd.) | 818-528-3500

"Loud" and "fun", this Encino Cajun channels "the real NOLA" with live R&B (Thursday–Sunday), "strong specialty drinks" and "N'Awlins"-style eats like gumbo and jambalaya; foes find the "too-expensive" food "takes a back seat" to the "entertainment" and add that "service could use some attention" as well.

| | FOOD | DECOR | SERVICE | COST |
|---|---|---|---|---|

### Stinking Rose, The *Italian*

16 | 18 | 18 | $35

**Beverly Hills** | 55 N. La Cienega Blvd. (Wilshire Blvd.) | 310-652-7673 | www.thestinkingrose.com

"You'll be missing kisses for a week" after a visit to this Beverly Hills Italian chain outpost where diners "sweat out all their toxins" with the aid of "garlic-centric" dishes like signature 40-clove chicken and herb-roasted prime rib; "kitschy" themed rooms strike some as a bit "Disneyland", but even detractors who dismiss it as "gimmicky" concede the "lively atmosphere" still works for "group dinners" and "out-of-town guests."

### Stonefire Grill *BBQ*

20 | 13 | 14 | $17

**West Hills** | Fallbrook Ctr. | 6405 Fallbrook Ave. (Victory Blvd.) | 818-887-4145
**Valencia** | Cinema Park Plaza | 23300 Cinema Dr. (Boquet Canyon Rd.) | 661-799-8282
www.stonefiregrill.com

"Flavorful' BBQ may be the prime focus at this "casual" SoCal chain, but pizzas, breadsticks and "amazing salads" perfect for "sharing" also have a strong fan following; service is of the "order-at-the-counter" variety while the "family-oriented" atmosphere means that noise levels "can drown out fighter jets", making "takeout" an appealing option.

### NEW Suki 7 ⊠ *Japanese*

- | - | - | M

**Westlake Village** | 925 Westlake Blvd. (Agoura Rd.) | 805-777-7579 | www.suki7lounge.com

From the team responsible for nearby ultratrendies P6 and Chapter 8, this midpriced Japanese has settled into a dazzling, modern Westlake space accented with live bamboo, a flowing water wall and a river-rock sushi bar with plush chartreuse leather chairs; located just off the freeway, it also sports a robata and dance floor.

### Sunnin *Lebanese*

24 | 6 | 15 | $15

**Westwood** | 1779 Westwood Blvd. (Santa Monica Blvd.) | 310-477-2358
**Long Beach** | 5110 E. Second St. (bet. Granada & Nieto Aves.) | 562-433-9000
www.sunnin.com

"Don't let the looks scare you off" of these "zero-atmosphere" Lebanese sibs in Long Beach and Westwood where cognoscenti overlook "harsh lighting", "tight quarters" and "Styrofoam plates" for "fantastic", "flavorful" kebabs and "addictive" hummus delivered by staffers that "clearly take pride" in their establishments; it's all "well priced" to the point that "you'd have to make an effort to spend more than $15" here.

### Sur *Californian/Mediterranean*

21 | 24 | 21 | $39

**West Hollywood** | 606 N. Robertson Blvd. (Melrose Ave.) | 310-289-2824 | www.sur-restaurant.com

"The ambiance is killer" at this relatively new West Hollywood boîte where the "gorgeous" white-on-white candlelit room is likened to a "five-star wedding" and enhanced by equally "attractive" servers; the Cal-Med fare strikes admirers as "tasty" and "inventive", and although critics contend it "doesn't know what it wants to be", even they concede some that "huge portions" (including "two sides") mean it's "a great value."

| | FOOD | DECOR | SERVICE | COST |
|---|---|---|---|---|

### Surya India  *Indian*
23 | 17 | 22 | $31

**Third Street** | 8048 W. Third St. (bet. S. Crescent Heights Blvd. & S. Laurel Ave.) | 323-653-5151

"Refined" flavors define this "lovely" Third Street Indian where "sumptuous" curries "deliver" and "the tandoori sea bass is fantastic" but will increase an already "pricey" experience; it's a "welcoming" spot, though, with a "wonderfully sweet staff" and "casual but classy" modern decor done up in deep reds and oranges, which wins many fans amongst well-heeled locals.

### Sushi Dokoro Ki Ra La  *Japanese*
▽ 24 | 17 | 22 | $50

**Beverly Hills** | 9777 S. Santa Monica Blvd. (Wilshire Blvd.) | 310-275-9003

"Each customer is welcomed like an honored guest" at this "classy", "little" space in Beverly Hills where chefs slice "amazingly fresh fish" into "generous" bites of sushi that's wolfed down by "agents" and industry types "brokering the next big deal" at their table; fans find it "a cut above" other neighborhood spots and vow they're "definitely going back."

### Sushi Duke  *Japanese*
▽ 25 | 20 | 19 | $27

**Hermosa Beach** | 201 Hermosa Ave. (2nd St.) | 310-406-8986

This "neighborhood" Japanese in Hermosa Beach offers "high-quality" sushi "with a kick" served in "quiet" but still stylish surroundings with a wraparound patio; insiders say the best service can be had "sitting at the bar", while happy-hour specials (5:30–6:30 PM every day) promise "good value."

### Sushi Mac  ⊘ *Japanese*
17 | 7 | 16 | $15

**Third Street** | 8474 W. Third St. (La Cienega Blvd.) | 323-653-3959
**West LA** | 2222A Sawtelle Blvd. (Olympic Blvd.) | 310-481-9954
**Sherman Oaks** | 15030 Ventura Blvd. (Lemona Ave.) | 818-986-6450

"Cheap-o" sushi is the draw at this "crowded" Japanese mini-chain where the fin fare is "fresh", if "not exactly high-quality", and there's "no ambiance", unless you count the "loud, hip grooves" issuing from the stereo speakers; "very fast" "counter service" has replaced the former conveyor-belt system; N.B. cash only.

### Sushi Masu  Ⓜ *Japanese*
▽ 26 | 13 | 23 | $40

**West LA** | 1911 Westwood Blvd. (bet. La Grange & Missouri Aves.) | 310-446-4368

"Destination-quality sushi" in a "neighborhood setting" lures West LA locals to this "under-the-radar" outpost for "intriguing presentations" of "amazingly fresh" fish; "personable chef" Masu lights up somewhat "drab quarters", while relatively "affordable" tabs add to the "enjoyment."

### Sushi Mon  *Japanese*
19 | 13 | 15 | $30

**Third Street** | 8562 W. Third St. (Holt Ave.) | 310-246-9230
**Santa Monica** | 401 Santa Monica Blvd. (4th St.) | 310-576-7011 | www.sushimon.net

"Huge pieces" of sushi and "unique rolls" are the hallmarks of this "quick and casual" Japanese duo in Santa Monica and on Third Street, where "fantastic lunch combos" are the best "bargain"; on the downside is "tired" decor and service "so inconsistent, it's amusing."

| | FOOD | DECOR | SERVICE | COST |
|---|---|---|---|---|

### ☑ Sushi Nozawa 🖻 *Japanese*

| 27 | 6 | 15 | $58 |

**Studio City** | 11288 Ventura Blvd. (bet. Arch & Tropical Drs.) | 818-508-7017

"Master" chef-owner Kazunori Nozawa continues to "rule with an iron fist" at this "outstanding" Studio City "strip-mall" spot where the "famously nonexistent decor" is "part of the shtick", as is the somewhat "intimidating" man behind the counter who doles out "melt-in-your-mouth perfect" slabs of "buttery" fish on "warm rice" (but "no California rolls"); "purists" know to simply "order the omakase", "shut up" and "revel in the experience" – it's "worth the punishment" "at least once."

### Sushi Ozekii *Japanese*

| - | - | - | M |

**NEW Beverly Hills** | 480 S. San Vicente Blvd. (La Cienega Blvd.) | 323-852-1799
**Agoura Hills** | 5653 Kanan Rd. (Agoura Rd.) | 818-991-4345 🖻
**Camarillo** | 4421 E. Las Posas Rd., Ste. E (Lewis Rd.) | 805-389-1164 🖻
www.ozekii.com

This small stylish sushi chain offers well-priced lunch specials as well as soju cocktails to supplement its menu of maki, sashimi, salads and combo platters; patio seating (at the Beverly Hills branch) and moderate prices are additional enticements.

### Sushi Roku *Japanese*

| 22 | 22 | 19 | $48 |

**Third Street** | 8445 W. Third St. (bet. Croft Ave. & La Cienega Blvd.) | 323-655-6767 ◗
**Santa Monica** | 1401 Ocean Ave. (Santa Monica Blvd.) | 310-458-4771 ◗
**Pasadena** | One Colorado | 33 Miller Alley (bet. Colorado & Fair Oaks Blvds.) | 626-683-3000
www.sushiroku.com

"So deliciously LA", this "chic" Japanese eatery has three locations, all offering similarly "creative" raw and cooked cuisine for those willing to shell out the "big bucks", including "buttery" fish, "inventive rolls" and "a sake list to drool over"; service swings between "courteous" and "snooty" while a "young, über-hip, industry" crowd digs the "spectacular, sexy" vibe; "even the room works the room" here; N.B. they're planning to add a robata bar at the Santa Monica outpost.

### Sushi Sasabune 🖻 *Japanese*

| 26 | 13 | 18 | $63 |

**West LA** | 12400 Wilshire Blvd. (Centinela Ave.) | 310-268-8380

"Perfect harmony" is achieved via the "divine" combination of "unbelievably tender" fish and "warm rice" at this "top-tier" West LA Japanese "destination" where the "exceptionally fresh" sushi is presented omakase-style in "upgraded" digs; though a few longtimers lament the "loss of intimacy" and "assembly-line" service in the "expansive" new space, it's ultimately "not about atmosphere – it's strictly about sublime fare" that's "a must" at least once, "even if you have to brown-bag it for the rest of the week."

### Sushi Sushi 🖻 *Japanese*

| ▽ 25 | 14 | 18 | $52 |

**Beverly Hills** | 326½ S. Beverly Dr. (bet. Gregory Way & Olympic Blvd.) | 310-277-1165

"Frequented by more Japanese than Trump's latest golf course", this "unassuming gem" in Beverly Hills proffers "traditional", "top-quality" sushi "beautifully" cut in "a long and slender fashion" by "amazing" chef-owner Hiroshige Yamada; contented diners declare it's the "closest you can get to Tokyo without leaving LA", so who cares if "you'll need a second mortgage for those two pieces of toro"?

### Susina Bakery  *Bakery*
23 | 21 | 19 | $15

**La Brea** | 7122 Beverly Blvd. (La Brea Ave.) | 323-934-7900 | www.susinabakery.com

"Heavenly desserts" (including "brioche bread pudding to thank your lucky stars for") keep crowds coming to this La Brea "sweet shop" where "perfect" panini, salads and sandwiches have a smaller but still-loyal following; "hospitable" counter service and a "quaint" "Parisian patisserie" ambiance make it work for both "Sunday mornings" or "date night", especially now that they're open till 11 PM.

### ☑ Sweet Lady Jane ●☒ *Bakery*
25 | 14 | 15 | $17

**Melrose** | 8360 Melrose Ave. (bet. N. Kings Rd. & N. Orlando Ave.) | 323-653-7145 | www.sweetladyjane.com

"Ignore the zillion calories and enjoy" the "beautifully decorated" cakes and other "delectable" confections at this Melrose bakery where soups and other lunchtime savories are also solid; the disgruntled dis "steep pricing" and somewhat "shoddy" service that's slow as "molasses" but even still, it's always "jammed", meaning unless you're "lucky" enough to snag one of the few tables, your "best bet is takeout."

### Swingers ● *Diner*
17 | 16 | 16 | $16

**Beverly Boulevard** | Beverly Laurel Motor Hotel | 8020 Beverly Blvd. (Laurel Ave.) | 323-653-5858
**Santa Monica** | 802 Broadway (Lincoln Blvd.) | 310-393-9793

The "classic diner" gets the LA "hipster" treatment at these "too-cool-for-school" spots on Beverly Boulevard and in Santa Monica "open till the wee hours" where a "young Hollywood" crowd chows down on "coffee shop fare" "with a bit of an edge"; "tattooed" servers provide "iffy" service while the "kick-ass jukebox" means you can have a side of "Sex Pistols" while you're nursing your "hangover."

### Swinging Door ☒ *BBQ*
- | - | - | I

**North Hollywood** | 11018 Vanowen St. (Vineland St.) | 818-763-8996 | www.swingingdoorbbq.com

"Fine barbecue" and "superb" fixin's are the lure at this well-priced North Hollywood newcomer where the "tasty" Texas-style fare makes up for the "truck-stop" decor ("you wouldn't want white tablecloths anyway"); the "friendly owner" is improving the scene with new a/c and live music on Friday nights.

### Table 8 ☒ *Californian*
24 | 20 | 21 | $58

**Melrose** | 7661 Melrose Ave. (bet. Spaulding & Stanley Aves.) | 323-782-8258 | www.table8la.com

The off-the-menu "secret" salt-encrusted porterhouse is "still king" (and "worth every penny" of its $88 price tag) at "sexy" chef Govind Armstrong's "swanky" Melrose eatery where a "pleasant" (if sometimes "rushed") staff delivers "delicious", "unusual" takes on Californian cuisine; diners divide on the recent remodel that imparts a "dark", "slightly Goth" vibe ("stunning" vs. "off-putting") while the "crowded, noisy" room strikes several as better-suited to "a club than fine dining."

|  | FOOD | DECOR | SERVICE | COST |
|---|---|---|---|---|

## Taiko *Japanese* | 21 | 15 | 18 | $26 |

**Brentwood** | Brentwood Gdns. | 11677 San Vicente Blvd. (Barrington Ave.) | 310-207-7782

**El Segundo** | 2041 Rosecrans Ave. (Sepulveda Blvd.) | 310-647-3100

"A robust menu of Japanese staples" like "slurpable" noodles, "decent" sushi and "myriad combos" keeps families coming to this "casual", "no-nonsense" pair in Brentwood and El Segundo; service is "attentive", though some disdain the "dinerlike" decor and add that the "noise can be deafening" at times.

## Taix *French* | 16 | 15 | 19 | $30 |

**Echo Park** | 1911 Sunset Blvd. (Glendale Blvd.) | 213-484-1265 | www.taixfrench.com

"Basic" French fare gets a boost from a complimentary tureen of "good, hot soup" at this Echo Park eatery open since 1927; if the "time warp" ambiance feels a bit "tired", equally "old-fashioned" prices and appropriately "hospitable" servers are appealing to the "senior" crowd.

## NEW Takami Sushi & Robata Ⓢ Ⓜ *Japanese* | – | – | – | M |

**Downtown** | 811 Wilshire Blvd. (8th St.) | 213-236-9600 | www.takamisushi.com

Situated 21 stories above the Financial District, adjacent to the Elevate Lounge, this ambitious, hyper-modern Japanese offers further proof that Downtown is reviving; with a long sake and soju list, an assortment of exotic cocktails and a menu including Tokyo tacos and rock shrimp tempura purses, it's sure to draw Westside sushi aficionados east for a taste of the high life.

## Takao *Japanese* | 25 | 12 | 21 | $50 |

**Brentwood** | 11656 San Vicente Blvd. (bet. Barrington & Darlington Aves.) | 310-207-8636

"Who needs ambiance with food like this?" ask those enchanted with Takao Izumida's "unique approach" that "stretches the definition of Japanese food" with "artistic" sushi and cooked dishes and overcomes the "sparse", "brightly lit" Brentwood setting; no surprise, tabs are "expensive" but offset by the "warm hosts" and a "devoted" staff.

## Talésai *Thai* | 22 | 17 | 19 | $34 |

**West Hollywood** | 9043 Sunset Blvd. (Doheny Dr.) | 310-275-9724 | www.talesai.com

**Beverly Hills** | 9198 Olympic Blvd. (Oakhurst Dr.) | 310-271-9345 | www.talesai.com

**Studio City** | 11744 Ventura Blvd. (bet. Colfax Ave. & Laurel Canyon Blvd.) | 818-753-1001 Ⓢ

It may not be "authentic", but this separately owned "upscale" Thai trio is a "nice change of pace" that "pleases" for more "elegant", "flavorful" creations served in "contemporary" quarters; considering the "modern" "white-tablecloth" setting and "nice" service, "the little extra on the tab is well worth it."

## Talia's *Italian* | 25 | 24 | 23 | $41 |

**Manhattan Beach** | 1148 Manhattan Ave. (12th St.) | 310-545-6884 | www.taliasrestaurant.com

A "romantic" atmosphere prevails at this "incredible" Italian trattoria in Manhattan Beach that's a "charming" "jewel box of a place" and a "favorite date spot" for many "locals"; the "accommodating" service and moderate check make up for "fishbowl"-style crowding in the "tiny" dining room.

## Tama Sushi *Japanese*

24 | 18 | 20 | $40

**Studio City** | 11920 Ventura Blvd. (bet. Carpenter Ave. & Laurel Canyon Blvd.) | 818-760-4585 | www.tamasushi.net

"A sushi sanctuary" that's "slightly under the radar", this "low-key" Studio City Japanese by Katsu Michite pleases with "nothing hip or trendy" just "simple, outstanding" fare served in "serene" environs with plenty of "space between the tables"; a few save it "for when other places are full", but supporters say they're "glad the crowds go elsewhere", leaving this reasonably priced spot "without the waits" of its Ventura Boulevard neighbors.

## Tamayo 🗷 *Mexican*

▽ 21 | 25 | 22 | $25

**East LA** | 5300 E. Olympic Blvd. (bet. Amalia & S. Hillview Aves.) | 323-260-4700

"Incredible original artwork" by the late Rufino Tamayo covers the walls at this spacious "museum"-like East LA Mexican set in a restored 1928 hacienda; regional fare is "tasty" while the "warm and welcoming" service, "reasonable" prices and occasional live music add to the "great atmosphere."

## Tam O'Shanter Inn *Scottish*

21 | 22 | 22 | $35

**Atwater Village** | 2980 Los Feliz Blvd. (Boyce Ave.) | 323-664-0228 | www.lawrysonline.com

2007 marks the 85th year in business for this Atwater Village "time warp" (and "Lawry's older brother") where supporters settle in for "consistently great prime rib" and other Scottish vittles washed down with a "wee dram of whiskey"; traditional country pub decor is "like a visit to the British isles" (though some say "it's a bit long in the tooth") while "top-notch", "old-fashioned service" contributes to the "rustic", "inviting" ambiance.

## Tanino *Italian*

22 | 22 | 21 | $43

**Westwood** | 1043 Westwood Blvd. (bet. Kinross & Weyburn Aves.) | 310-208-0444 | www.tanino.com

"Pasta is the sure thing" declare fans who gobble up the "sensational" signature pumpkin tortellini along with other "memorable" Southern Italian dishes at chef-owner Tanino Drago's moderately priced Westside "standout"; the "Medici" decor in the two-story space with a black-and-white marble floor strikes some as "kitschy" and others as "delightful", while the location near the "movies and the Geffen Playhouse" is a boon to theatergoers.

## Tantra 🅼 *Indian*

21 | 25 | 18 | $35

**Silver Lake** | 3705 W. Sunset Blvd. (Edgecliffe Dr.) | 323-663-8268 | www.tantrasunset.com

This "dark, sexy" Silver Lake Indian draws a "hip" crowd of "groovy youngsters" for a mix of "inventive cocktails" and "intriguing" Indian fare (though in "minuscule portions") served in "chic", saffron-colored quarters with "Bollywood films" screened on plasma TVs; a few find it "overpriced" for what it is, adding that the "dark, clubby" feel is more suited to a "nightspot" than a restaurant.

| | FOOD | DECOR | SERVICE | COST |
|---|---|---|---|---|

**NEW** **Tanzore** *Indian* — | — | — | M

**Beverly Hills** | 50 N. La Cienega Blvd. (Wilshire Blvd.) | 310-652-3838 | www.tanzore.com

In a Beverly Hills location that's been home to Gaylord of India and The Raj comes this mega-stylish yet moderately priced Indian; designer Sat Garg has turned the space into a palace worthy of a maharajah with hand-carved wooden doors, a 'river' and a color palette intended to reflect the flavors of subcontinental cooking.

**Tart** *American* ∇ 18 | 17 | 18 | $26

**Fairfax** | Farmer's Daughter Hotel | 115 S. Fairfax Ave. (bet. Beverly Blvd. & W. 3rd St.) | 323-937-3930 | www.farmersdaughterhotel.com

After a few chef and concept changes, this "adorable" retro spot in the Farmer's Daughter Hotel (across the street from the Farmers Market) "may have finally found its groove" report reviewers who rate the New American "comfort" eats "enjoyable" and give a special shout-out to the "must-have" "mini-burgers"; service is "eager, but often incompetent", though even the "underwhelmed" have to admit it's a "cute" place.

**Tasca Winebar** *Spanish* ∇ 21 | 19 | 22 | $34

**Third Street** | 8108 W. Third St. (Crescent Heights Blvd.) | 323-951-9890 | www.tascawinebar.com

"Wow, what a find" exclaim Third Street denizens who've stumbled upon this "satisfying" new tapas joint serving "well-thought-out plates" and 20 wines-by-the-glass in a "low-lit", "intimate" setting; reviewers report "it's still finding its legs", but is already shaping up to be a "great" moderately priced "alternative" to other spots in the area.

**Taste** *American* 20 | 19 | 19 | $35

**West Hollywood** | 8454 Melrose Ave. (La Cienega Blvd.) | 323-852-6888 | www.ilovetaste.com

Deemed "tasteful", if somewhat "mundane", by West Hollywoodites, this "laid-back" New American does "decent plates" of seasonal fare in a "cozy", "understated" converted-bungalow setting; service is "consistent" and tabs "a bargain", especially on Wine Discovery Mondays when bottles are half off.

**Taste Chicago** *Italian* ∇ 19 | 8 | 14 | $12

**Burbank** | 603 N. Hollywood Way (W. Verdugo Ave.) | 818-563-2800 | www.tastechicago.biz

Actor-owner Joe Mantegna's "homage to the Windy City" appeals to "displaced Midwesterners" with "guilty pleasures" like Italian beef sandwiches, Vienna red hots and Chicago-style pizza served out of "casual" cafeteria-style quarters in Burbank; a few diehards declare it "doesn't compare" to the real thing, but for LA it's pretty darn "close."

**Taverna Tony** *Greek* 21 | 20 | 21 | $38

**Malibu** | Malibu Country Mart | 23410 Civic Center Way (Cross Creek Rd.) | 310-317-9667 | www.tavernatony.com

"More fun than you can shake a lamb shank at", this "festive" bit of "Mykonos" in Malibu serves up "hearty" fare in "generous helpings"; "live music" and "dancing" waiters are a "plus" to partiers, but "border on annoying" to more sedate sorts who prefer the quieter patio with its "charming outdoor tables, lights and heating lamps."

| | FOOD | DECOR | SERVICE | COST |
|---|---|---|---|---|

### Taylor's Steak House  *Steak*   | 21 | 17 | 20 | $36 |

**Koreatown** | 3361 W. Eighth St. (Ardmore Ave.) | 213-382-8449
**La Cañada Flintridge** | 901 Foothill Blvd. (Beulah Dr.) |
818-790-7668
www.taylorssteakhouse.com

"Dim lighting", "mahogany paneling" and "red furnishings" characterize these "old-fashioned" "beef and booze" houses in Koreatown and
La Cañada Flintridge that fans favor for "perfectly done" steaks and
chops and "warm" service; if some complain that "quality doesn't
stand up" to some of its competitors, they also admit they dig the
"refreshingly restrained prices."

### Tender Greens  *American*   | 23 | 16 | 18 | $17 |

**Culver City** | 9523 Culver Blvd. (Cardiff Ave.) | 310-842-8300 |
www.tendergreensfood.com

Culver City continues to "boom" with this "cute", "casual" New
American arrival that provides a "broad" selection of "delicious",
"farm-fresh" salads, soups and sandwiches made from "locally
grown" ingredients and served in a "hip", "cafeteria" setting
that seems straight out of *Dwell* magazine; despite counter service
that "needs some work", "lines out the door" and "limited seating"
supporters are still hailing it as "a hit" and "one of LA's best
values" to boot.

### Tengu  *Japanese*   | 22 | 21 | 19 | $45 |

**NEW** **Santa Monica** | 1541 Ocean Ave. (bet. B'way & Colorado Ave.) |
310-587-2222
**Westwood** | 10853 Lindbrook Dr. (Tiverton Ave.) | 310-209-0071
www.tengu.com

"Super-fresh" "LA-style" sushi, "strong cocktails" and "über-chic" environs lure "the young and beautiful" to these "sceney" twins in Santa
Monica (new) and Westwood where Asian fusion dishes round out
the "creative" menu; the "hip" vibe is enhanced by "on-site DJs", but
"uneven" service and "ridiculous" prices leave a few wondering
whether or not it's "worth it."

### Teru Sushi  *Japanese*   | 20 | 18 | 18 | $38 |

**Studio City** | 11940 Ventura Blvd. (bet. Carpenter & Radford Aves.) |
818-763-6201 | www.terusushi.com

Still "going strong" after almost 30 years, this "reliable" Japanese
offers a "large selection" of "high-quality" sushi plus "innovative" rolls
served by a staff that "makes an effort to get to know the regulars"; the
"tired looking" decor is brightened up by the occasional "star sighting", though a few lament this "Valley hangout" is "not as good as it
used to be."

### Tesoro Trattoria  *Italian*   | 18 | 17 | 17 | $35 |

**Downtown** | California Plaza | 300 S. Grand Ave. (3rd St.) | 213-680-0000 |
www.tesorotrattoria.com

"Value Italian" "conveniently located" near the Music Center draws
diners to this "lobby level" pre-theater spot set in "an office building";
though cuisine quality is "inconsistent", service is "sensitive to curtain
times" and the "comfortable" dining room with "lovely views" of the
courtyard waterfall is also "pleasant"; N.B. the Food score might not
reflect an April 2007 chef change.

| | FOOD | DECOR | SERVICE | COST |
|---|---|---|---|---|

## Thai Dishes  *Thai*

| 18 | 11 | 17 | $18 |

**Culver City** | 9901 Washington Blvd. (Hughes Ave.) | 310-559-0987
**Malibu** | 22333 PCH (Carbon Canyon Rd.) | 310-456-6592
**Santa Monica** | 111 Santa Monica Blvd. (Ocean Ave.) | 310-394-6189
**Santa Monica** | 1910 Wilshire Blvd. (19th St.) | 310-828-5634
**El Segundo** | 150 S. Sepulveda Blvd. (El Segundo Blvd.) | 310-416-1080 🗲
**Inglewood** | 11934 Aviation Blvd. (W. 119th Pl.) | 310-643-6199 🗲
**LAX** | 6234 W. Manchester Ave. (Sepulveda Blvd.) | 310-342-0046
**Manhattan Beach** | 1015 N. Sepulveda Blvd. (10th St.) | 310-546-4147
**Pasadena** | 239 E. Colorado Blvd. (bet. Garfield & Marengo Sts.) | 626-304-9975
**Valencia** | 23328 Valencia Blvd. (bet. Bouquet Canyon Rd. & Cinema Dr.) | 661-253-3663
Additional locations throughout Southern California
"Pretty tasty" Thai food "on the cheap" defines this "reliable" LA-area chain of separately owned spots serving up "not-too-spicy" fare that fans favor for a "quick" meal or "takeout" (delivery is available at some branches too); "decor varies dramatically by location", but the "convenience" is consistent all around.

## Thaitalian Cooking Duet  *Italian/Thai*

| ▽ 17 | 18 | 21 | $23 |

**Pasadena** | 49 E. Colorado Blvd. (bet. N. Fair Oaks & Raymond Aves.) | 626-585-8808 | www.thaitalian.com
"Attentive service" is the strongest suit at this Pasadena Italian-Thai "fusion" whose somewhat "muddled" "concept" (green curry linguini, anyone?) "falls short on execution", though some say it's "tasty" when it hits its mark; "pleasant" decor includes sidewalk seating and a view of the open kitchen while prices are "just right."

## 3rd Stop  ● *Italian*

| 20 | 17 | 16 | $21 |

**West Hollywood** | 8636 W. Third St. (S. Williams Dr.) | 310-273-3605
"For an easy drink and a bite after work", this WeHo pub offers "varied" small plates and "excellent" bar classics as well as Italian choices to go with its "exotic" beers (on a 30-plus list) and "neighborhood" feel; "on weekends it's a madhouse", but it's "casual" and "low-key" during the week.

## Thousand Cranes, A  *Japanese*

| 23 | 24 | 23 | $49 |

**Little Tokyo** | New Otani | 120 S. Los Angeles St. (bet. 1st & 2nd Sts.) | 213-253-9255 | www.newotani.com
"Exquisitely prepared" sushi and *kaiseki*-style dishes are "served like pieces of art" at this Little Tokyo Japanese set inside the New Otani hotel offering views of "waterfalls" and an outdoor "garden" area; considering the "attention to detail", service is appropriately "formal" and "professional" while "steep prices" mean it's "geared toward expense-account" types; P.S. some suggest you "go for the champagne Sunday brunch."

## Three on Fourth  🗲 *American/Japanese*

| ▽ 16 | 16 | 21 | $41 |

**Santa Monica** | 1432-A Fourth St. (Santa Monica Blvd.) | 310-395-6765 | www.3onfourth.com
Diners are split on this moderately priced relative newcomer in Santa Monica, where a "nice assortment" of American, Asian and European dishes are paired with international beers, sakes and wines and served in sleek quarters with a communal table; while some find the fare "interesting", others deem it "not memorable" in spite of the unique "concept."

| | FOOD | DECOR | SERVICE | COST |
|---|---|---|---|---|

### NEW 3 Square

**Cafe + Bakery**  *Bakery/Sandwiches*  ▽ 21 | 18 | 19 | $18

**Venice** | 1121 Abbot Kinney Blvd. (bet. San Juan & Westminster Aves.) | 310-399-6504

Early samplers insist that "Hans down", "Röckenwagner's new cafe is right on the beat", offering "marvelous" pastries, "super" brunches and a pretzel burger that "shouldn't be missed"; though the staff is still "working out the kinks" and the space can feel a little "chilly on foggy Venice mornings", it has a "community atmosphere" that civic surveyors say is "badly needed on Abbot Kinney."

### Tiara Cafe  *American*  ▽ 20 | 22 | 20 | $21

**Downtown** | 127 E. Ninth St. (Main St.) | 213-623-3663 | www.tiara-cafe.com

"Creative" chef-owner Fred Eric (of Fred 62) "has done it again" enthuse fans of this fanciful Downtown eatery in the New Mart Building that sets the scene with "precious" purple and rose-colored walls and "waitresses wearing tiaras"; a "gourmet" American menu of salads, sandwiches and pizzettes includes "some new twists on old favorites", while their take-out area specializes in prepared foods and drinks; N.B. breakfast and lunch only, though dinner service is reportedly in the works.

### Tibet Nepal House  *Nepalese/Tibetan*  ▽ 19 | 18 | 20 | $22

**Pasadena** | 36 E. Holly St. (N. Fair Oaks Ave.) | 5626-585-0955 | www.tibetnepalhouse.com

The "best yak in Southern California" say straight-faced supporters of this "undoubtedly authentic" Pasadena Nepalese-Tibetan eatery with "simple", "soulful" fare (some say it "tastes like a cross between Indian and Chinese food") that's washed down with "warm butter tea"; decor "isn't fancy", with "prayer flags hanging from the rafters", but it's "quiet", while "attentive" service adds an additionally "calming" touch.

### Tiger Lily  *Asian/Eclectic*  ▽ 19 | 23 | 17 | $35

**Los Feliz** | 1745 N. Vermont Ave. (Prospect Ave.) | 323-661-5900 | www.tigerlilyrestaurant.com

"Swanky" *Enter the Dragon*–style decor defines this "decked out" Los Feliz eatery that "turns into a sexy lounge at night" where hipsters sip on "to-die-for" martinis and saketinis; some say "it's too bad they didn't spend as much attention on the food" as the Asian-Eclectic eats are "tasty, but "inconsistent", while the "staff needs lessons in the art of service"; N.B. the Food score might not reflect a 2006 chef change.

### Tlapazola Grill  *Mexican*  24 | 15 | 23 | $28

**Marina del Rey** | 4059 Lincoln Blvd. (Beach Ave.) | 310-822-7561 Ⓜ
**West LA** | 11676 Gateway Blvd. (Barrington Ave.) | 310-477-1577

With locations in Marina del Rey and West LA, this Mexican duo woos Westsiders with "exceptional" Oaxacan dishes served with "enthusiasm" by a "gracious" staff; though both are set in "strip malls", the newer MdR outpost is "cuter than its cousin", while the original location wins points for its "terrific margaritas" and 100-bottle tequila selection.

### Toast  *American*  20 | 14 | 16 | $20

**Third Street** | 8221 W. Third St. (bet. S. Harper & S. La Jolla Aves.) | 323-655-5018 | www.toastbakerycafe.net

Surveyors say "the scene is the best (or worst) thing about" this Third Street American bakery where the "amazing brunch" and "must-try"

|  | FOOD | DECOR | SERVICE | COST |
|--|------|-------|---------|------|

cupcakes are upstaged by "tragically hip" "boys and girls" with their "trendy little dogs" and plenty of "stars in their pajamas"; in spite of the "tasty" fare, "long lines" and "a lot of attitude" from a "blasé staff" leave plenty of people "burned out."

### NEW Tokyo Table ● *Japanese*

▽ | 16 | 22 | 19 | $34

**Beverly Hills** | 50 N. La Cienega Blvd. (bet. Clifton Way & Wilshire Blvd.) | 310-657-9500 | www.tokyotable.com

This Beverly Hills newcomer offers an "interesting menu" of Japanese fare, though diners divide on whether it constitutes "affordable Asian fusion" or "fast food", while the "blend between trendy and family-friendly" confuses others; servers are "friendly" but not always "professional", though everyone agrees, "great drinks" – like fruit-infused sake – are a definite plus.

### NEW Tommy Ray's *Californian*

▽ | 18 | 20 | 19 | $34

**Studio City** | 12345 Ventura Blvd. (Whitsett Ave.) | 818-506-2412 | www.tommyrayscafe.com

Hailed as "a welcome addition to Ventura Boulevard", this "promising" new Studio City "hangout" features a "lovely" tree-shaded patio, "personable" staff and "reasonable prices"; the "short, but innovative" menu of Californian cuisine suffers from problems of "consistency", but supporters suggest you "give it a chance", saying it's a "promising" spot that they hope will blossom into a local "destination."

### Tommy's ●🍴 *Hamburgers/Hot Dogs*

22 | 6 | 15 | $8

**Downtown** | 2575 W. Beverly Blvd. (bet. Coronado St. & Rampart Blvd.) | 213-389-9060 | www.originaltommys.com

"Oh, to have an iron stomach" say those in awe of the "sloppy", "gut-busting" chili burgers at this "beloved" 24/7 Downtown dog and patty stand where "locals" and "tourists" queue up and chow down at all hours, some swearing that everything "tastes better at 3 AM" (it's also "a must after Dodgers games"); diehards declare the "mean streets" locale and "parking lot" decor actually "enhance the food", while others note that "it may be cheap, but you'll pay for it for days"; N.B. cash only.

### Tongdang Thai Kitchen *Thai*

18 | 18 | 21 | $23

**San Marino** | 932 Huntington Dr. (S. Oak Knoll Ave.) | 626-300-1010 | www.tongdang.com

San Marino denizens choose this "neighborhood Thai" for its "generous portions" that make for a "solid" "last-minute dinner"; others call it "nothing special" but say the "pleasant service" and "affordable" tabs means it still works "in an area without many other options"; N.B. the Brentwood location has closed.

### Tony P's Dockside Grill *American*

17 | 18 | 18 | $26

**Marina del Rey** | 4445 Admiralty Way (bet. Bali Way & Via Marina) | 310-823-4534 | www.tonyps.com

The "wonderful location" right on the water is the most memorable thing about this rather "ordinary" Marina del Rey American eatery; the fare is "standard", but "large portions" are its saving grace, particularly since the venue – done up in a nautical theme with a "huge, noisy sports bar" and "semi-enclosed patio" – caters to a "family-friendly" crowd.

| | FOOD | DECOR | SERVICE | COST |
|---|---|---|---|---|

### Tony's Bella Vista  *Italian*
▽ 22 | 9 | 17 | $21

**Burbank** | 3116 W. Magnolia Blvd. (Fairview St.) | 818-843-0164 | www.tonysbellavista.com

A "longtime" Burbank "neighborhood favorite", this Italian keeps "locals" "coming back" with "homey pastas" and "delicious" "thin-crust" pizzas served in a low-lit room with "old-school red leather booths" and murals of the old country decorating the walls; the nice price means it gets "crowded", especially on "weekends."

### Torafuku  *Japanese*
22 | 19 | 19 | $44

**West LA** | 10914 W. Pico Blvd. (Westwood Blvd.) | 310-470-0014 | www.torafuku-usa.com

"Authentic", "well-executed" sushi and cooked dishes draw the proudly self-styled "anti-Nobu crowd" to this "serene" Tokyo import in West LA, which proves its pedigree by serving "pearllike" Kamado rice that cognoscenti cherish for its "subtle flavor"; service is typically "pleasant" while the "refined" setting suits the "urbane" cuisine.

### Toscana  *Italian*
24 | 17 | 21 | $53

**Brentwood** | 11633 San Vicente Blvd. (Darlington Ave.) | 310-820-2448

"See celebrities in their natural habitat" at this "bustling" Brentwood "standby" serving "fabulous" Northern Italian dishes that are priced in step with the "movie mogul" clientele; servers are "charming" (more so to "regulars"), and if some call it "overloud" and "overrated", most say "it's always a fun time" – just "bring earplugs."

### Tower Bar  *Californian*
▽ 22 | 27 | 22 | $63

**West Hollywood** | Sunset Tower Hotel | 8358 Sunset Blvd. (bet. La Cienega Blvd. & Sweetzer Ave.) | 323-848-6677 | www.sunsettowerhotel.com

This "sophisticated" spot atop the Sunset Tower Hotel "feels like an exclusive NYC club" insist insiders who also appreciate the "delicious", "straightforward" Californian cuisine, though a few quibble it "doesn't meet the ambitions" of the "historic" art deco setting; "aspiring-actor waiters" add to the "old-Hollywood" "look and feel" that includes walnut-paneled walls, a sleek piano and "breathtaking views" of the city.

### Towne  *Californian*
▽ 19 | 21 | 17 | $45

**Manhattan Beach** | 1142 Manhattan Ave. (Manhattan Beach Blvd.) | 310-545-5405 | www.townebythesea.com

"Lively", "hip" and right in the heart of Manhattan Beach, this local "hangout" is Californian not only in cuisine, but in "vibe" too; seasonal fare is "hearty with flair" (though perhaps "not terribly inspiring" for foodies), while the owner is a "charming, attentive host", who skillfully orchestrates the every-weekend transition from "upscale" eatery to "trendy pickup hangout."

### NEW  Tracht's  🅂 🅼  *American*
– | – | – | M

**Long Beach** | Renaissance Long Beach Hotel | 111 E. Ocean Blvd. (Pine Ave.) | 562-499-2533 | www.renaissancehotels.com

Chef Suzanne Tracht brings her brand of New American cuisine to the South Bay with this midpriced, hotel version of Jar in the lobby of the Renaissance Long Beach; its dramatic space with an atrium ceiling and glass walls is complemented by its spacious outdoor patio, complete with a fire pit and a fine view of the harbor.

### Tra Di Noi  *Italian*

22 | 19 | 20 | $44

**Malibu** | Malibu Country Mart | 3835 Cross Creek Rd. (PCH) | 310-456-0169

"Beautiful people" (including a "celeb" or two) congregate at this "sceney" Italian "hidden" behind the Malibu Country Mart, where a seat on the "patio" on a "summer night" provides a truly "pleasant" experience; fare is "imaginative", if "overpriced", while "professional" service extends from the dining room to the express take-out window.

### Trails, The  Ⓜ✄  *American/Vegan*

▽ 18 | 21 | 14 | $11

**Los Feliz** | Griffith Park | 2333 Fern Dell Dr. (Los Feliz Blvd.) | 323-871-2102 | www.thetrailslosfeliz.com

Los Feliz denizens say this "adorable little shack" in the middle of Griffith Park is "great after a hike" for a "cup of coffee" or a "healthy snack" from the menu of inexpensive American-vegan offerings; patio seating is appropriately "rustic", though WiFi capability means you can stay connected, even when enjoying "mother nature."

### Trastevere  *Italian*

18 | 18 | 18 | $33

**Hollywood** | Hollywood & Highland Complex | 6801 Hollywood Blvd. (Highland Ave.) | 323-962-3261
**Santa Monica** | 1360 Third St. Promenade (Santa Monica Blvd.) | 310-319-1985
www.trastevereristorante.com

Prime "people-watching" is on offer at both branches of this "moderately priced" Italian trattoria in the Santa Monica Promenade and the Hollywood & Highland Complex where "tourists" and locals munch on "decent", if "very ordinary", pizzas and pastas; turnaround is usually "ultrafast", while the patio seating at both locations feels a bit "like being in Rome" to some surveyors.

### Traxx  Ⓩ  *American*

20 | 21 | 19 | $40

**Downtown** | Union Station | 800 N. Alameda St. (bet. Cesar Chavez Ave. & Rte. 101) | 213-625-1999 | www.traxxrestaurant.com

Downtown's "undiscovered gem" declare those enchanted by this "offbeat" New American eatery nestled in "historic" Union Station where the "elegant" "art deco" surroundings set the mood for chef Tara Thomas' "innovative" midpriced fare; service is "attentive", while garden seating provides the perfect opportunity to people-watch" and soak up a bit of the "old LA" atmosphere.

### Tre Venezie  Ⓜ  *Italian*

24 | 20 | 21 | $57

**Pasadena** | 119 W. Green St. (bet. De Lacey & Pasadena Aves.) | 626-795-4455

"Don't expect typical Italian fare" at this "unusual" ristorante in Pasadena, because it's "dedicated to the history" and "tradition" of the Boot's northeast, a region whose cuisine seems "exotic" to many and is delivered "artistically"; although some deem the "quaint, understated" dining room "stuffy", staffers who "seem to love their jobs" are breaths of fresh air.

### Trio Mediterranean Grill  *Mediterranean*

▽ 17 | 15 | 19 | $24

**Rolling Hills** | Peninsula Ctr. | 46B Peninsula Ctr. (Hawthorne Blvd.) | 310-265-5577 | www.triogrille.com

A "neighborhood find" in a Rolling Hills shopping center, this "reliable" Mediterranean is a "regular choice" for surveyors seeking a "quick, reasonably priced meal"; "lots of fans" create a "boisterous" ambiance, though a handful of dissenters declare its "popularity" is due to otherwise "limited dining options" in the area.

### Triumphal Palace  *Chinese*

24 | 18 | 18 | $28

**Alhambra** | 500 W. Main St. (5th St.) | 626-308-3222

"No carts" mean the "amazing variety" of "delicate", "tasty" dim sum comes "piping-hot" at this Alhambra Cantonese, whose kitchen also does dinner "sublimely" enough to "stand up to any celebrity chef"; though the service can "vary greatly from visit to visit", the somewhat "posh" surroundings (white tablecloths, lobster tank, Lucite bar) stand firm – "too bad" you "pay more for the nicer decor."

### Tropicalia Brazilian Grill ❶ *Brazilian*

19 | 11 | 18 | $21

**Los Feliz** | 1966 Hillhurst Ave. (Franklin Ave.) | 323-644-1798 | www.tropicaliabraziliangrill.com

"Simple", "solid" Brazilian food is served in "generous" portions at this Los Feliz "hang" with "fast" and "friendly" service; though the setting is "sparse", the "great" wine-by-the-glass selections from the adjacent wine bar fuel an "entertaining", "neighborhood" vibe; N.B. patio seating is a recent addition.

### Trump's Ⓜ *American*

23 | 25 | 24 | $56

**Rancho Palos Verdes** | Trump Nat'l Golf Course | 1 Ocean Trails Dr. (Palos Verdes Dr. S.) | 310-303-3260 | www.trumpgolf.com

"Donald Trump's seaside oasis" in ritzy Rancho Palos Verdes has changed its Continental menu to more Traditional American offerings, but the "spectacular panoramic views", highly rated service and "luxurious", "over-the-top" atmosphere remain (jackets suggested); to regulars' relief, the "do-not-miss" Sunday buffet brunch is also still available; N.B. the Food score may not reflect the recent cuisine change.

### Tsuji No Hana  *Japanese*

▽ 22 | 11 | 20 | $32

**Marina del Rey** | 4714 Lincoln Blvd. (Mindanao Way) | 310-827-1433

"Reliably fresh" sushi inspires devotees to "over order" at this "unpretentious" Marina del Rey "neighborhood" eatery; with a "welcoming" staff, "decent prices" and "minimal" but still "cozy" candlelit quarters, it's small wonder that "everyone here seems to be a regular."

### Tuk Tuk Thai  *Thai*

21 | 16 | 17 | $23

**Pico-Robertson** | 8875 W. Pico Blvd. (bet. Doheny Dr. & Robertson Blvd.) | 310-860-1872 | www.tuktukla.com

"Consistent" and "convenient" Thai food at "reasonable" prices has Pico-Robertson locals "addicted" to this "friendly" "neighborhood" "storefront" serving "well-presented" dishes tailored to diners' "tolerance for spice"; the recently renovated decor is "pleasant" with rose-hued walls and sleek wooden floors, though "fast take-out service" means many may order their meal to go.

### Tulipano Ⓜ *Italian*

▽ 23 | 13 | 24 | $28

**Azusa** | 530 S. Citrus Ave. (Gladstone St.) | 626-967-6670

Guests are greeted to "a warm welcome upon arrival" at this "tried-and-true" Azusa Italian that whips up "outstanding", "authentic" fare; if both of its two sides – a formal blue-and-pink dining room and a casual maroon trattoria – are "not much to look at" (its location in a "shady strip mall" doesn't help matters), take comfort in the fact that "prices would be 50-percent higher if they were located in the 'other' valley."

### ☑ Tuscany II Ristorante  *Italian*          27  22  24  $48

**Westlake Village** | Westlake Plaza | 968 S. Westlake Blvd. (Townsgate Rd.) | 805-495-2768 | www.tuscany-restaurant.com

Widely considered the "crème de la crème" for Westlake Village, this "outstanding" Italian kitchen presents creations that "taste as good as they look", including "fine specials" and a "good wine selection"; adding to the feel of "formal dining in a casual atmosphere" ("even better since the redesign") are "servers who genuinely care about making you happy", themselves overseen by "delightful owners."

### 25 Degrees ❶ *Hamburgers*          21  19  17  $25

**Hollywood** | Roosevelt Hotel | 7000 Hollywood Blvd. (N. Orange Dr.) | 323-785-7244 | www.25degreesrestaurant.com

Sure, the "juicy", "build-your-own" burgers at this "hyper-trendy" Roosevelt Hotel joint are "a little expensive", but the "wide assortment of sauces", "fancy cheeses" and other "tantalizing toppings", not to mention the "luscious" wines, "take it to the next level"; while aesthetes also dig the Dodd Mitchell–designed "retro setting with red flocked wallpaper", some sniff that the "waiters are more concerned with being seen than serving."

### 2117 Ⓜ *Asian/European*          24  14  21  $39

**West LA** | 2117 Sawtelle Blvd. (bet. Mississippi Ave. & Olympic Blvd.) | 310-477-1617 | www.restaurant2117.com

Loyalists laud the chef's "deft touch" with organic ingredients at this "tiny" West LA "foodie find" where "wonderful" "high-end" Asian-European fare (think penne with spicy crab) is offered at "fair prices"; add in "attentive service" and it's "a gem" in spite of "parking difficulty" and its somewhat "dowdy strip-mall setting."

### 22nd St. Landing Ⓜ *Seafood*          18  19  18  $32

**San Pedro** | 141A W. 22nd St. (Harbor Blvd.) | 310-548-4400 | www.22ndstlandingrestaurant.com

The "spectacular view" takes center stage at this San Pedro stalwart set in the Cabrillo Marina where "boats" and "local fishermen" provide an appropriate backdrop for "well-prepared" seafood dishes; though the menu "hasn't really changed in the last decade", customers can "count on" it for "relaxed" ambiance and moderate tabs.

### 26 Beach  *Californian*          20  18  19  $26

**Marina del Rey** | 3100 Washington Blvd. (Lincoln Blvd.) | 310-823-7526

"Gourmet burgers", "bountiful salads" and "scrumptious French toasts" anchor the Californian menu at this Marina del Rey "neighborhood cafe" whose guests gravitate to the "cheerful" tea garden with a fountain; despite the sometimes "sporadic service", most appreciate that it's "moderately priced" and maintains a "casual", "homey" feel.

### Twin Palms  *American*          17  21  17  $36

**Pasadena** | 101 W. Green St. (De Lacey Ave.) | 626-577-2567 | www.twin-palms.com

With seating "half-inside and half-outside" "under a tent and trees", this "ultracasual" yet "chic" Pasadena New American offers "pleasant" repasts, which are made "livelier" with bands on weekend evenings and the "fun" Sunday jazz brunch; the "reasonably priced" New American menu can range from "great to mediocre" (likewise, the staff can be "inconsistent"), but that may not matter much to the "singles" who create "quite a scene" at the bar.

### Twist *Californian* ▽ 19 | 20 | 19 | $39

**Hollywood** | Renaissance Hollywood Hotel | 1755 N. Highland Ave. (Hollywood Blvd.) | 323-491-1000 | www.renaissancehollywood.com

"It would be the hottest restaurant around were it in Beverly Hills" guess guests of the Renaissance Hollywood Hotel who appreciate this spot's geometric-centric midcentury-modern design and Asian-leaning Californian breakfasts, lunches and dinners; as it is now, it remains a "hidden treasure."

### Typhoon *Pan-Asian* 21 | 21 | 20 | $36

**Santa Monica** | Santa Monica Airport | 3221 Donald Douglas Loop S. (Airport Ave.) | 310-390-6565 | www.typhoon.biz

"A hidden gem", this Pan-Asian "hang" in the Santa Monica Airport has a "wildly interesting menu" offering everything from curries and deep-fried catfish to surprisingly "tasty" insect dishes like stir-fried crickets and stuffed waterbugs; service is "on top of it", and the room, while "as loud as" the "runway" it overlooks, works well for "larger groups" or as an "unusual date spot."

### Ugo *Italian* - | - | - | I

**Culver City** | 3865 Cardiff Ave. (Culver Blvd.) | 310-204-1222 | www.cafeugo.com

The latest arrival to the Culver City dining hub, this large Milanese-looking eatery, with a sizable outdoor patio, big open kitchen and lush lounge area, serves a reasonably priced Italian menu of antipasti and pastas; there's also an adjacent wine bar with self-sevice tastings.

### Ulysses Voyage *Greek* ▽ 20 | 16 | 18 | $30

**Fairfax** | The Grove at Farmers Mkt. | 6333 W. Third St. (Fairfax Ave.) | 323-939-9728 | www.ulyssesvoyage.com

Diners divide on the fare at this Greek "sit-down" restaurant at the Grove that some find "excellent" and others insist is "inconsistent"; still, "cheerful service", live music nightly and a "homey ambiance enhanced by a crackling fireplace" make it "a solid bet" for hungry Farmers Market patrons while the "patio is the place to be" in fine weather.

### NEW Ummba Grill *Brazilian* ▽ 16 | 14 | 14 | $23

**Century City** | Westfield Century City Shopping Ctr. | 10250 Santa Monica Blvd. (Ave. of the Stars) | 310-552-2014

"They weigh your plate and charge you accordingly" at this Century City churrascaria, which offers "self-service" Brazilian meats and a "nice salad bar selection" (the staff can also "bring the food" to you for "some extra bucks") in "utilitarian" environs, surprisingly augmented by a "patio" "lined with mini-trees"; some Westfield shoppers, however, dis it as a "just-ordinary" "part of the food court", while others allow "they are trying."

|  | FOOD | DECOR | SERVICE | COST |
|--|------|-------|---------|------|

### Uncle Bill's Pancake House *Diner* | 22 | 14 | 19 | $14 |

**Manhattan Beach** | 1305 Highland Ave. (13th St.) | 310-545-5177

This "hometown favorite" for "hangover"-busting breakfasts in Manhattan Beach serves up "delish" diner staples like "warm muffins" and bacon-cheddar waffles that are "worth getting out of bed early" for; service is "friendly" and tabs inexpensive, while the "joint" decor gets a boost from a patio with "ocean views."

### Uncle Darrow's *Cajun/Creole* | 19 | 10 | 18 | $14 |

**Marina del Rey** | 2560 S. Lincoln Blvd. (Washington Blvd.) | 310-306-4862 | www.uncledarrows.com

"They put plenty of care" into the Cajun-Creole cooking at this "solid" Marina del Rey joint with no beef or pork on the menu, but plenty of other "tasty" fare like seafood gumbo and jambalaya; the owners and staff get props for giving plenty of "personal attention" (and "free samples"), and though many people opt for takeout, the "friendly" "New Orleans" ambiance is tonic "if you've had a bad day."

### Upstairs 2 Ⓢ Ⓜ *Mediterranean* | 23 | 18 | 21 | $43 |

**West LA** | Wine House | 2311 Cotner Ave. (Olympic Blvd.) | 310-231-0316 | www.upstairs2.com

West LA diners dig the "sophisticated" small plates and "incredible selection" of "off-the-beaten-path" vintages at this Mediterranean newcomer "perched above" the Wine House retail shop and staffed with "intelligent" servers who "steer you" through the "ambitious" menu; though the "intimate", "high concept" decor and "expensive" tabs don't work for everyone, most find it "completely pleasant", especially for late-night "grazing" (they're open till 1 AM on weekends).

### Urasawa Ⓢ *Japanese* | ▽ 29 | 26 | 29 | $334 |

**Beverly Hills** | 218 N. Rodeo Dr. (Wilshire Blvd.) | 310-247-8939

"Who says you can't have it all in Beverly Hills?" – you can if you "scrape up the ducats" ("$275 per person before you order drinks") for the only-at-6-PM seating at this "slice of sushi heaven" where the "charming" Hiro Urasawa offers "personal attention" while creating omakase-only meals of about 30 "exquisite" courses featuring "some strange delights"; add presentation that's "nothing short of art", and you have a "unique culinary adventure" that's "unlike anything in LA."

### Urth Caffé *American* | 21 | 16 | 15 | $18 |

**West Hollywood** | 8565 Melrose Ave. (bet. La Cienega & Robertson Blvds.) | 310-659-0628

**Beverly Hills** | 267 S. Beverly Dr. (Gregory Way) | 310-205-9311 | www.urthcaffe.com ◑

**Santa Monica** | 2327 Main St. (bet. Ocean Park & Pico Blvds.) | 310-314-7040 | www.urthcaffe.com

A "health joint" with a "see-and-be-seen vibe", this American mini-chain attracts the "post-yoga crowd", "idle rich on BlackBerries", "tourists" and plenty of "celebs in baseball caps" for organic American fare like "light" salads and sandwiches, "fresh" baked goods and "strong lattes"; conditions are "crowded" both inside and out on the patios while "friendly" counter staffers try to impose a "method to the madness" of the ordering line.

| | FOOD | DECOR | SERVICE | COST |
|---|---|---|---|---|

### NEW uWink Bistro ⬤ *Californian*
▽ 14 | 17 | 13 | $21

**Woodland Hills** | Westfield Promenade | 6100 Topanga Canyon Blvd. (bet. Erwin & Oxnard Sts.) | 818-992-1100 | www.uwink.com

Owner Nolan Bushnell, founder of Atari and Chuck E. Cheese, had a "novel idea" with this high-tech "gimmick" inside the Westfield Promenade in Woodland Hills, where guests use a tabletop "touch screen to order food and then play games and trivia contests while waiting"; "parents who don't wish to talk to their kids" appreciate the "entertainment", but note "changing orders is a pain" and label the Californian eats "moderate" at best.

### Uzbekistan *Uzbeki*
▽ 18 | 12 | 16 | $30

**Hollywood** | 7077 Sunset Blvd. (La Brea Ave.) | 323-464-3663

"Exotic" Uzbeki cuisine raises eyebrows at this Hollywood strip-mall spot where "foreign flavors" infuse "wholesome" traditional dishes like *plov* (a rice pilaf made with tender lamb); decor is quirky and includes memorabilia and photos lining the walls, while "live music" on weekends makes it a festive "favorite" with the "local Russian community."

### U-Zen 🗷 *Japanese*
22 | 13 | 21 | $31

**West LA** | 11951 Santa Monica Blvd. (Brockton St.) | 310-477-1390

"Fresh" and "not over-the-top expensive" sushi is the draw at this West LA "local" where insiders insist the "friendly" chef-owner "will never steer you wrong"; fans find it "satisfies the urge", but even boosters beg the "modest" decor is "severely in need of updating."

### 🗷 Valentino 🗷 *Italian*
26 | 22 | 25 | $72

**Santa Monica** | 3115 Pico Blvd. (bet. 31st & 32nd Sts.) | 310-829-4313 | www.welovewine.com

Piero Selvaggio's Santa Monica "favorite" still sets "the standard" with its "incomparable" 3,000-label wine list, "consistently fantastic" Italian cuisine and "inspirational" tasting menus ("put yourself in the chef's hands" and "miracles will happen"); the "impeccably trained" staff "knows how to take care of you", and though a few feel the "over-the-top" decor with Murano glass chandeliers is "stuck in the '80s" – which may be why it's currently being remodeled – most find it an "elegant" respite that's well worth the final "credit-card-busting" bill.

### NEW Vault, The *American*
▽ 15 | 20 | 16 | $32

**Pasadena** | 2675 E. Colorado Blvd. (N. San Gabriel Blvd.) | 626-683-3344 | www.thevaultpasadena.com

The sports bar goes "chic" at this Pasadena newcomer set in a former bank building where the reasonably priced American menu plays second fiddle to the "cool" plasma TVs on the walls and the extensive cocktail menu; it's "trendy" for the neighborhood, with "cute waitresses" and Monday Night Football crowds contributing to the "great mood."

### Vegan Glory *Vegan*
▽ 24 | 11 | 23 | $16

**Beverly Boulevard** | 8393 Beverly Blvd. (Orlando Ave.) | 323-653-4900

"Surprisingly tasty" "Thai-inspired" vegan fare is served at this "healthy pit stop" on Beverly Boulevard where some dishes like spicy eggplant "appeal even to carnivores"; meanwhile, "simple" decor, "reasonable" prices and a "friendly" owner make first-timers "look forward" to visiting again.

|  | FOOD | DECOR | SERVICE | COST |
|---|---|---|---|---|

### Velvet Margarita Cantina ● *Mexican*    16 | 24 | 17 | $28

**Hollywood** | 1612 N. Cahuenga Blvd. (bet. Hollywood Blvd. & Selma Ave.) | 323-469-2000 | www.velvetmargarita.com

The atmosphere is like a cross between a "Tijuana brothel" and "the back of some dude's makeout van" at this "campy" "blacklit" Hollywood Mexican where the "kitschy" "velour paintings" and "Goth" decor are a big hit with the "rock 'n' roll" crowd; "friendly" staffers who seem to be "hired for their looks" watch over the "jam-packed" "bar scene" fueled by "great tastin' margaritas" and "merely average" food.

### vermont *American*    22 | 22 | 20 | $43

**Los Feliz** | 1714 N. Vermont Ave. (Prospect Ave.) | 323-661-6163 | www.vermontrestaurantonline.com

Los Feliz locals laud this "neighborhood favorite" for its "reliable", "delicious" New American menu and "warm, but not overbearing" service; a "hipster cocktail lounge" area offsets the "elegant", "white-tablecloth" dining room, and while tabs are "pricey", owners "Mike and Manny" are so nice, they "make the check go down easy."

### Versailles *Cuban*    21 | 9 | 17 | $18

**Mid-City** | 1415 S. La Cienega Blvd. (Pico Blvd.) | 310-289-0392
**Palms** | 10319 Venice Blvd. (Motor Ave.) | 310-558-3168
**Manhattan Beach** | 1000 N. Sepulveda Blvd. (10th St.) | 310-937-6829
**Encino** | 17410 Ventura Blvd. (bet. Louise & White Oak Aves.) | 818-906-0756
**Universal City** | Universal CityWalk | 1000 Universal Studios Blvd. (off Rte. 101) | 818-505-0093
www.versaillescuban.com

"Beware the cravings once you try" the "famous garlic chicken" warn addicts of this "no-nonsense" Cuban chain, which also serves "hearty portions" of "succulent, decadent" roast pork, beef and seafood "at incredible prices"; "nobody notices" the "dim lighting", "tired decor" or "average" service, looking up from their plates only to mumble "more plantains, please"; N.B. counter service only at Universal City.

### Vert *American/Californian*    21 | 20 | 19 | $42

**Hollywood** | Hollywood & Highland Complex | 6801 Hollywood Blvd., 4th fl. (Highland Ave.) | 323-491-1300 | www.wolfgangpuck.com

Wolfgang Puck's "casual" Californian–New American cafe and its colorful new lounge caters to Hollywood & Highland crowds with "inventive" cuisine and portions fit for "sharing"; service is "attentive" when it's "not too crazy", and though jaded critics dub it "Spago-lite" and say they "expect more" from the famous owner, it's still "good for out-of-town guests."

### NEW Vertical Wine Bistro Ⓜ *Eclectic/Mediterranean*    19 | 25 | 17 | $41

**Pasadena** | 70 N. Raymond Ave. (Union St.) | 626-795-3999 | www.verticalwinebistro.com

A "pricey, hip" addition to Pasadena, this wine bar (owned by film producer Gale Ann Hurd of the *Terminator* series) wins accolades for its "beautiful" yet "comfortable" interior done up in chocolate brown with wood furnishings; Eclectic-Mediterranean cuisine "has potential but isn't there yet", while several reviewers feel "staffers could be better trained" about the "amazing selection" of bottles.

|  | FOOD | DECOR | SERVICE | COST |
|---|---|---|---|---|

### ☒ Via Veneto  *Italian*                        26 | 19 | 21 | $56

**Santa Monica** | 3009 Main St. (bet. Marine St. & Pier Ave.) | 310-399-1843 | www.viaveneto.us

Foodies feel they've "struck gold" at this "stellar" Santa Monica Italian where "heavenly" signature dishes like "melt-in-your-mouth" ravioli are augmented each night by a "dizzying" list of specials; the "intimate" (read: cramped) "candlelit space" is presided over by "authentic" old country waiters making it all so "perfect" you might not mind the "shocker" of a bill.

### Vibrato Grill & Jazz  Ⓜ *American/Steak*        22 | 24 | 22 | $61

**Bel-Air** | 2930 Beverly Glen Circle (Mulholland Dr.) | 310-474-9400 | www.vibratogrilljazz.com

"Consistently strong live jazz" in a "beautiful" room "brilliantly engineered for acoustics", "delicious steaks" and other "first-rate" American fare and "attentive service that's respectful of musicians" "meld together effortlessly to create an experience for all the senses" at the legendary Herb Alpert's "ideal date spot" in Bel-Air; though food and drink prices are "high", "it's the performances you're paying for" since there's no separate music fee.

### NEW Village Idiot, The  ◐ *American*           19 | 20 | 18 | $25

**Melrose** | 7383 Melrose Ave. (Martel Ave.) | 323-655-3331 | www.villageidiotla.com

Melrose "needed a place like this forever": a spot that serves slightly "fancy" American "pub grub" at "unbelievably reasonable" prices in a "cool" loftlike space that's open late; while the "raucous" "London/New York" atmosphere gets "way too crowded" for some suburbanites, "serious drinkers" slur "as a neighborhood bar, this place is tops."

### Village Pizzeria  *Pizza*                      24 | 11 | 16 | $14

**Hancock Park** | 131 N. Larchmont Blvd. (bet. Beverly Blvd. & 1st St.) | 323-465-5566 | www.villagepizzeria.net

"Arguably the best pizza west of Brooklyn" say "self-avowed NYC 'za experts" of this Hancock Park "fixture" turning out "divine", "thin-crust" pies including an "addictive" clam-topped one; "excruciating waits" and "surly teen" counter staff do little to dissuade "locals" from "coming back", though some do opt for "delivery."

### Villa Piacere  *Eclectic*                      20 | 24 | 19 | $36

**Woodland Hills** | 22160 Ventura Blvd. (bet. Shoup Ave. & Topanga Canyon Blvd.) | 818-704-1185 | www.villapiacere.com

A "charming room with a cozy fireplace" and a "delightful backyard patio" make this Woodland Hills "beauty" a "romantic getaway" in any season; though the Eclectic eats are "usually good", they and the staff can be "inconsistent", leading some lovebirds to sigh "if only the food and service were as nice as the decor."

### Villa Sorriso  *Italian*                       18 | 20 | 17 | $32

**Pasadena** | 168 W. Colorado Blvd. (Pasadena Ave.) | 626-793-8008 | www.sorrisopasadena.com

"Dine under the stars" "while viewing old films projected on a wall" (on weekends) in the "softly lit", fountain-blessed "courtyard" of this "trendy" Italian in a "touristy" part of Pasadena; though it "sometimes reads better than it tastes", the Italian menu is mostly "dependable" –

| | FOOD | DECOR | SERVICE | COST |
|---|---|---|---|---|

not like the staff, which can be "inattentive", especially on "Friday and Saturday nights" when the bar area becomes a bit of a "scene."

## Vincenti 🖪 *Italian* | 25 | 23 | 23 | $60 |

**Brentwood** | 11930 San Vicente Blvd. (Montana Ave.) | 310-207-0127 | www.vincentiristorante.com

Nicola Mastronardi "continually surprises" with a "truly creative", "heavenly" seasonal menu, leading "pasta people" to proclaim him "the most underappreciated Italian chef" in LA – or at least in Brentwood where his "action-packed", "upscale" and "astronomically priced" kitchen continues to "delight" after more than 10 years; indeed, from "delightful co-owner/host" Maureen Vincenti's "warm" "welcome to the final sip of cappuccino, it's a memorable experience."

## Violet 🅼 *American* | 21 | 17 | 19 | $39 |

**Santa Monica** | 3221 Pico Blvd. (bet. 32nd & 33rd Sts.) | 310-453-9113 | www.violetrestaurant.com

"Singularly creative" New American small plates fit for "sharing" draw a "young, professional" crowd to this "ambitious" Santa Monica "find" helmed by "up-and-coming" chef-owner Jared Simons; it's an "appealing" spot with a "smart" wine list and "cozy", though "loud", atmosphere, and while critics complain they "end up spending more than expected", those in-the-know suggest you "go early" for the 7 by 7 "deal" ("seven plates at $7 each before 7 PM", Tuesday–Thursday).

## V.I.P. Harbor Seafood *Chinese/Seafood* | 18 | 13 | 14 | $22 |

**West LA** | 11701 Wilshire Blvd. (Barrington Ave.) | 310-979-3377

"Keep your expectations low" and you won't be disappointed at this West LA strip-mall Sino that "satisfies cravings" with a "wide variety" of dim sum and seafood dishes that are about "as authentic as you can get in the area"; there's "no atmosphere" to speak of and many feel "the staff could use a lesson in manners", but it "does the job" for "takeout" or a meal in the "neighborhood"; N.B. dim sum served at lunch only.

## Vitello's *Italian* | 14 | 14 | 18 | $27 |

**Studio City** | 4349 Tujunga Ave. (Moorpark St.) | 818-769-0905 | www.vitellosrestaurant.com

Red-sauce loyalists have been lauding this Studio City "spaghetti house" (open since 1976) for its affordable, "classic" Italian dishes ("there is nothing nouvelle" here) and "old-school" decor since "even before Robert Blake made it world-famous" during his high-profile trial; cynics, however, snipe "eliminate the morbid-curiosity factor, and all you're left with" is "mediocre" food and live entertainment (piano or jazz band nightly, comedy on Wednesdays and weekends).

## Vito *Italian* | 23 | 19 | 23 | $41 |

**Santa Monica** | 2807 Ocean Park Blvd. (28th St.) | 310-450-4999 | www.vitorestaurant.com

Dubbed "Little Italy in Santa Monica", this "old-style" establishment specializes in veal chops, osso buco and other "rich, heavy" classics dished out by "grumpy but lovable" tuxedo-clad waiters; the "comfortable" room with "white tablecloths" and "romantic" lighting exudes a "classic" "NYC" vibe that makes you feel like *The Godfather* could be sitting at the next table"; N.B. the Decor score may not reflect a June 2007 remodel.

| | FOOD | DECOR | SERVICE | COST |
|---|---|---|---|---|

### Vittorio's Ⓜ Italian

18 | 14 | 19 | $28

**Pacific Palisades** | 16646 Marquez Ave. (Sunset Blvd.) | 310-459-9316 |
www.vittoriosla.com

Pacific Palisades' Southern Italian "family" destination serves "simple", "red-sauce" dishes, pizzas and "tasty" garlic knots in a "cozy, neighborhood" setting with celebrity headshots lining the walls; some say "dine-in service is lacking" and opt for "takeout", while others insist they could "come here every week and never get bored."

### Viva Madrid Spanish

▽ 22 | 18 | 18 | $28

**Claremont** | 225 Yale Ave. (Bonita Ave.) | 909-624-5500 |
www.vivamadrid.com

"A fun stop" on the Claremont "dining circuit", this "interesting" Iberian serves "fantastic tapas" with "funky" "flair", "amazing sangria" and "excellent paella" entrees in an "authentic" environment that makes folks feel like they've "traveled to Spain"; though there are some reports of "erratic service", at least they vow not to close up shop until the last customer has had his fill.

### Vivoli Café & Trattoria Italian

25 | 16 | 24 | $34

**West Hollywood** | 7994 Sunset Blvd. (Laurel Ave.) | 323-656-5050 |
www.vivolicafe.com

"Jammed into" an "inauspicious" West Hollywood "mini-mall", this "totally unexpected" "slice of Italy" concocts "homemade pasta" "so good", it's practically "not fair to other restaurants" – and so "reasonably priced", it's "living proof that great Italian food doesn't need to be expensive"; the "cozy" dining room may be "overstuffed", but the "over-the-top thankful waiters" (many of whom sport "seductive accents") "welcome" everyone like "a longtime friend."

### Wa Ⓜ Japanese

▽ 27 | 11 | 21 | $53

**West Hollywood** | La Cienega Plaza | 1106 N. La Cienega Blvd.
(Holloway Dr.) | 310-854-7285

For "Nobu-like food in a very un-Nobu-like environment", ascend to this "nouvelle sushi" spot "on the second floor of a strip mall", where chefs who "trained under Matsuhisa" himself present "wonderfully fresh" and "creative" cuts exhibiting "refined yet intense flavors"; "occasional star sightings defy the locale", which does feature a "sort-of-good view" of "the WeHo skyline."

### Wabi-Sabi Asian Fusion

22 | 17 | 19 | $40

**Venice** | 1635 Abbot Kinney Blvd. (Venice Blvd.) | 310-314-2229 |
www.wabisabisushi.com

While the "creative sushi chefs" whip up "imaginative" fish dishes, even cooked food fans find plenty of "satisfying" fare – including vegan miso soup "containing every vegetable in the planet" – at this Asian fusion spot in Venice's "hip Abbot Kinney district"; though the modern space is "trendy", "noisy" and "always crowded", the "young" "regulars" still manage to find dinner here "relaxing."

### Wahib's Middle East Mideastern

21 | 13 | 19 | $21

**Alhambra** | 910 E. Main St. (Granada Ave.) | 626-576-1048 |
www.wahibsmiddleeast.com

"Be prepared to share" or settle for some "wonderful leftovers" at this "reasonably priced" Alhambra stalwart where the "delicious" Middle

Eastern fare like lamb kebabs and "exotic" quail and frog dishes comes in "heaping portions"; service is "quick and friendly" while the "cave-like" interior is enlivened by belly dancers and singers Friday and Saturday nights.

## Walter's Eclectic
| 19 | 18 | 19 | $25 |

**Claremont** | 308 Yale Ave. (Bonita Ave.) | 909-624-4914 | www.waltersrestaurant.net

"An institution" declare devotees of this rambling cafe in "picture-perfect" Claremont with a "beautiful patio" and a "multiculti" crowd that ranges from "college students" to "ladies who lunch"; "the menu is as diverse as the clientele" with "approachable" servers delivering a variety of "tasty" Eclectic fare that meshes Californian cuisine with "Afghani" and "Middle-Eastern" accents.

## Warszawa M Polish
| 21 | 16 | 20 | $34 |

**Santa Monica** | 1414 Lincoln Blvd. (Santa Monica Blvd.) | 310-393-8831 | www.warszawarestaurant.com

"Deliciously seasoned", albeit slightly "fancier than traditional", cuisine of Poland awaits at this "charming old Santa Monica home" where "strong signature martinis" precede "amazing potato pancakes", "incredible" crispy duck and the like, served in "various rooms" and on an "appealing" patio; the meals may be "heavy", but they offer "real value", making this the "best" "upscale Polish" restaurant in town - "ok, it's the only one", but still, it's "fab."

## NEW Watercress Eclectic
| - | - | - | I |

**Sherman Oaks** | 13565 Ventura Blvd. (Ventura Canyon Ave.) | 818-385-1448
From the owners behind the The Coffee Roaster next door (a Sherman Oaks caffeine institution), this bright and airy breakfast and lunch cafe offers mostly organic Eclectic fare like buttermilk pancakes, frittatas, panini, muffins and cookies; counter and waiter service are available while tabs tally on the low end.

## Z Water Grill Seafood
| 27 | 24 | 25 | $62 |

**Downtown** | 544 S. Grand Ave. (bet. 5th & 6th Sts.) | 213-891-0900 | www.watergrill.com

A "mind-boggling assortment" of fish prepared in a "brilliantly" "imaginative manner" is what you'll find at this Downtown "favorite", which surveyors have once again deemed the "best damned seafood" spot in LA; a "terrific selection" of international wines adds to the "classy", "clubby" ambiance, as do the "sophisticated", "well-informed" servers, putting it "at the top" of the "short list" "for special occasions, business dinners" and other events that merit "ocean-deep pockets."

## West Italian/Steak
| 18 | 22 | 17 | $55 |

**Brentwood** | Hotel Angeleno | 170 N. Church Ln., 17th fl. (I-405) | 310-476-6411 | www.westatangeleno.com

"Dizzying views of traffic flowing along the 405" are the most memorable parts of this newish Italian steakhouse atop Brentwood's Hotel Angeleno, although the "beautiful" room comes in a close second; however, "the food does not match up" and it "seems like they're still trying to figure out the service" - maybe the "hipster crowds" and "thumping techno" indicate this isn't meant to be the "grown-up" experience serious diners think it should be.

| | FOOD | DECOR | SERVICE | COST |

### Whale & Ale, The  *Pub Food*
▽ 16 | 17 | 16 | $25

**San Pedro** | 327 W. Seventh St. (bet. Centre & Mesa Sts.) | 310-832-0363 |
www.whaleandale.com

"Authentic" from its "old London" atmosphere to its "mighty fine
pints", this British pub in San Pedro is "ok for fish 'n' chips" – however,
some of "the more ambitious menu items don't fly"; still, there's "good
entertainment" on weekends and an owner who "puts his heart and
soul into" the endeavor – good thing too, because the rest of the service can be "excruciatingly slow."

### Wharo Korean BBQ  *Korean*
19 | 16 | 17 | $31

**Marina del Rey** | 4029 Lincoln Blvd. (Washington Blvd.) | 310-578-7114 |
www.wharo.com

"No need to drive to K-town for good Korean BBQ" when this spot is
conveniently located right in a Marina del Rey "strip mall"; "whole
families" and "hip, young" things "cook the food bit by bit" on a "little
grill", making for a "fun" experience, especially "when you want to savor the company" – but it is somewhat "expensive for what it is" and
can really "add up if people are hungry."

### Whisper Lounge, The  *American*
16 | 20 | 17 | $34

**Fairfax** | The Grove at Farmers Mkt. | 189 The Grove Dr. (bet. Fairfax Ave. &
3rd St.) | 323-931-0202 | www.whisperloungela.com

Grove shoppers "rest their feet" while Fairfax nine-to-fivers "unwind"
at this "stop-off", a "sexy" place for "drinks and nibbles" from an
American menu that "hits all of today's hot spots"; however, the "hip"
vibe, "live piano music" (Monday, Wednesday and Friday) and prices
that are "not so pleasing" "after happy hour ends" may make it "a
much better bar than restaurant."

### ☑ Whist  *Californian*
21 | 25 | 21 | $61

**Santa Monica** | Viceroy Santa Monica | 1819 Ocean Ave. (Pico Blvd.) |
310-260-7500 | www.viceroysantamonica.com

For being such a "trendy" "magnet for the young and beautiful", this
"cool" cafe in Santa Monica's Viceroy hotel serves "surprisingly good"
and "hearty" Californian eats; but it's the "contemporary" "mad-
hatter" interior (green walls trimmed with china plates) and
"hopping" patio – replete with "private cabanas", "white wing chairs"
and palm trees – that really "seduce."

### Wildflour Pizza  *Pizza*
▽ 18 | 11 | 15 | $14

**Santa Monica** | 2807 Main St. (bet. Ashland Ave. & Hill St.) | 310-392-3300
"In the old part" of Santa Monica, this "reliable pizza place" caters to
"students" who "order at the counter" and "spread out in the courtyard for pitchers", "huge diner-style salads" and "basic" though "enjoyable" pies; it's "kid-friendly" as well, making it "pleasant" for "a
casual night out or at home (they deliver too)."

### Wilshire  ●☑  *American*
21 | 25 | 20 | $58

**Santa Monica** | 2454 Wilshire Blvd. (bet. Chelsea Ave. & 25th St.) |
310-586-1707 | www.wilshirerestaurant.com

An "extraordinary" "tree-houselike" patio, sporting "fire pits" and "romantic lighting", is the highlight of the "dazzling decor" at this "sexy"
Santa Monica "scene"; regrettably, many foodies feel the fare is "an
afterthought", because though the "seasonal" New American dishes are

| | FOOD | DECOR | SERVICE | COST |
|---|---|---|---|---|

"beautifully presented", they're often "under-executed" and "overpriced" – but perhaps that matters not to the "hipsters" who "line up down the block" "after dinner" when it turns into a "nightspot."

### Wilson 🗷 Mediterranean
| 23 | 17 | 20 | $46 |

**Culver City** | 8631 Washington Blvd. (Sherbourne Dr.) | 310-287-2093 | www.wilsonfoodandwine.com

"More magic from the Piccolo–La Botte gang" "dazzles" guests at this "imaginative" new Culver City Med by chef/co-owner Michael Wilson (Beach Boy Dennis Wilson's son), who particularly impresses with "outstanding" dishes like "slow roasted pork"; some call the "art-gallery setting" with a patio "too cold but cool" and say the service is "casual for the price", but most appreciate that "care is taken in providing a unique experience", especially when you opt for a tasting menu.

### Wine Bistro Ⓜ French
| 23 | 20 | 22 | $40 |

**Studio City** | 11915 Ventura Blvd. (Laurel Canyon Blvd.) | 818-766-6233 | www.winebistro.net

*Amis* agree the "menu is fantastic now" that chef and partner Peter Roelant (ex the closed Four Oaks) is cooking "terrific" seasonal French food to pair with "lovely" wines by the glass at this "easygoing" bistro in Studio City; despite its "slightly dated" brass-accented decor, the front of the house "can be very romantic", and it's "well run" by owner J.B. Torchon who's "almost always on hand to chat."

### Wokcano Cafe Chinese/Japanese
| 17 | 14 | 16 | $26 |

**West Hollywood** | 8408 W. Third St. (Orlando Ave.) | 323-653-1998 ●
**Century City** | Century Club | 10131 Constellation Blvd. (Ave. of the Stars) | 310-551-6688 🗷
**Pasadena** | 33 S. Fair Oaks Ave. (bet. W. Colorado Blvd. & W. Green St.) | 626-578-1818 ●
NEW **Burbank** | 150 S. San Fernando Blvd. (Angeleno Ave.) | 818-524-2288 ●
www.wokcanocafe.com

"Nothing particularly stands out" at this "no-frills" Chinese-Japanese mini-chain, but it does offer an "easy menu with many choices", from "tempura" to "ribs and everything in between" – though the sushi may be strictly "for the uninitiated"; most are open for a "late-night" "bite" when hungry "vampires" create a "scary club vibe."

### Wolfgang Puck Cafe Californian
| 18 | 16 | 17 | $27 |

**Universal City** | Universal CityWalk | 1000 Universal Studios Blvd. (off Rte. 101) | 818-985-9653 | www.wolfgangpuck.com

"Shoppers" and "tourists" hit up this "lower-end Wolfgang Puck" duo in Costa Mesa and Universal City for "quick", "reasonably priced" meals of Cal cuisine like Chinois chicken salad and pizzas not unlike those "found in the freezer section of your local supermarket"; critics claim both service and decor could use some "updating", adding that the fare isn't as good as expected" given the "famous name" behind it.

### Wood Ranch BBQ & Grill BBQ
| 20 | 17 | 18 | $26 |

**Fairfax** | The Grove at Farmers Mkt. | 189 The Grove Dr. (bet. Fairfax Ave. & 3rd St.) | 323-937-6800
**Cerritos** | Cerritos Towne Ctr. | 12801 Towne Center Dr. (bet. Bloomfield Ave. & 183rd St.) | 562-865-0202

(continued)

*(continued)*

## Wood Ranch BBQ & Grill

**Arcadia** | Westfield Shoppingtown Santa Anita | 400 S. Baldwin Ave. (Huntington Dr.) | 626-447-4745

**Northridge** | Northridge Fashion Ctr. | 9301 Tampa Ave. (bet. Nordhoff & Plummer Sts.) | 818-886-6464

**Agoura Hills** | Whizins Plaza | 5050 Cornell Rd. (Roadside Dr.) | 818-597-8900

**Camarillo** | 1101 Daily Dr. (Lantana St.) | 805-482-1202

**Moorpark** | 540 New Los Angeles Ave. (Spring Rd.) | 805-523-7253

**Valencia** | Valencia Mktpl. | 25580 N. The Old Rd. (Constitution Ave.) | 661-222-9494

www.woodranch.com

"Families" flock to this American BBQ chain for "tender, slow-roasted" meats and "dynamite garlic rolls" ferried by "generally dependable" servers; a few report being "disappointed" by the "flavor" ("why have 'wood' in the name if you can't taste it?") but "the crowds don't seem to mind" judging from the "long waits" at "peak times"; P.S. "the take-out service can come in very handy after a long day at work."

## Woody's Bar-B-Que *BBQ*                    ▽ 21 | 6 | 16 | $17

**Leimert Park** | 3446 W. Slauson Ave. (Crenshaw Blvd.) | 323-294-9443

There's "soul in every bite" of the "finger lickin' good" "chicken, ribs and hot links" barbecued at this "classic" "joint" in Leimert Park; the area's "not so great" and there's "no place to sit down" inside, so it's probably best if you grabbed your stash and hightailed it home – just don't forget extra "sauce on the side."

## Woo Lae Oak *Korean*                    22 | 21 | 19 | $44

**Beverly Hills** | 170 N. La Cienega Blvd. (Clifton Way) | 310-652-4187

Korean barbecue "goes chic" at this "upscale" Beverly Hills grill where "Caucasian-friendly" versions of the traditional "marinated beef", chicken and seafood make for "fun, delicious" meals – and if they're burnt, "it's your own fault", because "you're the one cooking it"; the dining room is "prettier" and more "elegant" than many you'd "find in K-town", just as the prices are "higher."

## WP 🅶 *American*                    – | – | – | M

**West Hollywood** | Pacific Design Ctr. | 8687 Melrose Ave. (San Vicente Blvd.) | 310-652-3933 | www.wolfgangpuck.com

"Pacific Design Center clients lucked out" when Wolfgang Puck took over this West Hollywood "hidden gem", because when they stop by "to pick a fabric or finish", they can also sit down to "simple but well-done" American specialties for lunch; tables spaced "far apart and low noise levels" are also appreciated for making "conversations easy" – "now, if they could only speed up the service!"

## W's China Bistro *Chinese*                    21 | 21 | 19 | $31

**Redondo Beach** | 1410 S. PCH (Ave. F) | 310-792-1600 | www.wschinabistro.com

Bring "a date or the whole family" to this "upscale" Redondo Beach bistro for "creative", "fresh and well-seasoned" Chinese cooking "with a Californian influence"; the "fabulous Zen ambiance" is a "nice alternative to typical" spots for a sit-down meal, but its also a "great place for takeout" to boot.

### Xi'an *Chinese*    22 | 17 | 18 | $32

**Beverly Hills** | 362 N. Cañon Dr. (bet. Brighton & Dayton Ways) |
310-275-3345 | www.xian90210.com

Supporters "don't have to know how to pronounce the name" (it's
zhee-on) of this "chic" Beverly Hills "gourmet" Chinese in order to appreciate the "flavorful" fare with "many healthy options" like
Mandarin salad and moo shu made with egg whites only; for those
who find the "busy", "contemporary" room "noisy", insiders suggest
you "escape" to the "patio" on a "warm day."

### Xiomara *Nuevo Latino*    21 | 19 | 21 | $42

**Hollywood** | 6101 Melrose Ave. (Seward St.) | 323-461-0601 |
www.xiomararestaurant.com

Cuban chef-owner Xiomara Ardolina may have sold her original
Pasadena outpost, but this Hollywood sib still "satisfies" with her
"passionate" Nuevo Latino dishes and "knock-your-socks-off" mojitos
made with "fresh sugarcane juice"; "romantic" "Old Havana" decor
and "professional" service make it a "favorite" for "celebrations", but
a few take issue with tabs they find "kind of pricey."

### Yabu *Japanese*    23 | 16 | 19 | $30

**West Hollywood** | 521 N. La Cienega Blvd. (Melrose Ave.) |
310-854-0400
**West LA** | 11820 W. Pico Blvd. (bet. Barrington Ave. & Bundy Dr.) |
310-473-9757

At the West Hollywood location of this Japanese duo, the "delicious,
fresh" sushi is best enjoyed on the "cute, bamboo-lined patio"; the
West LA incarnation, which specializes in "excellent noodles", feels
like an "izakaya" you'd "stumble into off a side street in Shibuya" – it's
"not a place to relax", so just "eat and go."

### ⚡ Yamashiro *Asian/Californian*    18 | 27 | 20 | $46

**Hollywood** | 1999 N. Sycamore Ave. (Franklin Ave.) | 323-466-5125 |
www.yamashirorestaurant.com

"Fabulous" Hollywood views and a "breathtaking" garden setting with
an "authentic" Japanese pagoda keep this "pricey" Cal-Asian
"standby" at the top of the "most romantic" running; critics, however,
find the menu "uninspired" and say service skews from "wonderful" to
"so-so", leading them to suggest it "for drinks and appetizers", but not
necessarily a main-event meal.

### Yang Chow *Chinese*    23 | 11 | 18 | $22

**Chinatown** | 819 N. Broadway (bet. Alpine & College Sts.) |
213-625-0811
**Pasadena** | 3777 E. Colorado Blvd. (Rosemead Blvd.) | 626-432-6868
**Canoga Park** | 6443 Topanga Canyon Blvd. (Victory Blvd.) |
818-347-2610
www.yangchow.com

"The crowd-pleasing slippery shrimp" is "well-deserving of its stellar
reputation" at this "old-style" Chinese trio in Canoga Park, Chinatown
and Pasadena that's a "favorite" of "Dodgers fans", "politicians" and a
handful of "celebrities" for its "fantastic" (though some say
"Americanized") fare; servers are "efficient" while "the price is so
right" a few fanatics sigh it "almost makes you wish you could spend
more money" if only you weren't "so full" already.

### Yard House  *American*  | 19 | 18 | 17 | $26 |

**Long Beach** | Shoreline Vill. | 401 Shoreline Village Dr. (Shoreline Dr.) | 562-628-0455

**Pasadena** | Paseo Colorado | 330 E. Colorado Blvd. (bet. Fair Oaks & N. Los Robles Aves.) | 626-577-9273

www.yardhouse.com

"Beer connoisseurs" can't get enough of the "zillion" "international" suds and "microbrews on tap" at this burgeoning band of "slightly up-scale" brewpubs; though they serve an "impressive selection" of "full-flavored" American fare deemed "better than it needs to be", most go for the booze, the "young" and "pretty crowd" and the "amazing" happy hour, complete with "classic rock" that "booms over the speakers"; P.S. the patio at the Long Beach flagship offers "beautiful views" of "sunsets over the marina."

### NEW Yatai Asian Tapas Bar  *Pan-Asian*  | ▽ 19 | 18 | 21 | $30 |

**West Hollywood** | 8535 W. Sunset Blvd. (N. La Cienega Blvd.) | 310-289-0030 | www.yatai-bar.com

"A sliver of a restaurant", this relatively new West Hollywood "find" wins kudos for its "unique setting" with a "wonderful" courtyard as well as its "tasty" Pan-Asian small plates like spicy tuna tartar and crispy shrimp with black pepper and chile sauce; add in a "super-friendly" owner and "helpful" staff, and it's an experience "so good" that converts confide they "don't want it to get discovered."

### Yen Sushi & Sake Bar  *Japanese*  | ▽ 23 | 21 | 20 | $36 |

**Pico-Robertson** | 9618 W. Pico Blvd., Ste. 509 (Beverwil Dr.) | 310-278-0691

**West LA** | 11819 Wilshire Blvd., Ste. 101 (Granville Ave.) | 310-996-1313

**Long Beach** | 4905 E. Second St. (bet. Argonne & St. Joseph Aves.) | 562-434-5757

**Studio City** | 12930 Ventura Blvd. (Coldwater Canyon Ave.) | 818-907-6400

www.yensushiusa.com

"The sushi chefs know their stuff" at this LA chainlet offering both "traditional" dishes as well as "imaginative" "fusion" maki all washed down with "endless sake choices" and soju cocktails; a few find it "pricey for the quality", but others are willing to pay a little extra for "hip" environs and "excellent people-watching."

### Ye Olde King's Head  *Pub Food*  | 17 | 17 | 16 | $23 |

**Santa Monica** | 116 Santa Monica Blvd. (Ocean Ave.) | 310-451-1402 | www.yeoldekingshead.com

"Authentic English pub fare" and "Guinness on tap" are the draw for "expats", "Anglophiles" and "cheeky blighters" at this bit of "Brighton on the Pacific" in Santa Monica; service is "friendly" while the "comfy" atmosphere comes via the kitschy memorabilia-filled space and "real football" on the telly.

### NEW York, The ☻ *Eclectic*  | — | — | — | — |

**Highland Park** | 5018 York Blvd. (N. Ave. 50) | 323-255-9675 | www.theyorkonyork.com

Westsiders need MapQuest to figure out where Highland Park is, but Eastsiders have long known it as a fine destination for some of the most authentic Mexican food in town; these days, it's turning into a neighborhood of many galleries, and of colorful gastropubs like this newcomer, with its rough wood floors and bare brick walls, its good-sized assortment of beers (many on tap) and an Eclectic menu of dishes like warm olives with fried garbanzos, truffle-scented grilled cheese and a pulled pork Cuban sandwich; it's open nightly till 2 AM.

### NEW Yose Pan-Asian
▽ 22 | 21 | 21 | $31

**Santa Monica** | Edgemar | 2435 Main St. (Ocean Park Blvd.) | 310-255-0680 | www.yosedining.com

"Beautifully presented" Pan-Asian cuisine gets the nod from surveyors at this Santa Monica newcomer set in "beautiful" concrete and red-accented digs in the Frank Gehry–designed Edgemar Center; though some surmise the "unusual" menu with "too many selections" might need a bit more "focus", most dishes are deemed "tasty" and service is "gracious" – "it won't be long before this place is packed."

### Yujean Kang's Chinese
26 | 17 | 21 | $38

**Pasadena** | 67 N. Raymond Ave. (bet. Holly & Union Sts.) | 626-585-0855 | www.yujeankangs.com

Chinese cuisine goes "beyond the genre" with "outstanding", "delicately balanced" dishes at "artist" chef-owner Yujean Kang's "serene" Pasadena "favorite" that truly "stands out" with "haute" fare and a 50-label wine selection; sharp-eyed servers ensure "your teacup will never run dry", and if some find fault with the "dated" decor, most marvel that this "longtime" "favorite" "still has the right stuff."

### Yuzu Japanese
▽ 23 | 18 | 19 | $43

**Torrance** | 1231 Cabrillo Ave. (Torrance Blvd.) | 310-533-9898

"Real Japanese bar food" (aka "izakaya") is on order at this "authentic" Torrance eatery that pleases with "sophisticated" small plates and "traditional" "comfort" fare as well as 25 varieties of sake; service is "pleasant" if "slow", and if dinner prices are a little "steep", wallet-watchers suggest "lunch" as a better "bargain."

### Zankou Chicken Mediterranean
22 | 6 | 12 | $11

**East Hollywood** | 5065 W. Sunset Blvd. (Normandie Ave.) | 323-665-7845 ⊠
**West LA** | 1716 S. Sepulveda Blvd., Ste. 101 (Santa Monica Blvd.) | 310-444-0550
**Pasadena** | 1296 E. Colorado Blvd. (Hill Ave.) | 626-405-1502
**Burbank** | 1001 N. San Fernando Blvd., Ste. 100 (E. Walnut Ave.) | 818-238-0414
**Glendale** | 1415 E. Colorado Blvd., Ste. D (Verdugo Rd.) | 818-244-1937
**Van Nuys** | 5658 Sepulveda Blvd., Ste. 103 (Burbank Blvd.) | 818-781-0615
www.zankouchicken.com

"Zank-you!" say zealots to this Med chain for its "brilliant rotisserie chicken" "masterfully prepared" and served with "delectable garlic sauce" that's "out of this world" ("seriously, what planet is it from?"); "gruff" counter help and "ugly plastic benches" give it "all the charm of a gas station", and while a chorus of critics cry that recent "expansion" has "lowered quality", supporters shoot back – "if this counts as downhill, I don't mind the slide."

### Zazou Mediterranean
24 | 20 | 21 | $41

**Redondo Beach** | 1810 S. Catalina Ave. (bet. Ave. I & Vista Del Mar) | 310-540-4884 | www.zazourestaurant.com

This "sophisticated" Redondo Beach "special-occasion" standby is a "go-to" spot for "creative" Mediterranean cuisine that pairs well with glasses or flights from a 300-label wine list; a "fun" wait and a "friendly" regular crowd make this "little spot" "worth returning to" "especially for a date" or a late dinner (served until 11 PM on weekends).

### Zeidler's Café ⓂCalifornian
17 | 15 | 16 | $24

**Brentwood** | Skirball Cultural Ctr. | 2701 N. Sepulveda Blvd. (Mulholland Dr.) | 310-440-4515 | www.skirball.org

"Better than your average museum restaurant", this meatless Californian-Kosher in the Skirball Cultural Center offers "fresh and tasty" sandwiches, salads and frittatas that are "a cut above the ordinary"; service is "unsteady", but views of the courtyard still make this a "relaxing" spot that's "lovely for lunch" or "pre-concert."

### Zeke's Smokehouse BBQ
19 | 13 | 17 | $21

**West Hollywood** | West Hollywood Gateway Ctr. | 7100 Santa Monica Blvd. (Formosa Ave.) | 323-850-9353
**Montrose** | 2209 Honolulu Ave. (Verdugo Blvd.) | 818-957-7045
www.zekessmokehouse.com

"Solid enough 'cue" with "no skimping on the portions" characterizes this "no-frills" BBQ duo in Montrose and West Hollywood where "three different types of sauces" liven up the "finger-lickin'" fare; even if it's "a little pricy" and "doesn't compare to joints in Memphis or Kansas City", "locals" say it works as a "quick dinner" and add that it's "good for groups" too.

### Zen Grill Pan-Asian
20 | 13 | 16 | $25

**Third Street** | 8432 W. Third St. (bet. La Cienega Blvd. & Orlando Ave.) | 323-655-9991
**Beverly Hills** | 9111 W. Olympic Blvd. (Doheny Dr.) | 310-278-7773

"Easygoing" and "affordable", these Pan-Asian twins in Beverly Hills (under new ownership) and on Third Street offer "so much to choose from", making them a "low-key option" for "cheap dates" or "one of those nights when you can't decide" what to eat; comfort-hounds call the "pint-sized" spaces "uncomfortably close" and suggest they're best for "takeout" only.

### NEW Zin Bistro Americana American/French
▽ 21 | 23 | 18 | $42

**Westlake Village** | 32131 Lindero Canyon Rd. (bet. Lakeview Canyon Rd. & Ridgeford Dr.) | 818-865-0095 | www.zinbistroamericana.com

The "stunning alfresco setting" "overlooking the lake" wins top marks at this Westlake Village newcomer offering a "creative" menu of New American and French bistro cuisine; critics say it's "overpriced" and service is "a little too velvet-rope" for the locale, but a "terrific wine by the glass" list and "tasty" signatures like the chicken fried lobster still make this "a bright spot" in the Conejo Valley dining scene.

### Zip Fusion Japanese
18 | 16 | 17 | $29

**Downtown** | 744 E. Third St. (Rose St.) | 213-680-3770 Ⓢ
**West LA** | 11301 W. Olympic Blvd. (Sawtelle Blvd.) | 310-575-3636 ☾
www.zipfusion.com

"Novelty rolls" and a "strong" sake selection are the main draw at this Southland mini-chain; though some say it has "zip authenticity" and "slow" service to boot, the "cool" atmosphere and "bargain" prices make it "worth the tradeoff" for those seeking "funkier" raw fish options; N.B. the West LA branch has private karaoke rooms.

| | FOOD | DECOR | SERVICE | COST |
|---|---|---|---|---|

### Zita Trattoria & Bar 🗷 *Italian* ▽ 18 | 15 | 15 | $33

**Downtown** | TCW Bldg. | 865 S. Figueroa St. (W. Olympic Blvd.) |
213-488-0400

"Solid Italian" near the Staples Center and the Downtown business
district draws a "suited", "power-lunching" crowd for midday linguini,
panini and pizzas; detractors declare that "service can be
excruciatingly slow", while others find it "overpriced" for a merely
"decent" dining experience.

### Zucca Ristorante *Italian* 22 | 23 | 21 | $47

**Downtown** | 801 Tower | 801 S. Figueroa St. (8th St.) | 213-614-7800 |
www.patinagroup.com

At Joachim Splichal's "Downtown gem", "pumpkin reigns supreme" in
the signature homemade tortellini while other Italian dishes are
deemed "wonderful" and the 250-label wine list "deserves exploration"; the "gorgeous" space is antiques-furnished with old world im-
ports, and the "pleasant, accommodating" staff allows you to "take
your time or rush in and out", making it a "top choice" for local happy-
hour crowds, concert-goers or Staples Center attendees.

### NEW Zu Robata *Japanese* - | - | - | M

**West LA** | 12217 Wilshire Blvd. (Bundy Dr.) | 310-571-1920 |
www.zurobata.com

West LA gets another Japanese with ultramodern decor, this one featuring both sushi and robata-yaki (which roughly translates to many
small things grilled over coals); a whole wall is artfully covered by
oversized jars of fruit-infused soju, the fermented sake that's a popular ingredient in the cocktails served at its lively bar.

# LOS ANGELES
## INDEXES

## LOCATION MAPS

# Cuisines

Includes restaurant names, locations and Food ratings. ☒ indicates places with the highest ratings, popularity and importance.

## AMERICAN (NEW)

| | |
|---|---|
| NEW Abode \| **Santa Monica** | 23 |
| Avenue \| **Manhattan Bch** | 23 |
| NEW Baleen \| **Redondo Bch** | 22 |
| Beechwood \| **Venice** | 20 |
| ☒ Belvedere \| **Beverly Hills** | 25 |
| Blair's \| **Silver Lake** | 23 |
| bld \| **Beverly Blvd.** | 21 |
| NEW Bloom Cafe \| **Mid-City** | 23 |
| blue on blue \| **Beverly Hills** | 18 |
| NEW☒ Blue Velvet \| **Downtown** | 22 |
| boé \| **Beverly Hills** | 14 |
| Breadbar \| **multi. loc.** | 19 |
| Brentwood, The \| **Brentwood** | 21 |
| Café Pacific \| **Rancho Palos Verdes** | 24 |
| Caffe Latte \| **Mid-Wilshire** | 16 |
| NEW Charcoal \| **Hollywood** | - |
| NEW Circa 55 \| **Beverly Hills** | 21 |
| Citizen Smith \| **Hollywood** | 18 |
| Cooks Dbl. Dutch \| **Culver City** | 22 |
| NEW Craft \| **Century City** | - |
| eat. on sunset \| **Hollywood** | 19 |
| NEW Eleven \| **W Hollywood** | 21 |
| Farm/Bev. Hills \| **multi. loc.** | 19 |
| Firefly \| **Studio City** | 20 |
| Firefly Bistro \| **S Pasadena** | 19 |
| Ford's Filling Stat. \| **Culver City** | 19 |
| NEW Foundry/Melrose \| **Melrose** | - |
| ☒ Grace \| **Beverly Blvd.** | 25 |
| Hal's B&G \| **Venice** | 20 |
| ☒ Hatfield's \| **Beverly Blvd.** | 27 |
| Hugo's \| **W Hollywood** | 21 |
| Ivy/Shore \| **Santa Monica** | 21 |
| Jackson's Vill. \| **Hermosa Bch** | 23 |
| ☒ Jar \| **Beverly Blvd.** | 25 |
| John O'Groats \| **Rancho Pk** | 20 |
| ☒ Josie \| **Santa Monica** | 27 |
| NEW J Rest. \| **Downtown** | 13 |
| NEW Larchmont Grill \| **Hollywood** | 21 |
| Lola's \| **W Hollywood** | 18 |
| Magnolia \| **Hollywood** | 20 |
| ☒ Mélisse \| **Santa Monica** | 28 |
| NEW Mike & Anne's \| **S Pasadena** | 20 |

| | |
|---|---|
| Moonshadows \| **Malibu** | 17 |
| Napa Valley \| **Westwood** | 20 |
| Nic's \| **Beverly Hills** | 21 |
| Nine Thirty \| **Westwood** | 23 |
| Noé \| **Downtown** | 25 |
| Nook Bistro \| **West LA** | 24 |
| O-Bar \| **W Hollywood** | 20 |
| Ocean & Vine \| **Santa Monica** | 22 |
| NEW One Sunset \| **W Hollywood** | - |
| Palomino \| **Westwood** | 18 |
| ☒ Patina \| **Downtown** | 26 |
| NEW Penthouse \| **Santa Monica** | 20 |
| Pete's Cafe \| **Downtown** | 18 |
| ☒ Providence \| **Hollywood** | 27 |
| P6 Rest. \| **Westlake Vill** | 20 |
| NEW Punch Grill \| **Santa Monica** | 18 |
| NEW redwhite+bluezz \| **Pasadena** | 21 |
| ☒ Republic \| **W Hollywood** | 20 |
| NEW Royale \| **Mid-Wilshire** | 18 |
| ☒ Saddle Peak \| **Calabasas** | 26 |
| NEW Safire \| **Camarillo** | - |
| Second City Bistro \| **El Segundo** | 22 |
| Sky Room \| **Long Bch** | 21 |
| Tart \| **Fairfax** | 18 |
| Taste \| **W Hollywood** | 20 |
| Tender Greens \| **Culver City** | 23 |
| Tiara Cafe \| **Downtown** | 20 |
| NEW Tracht's \| **Long Bch** | - |
| Traxx \| **Downtown** | 20 |
| Twin Palms \| **Pasadena** | 17 |
| vermont \| **Los Feliz** | 22 |
| Vert \| **Hollywood** | 21 |
| Violet \| **Santa Monica** | 21 |
| Wilshire \| **Santa Monica** | 21 |
| WP \| **W Hollywood** | - |
| NEW Zin Bistro \| **Westlake Vill** | 21 |

## AMERICAN (TRADITIONAL)

| | |
|---|---|
| Abbey \| **W Hollywood** | 16 |
| Alcove \| **Los Feliz** | 22 |
| Apple Pan \| **West LA** | 22 |
| Auntie Em's \| **Eagle Rock** | - |

| | |
|---|---|
| Back on Beach \| **Santa Monica** | 14 |
| Bandera \| **West LA** | 22 |
| Beckham Grill \| **Pasadena** | 18 |
| Belmont Brew. \| **Long Bch** | 18 |
| BJ's \| **multi. loc.** | 17 |
| Bluewater Grill \| **Redondo Bch** | 20 |
| Bowery \| **Hollywood** | 21 |
| Brighton Coffee \| **Beverly Hills** | 16 |
| Buffalo Club \| **Santa Monica** | 19 |
| NEW Burger 90210 \| **Beverly Hills** | - |
| Cafe 50's \| **multi. loc.** | 15 |
| Cafe Surfas \| **Culver City** | 20 |
| Cali. Chicken \| **multi. loc.** | 21 |
| Carney's Express \| **multi. loc.** | 19 |
| NEW Central Park \| **Pasadena** | 18 |
| ☑ Cheesecake Fact. \| **multi. loc.** | 20 |
| Chili John's \| **Burbank** | 23 |
| City Bakery \| **Brentwood** | 18 |
| Claim Jumper \| **multi. loc.** | 19 |
| Clementine \| **Century City** | 24 |
| Club 41 \| **Pasadena** | 19 |
| Colony Cafe/Papa's Porch \| **West LA** | 18 |
| Daily Grill \| **multi. loc.** | 18 |
| Dish \| **La Cañada Flintridge** | 18 |
| Doughboys \| **multi. loc.** | 22 |
| Du-par's \| **multi. loc.** | 16 |
| Dusty's \| **Silver Lake** | 21 |
| Eat Well Cafe \| **multi. loc.** | 15 |
| Edendale Grill \| **Silver Lake** | 15 |
| Engine Co. 28 \| **Downtown** | 19 |
| Gordon Biersch \| **multi. loc.** | 17 |
| Griddle Cafe \| **Hollywood** | 22 |
| ☑ Grill on Alley \| **Beverly Hills** | 24 |
| Grill on Hollywood \| **Hollywood** | 19 |
| Grub \| **Hollywood** | 21 |
| Gulfstream \| **Century City** | 21 |
| Hamburger Mary's \| **W Hollywood** | 15 |
| Hamlet \| **multi. loc.** | 16 |
| Hard Rock \| **Universal City** | 14 |
| Heroes B&G \| **Claremont** | 16 |
| Hoboken \| **West LA** | 18 |
| ☑ Houston's \| **multi. loc.** | 21 |
| Islands \| **multi. loc.** | 16 |
| Jack n' Jill's \| **multi. loc.** | 19 |
| James' Bch. \| **Venice** | 18 |
| Jinky's \| **multi. loc.** | 20 |
| Joan's on Third \| **Third St.** | 24 |
| Johnny Rockets \| **multi. loc.** | 15 |
| Jones Hollywood \| **W Hollywood** | 18 |
| Kate Mantilini \| **multi. loc.** | 18 |
| NEW Ketchup \| **W Hollywood** | 16 |
| Kings Road \| **Beverly Blvd.** | 19 |
| Kitchen, The \| **Silver Lake** | 19 |
| Koo Koo Roo \| **multi. loc.** | 16 |
| LA Food Show \| **Manhattan Bch** | 19 |
| Lasher's \| **multi. loc.** | 24 |
| NEW Liberty Grill \| **Downtown** | - |
| Local Place \| **Torrance** | 17 |
| Lucky Devils \| **Hollywood** | 21 |
| Luna Park \| **La Brea** | 19 |
| Madame Matisse \| **Silver Lake** | 22 |
| Marmalade Café \| **multi. loc.** | 18 |
| Marston's \| **Pasadena** | 23 |
| Martha 22nd St. \| **Hermosa Bch** | 22 |
| Maxwell's Cafe \| **Venice** | 19 |
| Mel's Drive-In \| **multi. loc.** | 16 |
| NEW Meltdown Etc. \| **Culver City** | - |
| Mimi's Cafe \| **multi. loc.** | 17 |
| Monty's Steak \| **Woodland Hills** | 21 |
| Morton's \| **W Hollywood** | 23 |
| Mo's \| **Burbank** | 17 |
| Musso & Frank \| **Hollywood** | 19 |
| Neptune's Net \| **Malibu** | 17 |
| Off Vine \| **Hollywood** | 22 |
| NEW Oinkster, The \| **Eagle Rock** | 21 |
| Omelette Parlor \| **Santa Monica** | 18 |
| ☑ Original Pancake \| **Redondo Bch** | 23 |
| Original Pantry \| **Downtown** | 16 |
| Outlaws B&G \| **Playa del Rey** | 15 |
| Paradise Cove \| **Malibu** | 16 |
| Pike Rest. \| **Long Bch** | - |
| Rainforest Cafe \| **Ontario** | 13 |
| Ruby's \| **multi. loc.** | 16 |
| Russell's Burgers \| **Pasadena** | 17 |
| Shack, The \| **multi. loc.** | 18 |
| Simon LA \| **W Hollywood** | 21 |
| Smitty's Grill \| **Pasadena** | 21 |
| Souplantation \| **multi. loc.** | 16 |
| Spark Woodfire \| **multi. loc.** | 17 |
| Spin Rotisserie \| **Marina del Rey** | 17 |
| Square One Dining \| **E Hollywood** | 24 |
| Stand, The \| **multi. loc.** | 18 |
| Standard, The \| **Downtown** | 16 |
| Swingers \| **multi. loc.** | 17 |

| | |
|---|---|
| Three on Fourth \| **Santa Monica** | 16 |
| Toast \| **Third St.** | 20 |
| Tony P's Dock \| **Marina del Rey** | 17 |
| Trails, The \| **Los Feliz** | 18 |
| Trump's \| **Rancho Palos Verdes** | 23 |
| Urth Caffé \| **multi. loc.** | 21 |
| NEW Vault, The \| **Pasadena** | 15 |
| Vibrato \| **Bel-Air** | 22 |
| NEW Village Idiot \| **Melrose** | 19 |
| Whisper Lounge \| **Fairfax** | 16 |
| Wood Ranch BBQ \| **multi. loc.** | 20 |
| Yard House \| **multi. loc.** | 19 |

## ARGENTINEAN

| | |
|---|---|
| Carlitos Gardel \| **Melrose** | 23 |
| Gaucho Grill \| **multi. loc.** | 18 |

## ASIAN

| | |
|---|---|
| NEW Asia Los Feliz \| **Atwater Vill** | 20 |
| Chaya \| **W Hollywood** | 23 |
| Z Chinois/Main \| **Santa Monica** | 26 |
| Feast from East \| **West LA** | 21 |
| NEW Garden Cafe \| **Little Tokyo** | - |
| Gina Lee's Bistro \| **Redondo Bch** | 26 |
| Gordon Biersch \| **multi. loc.** | 17 |
| Z Mako \| **Beverly Hills** | 26 |
| Max \| **Sherman Oaks** | 24 |
| NEW Parc \| **Hollywood** | - |
| Tiger Lily \| **Los Feliz** | 19 |
| 2117 \| **West LA** | 24 |
| Vegan Glory \| **Beverly Blvd.** | 24 |
| Z Yamashiro \| **Hollywood** | 18 |

## ASIAN FUSION

| | |
|---|---|
| Ahi Sushi \| **Studio City** | 22 |
| Asia de Cuba \| **W Hollywood** | 24 |
| Chop Suey \| **Little Tokyo** | 11 |
| Z Crustacean \| **Beverly Hills** | 23 |
| Fat Fish \| **multi. loc.** | 20 |
| Formosa Cafe \| **W Hollywood** | 15 |
| Z Mako \| **Beverly Hills** | 26 |
| Max \| **Sherman Oaks** | 24 |
| MOZ Buddha \| **Agoura Hills** | 20 |
| NEW RA Sushi \| **Torrance** | 18 |
| Z Roy's \| **multi. loc.** | 24 |
| Saketini \| **Brentwood** | 20 |
| Tengu \| **multi. loc.** | 22 |
| Wabi-Sabi \| **Venice** | 22 |
| Zen Grill \| **multi. loc.** | 20 |

## AUSTRALIAN

| | |
|---|---|
| NEW Bondi BBQ \| **Venice** | - |

## BAKERIES

| | |
|---|---|
| A La Tarte \| **Pacific Palisades** | 18 |
| Breadbar \| **W Hollywood** | 19 |
| City Bakery \| **Brentwood** | 18 |
| Clementine \| **Century City** | 24 |
| Doña Rosa \| **multi. loc.** | 16 |
| Doughboys \| **Third St.** | 22 |
| Jack n' Jill's \| **Santa Monica** | 19 |
| Joan's on Third \| **Third St.** | 24 |
| L'Artiste Patisserie \| **Encino** | 20 |
| Le Pain Quotidien \| **multi. loc.** | 21 |
| Mäni's \| **multi. loc.** | 18 |
| Michel Richard \| **Beverly Hills** | 20 |
| Misto Caffé \| **Torrance** | 21 |
| Porto's Bakery \| **multi. loc.** | - |
| Susina Bakery \| **La Brea** | 23 |
| Z Sweet Lady Jane \| **Melrose** | 25 |
| NEW 3 Square \| **Venice** | 21 |

## BARBECUE

| | |
|---|---|
| Adobe Cantina \| **Agoura Hills** | 19 |
| Baby Blues BBQ \| **Venice** | 22 |
| Big Mama's \| **Pasadena** | 20 |
| NEW Bondi BBQ \| **Venice** | - |
| Boneyard Bistro \| **Sherman Oaks** | 20 |
| Dr. Hogly Wogly's \| **Van Nuys** | 23 |
| NEW Joey's Smokin' BBQ \| **Manhattan Bch** | - |
| Johnny Rebs' \| **multi. loc.** | 22 |
| JR's BBQ \| **Culver City** | 20 |
| NEW Kansas City BBQ \| **Studio City** | - |
| Lucille's BBQ \| **multi. loc.** | 22 |
| Mr. Cecil's Ribs \| **multi. loc.** | 18 |
| NEW Oinkster, The \| **Eagle Rock** | 21 |
| Original Texas BBQ \| **Downtown** | 20 |
| Z Phillips BBQ \| **multi. loc.** | 24 |
| Pig, The \| **La Brea** | 15 |
| Porky's BBQ \| **Inglewood** | - |
| Quincy's BBQ \| **Encino** | 15 |
| Reddi Chick BBQ \| **Brentwood** | 23 |
| Ribs USA \| **Burbank** | 20 |
| Robin's Woodfire BBQ \| **Pasadena** | 17 |
| Stonefire Grill \| **multi. loc.** | 20 |
| Swinging Door \| **N Hollywood** | - |
| Wood Ranch BBQ \| **multi. loc.** | 20 |
| Woody's BBQ \| **Leimert Pk** | 21 |
| Zeke's Smokehse. \| **multi. loc.** | 19 |

## BELGIAN

| Le Pain Quotidien | multi. loc. | 21 |

## BRAZILIAN

| Bossa Nova | multi. loc. | 21 |
| Café Brasil | multi. loc. | 19 |
| Fogo de Chão | Beverly Hills | 23 |
| Galletto | Westlake Vill | 23 |
| Green Field Churr. | multi. loc. | 23 |
| Picanha Churr. | Burbank | 19 |
| Porto Alegre | Pasadena | - |
| Tropicalia Brazil | Los Feliz | 19 |
| NEW Ummba Grill | Century City | 16 |

## BRITISH

| Whale & Ale | San Pedro | 16 |
| Ye Olde King's Head | Santa Monica | 17 |

## CAJUN

| Bourbon St. Shrimp | West LA | 16 |
| Gumbo Pot | Fairfax | 21 |
| Z Ragin' Cajun | Hermosa Bch | 21 |
| Stevie's Creole | Encino | 17 |
| Uncle Darrow's | Marina del Rey | 19 |

## CALIFORNIAN

| Akwa | Santa Monica | 19 |
| Ammo | Hollywood | 22 |
| Amori | Monrovia | 22 |
| Z A.O.C. | Third St. | 26 |
| NEW Asia Los Feliz | Atwater Vill | 20 |
| Axe | Venice | 22 |
| Babalu | Santa Monica | 20 |
| Bamboom | Agoura Hills | - |
| Barefoot B&G | Third St. | 18 |
| Barsac Brasserie | N Hollywood | 23 |
| Basix Cafe | W Hollywood | 18 |
| Bel-Air B&G | Bel-Air | 19 |
| Z Bistro 45 | Pasadena | 26 |
| Bistro 767 | Rolling Hills | 22 |
| Bistro 31 | Santa Monica | 23 |
| NEW Bloom Cafe | Mid-City | 23 |
| Blvd | Beverly Hills | 21 |
| Bono's | Long Bch | 21 |
| Bora Bora | Manhattan Bch | 23 |
| Breeze | Century City | 19 |
| Z Café Bizou | multi. loc. | 23 |
| Cafe Del Rey | Marina del Rey | 23 |
| Z Café 14 | Agoura Hills | 26 |

| Cafe Montana | Santa Monica | 20 |
| Café Mundial | Monrovia | 20 |
| Cafe Pinot | Downtown | 22 |
| Cafe Rodeo | Beverly Hills | 16 |
| Caioti Pizza | Studio City | 22 |
| Camden House | Beverly Hills | 15 |
| Camilo's | Eagle Rock | 20 |
| Z Campanile | La Brea | 26 |
| Canal Club | Venice | 18 |
| Castaway | Burbank | 17 |
| NEW Catch | Santa Monica | - |
| NEW Central Park | Pasadena | 18 |
| Cézanne | Santa Monica | 21 |
| Chateau Marmont | W Hollywood | 21 |
| Checkers | Downtown | 22 |
| Chef Melba's | Hermosa Bch | 23 |
| China Grill | Manhattan Bch | 20 |
| Chocolat | Melrose | 16 |
| Z Cicada | Downtown | 23 |
| NEW Circa 55 | Beverly Hills | 21 |
| Cliff's Edge | Silver Lake | 20 |
| NEW Coast | Santa Monica | - |
| Coral Tree | multi. loc. | 19 |
| Crocodile Cafe | multi. loc. | 16 |
| Z Derek's | Pasadena | 27 |
| Devon | Monrovia | 25 |
| NEW Dive, The | Hollywood | - |
| Doug Arango's | W Hollywood | 22 |
| Emle's | Northridge | 19 |
| Farm/Bev. Hills | Woodland Hills | 19 |
| Five Sixty-One | Pasadena | 19 |
| 410 Boyd | Downtown | 20 |
| Fritto Misto | multi. loc. | 21 |
| NEW Garden Cafe | Little Tokyo | - |
| Z Gardens | Beverly Hills | 25 |
| Gardens/Glendon | Westwood | 19 |
| Z Geoffrey's | Malibu | 22 |
| Getty Center | Brentwood | 22 |
| Gina Lee's Bistro | Redondo Bch | 26 |
| Gorikee | Woodland Hills | 21 |
| Hal's B&G | Venice | 20 |
| NEW Hampton's | Westlake Vill | 24 |
| Holly Street | Pasadena | 21 |
| Z Hotel Bel-Air | Bel-Air | 26 |
| Hugo's | multi. loc. | 21 |
| Z Inn/Seventh Ray | Topanga | 21 |
| Z Ivy, The | W Hollywood | 22 |
| Ivy/Shore | Santa Monica | 21 |
| Jack Sprat's | West LA | 19 |

| | |
|---|---|
| Jer-ne \| **Marina del Rey** | 22 |
| ⊠ JiRaffe \| **Santa Monica** | 26 |
| ⊠ Joe's \| **Venice** | 26 |
| L.A. Farm \| **Santa Monica** | 20 |
| NEW Larkin's \| **Eagle Rock** | – |
| ⊠ Leila's \| **Oak Pk** | 27 |
| Lemon Moon \| **West LA** | 20 |
| Literati \| **West LA** | 20 |
| Louise's Tratt. \| **multi. loc.** | 16 |
| Madeleine's \| **Pasadena** | 23 |
| Mark's \| **W Hollywood** | 16 |
| Marmalade Café \| **multi. loc.** | 18 |
| NEW Marty's \| **Highland Pk** | – |
| Mason Jar Cafe \| **W Hollywood** | 17 |
| Michael's \| **Santa Monica** | 24 |
| Milky Way \| **Pico-Robertson** | 18 |
| Mi Piace \| **multi. loc.** | 19 |
| Mirabelle \| **W Hollywood** | 20 |
| Misto Caffé \| **Torrance** | 21 |
| Morton's \| **W Hollywood** | 23 |
| Mr. Cecil's Ribs \| **West LA** | 18 |
| Napa Valley \| **Westwood** | 20 |
| Native Foods \| **Westwood** | 22 |
| Nicola's Kitchen \| **Woodland Hills** | 18 |
| Off Vine \| **Hollywood** | 22 |
| ⊠ One Pico \| **Santa Monica** | 23 |
| NEW On Sunset \| **Brentwood** | – |
| ⊠ Parkway Grill \| **Pasadena** | 25 |
| ⊠ Patina \| **Downtown** | 26 |
| Pat's \| **Pico-Robertson** | 22 |
| Paul's Cafe \| **Tarzana** | 18 |
| Pentimento \| **Mid-Wilshire** | 17 |
| ⊠ Polo Lounge \| **Beverly Hills** | 22 |
| Porta Via \| **Beverly Hills** | 22 |
| NEW Rack \| **Woodland Hills** | 15 |
| Raymond, The \| **Pasadena** | 24 |
| Reed's \| **Manhattan Bch** | 21 |
| ⊠ Ritz Huntington \| **Pasadena** | 26 |
| Rose Cafe \| **Venice** | 18 |
| NEW Rustic Canyon \| **Santa Monica** | 21 |
| ⊠ Sam's/Beach \| **Santa Monica** | 26 |
| 17th St. Cafe \| **Santa Monica** | 19 |
| ⊠ Sir Winston's \| **Long Bch** | 23 |
| Sona's \| **Encino** | 17 |
| ⊠ Spago \| **Beverly Hills** | 27 |
| Spazio \| **Sherman Oaks** | 19 |
| Stanley's \| **Sherman Oaks** | 19 |
| Sur \| **W Hollywood** | 21 |
| Table 8 \| **Melrose** | 24 |

| | |
|---|---|
| NEW Tommy Ray's \| **Studio City** | 18 |
| Tower Bar \| **W Hollywood** | 22 |
| Towne \| **Manhattan Bch** | 19 |
| 26 Beach \| **Marina del Rey** | 20 |
| Twist \| **Hollywood** | 19 |
| NEW uWink Bistro \| **Woodland Hills** | 14 |
| Vert \| **Hollywood** | 21 |
| ⊠ Whist \| **Santa Monica** | 21 |
| Wolfgang Puck \| **Universal City** | 18 |
| ⊠ Yamashiro \| **Hollywood** | 18 |
| Zeidler's \| **Brentwood** | 17 |

## CANADIAN

| | |
|---|---|
| Soleil Westwood \| **Westwood** | 20 |

## CARIBBEAN

| | |
|---|---|
| Bamboo \| **Culver City** | 19 |
| Cha Cha Cha \| **multi. loc.** | 20 |
| Cha Cha Chick. \| **Santa Monica** | 20 |
| ⊠ Prado \| **Hancock Pk** | 21 |

## CENTRAL AMERICAN

| | |
|---|---|
| Chichen Itza \| **Downtown** | 24 |

## CHEESE SPECIALISTS

| | |
|---|---|
| Artisan Cheese \| **Studio City** | 24 |
| CUBE \| **La Brea** | 25 |

## CHEESE STEAKS

| | |
|---|---|
| South Street \| **multi. loc.** | 18 |

## CHINESE

(* dim sum specialist)

| | |
|---|---|
| ABC Seafood* \| **Chinatown** | 19 |
| Bamboo Cuisine \| **Sherman Oaks** | 22 |
| Cali. Wok \| **multi. loc.** | 18 |
| Chi Dynasty \| **Los Feliz** | 23 |
| China Grill \| **Manhattan Bch** | 20 |
| Chin Chin* \| **multi. loc.** | 17 |
| Chung King \| **Monterey Pk** | – |
| Din Tai Fung \| **Arcadia** | 26 |
| NEW Dong Ting Spring \| **San Gabriel** | – |
| Empress Harbor* \| **Monterey Pk** | 22 |
| Empress Pavilion \| **Chinatown** | 21 |
| Fu-Shing \| **Pasadena** | 21 |
| Genghis Cohen \| **Fairfax** | 20 |
| Hop Li \| **multi. loc.** | 18 |
| Hop Woo \| **multi. loc.** | 19 |
| Hu's Szechwan \| **Palms** | 20 |
| Kung Pao \| **multi. loc.** | 19 |
| Lake Spring Shanghai \| **Monterey Pk** | 21 |

| | |
|---|---|
| Macau St. \| **Monterey Pk** | 20 |
| Mandarette \| **W Hollywood** | 18 |
| Mandarin Deli \| **multi. loc.** | 21 |
| Mission 261* \| **San Gabriel** | 22 |
| Mr. Chow \| **Beverly Hills** | 23 |
| NBC Seafood* \| **Monterey Pk** | 22 |
| New Flavors \| **Culver City** | 19 |
| New Moon \| **Montrose** | 22 |
| Ocean Seafood* \| **Chinatown** | 22 |
| Ocean Star* \| **Monterey Pk** | 22 |
| Panda Inn \| **multi. loc.** | 20 |
| ☑ P.F. Chang's \| **multi. loc.** | 19 |
| Sam Woo \| **multi. loc.** | 20 |
| Sea Empress* \| **Gardena** | 19 |
| ☑ Sea Harbour* \| **Rosemead** | 25 |
| Triumphal Palace* \| **Alhambra** | 24 |
| V.I.P. Harbor* \| **West LA** | 18 |
| Wokcano Cafe \| **multi. loc.** | 17 |
| W's China \| **Redondo Bch** | 21 |
| Xi'an \| **Beverly Hills** | 22 |
| Yang Chow \| **multi. loc.** | 23 |
| ☑ Yujean Kang's \| **Pasadena** | 26 |

## COFFEEHOUSES

| | |
|---|---|
| Caffe Latte \| **Mid-Wilshire** | 16 |
| NEW Caffe Luxxe \| **Santa Monica** | – |
| NEW Coupa Cafe \| **Beverly Hills** | 14 |
| Literati \| **West LA** | 20 |

## COFFEE SHOPS/DINERS

| | |
|---|---|
| Brighton Coffee \| **Beverly Hills** | 16 |
| Cafe 50's \| **multi. loc.** | 15 |
| Cora's Coffee \| **Santa Monica** | 21 |
| Duke's Coffee \| **W Hollywood** | 18 |
| Du-par's \| **multi. loc.** | 16 |
| Fred 62 \| **Los Feliz** | 18 |
| Hamburger Mary's \| **W Hollywood** | 15 |
| Jan's \| **W Hollywood** | 14 |
| Kate Mantilini \| **multi. loc.** | 18 |
| Mimi's Cafe \| **multi. loc.** | 17 |
| ☑ Original Pancake \| **Redondo Bch** | 23 |
| Original Pantry \| **Downtown** | 16 |
| Patrick's \| **Santa Monica** | 16 |
| Pie 'N Burger \| **Pasadena** | 20 |
| Rae's \| **Santa Monica** | 16 |
| Rocky Cola \| **multi. loc.** | – |
| Ruby's \| **multi. loc.** | 16 |
| Russell's Burgers \| **Pasadena** | 17 |

| | |
|---|---|
| Swingers \| **multi. loc.** | 17 |
| Uncle Bill's Pancake \| **Manhattan Bch** | 22 |

## CONTEMPORARY LOUISIANA

| | |
|---|---|
| NEW Magnolia Lounge \| **Pasadena** | 16 |

## CONTINENTAL

| | |
|---|---|
| Aphrodisiac \| **Century City** | 18 |
| ☑ Bistro Gdn./Coldwater \| **Studio City** | 20 |
| ☑ Brandywine \| **Woodland Hills** | 27 |
| ☑ Café 14 \| **Agoura Hills** | 26 |
| ☑ Dal Rae \| **Pico Rivera** | 26 |
| Fins \| **multi. loc.** | 22 |
| Harper's \| **Century City** | 16 |
| Mandevilla \| **Westlake Vill** | 23 |
| Odyssey \| **Granada Hills** | 14 |
| Patinette/MOCA \| **Downtown** | 16 |
| Pig 'n Whistle \| **Hollywood** | 15 |
| ☑ Polo Lounge \| **Beverly Hills** | 22 |
| ☑ Sir Winston's \| **Long Bch** | 23 |
| Trump's \| **Rancho Palos Verdes** | 23 |

## CREOLE

| | |
|---|---|
| Creole Chef \| **Baldwin Hills** | – |
| Harold & Belle's \| **Mid-City** | 24 |
| Uncle Darrow's \| **Marina del Rey** | 19 |

## CUBAN

| | |
|---|---|
| Cuban Bistro \| **Alhambra** | 20 |
| Versailles \| **multi. loc.** | 21 |

## DELIS

| | |
|---|---|
| Art's Deli \| **Studio City** | 19 |
| Barney Greengrass \| **Beverly Hills** | 21 |
| ☑ Brent's Deli \| **multi. loc.** | 26 |
| Broadway Deli \| **Santa Monica** | 14 |
| Canter's \| **Fairfax** | 18 |
| NEW Danny's Venice \| **Venice** | 18 |
| Factor's Deli \| **Pico-Robertson** | 16 |
| Fromin's Deli \| **multi. loc.** | 15 |
| Greenblatt's Deli \| **Hollywood** | 19 |
| Johnnie's Pastrami \| **Culver City** | 20 |
| Junior's \| **West LA** | 16 |
| La Bottega Marino \| **multi. loc.** | 20 |
| Langer's Deli \| **Downtown** | 25 |
| Nate 'n Al \| **Beverly Hills** | 21 |
| Roll 'n Rye \| **Culver City** | 18 |

## DESSERT

| | |
|---|---|
| A La Tarte \| **Pacific Palisades** | 18 |
| Alcove \| **Los Feliz** | 22 |

| | |
|---|---|
| Auntie Em's \| **Eagle Rock** | – |
| Babalu \| **Santa Monica** | 20 |
| 🅭 Café 14 \| **Agoura Hills** | 26 |
| Cafe Montana \| **Santa Monica** | 20 |
| 🅭 Campanile \| **La Brea** | 26 |
| 🅭 Cheesecake Fact. \| **multi. loc.** | 20 |
| Chocolat \| **Melrose** | 16 |
| Clementine \| **Century City** | 24 |
| NEW Coco Noche \| **Manhattan Bch** | 22 |
| Doughboys \| **multi. loc.** | 22 |
| Farm/Bev. Hills \| **multi. loc.** | 19 |
| 🅭 Grace \| **Beverly Blvd.** | 25 |
| Joan's on Third \| **Third St.** | 24 |
| Mäni's \| **multi. loc.** | 18 |
| Max \| **Sherman Oaks** | 24 |
| Melting Pot \| **multi. loc.** | 19 |
| Michel Richard \| **Beverly Hills** | 20 |
| Porto's Bakery \| **multi. loc.** | – |
| 🅭 Providence \| **Hollywood** | 27 |
| Simon LA \| **W Hollywood** | 21 |
| 🅭 Spago \| **Beverly Hills** | 27 |
| Susina Bakery \| **La Brea** | 23 |
| 🅭 Sweet Lady Jane \| **Melrose** | 25 |

## EASTERN EUROPEAN

| | |
|---|---|
| Danube Bulgarian \| **Westwood** | 15 |

## ECLECTIC

| | |
|---|---|
| NEW Ate-1-8 \| **Encino** | 15 |
| Barbara's/Brewery \| **Downtown** | 15 |
| Barefoot B&G \| **Third St.** | 18 |
| Bellavino \| **Westlake Vill** | 21 |
| 🅭 Bistro K \| **S Pasadena** | 26 |
| Broadway Deli \| **Santa Monica** | 14 |
| Buddha's Belly \| **Beverly Blvd.** | 20 |
| Buffet City \| **West LA** | 13 |
| Café/Tango \| **Universal City** | 20 |
| Canal Club \| **Venice** | 18 |
| NEW Celadon \| **Third St.** | 22 |
| Chaya \| **W Hollywood** | 23 |
| Chez Allez \| **Palos Verdes** | 21 |
| Chez Melange \| **Redondo Bch** | 25 |
| NEW Coco D'Amour \| **Simi Valley** | – |
| NEW Coco Noche \| **Manhattan Bch** | 22 |
| NEW Corkscrew Cafe \| **Manhattan Bch** | – |
| NEW Coupa Cafe \| **Beverly Hills** | 14 |
| Depot \| **Torrance** | 23 |
| NEW Dive, The \| **Hollywood** | – |

| | |
|---|---|
| Farm Stand \| **El Segundo** | 22 |
| Grand Lux \| **Beverly Hills** | 19 |
| Lazy Dog \| **Torrance** | 19 |
| Library Alehse. \| **Santa Monica** | 19 |
| Literati \| **West LA** | 20 |
| Lou \| **Hollywood** | 22 |
| Minibar \| **Universal City** | 23 |
| Minx \| **Glendale** | 19 |
| Mirabelle \| **W Hollywood** | 20 |
| Misto Caffé \| **Torrance** | 21 |
| Moroccan Room \| **Hollywood** | 18 |
| Native Foods \| **Westwood** | 22 |
| NEW Neomeze \| **Pasadena** | – |
| Nook Bistro \| **West LA** | 24 |
| Opus \| **Mid-Wilshire** | 22 |
| Patrick's \| **Santa Monica** | 16 |
| NEW Penthouse \| **Santa Monica** | 20 |
| Sona's \| **Encino** | 17 |
| Standard, The \| **W Hollywood** | 16 |
| Tiger Lily \| **Los Feliz** | 19 |
| NEW Vertical Wine \| **Pasadena** | 19 |
| Villa Piacere \| **Woodland Hills** | 20 |
| Walter's \| **Claremont** | 19 |
| NEW Watercress \| **Sherman Oaks** | – |
| NEW York, The \| **Highland Pk** | – |

## ETHIOPIAN

| | |
|---|---|
| Nyala Ethiopian \| **Fairfax** | 21 |

## EURASIAN

| | |
|---|---|
| NEW Celadon \| **Third St.** | 22 |

## EUROPEAN

| | |
|---|---|
| BIN 8945 \| **W Hollywood** | 21 |
| NEW BottleRock \| **Culver City** | 16 |
| Palomino \| **Westwood** | 18 |
| Three on Fourth \| **Santa Monica** | 16 |
| 2117 \| **West LA** | 24 |

## FILIPINO

| | |
|---|---|
| Alejandro's \| **Eagle Rock** | – |
| NEW Jollibee \| **Koreatown** | 12 |

## FONDUE

| | |
|---|---|
| La Fondue \| **Sherman Oaks** | 14 |
| Melting Pot \| **multi. loc.** | 19 |

## FRENCH

| | |
|---|---|
| A Cow Jumped \| **Beverly Hills** | 22 |
| A La Tarte \| **Pacific Palisades** | 18 |
| Amori \| **Monrovia** | 22 |
| 🅭 A.O.C. \| **Third St.** | 26 |
| Bowery \| **Hollywood** | 21 |

| | |
|---|---|
| Cafe Del Rey | **Marina del Rey** | 23 |
| Café Pierre | **Manhattan Bch** | 22 |
| Cafe Pinot | **Downtown** | 22 |
| Camden House | **Beverly Hills** | 15 |
| Cézanne | **Santa Monica** | 21 |
| Chameau | **Fairfax** | 24 |
| Chateau Marmont | **W Hollywood** | 21 |
| Chez Mimi | **Santa Monica** | 21 |
| ☑ Chinois/Main | **Santa Monica** | 26 |
| Chocolat | **Melrose** | 16 |
| Clafoutis | **W Hollywood** | 18 |
| ☑ Derek's | **Pasadena** | 27 |
| Devon | **Monrovia** | 25 |
| Dusty's | **Silver Lake** | 21 |
| Five Sixty-One | **Pasadena** | 19 |
| French Crêpe Co. | **multi. loc.** | 22 |
| **NEW** Hadaka Sushi | **W Hollywood** | – |
| **NEW** Hokusai | **Beverly Hills** | – |
| ☑ Hotel Bel-Air | **Bel-Air** | 26 |
| La Frite | **multi. loc.** | 20 |
| La Parisienne | **Monrovia** | 23 |
| La Rive Gauche | **Palos Verdes** | 22 |
| L'Artiste Patisserie | **Encino** | 20 |
| Le Chêne | **Saugus** | 25 |
| ☑ Lucques | **W Hollywood** | 27 |
| Madeleine Bistro | **Tarzana** | 22 |
| Maison Akira | **Pasadena** | 25 |
| ☑ Mélisse | **Santa Monica** | 28 |
| Morels French Steak | **Fairfax** | 19 |
| Orris | **West LA** | 26 |
| **NEW** Parc | **Hollywood** | – |
| Paul's Cafe | **Tarzana** | 18 |
| Petrossian | **W Hollywood** | – |
| Reed's | **Manhattan Bch** | 21 |
| **NEW** Salades/Provence | **W Hollywood** | – |
| ☑ Shiro | **S Pasadena** | 27 |
| Soleil Westwood | **Westwood** | 20 |
| Standard, The | **Downtown** | 16 |
| Taix | **Echo Pk** | 16 |

## FRENCH (BISTRO)

| | |
|---|---|
| Angelique Cafe | **Downtown** | 22 |
| Bistro de la Gare | **S Pasadena** | 20 |
| Bistro Provence | **Burbank** | 22 |
| Brass.-Cap. | **Santa Monica** | 19 |
| ☑ Café Bizou | **multi. loc.** | 23 |
| Cafe des Artistes | **Hollywood** | 19 |
| Cafe Stella | **Silver Lake** | 21 |
| CrêpeVine | **Pasadena** | 21 |

| | |
|---|---|
| Figaro Bistrot | **Los Feliz** | 18 |
| French 75 | **multi. loc.** | 21 |
| ☑ Frenchy's Bistro | **Long Bch** | 27 |
| Julienne | **San Marino** | 25 |
| La Crêperie | **Long Bch** | 23 |
| La Dijonaise | **Culver City** | 18 |
| Le Marmiton | **multi. loc.** | 18 |
| Le Petit Bistro | **W Hollywood** | 21 |
| Le Petit Cafe | **Santa Monica** | 21 |
| Le Petit Four | **W Hollywood** | 19 |
| Le Petit Rest. | **Sherman Oaks** | 21 |
| Lilly's French Cafe | **Venice** | 20 |
| Michel Richard | **Beverly Hills** | 20 |
| Mimosa | **Beverly Blvd.** | 22 |
| Mistral | **Sherman Oaks** | 25 |
| Monsieur Marcel | **Fairfax** | 19 |
| Morels First Floor | **Fairfax** | 17 |
| Pastis | **Beverly Blvd.** | 22 |
| Patinette/MOCA | **Downtown** | 16 |
| Pinot Bistro | **Studio City** | 23 |
| Rive Gauche | **Sherman Oaks** | 20 |
| **NEW** 750 ml | **S Pasadena** | – |
| Wine Bistro | **Studio City** | 23 |
| **NEW** Zin Bistro | **Westlake Vill** | 21 |

## FRENCH (BRASSERIE)

| | |
|---|---|
| Barsac Brasserie | **N Hollywood** | 23 |
| Kendall's Brass. | **Downtown** | 17 |

## FRENCH (NEW)

| | |
|---|---|
| ☑ Joe's | **Venice** | 26 |
| ☑ La Cachette | **Century City** | 27 |
| Le Sanglier | **Tarzana** | 22 |
| Ortolan | **Third St.** | 25 |
| ☑ Sona | **W Hollywood** | 27 |

## GASTROPUB

| | |
|---|---|
| Ford's Filling Stat. | **Amer.** | **Culver City** | 19 |
| **NEW** York, The | **Eclectic** | **Highland Pk** | – |

## GREEK

| | |
|---|---|
| Delphi Greek | **Westwood** | 17 |
| George's Greek | **multi. loc.** | 20 |
| Great Greek | **Sherman Oaks** | 21 |
| Joseph's Cafe | **Hollywood** | 18 |
| Le Petit Greek | **Hancock Pk** | 21 |
| Papa Cristo's | **Mid-City** | 22 |
| Papadakis Tav. | **San Pedro** | 22 |
| ☑ Petros | **Manhattan Bch** | 23 |
| Sofi | **Third St.** | 19 |
| Taverna Tony | **Malibu** | 21 |
| Ulysses Voyage | **Fairfax** | 20 |

## HAMBURGERS

| | |
|---|---|
| Apple Pan \| **West LA** | 22 |
| Astro Burger \| **multi. loc.** | 20 |
| Barney's Hamburgers \| **multi. loc.** | 21 |
| Burger Continental \| **Pasadena** | 16 |
| NEW Burger 90210 \| **Beverly Hills** | – |
| Cassell's \| **Koreatown** | 21 |
| Counter, The \| **Santa Monica** | 21 |
| ☑ Father's Office \| **Santa Monica** | 24 |
| Hamburger Mary's \| **W Hollywood** | 15 |
| ☑ In-N-Out Burger \| **multi. loc.** | 24 |
| Islands \| **multi. loc.** | 16 |
| Johnny Rockets \| **multi. loc.** | 15 |
| Mo's \| **Burbank** | 17 |
| Outlaws B&G \| **Playa del Rey** | 15 |
| Pie 'N Burger \| **Pasadena** | 20 |
| Ruby's \| **multi. loc.** | 16 |
| Russell's Burgers \| **Pasadena** | 17 |
| Shack, The \| **multi. loc.** | 18 |
| Tommy's \| **Downtown** | 22 |
| 25 Degrees \| **Hollywood** | 21 |
| 26 Beach \| **Marina del Rey** | 20 |

## HAWAIIAN

| | |
|---|---|
| Back Home/Lahaina \| **multi. loc.** | 17 |
| Local Place \| **Torrance** | 17 |
| Loft, The \| **multi. loc.** | 17 |
| New Flavors \| **Culver City** | 19 |
| Ohana BBQ \| **Studio City** | 19 |
| ☑ Roy's \| **multi. loc.** | 24 |

## HOT DOGS

| | |
|---|---|
| Carney's Express \| **multi. loc.** | 19 |
| Jody Maroni's \| **multi. loc.** | 19 |
| Pink's Chili Dogs \| **La Brea** | 19 |
| Stand, The \| **Encino** | 18 |
| Tommy's \| **Downtown** | 22 |

## INDIAN

| | |
|---|---|
| Addi's Tandoor \| **Redondo Bch** | 23 |
| Agra Cafe \| **Silver Lake** | 22 |
| Akbar \| **multi. loc.** | 20 |
| All India \| **multi. loc.** | 23 |
| Bombay Bite \| **Westwood** | 21 |
| ☑ Bombay Cafe \| **West LA** | 23 |
| Bombay Palace \| **Beverly Hills** | 21 |
| Chakra \| **Beverly Hills** | 21 |
| Clay Pit \| **Brentwood** | 22 |

| | |
|---|---|
| Electric Lotus \| **Los Feliz** | 19 |
| Flavor of India \| **W Hollywood** | 21 |
| Gate of India \| **Santa Monica** | 20 |
| NEW Holy Cow Indian \| **Third St.** | – |
| Hurry Curry \| **West LA** | 19 |
| India's Oven \| **Beverly Blvd.** | 20 |
| India's Tandoori \| **multi. loc.** | 19 |
| NEW Lal Mirch \| **Studio City** | – |
| Nawab of India \| **Santa Monica** | 22 |
| Nirvana \| **Beverly Hills** | 20 |
| Nizam \| **West LA** | 21 |
| NEW Raaga \| **Chatsworth** | – |
| Radhika's \| **Pasadena** | 18 |
| Surya India \| **Third St.** | 23 |
| Tantra \| **Silver Lake** | 21 |
| NEW Tanzore \| **Beverly Hills** | – |

## INDONESIAN

| | |
|---|---|
| Indo Cafe \| **Palms** | 19 |
| NEW Simpang Asia \| **West LA** | – |

## IRISH

| | |
|---|---|
| Auld Dubliner \| **Long Bch** | 21 |

## ITALIAN

(N=Northern; S=Southern)

| | |
|---|---|
| Adagio \| N \| **Woodland Hills** | 23 |
| Ago \| N \| **W Hollywood** | 21 |
| Alejo's \| **multi. loc.** | 21 |
| Alessio \| **multi. loc.** | 22 |
| NEW All' Angelo \| **Hollywood** | 26 |
| Allegria \| **Malibu** | 21 |
| Amalfi \| **La Brea** | 18 |
| Amici \| **multi. loc.** | 21 |
| Angeli Caffe \| **Melrose** | 23 |
| ☑ Angelini Osteria \| **Beverly Blvd.** | 27 |
| Angolo DiVino \| **West LA** | 23 |
| Anna's \| S \| **West LA** | 14 |
| Antica Pizzeria \| **Marina del Rey** | 20 |
| Aroma \| **Silver Lake** | – |
| Basix Cafe \| **W Hollywood** | 18 |
| Bella Cucina \| S \| **Hollywood** | 19 |
| NEW Bella Roma \| **Pico-Robertson** | – |
| Berri's Pizza \| **multi. loc.** | 17 |
| Bravo \| **Santa Monica** | 18 |
| NEW Briganti \| S **Pasadena** | 22 |
| Buca di Beppo \| S \| **multi. loc.** | 15 |
| Buona Sera \| **Redondo Bch** | 22 |
| Ca'Brea \| N \| **La Brea** | 22 |
| Ca' del Sole \| N \| **N Hollywood** | 22 |
| Cafe Med \| **W Hollywood** | 17 |
| Caffé Delfini \| **Santa Monica** | 23 |

Caffe Pinguini | **Playa del Rey** — 22

**NEW** Caffe Primo | **W Hollywood** — 17

Caffe Roma | **Beverly Hills** — 16

C & O | **Marina del Rey** — 19

☑ Capo | **Santa Monica** — 26

Carmine's Italian | **multi. loc.** — 18

Casa Bianca | **Eagle Rock** — 23

Celestino | N | **Pasadena** — 23

Cheebo | **Hollywood** — 19

Christy's | N | **Long Bch** — 24

Ciao Tratt. | **Downtown** — 19

☑ Cicada | **Downtown** — 23

Clafoutis | **W Hollywood** — 18

Cliff's Edge | **Silver Lake** — 20

**NEW** Coccole Lab. | **Redondo Bch** — 21

Coral Tree | **multi. loc.** — 19

Crescendo/Fred Segal | **Santa Monica** — 17

CUBE | **La Brea** — 25

Cucina Paradiso | N | **Palms** — 21

Dan Tana's | **W Hollywood** — 21

Da Pasquale | **Beverly Hills** — 21

Divino | **Brentwood** — 23

Dolce Enoteca | **Melrose** — 16

Dominick's | **Beverly Blvd.** — 20

Doug Arango's | **W Hollywood** — 22

Drago | **Santa Monica** — 24

**NEW** E. Baldi | N | **Beverly Hills** — 21

Enoteca Drago | **Beverly Hills** — 21

Enoteca Toscana | N | **Camarillo** — 18

Enzo & Angela | **West LA** — 21

Fabiolus Café | N | **Hollywood** — 19

Farfalla Trattoria | **Los Feliz** — 22

Far Niente | N | **Glendale** — 25

**NEW** Forte | **Beverly Hills** — –

Fresco | **Glendale** — 22

Fritto Misto | **multi. loc.** — 21

Gale's | N | **Pasadena** — 21

Galletto | **Westlake Vill** — 23

Gennaro's | **Glendale** — 24

Giorgio Baldi | **Santa Monica** — 24

Girasole Cucina | **Hancock Pk** — 24

Guido's | N | **multi. loc.** — 20

Harper's | **Century City** — 16

Hoboken | **West LA** — 18

i Cugini | **Santa Monica** — 21

Il Boccaccio | N | **Hermosa Bch** — 22

Il Buco | **Beverly Hills** — 22

Il Capriccio | **Los Feliz** — 22

Il Chianti | **Lomita** — 25

☑ Il Cielo | N | **Beverly Hills** — 21

☑ Il Fornaio | **multi. loc.** — 20

Il Forno | N | **Santa Monica** — 20

Il Forno Caldo | **Beverly Hills** — 20

Il Grano | **West LA** — 25

Il Moro | **West LA** — 22

Il Pastaio | **Beverly Hills** — 25

Il Sole | **W Hollywood** — 23

Il Tiramisù | N | **Sherman Oaks** — 22

Il Tramezzino | **multi. loc.** — 21

Jacopo's | **multi. loc.** — 17

Jones Hollywood | **W Hollywood** — 18

La Botte | **Santa Monica** — 24

La Bottega Marino | **multi. loc.** — 20

La Bruschetta | **Westwood** — 21

La Dolce Vita | **Beverly Hills** — 20

La Loggia | **Studio City** — 20

La Luna | **Hancock Pk** — 22

La Maschera | N | **Pasadena** — 22

La Pergola | **Sherman Oaks** — 23

La Piazza | **Fairfax** — 18

La Scala | **multi. loc.** — 20

La Sosta | **Hermosa Bch** — 27

La Terza | **Third St.** — 22

La Vecchia | **Santa Monica** — 21

Lido/Manhattan | **Manhattan Bch** — 21

Locanda/Lago | N | **Santa Monica** — 20

Locanda Veneta | N | **Third St.** — 25

L'Opera | N | **Long Bch** — 24

**NEW** Los Angeles Pizza | **Downtown** — –

Louise's Tratt. | **multi. loc.** — 16

Lucia's | **Pacific Palisades** — 18

Madeo | N | **W Hollywood** — 26

Maggiano's | **multi. loc.** — 19

Mama D's | **Manhattan Bch** — 22

Maria's Italian | **multi. loc.** — 17

Marino | **Hollywood** — 24

Market City | S | **Burbank** — 18

Massimo | N | **Beverly Hills** — 22

Matteo's | **West LA** — 19

Miceli's | S | **multi. loc.** — 17

Mio Babbo's | **Westwood** — 21

Mi Piace | **multi. loc.** — 19

Modo Mio | **Pacific Palisades** — 22

Mulberry St. Pizzeria | **multi. loc.** — 23

| | |
|---|---|
| Nicola's Kitchen \| **Woodland Hills** | 18 |
| Oliva \| N \| **Sherman Oaks** | 22 |
| Orso \| **Third St.** | 21 |
| Osteria Latini \| **Brentwood** | 25 |
| NEW Osteria Mozza \| **Hollywood** | - |
| Pace \| **Laurel Canyon** | 22 |
| Padri \| **Agoura Hills** | 21 |
| Palermo \| **Los Feliz** | 17 |
| Palmeri \| S \| **Brentwood** | 24 |
| Pane e Vino \| **Beverly Blvd.** | 21 |
| NEW Panini Cafe \| **Beverly Hills** | 16 |
| Panzanella \| S \| **Sherman Oaks** | 23 |
| Pastina \| S \| **West LA** | 21 |
| Pat's \| **Pico-Robertson** | 22 |
| Pecorino \| **Brentwood** | 20 |
| Peppone \| **Brentwood** | 21 |
| Petrelli's Steak \| **Culver City** | 17 |
| Piatti \| **Thousand Oaks** | 20 |
| Z Piccolo \| **Venice** | 27 |
| Piccolo Paradiso \| **Beverly Hills** | 24 |
| NEW Z Pizzeria Mozza \| **Hollywood** | 26 |
| Pizzicotto \| **Brentwood** | 23 |
| Pomodoro \| **multi. loc.** | 17 |
| Prizzi's Piazza \| **Hollywood** | 22 |
| Prosecco \| N \| **Toluca Lake** | 25 |
| Riviera Rest. \| **Calabasas** | 24 |
| Romano's Macaroni \| **multi. loc.** | 17 |
| Rosti \| N \| **multi. loc.** | 17 |
| Rustico \| **Westlake Vill** | 23 |
| NEW Saluzzi \| **Rancho Palos Verdes** | - |
| San Gennaro \| **Brentwood** | 16 |
| Sapori \| **Marina del Rey** | 24 |
| SHU \| **Bel-Air** | 20 |
| Sisley Italian \| **multi. loc.** | 18 |
| Sor Tino \| **Brentwood** | 19 |
| Spumoni \| **multi. loc.** | 23 |
| Stinking Rose \| **Beverly Hills** | 16 |
| Talia's \| **Manhattan Bch** | 25 |
| Tanino \| S \| **Westwood** | 22 |
| Taste Chicago \| **Burbank** | 19 |
| Tesoro Tratt. \| **Downtown** | 18 |
| Thaitalian \| **Pasadena** | 17 |
| 3rd Stop \| **W Hollywood** | 20 |
| Tony's Bella Vista \| **Burbank** | 22 |
| Toscana \| N \| **Brentwood** | 24 |
| Tra Di Noi \| **Malibu** | 22 |
| Trastevere \| **multi. loc.** | 18 |

| | |
|---|---|
| Tre Venezie \| N \| **Pasadena** | 24 |
| Tulipano \| **Azusa** | 23 |
| Z Tuscany \| **Westlake Vill** | 27 |
| Ugo \| **Culver City** | - |
| Z Valentino \| **Santa Monica** | 26 |
| Z Via Veneto \| **Santa Monica** | 26 |
| Villa Sorriso \| **Pasadena** | 18 |
| Vincenti \| **Brentwood** | 25 |
| Vitello's \| **Studio City** | 14 |
| Vito \| **Santa Monica** | 23 |
| Vittorio's \| S \| **Pacific Palisades** | 18 |
| Vivoli Café \| **W Hollywood** | 25 |
| West \| **Brentwood** | 18 |
| Zita Tratt. \| **Downtown** | 18 |
| Zucca \| **Downtown** | 22 |

## JAPANESE

(* sushi specialist)

| | |
|---|---|
| Ahi Sushi* \| **Studio City** | 22 |
| Ajisen Ramen \| **San Gabriel** | 17 |
| Asahi Ramen \| **West LA** | 21 |
| Asaka* \| **Rancho Palos Verdes** | 20 |
| Asakuma* \| **multi. loc.** | 21 |
| Z Asanebo* \| **Studio City** | 28 |
| Asuka* \| **Westwood** | 20 |
| Azami* \| **Hollywood** | - |
| Banzai Sushi* \| **Calabasas** | 22 |
| NEW Bar Hayama \| **West LA** | - |
| Benihana* \| **multi. loc.** | 18 |
| Blowfish Sushi* \| **W Hollywood** | 20 |
| Boiling Pot \| **Pasadena** | 16 |
| Boss Sushi* \| **Beverly Hills** | 24 |
| Cafe Sushi* \| **Beverly Blvd.** | 19 |
| NEW Catch* \| **Santa Monica** | - |
| Chabuya Tokyo \| **West LA** | 21 |
| Chaya \| **Venice** | 23 |
| Crazy Fish* \| **Beverly Hills** | 17 |
| Ebizo's Skewer \| **Manhattan Bch** | 16 |
| Echigo* \| **West LA** | - |
| Fat Fish* \| **multi. loc.** | 20 |
| Fusion Sushi* \| **multi. loc.** | 16 |
| Geisha House* \| **Hollywood** | 19 |
| NEW Gonpachi \| **Beverly Hills** | - |
| Gyu-Kaku \| **multi. loc.** | 20 |
| NEW Hadaka Sushi* \| **W Hollywood** | - |
| Z Hamasaku* \| **West LA** | 27 |
| Hama Sushi* \| **Venice** | 21 |
| Hayakawa \| **Covina** | 26 |
| Hide Sushi* \| **West LA** | 24 |
| Hirosuke* \| **Encino** | 24 |

| | |
|---|---|
| Hirozen* | **Beverly Blvd.** | 25 |
| NEW Hokusai* | **Beverly Hills** | – |
| Hump, The* | **Santa Monica** | 25 |
| Hurry Curry/Tokyo | **multi. loc.** | 17 |
| Iroha* | **Studio City** | 24 |
| Ita-Cho | **Beverly Blvd.** | 24 |
| NEW Izaka-Ya* | **Third St.** | 25 |
| NEW Izakaya | **W Hollywood** | – |
| Izayoi* | **Little Tokyo** | 23 |
| Japon Bistro* | **Pasadena** | 23 |
| Kanpai* | **Westchester** | 22 |
| Katana* | **W Hollywood** | 23 |
| Z Katsu-ya* | **multi. loc.** | 27 |
| Katsuya* | **Brentwood** | 24 |
| Koi* | **W Hollywood** | 24 |
| K-Zo* | **Culver City** | – |
| NEW Little Tokyo Shabu | **Rowland Hts** | – |
| Maison Akira | **Pasadena** | 25 |
| Z Matsuhisa* | **Beverly Hills** | 27 |
| Mia Sushi* | **Eagle Rock** | 20 |
| Mishima | **Third St.** | 21 |
| Momoyama* | **Redondo Bch** | 21 |
| Z Mori Sushi* | **West LA** | 26 |
| NEW Mubee* | **W Hollywood** | – |
| Musha | **multi. loc.** | 25 |
| Natalee* | **Palms** | 19 |
| Nishimura* | **W Hollywood** | 28 |
| Z Nobu Malibu* | **Malibu** | 28 |
| O-Dae San* | **Koreatown** | 19 |
| Omino Sushi* | **Chatsworth** | 23 |
| O-Nami* | **multi. loc.** | 16 |
| Orris | **West LA** | 26 |
| Pearl Dragon* | **Pacific Palisades** | 19 |
| NEW RA Sushi* | **Torrance** | 18 |
| R23* | **Little Tokyo** | 26 |
| Sai Sai* | **Downtown** | 17 |
| Saito's Sushi* | **Silver Lake** | 25 |
| Shabu Shabu Hse. | **Little Tokyo** | 23 |
| NEW Shabu Shabu Ya | **La Brea** | 15 |
| Shima | **Venice** | 25 |
| Z Shiro | **S Pasadena** | 27 |
| SHU* | **Bel-Air** | 20 |
| NEW Suki 7 | **Westlake Vill** | – |
| Sushi Dokoro* | **Beverly Hills** | 24 |
| Sushi Duke* | **Hermosa Bch** | 25 |
| Sushi Mac* | **multi. loc.** | 17 |
| Sushi Masu* | **West LA** | 26 |
| Sushi Mon* | **multi. loc.** | 19 |
| Z Sushi Nozawa* | **Studio City** | 27 |
| Sushi Ozekii* | **multi. loc.** | – |

| | |
|---|---|
| Sushi Roku* | **multi. loc.** | 22 |
| Sushi Sasabune* | **West LA** | 26 |
| Sushi Sushi* | **Beverly Hills** | 25 |
| Taiko* | **multi. loc.** | 21 |
| NEW Takami | **Downtown** | – |
| Takao* | **Brentwood** | 25 |
| Tama Sushi* | **Studio City** | 24 |
| Tengu* | **multi. loc.** | 22 |
| Teru Sushi* | **Studio City** | 20 |
| Thousand Cranes* | **Little Tokyo** | 23 |
| Three on Fourth | **Santa Monica** | 16 |
| NEW Tokyo Table | **Beverly Hills** | 16 |
| Torafuku* | **West LA** | 22 |
| Tsuji No Hana* | **Marina del Rey** | 22 |
| Urasawa* | **Beverly Hills** | 29 |
| U-Zen* | **West LA** | 22 |
| Wa* | **W Hollywood** | 27 |
| Wabi-Sabi* | **Venice** | 22 |
| Wokcano Cafe* | **multi. loc.** | 17 |
| Yabu* | **multi. loc.** | 23 |
| Yen Sushi* | **multi. loc.** | 23 |
| Yuzu* | **Torrance** | 23 |
| Zip Fusion* | **multi. loc.** | 18 |
| NEW Zu Robata | **West LA** | – |

## JEWISH

| | |
|---|---|
| Z Brent's Deli | **multi. loc.** | 26 |
| Canter's | **Fairfax** | 18 |
| Greenblatt's Deli | **Hollywood** | 19 |
| Nate 'n Al | **Beverly Hills** | 21 |

## KOREAN

(* barbecue specialist)

| | |
|---|---|
| NEW Asian-Ya Soy | **West LA** | – |
| BCD Tofu | **multi. loc.** | 20 |
| ChoSun Galbee* | **Koreatown** | – |
| Manna* | **Koreatown** | 18 |
| Nak Won* | **Koreatown** | 14 |
| O-Dae San* | **Koreatown** | 19 |
| Ohana BBQ* | **Studio City** | 19 |
| Seoul Jung* | **Downtown** | 22 |
| Soot Bull Jeep* | **Koreatown** | 24 |
| Wharo* | **Marina del Rey** | 19 |
| Woo Lae Oak | **Beverly Hills** | 22 |

## KOSHER

| | |
|---|---|
| A Cow Jumped | **Beverly Hills** | 22 |
| BBC | **multi. loc.** | 20 |
| Fish Grill | **multi. loc.** | 19 |
| Magic Carpet | **Pico-Robertson** | 22 |
| Milky Way | **Pico-Robertson** | 18 |
| O4U | **Beverly Hills** | – |

| | |
|---|---|
| Pat's \| **Pico-Robertson** | 22 |
| NEW Prime Grill \| **Beverly Hills** | 21 |
| Sassi Med. \| **Encino** | 19 |
| Zeidler's \| **Brentwood** | 17 |

## LEBANESE

| | |
|---|---|
| Carnival \| **Sherman Oaks** | 23 |
| Gaby's Med. \| **multi. loc.** | – |
| Marouch \| **E Hollywood** | 24 |
| NEW Phoenicia \| **Glendale** | – |
| Sunnin \| **multi. loc.** | 24 |

## MEDITERRANEAN

| | |
|---|---|
| Aioli \| **Torrance** | 17 |
| BBC \| **multi. loc.** | 20 |
| Beau Rivage \| **Malibu** | 20 |
| Café Mundial \| **Monrovia** | 20 |
| Café Santorini \| **Pasadena** | 20 |
| Z Campanile \| **La Brea** | 26 |
| NEW Canele \| **Atwater Vill** | 24 |
| Chaya \| **Venice** | 23 |
| Christine \| **Torrance** | 25 |
| NEW Eight-18 \| **Toluca Lake** | – |
| NEW Elf Café \| **Echo Pk** | – |
| Emle's \| **Northridge** | 19 |
| NEW Fraiche \| **Culver City** | – |
| Gaby's Med. \| **multi. loc.** | – |
| Z Gardens \| **Beverly Hills** | 25 |
| NEW J Rest. \| **Downtown** | 13 |
| Lemon Moon \| **West LA** | 20 |
| Lido/Manhattan \| **Manhattan Bch** | 21 |
| Z Little Door \| **Third St.** | 23 |
| Lou \| **Hollywood** | 22 |
| Z Lucques \| **W Hollywood** | 27 |
| Mediterraneo \| **Hermosa Bch** | 20 |
| NEW Mediterraneo/Westlake \| **Westlake Vill** | 21 |
| NEW Murano \| **W Hollywood** | – |
| Z One Pico \| **Santa Monica** | 23 |
| NEW Panini Cafe \| **Beverly Hills** | 16 |
| Pentimento \| **Mid-Wilshire** | 17 |
| Primitivo \| **Venice** | 21 |
| NEW Rustic Canyon \| **Santa Monica** | 21 |
| Z Sam's/Beach \| **Santa Monica** | 26 |
| Sassi Med. \| **Encino** | 19 |
| Spazio \| **Sherman Oaks** | 19 |
| Sur \| **W Hollywood** | 21 |
| Trio Med. \| **Rolling Hills** | 17 |
| Upstairs 2 \| **West LA** | 23 |
| NEW Vertical Wine \| **Pasadena** | 19 |
| Wilson \| **Culver City** | 23 |

| | |
|---|---|
| Zankou Chicken \| **multi. loc.** | 22 |
| Zazou \| **Redondo Bch** | 24 |

## MEXICAN

| | |
|---|---|
| Adobe Cantina \| **Agoura Hills** | 19 |
| Alegria/Sunset \| **Silver Lake** | 22 |
| Antonio's \| **Melrose** | 22 |
| Z Babita \| **San Gabriel** | 27 |
| Baja Fresh Mex. \| **multi. loc.** | 18 |
| Border Grill \| **Santa Monica** | 22 |
| Cabo Cantina \| **multi. loc.** | 12 |
| Casablanca \| **Venice** | 18 |
| Casa Vega \| **Sherman Oaks** | 18 |
| Chichen Itza \| **Downtown** | 24 |
| Chipotle \| **multi. loc.** | 19 |
| Cozymel's \| **El Segundo** | 14 |
| Doña Rosa \| **multi. loc.** | 16 |
| El Cholo \| **multi. loc.** | 18 |
| El Coyote \| **Beverly Blvd.** | 13 |
| El Tepeyac \| **East LA** | 24 |
| El Torito \| **multi. loc.** | 15 |
| El Torito Grill \| **multi. loc.** | 18 |
| Guelaguetza \| **multi. loc.** | 21 |
| Kay 'n Dave's \| **multi. loc.** | 18 |
| La Huasteca \| **Lynwood** | 22 |
| La Serenata \| **multi. loc.** | 23 |
| Z Lotería! \| **Fairfax** | 24 |
| Malo \| **Silver Lake** | 17 |
| Mexicali \| **Studio City** | 16 |
| Mexico City \| **Los Feliz** | 17 |
| Mi Ranchito \| **Culver City** | 16 |
| Monte Alban \| **West LA** | 22 |
| Pacifico's \| **Culver City** | 16 |
| Paco's Tacos \| **multi. loc.** | 18 |
| NEW Pink Taco \| **Century City** | – |
| Poquito Más \| **multi. loc.** | 22 |
| Señor Fred \| **Sherman Oaks** | 17 |
| Sharky's Mex. \| **multi. loc.** | 17 |
| Spanish Kitchen \| **W Hollywood** | 17 |
| Tamayo \| **East LA** | 21 |
| Tlapazola Grill \| **multi. loc.** | 24 |
| Velvet Margarita \| **Hollywood** | 16 |

## MIDDLE EASTERN

| | |
|---|---|
| Burger Continental \| **Pasadena** | 16 |
| Z Carousel \| **multi. loc.** | 24 |
| Falafel King \| **multi. loc.** | 18 |
| NEW Hummus Bar \| **Tarzana** | – |
| Magic Carpet \| **Pico-Robertson** | 22 |
| Moishe's \| **Fairfax** | 21 |
| O4U \| **Beverly Hills** | – |
| Wahib's Mid-East \| **Alhambra** | 21 |

## MOROCCAN

| | |
|---|---|
| Chameau | **Fairfax** | 24 |
| Dar Maghreb | **Hollywood** | 18 |
| Koutoubia | **Westwood** | 20 |
| Marrakesh | **Studio City** | 19 |

## NEPALESE

| | |
|---|---|
| Tibet Nepal | **Pasadena** | 19 |

## NOODLE SHOPS

| | |
|---|---|
| Ajisen Ramen | **San Gabriel** | 17 |
| Asahi Ramen | **West LA** | 21 |
| Chabuya Tokyo | **West LA** | 21 |
| Mishima | **Third St.** | 21 |
| Pho Café | **Silver Lake** | 22 |

## NUEVO LATINO

| | |
|---|---|
| Alegria | **Long Bch** | 21 |
| Ciudad | **Downtown** | 21 |
| Xiomara | **Hollywood** | 21 |

## PACIFIC RIM

| | |
|---|---|
| Christine | **Torrance** | 25 |
| Duke's | **Malibu** | 17 |

## PAN-ASIAN

| | |
|---|---|
| Beacon | **Culver City** | 22 |
| Bite | **Marina del Rey** | 16 |
| Buddha's Belly | **Beverly Blvd.** | 20 |
| Chin Chin | **W Hollywood** | 17 |
| NEW Happi Songs | **La Brea** | - |
| NEW Liliya | **Downtown** | - |
| Mirü8691 | **Beverly Hills** | 24 |
| Monsoon Cafe | **Santa Monica** | 17 |
| Pearl Dragon | **Pacific Palisades** | 19 |
| Pei Wei Diner | **multi. loc.** | 16 |
| NEW Prana Cafe | **W Hollywood** | 22 |
| Red Pearl | **Hollywood** | 19 |
| NEW Red Seven | **W Hollywood** | - |
| Typhoon | **Santa Monica** | 21 |
| NEW Yatai Asian Tapas | **W Hollywood** | 19 |
| NEW Yose | **Santa Monica** | 22 |
| Zen Grill | **multi. loc.** | 20 |

## PAN-LATIN

| | |
|---|---|
| NEW Limon Latin Grill | **Simi Valley** | - |

## PERSIAN

| | |
|---|---|
| NEW Baran | **Westwood** | 20 |
| Javan | **West LA** | 21 |
| Pistachio Grill | **Beverly Hills** | 23 |
| Shaherzad | **Westwood** | 22 |

## PERUVIAN

| | |
|---|---|
| El Pollo Inka | **multi. loc.** | 19 |
| Los Balcones/Peru | **Hollywood** | 21 |
| Z Mario Peruvian | **Hollywood** | 25 |
| NEW Qusqo | **West LA** | - |

## PIZZA

| | |
|---|---|
| Abbot's Pizza | **multi. loc.** | 23 |
| Albano's | **Melrose** | 23 |
| Antica Pizzeria | **Marina del Rey** | 20 |
| Berri's Pizza | **multi. loc.** | 17 |
| BJ's | **multi. loc.** | 17 |
| Bravo | **Santa Monica** | 18 |
| Caioti Pizza | **Studio City** | 22 |
| Cali. Pizza Kitchen | **multi. loc.** | 18 |
| Casa Bianca | **Eagle Rock** | 23 |
| Cheebo | **Hollywood** | 19 |
| D'Amore's Pizza | **multi. loc.** | 21 |
| Farfalla Trattoria | **Los Feliz** | 22 |
| Il Capriccio | **Hollywood** | 22 |
| Jacopo's | **multi. loc.** | 17 |
| Johnnie's NY | **multi. loc.** | 18 |
| La Bottega Marino | **multi. loc.** | 20 |
| La Luna | **Hancock Pk** | 22 |
| Lamonica's NY Pizza | **Westwood** | 22 |
| NEW Los Angeles Pizza | **Downtown** | - |
| Mulberry St. Pizzeria | **multi. loc.** | 23 |
| Pace | **Laurel Canyon** | 22 |
| Pizza Rustica | **multi. loc.** | 17 |
| NEW Z Pizzeria Mozza | **Hollywood** | 26 |
| Prizzi's Piazza | **Hollywood** | 22 |
| Village Pizzeria | **Hancock Pk** | 24 |
| Wildflour Pizza | **Santa Monica** | 18 |
| Wolfgang Puck | **Universal City** | 18 |

## POLISH

| | |
|---|---|
| Warszawa | **Santa Monica** | 21 |

## POLYNESIAN

| | |
|---|---|
| Bora Bora | **Manhattan Bch** | 23 |
| NEW Coco D'Amour | **Simi Valley** | - |

## PUB FOOD

| | |
|---|---|
| Auld Dubliner | **Long Bch** | 21 |
| BJ's | **multi. loc.** | 17 |
| Gordon Biersch | **Pasadena** | 17 |
| Heroes B&G | **Claremont** | 16 |
| Whale & Ale | **San Pedro** | 16 |
| Ye Olde King's Head | **Santa Monica** | 17 |

## PUERTO RICAN

Madre's | **Pasadena** — 14

## RUSSIAN

**NEW** Romanov | **Studio City** — –

## SANDWICHES

| | |
|---|---|
| Artisan Cheese | **Studio City** | 24 |
| Art's Deli | **Studio City** | 19 |
| Barney Greengrass | **Beverly Hills** | 21 |
| Breadbar | **W Hollywood** | 19 |
| Canter's | **Fairfax** | 18 |
| Chez Allez | **Palos Verdes** | 21 |
| Joan's on Third | **Third St.** | 24 |
| Johnnie's Pastrami | **Culver City** | 20 |
| Junior's | **West LA** | 16 |
| Langer's Deli | **Downtown** | 25 |
| **NEW** Meltdown Etc. | **Culver City** | – |
| Nate 'n Al | **Beverly Hills** | 21 |
| Nicola's Kitchen | **Woodland Hills** | 18 |
| Noah's NY Bagels | **multi. loc.** | 18 |
| Philippe/Orig. | **Chinatown** | 21 |
| Porto's Bakery | **multi. loc.** | – |
| Roll 'n Rye | **Culver City** | 18 |
| Sandbag Sandwich | **multi. loc.** | 18 |
| **NEW** 3 Square | **Venice** | 21 |

## SCOTTISH

Tam O'Shanter | **Atwater Vill** — 21

## SEAFOOD

| | |
|---|---|
| ABC Seafood | **Chinatown** | 19 |
| Admiral Risty | **Rancho Palos Verdes** | 21 |
| **NEW** Baleen | **Redondo Bch** | 22 |
| Bluewater Grill | **Redondo Bch** | 20 |
| Breeze | **Century City** | 19 |
| Buggy Whip | **Westchester** | 19 |
| **NEW** Catch | **Santa Monica** | – |
| Chart House | **multi. loc.** | 19 |
| Delmonico's Lobster | **Encino** | 21 |
| Duke's | **Malibu** | 17 |
| Enterprise Fish | **Santa Monica** | 18 |
| Fins | **multi. loc.** | 22 |
| Fish Grill | **multi. loc.** | 19 |
| Fonz's | **Manhattan Bch** | 22 |
| Galley, The | **Santa Monica** | 18 |
| Gladstone's | **Pacific Palisades** | 15 |
| Gulfstream | **Century City** | 21 |
| Hop Woo | **Alhambra** | 19 |

| | |
|---|---|
| Hungry Cat | **Hollywood** | 24 |
| i Cugini | **Santa Monica** | 21 |
| Joe's Crab | **multi. loc.** | 13 |
| Killer Shrimp | **multi. loc.** | 21 |
| Kincaid's | **Redondo Bch** | 21 |
| King's Fish Hse. | **multi. loc.** | 21 |
| La Serenata | **multi. loc.** | 23 |
| ☑ Lobster, The | **Santa Monica** | 23 |
| ☑ Madison, The | **Long Bch** | 21 |
| Malibu Seafood | **Malibu** | 21 |
| McCormick/Schmick | **multi. loc.** | 19 |
| McKenna's | **Long Bch** | 20 |
| NBC Seafood | **Monterey Pk** | 22 |
| Neptune's Net | **Malibu** | 17 |
| Ocean Ave. | **Santa Monica** | 23 |
| Ocean Seafood | **Chinatown** | 22 |
| O-Dae San | **Koreatown** | 19 |
| Odyssey | **Granada Hills** | 14 |
| O-Nami | **Torrance** | 16 |
| Pacifico's | **Culver City** | 16 |
| ☑ Palm, The | **multi. loc.** | 24 |
| Paradise Cove | **Malibu** | 16 |
| Parker's Lighthse. | **Long Bch** | 18 |
| ☑ Providence | **Hollywood** | 27 |
| Reel Inn | **Malibu** | 20 |
| Rock 'N Fish | **Manhattan Bch** | 21 |
| ☑ Sea Harbour | **Rosemead** | 25 |
| 22nd St. Landing | **San Pedro** | 18 |
| V.I.P. Harbor | **West LA** | 18 |
| ☑ Water Grill | **Downtown** | 27 |

## SMALL PLATES

(See also Spanish tapas specialist)

| | |
|---|---|
| ☑ A.O.C. | Calif./French | **Third St.** | 26 |
| **NEW** Bar Hayama | Jap. | **West LA** | – |
| Beacon | Pan-Asian | **Culver City** | 22 |
| Bite | Pan-Asian | **Marina del Rey** | 16 |
| **NEW** BottleRock | Euro. | **Culver City** | 16 |
| Broadway Deli | Eclectic | **Santa Monica** | 14 |
| Buddha's Belly | Eclectic | **Beverly Blvd.** | 20 |
| Café/Tango | Eclectic | **Universal City** | 20 |
| **NEW** Coco Noche | Eclectic | **Manhattan Bch** | 22 |

| | |
|---|---|
| NEW Corkscrew Cafe \| Eclectic \| **Manhattan Bch** | — |
| CUBE \| Italian \| **La Brea** | 25 |
| NEW Eight-18 \| Med. \| **Toluca Lake** | — |
| Enoteca Drago \| Italian \| **Beverly Hills** | 21 |
| NEW Happi Songs \| Pan-Asian \| **La Brea** | — |
| Ita-Cho \| Jap. \| **Beverly Blvd.** | 24 |
| NEW Izaka-Ya \| Jap. \| **Third St.** | 25 |
| NEW Izakaya \| Jap. \| **W Hollywood** | — |
| Jer-ne \| Calif. \| **Marina del Rey** | 22 |
| K-Zo \| Jap. \| **Culver City** | — |
| La Sosta \| Italian \| **Hermosa Bch** | 27 |
| Lou \| Med. \| **Hollywood** | 22 |
| ☑ Mako \| Asian Fusion \| **Beverly Hills** | 26 |
| Minibar \| Eclectic \| **Universal City** | 23 |
| Musha \| Jap. \| **multi. loc.** | 25 |
| Orris \| French/Jap. \| **West LA** | 26 |
| Primitivo \| Med. \| **Venice** | 21 |
| Red Pearl \| Pan-Asian \| **Hollywood** | 19 |
| NEW Rustic Canyon \| Med. \| **Santa Monica** | 21 |
| 3rd Stop \| Italian \| **W Hollywood** | 20 |
| Upstairs 2 \| Med. \| **West LA** | 23 |
| NEW Vertical Wine \| Eclectic/Med. \| **Pasadena** | 19 |
| Violet \| Amer. \| **Santa Monica** | 21 |
| NEW Yatai Asian Tapas \| Pan-Asian \| **W Hollywood** | 19 |
| Yuzu \| Jap. \| **Torrance** | 23 |

## SOUL FOOD

| | |
|---|---|
| Big Mama's \| **Pasadena** | 20 |
| NEW Larkin's \| **Eagle Rock** | — |
| ☑ Roscoe's \| **multi. loc.** | 22 |

## SOUTHERN

| | |
|---|---|
| Angelena's Southern \| **Alhambra** | 15 |
| Aunt Kizzy's \| **Marina del Rey** | 20 |
| Baby Blues BBQ \| **Venice** | 22 |
| House of Blues \| **W Hollywood** | 15 |
| Johnny Rebs' \| **multi. loc.** | 22 |
| Kokomo Cafe \| **Fairfax** | 20 |
| NEW Larkin's \| **Eagle Rock** | — |
| Les Sisters \| **Chatsworth** | 25 |
| Lucille's BBQ \| **multi. loc.** | 22 |
| Memphis \| **Hollywood** | 17 |

## SOUTHWESTERN

| | |
|---|---|
| Bandera \| **West LA** | 22 |
| Chili My Soul \| **Encino** | 22 |
| Coyote Cantina \| **Redondo Bch** | 20 |
| Jinky's \| **multi. loc.** | 20 |
| Sagebrush Cantina \| **Calabasas** | 14 |
| Sonora Cafe \| **La Brea** | 21 |

## SPANISH

(* tapas specialist)

| | |
|---|---|
| Aioli* \| **Torrance** | 17 |
| Bar Celona* \| **Pasadena** | 16 |
| Cobras/Matadors* \| **multi. loc.** | 21 |
| Courtyard* \| **W Hollywood** | 17 |
| Enoteca Toscana \| **Camarillo** | 18 |
| La Paella* \| **Beverly Hills** | 22 |
| NEW Minotaure* \| **Playa del Rey** | 19 |
| Next Door/La Loggia* \| **Studio City** | 20 |
| Olé! Tapas Bar* \| **Studio City** | 17 |
| Tasca Winebar* \| **Third St.** | 21 |
| Viva Madrid* \| **Claremont** | 22 |

## STEAKHOUSES

| | |
|---|---|
| ☑ Arnie Morton's Steak \| **multi. loc.** | 25 |
| Arroyo Chop Hse. \| **Pasadena** | 25 |
| Beckham Grill \| **Pasadena** | 18 |
| Benihana \| **multi. loc.** | 18 |
| Billingsley's \| **West LA** | 14 |
| Boa \| **multi. loc.** | 23 |
| Buggy Whip \| **Westchester** | 19 |
| Carlitos Gardel \| **Melrose** | 23 |
| Chapter 8 Steak \| **Agoura Hills** | 18 |
| Chart House \| **multi. loc.** | 19 |
| Chez Jay \| **Santa Monica** | 16 |
| Club 41 \| **Pasadena** | 19 |
| ☑ Cut \| **Beverly Hills** | 26 |
| Dakota \| **Hollywood** | 22 |
| Damon's Steak \| **Glendale** | 16 |
| Derby \| **Arcadia** | 24 |
| NEW e3rd Steak \| **Downtown** | 20 |
| 555 East \| **Long Bch** | 25 |
| Fleming Prime \| **multi. loc.** | 25 |
| Fogo de Chão \| **Beverly Hills** | 23 |
| Fonz's \| **Manhattan Bch** | 22 |
| Galley, The \| **Santa Monica** | 18 |
| Gaucho Grill \| **multi. loc.** | 18 |
| NEW Holdren's Steak \| **Thousand Oaks** | — |
| ☑ Jar \| **Beverly Blvd.** | 25 |
| JJ Steak \| **Pasadena** | 20 |

| | |
|---|---|
| Kincaid's \| **Redondo Bch** | 21 |
| Lasher's \| **Burbank** | 24 |
| Z Lawry's Prime \| **Beverly Hills** | 25 |
| Lodge Steak \| **Beverly Hills** | 20 |
| Z Madison, The \| **Long Bch** | 21 |
| Z Mastro's Steak \| **multi. loc.** | 25 |
| McKenna's \| **Long Bch** | 20 |
| Monty's Steak \| **Woodland Hills** | 21 |
| Morels French Steak \| **Fairfax** | 19 |
| Nick & Stef's Steak \| **Downtown** | 22 |
| Outback Steak \| **multi. loc.** | 17 |
| Pacific Dining Car \| **multi. loc.** | 22 |
| Z Palm, The \| **multi. loc.** | 24 |
| Petrelli's Steak \| **Culver City** | 17 |
| Porterhouse \| **Beverly Hills** | 20 |
| Porto Alegre \| **Pasadena** | – |
| NEW Prime Grill \| **Beverly Hills** | 21 |
| NEW Riordan's Tavern \| **Downtown** | – |
| Rock 'N Fish \| **Manhattan Bch** | 21 |
| Z Ruth's Chris \| **multi. loc.** | 25 |
| Saddle Ranch Chop \| **multi. loc.** | 16 |
| Salt Creek \| **multi. loc.** | 18 |
| Smoke House \| **Burbank** | 19 |
| Taylor's Steak \| **multi. loc.** | 21 |
| Vibrato \| **Bel-Air** | 22 |
| West \| **Brentwood** | 18 |

### TEX-MEX

| | |
|---|---|
| Chili My Soul \| **Encino** | 22 |
| Marix Tex Mex \| **multi. loc.** | 17 |

### THAI

| | |
|---|---|
| NEW Bulan Thai Veg. \| **Melrose** | – |
| Chaba \| **Redondo Bch** | 20 |
| Z Chadaka \| **Burbank** | 24 |
| Chan Dara \| **multi. loc.** | 19 |
| Chao Krung \| **Fairfax** | 21 |
| Cholada \| **Malibu** | 26 |
| Jitlada \| **E Hollywood** | 21 |
| Naraya Thai \| **Pico-Robertson** | 19 |
| Natalee \| **multi. loc.** | 19 |
| Palms Thai \| **E Hollywood** | 23 |
| Rambutan Thai \| **Silver Lake** | 22 |
| Red Corner Asia \| **E Hollywood** | 22 |
| NEW Ruen Pair \| **E Hollywood** | 21 |
| Saladang \| **Pasadena** | 24 |
| NEW Spice Basil \| **Alhambra** | – |

| | |
|---|---|
| Talésai \| **multi. loc.** | 22 |
| Thai Dishes \| **multi. loc.** | 18 |
| Thaitalian \| **Pasadena** | 17 |
| Tongdang Thai \| **San Marino** | 18 |
| Tuk Tuk Thai \| **Pico-Robertson** | 21 |

### TIBETAN

| | |
|---|---|
| Tibet Nepal \| **Pasadena** | 19 |

### TUNISIAN

| | |
|---|---|
| Moun of Tunis \| **Hollywood** | 20 |

### UZBEKI

| | |
|---|---|
| Uzbekistan \| **Hollywood** | 18 |

### VEGETARIAN

(* vegan)

| | |
|---|---|
| A Votre Sante* \| **Brentwood** | 20 |
| NEW Bulan Thai Veg. \| **Melrose** | – |
| NEW Elf Café \| **Echo Pk** | – |
| Fatty's & Co. \| **Eagle Rock** | 20 |
| Z Inn/Seventh Ray* \| **Topanga** | 21 |
| Jack Sprat's \| **West LA** | 19 |
| Juliano's Raw* \| **Santa Monica** | 21 |
| Leaf Cuisine* \| **multi. loc.** | – |
| Madeleine Bistro* \| **Tarzana** | 22 |
| Mäni's* \| **multi. loc.** | 18 |
| Z M Café de Chaya \| **Melrose** | 23 |
| Native Foods* \| **Westwood** | 22 |
| Newsroom Café \| **W Hollywood** | 19 |
| Real Food Daily* \| **multi. loc.** | 21 |
| Trails, The* \| **Los Feliz** | 18 |
| Urth Caffé* \| **multi. loc.** | 21 |
| Vegan Glory* \| **Beverly Blvd.** | 24 |

### VIETNAMESE

| | |
|---|---|
| Absolutely Pho \| **W Hollywood** | 19 |
| Benley Viet. \| **Long Bch** | 26 |
| Blossom \| **Downtown** | 22 |
| Blue Hen \| **Eagle Rock** | 16 |
| China Beach \| **Venice** | 18 |
| Z Crustacean \| **Beverly Hills** | 23 |
| Gingergrass \| **Silver Lake** | 22 |
| Golden Deli \| **San Gabriel** | 23 |
| Indochine Vien \| **Atwater Vill** | 18 |
| Le Saigon \| **West LA** | 21 |
| Michelia \| **Third St.** | 23 |
| Pho Café \| **Silver Lake** | 22 |
| Pho 79 \| **Alhambra** | 21 |

# Locations

Includes restaurant names, cuisines, Food ratings and, for locations that are mapped, top list and map coordinates. ☑ indicates places with the highest ratings, popularity and importance.

## LA Central

### ATWATER VILLAGE

| | |
|---|---|
| **NEW** Asia Los Feliz \| *Asian/Calif.* | 20 |
| **NEW** Canele \| *Med.* | 24 |
| Indochine Vien \| *Viet.* | 18 |
| Mimi's Cafe \| *Diner* | 17 |
| Tam O'Shanter \| *Scottish* | 21 |

### BEVERLY BLVD.

(bet. La Brea & La Cienega; see map on back of gatefold)

#### TOP FOOD

| | |
|---|---|
| Angelini Osteria \| *Italian* \| **D8** | 27 |
| Hatfield's \| *Amer.* \| **D7** | 27 |
| Hirozen \| *Jap.* \| **D5** | 25 |
| Jar \| *Amer./Steak* \| **E6** | 25 |
| Grace \| *Amer.* \| **E8** | 25 |

#### LISTING

| | |
|---|---|
| ☑ Angelini Osteria \| *Italian* | 27 |
| bld \| *Amer.* | 21 |
| Buddha's Belly \| *Pan-Asian* | 20 |
| Cafe Sushi \| *Jap.* | 19 |
| Cobras/Matadors \| *Spanish* | 21 |
| Dominick's \| *Italian* | 20 |
| Eat Well Cafe \| *Amer.* | 15 |
| El Coyote \| *Mex.* | 13 |
| Fish Grill \| *Seafood* | 19 |
| ☑ Grace \| *Amer.* | 25 |
| ☑ Hatfield's \| *Amer.* | 27 |
| Hirozen \| *Jap.* | 25 |
| India's Oven \| *Indian* | 20 |
| Ita-Cho \| *Jap.* | 24 |
| ☑ Jar \| *Amer./Steak* | 25 |
| Kings Road \| *Amer.* | 19 |
| Mimosa \| *French* | 22 |
| Pane e Vino \| *Italian* | 21 |
| Pastis \| *French* | 22 |
| Swingers \| *Diner* | 17 |
| Vegan Glory \| *Vegan* | 24 |

### CHINATOWN

| | |
|---|---|
| ABC Seafood \| *Chinese/Seafood* | 19 |
| Empress Pavilion \| *Chinese* | 21 |
| Hop Li \| *Chinese* | 18 |
| Hop Woo \| *Chinese* | 19 |
| Ocean Seafood \| *Chinese/Seafood* | 22 |
| Philippe/Orig. \| *Sandwiches* | 21 |
| Sam Woo \| *Chinese* | 20 |
| Yang Chow \| *Chinese* | 23 |

### DOWNTOWN

(See map on page 272)

#### TOP FOOD

| | |
|---|---|
| Water Grill \| *Seafood* \| **F3** | 27 |
| Patina \| *Amer./Calif.* \| **E3** | 26 |
| Noé \| *Amer.* \| **E3** | 25 |
| Arnie Morton's Steak \| *Steak* \| **F1** | 25 |
| Langer's Deli \| *Deli* \| **F1** | 25 |
| Roy's \| *Hawaiian* \| **F1** | 24 |
| Palm, The \| *Seafood/Steak* \| **G1** | 24 |
| Cicada \| *Calif./Italian* \| **G2** | 23 |
| Cafe Pinot \| *Calif./French* \| **F2** | 22 |
| Pacific Dining Car \| *Steak* \| **E1** | 22 |
| Nick & Stef's Steak \| *Steak* \| **E3** | 22 |
| Angelique Cafe \| *French* \| **H2** | 22 |
| Blue Velvet \| *Amer.* \| **F1** | 22 |
| Tommy's \| *Hamburgers/Hot Dogs* \| **C1** | 22 |
| Checkers \| *Calif.* \| **F2** | 22 |

#### LISTING

| | |
|---|---|
| Angelique Cafe \| *French* | 22 |
| ☑ Arnie Morton's Steak \| *Steak* | 25 |
| Barbara's/Brewery \| *Eclectic* | 15 |
| BCD Tofu \| *Korean* | 20 |
| Blossom \| *Viet.* | 22 |
| **NEW** ☑ Blue Velvet \| *Amer.* | 22 |
| Cafe Pinot \| *Calif./French* | 22 |
| Cali. Pizza Kitchen \| *Pizza* | 18 |
| Checkers \| *Calif.* | 22 |
| Chichen Itza \| *Mex.* | 24 |
| Ciao Tratt. \| *Italian* | 19 |
| ☑ Cicada \| *Calif./Italian* | 23 |
| Ciudad \| *Nuevo Latino* | 21 |
| Engine Co. 28 \| *Amer.* | 19 |
| **NEW** e3rd Steak \| *Steak* | 20 |
| 410 Boyd \| *Calif.* | 20 |
| George's Greek \| *Greek* | 20 |
| **NEW** J Rest. \| *Amer./Med.* | 13 |
| Kendall's Brass. \| *French* | 17 |
| Koo Koo Roo \| *Amer.* | 16 |

| | | |
|---|---|---|
| Langer's Deli \| Deli | 25 | |
| **NEW** Liberty Grill \| Amer. | – | |
| **NEW** Liliya \| Pan-Asian | – | |
| **NEW** Los Angeles Pizza \| Pizza | – | |
| McCormick/Schmick \| Seafood | 19 | |
| Nick & Stef's Steak \| Steak | 22 | |
| Noé \| Amer. | 25 | |
| Original Pantry \| Diner | 16 | |
| Original Texas BBQ \| BBQ | 20 | |
| Pacific Dining Car \| Steak | 22 | |
| 🅩 Palm, The \| Seafood/Steak | 24 | |
| 🅩 Patina \| Amer./Calif. | 26 | |
| Patinette/MOCA \| Continental/French | 16 | |
| Pete's Cafe \| Amer. | 18 | |
| Pizza Rustica \| Pizza | 17 | |
| **NEW** Riordan's Tavern \| Steak | – | |
| 🅩 Roy's \| Hawaiian | 24 | |
| Sai Sai \| Jap. | 17 | |
| Sandbag Sandwich \| Sandwiches | 18 | |
| Seoul Jung \| Korean | 22 | |
| Standard, The \| Eclectic | 16 | |
| **NEW** Takami \| Jap. | – | |
| Tesoro Tratt. \| Italian | 18 | |
| Tiara Cafe \| Amer. | 20 | |
| Tommy's \| Hamburgers/Hot Dogs | 22 | |
| Traxx \| Amer. | 20 | |
| 🅩 Water Grill \| Seafood | 27 | |
| Zip Fusion \| Jap. | 18 | |
| Zita Tratt. \| Italian | 18 | |
| Zucca \| Italian | 22 | |

**EAST HOLLYWOOD**

| | |
|---|---|
| 🅩 Carousel \| Mideast. | 24 |
| Jitlada \| Thai | 21 |
| Marouch \| Lebanese | 24 |
| Palms Thai \| Thai | 23 |
| Red Corner Asia \| Thai | 22 |
| **NEW** Ruen Pair \| Thai | 21 |
| Square One Dining \| Amer. | 24 |
| Zankou Chicken \| Med. | 22 |

**ECHO PARK**

| | |
|---|---|
| **NEW** Elf Café \| Med./Veg. | – |
| Taix \| French | 16 |

**FAIRFAX**

| | |
|---|---|
| Canter's \| Deli | 18 |
| Chameau \| French/Moroccan | 24 |
| Chao Krung \| Thai | 21 |
| Chipotle \| Mex. | 19 |
| Du-par's \| Diner | 16 |

| | |
|---|---|
| Farm/Bev. Hills \| Amer. | 19 |
| French Crêpe Co. \| French | 22 |
| Genghis Cohen \| Chinese | 20 |
| Gumbo Pot \| Cajun | 21 |
| Johnny Rockets \| Hamburgers | 15 |
| Kokomo Cafe \| Southern | 20 |
| La Piazza \| Italian | 18 |
| 🅩 Lotería! \| Mex. | 24 |
| Maggiano's \| Italian | 19 |
| Mäni's \| Bakery/Vegan | 18 |
| Moishe's \| Mideast. | 21 |
| Monsieur Marcel \| French | 19 |
| Morels First Floor \| French | 17 |
| Morels French Steak \| French/Steak | 19 |
| Nyala Ethiopian \| Ethiopian | 21 |
| Tart \| Amer. | 18 |
| Ulysses Voyage \| Greek | 20 |
| Whisper Lounge \| Amer. | 16 |
| Wood Ranch BBQ \| BBQ | 20 |

**HANCOCK PARK/ LARCHMONT VILLAGE**

| | |
|---|---|
| Chan Dara \| Thai | 19 |
| Girasole Cucina \| Italian | 24 |
| Koo Koo Roo \| Amer. | 16 |
| La Bottega Marino \| Italian | 20 |
| La Luna \| Italian | 22 |
| Le Petit Greek \| Greek | 21 |
| Louise's Tratt. \| Calif./Italian | 16 |
| Noah's NY Bagels \| Sandwiches | 18 |
| 🅩 Prado \| Carib. | 21 |
| Village Pizzeria \| Pizza | 24 |

**HIGHLAND PARK**

| | |
|---|---|
| **NEW** Marty's \| Calif. | – |
| **NEW** York, The \| Eclectic | – |

**HOLLYWOOD**

(See map on page 271)

**TOP FOOD**

| | |
|---|---|
| Providence \| Amer./Seafood \| **E8** | 27 |
| Pizzeria Mozza \| Pizza \| **E7** | 26 |
| Mario Peruvian \| Peruvian \| **E8** | 25 |
| Hungry Cat \| Seafood \| **B8** | 24 |
| In-N-Out Burger \| Hamburgers \| **B6** | 24 |
| Marino \| Italian \| **E8** | 24 |
| Prizzi's Piazza \| Italian \| **A9** | 22 |
| Roscoe's \| Soul Food \| **B9** | 22 |
| Dakota \| Steak \| **B6** | 22 |
| Lou \| Eclectic/Med. \| **E8** | 22 |
| Ammo \| Calif. \| **C7** | 22 |

**LOS ANGELES**

**LOCATIONS**

## LITTLE TOKYO

| | |
|---|---|
| Chop Suey | *Asian Fusion* | 11 |
| NEW Garden Cafe | *Asian/Calif.* | - |
| Izayoi | *Jap.* | 23 |
| R23 | *Jap.* | 26 |
| Shabu Shabu Hse. | *Jap.* | 23 |
| Thousand Cranes | *Jap.* | 23 |

## LOS FELIZ

| | |
|---|---|
| Alcove | *Amer.* | 22 |
| Chi Dynasty | *Chinese* | 23 |
| Cobras/Matadors | *Spanish* | 21 |
| Electric Lotus | *Indian* | 19 |
| Farfalla Trattoria | *Italian* | 22 |
| Figaro Bistrot | *French* | 18 |
| Fred 62 | *Diner* | 18 |
| Il Capriccio | *Italian/Pizza* | 22 |
| Louise's Tratt. | *Calif./Italian* | 16 |
| Mexico City | *Mex.* | 17 |
| Palermo | *Italian* | 17 |
| Tiger Lily | *Asian/Eclectic* | 19 |
| Trails, The | *Amer./Vegan* | 18 |
| Tropicalia Brazil | *Brazilian* | 19 |
| vermont | *Amer.* | 22 |

## MELROSE

(See map on page 271)

### TOP FOOD

| | |
|---|---|
| Sweet Lady Jane | *Bakery* | **C5** | 25 |
| Table 8 | *Calif.* | **C7** | 24 |
| Carlitos Gardel | *Argent./Steak* | **C6** | 23 |

### LISTING

| | |
|---|---|
| Albano's | *Pizza* | 23 |
| Angeli Caffe | *Italian* | 23 |
| Antonio's | *Mex.* | 22 |
| NEW Bulan Thai Veg. | *Thai* | - |
| Carlitos Gardel | *Argent./Steak* | 23 |
| Chocolat | *Calif./French* | 16 |
| Dolce Enoteca | *Italian* | 16 |
| NEW Foundry/Melrose | *Amer.* | - |
| Johnny Rockets | *Hamburgers* | 15 |
| Louise's Tratt. | *Calif./Italian* | 16 |
| ☑ M Café de Chaya | *Veg.* | 23 |
| ☑ Sweet Lady Jane | *Bakery* | 25 |
| Table 8 | *Calif.* | 24 |
| NEW Village Idiot | *Amer.* | 19 |

## MID-CITY

| | |
|---|---|
| NEW Bloom Cafe | *Amer./Calif.* | 23 |
| El Cholo | *Mex.* | 18 |
| Harold & Belle's | *Creole* | 24 |
| India's Tandoori | *Indian* | 19 |

| | |
|---|---|
| Koo Koo Roo | *Amer.* | 16 |
| Papa Cristo's | *Greek* | 22 |
| ☑ Phillips BBQ | *BBQ* | 24 |
| ☑ Roscoe's | *Soul Food* | 22 |
| Versailles | *Cuban* | 21 |

## MID-WILSHIRE

| | |
|---|---|
| Caffe Latte | *Amer.* | 16 |
| Johnnie's NY | *Pizza* | 18 |
| Opus | *Eclectic* | 22 |
| Pentimento | *Calif./Med.* | 17 |
| NEW Royale | *Amer.* | 18 |
| Sandbag Sandwich | *Sandwiches* | 18 |

## PICO-ROBERTSON

| | |
|---|---|
| NEW Bella Roma | *Italian* | - |
| Bossa Nova | *Brazilian* | 21 |
| Factor's Deli | *Deli* | 16 |
| Fish Grill | *Seafood* | 19 |
| Magic Carpet | *Mideast.* | 22 |
| Milky Way | *Calif.* | 18 |
| Naraya Thai | *Thai* | 19 |
| Pat's | *Calif./Italian* | 22 |
| Spark Woodfire | *Amer.* | 17 |
| Tuk Tuk Thai | *Thai* | 21 |
| Yen Sushi | *Jap.* | 23 |

## SILVER LAKE

| | |
|---|---|
| Agra Cafe | *Indian* | 22 |
| Alegria/Sunset | *Mex.* | 22 |
| Aroma | *Italian* | - |
| Blair's | *Amer.* | 23 |
| Cafe Stella | *French* | 21 |
| Cha Cha Cha | *Carib.* | 20 |
| Cliff's Edge | *Calif./Italian* | 20 |
| Dusty's | *Amer./French* | 21 |
| Eat Well Cafe | *Amer.* | 15 |
| Edendale Grill | *Amer.* | 15 |
| Gingergrass | *Viet.* | 22 |
| Kitchen, The | *Amer.* | 19 |
| Madame Matisse | *Amer.* | 22 |
| Malo | *Mex.* | 17 |
| Pho Café | *Viet.* | 22 |
| Rambutan Thai | *Thai* | 22 |
| Saito's Sushi | *Jap.* | 25 |
| Tantra | *Indian* | 21 |

## THIRD STREET

(bet. La Brea & La Cienega; see map on back of gatefold)

### TOP FOOD

| | |
|---|---|
| A.O.C. | *Calif./French* | **E6** | 26 |
| Locanda Veneta | *Italian* | **E4** | 25 |

LOS ANGELES

LOCATIONS

| | |
|---|---|
| Mandarette \| *Chinese* | 18 |
| Marix Tex Mex \| *Tex-Mex* | 17 |
| Mark's \| *Calif.* | 16 |
| Mason Jar Cafe \| *Calif.* | 17 |
| Mel's Drive-In \| *Amer.* | 16 |
| Mirabelle \| *Calif./Eclectic* | 20 |
| Morton's \| *Amer./Calif.* | 23 |
| NEW Mubee \| *Jap.* | - |
| NEW Murano \| *Med.* | - |
| Newsroom Café \| *Veg.* | 19 |
| Nishimura \| *Jap.* | 28 |
| O-Bar \| *Amer.* | 20 |
| NEW One Sunset \| *Amer.* | - |
| Z Palm, The \| *Seafood/Steak* | 24 |
| Petrossian \| *French* | - |
| Pizza Rustica \| *Pizza* | 17 |
| Pomodoro \| *Italian* | 17 |
| Poquito Más \| *Mex.* | 22 |
| NEW Prana Cafe \| *Pan-Asian* | 22 |
| Real Food Daily \| *Vegan* | 21 |
| NEW Red Seven \| *Pan-Asian* | - |
| Z Republic \| *Amer.* | 20 |
| Saddle Ranch Chop \| *Steak* | 16 |
| NEW Salades/Provence \| *French* | - |
| Sandbag Sandwich \| *Sandwiches* | 18 |
| Simon LA \| *Amer.* | 21 |
| Z Sona \| *French* | 27 |
| Spanish Kitchen \| *Mex.* | 17 |
| Standard, The \| *Eclectic* | 16 |
| Sur \| *Calif./Med.* | 21 |
| Talésai \| *Thai* | 22 |
| Taste \| *Amer.* | 20 |
| 3rd Stop \| *Italian* | 20 |
| Tower Bar \| *Calif.* | 22 |
| Urth Caffé \| *Amer.* | 21 |
| Vivoli Café \| *Italian* | 25 |
| Wa \| *Jap.* | 27 |
| Wokcano Cafe \| *Chinese/Jap.* | 17 |
| WP \| *Amer.* | - |
| Yabu \| *Jap.* | 23 |
| NEW Yatai Asian Tapas \| *Pan-Asian* | 19 |
| Zeke's Smokehse. \| *BBQ* | 19 |

## LA East

### BOYLE HEIGHTS

| | |
|---|---|
| La Serenata \| *Mex./Seafood* | 23 |

### EAST LA

| | |
|---|---|
| El Tepeyac \| *Mex.* | 24 |
| Tamayo \| *Mex.* | 21 |

## LA South

### BELLFLOWER

| | |
|---|---|
| Johnny Rebs' \| *BBQ* | 22 |

### CARSON

| | |
|---|---|
| Back Home/Lahaina \| *Hawaiian* | 17 |

### CERRITOS

| | |
|---|---|
| BCD Tofu \| *Korean* | 20 |
| BJ's \| *Pub* | 17 |
| Loft, The \| *Hawaiian* | 17 |
| Mimi's Cafe \| *Diner* | 17 |
| Romano's Macaroni \| *Italian* | 17 |
| Sam Woo \| *Chinese* | 20 |
| Wood Ranch BBQ \| *BBQ* | 20 |

### HAWTHORNE

| | |
|---|---|
| El Torito \| *Mex.* | 15 |
| India's Tandoori \| *Indian* | 19 |

### LAKEWOOD

| | |
|---|---|
| Outback Steak \| *Steak* | 17 |
| Souplantation \| *Amer.* | 16 |

### LAWNDALE

| | |
|---|---|
| El Pollo Inka \| *Peruvian* | 19 |

### LOMITA

| | |
|---|---|
| Il Chianti \| *Italian* | 25 |

### LYNWOOD

| | |
|---|---|
| Guelaguetza \| *Mex.* | 21 |
| La Huasteca \| *Mex.* | 22 |

### PALOS VERDES PENINSULA/ROLLING HILLS

| | |
|---|---|
| Admiral Risty \| *Seafood* | 21 |
| Asaka \| *Jap.* | 20 |
| Bistro 767 \| *Calif.* | 22 |
| Café Pacific \| *Amer.* | 24 |
| Chez Allez \| *Eclectic/ Sandwiches* | 21 |
| La Rive Gauche \| *French* | 22 |
| Marmalade Café \| *Amer./Calif.* | 18 |
| Noah's NY Bagels \| *Sandwiches* | 18 |
| Ruby's \| *Diner* | 16 |
| NEW Saluzzi \| *Italian* | - |
| Trio Med. \| *Med.* | 17 |
| Trump's \| *American* | 23 |

## LA West

### BEL-AIR

| | |
|---|---|
| Bel-Air B&G \| *Calif.* | 19 |
| Z Hotel Bel-Air \| *Calif./French* | 26 |

| | |
|---|---|
| SHU | *Italian/Jap.* | 20 |
| Vibrato | *Amer./Steak* | 22 |

## BEVERLY HILLS

(See map on back of gatefold)

## TOP FOOD

| | |
|---|---|
| Matsuhisa | *Jap.* | **F5** | 27 |
| Spago | *Calif.* | **F2** | 27 |
| Mako | *Asian Fusion* | **F2** | 26 |
| Cut | *Steak* | **F2** | 26 |
| Mastro's Steak | *Steak* | **F2** | 25 |
| Belvedere | *Amer.* | **F1** | 25 |
| Arnie Morton's Steak | *Steak* | **E5** | 25 |
| Ruth's Chris | *Steak* | **F2** | 25 |
| Il Pastaio | *Italian* | **E2** | 25 |
| Lawry's Prime | *Steak* | **F5** | 25 |
| Gardens | *Calif./Med.* | **F3** | 25 |
| Grill on Alley | *Amer.* | **F2** | 24 |
| Piccolo Paradiso | *Italian* | **F2** | 24 |
| Crustacean | *Asian Fusion/ Viet.* | **E2** | 23 |
| Mulberry St. Pizzeria | *Pizza* | **E2** | **F2** | 23 |

## LISTING

| | |
|---|---|
| A Cow Jumped | *French* | 22 |
| Amici | *Italian* | 21 |
| ⊠ Arnie Morton's Steak | *Steak* | 25 |
| Asakuma | *Jap.* | 21 |
| Baja Fresh Mex. | *Mex.* | 18 |
| Barney Greengrass | *Deli* | 21 |
| BBC | *Med.* | 20 |
| ⊠ Belvedere | *Amer.* | 25 |
| Benihana | *Jap.* | 18 |
| blue on blue | *Amer.* | 18 |
| Blvd | *Calif.* | 21 |
| boé | *Amer.* | 14 |
| Bombay Palace | *Indian* | 21 |
| Bossa Nova | *Brazilian* | 21 |
| Boss Sushi | *Jap.* | 24 |
| Brighton Coffee | *Diner* | 16 |
| NEW Burger 90210 | *Hamburgers* | – |
| Cafe Rodeo | *Calif.* | 16 |
| Caffe Roma | *Italian* | 16 |
| Cali. Pizza Kitchen | *Pizza* | 18 |
| Camden House | *Calif./French* | 15 |
| Chakra | *Indian* | 21 |
| ⊠ Cheesecake Fact. | *Amer.* | 20 |
| Chin Chin | *Chinese* | 17 |
| Chipotle | *Mex.* | 19 |
| NEW Circa 55 | *Amer./Calif.* | 21 |
| NEW Coupa Cafe | *Eclectic* | 14 |

| | |
|---|---|
| Crazy Fish | *Jap.* | 17 |
| ⊠ Crustacean | *Asian Fusion/Viet.* | 23 |
| ⊠ Cut | *Steak* | 26 |
| Da Pasquale | *Italian* | 21 |
| NEW E. Baldi | *Italian* | 21 |
| El Torito Grill | *Mex.* | 18 |
| Enoteca Drago | *Italian* | 21 |
| Farm/Bev. Hills | *Amer.* | 19 |
| Fogo de Chão | *Brazilian* | 23 |
| NEW Forte | *Italian* | – |
| ⊠ Gardens | *Calif./Med.* | 25 |
| NEW Gonpachi | *Jap.* | – |
| Grand Lux | *Eclectic* | 19 |
| ⊠ Grill on Alley | *Amer.* | 24 |
| Gyu-Kaku | *Jap.* | 20 |
| NEW Hokusai | *French/Jap.* | – |
| Il Buco | *Italian* | 22 |
| ⊠ Il Cielo | *Italian* | 21 |
| ⊠ Il Fornaio | *Italian* | 20 |
| Il Forno Caldo | *Italian* | 20 |
| Il Pastaio | *Italian* | 25 |
| Il Tramezzino | *Italian* | 21 |
| Islands | *Amer.* | 16 |
| Jack n' Jill's | *Amer.* | 19 |
| Jacopo's | *Pizza* | 17 |
| Kate Mantilini | *Diner* | 18 |
| Koo Koo Roo | *Amer.* | 16 |
| La Dolce Vita | *Italian* | 20 |
| La Paella | *Spanish* | 22 |
| La Scala | *Italian* | 20 |
| ⊠ Lawry's Prime | *Steak* | 25 |
| Le Pain Quotidien | *Bakery/Belgian* | 21 |
| Lodge Steak | *Steak* | 20 |
| ⊠ Mako | *Asian Fusion* | 26 |
| Massimo | *Italian* | 22 |
| ⊠ Mastro's Steak | *Steak* | 25 |
| ⊠ Matsuhisa | *Jap.* | 27 |
| McCormick/Schmick | *Seafood* | 19 |
| Michel Richard | *Bakery/French* | 20 |
| Mirü8691 | *Pan-Asian* | 24 |
| Mr. Chow | *Chinese* | 23 |
| Mulberry St. Pizzeria | *Pizza* | 23 |
| Natalee | *Thai* | 19 |
| Nate 'n Al | *Deli* | 21 |
| Nic's | *Amer.* | 21 |
| Nirvana | *Indian* | 20 |
| O4U | *Mideast.* | – |
| NEW Panini Cafe | *Italian/Med.* | 16 |
| ⊠ P.F. Chang's | *Chinese* | 19 |
| Piccolo Paradiso | *Italian* | 24 |
| Pistachio Grill | *Persian* | 23 |

| | |
|---|---|
| Pizza Rustica | *Pizza* | 17 |
| ☑ Polo Lounge | *Calif./Continental* | 22 |
| Porta Via | *Calif.* | 22 |
| Porterhouse | *Steak* | 20 |
| NEW Prime Grill | *Steak* | 21 |
| Rosti | *Italian* | 17 |
| ☑ Ruth's Chris | *Steak* | 25 |
| Sandbag Sandwich | *Sandwiches* | 18 |
| Sharky's Mex. | *Mex.* | 17 |
| ☑ Spago | *Calif.* | 27 |
| Stinking Rose | *Italian* | 16 |
| Sushi Dokoro | *Jap.* | 24 |
| Sushi Ozekii | *Jap.* | - |
| Sushi Sushi | *Jap.* | 25 |
| Talésai | *Thai* | 22 |
| NEW Tanzore | *Indian* | - |
| NEW Tokyo Table | *Jap.* | 16 |
| Urasawa | *Jap.* | 29 |
| Urth Caffé | *Amer.* | 21 |
| Woo Lae Oak | *Korean* | 22 |
| Xi'an | *Chinese* | 22 |
| Zen Grill | *Pan-Asian* | 20 |

## BRENTWOOD

| | |
|---|---|
| Amici | *Italian* | 21 |
| A Votre Sante | *Veg.* | 20 |
| Baja Fresh Mex. | *Mex.* | 18 |
| Barney's Hamburgers | *Hamburgers* | 21 |
| Brentwood, The | *Amer.* | 21 |
| Cali. Wok | *Chinese* | 18 |
| ☑ Cheesecake Fact. | *Amer.* | 20 |
| Chin Chin | *Chinese* | 17 |
| City Bakery | *Bakery* | 18 |
| Clay Pit | *Indian* | 22 |
| Coral Tree | *Calif./Italian* | 19 |
| Daily Grill | *Amer.* | 18 |
| Divino | *Italian* | 23 |
| Fish Grill | *Seafood* | 19 |
| Gaucho Grill | *Argent./Steak* | 18 |
| Getty Center | *Calif.* | 22 |
| Hamlet | *Amer.* | 16 |
| Katsuya | *Jap.* | 24 |
| La Scala | *Italian* | 20 |
| Le Pain Quotidien | *Bakery/Belgian* | 21 |
| Louise's Tratt. | *Calif./Italian* | 16 |
| Maria's Italian | *Italian* | 17 |
| Noah's NY Bagels | *Sandwiches* | 18 |
| NEW On Sunset | *Calif.* | - |
| Osteria Latini | *Italian* | 25 |

| | |
|---|---|
| Palmeri | *Italian* | 24 |
| Pecorino | *Italian* | 20 |
| Peppone | *Italian* | 21 |
| Pizzicotto | *Italian* | 23 |
| Reddi Chick BBQ | *BBQ* | 23 |
| Saketini | *Asian Fusion* | 20 |
| Sandbag Sandwich | *Sandwiches* | 18 |
| San Gennaro | *Italian* | 16 |
| Sor Tino | *Italian* | 19 |
| Souplantation | *Amer.* | 16 |
| Taiko | *Jap.* | 21 |
| Takao | *Jap.* | 25 |
| Toscana | *Italian* | 24 |
| Vincenti | *Italian* | 25 |
| West | *Italian/Steak* | 18 |
| Zeidler's | *Calif.* | 17 |

## CENTURY CITY

| | |
|---|---|
| Aphrodisiac | *Continental* | 18 |
| Breadbar | *Amer./Bakery* | 19 |
| Breeze | *Calif./Seafood* | 19 |
| Clementine | *Bakery* | 24 |
| Coral Tree | *Calif./Italian* | 19 |
| NEW Craft | *Amer.* | - |
| French 75 | *French* | 21 |
| Gulfstream | *Amer./Seafood* | 21 |
| Harper's | *Continental/Italian* | 16 |
| ☑ Houston's | *Amer.* | 21 |
| Johnnie's NY | *Pizza* | 18 |
| ☑ La Cachette | *French* | 27 |
| NEW Pink Taco | *Mex.* | - |
| Stand, The | *Hot Dogs* | 18 |
| NEW Ummba Grill | *Brazilian* | 16 |
| Wokcano Cafe | *Chinese/Jap.* | 17 |

## CULVER CITY

| | |
|---|---|
| Bamboo | *Carib.* | 19 |
| Beacon | *Pan-Asian* | 22 |
| NEW BottleRock | *Euro.* | 16 |
| Cafe Surfas | *Amer.* | 20 |
| Cooks Dbl. Dutch | *Amer.* | 22 |
| Ford's Filling Stat. | *Gastropub* | 19 |
| NEW Fraiche | *Med.* | - |
| ☑ In-N-Out Burger | *Hamburgers* | 24 |
| Jody Maroni's | *Hot Dogs* | 19 |
| Johnnie's Pastrami | *Deli* | 20 |
| Johnny Rockets | *Hamburgers* | 15 |
| JR's BBQ | *BBQ* | 20 |
| K-Zo | *Jap.* | - |
| La Dijonaise | *French* | 18 |
| Leaf Cuisine | *Vegan* | - |

| | |
|---|---|
| NEW Meltdown Etc. | *Amer.* | ⌐ |
| Mi Ranchito | *Mex.* | 16 |
| New Flavors | *Chinese/Hawaiian* | 19 |
| Pacifico's | *Mex./Seafood* | 16 |
| Petrelli's Steak | *Italian/Steak* | 17 |
| Roll 'n Rye | *Deli* | 18 |
| Tender Greens | *Amer.* | 23 |
| Thai Dishes | *Thai* | 18 |
| Ugo | *Italian* | ⌐ |
| Wilson | *Med.* | 23 |

## MALIBU

| | |
|---|---|
| Allegria | *Italian* | 21 |
| BBC | *Med.* | 20 |
| Beau Rivage | *Med.* | 20 |
| Chart House | *Seafood/Steak* | 19 |
| Cholada | *Thai* | 26 |
| D'Amore's Pizza | *Pizza* | 21 |
| Duke's | *Pac. Rim* | 17 |
| ☑ Geoffrey's | *Calif.* | 22 |
| Guido's | *Italian* | 20 |
| Johnnie's NY | *Pizza* | 18 |
| Malibu Seafood | *Seafood* | 21 |
| Marmalade Café | *Amer./Calif.* | 18 |
| Moonshadows | *Amer.* | 17 |
| Neptune's Net | *Seafood* | 17 |
| ☑ Nobu Malibu | *Jap.* | 28 |
| Paradise Cove | *Amer./Seafood* | 16 |
| Reel Inn | *Seafood* | 20 |
| Taverna Tony | *Greek* | 21 |
| Thai Dishes | *Thai* | 18 |
| Tra Di Noi | *Italian* | 22 |

## MARINA DEL REY

(See map on page 273)

### TOP FOOD

| | |
|---|---|
| Tlapazola Grill | *Mex.* | **J3** | 24 |
| Cafe Del Rey | *Calif./French* | **J3** | 23 |
| Jer-ne | *Calif.* | **J3** | 22 |
| Tsuji No Hana | *Jap.* | **K3** | 22 |
| Asakuma | *Jap.* | **J3** | 21 |

### LISTING

| | |
|---|---|
| Akbar | *Indian* | 20 |
| Alejo's | *Italian* | 21 |
| Antica Pizzeria | *Pizza* | 20 |
| Asakuma | *Jap.* | 21 |
| Aunt Kizzy's | *Southern* | 20 |
| Baja Fresh Mex. | *Mex.* | 18 |
| Bite | *Pan-Asian* | 16 |
| Cafe Del Rey | *Calif./French* | 23 |
| C & O | *Italian* | 19 |
| Chart House | *Seafood/Steak* | 19 |

| | |
|---|---|
| ☑ Cheesecake Fact. | *Amer.* | 20 |
| Chin Chin | *Chinese* | 17 |
| Chipotle | *Mex.* | 19 |
| El Torito | *Mex.* | 15 |
| Gaby's Med. | *Lebanese/Med.* | ⌐ |
| Islands | *Amer.* | 16 |
| Jer-ne | *Calif.* | 22 |
| Johnnie's NY | *Pizza* | 18 |
| Killer Shrimp | *Seafood* | 21 |
| Koo Koo Roo | *Amer.* | 16 |
| Le Marmiton | *French* | 18 |
| Noah's NY Bagels | *Sandwiches* | 18 |
| Sapori | *Italian* | 24 |
| Souplantation | *Amer.* | 16 |
| Spin Rotisserie | *Amer.* | 17 |
| Tlapazola Grill | *Mex.* | 24 |
| Tony P's Dock | *Amer.* | 17 |
| Tsuji No Hana | *Jap.* | 22 |
| 26 Beach | *Calif.* | 20 |
| Uncle Darrow's | *Cajun/Creole* | 19 |
| Wharo | *Korean* | 19 |

## MAR VISTA

| | |
|---|---|
| Paco's Tacos | *Mex.* | 18 |

## PACIFIC PALISADES

| | |
|---|---|
| A La Tarte | *Bakery/French* | 18 |
| Gladstone's | *Seafood* | 15 |
| Jacopo's | *Pizza* | 17 |
| Kay 'n Dave's | *Mex.* | 18 |
| Lucia's | *Italian* | 18 |
| Modo Mio | *Italian* | 22 |
| Pearl Dragon | *Pan-Asian* | 19 |
| Vittorio's | *Italian* | 18 |

## PALMS

| | |
|---|---|
| Café Brasil | *Brazilian* | 19 |
| Cucina Paradiso | *Italian* | 21 |
| Guelaguetza | *Mex.* | 21 |
| Hu's Szechwan | *Chinese* | 20 |
| Indo Cafe | *Indonesian* | 19 |
| Natalee | *Thai* | 19 |
| Versailles | *Cuban* | 21 |

## PLAYA DEL REY

| | |
|---|---|
| Berri's Pizza | *Pizza* | 17 |
| Caffe Pinguini | *Italian* | 22 |
| NEW Minotaure | *Spanish* | 19 |
| Outlaws B&G | *Amer.* | 15 |
| Shack, The | *Amer.* | 18 |

## RANCHO PARK

| | |
|---|---|
| John O'Groats | *Amer.* | 20 |
| Kay 'n Dave's | *Mex.* | 18 |

## TOP FOOD

| | |
|---|---|
| Mélisse | *Amer./French* | **D2** | 28 |
| Josie | *Amer.* | **F4** | 27 |
| Capo | *Italian* | **E1** | 26 |
| Chinois/Main | *Asian/French* | **G1** | 26 |
| Valentino | *Italian* | **F5** | 26 |
| Via Veneto | *Italian* | **G1** | 26 |
| JiRaffe | *Calif.* | **D2** | 26 |
| Sam's/Beach | *Calif./Med.* | **B1** | 26 |
| Musha | *Jap.* | **D2** | 25 |
| Hump, The | *Jap.* | **G5** | 25 |
| Drago | *Italian* | **D5** | 24 |
| La Botte | *Italian* | **D2** | 24 |
| Michael's | *Calif.* | **D1** | 24 |
| Father's Office | *Hamburgers* | **C2** | 24 |
| Giorgio Baldi | *Italian* | **B1** | 24 |

## LISTING

| | |
|---|---|
| Abbot's Pizza | *Pizza* | 23 |
| **NEW** Abode | *Amer.* | 23 |
| Akbar | *Indian* | 20 |
| Akwa | *Calif.* | 19 |
| Babalu | *Calif.* | 20 |
| Back on Beach | *Amer.* | 14 |
| Benihana | *Jap.* | 18 |
| Bistro 31 | *Calif.* | 23 |
| Boa | *Steak* | 23 |
| Border Grill | *Mex.* | 22 |
| Brass.-Cap. | *French* | 19 |
| Bravo | *Italian/Pizza* | 18 |
| Broadway Deli | *Deli* | 14 |
| Buca di Beppo | *Italian* | 15 |
| Buffalo Club | *Amer.* | 19 |
| Cafe Montana | *Calif.* | 20 |
| Caffé Delfini | *Italian* | 23 |
| **NEW** Caffe Luxxe | *Coffee* | – |
| Cali. Chicken | *Amer.* | 21 |
| Cali. Pizza Kitchen | *Pizza* | 18 |
| **Z** Capo | *Italian* | 26 |
| **NEW** Catch | *Seafood* | – |
| Cézanne | *Calif./French* | 21 |
| Cha Cha Chick. | *Carib.* | 20 |
| Chez Jay | *Steak* | 16 |
| Chez Mimi | *French* | 21 |
| **Z** Chinois/Main | *Asian/French* | 26 |
| **NEW** Coast | *Calif.* | – |
| Cora's Coffee | *Diner* | 21 |
| Counter, The | *Hamburgers* | 21 |
| Crescendo/Fred Segal | *Italian* | 17 |
| Drago | *Italian* | 24 |

| | |
|---|---|
| El Cholo | *Mex.* | 18 |
| Enterprise Fish | *Seafood* | 18 |
| Falafel King | *Mideast.* | 18 |
| **Z** Father's Office | *Hamburgers* | 24 |
| Fritto Misto | *Italian* | 21 |
| Fromin's Deli | *Deli* | 15 |
| Galley, The | *Seafood/Steak* | 18 |
| Gate of India | *Indian* | 20 |
| Gaucho Grill | *Argent./Steak* | 18 |
| Giorgio Baldi | *Italian* | 24 |
| **Z** Houston's | *Amer.* | 21 |
| Hump, The | *Jap.* | 25 |
| i Cugini | *Italian/Seafood* | 21 |
| **Z** Il Fornaio | *Italian* | 20 |
| Il Forno | *Italian* | 20 |
| Ivy/Shore | *Calif.* | 21 |
| Jack n' Jill's | *Amer.* | 19 |
| Jinky's | *SW* | 20 |
| **Z** JiRaffe | *Calif.* | 26 |
| **Z** Josie | *Amer.* | 27 |
| Juliano's Raw | *Vegan* | 21 |
| Kay 'n Dave's | *Mex.* | 18 |
| La Botte | *Italian* | 24 |
| L.A. Farm | *Calif.* | 20 |
| La Serenata | *Mex./Seafood* | 23 |
| La Vecchia | *Italian* | 21 |
| Le Marmiton | *French* | 18 |
| Le Pain Quotidien | *Bakery/Belgian* | 21 |
| Le Petit Cafe | *French* | 21 |
| Library Alehse. | *Eclectic* | 19 |
| **Z** Lobster, The | *Seafood* | 23 |
| Locanda/Lago | *Italian* | 20 |
| Louise's Tratt. | *Calif./Italian* | 16 |
| Mäni's | *Bakery/Vegan* | 18 |
| Marix Tex Mex | *Tex-Mex* | 17 |
| Marmalade Café | *Amer./Calif.* | 18 |
| **Z** Mélisse | *Amer./French* | 28 |
| Michael's | *Calif.* | 24 |
| Monsoon Cafe | *Pan-Asian* | 17 |
| Musha | *Jap.* | 25 |
| Nawab of India | *Indian* | 22 |
| Ocean & Vine | *Amer.* | 22 |
| Ocean Ave. | *Seafood* | 23 |
| Omelette Parlor | *Amer.* | 18 |
| **Z** One Pico | *Calif./Med.* | 23 |
| Pacific Dining Car | *Steak* | 22 |
| Patrick's | *Diner* | 16 |
| **NEW** Penthouse | *Amer.* | 20 |
| **Z** P.F. Chang's | *Chinese* | 19 |
| **NEW** Punch Grill | *Amer.* | 18 |

**LOS ANGELES**

**LOCATIONS**

| | |
|---|---|
| Hurry Curry/Tokyo \| *Jap.* | 17 |
| Il Grano \| *Italian* | 25 |
| Il Moro \| *Italian* | 22 |
| India's Tandoori \| *Indian* | 19 |
| ☑ In-N-Out Burger \| *Hamburgers* | 24 |
| Islands \| *Amer.* | 16 |
| Jack Sprat's \| *Calif.* | 19 |
| Javan \| *Persian* | 21 |
| Junior's \| *Deli* | 16 |
| Koo Koo Roo \| *Amer.* | 16 |
| La Bottega Marino \| *Italian* | 20 |
| La Serenata \| *Mex./Seafood* | 23 |
| Lemon Moon \| *Calif./Med.* | 20 |
| Le Saigon \| *Viet.* | 21 |
| Literati \| *Calif./Eclectic* | 20 |
| Louise's Tratt. \| *Calif./Italian* | 16 |
| Maria's Italian \| *Italian* | 17 |
| Matteo's \| *Italian* | 19 |
| Monte Alban \| *Mex.* | 22 |
| ☑ Mori Sushi \| *Jap.* | 26 |
| Mr. Cecil's Ribs \| *BBQ* | 18 |
| Nizam \| *Indian* | 21 |
| Nook Bistro \| *Amer./Eclectic* | 24 |
| Orris \| *French/Jap.* | 26 |
| Pastina \| *Italian* | 21 |
| Poquito Más \| *Mex.* | 22 |
| NEW Qusqo \| *Peruvian* | - |
| NEW Simpang Asia \| *Indonesian* | - |
| Sisley Italian \| *Italian* | 18 |
| Sushi Mac \| *Jap.* | 17 |
| Sushi Masu \| *Jap.* | 26 |
| Sushi Sasabune \| *Jap.* | 26 |
| Tlapazola Grill \| *Mex.* | 24 |
| Torafuku \| *Jap.* | 22 |
| 2117 \| *Asian/Euro.* | 24 |
| Upstairs 2 \| *Med.* | 23 |
| U-Zen \| *Jap.* | 22 |
| V.I.P. Harbor \| *Chinese/Seafood* | 18 |
| Yabu \| *Jap.* | 23 |
| Yen Sushi \| *Jap.* | 23 |
| Zankou Chicken \| *Med.* | 22 |
| Zip Fusion \| *Jap.* | 18 |
| NEW Zu Robata \| *Jap.* | - |

## WESTWOOD

| | |
|---|---|
| Asuka \| *Jap.* | 20 |
| Baja Fresh Mex. \| *Mex.* | 18 |
| NEW Baran \| *Persian* | 20 |
| BJ's \| *Pub* | 17 |
| Bombay Bite \| *Indian* | 21 |

| | |
|---|---|
| Cali. Pizza Kitchen \| *Pizza* | 18 |
| D'Amore's Pizza \| *Pizza* | 21 |
| Danube Bulgarian \| *Bulgarian* | 15 |
| Delphi Greek \| *Greek* | 17 |
| Falafel King \| *Mideast.* | 18 |
| Gardens/Glendon \| *Calif.* | 19 |
| ☑ In-N-Out Burger \| *Hamburgers* | 24 |
| Koutoubia \| *Moroccan* | 20 |
| La Bruschetta \| *Italian* | 21 |
| Lamonica's NY Pizza \| *Pizza* | 22 |
| Le Pain Quotidien \| *Bakery/Belgian* | 21 |
| Mio Babbo's \| *Italian* | 21 |
| Napa Valley \| *Calif.* | 20 |
| Native Foods \| *Calif./Eclectic* | 22 |
| Nine Thirty \| *Amer.* | 23 |
| Noah's NY Bagels \| *Sandwiches* | 18 |
| Palomino \| *Amer./Euro.* | 18 |
| Sandbag Sandwich \| *Sandwiches* | 18 |
| Shaherzad \| *Persian* | 22 |
| Soleil Westwood \| *Canadian/French* | 20 |
| South Street \| *Cheese Stks.* | 18 |
| Sunnin \| *Lebanese* | 24 |
| Tanino \| *Italian* | 22 |
| Tengu \| *Jap.* | 22 |

# South Bay

## BALDWIN HILLS

| | |
|---|---|
| Creole Chef \| *Creole* | - |

## DOWNEY

| | |
|---|---|
| Mimi's Cafe \| *Diner* | 17 |

## EL SEGUNDO

| | |
|---|---|
| Cozymel's \| *Mex.* | 14 |
| Daily Grill \| *Amer.* | 18 |
| Farm Stand \| *Eclectic* | 22 |
| Fleming Prime \| *Steak* | 25 |
| Marmalade Café \| *Amer./Calif.* | 18 |
| McCormick/Schmick \| *Seafood* | 19 |
| ☑ P.F. Chang's \| *Chinese* | 19 |
| Romano's Macaroni \| *Italian* | 17 |
| Salt Creek \| *Steak* | 18 |
| Second City Bistro \| *Amer.* | 22 |
| Taiko \| *Jap.* | 21 |
| Thai Dishes \| *Thai* | 18 |

## GARDENA

| | |
|---|---|
| El Pollo Inka \| *Peruvian* | 19 |
| Sea Empress \| *Chinese* | 19 |

## HERMOSA BEACH

| | |
|---|---|
| Akbar | *Indian* | 20 |
| Chef Melba's | *Calif.* | 23 |
| El Pollo Inka | *Peruvian* | 19 |
| Fritto Misto | *Italian* | 21 |
| Fusion Sushi | *Jap.* | 16 |
| Il Boccaccio | *Italian* | 22 |
| Jackson's Vill. | *Amer.* | 23 |
| La Sosta | *Italian* | 27 |
| Martha 22nd St. | *Amer.* | 22 |
| Mediterraneo | *Med.* | 20 |
| ☑ Ragin' Cajun | *Cajun* | 21 |
| Rocky Cola | *Diner* | – |
| Sushi Duke | *Jap.* | 25 |

## INGLEWOOD

| | |
|---|---|
| ☑ Phillips BBQ | *BBQ* | 24 |
| Porky's BBQ | *BBQ* | – |
| Thai Dishes | *Thai* | 18 |

## LAX

| | |
|---|---|
| Daily Grill | *Amer.* | 18 |
| El Cholo | *Mex.* | 18 |
| Jody Maroni's | *Hot Dogs* | 19 |
| Ruby's | *Diner* | 16 |
| Thai Dishes | *Thai* | 18 |

## LONG BEACH

| | |
|---|---|
| Alegria | *Nuevo Latino* | 21 |
| Auld Dubliner | *Pub* | 21 |
| Baja Fresh Mex. | *Mex.* | 18 |
| Belmont Brew. | *Amer.* | 18 |
| Benley Viet. | *Viet.* | 26 |
| BJ's | *Pub* | 17 |
| Bono's | *Calif.* | 21 |
| Christy's | *Italian* | 24 |
| Claim Jumper | *Amer.* | 19 |
| El Torito | *Mex.* | 15 |
| 555 East | *Steak* | 25 |
| ☑ Frenchy's Bistro | *French* | 27 |
| Fusion Sushi | *Jap.* | 16 |
| George's Greek | *Greek* | 20 |
| Green Field Churr. | *Brazilian* | 23 |
| Joe's Crab | *Seafood* | 13 |
| Johnny Rebs' | *BBQ* | 22 |
| Johnny Rockets | *Hamburgers* | 15 |
| King's Fish Hse. | *Seafood* | 21 |
| La Crêperie | *French* | 23 |
| Lasher's | *Amer.* | 24 |
| L'Opera | *Italian* | 24 |
| Lucille's BBQ | *BBQ* | 22 |
| ☑ Madison, The | *Seafood/Steak* | 21 |
| McKenna's | *Seafood/Steak* | 20 |
| Mimi's Cafe | *Diner* | 17 |
| Parker's Lighthse. | *Seafood* | 18 |
| Pike Rest. | *Amer.* | – |
| ☑ Roscoe's | *Soul Food* | 22 |
| Sandbag Sandwich | *Sandwiches* | 18 |
| Sharky's Mex. | *Mex.* | 17 |
| ☑ Sir Winston's | *Continental* | 23 |
| Sky Room | *Amer.* | 21 |
| Sunnin | *Lebanese* | 24 |
| NEW Tracht's | *Amer.* | – |
| Yard House | *Amer.* | 19 |
| Yen Sushi | *Jap.* | 23 |

## MANHATTAN BEACH

| | |
|---|---|
| Avenue | *Amer.* | 23 |
| Back Home/Lahaina | *Hawaiian* | 17 |
| Bora Bora | *Calif./Polynesian* | 23 |
| Café Pierre | *French* | 22 |
| Cali. Pizza Kitchen | *Pizza* | 18 |
| China Grill | *Calif./Chinese* | 20 |
| NEW Coco Noche | *Dessert/Eclectic* | 22 |
| NEW Corkscrew Cafe | *Eclectic* | – |
| Ebizo's Skewer | *Jap.* | 16 |
| Fonz's | *Seafood/Steak* | 22 |
| Fusion Sushi | *Jap.* | 16 |
| ☑ Houston's | *Amer.* | 21 |
| ☑ Il Fornaio | *Italian* | 20 |
| Islands | *Amer.* | 16 |
| NEW Joey's Smokin' BBQ | *BBQ* | – |
| Johnny Rockets | *Hamburgers* | 15 |
| Koo Koo Roo | *Amer.* | 16 |
| LA Food Show | *Amer.* | 19 |
| Le Pain Quotidien | *Bakery/Belgian* | 21 |
| Lido/Manhattan | *Italian/Med.* | 21 |
| Mama D's | *Italian* | 22 |
| Noah's NY Bagels | *Sandwiches* | 18 |
| ☑ Petros | *Greek* | 23 |
| Pomodoro | *Italian* | 17 |
| Reed's | *Calif./French* | 21 |
| Rock 'N Fish | *Seafood/Steak* | 21 |
| Talia's | *Italian* | 25 |
| Thai Dishes | *Thai* | 18 |
| Towne | *Calif.* | 19 |
| Uncle Bill's Pancake | *Diner* | 22 |
| Versailles | *Cuban* | 21 |

## REDONDO BEACH

| | |
|---|---|
| Addi's Tandoor | *Indian* | 23 |
| NEW Baleen | *Amer.* | 22 |

| | |
|---|---|
| Bluewater Grill | *Amer./Seafood* | 20 |
| Buca di Beppo | *Italian* | 15 |
| Buona Sera | *Italian* | 22 |
| Chaba | *Thai* | 20 |
| Chart House | *Seafood/Steak* | 19 |
| Ⓩ Cheesecake Fact. | *Amer.* | 20 |
| Chez Melange | *Eclectic* | 25 |
| NEW Coccole Lab. | *Italian* | 21 |
| Coyote Cantina | *SW* | 20 |
| El Torito | *Mex.* | 15 |
| Gina Lee's Bistro | *Asian/Calif.* | 26 |
| Joe's Crab | *Seafood* | 13 |
| Kincaid's | *Seafood/Steak* | 21 |
| Momoyama | *Jap.* | 21 |
| Ⓩ Original Pancake | *Diner* | 23 |
| Ruby's | *Diner* | 16 |
| W's China | *Chinese* | 21 |
| Zazou | *Med.* | 24 |

### SAN PEDRO

| | |
|---|---|
| Papadakis Tav. | *Greek* | 22 |
| 22nd St. Landing | *Seafood* | 18 |
| Whale & Ale | *Pub* | 16 |

### TORRANCE

| | |
|---|---|
| Aioli | *Med./Spanish* | 17 |
| BCD Tofu | *Korean* | 20 |
| Chipotle | *Mex.* | 19 |
| Christine | *Med./Pac. Rim* | 25 |
| Claim Jumper | *Amer.* | 19 |
| Depot | *Eclectic* | 23 |
| El Pollo Inka | *Peruvian* | 19 |
| El Torito Grill | *Mex.* | 18 |
| Fusion Sushi | *Jap.* | 16 |
| Gyu-Kaku | *Jap.* | 20 |
| Islands | *Amer.* | 16 |
| Jody Maroni's | *Hot Dogs* | 19 |
| Lazy Dog | *Eclectic* | 19 |
| Local Place | *Amer./Hawaiian* | 17 |
| Loft, The | *Hawaiian* | 17 |
| Lucille's BBQ | *BBQ* | 22 |
| Mimi's Cafe | *Diner* | 17 |
| Misto Caffé | *Calif.* | 21 |
| Musha | *Jap.* | 25 |
| O-Nami | *Jap.* | 16 |
| Outback Steak | *Steak* | 17 |
| Pei Wei Diner | *Pan-Asian* | 16 |
| Poquito Más | *Mex.* | 22 |
| NEW RA Sushi | *Jap.* | 18 |
| Romano's Macaroni | *Italian* | 17 |
| Yuzu | *Jap.* | 23 |

### WESTCHESTER

| | |
|---|---|
| Alejo's | *Italian* | 21 |
| Buggy Whip | *Seafood/Steak* | 19 |
| Ⓩ In-N-Out Burger |  | 24 |
| *Hamburgers* | |
| Kanpai | *Jap.* | 22 |
| Paco's Tacos | *Mex.* | 18 |

## Inland Empire

### MORENO VALLEY

| | |
|---|---|
| BJ's | *Pub* | 17 |

### ONTARIO

| | |
|---|---|
| Benihana | *Jap.* | 18 |
| Panda Inn | *Chinese* | 20 |
| Rainforest Cafe | *Amer.* | 13 |

## Pasadena & Environs

### ARCADIA

| | |
|---|---|
| BJ's | *Pub* | 17 |
| Carmine's Italian | *Italian* | 18 |
| Derby | *Steak* | 24 |
| Din Tai Fung | *Chinese* | 26 |
| Doña Rosa | *Bakery/Mex.* | 16 |
| Hop Li | *Chinese* | 18 |
| Johnny Rockets | *Hamburgers* | 15 |
| Outback Steak | *Steak* | 17 |
| Souplantation | *Amer.* | 16 |
| Wood Ranch BBQ | *BBQ* | 20 |

### EAGLE ROCK

| | |
|---|---|
| Alejandro's | *Filipino* | - |
| Auntie Em's | *Amer.* | - |
| Blue Hen | *Viet.* | 16 |
| Café Beaujolais | *French* | - |
| Camilo's | *Calif.* | 20 |
| Casa Bianca | *Pizza* | 23 |
| Fatty's & Co. | *Veg.* | 20 |
| NEW Larkin's | *Southern* | - |
| Mia Sushi | *Jap.* | 20 |
| NEW Oinkster, The | *BBQ* | 21 |

### LA CAÑADA FLINTRIDGE

| | |
|---|---|
| Dish | *Amer.* | 18 |
| Taylor's Steak | *Steak* | 21 |

### MONROVIA

| | |
|---|---|
| Amori | *Calif./French* | 22 |
| Café Mundial | *Calif./Med.* | 20 |
| Claim Jumper | *Amer.* | 19 |
| Devon | *Calif./French* | 25 |
| La Parisienne | *French* | 23 |

| | | | |
|---|---|---|---|
| Mimi's Cafe | *Diner* | | 17 |
| Romano's Macaroni | *Italian* | | 17 |

## MONTROSE

| | | | |
|---|---|---|---|
| New Moon | *Chinese* | | 22 |
| Rocky Cola | *Diner* | | – |
| Zeke's Smokehse. | *BBQ* | | 19 |

## PASADENA

(See map on page 274)

### TOP FOOD

| | | | |
|---|---|---|---|
| Derek's | *Calif./French* | **H3** | 27 |
| Ritz Huntington | *Calif.* | **I5** | 26 |
| Yujean Kang's | *Chinese* | **D1** | 26 |
| Bistro 45 | *Calif.* | **D5** | 26 |
| Maison Akira | *French/Jap.* | **D4** | 25 |
| Parkway Grill | *Calif.* | **F2** | 25 |
| Ruth's Chris | *Steak* | **D3** | 25 |
| Arroyo Chop Hse. | *Steak* | **F2** | 25 |
| Tre Venezie | *Italian* | **D2** | 24 |
| Saladang | *Thai* | **E1** | **E2** | 24 |
| Raymond, The | *Calif.* | **H2** | 24 |
| Madeleine's | *Calif.* | **D5** | 23 |
| Yang Chow | *Chinese* | **D5** | 23 |
| Café Bizou | *Calif./French* | **D2** | 23 |
| All India | *Indian* | **D2** | 23 |

### LISTING

| | | | |
|---|---|---|---|
| Akbar | *Indian* | | 20 |
| All India | *Indian* | | 23 |
| Arroyo Chop Hse. | *Steak* | | 25 |
| Baja Fresh Mex. | *Mex.* | | 18 |
| Bar Celona | *Spanish* | | 16 |
| Beckham Grill | *Amer.* | | 18 |
| Big Mama's | *BBQ/Soul Food* | | 20 |
| ⧉ Bistro 45 | *Calif.* | | 26 |
| Boiling Pot | *Jap.* | | 16 |
| NEW Briganti | *Italian* | | 22 |
| Buca di Beppo | *Italian* | | 15 |
| Burger Continental | *Mideast.* | | 16 |
| ⧉ Café Bizou | *Calif./French* | | 23 |
| Café Santorini | *Med.* | | 20 |
| Cali. Pizza Kitchen | *Pizza* | | 18 |
| Celestino | *Italian* | | 23 |
| NEW Central Park | *Amer./Calif.* | | 18 |
| ⧉ Cheesecake Fact. | *Amer.* | | 20 |
| Chipotle | *Mex.* | | 19 |
| Club 41 | *Steak* | | 19 |
| CrêpeVine | *French* | | 21 |
| Crocodile Cafe | *Calif.* | | 16 |
| ⧉ Derek's | *Calif./French* | | 27 |
| Doña Rosa | *Bakery/Mex.* | | 16 |
| El Cholo | *Mex.* | | 18 |

| | | | |
|---|---|---|---|
| El Torito | *Mex.* | | 15 |
| Five Sixty-One | *Calif./French* | | 19 |
| Fu-Shing | *Chinese* | | 21 |
| Gale's | *Italian* | | 21 |
| Gaucho Grill | *Argent./Steak* | | 18 |
| Gordon Biersch | *Pub* | | 17 |
| Gyu-Kaku | *Jap.* | | 20 |
| Hamlet | *Amer.* | | 16 |
| Holly Street | *Calif.* | | 21 |
| ⧉ Houston's | *Amer.* | | 21 |
| Hurry Curry/Tokyo | *Jap.* | | 17 |
| ⧉ Il Fornaio | *Italian* | | 20 |
| Islands | *Amer.* | | 16 |
| Japon Bistro | *Jap.* | | 23 |
| JJ Steak | *Steak* | | 20 |
| Koo Koo Roo | *Amer.* | | 16 |
| La Maschera | *Italian* | | 22 |
| Louise's Tratt. | *Calif./Italian* | | 16 |
| Madeleine's | *Calif.* | | 23 |
| Madre's | *Puerto Rican* | | 14 |
| NEW Magnolia Lounge | *Contemp. LA* | | 16 |
| Maison Akira | *French/Jap.* | | 25 |
| Maria's Italian | *Italian* | | 17 |
| Marston's | *Amer.* | | 23 |
| McCormick/Schmick | *Seafood* | | 19 |
| Melting Pot | *Fondue* | | 19 |
| Mi Piace | *Calif./Italian* | | 19 |
| NEW Neomeze | *Eclectic* | | – |
| Noah's NY Bagels | *Sandwiches* | | 18 |
| Panda Inn | *Chinese* | | 20 |
| ⧉ Parkway Grill | *Calif.* | | 25 |
| Pei Wei Diner | *Pan-Asian* | | 16 |
| ⧉ P.F. Chang's | *Chinese* | | 19 |
| Pie 'N Burger | *Diner* | | 20 |
| Porto Alegre | *Brazilian/Steak* | | – |
| Radhika's | *Indian* | | 18 |
| Raymond, The | *Calif.* | | 24 |
| NEW redwhite+bluezz | *Amer.* | | 21 |
| ⧉ Ritz Huntington | *Calif.* | | 26 |
| Robin's Woodfire BBQ | *BBQ* | | 17 |
| ⧉ Roscoe's | *Soul Food* | | 22 |
| Russell's Burgers | *Diner* | | 17 |
| ⧉ Ruth's Chris | *Steak* | | 25 |
| Saladang | *Thai* | | 24 |
| Sharky's Mex. | *Mex.* | | 17 |
| Smitty's Grill | *Amer.* | | 21 |
| Souplantation | *Amer.* | | 16 |
| Sushi Roku | *Jap.* | | 22 |
| Thai Dishes | *Thai* | | 18 |
| Thaitalian | *Italian/Thai* | | 17 |

| | | |
|---|---|---|
| Tibet Nepal | *Nepalese/Tibetan* | 19 |
| Tre Venezie | *Italian* | 24 |
| Twin Palms | *Amer.* | 17 |
| NEW Vault, The | *Amer.* | 15 |
| NEW Vertical Wine | *Eclectic/Med.* | 19 |
| Villa Sorriso | *Italian* | 18 |
| Wokcano Cafe | *Chinese/Jap.* | 17 |
| Yang Chow | *Chinese* | 23 |
| Yard House | *Amer.* | 19 |
| Z Yujean Kang's | *Chinese* | 26 |
| Zankou Chicken | *Med.* | 22 |

## SAN MARINO

| | | |
|---|---|---|
| Julienne | *French* | 25 |
| Tongdang Thai | *Thai* | 18 |

## SOUTH PASADENA

| | | |
|---|---|---|
| Bistro de la Gare | *French* | 20 |
| Z Bistro K | *Eclectic* | 26 |
| NEW Briganti | *Italian* | 22 |
| Carmine's Italian | *Italian* | 18 |
| Firefly Bistro | *Amer.* | 19 |
| NEW Mike & Anne's | *Amer.* | 20 |
| NEW 750 ml | *French* | - |
| Z Shiro | *French/Jap.* | 27 |

# San Fernando Valley & Burbank

## BURBANK

| | | |
|---|---|---|
| Z Arnie Morton's Steak | *Steak* | 25 |
| Baja Fresh Mex. | *Mex.* | 18 |
| Bistro Provence | *French* | 22 |
| BJ's | *Pub* | 17 |
| Cali. Pizza Kitchen | *Pizza* | 18 |
| Castaway | *Calif.* | 17 |
| Z Chadaka | *Thai* | 24 |
| Chili John's | *Amer.* | 23 |
| Chipotle | *Mex.* | 19 |
| Daily Grill | *Amer.* | 18 |
| El Torito | *Mex.* | 15 |
| French 75 | *French* | 21 |
| Gordon Biersch | *Pub* | 17 |
| India's Tandoori | *Indian* | 19 |
| Islands | *Amer.* | 16 |
| Johnny Rockets | *Hamburgers* | 15 |
| Lasher's | *Amer.* | 24 |
| Market City | *Calif./Italian* | 18 |
| McCormick/Schmick | *Seafood* | 19 |
| Mo's | *Amer.* | 17 |
| Outback Steak | *Steak* | 17 |

| | | |
|---|---|---|
| Picanha Churr. | *Brazilian* | 19 |
| Pomodoro | *Italian* | 17 |
| Poquito Más | *Mex.* | 22 |
| Porto's Bakery | *Bakery* | - |
| Ribs USA | *BBQ* | 20 |
| Sharky's Mex. | *Mex.* | 17 |
| Smoke House | *Steak* | 19 |
| South Street | *Cheese Stks.* | 18 |
| Taste Chicago | *Italian* | 19 |
| Tony's Bella Vista | *Italian* | 22 |
| Wokcano Cafe | *Chinese/Jap.* | 17 |
| Zankou Chicken | *Med.* | 22 |

## CALABASAS

| | | |
|---|---|---|
| Banzai Sushi | *Jap.* | 22 |
| Fins | *Continental/Seafood* | 22 |
| King's Fish Hse. | *Seafood* | 21 |
| Marmalade Café | *Amer./Calif.* | 18 |
| Mi Piace | *Calif./Italian* | 19 |
| Riviera Rest. | *Italian* | 24 |
| Z Saddle Peak | *Amer.* | 26 |
| Sagebrush Cantina | *SW* | 14 |
| Sharky's Mex. | *Mex.* | 17 |
| Spumoni | *Italian* | 23 |

## CANOGA PARK

| | | |
|---|---|---|
| D'Amore's Pizza | *Pizza* | 21 |
| Gyu-Kaku | *Jap.* | 20 |
| Yang Chow | *Chinese* | 23 |

## CHATSWORTH

| | | |
|---|---|---|
| Les Sisters | *Southern* | 25 |
| Mimi's Cafe | *Diner* | 17 |
| Omino Sushi | *Jap.* | 23 |
| NEW Raaga | *Indian* | - |

## ENCINO

| | | |
|---|---|---|
| NEW Ate-1-8 | *Eclectic* | 15 |
| Benihana | *Jap.* | 18 |
| Buca di Beppo | *Italian* | 15 |
| Cali. Chicken | *Amer.* | 21 |
| Cali. Wok | *Chinese* | 18 |
| Chili My Soul | *SW/Tex-Mex* | 22 |
| Coral Tree | *Calif./Italian* | 19 |
| D'Amore's Pizza | *Pizza* | 21 |
| Delmonico's Lobster | *Seafood* | 21 |
| Fromin's Deli | *Deli* | 15 |
| Hirosuke | *Jap.* | 24 |
| Islands | *Amer.* | 16 |
| Johnny Rockets | *Hamburgers* | 15 |
| Z Katsu-ya | *Jap.* | 27 |
| L'Artiste Patisserie | *Bakery* | 20 |
| Maria's Italian | *Italian* | 17 |

Mulberry St. Pizzeria | *Pizza* — 23

Quincy's BBQ | *BBQ* — 15

Rosti | *Italian* — 17

Sassi Med. | *Med.* — 19

Sona's | *Calif./Eclectic* — 17

Stand, The | *Hot Dogs* — 18

Stevie's Creole | *Cajun* — 17

Versailles | *Cuban* — 21

## GLENDALE

Ⓩ Carousel | *Mideast.* — 24

Crocodile Cafe | *Calif.* — 16

Damon's Steak | *Steak* — 16

Far Niente | *Italian* — 25

Fresco | *Italian* — 22

Gennaro's | *Italian* — 24

Islands | *Amer.* — 16

Minx | *Eclectic* — 19

Panda Inn | *Chinese* — 20

NEW Phoenicia | *Lebanese* — –

Porto's Bakery | *Bakery* — –

Sandbag Sandwich | *Sandwiches* — 18

Zankou Chicken | *Med.* — 22

## GRANADA HILLS

Odyssey | *Continental/Seafood* — 14

## NORTH HOLLYWOOD

Barsac Brasserie | *Calif./French* — 23

Ca' del Sole | *Italian* — 22

Ⓩ In-N-Out Burger | *Hamburgers* — 24

Poquito Más | *Mex.* — 22

Swinging Door | *BBQ* — –

## NORTHRIDGE

Alessio | *Italian* — 22

Ⓩ Brent's Deli | *Deli* — 26

Cali. Chicken | *Amer.* — 21

Claim Jumper | *Amer.* — 19

El Torito | *Mex.* — 15

Emle's | *Calif./Med.* — 19

Mandarin Deli | *Chinese* — 21

Maria's Italian | *Italian* — 17

Outback Steak | *Steak* — 17

Romano's Macaroni | *Italian* — 17

Souplantation | *Amer.* — 16

Wood Ranch BBQ | *BBQ* — 20

## RESEDA

BCD Tofu | *Korean* — 20

## SHERMAN OAKS

Bamboo Cuisine | *Chinese* — 22

Barney's Hamburgers | *Hamburgers* — 21

Boneyard Bistro | *BBQ* — 20

Ⓩ Café Bizou | *Calif./French* — 23

Cafe 50's | *Diner* — 15

Carnival | *Lebanese* — 23

Casa Vega | *Mex.* — 18

Ⓩ Cheesecake Fact. | *Amer.* — 20

D'Amore's Pizza | *Pizza* — 21

El Torito | *Mex.* — 15

El Torito Grill | *Mex.* — 18

Great Greek | *Greek* — 21

Gyu-Kaku | *Jap.* — 20

Hamlet | *Amer.* — 16

Il Tiramisù | *Italian* — 22

Ⓩ In-N-Out Burger | *Hamburgers* — 24

Jinky's | *SW* — 20

Kung Pao | *Chinese* — 19

La Fondue | *Fondue* — 14

La Frite | *French* — 20

La Pergola | *Italian* — 23

Leaf Cuisine | *Vegan* — –

Le Petit Rest. | *French* — 21

Maria's Italian | *Italian* — 17

Marmalade Café | *Amer./Calif.* — 18

Max | *Asian Fusion* — 24

Mel's Drive-In | *Amer.* — 16

Mistral | *French* — 25

Mr. Cecil's Ribs | *BBQ* — 18

Noah's NY Bagels | *Sandwiches* — 18

Oliva | *Italian* — 22

Panzanella | *Italian* — 23

Ⓩ P.F. Chang's | *Chinese* — 19

Pizza Rustica | *Pizza* — 17

Pomodoro | *Italian* — 17

Rive Gauche | *French* — 20

Señor Fred | *Mex.* — 17

Sharky's Mex. | *Mex.* — 17

Sisley Italian | *Italian* — 18

Spazio | *Calif./Med.* — 19

Spumoni | *Italian* — 23

Stanley's | *Calif.* — 19

Sushi Mac | *Jap.* — 17

NEW Watercress | *Eclectic* — –

## STUDIO CITY

Ahi Sushi | *Jap.* — 22

Artisan Cheese | *Cheese/Sandwiches* — 24

Art's Deli | *Deli* — 19

Ⓩ Asanebo | *Jap.* — 28

Baja Fresh Mex. | *Mex.* — 18

Ⓩ Bistro Gdn./Coldwater | *Continental* — 20

| | |
|---|---|
| Caioti Pizza | *Pizza* | 22 |
| Cali. Pizza Kitchen | *Pizza* | 18 |
| Carney's Express | *Hot Dogs* | 19 |
| Chin Chin | *Chinese* | 17 |
| Daily Grill | *Amer.* | 18 |
| Du-par's | *Diner* | 16 |
| Firefly | *Amer.* | 20 |
| Gaucho Grill | *Argent./Steak* | 18 |
| Hugo's | *Calif.* | 21 |
| Il Tramezzino | *Italian* | 21 |
| ☑ In-N-Out Burger | *Hamburgers* | 24 |
| Iroha | *Jap.* | 24 |
| NEW Kansas City BBQ | *BBQ* | – |
| ☑ Katsu-ya | *Jap.* | 27 |
| Killer Shrimp | *Seafood* | 21 |
| Kung Pao | *Chinese* | 19 |
| NEW Lal Mirch | *Indian* | – |
| La Loggia | *Italian* | 20 |
| Le Pain Quotidien | *Bakery/Belgian* | 21 |
| Louise's Tratt. | *Calif./Italian* | 16 |
| Marrakesh | *Moroccan* | 19 |
| Mexicali | *Mex.* | 16 |
| Next Door/La Loggia | *Spanish* | 20 |
| Ohana BBQ | *Korean* | 19 |
| Olé! Tapas Bar | *Spanish* | 17 |
| Pinot Bistro | *French* | 23 |
| Poquito Más | *Mex.* | 22 |
| NEW Romanov | *Russian/Steak* | – |
| Spark Woodfire | *Amer.* | 17 |
| ☑ Sushi Nozawa | *Jap.* | 27 |
| Talésai | *Thai* | 22 |
| Tama Sushi | *Jap.* | 24 |
| Teru Sushi | *Jap.* | 20 |
| NEW Tommy Ray's | *Calif.* | 18 |
| Vitello's | *Italian* | 14 |
| Wine Bistro | *French* | 23 |
| Yen Sushi | *Jap.* | 23 |

### TARZANA

| | |
|---|---|
| NEW Hummus Bar | *Mideast.* | – |
| India's Tandoori | *Indian* | 19 |
| Le Sanglier | *French* | 22 |
| Madeleine Bistro | *French/Vegan* | 22 |
| Paul's Cafe | *Calif./French* | 18 |
| Sharky's Mex. | *Mex.* | 17 |

### TOLUCA LAKE

| | |
|---|---|
| NEW Eight-18 | *Med.* | – |
| Prosecco | *Italian* | 25 |

### UNIVERSAL CITY

| | |
|---|---|
| Buca di Beppo | *Italian* | 15 |
| Café/Tango | *Eclectic* | 20 |
| Daily Grill | *Amer.* | 18 |
| Hard Rock | *Amer.* | 14 |
| Jody Maroni's | *Hot Dogs* | 19 |
| Miceli's | *Italian* | 17 |
| Minibar | *Eclectic* | 23 |
| Saddle Ranch Chop | *Steak* | 16 |
| Versailles | *Cuban* | 21 |
| Wolfgang Puck | *Calif.* | 18 |

### VAN NUYS

| | |
|---|---|
| Dr. Hogly Wogly's | *BBQ* | 23 |
| ☑ In-N-Out Burger | *Hamburgers* | 24 |
| Sam Woo | *Chinese* | 20 |
| Zankou Chicken | *Med.* | 22 |

### WEST HILLS

| | |
|---|---|
| Alessio | *Italian* | 22 |
| Stonefire Grill | *BBQ* | 20 |

### WOODLAND HILLS

| | |
|---|---|
| Adagio | *Italian* | 23 |
| Baja Fresh Mex. | *Mex.* | 18 |
| BJ's | *Pub* | 17 |
| ☑ Brandywine | *Continental* | 27 |
| Cali. Chicken | *Amer.* | 21 |
| ☑ Cheesecake Fact. | *Amer.* | 20 |
| El Torito | *Mex.* | 15 |
| Farm/Bev. Hills | *Amer.* | 19 |
| Fleming Prime | *Steak* | 25 |
| Gaucho Grill | *Argent./Steak* | 18 |
| Gorikee | *Calif.* | 21 |
| ☑ In-N-Out Burger | *Hamburgers* | 24 |
| Islands | *Amer.* | 16 |
| Kate Mantilini | *Diner* | 18 |
| La Frite | *French* | 20 |
| Maggiano's | *Italian* | 19 |
| Maria's Italian | *Italian* | 17 |
| Monty's Steak | *Steak* | 21 |
| Nicola's Kitchen | *Calif./Italian* | 18 |
| ☑ P.F. Chang's | *Chinese* | 19 |
| Pomodoro | *Italian* | 17 |
| Poquito Más | *Mex.* | 22 |
| NEW Rack | *Calif.* | 15 |
| ☑ Roy's | *Hawaiian* | 24 |
| Ruby's | *Diner* | 16 |
| ☑ Ruth's Chris | *Steak* | 25 |
| NEW uWink Bistro | *Calif.* | 14 |
| Villa Piacere | *Eclectic* | 20 |

# San Gabriel Valley

## ALHAMBRA

| | |
|---|---|
| Angelena's Southern | *Southern* | 15 |
| Cuban Bistro | *Cuban* | 20 |
| Hop Woo | *Chinese* | 19 |
| Johnny Rockets | *Hamburgers* | 15 |
| Pho 79 | *Viet.* | 21 |
| Sam Woo | *Chinese* | 20 |
| Souplantation | *Amer.* | 16 |
| NEW Spice Basil | *Thai* | - |
| Triumphal Palace | *Chinese* | 24 |
| Wahib's Mid-East | *Mideast.* | 21 |

## AZUSA

| | |
|---|---|
| Tulipano | *Italian* | 23 |

## CITY OF INDUSTRY

| | |
|---|---|
| Benihana | *Jap.* | 18 |
| Claim Jumper | *Amer.* | 19 |
| Joe's Crab | *Seafood* | 13 |
| Mimi's Cafe | *Diner* | 17 |
| Outback Steak | *Steak* | 17 |
| Souplantation | *Amer.* | 16 |

## CLAREMONT

| | |
|---|---|
| Buca di Beppo | *Italian* | 15 |
| Heroes B&G | *Pub* | 16 |
| Viva Madrid | *Spanish* | 22 |
| Walter's | *Eclectic* | 19 |

## COVINA/WEST COVINA

| | |
|---|---|
| BJ's | *Pub* | 17 |
| Green Field Churr. | *Brazilian* | 23 |
| Hayakawa | *Jap.* | 26 |
| O-Nami | *Jap.* | 16 |
| Outback Steak | *Steak* | 17 |

## MONTEBELLO

| | |
|---|---|
| Astro Burger | *Hamburgers* | 20 |
| Sam Woo | *Chinese* | 20 |

## MONTEREY PARK

| | |
|---|---|
| Chung King | *Chinese* | - |
| Empress Harbor | *Chinese* | 22 |
| Lake Spring Shanghai | *Chinese* | 21 |
| Macau St. | *Chinese* | 20 |
| Mandarin Deli | *Chinese* | 21 |
| NBC Seafood | *Chinese/Seafood* | 22 |
| Ocean Star | *Chinese* | 22 |
| Sam Woo | *Chinese* | 20 |

## PICO RIVERA

| | |
|---|---|
| Z Dal Rae | *Continental* | 26 |

## ROSEMEAD

| | |
|---|---|
| Z Sea Harbour | *Chinese/Seafood* | 25 |

## ROWLAND HEIGHTS

| | |
|---|---|
| BCD Tofu | *Korean* | 20 |
| NEW Little Tokyo Shabu | *Jap.* | - |

## SAN GABRIEL

| | |
|---|---|
| Ajisen Ramen | *Jap.* | 17 |
| Z Babita | *Mex.* | 27 |
| NEW Dong Ting Spring | *Chinese* | - |
| Golden Deli | *Viet.* | 23 |
| Mission 261 | *Chinese* | 22 |
| Sam Woo | *Chinese* | 20 |

## WHITTIER

| | |
|---|---|
| Mimi's Cafe | *Diner* | 17 |
| Rocky Cola | *Diner* | - |
| Ruby's | *Diner* | 16 |

# Conejo Valley/
# Simi Valley & Environs

## AGOURA HILLS/OAK PARK

| | |
|---|---|
| Adobe Cantina | *BBQ/Mex.* | 19 |
| Bamboom | *Calif.* | - |
| Z Café 14 | *Calif.* | 26 |
| Chapter 8 Steak | *Steak* | 18 |
| Z Leila's | *Calif.* | 27 |
| Maria's Italian | *Italian* | 17 |
| MOZ Buddha | *Asian Fusion* | 20 |
| Padri | *Italian* | 21 |
| Sushi Ozekii | *Jap.* | - |
| Wood Ranch BBQ | *BBQ* | 20 |

## CAMARILLO

| | |
|---|---|
| Enoteca Toscana | *Italian/Spanish* | 18 |
| Jody Maroni's | *Hot Dogs* | 19 |
| NEW Safire | *Amer.* | - |
| Souplantation | *Amer.* | 16 |
| Spumoni | *Italian* | 23 |
| Sushi Ozekii | *Jap.* | - |
| Wood Ranch BBQ | *BBQ* | 20 |

## MOORPARK

| | |
|---|---|
| Wood Ranch BBQ | *BBQ* | 20 |

## SIMI VALLEY

| | |
|---|---|
| NEW Coco D'Amour | *Eclectic* | - |
| NEW Limon Latin Grill | *Pan-Latin* | - |
| Sharky's Mex. | *Mex.* | 17 |

## THOUSAND OAKS

Buca di Beppo | *Italian* — 15
🅩 Cheesecake Fact. | *Amer.* — 20
D'Amore's Pizza | *Pizza* — 21
Du-par's | *Diner* — 16
El Torito | *Mex.* — 15
NEW Holdren's Steak | *Steak* — -
🅩 Mastro's Steak | *Steak* — 25
Outback Steak | *Steak* — 17
Piatti | *Italian* — 20
Romano's Macaroni | *Italian* — 17
Sisley Italian | *Italian* — 18

## WESTLAKE VILLAGE

Alessio | *Italian* — 22
Bellavino | *Eclectic* — 21
BJ's | *Pub* — 17
🅩 Brent's Deli | *Deli* — 26
Fins | *Continental/Seafood* — 22
Galletto | *Brazilian/Italian* — 23
NEW Hampton's | *Calif.* — 24
Louise's Tratt. | *Calif./Italian* — 16
Mandevilla | *Continental* — 23
Marmalade Café | *Amer./Calif.* — 18
NEW Mediterraneo/Westlake | *Med.* — 21
Melting Pot | *Fondue* — 19
P6 Rest. | *Amer.* — 20
Rosti | *Italian* — 17

Rustico | *Italian* — 23
Sharky's Mex. | *Mex.* — 17
NEW Suki 7 | *Jap.* — -
🅩 Tuscany | *Italian* — 27
NEW Zin Bistro | *Amer./French* — 21

# Santa Clarita Valley & Environs

## SANTA CLARITA

Mimi's Cafe | *Diner* — 17
Pei Wei Diner | *Pan-Asian* — 16
Romano's Macaroni | *Italian* — 17

## SAUGUS/NEWHALL

Le Chêne | *French* — 25

## STEVENSON RANCH

Spumoni | *Italian* — 23

## VALENCIA

BJ's | *Pub* — 17
Buca di Beppo | *Italian* — 15
Claim Jumper | *Amer.* — 19
Outback Steak | *Steak* — 17
Poquito Más | *Mex.* — 22
Salt Creek | *Steak* — 18
Sisley Italian | *Italian* — 18
Stonefire Grill | *BBQ* — 20
Thai Dishes | *Thai* — 18
Wood Ranch BBQ | *BBQ* — 20

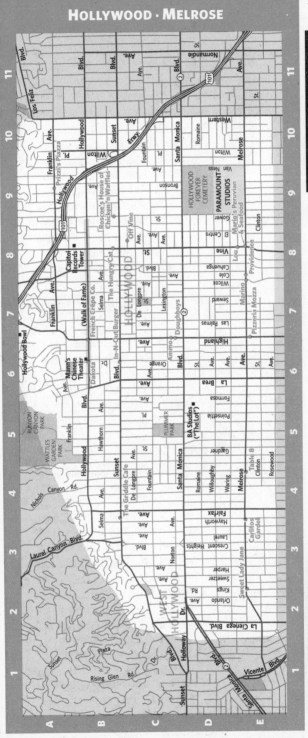

MAPS

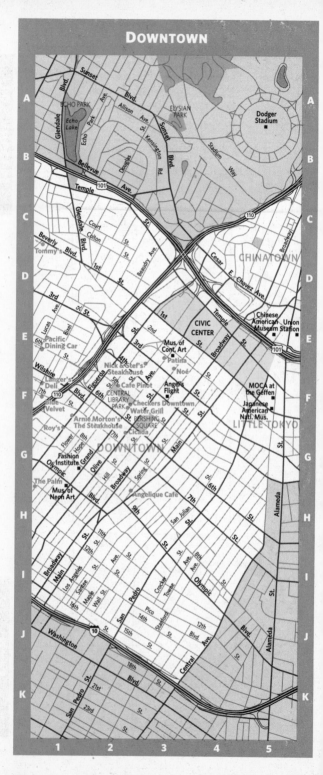

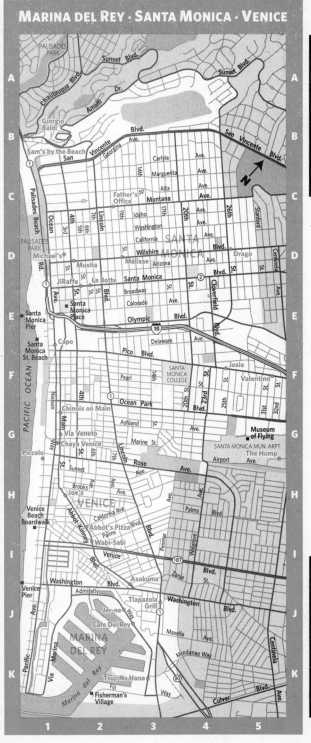

# PASADENA

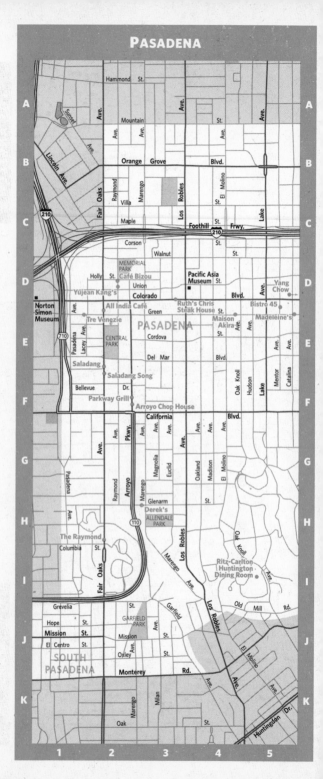

# Special Features

Listings cover the best in each category and include restaurant names, locations and Food ratings. Multi-location restaurants' features may vary by branch. ⊠ indicates places with the highest ratings, popularity and importance.

## BREAKFAST

(See also Hotel Dining)

| | |
|---|---|
| Alcove | **Los Feliz** | 22 |
| Art's Deli | **Studio City** | 19 |
| Barney Greengrass | **Beverly Hills** | 21 |
| bld | **Beverly Blvd.** | 21 |
| Brighton Coffee | **Beverly Hills** | 16 |
| City Bakery | **Brentwood** | 18 |
| Cora's Coffee | **Santa Monica** | 21 |
| Doughboys | **multi. loc.** | 22 |
| Duke's Coffee | **W Hollywood** | 18 |
| Du-par's | **multi. loc.** | 16 |
| Farm/Bev. Hills | **multi. loc.** | 19 |
| Fred 62 | **Los Feliz** | 18 |
| Griddle Cafe | **Hollywood** | 22 |
| Kate Mantilini | **Beverly Hills** | 18 |
| Lemon Moon | **West LA** | 20 |
| Le Pain Quotidien | **multi. loc.** | 21 |
| Literati | **West LA** | 20 |
| ⊠ Lotería! | **Fairfax** | 24 |
| Mäni's | **multi. loc.** | 18 |
| Marmalade Café | **multi. loc.** | 18 |
| Mel's Drive-In | **Hollywood** | 16 |
| Mimi's Cafe | **Atwater Vill** | 17 |
| Newsroom Café | **W Hollywood** | 19 |
| Pacific Dining Car | **multi. loc.** | 22 |
| Patrick's | **Santa Monica** | 16 |
| ⊠ Roscoe's | **Mid-City** | 22 |
| Ruby's | **multi. loc.** | 16 |
| Square One Dining | **E Hollywood** | 24 |
| Susina Bakery | **La Brea** | 23 |
| ⊠ Sweet Lady Jane | **Melrose** | 25 |
| Swingers | **Santa Monica** | 17 |
| Toast | **Third St.** | 20 |
| Uncle Bill's Pancake | **Manhattan Bch** | 22 |
| Urth Caffé | **multi. loc.** | 21 |

## BRUNCH

| | |
|---|---|
| Abbey | **W Hollywood** | 16 |
| ABC Seafood | **Chinatown** | 19 |
| NEW Abode | **Santa Monica** | 23 |
| A La Tarte | **Pacific Palisades** | 18 |
| ⊠ Belvedere | **Beverly Hills** | 25 |
| ⊠ Campanile | **La Brea** | 26 |
| Cliff's Edge | **Silver Lake** | 20 |
| Dusty's | **Silver Lake** | 21 |
| Firefly Bistro | **S Pasadena** | 19 |
| ⊠ Hotel Bel-Air | **Bel-Air** | 26 |
| Jer-ne | **Marina del Rey** | 22 |
| ⊠ Joe's | **Venice** | 26 |
| Lilly's French Cafe | **Venice** | 20 |
| Massimo | **Beverly Hills** | 22 |
| McCormick/Schmick | **El Segundo** | 19 |
| Morels First Floor | **Fairfax** | 17 |
| Napa Valley | **Westwood** | 20 |
| Nine Thirty | **Westwood** | 23 |
| Ocean Ave. | **Santa Monica** | 23 |
| Ocean Seafood | **Chinatown** | 22 |
| ⊠ One Pico | **Santa Monica** | 23 |
| ⊠ Polo Lounge | **Beverly Hills** | 22 |
| NEW Prana Cafe | **W Hollywood** | 22 |
| Raymond, The | **Pasadena** | 24 |
| ⊠ Saddle Peak | **Calabasas** | 26 |
| Twin Palms | **Pasadena** | 17 |
| ⊠ Whist | **Santa Monica** | 21 |

## BUFFET

(Check availability)

| | |
|---|---|
| Akbar | **Hermosa Bch** | 20 |
| All India | **West LA** | 23 |
| Aunt Kizzy's | **Marina del Rey** | 20 |
| Bombay Palace | **Beverly Hills** | 21 |
| Buffet City | **West LA** | 13 |
| Burger Continental | **Pasadena** | 16 |
| Café Pacific | **Rancho Palos Verdes** | 24 |
| Castaway | **Burbank** | 17 |
| Chao Krung | **Fairfax** | 21 |
| NEW Circa 55 | **Beverly Hills** | 21 |
| Clay Pit | **Brentwood** | 22 |
| Delmonico's Lobster | **Encino** | 21 |
| El Torito | **Woodland Hills** | 15 |
| El Torito Grill | **Torrance** | 18 |
| Flavor of India | **W Hollywood** | 21 |
| Fogo de Chão | **Beverly Hills** | 23 |
| Gate of India | **Santa Monica** | 20 |
| Green Field Churr. | **multi. loc.** | 23 |
| House of Blues | **W Hollywood** | 15 |

| | |
|---|---|
| i Cugini \| **Santa Monica** | 21 |
| India's Tandoori \| **multi. loc.** | 19 |
| ☑ Inn/Seventh Ray \| **Topanga** | 21 |
| Jer-ne \| **Marina del Rey** | 22 |
| La Huasteca \| **Lynwood** | 22 |
| Locanda/Lago \| **Santa Monica** | 20 |
| Maison Akira \| **Pasadena** | 25 |
| NEW Mediterraneo/Westlake \| **Westlake Vill** | 21 |
| Nawab of India \| **Santa Monica** | 22 |
| Nizam \| **West LA** | 21 |
| Odyssey \| **Granada Hills** | 14 |
| O-Nami \| **multi. loc.** | 16 |
| Panda Inn \| **Pasadena** | 20 |
| Picanha Churr. \| **Burbank** | 19 |
| NEW Raaga \| **Chatsworth** | - |
| Radhika's \| **Pasadena** | 18 |
| Sagebrush Cantina \| **Calabasas** | 14 |
| Salt Creek \| **Valencia** | 18 |
| Smoke House \| **Burbank** | 19 |
| Souplantation \| **multi. loc.** | 16 |
| Tamayo \| **East LA** | 21 |
| Thousand Cranes \| **Little Tokyo** | 23 |
| Tibet Nepal \| **Pasadena** | 19 |
| Tra Di Noi \| **Malibu** | 22 |
| Twin Palms \| **Pasadena** | 17 |
| Vitello's \| **Studio City** | 14 |

## BUSINESS DINING

| | |
|---|---|
| Ago \| **W Hollywood** | 21 |
| Alessio \| **Northridge** | 22 |
| Angolo DiVino \| **West LA** | 23 |
| Aphrodisiac \| **Century City** | 18 |
| ☑ Arnie Morton's Steak \| **multi. loc.** | 25 |
| Arroyo Chop Hse. \| **Pasadena** | 25 |
| NEW Baleen \| **Redondo Bch** | 22 |
| Barney Greengrass \| **Beverly Hills** | 21 |
| ☑ Belvedere \| **Beverly Hills** | 25 |
| BIN 8945 \| **W Hollywood** | 21 |
| ☑ Bistro 45 \| **Pasadena** | 26 |
| Bistro Provence \| **Burbank** | 22 |
| bld \| **Beverly Blvd.** | 21 |
| Blvd \| **Beverly Hills** | 21 |
| Breeze \| **Century City** | 19 |
| Buffalo Club \| **Santa Monica** | 19 |
| Cafe Del Rey \| **Marina del Rey** | 23 |
| Caffe Roma \| **Beverly Hills** | 16 |
| ☑ Campanile \| **La Brea** | 26 |
| NEW Catch \| **Santa Monica** | - |
| Celestino \| **Pasadena** | 23 |

| | |
|---|---|
| Chapter 8 Steak \| **Agoura Hills** | 18 |
| NEW Charcoal \| **Hollywood** | - |
| Checkers \| **Downtown** | 22 |
| ☑ Cicada \| **Downtown** | 23 |
| NEW Coast \| **Santa Monica** | - |
| NEW Craft \| **Century City** | - |
| ☑ Crustacean \| **Beverly Hills** | 23 |
| ☑ Cut \| **Beverly Hills** | 26 |
| Dakota \| **Hollywood** | 22 |
| Dan Tana's \| **W Hollywood** | 21 |
| Doug Arango's \| **W Hollywood** | 22 |
| Drago \| **Santa Monica** | 24 |
| eat. on sunset \| **Hollywood** | 19 |
| 555 East \| **Long Bch** | 25 |
| Five Sixty-One \| **Pasadena** | 19 |
| Fleming Prime \| **Woodland Hills** | 25 |
| Fogo de Chão \| **Beverly Hills** | 23 |
| NEW Fraiche \| **Culver City** | - |
| French 75 \| **Burbank** | 21 |
| ☑ Gardens \| **Beverly Hills** | 25 |
| ☑ Grace \| **Beverly Blvd.** | 25 |
| ☑ Grill on Alley \| **Beverly Hills** | 24 |
| Grill on Hollywood \| **Hollywood** | 19 |
| NEW Hampton's \| **Westlake Vill** | 24 |
| Harper's \| **Century City** | 16 |
| ☑ Hatfield's \| **Beverly Blvd.** | 27 |
| Il Grano \| **West LA** | 25 |
| Il Moro \| **West LA** | 22 |
| ☑ Jar \| **Beverly Blvd.** | 25 |
| ☑ Josie \| **Santa Monica** | 27 |
| Kincaid's \| **Redondo Bch** | 21 |
| La Botte \| **Santa Monica** | 24 |
| ☑ La Cachette \| **Century City** | 27 |
| Madeo \| **W Hollywood** | 26 |
| McCormick/Schmick \| **multi. loc.** | 19 |
| ☑ Mélisse \| **Santa Monica** | 28 |
| Michael's \| **Santa Monica** | 24 |
| Mistral \| **Sherman Oaks** | 25 |
| Nick & Stef's Steak \| **Downtown** | 22 |
| Nic's \| **Beverly Hills** | 21 |
| Ocean & Vine \| **Santa Monica** | 22 |
| ☑ One Pico \| **Santa Monica** | 23 |
| NEW On Sunset \| **Brentwood** | - |
| Opus \| **Mid-Wilshire** | 22 |
| Ortolan \| **Third St.** | 25 |
| ☑ Patina \| **Downtown** | 26 |
| NEW Penthouse \| **Santa Monica** | 20 |
| Peppone \| **Brentwood** | 21 |

| | |
|---|---|
| 🅉 Petros | **Manhattan Bch** | 23 |
| Pinot Bistro | **Studio City** | 23 |
| 🅉 Polo Lounge | **Beverly Hills** | 22 |
| 🅉 Providence | **Hollywood** | 27 |
| NEW Punch Grill | **Santa Monica** | 18 |
| NEW Red Seven | **W Hollywood** | -| |
| NEW Riordan's Tavern | **Downtown** | -| |
| 🅉 Ritz Huntington | **Pasadena** | 26 |
| 🅉 Roy's | **Downtown** | 24 |
| NEW Rustic Canyon | **Santa Monica** | 21 |
| 🅉 Ruth's Chris | **multi. loc.** | 25 |
| NEW Safire | **Camarillo** | -| |
| Salt Creek | **El Segundo** | 18 |
| Simon LA | **W Hollywood** | 21 |
| 🅉 Spago | **Beverly Hills** | 27 |
| Sur | **W Hollywood** | 21 |
| Sushi Dokoro | **Beverly Hills** | 24 |
| NEW Takami | **Downtown** | -| |
| NEW Tanzore | **Beverly Hills** | -| |
| Taylor's Steak | **multi. loc.** | 21 |
| Thousand Cranes | **Little Tokyo** | 23 |
| NEW Tracht's | **Long Bch** | -| |
| Triumphal Palace | **Alhambra** | 24 |
| Twist | **Hollywood** | 19 |
| Ugo | **Culver City** | -| |
| 🅉 Valentino | **Santa Monica** | 26 |
| Vert | **Hollywood** | 21 |
| NEW Vertical Wine | **Pasadena** | 19 |
| Vincenti | **Brentwood** | 25 |
| 🅉 Water Grill | **Downtown** | 27 |
| West | **Brentwood** | 18 |
| Wilshire | **Santa Monica** | 21 |
| 🅉 Yujean Kang's | **Pasadena** | 26 |
| Zucca | **Downtown** | 22 |

## CHEESE TRAYS

| | |
|---|---|
| Amori | **Monrovia** | 22 |
| 🅉 Angelini Osteria | **Beverly Blvd.** | 27 |
| 🅉 A.O.C. | **Third St.** | 26 |
| Artisan Cheese | **Studio City** | 24 |
| Avenue | **Manhattan Bch** | 23 |
| 🅉 Belvedere | **Beverly Hills** | 25 |
| 🅉 Bistro 45 | **Pasadena** | 26 |
| NEW BottleRock | **Culver City** | 16 |
| Chateau Marmont | **W Hollywood** | 21 |
| Checkers | **Downtown** | 22 |
| Chez Mimi | **Santa Monica** | 21 |

| | |
|---|---|
| 🅉 Cicada | **Downtown** | 23 |
| Cobras/Matadors | **multi. loc.** | 21 |
| NEW Coco Noche | **Manhattan Bch** | 22 |
| 🅉 Derek's | **Pasadena** | 27 |
| Devon | **Monrovia** | 25 |
| Enzo & Angela | **West LA** | 21 |
| Figaro Bistrot | **Los Feliz** | 18 |
| Firefly | **Studio City** | 20 |
| Five Sixty-One | **Pasadena** | 19 |
| Fleming Prime | **El Segundo** | 25 |
| NEW Fraiche | **Culver City** | -| |
| French 75 | **Burbank** | 21 |
| 🅉 Frenchy's Bistro | **Long Bch** | 27 |
| Gale's | **Pasadena** | 21 |
| Galletto | **Westlake Vill** | 23 |
| Getty Center | **Brentwood** | 22 |
| 🅉 Grace | **Beverly Blvd.** | 25 |
| 🅉 Hotel Bel-Air | **Bel-Air** | 26 |
| 🅉 Il Cielo | **Beverly Hills** | 21 |
| Il Grano | **West LA** | 25 |
| Il Moro | **West LA** | 22 |
| Kendall's Brass. | **Downtown** | 17 |
| La Sosta | **Hermosa Bch** | 27 |
| Le Chêne | **Saugus** | 25 |
| Le Sanglier | **Tarzana** | 22 |
| Lodge Steak | **Beverly Hills** | 20 |
| Lou | **Hollywood** | 22 |
| 🅉 Mélisse | **Santa Monica** | 28 |
| NEW Mike & Anne's | **S Pasadena** | 20 |
| Mimosa | **Beverly Blvd.** | 22 |
| Monsieur Marcel | **Fairfax** | 19 |
| NEW Murano | **W Hollywood** | -| |
| Napa Valley | **Westwood** | 20 |
| Noé | **Downtown** | 25 |
| Opus | **Mid-Wilshire** | 22 |
| Ortolan | **Third St.** | 25 |
| NEW Parc | **Hollywood** | -| |
| Pastis | **Beverly Blvd.** | 22 |
| 🅉 Patina | **Downtown** | 26 |
| Petrossian | **W Hollywood** | -| |
| 🅉 Polo Lounge | **Beverly Hills** | 22 |
| 🅉 Providence | **Hollywood** | 27 |
| 🅉 Ritz Huntington | **Pasadena** | 26 |
| NEW Rustic Canyon | **Santa Monica** | 21 |
| 🅉 Saddle Peak | **Calabasas** | 26 |
| 🅉 Spago | **Beverly Hills** | 27 |
| Table 8 | **Melrose** | 24 |
| Taste | **W Hollywood** | 20 |

Tre Venezie | **Pasadena** 24
Ⓩ Tuscany | **Westlake Vill** 27
Ⓩ Via Veneto | **Santa Monica** 26
Vibrato | **Bel-Air** 22
Villa Piacere | **Woodland Hills** 20
Violet | **Santa Monica** 21
Whisper Lounge | **Fairfax** 16
Ⓩ Whist | **Santa Monica** 21
Wine Bistro | **Studio City** 23

## CHEF'S TABLE

blue on blue | **Beverly Hills** 18
Chez Melange | **Redondo Bch** 25
Depot | **Torrance** 23
Fleming Prime | **multi. loc.** 25
French 75 | **Century City** 21
NEW Hadaka Sushi | **W Hollywood** –
NEW Hampton's | **Westlake Vill** 24
Ⓩ Hotel Bel-Air | **Bel-Air** 26
Il Grano | **West LA** 25
Il Pastaio | **Beverly Hills** 25
L'Opera | **Long Bch** 24
Ⓩ Patina | **Downtown** 26
Ⓩ Providence | **Hollywood** 27
NEW Safire | **Camarillo** –

## COOL LOOS

NEW Ⓩ Blue Velvet | **Downtown** 22
Chapter 8 Steak | **Agoura Hills** 18
Firefly | **Studio City** 20
Ⓩ Grace | **Beverly Blvd.** 25
Katsuya | **Brentwood** 24
LA Food Show | **Manhattan Bch** 19
Ortolan | **Third St.** 25
Ⓩ Patina | **Downtown** 26
NEW Penthouse | **Santa Monica** 20
Ⓩ Roy's | **Downtown** 24
Smitty's Grill | **Pasadena** 21
Ⓩ Sona | **W Hollywood** 27
Ⓩ Spago | **Beverly Hills** 27

## CRITIC-PROOF

(Gets lots of business despite so-so food)

Broadway Deli | **Santa Monica** 14
El Coyote | **Beverly Blvd.** 13
Joe's Crab | **multi. loc.** 13
Rainforest Cafe | **Ontario** 13

## DANCING

Alegria | **Long Bch** 21
Alessio | **Westlake Vill** 22

Buffalo Club | **Santa Monica** 19
Café/Tango | **Universal City** 20
Carmine's Italian | **S Pasadena** 18
NEW Catch | **Santa Monica** –
Cuban Bistro | **Alhambra** 20
Ⓩ Dal Rae | **Pico Rivera** 26
El Pollo Inka | **Gardena** 19
Joseph's Cafe | **Hollywood** 18
NEW J Rest. | **Downtown** 13
La Huasteca | **Lynwood** 22
Ⓩ Madison, The | **Long Bch** 21
Minibar | **Universal City** 23
Minx | **Glendale** 19
Padri | **Agoura Hills** 21
P6 Rest. | **Westlake Vill** 20
Saddle Ranch Chop | **Universal City** 16
Sky Room | **Long Bch** 21
Smoke House | **Burbank** 19
Taverna Tony | **Malibu** 21
Tiger Lily | **Los Feliz** 19
Twin Palms | **Pasadena** 17
Villa Sorriso | **Pasadena** 18

## DESSERT

A La Tarte | **Pacific Palisades** 18
Alessio | **Northridge** 22
Angelena's Southern | **Alhambra** 15
Auntie Em's | **Eagle Rock** –
Ⓩ Café 14 | **Agoura Hills** 26
Ⓩ Campanile | **La Brea** 26
Ⓩ Cheesecake Fact. | **multi. loc.** 20
City Bakery | **Brentwood** 18
Clementine | **Century City** 24
NEW Coco Noche | **Manhattan Bch** 22
Doña Rosa | **Arcadia** 16
Doughboys | **multi. loc.** 22
Farm/Bev. Hills | **multi. loc.** 19
Ⓩ Grace | **Beverly Blvd.** 25
Jack n' Jill's | **Santa Monica** 19
Joan's on Third | **Third St.** 24
La Crêperie | **Long Bch** 23
Le Marmiton | **Marina del Rey** 18
Magnolia | **Hollywood** 20
Mäni's | **multi. loc.** 18
Max | **Sherman Oaks** 24
Melting Pot | **multi. loc.** 19
Michel Richard | **Beverly Hills** 20
Porto's Bakery | **multi. loc.** –
Ⓩ Providence | **Hollywood** 27

Simon LA | **W Hollywood** 21

☑ Sona | **W Hollywood** 27

☑ Spago | **Beverly Hills** 27

Susina Bakery | **La Brea** 23

☑ Sweet Lady Jane | **Melrose** 25

Tart | **Fairfax** 18

## ENTERTAINMENT

(Call for days and times of performances)

Alegria | varies | **Long Bch** 21

Alessio | varies | **Westlake Vill** 22

Amalfi | varies | **La Brea** 18

Antonio's | guitar | **Melrose** 22

Arroyo Chop Hse. | piano | **Pasadena** 25

Auld Dubliner | Irish | **Long Bch** 21

Bandera | jazz | **West LA** 22

☑ Brandywine | guitar | **Woodland Hills** 27

Buffalo Club | varies | **Santa Monica** 19

Buggy Whip | piano | **Westchester** 19

Cafe Del Rey | guitar/piano | **Marina del Rey** 23

Cafe des Artistes | DJ | **Hollywood** 19

Café/Tango | varies | **Universal City** 20

Canal Club | DJ | **Venice** 18

Canter's | varies | **Fairfax** 18

Carlitos Gardel | piano/violin | **Melrose** 23

Carmine's Italian | varies | **S Pasadena** 18

☑ Carousel | varies | **Glendale** 24

Casablanca | Latin guitar | **Venice** 18

**NEW** Catch | varies | **Santa Monica** -

Ciudad | flamenco | **Downtown** 21

Club 41 | varies | **Pasadena** 19

☑ Crustacean | jazz/piano | **Beverly Hills** 23

Cuban Bistro | Latin bands | **Alhambra** 20

Dar Maghreb | belly dancing | **Hollywood** 18

El Cholo | varies | **Pasadena** 18

Electric Lotus | DJ | **Los Feliz** 19

El Pollo Inka | varies | **multi. loc.** 19

Fins | varies | **multi. loc.** 22

☑ Frenchy's Bistro | jazz | **Long Bch** 27

Galletto | varies | **Westlake Vill** 23

Geisha House | DJ | **Hollywood** 19

Genghis Cohen | varies | **Fairfax** 20

Great Greek | Greek | **Sherman Oaks** 21

Hal's B&G | jazz | **Venice** 20

House of Blues | varies | **W Hollywood** 15

Joseph's Cafe | DJ | **Hollywood** 18

Koutoubia | belly dancing | **Westwood** 20

Lucille's BBQ | blues | **Long Bch** 22

☑ Madison, The | piano | **Long Bch** 21

Market City | strings | **Burbank** 18

Marouch | belly dancing | **E Hollywood** 24

Marrakesh | belly dancing | **Studio City** 19

☑ Mastro's Steak | piano/vocals | **Beverly Hills** 25

Moonshadows | DJ | **Malibu** 17

Morels French Steak | jazz band | **Fairfax** 19

Moun of Tunis | belly dancing | **Hollywood** 20

Nic's | bands | **Beverly Hills** 21

☑ One Pico | bass/piano | **Santa Monica** 23

Padri | varies | **Agoura Hills** 21

Papa Cristo's | belly dancing | **Mid-City** 22

Papadakis Tav. | varies | **San Pedro** 22

Parker's Lighthse. | jazz | **Long Bch** 18

☑ Parkway Grill | piano | **Pasadena** 25

Pig 'n Whistle | varies | **Hollywood** 15

☑ Polo Lounge | piano | **Beverly Hills** 22

P6 Rest. | DJ | **Westlake Vill** 20

☑ Ritz Huntington | varies | **Pasadena** 26

Romano's Macaroni | varies | **multi. loc.** 17

Saddle Ranch Chop | varies | **multi. loc.** 16

☑ Sir Winston's | piano/vocals | **Long Bch** 23

Sky Room | varies | **Long Bch** 21

Twin Palms | varies | **Pasadena** 17

LOS ANGELES

SPECIAL FEATURES

Velvet Margarita | DJ | **Hollywood** _16_

Vibrato | jazz | **Bel-Air** _22_

Villa Sorriso | DJ | **Pasadena** _18_

Whisper Lounge | jazz/piano | **Fairfax** _16_

Zip Fusion | karaoke | **West LA** _18_

## FAMILY-STYLE

Benihana | multi. loc. _18_

Blue Hen | **Eagle Rock** _16_

Buca di Beppo | multi. loc. _15_

Buddha's Belly | **Beverly Blvd.** _20_

Café Brasil | **Palms** _19_

☑ Campanile | **La Brea** _26_

C & O | **Marina del Rey** _19_

☑ Carousel | multi. loc. _24_

Chop Suey | **Little Tokyo** _11_

☑ Crustacean | **Beverly Hills** _23_

Danube Bulgarian | **Westwood** _15_

Gingergrass | **Silver Lake** _22_

Ita-Cho | **Beverly Blvd.** _24_

Koo Koo Roo | multi. loc. _16_

Lamonica's NY Pizza | **Westwood** _22_

Les Sisters | **Chatsworth** _25_

Loft, The | **Torrance** _17_

Lucille's BBQ | **Long Bch** _22_

Maggiano's | multi. loc. _19_

Mandarette | **W Hollywood** _18_

Maria's Italian | multi. loc. _17_

Miceli's | multi. loc. _17_

Mission 261 | **San Gabriel** _22_

Musha | multi. loc. _25_

Ocean Seafood | **Chinatown** _22_

Ocean Star | **Monterey Pk** _22_

☑ P.F. Chang's | multi. loc. _19_

Riviera Rest. | **Calabasas** _24_

Robin's Woodfire BBQ | **Pasadena** _17_

Romano's Macaroni | multi. loc. _17_

Sapori | **Marina del Rey** _24_

Sea Empress | **Gardena** _19_

South Street | **Burbank** _18_

Spumoni | **Sherman Oaks** _23_

Stonefire Grill | multi. loc. _20_

Toscana | **Brentwood** _24_

Tra Di Noi | **Malibu** _22_

Woody's BBQ | **Leimert Pk** _21_

Xi'an | **Beverly Hills** _22_

Zeke's Smokehse. | multi. loc. _19_

## FIREPLACES

Abbey | **W Hollywood** _16_

Admiral Risty | **Rancho Palos Verdes** _21_

Amalfi | **La Brea** _18_

Axe | **Venice** _22_

NEW Baleen | **Redondo Bch** _22_

Barefoot B&G | **Third St.** _18_

Beau Rivage | **Malibu** _20_

Beckham Grill | **Pasadena** _18_

Bel-Air B&G | **Bel-Air** _19_

☑ Bistro Gdn./Coldwater | **Studio City** _20_

NEW ☑ Blue Velvet | **Downtown** _22_

Bluewater Grill | **Redondo Bch** _20_

boé | **Beverly Hills** _14_

Ca' del Sole | **N Hollywood** _22_

Cafe Del Rey | **Marina del Rey** _23_

Cafe des Artistes | **Hollywood** _19_

☑ Capo | **Santa Monica** _26_

NEW Catch | **Santa Monica** _-_

NEW Celadon | **Third St.** _22_

Chapter 8 Steak | **Agoura Hills** _18_

NEW Charcoal | **Hollywood** _-_

Chart House | multi. loc. _19_

Checkers | **Downtown** _22_

Chez Mimi | **Santa Monica** _21_

Christy's | **Long Bch** _24_

Claim Jumper | multi. loc. _19_

NEW Coupa Cafe | **Beverly Hills** _14_

Crocodile Cafe | multi. loc. _16_

☑ Dal Rae | **Pico Rivera** _26_

Dan Tana's | **W Hollywood** _21_

Derby | **Arcadia** _24_

☑ Derek's | **Pasadena** _27_

Dish | **La Cañada Flintridge** _18_

Dominick's | **Beverly Blvd.** _20_

Doug Arango's | **W Hollywood** _22_

eat. on sunset | **Hollywood** _19_

El Cholo | multi. loc. _18_

El Coyote | **Beverly Blvd.** _13_

NEW Eleven | **W Hollywood** _21_

Fins | **Calabasas** _22_

NEW Foundry/Melrose | **Melrose** _-_

Gardens/Glendon | **Westwood** _19_

Geisha House | **Hollywood** _19_

Gennaro's | **Glendale** _24_

Green Field Churr. | **W Covina** _23_

Guido's | **West LA** _20_

Gulfstream | **Century City** _21_

| | | |
|---|---|---|
| NEW Hadaka Sushi \| W Hollywood | – | |
| Hamlet \| Pasadena | 16 | |
| Z Hotel Bel-Air \| Bel-Air | 26 | |
| Z Houston's \| multi. loc. | 21 | |
| Z Il Cielo \| Beverly Hills | 21 | |
| Z Il Fornaio \| multi. loc. | 20 | |
| Il Pastaio \| Beverly Hills | 25 | |
| Z Inn/Seventh Ray \| Topanga | 21 | |
| Z Ivy, The \| W Hollywood | 22 | |
| James' Bch. \| Venice | 18 | |
| Jer-ne \| Marina del Rey | 22 | |
| JJ Steak \| Pasadena | 20 | |
| Z Josie \| Santa Monica | 27 | |
| Koi \| W Hollywood | 24 | |
| La Parisienne \| Monrovia | 23 | |
| NEW Larchmont Grill \| Hollywood | 21 | |
| La Rive Gauche \| Palos Verdes | 22 | |
| Lasher's \| Long Bch | 24 | |
| Z Lawry's Prime \| Beverly Hills | 25 | |
| Literati \| West LA | 20 | |
| Z Little Door \| Third St. | 23 | |
| Lodge Steak \| Beverly Hills | 20 | |
| Z Lucques \| W Hollywood | 27 | |
| Madeleine's \| Pasadena | 23 | |
| Madre's \| Pasadena | 14 | |
| Maison Akira \| Pasadena | 25 | |
| Marrakesh \| Studio City | 19 | |
| McCormick/Schmick \| multi. loc. | 19 | |
| Z Mélisse \| Santa Monica | 28 | |
| Memphis \| Hollywood | 17 | |
| Michael's \| Santa Monica | 24 | |
| Minx \| Glendale | 19 | |
| Mission 261 \| San Gabriel | 22 | |
| Monty's Steak \| Woodland Hills | 21 | |
| Moroccan Room \| Hollywood | 18 | |
| MOZ Buddha \| Agoura Hills | 20 | |
| Napa Valley \| Westwood | 20 | |
| Next Door/La Loggia \| Studio City | 20 | |
| Nirvana \| Beverly Hills | 20 | |
| Ocean & Vine \| Santa Monica | 22 | |
| Off Vine \| Hollywood | 22 | |
| Z One Pico \| Santa Monica | 23 | |
| Ortolan \| Third St. | 25 | |
| Padri \| Agoura Hills | 21 | |
| Panda Inn \| Ontario | 20 | |
| Paradise Cove \| Malibu | 16 | |
| Z Parkway Grill \| Pasadena | 25 | |

| | |
|---|---|
| Paul's Cafe \| Tarzana | 18 |
| Petrelli's Steak \| Culver City | 17 |
| Piatti \| Thousand Oaks | 20 |
| P6 Rest. \| Westlake Vill | 20 |
| Raymond, The \| Pasadena | 24 |
| Reel Inn \| Malibu | 20 |
| Rive Gauche \| Sherman Oaks | 20 |
| Romano's Macaroni \| multi. loc. | 17 |
| NEW Romanov \| Studio City | – |
| Z Saddle Peak \| Calabasas | 26 |
| NEW Safire \| Camarillo | – |
| Salt Creek \| El Segundo | 18 |
| Smoke House \| Burbank | 19 |
| Sonora Cafe \| La Brea | 21 |
| Spanish Kitchen \| W Hollywood | 17 |
| Spazio \| Sherman Oaks | 19 |
| Stinking Rose \| Beverly Hills | 16 |
| NEW Suki 7 \| Westlake Vill | – |
| Taix \| Echo Pk | 16 |
| Tam O'Shanter \| Atwater Vill | 21 |
| Tanino \| Westwood | 22 |
| Taverna Tony \| Malibu | 21 |
| Tower Bar \| W Hollywood | 22 |
| Ulysses Voyage \| Fairfax | 20 |
| Urth Caffé \| multi. loc. | 21 |
| NEW Vertical Wine \| Pasadena | 19 |
| Vibrato \| Bel-Air | 22 |
| Villa Piacere \| Woodland Hills | 20 |
| Whale & Ale \| San Pedro | 16 |
| Wilshire \| Santa Monica | 21 |
| Woo Lae Oak \| Beverly Hills | 22 |
| NEW Yatai Asian Tapas \| W Hollywood | 19 |
| Ye Olde King's Head \| Santa Monica | 17 |
| NEW Zin Bistro \| Westlake Vill | 21 |

## HISTORIC PLACES

| (Year opened; * building) | |
|---|---|
| 1900 \| Raymond, The* \| Pasadena | 24 |
| 1900 \| Saddle Peak* \| Calabasas | 26 |
| 1906 \| Pete's Cafe* \| Downtown | 18 |
| 1908 \| Off Vine* \| Hollywood | 22 |
| 1908 \| Philippe/Orig. \| Chinatown | 21 |
| 1910 \| Via Veneto* \| Santa Monica | 26 |
| 1910 \| Warszawa* \| Santa Monica | 21 |
| 1911 \| Larkin's* \| Eagle Rock | – |
| 1912 \| Engine Co. 28* \| Downtown | 19 |

| Year | Name | Location | Rating |
|------|------|----------|--------|
| 1912 | Polo Lounge* | Beverly Hills | 22 |
| 1913 | Holly Street* | Pasadena | 21 |
| 1916 | Madison, The* | Long Bch | 21 |
| 1919 | Musso & Frank* | Hollywood | 19 |
| 1920 | Clafoutis* | W Hollywood | 18 |
| 1920 | Farm/Bev. Hills* | Beverly Hills | 19 |
| 1920 | La Paella* | Beverly Hills | 22 |
| 1920 | Lasher's* | Long Bch | 24 |
| 1921 | Pacific Dining Car | Downtown | 22 |
| 1922 | Derby* | Arcadia | 24 |
| 1922 | Second City Bistro* | El Segundo | 22 |
| 1922 | Tam O'Shanter | Atwater Vill | 21 |
| 1923 | El Cholo | Mid-City | 18 |
| 1923 | Farfalla Trattoria* | Los Feliz | 22 |
| 1923 | Lobster, The | Santa Monica | 23 |
| 1924 | Canter's | Fairfax | 18 |
| 1924 | Edendale Grill* | Silver Lake | 15 |
| 1924 | Grub* | Hollywood | 21 |
| 1924 | Original Pantry | Downtown | 16 |
| 1925 | Palm, The* | Downtown | 24 |
| 1925 | Taste* | W Hollywood | 20 |
| 1926 | Greenblatt's Deli | Hollywood | 19 |
| 1926 | Sky Room* | Long Bch | 21 |
| 1927 | Benihana* | Santa Monica | 18 |
| 1927 | Far Niente* | Glendale | 25 |
| 1927 | Pig 'n Whistle* | Hollywood | 15 |
| 1927 | Taix | Echo Pk | 16 |
| 1928 | Cafe Stella* | Silver Lake | 21 |
| 1928 | Ciao Tratt.* | Downtown | 19 |
| 1928 | Tamayo* | East LA | 21 |
| 1929 | Campanile* | La Brea | 26 |
| 1929 | Chateau Marmont* | W Hollywood | 21 |
| 1929 | Tanino* | Westwood | 22 |
| 1929 | Tower Bar* | W Hollywood | 22 |
| 1930 | Brighton Coffee | Beverly Hills | 16 |
| 1931 | El Coyote | Beverly Blvd. | 13 |
| 1931 | Lucques* | W Hollywood | 27 |
| 1931 | Petrelli's Steak | Culver City | 17 |
| 1932 | Fatty's & Co.* | Eagle Rock | 20 |
| 1934 | Galley, The* | Santa Monica | 18 |
| 1936 | Sir Winston's* | Long Bch | 23 |
| 1937 | Damon's Steak | Glendale | 16 |
| 1937 | Traxx | Downtown | 20 |
| 1938 | Du-par's | Fairfax | 16 |
| 1938 | Lawry's Prime | Beverly Hills | 25 |
| 1938 | Paul's Cafe* | Tarzana | 18 |
| 1939 | Formosa Cafe | W Hollywood | 15 |
| 1939 | Luna Park* | La Brea | 19 |
| 1939 | Pink's Chili Dogs | La Brea | 19 |
| 1940 | Il Cielo* | Beverly Hills | 21 |
| 1942 | Mr. Cecil's Ribs* | West LA | 18 |
| 1945 | Dominick's | Beverly Blvd. | 20 |
| 1945 | Nate 'n Al | Beverly Hills | 21 |
| 1946 | Billingsley's | West LA | 14 |
| 1946 | Chili John's | Burbank | 23 |
| 1946 | Hotel Bel-Air | Bel-Air | 26 |
| 1946 | Paradise Cove* | Malibu | 16 |
| 1946 | Smoke House | Burbank | 19 |
| 1946 | Tommy's* | Downtown | 22 |
| 1946 | Uncle Bill's Pancake | Manhattan Bch | 22 |
| 1947 | Apple Pan | West LA | 22 |
| 1947 | Langer's Deli | Downtown | 25 |
| 1948 | Cassell's | Koreatown | 21 |
| 1948 | Factor's Deli | Pico-Robertson | 16 |
| 1948 | Papa Cristo's | Mid-City | 22 |
| 1948 | Reddi Chick BBQ | Brentwood | 23 |
| 1949 | Miceli's | Hollywood | 17 |
| 1950 | Hamlet | W Hollywood | 16 |
| 1952 | Buggy Whip | Westchester | 19 |
| 1952 | Cafe 50's* | West LA | 15 |
| 1952 | Johnnie's Pastrami | Culver City | 20 |
| 1953 | Father's Office | Santa Monica | 24 |
| 1953 | Taylor's Steak | Koreatown | 21 |
| 1954 | El Torito | multi. loc. | 15 |

Peninsula Hotel of Beverly Hills
  🅩 Belvedere | **Beverly Hills**    25

Portofino Hotel & Yacht Club
  NEW Baleen | **Redondo Bch**    22

RenaissancE Hollywood Hotel
  Twist | **Hollywood**    19

Renisssance Long Beach Hotel
  NEW Tracht's | **Long Bch**    ⌐

Ritz-Carlton Huntington
  🅩 Ritz Huntington |    26
  **Pasadena**

Ritz-Carlton Marina del Rey
  Jer-ne | **Marina del Rey**    22

Roosevelt Hotel
  Dakota | **Hollywood**    22
  25 Degrees | **Hollywood**    21

Shutters on the Bch.
  🅩 One Pico | **Santa Monica**    23

Shutters on the Beach
  NEW Coast | **Santa Monica**    ⌐

Sofitel Los Angeles
  Simon LA | **W Hollywood**    21

Standard
  Standard, The | **multi. loc.**    16

Sunset Tower Hotel
  Tower Bar | **W Hollywood**    22

Viceroy Santa Monica
  🅩 Whist | **Santa Monica**    21

Westlake Village Inn
  NEW Mediterraneo/    21
  Westlake | **Westlake Vill**

Wilshire Grand
  Seoul Jung | **Downtown**    22

Wilshire Royale Hotel
  NEW Royale | **Mid-Wilshire**    18

W Los Angeles Westwood
  Nine Thirty | **Westwood**    23

## LATE DINING

(Weekday closing hour)

Abbey | 2 AM | **W Hollywood**    16
Apple Pan | 12 AM | **West LA**    22
Astro Burger | varies |    20
  **multi. loc.**
NEW Ate-1-8 | 12 AM | **Encino**    15
BCD Tofu | varies | **multi. loc.**    20
Berri's Pizza | varies | **Third St.**    17
BIN 8945 | 2 AM | **W Hollywood**    21
Bite | 1 AM | **Marina del Rey**    16
BJ's | 12 AM, varies | **multi. loc.**    17
Bossa Nova | varies | **multi. loc.**    21
Bowery | 2 AM | **Hollywood**    21

Brass.-Cap. | 12 AM |    19
  **Santa Monica**
Cabo Cantina | 12 AM |    12
  **West LA**
Cafe 50's | varies | **multi. loc.**    15
Cafe Sushi | 12 AM |    19
  **Beverly Blvd.**
Canter's | 24 hrs. | **Fairfax**    18
Carney's Express | varies |    19
  **W Hollywood**
Casa Bianca | 12 AM |    23
  **Eagle Rock**
Casa Vega | 1 AM |    18
  **Sherman Oaks**
NEW Charcoal | 12 AM |    ⌐
  **Hollywood**
Citizen Smith | 4 AM |    18
  **Hollywood**
Clafoutis | 12 AM |    18
  **W Hollywood**
Courtyard | 12 AM |    17
  **W Hollywood**
Dan Tana's | 1 AM |    21
  **W Hollywood**
NEW Dive, The | 12 AM |    ⌐
  **Hollywood**
Doña Rosa | varies | **Pasadena**    16
Doughboys | 12 AM | **multi. loc.**    22
Du-par's | varies | **multi. loc.**    16
Electric Lotus | 12 AM |    19
  **Los Feliz**
NEW e3rd Steak | 1 AM |    20
  **Downtown**
Firefly | 12 AM | **Studio City**    20
Fred 62 | 24 hrs. | **Los Feliz**    18
Gaby's Med. | varies |    ⌐
  **multi. loc.**
Geisha House | 12 AM |    19
  **Hollywood**
Greenblatt's Deli | 1:30 AM |    19
  **Hollywood**
NEW Hadaka Sushi | 12 AM |    ⌐
  **W Hollywood**
Hal's B&G | 12:30 AM | **Venice**    20
Hamburger Mary's | 12 AM |    15
  **W Hollywood**
NEW Happi Songs | 12 AM |    ⌐
  **La Brea**
Hop Li | varies | **Arcadia**    18
Hop Woo | varies | **Chinatown**    19
Hungry Cat | 12 AM |    24
  **Hollywood**
Il Capriccio | 12 AM |    22
  **Hollywood**

In-N-Out Burger | 1 AM | multi. loc. `24`

Iroha | 12 AM | **Studio City** `24`

Jan's | 2 AM | **W Hollywood** `14`

Johnnie's Pastrami | varies | **Culver City** `20`

Jones Hollywood | 1:30 AM | **W Hollywood** `18`

Katana | 12 AM | **W Hollywood** `23`

Kate Mantilini | varies | **Beverly Hills** `18`

Kitchen, The | 12 AM | **Silver Lake** `19`

La Dolce Vita | 12 AM | **Beverly Hills** `20`

Lamonica's NY Pizza | varies | **Westwood** `22`

Lola's | 1:30 AM | **W Hollywood** `18`

Lou | 12 AM | **Hollywood** `22`

Macau St. | 12 AM | **Monterey Pk** `20`

Madison, The | 12 AM | **Long Bch** `21`

Magnolia | 3 AM | **Hollywood** `20`

Mäni's | 12 AM | **Fairfax** `18`

Mel's Drive-In | varies | multi. loc. `16`

Memphis | 1 AM | **Hollywood** `17`

Mexicali | 1 AM | **Studio City** `16`

Minibar | 2 AM | **Universal City** `23`

NEW Minotaure | 12 AM | **Playa del Rey** `19`

Mi Piace | varies | **Pasadena** `19`

Mirabelle | 12:30 AM | **W Hollywood** `20`

Monte Alban | 12 AM | **West LA** `22`

Nak Won | 24 hrs. | **Koreatown** `14`

NEW Neomeze | varies | **Pasadena** `-`

Next Door/La Loggia | 12 AM | **Studio City** `20`

Nirvana | 2 AM | **Beverly Hills** `20`

O-Bar | varies | **W Hollywood** `20`

NEW One Sunset | 2 AM | **W Hollywood** `-`

Original Pantry | 24 hrs. | **Downtown** `16`

NEW Osteria Mozza | 12 AM | **Hollywood** `-`

Pacific Dining Car | 24 hrs. | multi. loc. `22`

Palms Thai | 12 AM | **E Hollywood** `23`

Pete's Cafe | 2 AM | **Downtown** `18`

Pho Café | 12 AM | **Silver Lake** `22`

Pike Rest. | 12 AM | **Long Bch** `-`

Pink's Chili Dogs | 2 AM | **La Brea** `19`

Pizza Rustica | varies | **W Hollywood** `17`

NEW Pizzeria Mozza | 12 AM | **Hollywood** `26`

Polo Lounge | 1 AM | **Beverly Hills** `22`

Poquito Más | varies | **Studio City** `22`

NEW Rack | varies | **Woodland Hills** `15`

Rocky Cola | 12 AM | **Hermosa Bch** `-`

Roscoe's | varies | multi. loc. `22`

NEW Ruen Pair | 4 AM | **E Hollywood** `21`

Saddle Ranch Chop | varies | multi. loc. `16`

Sam Woo | 12 AM | multi. loc. `20`

Standard, The | 24 hrs. | multi. loc. `16`

Swingers | varies | multi. loc. `17`

3rd Stop | 12 AM | **W Hollywood** `20`

NEW Tokyo Table | 1 AM | **Beverly Hills** `16`

Tommy's | 24 hrs. | **Downtown** `22`

25 Degrees | 1:30 AM | **Hollywood** `21`

NEW uWink Bistro | 12 AM | **Woodland Hills** `14`

Velvet Margarita | 2 AM | **Hollywood** `16`

NEW Village Idiot | 12 AM | **Melrose** `19`

Wilshire | varies | **Santa Monica** `21`

Wokcano Cafe | 2 AM, varies | multi. loc. `17`

NEW York, The | 2 AM | **Highland Pk** `-`

## LOCAL FAVORITES

Addi's Tandoor | **Redondo Bch** `23`

Amici | **Brentwood** `21`

A.O.C. | **Third St.** `26`

Artisan Cheese | **Studio City** `24`

Babalu | **Santa Monica** `20`

Back Home/Lahaina | **Manhattan Bch** `17`

BCD Tofu | **Downtown** `20`

Beau Rivage | **Malibu** `20`

Bella Cucina | **Hollywood** `19`

| | |
|---|---|
| Bistro de la Gare \| **S Pasadena** | 20 |
| Boneyard Bistro \| **Sherman Oaks** | 20 |
| Bowery \| **Hollywood** | 21 |
| Breadbar \| **W Hollywood** | 19 |
| Buca di Beppo \| **multi. loc.** | 15 |
| Buddha's Belly \| **Beverly Blvd.** | 20 |
| Café Pierre \| **Manhattan Bch** | 22 |
| Café Santorini \| **Pasadena** | 20 |
| Carmine's Italian \| **S Pasadena** | 18 |
| Chaba \| **Redondo Bch** | 20 |
| Chaya \| **Venice** | 23 |
| Christy's \| **Long Bch** | 24 |
| Derby \| **Arcadia** | 24 |
| Doug Arango's \| **W Hollywood** | 22 |
| Dusty's \| **Silver Lake** | 21 |
| Edendale Grill \| **Silver Lake** | 15 |
| El Pollo Inka \| **Lawndale** | 19 |
| El Tepeyac \| **East LA** | 24 |
| Falafel King \| **Westwood** | 18 |
| Fred 62 \| **Los Feliz** | 18 |
| ☑ Frenchy's Bistro \| **Long Bch** | 27 |
| Gale's \| **Pasadena** | 21 |
| Galletto \| **Westlake Vill** | 23 |
| Gladstone's \| **Pacific Palisades** | 15 |
| Hal's B&G \| **Venice** | 20 |
| Harper's \| **Century City** | 16 |
| Il Capriccio \| **Los Feliz** | 22 |
| ☑ Il Fornaio \| **Pasadena** | 20 |
| Il Forno Caldo \| **Beverly Hills** | 20 |
| Indochine Vien \| **Atwater Vill** | 18 |
| Iroha \| **Studio City** | 24 |
| Izayoi \| **Little Tokyo** | 23 |
| Jack n' Jill's \| **Santa Monica** | 19 |
| Jinky's \| **Sherman Oaks** | 20 |
| La Botte \| **Santa Monica** | 24 |
| La Bottega Marino \| **Hancock Pk** | 20 |
| La Crêperie \| **Long Bch** | 23 |
| La Scala \| **Beverly Hills** | 20 |
| La Serenata \| **Boyle Hts** | 23 |
| Les Sisters \| **Chatsworth** | 25 |
| ☑ Lotería! \| **Fairfax** | 24 |
| Lucille's BBQ \| **Long Bch** | 22 |
| Magnolia \| **Hollywood** | 20 |
| Mandevilla \| **Westlake Vill** | 23 |
| Mediterraneo \| **Hermosa Bch** | 20 |
| Mio Babbo's \| **Westwood** | 21 |
| Mission 261 \| **San Gabriel** | 22 |
| Mr. Cecil's Ribs \| **West LA** | 18 |
| Mulberry St. Pizzeria \| **Encino** | 23 |

| | |
|---|---|
| Next Door/La Loggia \| **Studio City** | 20 |
| O-Nami \| **Torrance** | 16 |
| Padri \| **Agoura Hills** | 21 |
| Peppone \| **Brentwood** | 21 |
| Petrelli's Steak \| **Culver City** | 17 |
| ☑ Petros \| **Manhattan Bch** | 23 |
| Roll 'n Rye \| **Culver City** | 18 |
| Rose Cafe \| **Venice** | 18 |
| Saladang \| **Pasadena** | 24 |
| Salt Creek \| **Valencia** | 18 |
| ☑ Shiro \| **S Pasadena** | 27 |
| ☑ Sir Winston's \| **Long Bch** | 23 |
| Stand, The \| **Encino** | 18 |
| Stanley's \| **Sherman Oaks** | 19 |
| Takao \| **Brentwood** | 25 |
| Talésai \| **Studio City** | 22 |
| Toast \| **Third St.** | 20 |
| Trastevere \| **Santa Monica** | 18 |
| Tropicalia Brazil \| **Los Feliz** | 19 |
| 2117 \| **West LA** | 24 |
| Wood Ranch BBQ \| **multi. loc.** | 20 |
| Woody's BBQ \| **Leimert Pk** | 21 |
| W's China \| **Redondo Bch** | 21 |
| Yuzu \| **Torrance** | 23 |
| Zankou Chicken \| **Burbank** | 22 |

### MICROBREWERIES

| | |
|---|---|
| Belmont Brew. \| **Long Bch** | 18 |
| BJ's \| **multi. loc.** | 17 |
| Gordon Biersch \| **multi. loc.** | 17 |
| Heroes B&G \| **Claremont** | 16 |
| Yard House \| **multi. loc.** | 19 |

### NATURAL/ORGANIC

(These restaurants often or always use organic, local ingredients)

| | |
|---|---|
| **NEW** Abode \| **Santa Monica** | 23 |
| A La Tarte \| **Pacific Palisades** | 18 |
| Ammo \| **Hollywood** | 22 |
| A Votre Sante \| **Brentwood** | 20 |
| Baja Fresh Mex. \| **multi. loc.** | 18 |
| **NEW** Baleen \| **Redondo Bch** | 22 |
| **NEW** Bar Hayama \| **West LA** | – |
| BBC \| **multi. loc.** | 20 |
| Beechwood \| **Venice** | 20 |
| Berri's Pizza \| **Playa del Rey** | 17 |
| ☑ Bistro 45 \| **Pasadena** | 26 |
| Bistro 767 \| **Rolling Hills** | 22 |
| **NEW** Bloom Cafe \| **Mid-City** | 23 |
| Blue Hen \| **Eagle Rock** | 16 |
| **NEW** ☑ Blue Velvet \| **Downtown** | 22 |

| | |
|---|---|
| boé \| **Beverly Hills** | 14 |
| Border Grill \| **Santa Monica** | 22 |
| Breeze \| **Century City** | 19 |
| Brentwood, The \| **Brentwood** | 21 |
| ☑ Café 14 \| **Agoura Hills** | 26 |
| Cafe Stella \| **Silver Lake** | 21 |
| **NEW** Canele \| **Atwater Vill** | 24 |
| ☑ Capo \| **Santa Monica** | 26 |
| Cézanne \| **Santa Monica** | 21 |
| Chameau \| **Fairfax** | 24 |
| Chan Dara \| **Hollywood** | 19 |
| Chaya \| **W Hollywood** | 23 |
| Chaya \| **Venice** | 23 |
| Cheebo \| **Hollywood** | 19 |
| Chef Melba's \| **Hermosa Bch** | 23 |
| Chez Allez \| **Palos Verdes** | 21 |
| Chez Melange \| **Redondo Bch** | 25 |
| Chez Mimi \| **Santa Monica** | 21 |
| Chi Dynasty \| **Los Feliz** | 23 |
| Chipotle \| **multi. loc.** | 19 |
| Christy's \| **Long Bch** | 24 |
| ☑ Cicada \| **Downtown** | 23 |
| City Bakery \| **Brentwood** | 18 |
| Ciudad \| **Downtown** | 21 |
| Cooks Dbl. Dutch \| **Culver City** | 22 |
| Coral Tree \| **multi. loc.** | 19 |
| **NEW** Corkscrew Cafe \| **Manhattan Bch** | – |
| Counter, The \| **Santa Monica** | 21 |
| CUBE \| **La Brea** | 25 |
| ☑ Derek's \| **Pasadena** | 27 |
| Dish \| **La Cañada Flintridge** | 18 |
| Dusty's \| **Silver Lake** | 21 |
| eat. on sunset \| **Hollywood** | 19 |
| Farm/Bev. Hills \| **multi. loc.** | 19 |
| Figaro Bistrot \| **Los Feliz** | 18 |
| Ford's Filling Stat. \| **Culver City** | 19 |
| Getty Center \| **Brentwood** | 22 |
| ☑ Hotel Bel-Air \| **Bel-Air** | 26 |
| Hugo's \| **multi. loc.** | 21 |
| Il Grano \| **West LA** | 25 |
| ☑ Inn/Seventh Ray \| **Topanga** | 21 |
| ☑ Ivy, The \| **W Hollywood** | 22 |
| Ivy/Shore \| **Santa Monica** | 21 |
| Jack Sprat's \| **West LA** | 19 |
| ☑ Jar \| **Beverly Blvd.** | 25 |
| ☑ Joe's \| **Venice** | 26 |
| ☑ Josie \| **Santa Monica** | 27 |
| Juliano's Raw \| **Santa Monica** | 21 |
| Kokomo Cafe \| **Fairfax** | 20 |
| La Pergola \| **Sherman Oaks** | 23 |
| Leaf Cuisine \| **multi. loc.** | – |
| Le Pain Quotidien \| **multi. loc.** | 21 |
| Literati \| **West LA** | 20 |
| ☑ Lucques \| **W Hollywood** | 27 |
| Madeleine Bistro \| **Tarzana** | 22 |
| ☑ Mako \| **Beverly Hills** | 26 |
| Mäni's \| **multi. loc.** | 18 |
| Marston's \| **Pasadena** | 23 |
| Mason Jar Cafe \| **W Hollywood** | 17 |
| Massimo \| **Beverly Hills** | 22 |
| Max \| **Sherman Oaks** | 24 |
| ☑ M Café de Chaya \| **Melrose** | 23 |
| ☑ Mélisse \| **Santa Monica** | 28 |
| Michael's \| **Santa Monica** | 24 |
| **NEW** Mike & Anne's \| **S Pasadena** | 20 |
| Mirü8691 \| **Beverly Hills** | 24 |
| Moonshadows \| **Malibu** | 17 |
| Moroccan Room \| **Hollywood** | 18 |
| Morton's \| **W Hollywood** | 23 |
| Napa Valley \| **Westwood** | 20 |
| Native Foods \| **Westwood** | 22 |
| Newsroom Café \| **W Hollywood** | 19 |
| Nic's \| **Beverly Hills** | 21 |
| ☑ One Pico \| **Santa Monica** | 23 |
| **NEW** One Sunset \| **W Hollywood** | – |
| Orris \| **West LA** | 26 |
| Ortolan \| **Third St.** | 25 |
| ☑ Parkway Grill \| **Pasadena** | 25 |
| Pentimento \| **Mid-Wilshire** | 17 |
| ☑ Petros \| **Manhattan Bch** | 23 |
| Piatti \| **Thousand Oaks** | 20 |
| Piccolo Paradiso \| **Beverly Hills** | 24 |
| **NEW** Prana Cafe \| **W Hollywood** | 22 |
| Real Food Daily \| **multi. loc.** | 21 |
| Rose Cafe \| **Venice** | 18 |
| R23 \| **Little Tokyo** | 26 |
| **NEW** Saluzzi \| **Rancho Palos Verdes** | – |
| ☑ Sam's/Beach \| **Santa Monica** | 26 |
| 17th St. Cafe \| **Santa Monica** | 19 |
| Sharky's Mex. \| **multi. loc.** | 17 |
| Shima \| **Venice** | 25 |
| ☑ Sona \| **W Hollywood** | 27 |
| ☑ Spago \| **Beverly Hills** | 27 |
| Table 8 \| **Melrose** | 24 |
| Tender Greens \| **Culver City** | 23 |
| Urasawa \| **Beverly Hills** | 29 |
| Urth Caffé \| **multi. loc.** | 21 |

LOS ANGELES

SPECIAL FEATURES

| | | |
|---|---|---|
| Prime Grill | **Beverly Hills** | 21 |
| Punch Grill | **Santa Monica** | 18 |
| Qusqo | **West LA** | - |
| Raaga | **Chatsworth** | - |
| Rack | **Woodland Hills** | 15 |
| RA Sushi | **Torrance** | 18 |
| Red Seven | **W Hollywood** | - |
| redwhite+bluezz | **Pasadena** | 21 |
| Riordan's Tavern | **Downtown** | - |
| Romanov | **Studio City** | - |
| Royale | **Mid-Wilshire** | 18 |
| Ruen Pair | **E Hollywood** | 21 |
| Rustic Canyon | **Santa Monica** | 21 |
| Safire | **Camarillo** | - |
| Salades/Provence | **W Hollywood** | - |
| Saluzzi | **Rancho Palos Verdes** | - |
| 750 ml | **S Pasadena** | - |
| Shabu Shabu Ya | **La Brea** | 15 |
| Simpang Asia | **West LA** | - |
| Spice Basil | **Alhambra** | - |
| Suki 7 | **Westlake Vill** | - |
| Takami | **Downtown** | - |
| Tanzore | **Beverly Hills** | - |
| 3 Square | **Venice** | 21 |
| Tokyo Table | **Beverly Hills** | 16 |
| Tommy Ray's | **Studio City** | 18 |
| Tracht's | **Long Bch** | - |
| Ummba Grill | **Century City** | 16 |
| uWink Bistro | **Woodland Hills** | 14 |
| Vault, The | **Pasadena** | 15 |
| Vertical Wine | **Pasadena** | 19 |
| Village Idiot | **Melrose** | 19 |
| Watercress | **Sherman Oaks** | - |
| Yatai Asian Tapas | **W Hollywood** | 19 |
| York, The | **Highland Pk** | - |
| Yose | **Santa Monica** | 22 |
| Zin Bistro | **Westlake Vill** | 21 |
| Zu Robata | **West LA** | - |

## OUTDOOR DINING

(G=garden; P=patio; S=sidewalk; T=terrace)

| | | |
|---|---|---|
| A La Tarte | T | **Pacific Palisades** | 18 |
| Alcove | P | **Los Feliz** | 22 |
| Antonio's | S | **Melrose** | 22 |
| Asia de Cuba | P | **W Hollywood** | 24 |
| Babalu | S | **Santa Monica** | 20 |
| Back on Beach | P | **Santa Monica** | 14 |
| Barefoot B&G | P | **Third St.** | 18 |

| | | |
|---|---|---|
| Barney Greengrass | T | **Beverly Hills** | 21 |
| Barney's Hamburgers | P | **Brentwood** | 21 |
| Beacon | P | **Culver City** | 22 |
| Beau Rivage | P | **Malibu** | 20 |
| Beechwood | P | **Venice** | 20 |
| Bel-Air B&G | P | **Bel-Air** | 19 |
| ☑ Belvedere | G, P | **Beverly Hills** | 25 |
| ☑ Bistro K | P | **S Pasadena** | 26 |
| bld | P | **Beverly Blvd.** | 21 |
| blue on blue | T | **Beverly Hills** | 18 |
| NEW BottleRock | P | **Culver City** | 16 |
| Bravo | P | **Santa Monica** | 18 |
| Breadbar | P | **multi. loc.** | 19 |
| Burger Continental | P | **Pasadena** | 16 |
| Ca' del Sole | P | **N Hollywood** | 22 |
| Cafe des Artistes | G | **Hollywood** | 19 |
| Cafe Med | P | **W Hollywood** | 17 |
| Cafe Pinot | P | **Downtown** | 22 |
| Café Santorini | P | **Pasadena** | 20 |
| C & O | P | **Marina del Rey** | 19 |
| Cha Cha Chick. | P | **Santa Monica** | 20 |
| Chapter 8 Steak | P | **Agoura Hills** | 18 |
| Chez Allez | P | **Palos Verdes** | 21 |
| Chez Mimi | G, P | **Santa Monica** | 21 |
| China Grill | P | **Manhattan Bch** | 20 |
| Chocolat | G, P | **Melrose** | 16 |
| Clementine | P, S | **Century City** | 24 |
| Cliff's Edge | G, P | **Silver Lake** | 20 |
| Coral Tree | P | **multi. loc.** | 19 |
| Cora's Coffee | P | **Santa Monica** | 21 |
| Courtyard | P | **W Hollywood** | 17 |
| Dominick's | G | **Beverly Blvd.** | 20 |
| eat. on sunset | P | **Hollywood** | 19 |
| Farm/Bev. Hills | P, S | **multi. loc.** | 19 |
| Fat Fish | P | **W Hollywood** | 20 |
| Fins | P | **multi. loc.** | 22 |
| Firefly | P | **Studio City** | 20 |
| Firefly Bistro | P | **S Pasadena** | 19 |
| Ford's Filling Stat. | S | **Culver City** | 19 |
| NEW Foundry/Melrose | G | **Melrose** | - |
| NEW Fraiche | P | **Culver City** | - |
| ☑ Gardens | G, T | **Beverly Hills** | 25 |

| | |
|---|---|
| ☑ Geoffrey's \| G, P \| **Malibu** | 22 |
| Gladstone's \| T \|<br>**Pacific Palisades** | 15 |
| Gumbo Pot \| P \| **Fairfax** | 21 |
| ☑ Hotel Bel-Air \| T \| **Bel-Air** | 26 |
| Hungry Cat \| P \| **Hollywood** | 24 |
| i Cugini \| P \| **Santa Monica** | 21 |
| ☑ Il Cielo \| G, P \| **Beverly Hills** | 21 |
| Il Moro \| P \| **West LA** | 22 |
| ☑ Inn/Seventh Ray \| G \|<br>**Topanga** | 21 |
| ☑ Ivy, The \| G, P \| **W Hollywood** | 22 |
| Ivy/Shore \| P, T \| **Santa Monica** | 21 |
| James' Bch. \| P \| **Venice** | 18 |
| ☑ Joe's \| P \| **Venice** | 26 |
| Katana \| P \| **W Hollywood** | 23 |
| Koi \| G, P \| **W Hollywood** | 24 |
| L.A. Farm \| G, P \| **Santa Monica** | 20 |
| Lasher's \| P \| **Burbank** | 24 |
| Library Alehse. \| P \|<br>**Santa Monica** | 19 |
| Lilly's French Cafe \| P \| **Venice** | 20 |
| ☑ Little Door \| G, P \| **Third St.** | 23 |
| Locanda/Lago \| P \| **Santa Monica** | 20 |
| ☑ Lotería! \| P \| **Fairfax** | 24 |
| ☑ Lucques \| P \| **W Hollywood** | 27 |
| Marix Tex Mex \| P \| **W Hollywood** | 17 |
| Martha 22nd St. \| S \|<br>**Hermosa Bch** | 22 |
| Mediterraneo \| P \| **Hermosa Bch** | 20 |
| NEW Mediterraneo/Westlake \|<br>T \| **Westlake Vill** | 21 |
| Michael's \| G, P \| **Santa Monica** | 24 |
| Minx \| P, T \| **Glendale** | 19 |
| Mi Piace \| P \| **multi. loc.** | 19 |
| Moonshadows \| T \| **Malibu** | 17 |
| Morels First Floor \| P \| **Fairfax** | 17 |
| NEW Neomeze \| P \| **Pasadena** | – |
| Neptune's Net \| P \| **Malibu** | 17 |
| ☑ Nobu Malibu \| P \| **Malibu** | 28 |
| Noé \| T \| **Downtown** | 25 |
| Off Vine \| G \| **Hollywood** | 22 |
| Padri \| P \| **Agoura Hills** | 21 |
| Pane e Vino \| G, P \| **Beverly Blvd.** | 21 |
| Pink's Chili Dogs \| P \| **La Brea** | 19 |
| ☑ Polo Lounge \| G, P \|<br>**Beverly Hills** | 22 |
| Pomodoro \| P \| **multi. loc.** | 17 |
| Porto's Bakery \| S \| **multi. loc.** | – |
| P6 Rest. \| P \| **Westlake Vill** | 20 |
| Raymond, The \| G, P \| **Pasadena** | 24 |
| Reel Inn \| P \| **Malibu** | 20 |

| | |
|---|---|
| ☑ Ritz Huntington \| G, P \|<br>**Pasadena** | 26 |
| Rose Cafe \| P \| **Venice** | 18 |
| ☑ Saddle Peak \| P, T \|<br>**Calabasas** | 26 |
| NEW Safire \| P \| **Camarillo** | – |
| Salt Creek \| P \| **multi. loc.** | 18 |
| Shack, The \| P \| **multi. loc.** | 18 |
| Sor Tino \| P \| **Brentwood** | 19 |
| ☑ Spago \| P \| **Beverly Hills** | 27 |
| Stand, The \| G, P \| **multi. loc.** | 18 |
| Standard, The \| P \| **multi. loc.** | 16 |
| NEW Suki 7 \| P \| **Westlake Vill** | – |
| Taverna Tony \| P \| **Malibu** | 21 |
| Thousand Cranes \| P \|<br>**Little Tokyo** | 23 |
| Tony P's Dock \| P \|<br>**Marina del Rey** | 17 |
| Tra Di Noi \| P \| **Malibu** | 22 |
| Traxx \| P \| **Downtown** | 20 |
| Twin Palms \| G, P, T \| **Pasadena** | 17 |
| NEW Ummba Grill \| P \|<br>**Century City** | 16 |
| Urth Caffé \| P, S \| **multi. loc.** | 21 |
| Villa Piacere \| P \|<br>**Woodland Hills** | 20 |
| ☑ Whist \| T \| **Santa Monica** | 21 |
| Wood Ranch BBQ \| P \|<br>**multi. loc.** | 20 |
| ☑ Yamashiro \| G \| **Hollywood** | 18 |
| NEW Zin Bistro \| P \|<br>**Westlake Vill** | 21 |

## PEOPLE-WATCHING

| | |
|---|---|
| Abbey \| **W Hollywood** | 16 |
| NEW Abode \| **Santa Monica** | 23 |
| Akwa \| **Santa Monica** | 19 |
| Alcove \| **Los Feliz** | 22 |
| ☑ A.O.C. \| **Third St.** | 26 |
| Asia de Cuba \| **W Hollywood** | 24 |
| Auntie Em's \| **Eagle Rock** | – |
| NEW Bar Hayama \| **West LA** | – |
| Barney Greengrass \|<br>**Beverly Hills** | 21 |
| Beechwood \| **Venice** | 20 |
| Bella Cucina \| **Hollywood** | 19 |
| BIN 8945 \| **W Hollywood** | 21 |
| bld \| **Beverly Blvd.** | 21 |
| NEW ☑ Blue Velvet \| **Downtown** | 22 |
| Blvd \| **Beverly Hills** | 21 |
| Bono's \| **Long Bch** | 21 |
| Bowery \| **Hollywood** | 21 |
| Cabo Cantina \| **West LA** | 12 |

subscribe to zagat.com

| | |
|---|---|
| Standard, The \| **W Hollywood** | 16 |
| Sur \| **W Hollywood** | 21 |
| Sushi Roku \| **multi. loc.** | 22 |
| **NEW** Takami \| **Downtown** | – |
| Tasca Winebar \| **Third St.** | 21 |
| Three on Fourth \| **Santa Monica** | 16 |
| **NEW** 3 Square \| **Venice** | 21 |
| Tiger Lily \| **Los Feliz** | 19 |
| **NEW** Tracht's \| **Long Bch** | – |
| 25 Degrees \| **Hollywood** | 21 |
| Ugo \| **Culver City** | – |
| **NEW** Vertical Wine \| **Pasadena** | 19 |
| **NEW** Village Idiot \| **Melrose** | 19 |
| West \| **Brentwood** | 18 |
| Wilshire \| **Santa Monica** | 21 |
| Wilson \| **Culver City** | 23 |
| **NEW** York, The \| **Highland Pk** | – |

## POWER SCENES

| | |
|---|---|
| Ago \| **W Hollywood** | 21 |
| ☑ Angelini Osteria \| **Beverly Blvd.** | 27 |
| ☑ A.O.C. \| **Third St.** | 26 |
| Barney Greengrass \| **Beverly Hills** | 21 |
| ☑ Belvedere \| **Beverly Hills** | 25 |
| BIN 8945 \| **W Hollywood** | 21 |
| bld \| **Beverly Blvd.** | 21 |
| Blvd \| **Beverly Hills** | 21 |
| Chapter 8 Steak \| **Agoura Hills** | 18 |
| **NEW** Craft \| **Century City** | – |
| ☑ Cut \| **Beverly Hills** | 26 |
| Dominick's \| **Beverly Blvd.** | 20 |
| eat. on sunset \| **Hollywood** | 19 |
| Giorgio Baldi \| **Santa Monica** | 24 |
| **NEW** Gonpachi \| **Beverly Hills** | – |
| ☑ Grace \| **Beverly Blvd.** | 25 |
| ☑ Grill on Alley \| **Beverly Hills** | 24 |
| ☑ Hamasaku \| **West LA** | 27 |
| ☑ Hotel Bel-Air \| **Bel-Air** | 26 |
| ☑ La Cachette \| **Century City** | 27 |
| ☑ Mastro's Steak \| **Beverly Hills** | 25 |
| ☑ Matsuhisa \| **Beverly Hills** | 27 |
| Moroccan Room \| **Hollywood** | 18 |
| Morton's \| **W Hollywood** | 23 |
| Nick & Stef's Steak \| **Downtown** | 22 |
| Ortolan \| **Third St.** | 25 |
| **NEW** Osteria Mozza \| **Hollywood** | – |
| ☑ Palm, The \| **W Hollywood** | 24 |
| ☑ Patina \| **Downtown** | 26 |

| | |
|---|---|
| **NEW** ☑ Pizzeria Mozza \| **Hollywood** | 26 |
| ☑ Providence \| **Hollywood** | 27 |
| ☑ Republic \| **W Hollywood** | 20 |
| Simon LA \| **W Hollywood** | 21 |
| ☑ Sona \| **W Hollywood** | 27 |
| ☑ Spago \| **Beverly Hills** | 27 |
| Sur \| **W Hollywood** | 21 |
| **NEW** Takami \| **Downtown** | – |
| Toscana \| **Brentwood** | 24 |
| **NEW** Tracht's \| **Long Bch** | – |
| ☑ Valentino \| **Santa Monica** | 26 |
| ☑ Water Grill \| **Downtown** | 27 |
| West \| **Brentwood** | 18 |

## PRIVATE ROOMS

(Restaurants charge less at off times; call for capacity)

| | |
|---|---|
| Admiral Risty \| **Rancho Palos Verdes** | 21 |
| Aioli \| **Torrance** | 17 |
| Antonio's \| **Melrose** | 22 |
| ☑ A.O.C. \| **Third St.** | 26 |
| ☑ Arnie Morton's Steak \| **multi. loc.** | 25 |
| Arroyo Chop Hse. \| **Pasadena** | 25 |
| Back on Beach \| **Santa Monica** | 14 |
| Banzai Sushi \| **Calabasas** | 22 |
| Barefoot B&G \| **Third St.** | 18 |
| Beau Rivage \| **Malibu** | 20 |
| Beckham Grill \| **Pasadena** | 18 |
| ☑ Belvedere \| **Beverly Hills** | 25 |
| ☑ Bistro Gdn./Coldwater \| **Studio City** | 20 |
| Bluewater Grill \| **Redondo Bch** | 20 |
| Boa \| **W Hollywood** | 23 |
| boé \| **Beverly Hills** | 14 |
| Bravo \| **Santa Monica** | 18 |
| Buca di Beppo \| **multi. loc.** | 15 |
| Buffalo Club \| **Santa Monica** | 19 |
| Buggy Whip \| **Westchester** | 19 |
| Buona Sera \| **Redondo Bch** | 22 |
| Ca'Brea \| **La Brea** | 22 |
| Ca' del Sole \| **N Hollywood** | 22 |
| ☑ Café Bizou \| **multi. loc.** | 23 |
| Cafe Del Rey \| **Marina del Rey** | 23 |
| Cafe Pinot \| **Downtown** | 22 |
| Café Santorini \| **Pasadena** | 20 |
| ☑ Campanile \| **La Brea** | 26 |
| Canal Club \| **Venice** | 18 |
| C & O \| **Marina del Rey** | 19 |
| Carmine's Italian \| **S Pasadena** | 18 |

| | | | | |
|---|---|---|---|---|
| Castaway | **Burbank** | 17 | ☑ Madison, The | **Long Bch** | 21 |
| Cézanne | **Santa Monica** | 21 | Maggiano's | **multi. loc.** | 19 |
| Chart House | **Redondo Bch** | 19 | Marino | **Hollywood** | 24 |
| Checkers | **Downtown** | 22 | Massimo | **Beverly Hills** | 22 |
| Chez Jay | **Santa Monica** | 16 | ☑ Mastro's Steak | **Beverly Hills** | 25 |
| Chez Melange | **Redondo Bch** | 25 | ☑ Matsuhisa | **Beverly Hills** | 27 |
| Chez Mimi | **Santa Monica** | 21 | McCormick/Schmick | **multi. loc.** | 19 |
| Christine | **Torrance** | 25 | | |
| ☑ Cicada | **Downtown** | 23 | McKenna's | **Long Bch** | 20 |
| Club 41 | **Pasadena** | 19 | Michael's | **Santa Monica** | 24 |
| Courtyard | **W Hollywood** | 17 | Monsoon Cafe | **Santa Monica** | 17 |
| Cucina Paradiso | **Palms** | 21 | Moonshadows | **Malibu** | 17 |
| ☑ Dal Rae | **Pico Rivera** | 26 | Morels French Steak | **Fairfax** | 19 |
| Dar Maghreb | **Hollywood** | 18 | Mr. Chow | **Beverly Hills** | 23 |
| Depot | **Torrance** | 23 | Napa Valley | **Westwood** | 20 |
| Derby | **Arcadia** | 24 | Nick & Stef's Steak | **Downtown** | 22 |
| ☑ Derek's | **Pasadena** | 27 | Nirvana | **Beverly Hills** | 20 |
| Devon | **Monrovia** | 25 | Off Vine | **Hollywood** | 22 |
| Drago | **Santa Monica** | 24 | ☑ One Pico | **Santa Monica** | 23 |
| Duke's | **Malibu** | 17 | Ortolan | **Third St.** | 25 |
| El Cholo | **multi. loc.** | 18 | Pacific Dining Car | **multi. loc.** | 22 |
| El Torito | **multi. loc.** | 15 | ☑ Palm, The | **multi. loc.** | 24 |
| Enoteca Drago | **Beverly Hills** | 21 | ☑ Parkway Grill | **Pasadena** | 25 |
| Fleming Prime | **El Segundo** | 25 | ☑ Patina | **Downtown** | 26 |
| Gaucho Grill | **Studio City** | 18 | Pinot Bistro | **Studio City** | 23 |
| Geisha House | **Hollywood** | 19 | ☑ Polo Lounge | **Beverly Hills** | 22 |
| Giorgio Baldi | **Santa Monica** | 24 | P6 Rest. | **Westlake Vill** | 20 |
| Gladstone's | **Pacific Palisades** | 15 | ☑ Ritz Huntington | **Pasadena** | 26 |
| Gordon Biersch | **multi. loc.** | 17 | R23 | **Little Tokyo** | 26 |
| ☑ Grace | **Beverly Blvd.** | 25 | ☑ Ruth's Chris | **Beverly Hills** | 25 |
| Hal's B&G | **Venice** | 20 | NEW Safire | **Camarillo** | – |
| House of Blues | **W Hollywood** | 15 | Simon LA | **W Hollywood** | 21 |
| ☑ Il Cielo | **Beverly Hills** | 21 | Smitty's Grill | **Pasadena** | 21 |
| ☑ Il Fornaio | **multi. loc.** | 20 | ☑ Sona | **W Hollywood** | 27 |
| Il Moro | **West LA** | 22 | Sonora Cafe | **La Brea** | 21 |
| Il Sole | **W Hollywood** | 23 | ☑ Spago | **Beverly Hills** | 27 |
| ☑ Inn/Seventh Ray | **Topanga** | 21 | NEW Suki 7 | **Westlake Vill** | – |
| James' Bch. | **Venice** | 18 | Tanino | **Westwood** | 22 |
| Joe's Crab | **Long Bch** | 13 | Tantra | **Silver Lake** | 21 |
| John O'Groats | **Rancho Pk** | 20 | Thousand Cranes | **Little Tokyo** | 23 |
| Jones Hollywood | **W Hollywood** | 18 | Urasawa | **Beverly Hills** | 29 |
| Katana | **W Hollywood** | 23 | ☑ Valentino | **Santa Monica** | 26 |
| Kate Mantilini | **Beverly Hills** | 18 | Vibrato | **Bel-Air** | 22 |
| Kendall's Brass. | **Downtown** | 17 | Villa Sorriso | **Pasadena** | 18 |
| King's Fish Hse. | **Long Bch** | 21 | Woo Lae Oak | **Beverly Hills** | 22 |
| ☑ La Cachette | **Century City** | 27 | ☑ Yamashiro | **Hollywood** | 18 |
| La Terza | **Third St.** | 22 | Zucca | **Downtown** | 22 |
| ☑ Lawry's Prime | **Beverly Hills** | 25 | | |
| ☑ Little Door | **Third St.** | 23 | | |
| Lola's | **W Hollywood** | 18 | | |
| L'Opera | **Long Bch** | 24 | | |

## QUIET CONVERSATION

| | | |
|---|---|---|
| A Cow Jumped | **Beverly Hills** | 22 |
| Angolo DiVino | **West LA** | 23 |

| | |
|---|---|
| Asaka | **Rancho Palos Verdes** | 20 |
| NEW Ate-1-8 | **Encino** | 15 |
| NEW Baleen | **Redondo Bch** | 22 |
| NEW Bella Roma | **Pico-Robertson** | – |
| Z Belvedere | **Beverly Hills** | 25 |
| BIN 8945 | **W Hollywood** | 21 |
| NEW Bloom Cafe | **Mid-City** | 23 |
| Blossom | **Downtown** | 22 |
| Blvd | **Beverly Hills** | 21 |
| boé | **Beverly Hills** | 14 |
| Breeze | **Century City** | 19 |
| Z Café 14 | **Agoura Hills** | 26 |
| NEW Caffe Primo | **W Hollywood** | 17 |
| Caffe Roma | **Beverly Hills** | 16 |
| Camden House | **Beverly Hills** | 15 |
| Z Capo | **Santa Monica** | 26 |
| NEW Celadon | **Third St.** | 22 |
| Cézanne | **Santa Monica** | 21 |
| Chaba | **Redondo Bch** | 20 |
| Z Chadaka | **Burbank** | 24 |
| Checkers | **Downtown** | 22 |
| Chez Allez | **Palos Verdes** | 21 |
| Chez Mimi | **Santa Monica** | 21 |
| NEW Circa 55 | **Beverly Hills** | 21 |
| NEW Coast | **Santa Monica** | – |
| NEW Coco Noche | **Manhattan Bch** | 22 |
| NEW Corkscrew Cafe | **Manhattan Bch** | – |
| NEW Coupa Cafe | **Beverly Hills** | 14 |
| CrêpeVine | **Pasadena** | 21 |
| CUBE | **La Brea** | 25 |
| Cucina Paradiso | **Palms** | 21 |
| Dakota | **Hollywood** | 22 |
| Z Derek's | **Pasadena** | 27 |
| Drago | **Santa Monica** | 24 |
| Dusty's | **Silver Lake** | 21 |
| eat. on sunset | **Hollywood** | 19 |
| Enzo & Angela | **West LA** | 21 |
| Five Sixty-One | **Pasadena** | 19 |
| NEW Fraiche | **Culver City** | – |
| Z Gardens | **Beverly Hills** | 25 |
| Z Grace | **Beverly Blvd.** | 25 |
| NEW Hampton's | **Westlake Vill** | 24 |
| Z Hatfield's | **Beverly Blvd.** | 27 |
| NEW Holdren's Steak | **Thousand Oaks** | – |
| Z Hotel Bel-Air | **Bel-Air** | 26 |
| Il Grano | **West LA** | 25 |

| | |
|---|---|
| JJ Steak | **Pasadena** | 20 |
| La Botte | **Santa Monica** | 24 |
| Z La Cachette | **Century City** | 27 |
| La Maschera | **Pasadena** | 22 |
| La Parisienne | **Monrovia** | 23 |
| NEW Larkin's | **Eagle Rock** | – |
| La Sosta | **Hermosa Bch** | 27 |
| Madeleine's | **Pasadena** | 23 |
| Madeo | **W Hollywood** | 26 |
| NEW Magnolia Lounge | **Pasadena** | 16 |
| Marino | **Hollywood** | 24 |
| Z Mélisse | **Santa Monica** | 28 |
| Michael's | **Santa Monica** | 24 |
| Michelia | **Third St.** | 23 |
| Mirü8691 | **Beverly Hills** | 24 |
| Naraya Thai | **Pico-Robertson** | 19 |
| NEW Neomeze | **Pasadena** | – |
| Ocean & Vine | **Santa Monica** | 22 |
| O-Dae San | **Koreatown** | 19 |
| Z One Pico | **Santa Monica** | 23 |
| NEW One Sunset | **W Hollywood** | – |
| NEW On Sunset | **Brentwood** | – |
| Ortolan | **Third St.** | 25 |
| NEW Parc | **Hollywood** | – |
| Z Polo Lounge | **Beverly Hills** | 22 |
| Porto Alegre | **Pasadena** | – |
| NEW Prime Grill | **Beverly Hills** | 21 |
| Z Providence | **Hollywood** | 27 |
| NEW Punch Grill | **Santa Monica** | 18 |
| Raymond, The | **Pasadena** | 24 |
| Red Corner Asia | **E Hollywood** | 22 |
| NEW Riordan's Tavern | **Downtown** | – |
| Z Ritz Huntington | **Pasadena** | 26 |
| Z Ruth's Chris | **Pasadena** | 25 |
| Salt Creek | **El Segundo** | 18 |
| NEW Saluzzi | **Rancho Palos Verdes** | – |
| NEW 750 ml | **S Pasadena** | – |
| Z Sona | **W Hollywood** | 27 |
| Sona's | **Encino** | 17 |
| Sur | **W Hollywood** | 21 |
| Sushi Ozekii | **Beverly Hills** | – |
| NEW Tanzore | **Beverly Hills** | – |
| Tasca Winebar | **Third St.** | 21 |
| 3rd Stop | **W Hollywood** | 20 |
| Thousand Cranes | **Little Tokyo** | 23 |
| Three on Fourth | **Santa Monica** | 16 |
| Tower Bar | **W Hollywood** | 22 |

NEW Tracht's | **Long Bch** | – |
Trails, The | **Los Feliz** | 18 |
Tre Venezie | **Pasadena** | 24 |
Trump's | **Rancho Palos Verdes** | 23 |
Twist | **Hollywood** | 19 |
Ugo | **Culver City** | – |
Upstairs 2 | **West LA** | 23 |
🅩 Valentino | **Santa Monica** | 26 |
Vito | **Santa Monica** | 23 |
NEW Watercress | **Sherman Oaks** | – |
Wilshire | **Santa Monica** | 21 |
Wilson | **Culver City** | 23 |
NEW York, The | **Highland Pk** | – |

## RAW BARS

Bluewater Grill | **Redondo Bch** | 20 |
Canal Club | **Venice** | 18 |
Gladstone's | **Pacific Palisades** | 15 |
Gulfstream | **Century City** | 21 |
Hungry Cat | **Hollywood** | 24 |
Kendall's Brass. | **Downtown** | 17 |
King's Fish Hse. | **multi. loc.** | 21 |
McKenna's | **Long Bch** | 20 |
Neptune's Net | **Malibu** | 17 |
Ocean Ave. | **Santa Monica** | 23 |
Pacifico's | **Culver City** | 16 |
Spanish Kitchen | **W Hollywood** | 17 |
Teru Sushi | **Studio City** | 20 |
🅩 Water Grill | **Downtown** | 27 |

## ROMANTIC PLACES

Adagio | **Woodland Hills** | 23 |
Aphrodisiac | **Century City** | 18 |
NEW Baleen | **Redondo Bch** | 22 |
Beau Rivage | **Malibu** | 20 |
Bella Cucina | **Hollywood** | 19 |
NEW Bella Roma | **Pico-Robertson** | – |
🅩 Belvedere | **Beverly Hills** | 25 |
Bistro de la Gare | **S Pasadena** | 20 |
🅩 Bistro 45 | **Pasadena** | 26 |
Blvd | **Beverly Hills** | 21 |
🅩 Brandywine | **Woodland Hills** | 27 |
Brentwood, The | **Brentwood** | 21 |
Cafe Del Rey | **Marina del Rey** | 23 |
Cafe des Artistes | **Hollywood** | 19 |
Caffe Roma | **Beverly Hills** | 16 |
Camden House | **Beverly Hills** | 15 |
🅩 Capo | **Santa Monica** | 26 |
NEW Catch | **Santa Monica** | – |
NEW Celadon | **Third St.** | 22 |

Cézanne | **Santa Monica** | 21 |
Checkers | **Downtown** | 22 |
Chez Mimi | **Santa Monica** | 21 |
Courtyard | **W Hollywood** | 17 |
NEW Craft | **Century City** | – |
CrêpeVine | **Pasadena** | 21 |
Cucina Paradiso | **Palms** | 21 |
🅩 Derek's | **Pasadena** | 27 |
Dominick's | **Beverly Blvd.** | 20 |
NEW Foundry/Melrose | **Melrose** | – |
NEW Fraiche | **Culver City** | – |
French 75 | **Burbank** | 21 |
🅩 Gardens | **Beverly Hills** | 25 |
🅩 Geoffrey's | **Malibu** | 22 |
Getty Center | **Brentwood** | 22 |
🅩 Grace | **Beverly Blvd.** | 25 |
NEW Hampton's | **Westlake Vill** | 24 |
🅩 Hatfield's | **Beverly Blvd.** | 27 |
🅩 Hotel Bel-Air | **Bel-Air** | 26 |
🅩 Il Cielo | **Beverly Hills** | 21 |
Il Sole | **W Hollywood** | 23 |
🅩 Inn/Seventh Ray | **Topanga** | 21 |
Jer-ne | **Marina del Rey** | 22 |
🅩 Joe's | **Venice** | 26 |
🅩 Josie | **Santa Monica** | 27 |
La Botte | **Santa Monica** | 24 |
🅩 La Cachette | **Century City** | 27 |
L.A. Farm | **Santa Monica** | 20 |
La Maschera | **Pasadena** | 22 |
La Parisienne | **Monrovia** | 23 |
La Sosta | **Hermosa Bch** | 27 |
Le Chêne | **Saugus** | 25 |
Le Marmiton | **Marina del Rey** | 18 |
🅩 Little Door | **Third St.** | 23 |
Lou | **Hollywood** | 22 |
🅩 Lucques | **W Hollywood** | 27 |
Madeleine's | **Pasadena** | 23 |
🅩 Mélisse | **Santa Monica** | 28 |
Michael's | **Santa Monica** | 24 |
Noé | **Downtown** | 25 |
Ortolan | **Third St.** | 25 |
NEW Parc | **Hollywood** | – |
🅩 Patina | **Downtown** | 26 |
🅩 Piccolo | **Venice** | 27 |
Pinot Bistro | **Studio City** | 23 |
Porto Alegre | **Pasadena** | – |
NEW Prime Grill | **Beverly Hills** | 21 |
🅩 Providence | **Hollywood** | 27 |

| | |
|---|---|
| **NEW** Punch Grill \| **Santa Monica** | 18 |
| Raymond, The \| **Pasadena** | 24 |
| **NEW** Red Seven \| **W Hollywood** | – |
| **Z** Ritz Huntington \| **Pasadena** | 26 |
| **NEW** Royale \| **Mid-Wilshire** | 18 |
| **NEW** Rustic Canyon \| **Santa Monica** | 21 |
| **Z** Saddle Peak \| **Calabasas** | 26 |
| Salt Creek \| **El Segundo** | 18 |
| **NEW** 750 ml \| **S Pasadena** | – |
| Simon LA \| **W Hollywood** | 21 |
| **Z** Sir Winston's \| **Long Bch** | 23 |
| Sky Room \| **Long Bch** | 21 |
| **Z** Sona \| **W Hollywood** | 27 |
| Sur \| **W Hollywood** | 21 |
| **NEW** Takami \| **Downtown** | – |
| **NEW** Tanzore \| **Beverly Hills** | – |
| Taste \| **W Hollywood** | 20 |
| Tower Bar \| **W Hollywood** | 22 |
| **NEW** Tracht's \| **Long Bch** | – |
| Trump's \| **Rancho Palos Verdes** | 23 |
| **Z** Valentino \| **Santa Monica** | 26 |
| **NEW** Vertical Wine \| **Pasadena** | 19 |
| Vito \| **Santa Monica** | 23 |
| West \| **Brentwood** | 18 |
| **Z** Yamashiro \| **Hollywood** | 18 |

## SINGLES SCENES

| | |
|---|---|
| Abbey \| **W Hollywood** | 16 |
| Beechwood \| **Venice** | 20 |
| BIN 8945 \| **W Hollywood** | 21 |
| bld \| **Beverly Blvd.** | 21 |
| **NEW Z** Blue Velvet \| **Downtown** | 22 |
| Boa \| **W Hollywood** | 23 |
| Border Grill \| **Santa Monica** | 22 |
| **NEW** BottleRock \| **Culver City** | 16 |
| Bowery \| **Hollywood** | 21 |
| Café Santorini \| **Pasadena** | 20 |
| Caffe Roma \| **Beverly Hills** | 16 |
| Canal Club \| **Venice** | 18 |
| **NEW** Celadon \| **Third St.** | 22 |
| Chapter 8 Steak \| **Agoura Hills** | 18 |
| **NEW** Charcoal \| **Hollywood** | – |
| Chaya \| **W Hollywood** | 23 |
| Chaya \| **Venice** | 23 |
| Cheebo \| **Hollywood** | 19 |
| Chez Jay \| **Santa Monica** | 16 |
| Citizen Smith \| **Hollywood** | 18 |
| Ciudad \| **Downtown** | 21 |
| **NEW** Craft \| **Century City** | – |

| | |
|---|---|
| Dominick's \| **Beverly Blvd.** | 20 |
| El Coyote \| **Beverly Blvd.** | 13 |
| Electric Lotus \| **Los Feliz** | 19 |
| **NEW** Eleven \| **W Hollywood** | 21 |
| **Z** Father's Office \| **Santa Monica** | 24 |
| Ford's Filling Stat. \| **Culver City** | 19 |
| Formosa Cafe \| **W Hollywood** | 15 |
| **NEW** Foundry/Melrose \| **Melrose** | – |
| French 75 \| **Burbank** | 21 |
| Geisha House \| **Hollywood** | 19 |
| Gordon Biersch \| **multi. loc.** | 17 |
| Hal's B&G \| **Venice** | 20 |
| Hama Sushi \| **Venice** | 21 |
| i Cugini \| **Santa Monica** | 21 |
| James' Bch. \| **Venice** | 18 |
| Jones Hollywood \| **W Hollywood** | 18 |
| Katsuya \| **Brentwood** | 24 |
| **NEW** Ketchup \| **W Hollywood** | 16 |
| Koi \| **W Hollywood** | 24 |
| **NEW** Liberty Grill \| **Downtown** | – |
| Lola's \| **W Hollywood** | 18 |
| Magnolia \| **Hollywood** | 20 |
| **NEW** Magnolia Lounge \| **Pasadena** | 16 |
| **NEW** Marty's \| **Highland Pk** | – |
| **Z** Mastro's Steak \| **Beverly Hills** | 25 |
| McCormick/Schmick \| **multi. loc.** | 19 |
| Memphis \| **Hollywood** | 17 |
| Minx \| **Glendale** | 19 |
| Moonshadows \| **Malibu** | 17 |
| Moroccan Room \| **Hollywood** | 18 |
| Morton's \| **W Hollywood** | 23 |
| Next Door/La Loggia \| **Studio City** | 20 |
| Nick & Stef's Steak \| **Downtown** | 22 |
| Ocean Ave. \| **Santa Monica** | 23 |
| **Z** Palm, The \| **W Hollywood** | 24 |
| **NEW** Parc \| **Hollywood** | – |
| **Z** Parkway Grill \| **Pasadena** | 25 |
| **NEW** Penthouse \| **Santa Monica** | 20 |
| **NEW Z** Pizzeria Mozza \| **Hollywood** | 26 |
| Primitivo \| **Venice** | 21 |
| P6 Rest. \| **Westlake Vill** | 20 |
| **NEW** Punch Grill \| **Santa Monica** | 18 |

| | |
|---|---|
| NEW Rack | **Woodland Hills** | 15 |
| NEW RA Sushi | **Torrance** | 18 |
| Rock 'N Fish | **Manhattan Bch** | 21 |
| NEW Royale | **Mid-Wilshire** | 18 |
| NEW Rustic Canyon | **Santa Monica** | 21 |
| NEW Safire | **Camarillo** | – |
| Salt Creek | **El Segundo** | 18 |
| NEW 750 ml | **S Pasadena** | – |
| Simon LA | **W Hollywood** | 21 |
| Standard, The | **W Hollywood** | 16 |
| Stanley's | **Sherman Oaks** | 19 |
| NEW Suki 7 | **Westlake Vill** | – |
| Sushi Roku | **multi. loc.** | 22 |
| Swingers | **Beverly Blvd.** | 17 |
| NEW Takami | **Downtown** | – |
| NEW Tanzore | **Beverly Hills** | – |
| Tasca Winebar | **Third St.** | 21 |
| Tengu | **Westwood** | 22 |
| NEW Tracht's | **Long Bch** | – |
| 25 Degrees | **Hollywood** | 21 |
| Twin Palms | **Pasadena** | 17 |
| Urth Caffé | **W Hollywood** | 21 |
| NEW Vault, The | **Pasadena** | 15 |
| NEW Village Idiot | **Melrose** | 19 |
| Wabi-Sabi | **Venice** | 22 |
| West | **Brentwood** | 18 |
| Wilshire | **Santa Monica** | 21 |
| NEW Yatai Asian Tapas | **W Hollywood** | 19 |
| Ye Olde King's Head | **Santa Monica** | – |
| NEW York, The | **Highland Pk** | – |

## SLEEPERS

(Good to excellent food, but little known)

| | |
|---|---|
| NEW Abode | **Santa Monica** | 23 |
| A Cow Jumped | **Beverly Hills** | 22 |
| Agra Cafe | **Silver Lake** | 22 |
| Ahi Sushi | **Studio City** | 22 |
| Albano's | **Melrose** | 23 |
| NEW All' Angelo | **Hollywood** | 26 |
| Amori | **Monrovia** | 22 |
| Angolo DiVino | **West LA** | 23 |
| Antonio's | **Melrose** | 22 |
| NEW Baleen | **Redondo Bch** | 22 |
| Barsac Brasserie | **N Hollywood** | 23 |
| Benley Viet. | **Long Bch** | 26 |
| Bistro 767 | **Rolling Hills** | 22 |
| Bistro 31 | **Santa Monica** | 23 |
| NEW Bloom Cafe | **Mid-City** | 23 |

| | |
|---|---|
| Blossom | **Downtown** | 22 |
| Bora Bora | **Manhattan Bch** | 23 |
| Boss Sushi | **Beverly Hills** | 24 |
| NEW Briganti | **S Pasadena** | 22 |
| Buona Sera | **Redondo Bch** | 22 |
| Café Pacific | **Rancho Palos Verdes** | 24 |
| Chef Melba's | **Hermosa Bch** | 23 |
| Chichen Itza | **Downtown** | 24 |
| Chili John's | **Burbank** | 23 |
| Cholada | **Malibu** | 26 |
| NEW Coco Noche | **Manhattan Bch** | 22 |
| CUBE | **La Brea** | 25 |
| Derby | **Arcadia** | 24 |
| Devon | **Monrovia** | 25 |
| Fresco | **Glendale** | 22 |
| Gennaro's | **Glendale** | 24 |
| NEW Hampton's | **Westlake Vill** | 24 |
| Harold & Belle's | **Mid-City** | 24 |
| Hayakawa | **Covina** | 26 |
| Il Boccaccio | **Hermosa Bch** | 22 |
| Il Chianti | **Lomita** | 25 |
| NEW Izaka-Ya | **Third St.** | 25 |
| Jackson's Vill. | **Hermosa Bch** | 23 |
| Japon Bistro | **Pasadena** | 23 |
| Kanpai | **Westchester** | 22 |
| La Maschera | **Pasadena** | 22 |
| La Parisienne | **Monrovia** | 23 |
| La Sosta | **Hermosa Bch** | 27 |
| Le Chêne | **Saugus** | 25 |
| Le Sanglier | **Tarzana** | 22 |
| Les Sisters | **Chatsworth** | 25 |
| Madeleine Bistro | **Tarzana** | 22 |
| Magic Carpet | **Pico-Robertson** | 22 |
| Marouch | **E Hollywood** | 24 |
| Minibar | **Universal City** | 23 |
| Mirü8691 | **Beverly Hills** | 24 |
| Nine Thirty | **Westwood** | 23 |
| Nishimura | **W Hollywood** | 28 |
| Omino Sushi | **Chatsworth** | 23 |
| Pat's | **Pico-Robertson** | 22 |
| Pistachio Grill | **Beverly Hills** | 23 |
| NEW Prana Cafe | **W Hollywood** | 22 |
| Prosecco | **Toluca Lake** | 25 |
| Red Corner Asia | **E Hollywood** | 22 |
| Saito's Sushi | **Silver Lake** | 25 |
| Sapori | **Marina del Rey** | 24 |
| Seoul Jung | **Downtown** | 22 |

| | |
|---|---|
| Shima \| **Venice** | 25 |
| Spumoni \| **multi. loc.** | 23 |
| Square One Dining \| **E Hollywood** | 24 |
| Sushi Dokoro \| **Beverly Hills** | 24 |
| Sushi Duke \| **Hermosa Bch** | 25 |
| Sushi Masu \| **West LA** | 26 |
| Sushi Sushi \| **Beverly Hills** | 25 |
| Tony's Bella Vista \| **Burbank** | 22 |
| Tower Bar \| **W Hollywood** | 22 |
| Tsuji No Hana \| **Marina del Rey** | 22 |
| Tulipano \| **Azusa** | 23 |
| Urasawa \| **Beverly Hills** | 29 |
| Vegan Glory \| **Beverly Blvd.** | 24 |
| Viva Madrid \| **Claremont** | 22 |
| Wa \| **W Hollywood** | 27 |
| Yen Sushi \| **multi. loc.** | 23 |
| NEW Yose \| **Santa Monica** | 22 |
| Yuzu \| **Torrance** | 23 |

## SPECIAL OCCASIONS

| | |
|---|---|
| NEW Baleen \| **Redondo Bch** | 22 |
| NEW Bella Roma \| **Pico-Robertson** | – |
| Z Belvedere \| **Beverly Hills** | 25 |
| Z Bistro 45 \| **Pasadena** | 26 |
| NEW Z Blue Velvet \| **Downtown** | 22 |
| Blvd \| **Beverly Hills** | 21 |
| Chapter 8 Steak \| **Agoura Hills** | 18 |
| Z Chinois/Main \| **Santa Monica** | 26 |
| Z Cicada \| **Downtown** | 23 |
| NEW Circa 55 \| **Beverly Hills** | 21 |
| NEW Coast \| **Santa Monica** | – |
| NEW Craft \| **Century City** | – |
| Z Cut \| **Beverly Hills** | 26 |
| Drago \| **Santa Monica** | 24 |
| NEW E. Baldi \| **Beverly Hills** | 21 |
| Fleming Prime \| **Woodland Hills** | 25 |
| NEW Foundry/Melrose \| **Melrose** | – |
| NEW Fraiche \| **Culver City** | – |
| French 75 \| **Burbank** | 21 |
| Z Grace \| **Beverly Blvd.** | 25 |
| NEW Hampton's \| **Westlake Vill** | 24 |
| Z Hatfield's \| **Beverly Blvd.** | 27 |
| Z Hotel Bel-Air \| **Bel-Air** | 26 |
| Z Jar \| **Beverly Blvd.** | 25 |
| Z Joe's \| **Venice** | 26 |
| Z Josie \| **Santa Monica** | 27 |
| La Botte \| **Santa Monica** | 24 |
| Z La Cachette \| **Century City** | 27 |

| | |
|---|---|
| La Maschera \| **Pasadena** | 22 |
| Madeleine's \| **Pasadena** | 23 |
| Marino \| **Hollywood** | 24 |
| Z Mastro's Steak \| **Beverly Hills** | 25 |
| Z Matsuhisa \| **Beverly Hills** | 27 |
| Minx \| **Glendale** | 19 |
| Moroccan Room \| **Hollywood** | 18 |
| Noé \| **Downtown** | 25 |
| Ocean & Vine \| **Santa Monica** | 22 |
| Z One Pico \| **Santa Monica** | 23 |
| Ortolan \| **Third St.** | 25 |
| NEW Osteria Mozza \| **Hollywood** | – |
| Z Palm, The \| **W Hollywood** | 24 |
| Z Patina \| **Downtown** | 26 |
| NEW Penthouse \| **Santa Monica** | 20 |
| Z Petros \| **Manhattan Bch** | 23 |
| NEW Phoenicia \| **Glendale** | – |
| Z Providence \| **Hollywood** | 27 |
| NEW Riordan's Tavern \| **Downtown** | – |
| NEW Royale \| **Mid-Wilshire** | 18 |
| Roy's \| **multi. loc.** | 24 |
| Ruth's Chris \| **Pasadena** | 25 |
| Z Saddle Peak \| **Calabasas** | 26 |
| NEW Safire \| **Camarillo** | – |
| Z Sona \| **W Hollywood** | 27 |
| Z Spago \| **Beverly Hills** | 27 |
| Tower Bar \| **W Hollywood** | 22 |
| NEW Tracht's \| **Long Bch** | – |
| Trump's \| **Rancho Palos Verdes** | 23 |
| Z Tuscany \| **Westlake Vill** | 27 |
| Urasawa \| **Beverly Hills** | 29 |
| Z Valentino \| **Santa Monica** | 26 |
| Z Water Grill \| **Downtown** | 27 |

## TASTING MENUS

| | |
|---|---|
| NEW Abode \| **Santa Monica** | 23 |
| Z Asanebo \| **Studio City** | 28 |
| Azami \| **Hollywood** | – |
| NEW Bar Hayama \| **West LA** | – |
| BIN 8945 \| **W Hollywood** | 21 |
| NEW Z Blue Velvet \| **Downtown** | 22 |
| Boss Sushi \| **Beverly Hills** | 24 |
| Brass.-Cap. \| **Santa Monica** | 19 |
| Cafe Pinot \| **Downtown** | 22 |
| Z Campanile \| **La Brea** | 26 |
| Z Capo \| **Santa Monica** | 26 |
| Z Carousel \| **Glendale** | 24 |
| Christine \| **Torrance** | 25 |

Cicada | **Downtown** 23
Derek's | **Pasadena** 27
Devon | **Monrovia** 25
NEW e3rd Steak | **Downtown** 20
NEW Foundry/Melrose | **Melrose** —
Grace | **Beverly Blvd.** 25
NEW Hadaka Sushi | **W Hollywood** —
Hamasaku | **West LA** 27
Hatfield's | **Beverly Blvd.** 27
Hayakawa | **Covina** 26
Hirozen | **Beverly Blvd.** 25
NEW Hokusai | **Beverly Hills** —
i Cugini | **Santa Monica** 21
Il Cielo | **Beverly Hills** 21
Il Grano | **West LA** 25
Inn/Seventh Ray | **Topanga** 21
Japon Bistro | **Pasadena** 23
Joe's | **Venice** 26
Katsuya | **Brentwood** 24
Koutoubia | **Westwood** 20
K-Zo | **Culver City** —
La Botte | **Santa Monica** 24
La Cachette | **Century City** 27
L.A. Farm | **Santa Monica** 20
La Maschera | **Pasadena** 22
Maison Akira | **Pasadena** 25
Matsuhisa | **Beverly Hills** 27
Mélisse | **Santa Monica** 28
Michael's | **Santa Monica** 24
Mori Sushi | **West LA** 26
Napa Valley | **Westwood** 20
Next Door/La Loggia | **Studio City** 20
Nobu Malibu | **Malibu** 28
Noé | **Downtown** 25
Opus | **Mid-Wilshire** 22
Ortolan | **Third St.** 25
Patina | **Downtown** 26
Piccolo | **Venice** 27
Polo Lounge | **Beverly Hills** 22
Raymond, The | **Pasadena** 24
Ritz Huntington | **Pasadena** 26
Seoul Jung | **Downtown** 22
Sona | **W Hollywood** 27
Spago | **Beverly Hills** 27
Sushi Roku | **Third St.** 22
Sushi Sasabune | **West LA** 26
Sushi Sushi | **Beverly Hills** 25
Taiko | **El Segundo** 21

Takao | **Brentwood** 25
Towne | **Manhattan Bch** 19
Tuscany | **Westlake Vill** 27
Urasawa | **Beverly Hills** 29
Valentino | **Santa Monica** 26
Vincenti | **Brentwood** 25
Wa | **W Hollywood** 27
Water Grill | **Downtown** 27
Wilson | **Culver City** 23
Yabu | **W Hollywood** 23
Yuzu | **Torrance** 23

## TRENDY

NEW Abode | **Santa Monica** 23
Ago | **W Hollywood** 21
Akwa | **Santa Monica** 19
NEW All' Angelo | **Hollywood** 26
Ammo | **Hollywood** 22
Aphrodisiac | **Century City** 18
Asia de Cuba | **W Hollywood** 24
NEW Ate-1-8 | **Encino** 15
Auntie Em's | **Eagle Rock** —
Beacon | **Culver City** 22
Beechwood | **Venice** 20
Bella Cucina | **Hollywood** 19
BIN 8945 | **W Hollywood** 21
Blair's | **Silver Lake** 23
bld | **Beverly Blvd.** 21
Blowfish Sushi | **W Hollywood** 20
blue on blue | **Beverly Hills** 18
NEW Blue Velvet | **Downtown** 22
Boa | **W Hollywood** 23
NEW BottleRock | **Culver City** 16
Bowery | **Hollywood** 21
Café Beaujolais | **Eagle Rock** —
Cafe Stella | **Silver Lake** 21
Caffe Roma | **Beverly Hills** 16
NEW Canele | **Atwater Vill** 24
NEW Celadon | **Third St.** 22
Chameau | **Fairfax** 24
Chapter 8 Steak | **Agoura Hills** 18
NEW Charcoal | **Hollywood** —
Chateau Marmont | **W Hollywood** 21
Chaya | **Venice** 23
NEW Circa 55 | **Beverly Hills** 21
Citizen Smith | **Hollywood** 18
Cliff's Edge | **Silver Lake** 20
NEW Coast | **Santa Monica** —
Cobras/Matadors | **Beverly Blvd.** 21

| Restaurant | Rating |
|---|---|
| NEW Coccole Lab. \| **Redondo Bch** | 21 |
| NEW Craft \| **Century City** | – |
| CUBE \| **La Brea** | 25 |
| Z Cut \| **Beverly Hills** | 26 |
| Dakota \| **Hollywood** | 22 |
| NEW Danny's Venice \| **Venice** | 18 |
| NEW Dive, The \| **Hollywood** | – |
| Dolce Enoteca \| **Melrose** | 16 |
| Doughboys \| **Hollywood** | 22 |
| Eat Well Cafe \| **Beverly Blvd.** | 15 |
| NEW E. Baldi \| **Beverly Hills** | 21 |
| Edendale Grill \| **Silver Lake** | 15 |
| Electric Lotus \| **Los Feliz** | 19 |
| NEW Eleven \| **W Hollywood** | 21 |
| NEW e3rd Steak \| **Downtown** | 20 |
| Ford's Filling Stat. \| **Culver City** | 19 |
| NEW Foundry/Melrose \| **Melrose** | – |
| NEW Fraiche \| **Culver City** | – |
| Geisha House \| **Hollywood** | 19 |
| Giorgio Baldi \| **Santa Monica** | 24 |
| NEW Gonpachi \| **Beverly Hills** | – |
| Griddle Cafe \| **Hollywood** | 22 |
| NEW Hadaka Sushi \| **W Hollywood** | – |
| Hama Sushi \| **Venice** | 21 |
| NEW Happi Songs \| **La Brea** | – |
| Z Hatfield's \| **Beverly Blvd.** | 27 |
| NEW Holy Cow Indian \| **Third St.** | – |
| Hump, The \| **Santa Monica** | 25 |
| Hungry Cat \| **Hollywood** | 24 |
| NEW Izaka-Ya \| **Third St.** | 25 |
| Z Jar \| **Beverly Blvd.** | 25 |
| Jones Hollywood \| **W Hollywood** | 18 |
| NEW J Rest. \| **Downtown** | 13 |
| Katana \| **W Hollywood** | 23 |
| Z Katsu-ya \| **multi. loc.** | 27 |
| Katsuya \| **Brentwood** | 24 |
| NEW Ketchup \| **W Hollywood** | 16 |
| Koi \| **W Hollywood** | 24 |
| Kokomo Cafe \| **Fairfax** | 20 |
| K-Zo \| **Culver City** | – |
| NEW Larchmont Grill \| **Hollywood** | 21 |
| NEW Larkin's \| **Eagle Rock** | – |
| NEW Liberty Grill \| **Downtown** | – |
| Literati \| **West LA** | 20 |
| Z Little Door \| **Third St.** | 23 |
| Lodge Steak \| **Beverly Hills** | 20 |
| Lou \| **Hollywood** | 22 |
| Lucky Devils \| **Hollywood** | 21 |
| Macau St. \| **Monterey Pk** | 20 |
| Madre's \| **Pasadena** | 14 |
| Magnolia \| **Hollywood** | 20 |
| NEW Magnolia Lounge \| **Pasadena** | 16 |
| Malo \| **Silver Lake** | 17 |
| NEW Marty's \| **Highland Pk** | – |
| Z Mastro's Steak \| **Beverly Hills** | 25 |
| Z M Café de Chaya \| **Melrose** | 23 |
| Memphis \| **Hollywood** | 17 |
| Mia Sushi \| **Eagle Rock** | 20 |
| Minibar \| **Universal City** | 23 |
| NEW Minotaure \| **Playa del Rey** | 19 |
| Minx \| **Glendale** | 19 |
| Moroccan Room \| **Hollywood** | 18 |
| NEW Murano \| **W Hollywood** | – |
| NEW Neomeze \| **Pasadena** | – |
| Next Door/La Loggia \| **Studio City** | 20 |
| Nine Thirty \| **Westwood** | 23 |
| Z Nobu Malibu \| **Malibu** | 28 |
| Nook Bistro \| **West LA** | 24 |
| NEW Oinkster, The \| **Eagle Rock** | 21 |
| NEW One Sunset \| **W Hollywood** | – |
| Orris \| **West LA** | 26 |
| Ortolan \| **Third St.** | 25 |
| NEW Osteria Mozza \| **Hollywood** | – |
| NEW Parc \| **Hollywood** | – |
| Pastis \| **Beverly Blvd.** | 22 |
| NEW Penthouse \| **Santa Monica** | 20 |
| NEW Pink Taco \| **Century City** | – |
| NEW Z Pizzeria Mozza \| **Hollywood** | 26 |
| NEW Prana Cafe \| **W Hollywood** | 22 |
| NEW Prime Grill \| **Beverly Hills** | 21 |
| P6 Rest. \| **Westlake Vill** | 20 |
| NEW Punch Grill \| **Santa Monica** | 18 |
| NEW RA Sushi \| **Torrance** | 18 |
| NEW Red Seven \| **W Hollywood** | – |
| Z Republic \| **W Hollywood** | 20 |
| NEW Riordan's Tavern \| **Downtown** | – |
| Rock 'N Fish \| **Manhattan Bch** | 21 |
| NEW Royale \| **Mid-Wilshire** | 18 |

subscribe to zagat.com

| | |
|---|---|
| R23 \| **Little Tokyo** | 26 |
| **NEW** Safire \| **Camarillo** | – |
| **NEW** 750 ml \| **S Pasadena** | – |
| SHU \| **Bel-Air** | 20 |
| Simon LA \| **W Hollywood** | 21 |
| **Z** Sona \| **W Hollywood** | 27 |
| Square One Dining \| **E Hollywood** | 24 |
| Standard, The \| **W Hollywood** | 16 |
| **NEW** Suki 7 \| **Westlake Vill** | – |
| Sur \| **W Hollywood** | 21 |
| Sushi Roku \| **multi. loc.** | 22 |
| Table 8 \| **Melrose** | 24 |
| **NEW** Takami \| **Downtown** | – |
| Tantra \| **Silver Lake** | 21 |
| Tasca Winebar \| **Third St.** | 21 |
| Taste \| **W Hollywood** | 20 |
| 3rd Stop \| **W Hollywood** | 20 |
| Three on Fourth \| **Santa Monica** | 16 |
| Tiger Lily \| **Los Feliz** | 19 |
| **NEW** Tokyo Table \| **Beverly Hills** | 16 |
| **NEW** Tracht's \| **Long Bch** | – |
| 25 Degrees \| **Hollywood** | 21 |
| Urth Caffé \| **W Hollywood** | 21 |
| **NEW** Vault, The \| **Pasadena** | 15 |
| Velvet Margarita \| **Hollywood** | 16 |
| **NEW** Vertical Wine \| **Pasadena** | 19 |
| **NEW** Village Idiot \| **Melrose** | 19 |
| Wabi-Sabi \| **Venice** | 22 |
| West \| **Brentwood** | 18 |
| Wilshire \| **Santa Monica** | 21 |
| Wilson \| **Culver City** | 23 |
| **NEW** Yatai Asian Tapas \| **W Hollywood** | 19 |
| **NEW** York, The \| **Highland Pk** | – |
| Zip Fusion \| **West LA** | 18 |
| **NEW** Zu Robata \| **West LA** | – |

## VIEWS

| | |
|---|---|
| Adagio \| **Woodland Hills** | 23 |
| Admiral Risty \| **Rancho Palos Verdes** | 21 |
| Alessio \| **Westlake Vill** | 22 |
| Asia de Cuba \| **W Hollywood** | 24 |
| Back on Beach \| **Santa Monica** | 14 |
| **NEW** Baleen \| **Redondo Bch** | 22 |
| Barney Greengrass \| **Beverly Hills** | 21 |
| Beau Rivage \| **Malibu** | 20 |
| Belmont Brew. \| **Long Bch** | 18 |
| Bite \| **Marina del Rey** | 16 |

| | |
|---|---|
| **NEW** **Z** Blue Velvet \| **Downtown** | 22 |
| Cafe Del Rey \| **Marina del Rey** | 23 |
| **NEW** Catch \| **Santa Monica** | – |
| Chart House \| **multi. loc.** | 19 |
| Clafoutis \| **W Hollywood** | 18 |
| Duke's \| **Malibu** | 17 |
| El Torito \| **Marina del Rey** | 15 |
| Fins \| **Calabasas** | 22 |
| **Z** Geoffrey's \| **Malibu** | 22 |
| Getty Center \| **Brentwood** | 22 |
| Gladstone's \| **Pacific Palisades** | 15 |
| **NEW** Hampton's \| **Westlake Vill** | 24 |
| Hump, The \| **Santa Monica** | 25 |
| **Z** Inn/Seventh Ray \| **Topanga** | 21 |
| Ivy/Shore \| **Santa Monica** | 21 |
| Jer-ne \| **Marina del Rey** | 22 |
| Kincaid's \| **Redondo Bch** | 21 |
| **Z** Lobster, The \| **Santa Monica** | 23 |
| Malibu Seafood \| **Malibu** | 21 |
| Martha 22nd St. \| **Hermosa Bch** | 22 |
| McKenna's \| **Long Bch** | 20 |
| **NEW** Mediterraneo/Westlake \| **Westlake Vill** | 21 |
| Minx \| **Glendale** | 19 |
| Moonshadows \| **Malibu** | 17 |
| Neptune's Net \| **Malibu** | 17 |
| Noé \| **Downtown** | 25 |
| Odyssey \| **Granada Hills** | 14 |
| **Z** One Pico \| **Santa Monica** | 23 |
| Paradise Cove \| **Malibu** | 16 |
| Parker's Lighthse. \| **Long Bch** | 18 |
| Patrick's \| **Santa Monica** | 16 |
| **NEW** Penthouse \| **Santa Monica** | 20 |
| Reel Inn \| **Malibu** | 20 |
| **Z** Saddle Peak \| **Calabasas** | 26 |
| **NEW** Saluzzi \| **Rancho Palos Verdes** | – |
| Sapori \| **Marina del Rey** | 24 |
| **Z** Sir Winston's \| **Long Bch** | 23 |
| Sky Room \| **Long Bch** | 21 |
| Taverna Tony \| **Malibu** | 21 |
| Thousand Cranes \| **Little Tokyo** | 23 |
| Tony P's Dock \| **Marina del Rey** | 17 |
| Tower Bar \| **W Hollywood** | 22 |
| 22nd St. Landing \| **San Pedro** | 18 |
| Typhoon \| **Santa Monica** | 21 |
| West \| **Brentwood** | 18 |
| **Z** Yamashiro \| **Hollywood** | 18 |
| Yard House \| **Long Bch** | 19 |

Zazou | **Redondo Bch** 24
NEW Zin Bistro | **Westlake Vill** 21

## VISITORS ON EXPENSE ACCOUNT

NEW Abode | **Santa Monica** 23
Ago | **W Hollywood** 21
Z A.O.C. | **Third St.** 26
Aphrodisiac | **Century City** 18
Z Arnie Morton's Steak | **multi. loc.** 25
Arroyo Chop Hse. | **Pasadena** 25
NEW Baleen | **Redondo Bch** 22
Z Belvedere | **Beverly Hills** 25
NEW Z Blue Velvet | **Downtown** 22
Blvd | **Beverly Hills** 21
Boa | **W Hollywood** 23
Brass.-Cap. | **Santa Monica** 19
Buffalo Club | **Santa Monica** 19
Z Campanile | **La Brea** 26
Z Capo | **Santa Monica** 26
NEW Catch | **Santa Monica** –
NEW Celadon | **Third St.** 22
Celestino | **Pasadena** 23
Chapter 8 Steak | **Agoura Hills** 18
Chaya | **W Hollywood** 23
Chaya | **Venice** 23
Checkers | **Downtown** 22
Z Chinois/Main | **Santa Monica** 26
Z Cicada | **Downtown** 23
NEW Circa 55 | **Beverly Hills** 21
NEW Craft | **Century City** –
Z Crustacean | **Beverly Hills** 23
Z Cut | **Beverly Hills** 26
Dakota | **Hollywood** 22
Devon | **Monrovia** 25
Dominick's | **Beverly Blvd.** 20
Drago | **Santa Monica** 24
eat. on sunset | **Hollywood** 19
NEW E. Baldi | **Beverly Hills** 21
Fogo de Chão | **Beverly Hills** 23
French 75 | **Burbank** 21
Z Gardens | **Beverly Hills** 25
Geisha House | **Hollywood** 19
Z Geoffrey's | **Malibu** 22
Z Grace | **Beverly Blvd.** 25
Grill on Hollywood | **Hollywood** 19
NEW Hampton's | **Westlake Vill** 24
Z Hatfield's | **Beverly Blvd.** 27

NEW Holdren's Steak | **Thousand Oaks** –
Hump, The | **Santa Monica** 25
Z Ivy, The | **W Hollywood** 22
Ivy/Shore | **Santa Monica** 21
Z Jar | **Beverly Blvd.** 25
Jer-ne | **Marina del Rey** 22
Z JiRaffe | **Santa Monica** 26
Z Joe's | **Venice** 26
Z Josie | **Santa Monica** 27
Z La Cachette | **Century City** 27
Z Little Door | **Third St.** 23
Z Lobster, The | **Santa Monica** 23
L'Opera | **Long Bch** 24
Z Lucques | **W Hollywood** 27
Madeleine's | **Pasadena** 23
Z Mako | **Beverly Hills** 26
Z Mastro's Steak | **Beverly Hills** 25
Z Matsuhisa | **Beverly Hills** 27
Z Mélisse | **Santa Monica** 28
Michael's | **Santa Monica** 24
Moroccan Room | **Hollywood** 18
Morton's | **W Hollywood** 23
Mr. Chow | **Beverly Hills** 23
Nick & Stef's Steak | **Downtown** 22
Nic's | **Beverly Hills** 21
Z Nobu Malibu | **Malibu** 28
Z One Pico | **Santa Monica** 23
NEW One Sunset | **W Hollywood** –
Opus | **Mid-Wilshire** 22
Ortolan | **Third St.** 25
NEW Osteria Mozza | **Hollywood** –
Pacific Dining Car | **multi. loc.** 22
Z Palm, The | **W Hollywood** 24
Z Parkway Grill | **Pasadena** 25
Z Patina | **Downtown** 26
NEW Penthouse | **Santa Monica** 20
Z Petros | **Manhattan Bch** 23
Z Polo Lounge | **Beverly Hills** 22
Z Providence | **Hollywood** 27
Raymond, The | **Pasadena** 24
Z Republic | **W Hollywood** 20
Z Ritz Huntington | **Pasadena** 26
NEW Romanov | **Studio City** –
Z Roy's | **multi. loc.** 24
Z Ruth's Chris | **Pasadena** 25
Z Saddle Peak | **Calabasas** 26
Salt Creek | **El Segundo** 18

| | |
|---|---|
| Shiro \| **S Pasadena** | 27 |
| SHU \| **Bel-Air** | 20 |
| Simon LA \| **W Hollywood** | 21 |
| Sona \| **W Hollywood** | 27 |
| Sur \| **W Hollywood** | 21 |
| Sushi Nozawa \| **Studio City** | 27 |
| Sushi Roku \| **multi. loc.** | 22 |
| Takao \| **Brentwood** | 25 |
| NEW Tracht's \| **Long Bch** | - |
| Trump's \| **Rancho Palos Verdes** | 23 |
| Valentino \| **Santa Monica** | 26 |
| Vincenti \| **Brentwood** | 25 |
| Water Grill \| **Downtown** | 27 |
| West \| **Brentwood** | 18 |
| Wilshire \| **Santa Monica** | 21 |
| Yujean Kang's \| **Pasadena** | 26 |

## WATERSIDE

| | |
|---|---|
| Back on Beach \| **Santa Monica** | 14 |
| NEW Baleen \| **Redondo Bch** | 22 |
| BBC \| **Malibu** | 20 |
| Belmont Brew. \| **Long Bch** | 18 |
| blue on blue \| **Beverly Hills** | 18 |
| Bluewater Grill \| **Redondo Bch** | 20 |
| Boa \| **Santa Monica** | 23 |
| Cafe Del Rey \| **Marina del Rey** | 23 |
| NEW Catch \| **Santa Monica** | - |
| Chart House \| **multi. loc.** | 19 |
| Cheesecake Fact. \| **Redondo Bch** | 20 |
| Duke's \| **Malibu** | 17 |
| El Torito \| **Redondo Bch** | 15 |
| Fins \| **Calabasas** | 22 |
| Gaby's Med. \| **Marina del Rey** | - |
| Geoffrey's \| **Malibu** | 22 |
| Gladstone's \| **Pacific Palisades** | 15 |
| Guido's \| **Malibu** | 20 |
| Il Boccaccio \| **Hermosa Bch** | 22 |
| Inn/Seventh Ray \| **Topanga** | 21 |
| Ivy/Shore \| **Santa Monica** | 21 |
| Jer-ne \| **Marina del Rey** | 22 |
| Jody Maroni's \| **Venice** | 19 |
| Joe's Crab \| **multi. loc.** | 13 |
| Kincaid's \| **Redondo Bch** | 21 |
| Le Marmiton \| **Marina del Rey** | 18 |
| Lobster, The \| **Santa Monica** | 23 |
| Malibu Seafood \| **Malibu** | 21 |
| Martha 22nd St. \| **Hermosa Bch** | 22 |
| McKenna's \| **Long Bch** | 20 |
| NEW Mediterraneo/Westlake \| **Westlake Vill** | 21 |

| | |
|---|---|
| Moonshadows \| **Malibu** | 17 |
| Neptune's Net \| **Malibu** | 17 |
| One Pico \| **Santa Monica** | 23 |
| Paradise Cove \| **Malibu** | 16 |
| Parker's Lighthse. \| **Long Bch** | 18 |
| Patrick's \| **Santa Monica** | 16 |
| NEW Penthouse \| **Santa Monica** | 20 |
| Ruby's \| **Redondo Bch** | 16 |
| NEW Saluzzi \| **Rancho Palos Verdes** | - |
| Sapori \| **Marina del Rey** | 24 |
| Sir Winston's \| **Long Bch** | 23 |
| Sky Room \| **Long Bch** | 21 |
| Tony P's Dock \| **Marina del Rey** | 17 |
| 22nd St. Landing \| **San Pedro** | 18 |
| Yard House \| **Long Bch** | 19 |
| NEW Zin Bistro \| **Westlake Vill** | 21 |

## WINE BARS

| | |
|---|---|
| Alessio \| **Northridge** | 22 |
| A.O.C. \| **Third St.** | 26 |
| Bellavino \| **Westlake Vill** | 21 |
| BIN 8945 \| **W Hollywood** | 21 |
| NEW BottleRock \| **Culver City** | 16 |
| Broadway Deli \| **Santa Monica** | 14 |
| Cafe Stella \| **Silver Lake** | 21 |
| C & O \| **Marina del Rey** | 19 |
| NEW Coco Noche \| **Manhattan Bch** | 22 |
| NEW Corkscrew Cafe \| **Manhattan Bch** | - |
| CrêpeVine \| **Pasadena** | 21 |
| Enoteca Drago \| **Beverly Hills** | 21 |
| Enoteca Toscana \| **Camarillo** | 18 |
| Fleming Prime \| **multi. loc.** | 25 |
| Frenchy's Bistro \| **Long Bch** | 27 |
| Hungry Cat \| **Hollywood** | 24 |
| La Sosta \| **Hermosa Bch** | 27 |
| Leila's \| **Oak Pk** | 27 |
| Lilly's French Cafe \| **Venice** | 20 |
| NEW Minotaure \| **Playa del Rey** | 19 |
| Monsieur Marcel \| **Fairfax** | 19 |
| NEW Neomeze \| **Pasadena** | - |
| Next Door/La Loggia \| **Studio City** | 20 |
| Petrossian \| **W Hollywood** | - |
| Primitivo \| **Venice** | 21 |
| NEW 750 ml \| **S Pasadena** | - |
| Tasca Winebar \| **Third St.** | 21 |
| Tropicalia Brazil \| **Los Feliz** | 19 |
| 25 Degrees \| **Hollywood** | 21 |

Upstairs 2 | **West LA** 23

NEW Vertical Wine | **Pasadena** 19

Violet | **Santa Monica** 21

Wine Bistro | **Studio City** 23

## WINNING WINE LISTS

NEW Abode | **Santa Monica** 23

A Cow Jumped | **Beverly Hills** 22

Ago | **W Hollywood** 21

NEW All' Angelo | **Hollywood** 26

Z A.O.C. | **Third St.** 26

Arroyo Chop Hse. | **Pasadena** 25

Avenue | **Manhattan Bch** 23

NEW Baleen | **Redondo Bch** 22

Beacon | **Culver City** 22

Beechwood | **Venice** 20

NEW Bella Roma | **Pico-Robertson** –

BIN 8945 | **W Hollywood** 21

Z Bistro 45 | **Pasadena** 26

Bistro Provence | **Burbank** 22

bld | **Beverly Blvd.** 21

NEW Z Blue Velvet | **Downtown** 22

Blvd | **Beverly Hills** 21

Boa | **Santa Monica** 23

NEW BottleRock | **Culver City** 16

Brass.-Cap. | **Santa Monica** 19

Cafe Del Rey | **Marina del Rey** 23

Cafe Pinot | **Downtown** 22

Z Campanile | **La Brea** 26

Checkers | **Downtown** 22

Chez Melange | **Redondo Bch** 25

Z Chinois/Main | **Santa Monica** 26

NEW Circa 55 | **Beverly Hills** 21

NEW Coccole Lab. | **Redondo Bch** 21

NEW Coco Noche | **Manhattan Bch** 22

NEW Craft | **Century City** –

Z Cut | **Beverly Hills** 26

Dakota | **Hollywood** 22

Drago | **Santa Monica** 24

eat. on sunset | **Hollywood** 19

NEW E. Baldi | **Beverly Hills** 21

555 East | **Long Bch** 25

Fleming Prime | **Woodland Hills** 25

NEW Foundry/Melrose | **Melrose** –

NEW Fraiche | **Culver City** –

French 75 | **Burbank** 21

NEW Gonpachi | **Beverly Hills** –

Z Grace | **Beverly Blvd.** 25

Z Grill on Alley | **Beverly Hills** 24

NEW Hampton's | **Westlake Vill** 24

Z Hatfield's | **Beverly Blvd.** 27

Z Hotel Bel-Air | **Bel-Air** 26

Il Moro | **West LA** 22

Z Ivy, The | **W Hollywood** 22

Jer-ne | **Marina del Rey** 22

Z JiRaffe | **Santa Monica** 26

Kendall's Brass. | **Downtown** 17

King's Fish Hse. | **Calabasas** 21

La Botte | **Santa Monica** 24

Z La Cachette | **Century City** 27

La Maschera | **Pasadena** 22

Z Lucques | **W Hollywood** 27

Madeleine's | **Pasadena** 23

Z Mélisse | **Santa Monica** 28

Michael's | **Santa Monica** 24

Minx | **Glendale** 19

Moroccan Room | **Hollywood** 18

Morton's | **W Hollywood** 23

Napa Valley | **Westwood** 20

NEW Neomeze | **Pasadena** –

Next Door/La Loggia | **Studio City** 20

Nick & Stef's Steak | **Downtown** 22

Ocean Ave. | **Santa Monica** 23

NEW One Sunset | **W Hollywood** –

NEW On Sunset | **Brentwood** –

Opus | **Mid-Wilshire** 22

Ortolan | **Third St.** 25

Pacific Dining Car | **multi. loc.** 22

NEW Parc | **Hollywood** –

Z Parkway Grill | **Pasadena** 25

Z Patina | **Downtown** 26

NEW Penthouse | **Santa Monica** 20

Peppone | **Brentwood** 21

Pinot Bistro | **Studio City** 23

Pizzicotto | **Brentwood** 23

Primitivo | **Venice** 21

Raymond, The | **Pasadena** 24

NEW redwhite+bluezz | **Pasadena** 21

Z Republic | **W Hollywood** 20

NEW Riordan's Tavern | **Downtown** –

Z Roy's | **Downtown** 24

Z Ruth's Chris | **Pasadena** 25

NEW Safire | **Camarillo** –

# ORANGE COUNTY

# Top Food

Ratings are to the left of names.

28 Basilic
Stonehill Tavern

27 Tradition/Pascal
Napa Rose
Hobbit, The

Studio

26 Tabu Grill
Cafe Zoolu
Golden Truffle
Ramos House

# Top Decor

27 Studio
162', Rest.
Stonehill Tavern

26 Summit House
First Cabin

Napa Rose

25 Mastro's Ocean Club
Splashes
Leatherby's Cafe Rouge
Chat Noir

# Top Service

28 Hobbit, The

27 Napa Rose

26 Studio
La Vie en Rose
Stonehill Tavern

25 Ritz Rest./Gdn.
Antonello
Tradition/Pascal
Basilic
Mr. Stox

# Best Buys

In order of Bang for the Buck rating.

1. In-N-Out Burger
2. Jerry's/Dogs
3. Portillo's Hot Dogs
4. Jody Maroni's
5. Baja Fresh Mex.
6. Taco Mesa
7. Pho 79
8. Original Pancake
9. Sharky's Mexican
10. Zankou Chicken

## BY LOCATION

ANAHEIM

27 Napa Rose
25 Morton's Steak
24 Mr. Stox

CORONA DEL MAR

24 Five Crowns
23 Oysters
22 Rothschild's

COSTA MESA

26 Golden Truffle
25 Mastro's Steak
Pinot Provence

IRVINE

25 Ruth's Chris
24 Bistango
Wasa

LAGUNA BEACH

27 Studio
26 Tabu Grill
Cafe Zoolu

NEWPORT BEACH

28 Basilic
27 Tradition/Pascal
25 Bayside

### Abe *Japanese*

| | 25 | 13 | 21 | $49 |

**Newport Beach** | 2900 Newport Blvd. (29th St.) | 949-675-1739 |
www.restaurantabe.com

This "nondescript" Balboa Peninsula sushi bar may be "easy to miss", but plenty of fin fans manage to wriggle in for "absolutely fabulous", "inventive" fare that's "precious and pleasing to the eye"; since founder Takashi Abe (now of Bluefin) is no longer attached, some lament the service is "spotty" and "it's just not the same", however, finatics note "it's still one of the best" "by far in OC, if not SoCal"; N.B. insiders tout the $28 omakase lunch.

### Agora Churrascaria *Brazilian*

| | 24 | 19 | 21 | $47 |

**Irvine** | 1830 Main St. (MacArthur Blvd.) | 949-222-9910 |
www.agoranow.com

"Juicy saber-skewered meats" are carved tableside "by gauchos" at this Brazilian "temple of meat" in Irvine where carnivores convene for "way, way too much food" ("pace yourself"), and a "bountiful" buffet of "salads and side dishes" satisfies those "who prefer lighter fare"; if it "seems a little pricey" even for "special occasions", penny-pinchers point to "lunch" as a "better deal."

### Aire *Eclectic*

| | 23 | 22 | 21 | $38 |

**Costa Mesa** | The Camp | 2937 Bristol St. (Rte. 73) | 714-751-7099 |
www.aireglobal.com

Tucked into the southern reaches of The Camp, this Costa Mesa "hipster hangout" with bamboo walls "almost feels like a trendy LA nightclub" say scenesters who are also wowed by chef Troy Furuta's "innovative" Eclectic dishes served in "tapas portions" ("go with a group to sample more food"); true, you may "pay less" elsewhere, but this "enjoyable" spot has a "great vibe" thanks in part to live DJs who keep the energy "upbeat and fun."

### Alvarado's Kitchen *Californian*

| | ▽ 22 | 14 | 19 | $31 |

**Anaheim Hills** | 430 S. Anaheim Hills Rd. (Nohl Ranch Rd.) | 714-279-0550

This "cozy" Anaheim Hills "jewel" lures a "loyal following" with Cal cuisine that's "very original for the area", and boosted by a "great wine selection"; add "welcoming" service plus fair pricing, and it's no wonder it generates the kind of "word-of-mouth advertising" that keeps it "always busy"; N.B. the Decor score does not reflect a recent move.

### Amazon Churrascaria *Brazilian*

| | ▽ 16 | 13 | 15 | $29 |

**Fullerton** | 1445 S. Lemon St. (bet. Orangethorpe Ave. & Rte. 91) |
714-447-1200 | www.amazonbbq.com

"One of the most reasonable Brazilian churrascarias in SoCal" awaits in freeway-adjacent Fullerton where "ample servings" of "about 15 kinds of meat" are sliced up in a rainforest setting that offers a "taste of the wild side"; carnivores may only have eyes for those sizzling skewers, but herbivores appreciate the "huge buffet of non-meat items" including a "fantastic, fresh" salad bar.

### Ambrosia 🅢Ⓜ *French*

| | ▽ 24 | 24 | 22 | $56 |

**Santa Ana** | OC Pavilion | 801 N. Main St. (8th St.) | 714-550-0880 |
www.ocpavilion.com

Arching palms, "comfy" leather booths, long-stemmed roses on the tables and "live jazz" create a "special occasion" aura at this Santa

Ana New French set in a repurposed bank, where chef Michael Rossi (ex Napa Rose) relies on "fresh, high-quality ingredients" and showy, tableside preparations come courtesy of a "top-notch" "cast of characters"; if dinner seems too "expensive", try "half-price appetizers and discounted drinks" at happy hour.

### Anaheim White House  *Italian*

24 | 22 | 24 | $54

**Anaheim** | 887 S. Anaheim Blvd. (Ball Rd.) | 714-772-1381 |
www.anaheimwhitehouse.com

A "go-to place" "when you want something special", this "stately" restored Anaheim manor house with silk-draped ceilings provides "over-the-top" meals of "divine" Northern Italian specialties plated in "eye-catching" presentations; hospitality is "polished" "beyond expectations" (owner "Bruno Serato is a maestro of charm"), and while protestors may balk at the price and find the setting overly "florid", they're outvoted by constituents who insist this "OC classic" "makes dining out an event."

### ☑ Antonello  ⬚ *Italian*

24 | 23 | 25 | $51

**Santa Ana** | 3800 Plaza Dr. (Sunflower Ave.) | 714-751-7153 |
www.antonello.com

South Coast Plaza's "inviting" Italian "perennial" pampers an "upscale" power-broker clientele with "polished, professional" service, "wonderfully authentic" fare and an extensive array of vintages (there's a "great grappa selection" too); though critics may find the ersatz piazza setting a bit "dated", supporters find the overall package "still head and shoulders" over most other trattorias in the area.

### Baja Fresh Mexican Grill  *Mexican*

18 | 10 | 14 | $10

**Brea** | 2445 Imperial Hwy. (Kraemer Blvd.) | 714-671-9992
**Costa Mesa** | 171 E. 17th St. (bet. Fullerton & Orange Aves.) |
949-722-2994
**Irvine** | Main Plaza | 2540 Main St. (Jamboree Rd.) |
949-261-2214 ⬚
**Laguna Hills** | 26548 Moulton Pkwy. (La Paz Rd.) | 949-360-4222
**Santa Ana** | 2220 E. 17th St. (Tustin Ave.) | 714-973-1943
www.bajafresh.com
Additional locations throughout Southern California
See review in Los Angeles Directory.

### bambu  *Californian*

– | – | – | VE

**Newport Beach** | Fairmont Newport Bch. | 4500 MacArthur Blvd.
(bet. Campus Dr. & Jamboree Rd.) | 949-476-2001 |
www.fairmont.com

The Fairmont Newport Beach's lobby-level dining room (formerly Accents) has been transformed with bamboo detailing and lush greenery to match the new Asian- and French-influenced Californian menu; premium cocktails and live music enliven the adjacent lounge while Sundays continue the location's enduring custom of the laying out a lavish champagne brunch buffet.

### Bandera  *American/Southwestern*

22 | 20 | 20 | $35

**Corona del Mar** | 3201 E. PCH (Marguerite Ave.) | 949-673-3524 |
www.hillstone.com
See review in Los Angeles Directory.

### ☑ Basilic ☒Ⓜ French/Swiss

| 28 | 20 | 25 | $53 |

**Newport Beach** | 217 Marine Ave. (Park Ave.) | 949-673-0570 |
www.basilicrestaurant.com

Francophile fans "don't want to share the secret" of this "cute, minute" Newport Beach bistro, voted No. 1 for Food in Orange County, but word's out that chef-owner Bernard Althaus "is a master" of "delicately prepared", "delectable" French-Swiss dishes while "five-star" service further polishes this "gem"; if a minority murmurs it "caters to the easily impressed" at "decidedly high prices", boosters boast that this *très romantique* spot "just gets better and better"; P.S. "limited seating" (24 maximum) makes "reservations necessary."

### Bayside American

| 25 | 23 | 23 | $50 |

**Newport Beach** | 900 Bayside Dr. (Jamboree Rd.) | 949-721-1222 |
www.baysiderestaurant.com

"Nothing on the menu fails to please" at this Newport "upscale" New American "favorite" where "imaginative" dishes are served in a sleek setting with bay views, rotating art exhibits, a "great patio" and a "scene at the bar"; usually "attentive" service "can be spotty" on "busy weekends" (especially during Sunday's champagne brunch) when the "elite" "over-40 OC crowd" holds court.

### BCD Tofu House ◗ Korean

| 20 | 10 | 12 | $15 |

**Garden Grove** | 9520 Garden Grove Blvd. (Gilbert St.) | 714-636-5599 |
www.bcdtofu.com

See review in Los Angeles Directory.

### Beachcomber Café, The Californian

| 17 | 21 | 17 | $30 |

**Newport Coast** | Crystal Cove State Bch. | 15 Crystal Cove (PCH) |
949-376-6900 | www.thebeachcombercafe.com

"It's all about the view" of the water and the "enchanting" location at historic Crystal Cove's converted cottage eatery that's "right on the sand" "with waves practically lapping at your feet"; the Californian cuisine "could be better", and a "too young" staff "needs help", but nevertheless, "long lines form at all hours" so savvy surveyors suggest "breakfast" is best; N.B. shuttles from the state lot provide access.

### BeachFire Californian

| 18 | 15 | 15 | $30 |

**San Clemente** | 204 Avenida Del Mar (N. Ola Vista St.) | 949-366-3232 |
www.beachfire.com

A "lively" scene and some "tasty bar food" attract "tourists, business locals" and a "younger beach-going crowd" to this "cool" Californian hang on San Clemente's "quaint" Del Mar; critics cite "inconsistent" eats and "tacky" decor, but at least it's a "fun" place to "meet friends" (there's live music Tuesday–Saturday) or bask on the patio on "sunny afternoons", which are "the norm here."

### Benihana Japanese

| 18 | 16 | 19 | $36 |

**Anaheim** | 2100 E. Ball Rd. (State College Blvd.) | 714-774-4940
**Newport Beach** | 4250 Birch St. (bet. Corinthian Way & Dove St.) |
949-955-0822
www.benihana.com

See review in Los Angeles Directory.

| | FOOD | DECOR | SERVICE | COST |
|---|---|---|---|---|

### Bistango  *American* 

| 24 | 24 | 22 | $46 |

**Irvine** | 19100 Von Karman Ave. (bet. Campus Dr. & DuPont Ave.) | 949-752-5222 | www.bistango.com

"Wild modern art on the walls" and "scrumptious" New American "art on the plate" set the scene at Irvine's "hip" atrium where luxe touches like the "superb" wine list, "wonderful" "fresh-baked" dessert soufflés and "accommodating" servers make it "spot on" for "yuppie" "business lunches" or "romantic dates"; there's a live soundtrack of "soft jazz" every night while "people-watching" provides additional entertainment.

### BJ's  *Pub Food*

| 17 | 16 | 16 | $19 |

**Brea** | 600 Brea Mall Dr. (Imperial Hwy.) | 714-990-2095
**Huntington Beach** | 200 Main St. (Walnut Ave.) | 714-374-2224
**Laguna Beach** | 280 S. Coast Hwy. (bet. Forest & Ocean Aves.) | 949-494-3802
**Laguna Hills** | 24032 El Toro Rd. (Paseo De Valencia) | 949-900-2670
**Newport Beach** | 106 Main St. (Balboa Blvd.) | 949-675-7560
www.bjsbrewhouse.com
Additional locations throughout Southern California
See review in Los Angeles Directory.

### Black Sheep Bistro  🗷 🅼 *French/Spanish*

| 24 | 16 | 21 | $40 |

**Tustin** | 303 El Camino Real (3rd St.) | 714-544-6060 | www.blacksheepbistro.com

"Tucked away" from the herd in vintage Old Town, this Tustin "neighborhood" "find" warms fans with "outstanding" Spanish-French bistro cuisine ("the paella is a must" but takes about an hour unless you request it in advance) and an "intelligent", "well-priced" wine list; yes, the "cozy" digs "may not be much to speak of", but "welcoming" owners Rick and Diana Bouffard keep followers coming b-a-a-a-ck.

### Blue Coral  *Seafood*

| 22 | 23 | 20 | $53 |

**Newport Beach** | Fashion Island | 451 Newport Center Dr. (bet. San Miguel & San Nicolas Drs.) | 949-856-2583 | www.bluecoralseafood.com

"Trendy" Newporters navigate "lively" waters at Fashion Island's "glam" seafooder serving "rich", "delicious" dishes and "stellar libations" concocted from the "impressive" vodka selection at the luminescent bar; although some find the menu and service "outmatched" by the "sophisticated" setting, and "expect more for the cost" in general, all agree it's "not your grandfather's fish restaurant."

### Bluefin  *Japanese*

| 25 | 20 | 21 | $57 |

**Newport Coast** | Crystal Cove Promenade | 7952 E. PCH (Crystal Heights Dr.) | 949-715-7373 | www.bluefinbyabe.com

Connoisseurs call the "cutting-edge" sushi and other Japanese creations from "master" chef-owner Takashi Abe "a marvel" at Crystal Cove's "sleek" spot for "world-class" feasts aided by "exquisite sakes" and a "slight view" of the Pacific; while guests can expect to "pay dearly" for the "unforgettable experience", insiders know the "lunch omakase" is a "gourmet bargain"; P.S. reservations are a "must" on weekends.

### Bluewater Grill  *American/Seafood*

| 20 | 18 | 19 | $33 |

**Newport Beach** | 630 Lido Park Dr. (Lafayette St.) | 949-675-3474 | www.bluewatergrill.com
See review in Los Angeles Directory.

| | FOOD | DECOR | SERVICE | COST |
|---|---|---|---|---|

### Britta's Café  *American*  | 20 | 17 | 17 | $34 |

**Irvine** | University Ctr. | 4237 Campus Dr. (Stanford Ct.) | 949-509-1211 | www.brittascafe.com

"Yes, there is a Britta!" gush Irvine admirers of chef-owner Britta Pulliam's American "home cookin'" with European accents fit for "foodies"; despite uneven service, the "pretty", sofa-dotted digs are inviting, especially for the "great Sunday brunch", as well as nights "before the Barclay" or "indie films playing next door."

### NEW  Brodard Chateau  *Vietnamese*  ▽ 24 | 17 | 17 | $22 |

**Garden Grove** | 9100 Trask Ave. (bet. Gilbert & Magnolia Sts.) | 714-899-8273 | www.brodard.net

"Dynamite Vietnamese" draws guests to Garden Grove's two-story "modern" manor offering a reasonably priced menu (even if it is a touch "more expensive than others" in the Little Saigon zone); diners advise "don't expect too much from the service", but you can count on "lots of variety" for "both vegetarians and carnivores", including "burrito-sized spring rolls" that some boast are the "best in OC."

### Brussels Bistro  *Belgian*  | 17 | 14 | 20 | $33 |

**Laguna Beach** | 222 Forest Ave., downstairs (S. PCH) | 949-376-7955 | www.brusselsbistro.com

A "knowledgeable staff" guides brew buffs through a "fantastic selection" of Belgian beers at this Laguna "basement" boîte; most don't mind that the "wonderful" pommes frites tend to outshine the otherwise "good bistro cuisine", since they're coming for a "cool hangout" where DJs and musicians stir up a "lively" vibe.

### Buca di Beppo  *Italian*  | 15 | 17 | 17 | $24 |

**Brea** | 1609 E. Imperial Hwy. (Associated Rd.) | 714-529-6262
**Garden Grove** | 11757 Harbor Blvd. (Wilken Way) | 714-740-2822
**Huntington Beach** | 7979 Center Ave. (off I-405) | 714-891-4666
**Irvine** | 13390 Jamboree Rd. (Irvine Blvd.) | 714-665-0800
www.bucadibeppo.com

See review in Los Angeles Directory.

### Bukhara  *Indian*  | - | - | - | M |

**Huntington Beach** | 7594 Edinger Ave. (bet. Gothard St. & Sher Ln.) | 714-842-3171

Huntington Beach's family-run Indian attracts local lunchers with its reasonable midday buffet and pulls dinner customers from farther afield with authentic cookery that doesn't skimp on spices; the small storefront digs won't win design awards but Sunday's champagne brunch is a reliable feast for low dough.

### Bungalow, The  *Seafood/Steak*  | 21 | 18 | 19 | $48 |

**Corona del Mar** | 2441 E. PCH (MacArthur Blvd.) | 949-673-6585 | www.thebungalowrestaurant.com

This posh CdM "staple" supplies well-heeled locals with "excellent" surf 'n' turf washed down with "tasty" martinis in a "dark" Craftsman-style space, decked out with velvet booths and a patio and staffed by "friendly" servers; critics judge it "a little tired" and "self-impressed", but that's no deterrent to "people-watching" in the "standing-room-only" bar – a "classic singles haunt."

|  | FOOD | DECOR | SERVICE | COST |
|---|---|---|---|---|

### Café Hidalgo  *Southwestern*
▽ 19 | 16 | 19 | $24

**Fullerton** | Villa del Sol | 305 N. Harbor Blvd. (bet. Chapman & Commonwealth Aves.) | 714-447-3202 | www.cafehidalgofullerton.com
Southwestern eats "match the atmosphere" at this "cozy" Fullerton hang where patrons relax in the "character-rich" Spanish courtyard, chow on steak chimichurri and sip "one of the best sangrias made in OC"; although critics cite "forgettable" fare, regulars report "never a bad experience."

### Café Hiro  Ⓜ *Asian*
▽ 24 | 12 | 20 | $25

**Cypress** | 10509 Valley View St. (Cerritos Ave.) | 714-527-6090
Regulars recommend "sitting at the bar" of this "extremely small" "hidden gem" in Cypress, where you can watch chef-owner Hiro Ohiwa prepare "fantastic" fusions of Asian, French and Italian dishes that you "can't get anywhere else", providing "Euro-Japanese at its best" for "Denny's prices."

### Café R&D  *American*
21 | 18 | 19 | $32

**Newport Beach** | Fashion Island | 555 Newport Center Dr. (San Miguel Dr.) | 949-219-0555 | www.hillstone.com
"The Houston's group has done it right" at this "chic" Newport Beach eatery serving a "small menu" of "smashingly good" American eats like "fabulous" salads and French dip sandwiches that cater to "post-shopping refueling" in Fashion Island; a "no-reservations policy" means "perpetual" waits to land one of the leather banquettes, but at least the "people-watching" helps tide patrons over.

### Café Tu Tu Tango  ❶ *Eclectic*
20 | 21 | 17 | $26

**Orange** | The Block at Orange | 20 City Blvd. W. (City Dr.) | 714-769-2222 | www.cafetututango.com
See review in Los Angeles Directory.

### ☑ Cafe Zoolu  Ⓜ *Californian*
26 | 13 | 20 | $40

**Laguna Beach** | 860 Glenneyre St. (bet. St. Anne's Dr. & Thalia St.) | 949-494-6825 | www.cafezoolu.com
"One of Laguna's few remaining old funky spots", this "tiny, out-of-the-way" Californian "sleeper" earns raves for "flavors that demand attention" in dishes such as the "unbelievably thick" charbroiled swordfish, which "reigns supreme here"; along with an "eclectic" staff, the "terrific" mom-and-pop owners make sure that their "in-the-know" diners are "happy as clams", but since the "campy", Polynesian-themed "bungalow" seats only 33, "don't try it without a reservation."

### Californian, The  *Californian*
▽ 23 | 21 | 22 | $52

**Huntington Beach** | Hyatt Regency Huntington Bch. | 21500 PCH (Beach Blvd.) | 714-845-4776 | www.huntingtonbeach.hyatt.com
"Couture" cuisine in a "beautiful", "casual setting" is the draw at this "contemporary" Californian in the Hyatt Regency Huntington Beach; its adept service and indoor/outdoor tables overlooking the courtyard set the stage for an "ocean view brunch", as well as dinners worth splurging on "when you want to impress *and* enjoy your food."

### California Pizza Kitchen  *Pizza*
18 | 14 | 16 | $20

**Brea** | Brea Mall | 1065 Brea Mall, upper level (Imperial Hwy.) | 714-672-0407
**Irvine** | Park Pl. | 2957 Michelson Dr. (Jamboree Rd.) | 949-975-1585

*(continued)*

## California Pizza Kitchen

**Mission Viejo** | 25513 Marguerite Pkwy. (bet. La Paz Rd. & Oso Pkwy.) | 949-951-5026

**Santa Ana** | Santa Ana Mainplace Mall | 2800 N. Main St., upper level (Town And Country Rd.) | 714-479-0604

**Tustin** | The Market Place | 3001 El Camino Real (Jamboree Rd.) | 714-838-5083

www.cpk.com

Additional locations throughout Southern California

See review in Los Angeles Directory.

## California Wok  *Chinese*            18 | 8 | 16 | $16

**Costa Mesa** | 3033 Bristol St. (bet. Baker St. & Paularino Ave.) | 714-751-0673

See review in Los Angeles Directory.

## Cannery Seafood of the Pacific  *Seafood*   22 | 23 | 20 | $46

**Newport Beach** | 3010 Lafayette Ave. (30th St.) | 949-566-0060 | www.cannerynewport.com

A "top choice" "overlooking the bay" in Newport, this "well-rounded" "upscale" seafooder housed in a former cannery pleases both travelers and locals with multiple dining areas to "fit any mood or palate" – among them a "cool" upstairs bar for "surprisingly good sushi", "excellent drinks" and lounging by the "toasty fire", a grill room for "satisfying", "inventive" fare and a patio dock that delights on "warm evenings"; slightly less swimming are the variable service and "high prices."

## Capriccio  *Italian*               ▽ 22 | 14 | 19 | $25

**Mission Viejo** | Village Center Shopping Ctr. | 25380 Marguerite Pkwy. (La Paz Rd.) | 949-855-6866

Mission Viejo's "charming" "neighborhood" Italian veteran earns praise for "veal and other exceptional dishes" that regulars recommend over the kitchen's red-sauce plates; amid its old-fashioned decor in "strip-mall" quarters, "pleasant" service and "fair prices" prevail.

## Catal Restaurant & Uva Bar  *Mediterranean*  22 | 21 | 21 | $38

**Anaheim** | Downtown Disney | 1580 S. Disneyland Dr. (Ball Rd.) | 714-774-4442 | www.patinagroup.com

"Unwind" from all the "Mickey madness" at this little slice of "culinary heaven in Downtown Disney" where an "approachable" menu of "nicely prepared" Mediterranean dishes brought out by "kid-friendly" servers makes it "hands-down one of the best choices" after a day at the park; a few critics cite "uneven" quality, but the majority insists it's a "great choice", especially "on a warm summer evening" when dining on the deck supplies "perfect people-watching."

## Cat & The Custard Cup, The  *American/Californian*   23 | 23 | 23 | $45

**La Habra** | 800 E. Whittier Blvd. (Harbor Blvd.) | 562-694-3812 | www.catandcustardcup.com

La Habra's "diamond in the rough", this "warm and inviting" "innlike" charmer is "still tops" for "quiet and romantic" meals in the antiques-laden dining rooms with crackling fireplaces and live piano (Tuesday-Saturday); the "delicious" Cal-New American cuisine is abetted by "solid" wine choices while "spot-on" service has fans purring "the cat never disappoints."

| | FOOD | DECOR | SERVICE | COST |
|---|---|---|---|---|

### Cedar Creek Inn *American*

19 | 20 | 19 | $33

**Brea** | 20 Pointe Dr. (Lambert Rd.) | 714-255-5600
**Laguna Beach** | 384 Forest Ave. (bet. 2nd & 3rd Sts.) | 949-497-8696
**Laguna Niguel** | 27321 La Paz Rd. (bet. Avila Rd. & Pacific Park Dr.) |
949-389-1800
**San Juan Capistrano** | Mission Promenade | 26860 Ortega Hwy.
(bet. Camino Capsitrano & Del Obispo St.) | 949-240-2229
www.cedarcreekinn.com
Favored for "power lunches" or "simple dinners", this "solid local chain"
feels "upscale without being uppity" and serves "high-quality" American
fare from a "broad" menu with "choices for both conservative and adventuresome diners"; "live music on weekends" is a "fun touch" to these
"hangouts" that count "older folks" as fans, but are "child-friendly" too;
N.B. the Palm Springs branch is separately owned.

### Cellar, The ⓜ *French*

23 | 23 | 24 | $52

**Fullerton** | Villa del Sol | 305 N. Harbor Blvd. (Wilshire Ave.) | 714-525-5682 |
www.cellardining.com
A "lovely" converted cellar with arched doorways and a fireplace is the
setting for this "special-occasion" place in Fullerton's historic Villa del
Sol with "pricey" classic French cuisine and an "extensive" wine selection
that "complements" the "excellent" fare; "pampering" service plus a
"low noise level" further enhance "what fine dining is meant to be."

### Chakra *Indian*

21 | 24 | 19 | $37

**Irvine** | University Ctr. | 4143 Campus Dr. (Bridge Rd.) | 949-854-0009 |
www.chakracuisine.com
See review in Los Angeles Directory.

### Chart House *Seafood/Steak*

19 | 22 | 19 | $41

**Dana Point** | 34442 St. of the Green Lantern (PCH) | 949-493-1183
**Newport Beach** | 2801 W. PCH (Riverside Dr.) | 949-548-5889
www.chart-house.com
See review in Los Angeles Directory.

### ⒵ Chat Noir *French*

21 | 25 | 21 | $50

**Costa Mesa** | 655 Anton Blvd. (Bristol St.) | 714-557-6647 |
www.culinaryadventures.com
The "opulent" atmosphere with "dark red tones" and deep leather
booths (think "1920s Paris brothel") "sets the tone" at David
Wilhelm's "fabulous" (and "costly") Costa Mesa bistro that's a "treat"
for "solid" French fare like steak au poivre, pommes frites and champagne cocktails; though a few kitties call the menu "lackluster",
they're won over by the "seductive jazz bar" that "rocks" with the
"young, rich and beautiful."

### ⒵ Cheesecake Factory *American*

20 | 18 | 18 | $26

**Brea** | Brea Mall | 120 Brea Mall (Imperial Hwy.) | 714-255-0115 ◗
**Irvine** | Irvine Spectrum Ctr. | 71 Fortune Dr. (Pacifica St.) | 949-788-9998
**Mission Viejo** | The Shops at Missions Viejo | 42 The Shops at Mission Viejo
(I-5 at Crown Valley Pkwy.) | 949-364-6200
**Newport Beach** | Fashion Island | 1141 Newport Center Dr.
(Santa Barbara Dr.) | 949-720-8333
www.thecheesecakefactory.com
Additional locations throughout Southern California
See review in Los Angeles Directory.

|  | FOOD | DECOR | SERVICE | COST |

## Chimayo at the Beach *Pacific Rim*

| 18 | 21 | 19 | $34 |

**Huntington Beach** | 315 PCH (Main St.) | 714-374-7273 | www.culinaryadventures.com

The "million-dollar view of the Pacific" "can't be beat" at Surf City's "festive" "beachside" player from David Wilhelm; the "tasty" (and "pricey") Pacific Rim chow "doesn't take itself too seriously", prompting some to label it "not up to Wilhelm standards", but the "amazing patio" is still "jumping" "at sunset."

## Citrus Cafe *Californian*

| 20 | 18 | 18 | $32 |

**Tustin** | 1481 Edinger Ave. (Red Hill Ave.) | 714-258-2404 | www.citruscafe.com

## Citrus City Grille 🛇 *Californian*

**Orange** | 122 N. Glassell St. (Chapman Ave.) | 714-639-9600 | www.citruscitygrille.com

These "casual", "fast-paced" cafes traffic in "tasty" Californian cuisine that "pleases everyone" and is served by an "attentive" staff, making them "great for a business lunch or dinner"; the "quieter" Tustin site boasts "better parking" and "one of the best breakfasts" around while the Orange address has a "good bar and outside seating", making it a juicy choice for "antiquing in the Orange Circle."

## Claes *Seafood*

| 23 | 24 | 22 | $44 |

**Laguna Beach** | Hotel Laguna | 425 S. PCH (Laguna Ave.) | 949-376-9283 | www.claesrestaurant.com

"Time the sunset correctly" to maximize the "killer ocean view" at this "refined" Laguna seafooder "hidden" in a somewhat "dumpy" "historic" hotel "right on the sand" at Main Beach; "creative preparations with "fusion" overtones come "artfully presented" in the "chic" room that's "great for a date" or a "nice Sunday brunch."

## Claim Jumper *American*

| 19 | 17 | 18 | $25 |

**Brea** | 190 S. State College Blvd. (Birch St.) | 714-529-9061
**Costa Mesa** | 3333 Bristol St. (Anton Blvd.) | 714-434-8479
**Irvine** | 3935 Alton Pkwy. (Culver Dr.) | 949-851-5085
**Laguna Hills** | 25322 McIntyre St. (La Paz Rd.) | 949-768-0662
**Santa Ana** | 2250 E. 17th St. (Tustin Ave.) | 714-836-6658
www.claimjumper.com
Additional locations throughout Southern California
See review in Los Angeles Directory.

## NEW Commonwealth Lounge & Grill Ⓜ *American*

| - | - | - | E |

**Fullerton** | 112 E. Commonwealth Ave. (N. Harbor Blvd.) | 714-525-8888 | www.commonwealthlounge.com

Downtown Fullerton's latest entry is this swanky joint where tin ceilings, low lighting and framed girlie pictures on the walls set the scene for cocktails and nibbles from the American menu; valet parking on weekends and bottle service are additional perks befitting the pricey tabs.

## Cottage, The *American*

| 17 | 18 | 17 | $24 |

**Laguna Beach** | 308 N. PCH (Aster St.) | 949-494-3023 | www.thecottagerestaurant.com

Laguna's "quintessential breakfast spot" retains its status as a "crowded" "perennial" for "classic" American "comfort food" like "fluffy pancakes" and "yummy omelets", though some reviewers report that "other meals are overrated"; still, its setting in a "converted Craftsman house" with an outdoor patio exudes "old-time charm", which makes up for shortcomings like "waits" and "slow" service.

### Coyote Grill *Mexican* | 19 | 15 | 18 | $23 |

**Laguna Beach** | 31621 South Coast Hwy. (bet. Eagle Rock Way & Sea Bluff Ln.) | 949-499-4033 | www.coyotegrill-lagunabeach.com

"Cheesy, messy plates" of "surfer-style" Mexican fare like eggs with enchiladas and swordfish tacos are "beach-shack" staples at South Laguna's "locals hangout"; a "friendly" staff presides over the "crowded" but still "laid-back" "joint" while the "year-round patio" with its "distant" view of the ocean is a constant reminder that "you're in California."

### Crab Cooker, The *Seafood* | 22 | 12 | 17 | $25 |

**Newport Beach** | 2200 Newport Blvd. (22nd St.) | 949-673-0100
**Tustin** | Enderle Ctr. | 17260 E. 17th St. (Yorba St.) | 714-573-1077
www.crabcooker.com

Get ready to "get your hands dirty" at this "no-frills" Newport Beach seafood "institution" where locals and tourists look past the "paper plates" and "no-nonsense service" for "fantastic deals" on "the freshest" fin fare and "excellent clam chowder"; be prepared to hunker down "on the curb" or "benches out front" because there's "always a line" "and for good reason"; N.B. the Tustin branch lacks the same "shabby" "flavor of the original" "but the food is just as good."

### Crab Cove *Seafood* | ▽ 19 | 19 | 16 | $49 |

**Monarch Beach** | Monarch Bay Plaza | 8 Monarch Bay Plaza (Crown Valley Pkwy.) | 949-240-4401 | www.crabcoverestaurant.com

"Good, but not outstanding" is the verdict on the Euro-Asian cooking at this Monarch Beach seafooder that gets a boost from a "neat" "river of koi" swimming beneath the glass floor; it works as a "date place", though the suburban setting can mean "walk-ins with kids."

### NEW Crystal Jade *Asian* | ▽ 20 | 20 | 16 | $23 |

**Irvine** | Quail Hill Village Shopping Ctr. | 6511 Quail Hill Pkwy. (Shady Canyon Dr.) | 949-725-3368

Early admirers of this new Asian "gem" praise the "surprisingly authentic" Chinese dishes like "fabulous noodles" and dim sum – a "rarity in these parts" of glossy Irvine; the "upscale" shopping-center quarters are "comfortable", but "disorganized" service can detract; still, it's "fun for a big group" or as a "weekday lunch spot."

### Daily Grill *American* | 18 | 17 | 18 | $30 |

**Irvine** | Jamboree Promenade | 2636 Dupont Dr. (Jamboree Rd.) | 949-474-2223
**Newport Beach** | Fashion Island | 957 Newport Center Dr. (Santa Barbara Dr.) | 949-644-2223
www.dailygrill.com
See review in Los Angeles Directory.

### Darya *Persian* | 23 | 21 | 22 | $32 |

**Santa Ana** | South Coast Plaza Vill. | 1611 W. Sunflower Ave. (bet. Bear & Bristol Sts.) | 714-557-6600 | www.daryasouthcoastplaza.com

"Exquisitely prepared" Persian cuisine exuding "exotic, subtle" flavors makes for an "enjoyable feast" at South Coast Plaza's "beautiful", "cavernous" chandeliered palace that's made more "comfortable" by "attentive, respectful" servers; prices may be "expensive", but "large portions" (even on lunch specials) appease the budget-conscious.

### Dizz's As Is ☒ *Eclectic* 23 | 18 | 24 | $45

**Laguna Beach** | 2794 SCH (Nyes Pl.) | 949-494-5250

"Old Laguna in the best sense" say dizzy devotees of this "mainstay" for "superb" Eclectic dining "off the beaten path" in "romantic", "kitschy" digs with "1930s flashback" decor; nonbelievers deem it "weird", but that's no matter to "locals" who overlook its "quirks" – including a "no reservations policy" and "nightmare parking" – in order to enjoy an "old-time place" that "hasn't lost its appeal."

### Dolce Ristorante *Italian* 18 | 18 | 18 | $47

**Newport Beach** | 800 WCH (Dover Dr.) | 949-631-4334 | www.dolcenb.net

Supporters salute this "traditional" Northern Italian for its "romantic" seating area "near the fireplace", lively bar and "great patio" attended to by "personable" staff; however, critics who find the fare "unmemorable" ponder if it's "better for the scene than the food", contending that "it's overpriced for what you get."

### Duke's *Pacific Rim* 17 | 21 | 18 | $32

**Huntington Beach** | 317 PCH (Main St.) | 714-374-6446 | www.hulapie.com

See review in Los Angeles Directory.

### El Cholo Cafe *Mexican* 18 | 18 | 18 | $23

**La Habra** | 840 E. Whittier Blvd. (Harbor Blvd.) | 562-691-4618

### El Cholo Cantina *Mexican*

**Irvine** | Alton Sq. | 5465 Alton Pkwy. (Jeffrey Rd.) | 949-451-0044

www.elcholo.com

See review in Los Angeles Directory.

### El Torito *Mexican* 15 | 15 | 16 | $21

**Anaheim** | 2020 E. Ball Rd. (State College Blvd.) | 714-956-4880

**Orange** | Block at Orange | 3520 The City Way E. (The City Dr. S.) | 714-939-6711

**Tustin** | Enderle Center | 17420 17th St. (Yorba St.) | 714-838-6630

**Yorba Linda** | 22699 Oakcrest Circle (Yorba Linda Blvd.) | 714-921-2335

www.eltorito.com

Additional locations throughout Southern California

See review in Los Angeles Directory.

### El Torito Grill *Mexican* 18 | 17 | 17 | $25

**Brea** | 555 Pointe Dr. (bet. Lambert Rd. & Rte. 57) | 714-990-2411

**Irvine** | 1910 Main St. (Mercantile St.) | 949-975-1220

**Mission Viejo** | Kaleidoscope | 27741 Crown Valley Pkwy. (I-5) | 949-367-1567

**Newport Beach** | Fashion Island | 951 Newport Center Dr. (Santa Barbara Dr.) | 949-640-2875

www.eltorito.com

See review in Los Angeles Directory.

### NEW Eno ◑ *Eclectic* - | - | - | M

**Laguna Niguel** | Ritz-Carlton | 1 Ritz-Carlton Dr. (PCH) | 949-240-2000 | www.ritzcarlton.com

This national tasting room chainlet, which boasts a selection of hundreds of wines and some 50 cheeses and chocolates, has carved out a woodsy, candlelit space in the Ritz-Carlton Laguna Niguel; sybarites seeking to better understand the pleasures of the palate may want to look into the courses offered at its in-house 'Enoversity.'

### 55 Steakhouse & Lounge  *Steak*  ▽ 23 | 23 | 22 | $42
### (fka Granville's)

**Anaheim** | Disneyland Hotel | 1150 Magic Way (Downtown Dr.) | 714-778-6600

A hi-glam remodel lures chophouse fans to this steakhouse in Anaheim's Disneyland Hotel for a "fine-dining extravaganza" where "wonderful old photos" on the walls spotlight Walt's 'after dark' escapades with Hollywood royalty; the "friendly staff" ensures you're well treated, but even enthusiasts find the fare "a bit pricey" while foes say it "doesn't dazzle."

### Filling Station  *Diner*  17 | 15 | 14 | $18

**Orange** | 201 N. Glassell St. (W. Maple Ave.) | 714-289-9714

"Nicely hidden" "off the circle" in Orange's quaint "antiques district", this American diner set in a converted "1930 gas station" dispenses "big portions" of "dependable breakfast fare" and "home-cooked" lunches to shoppers and "university students" drawn to the "relaxing" patio seating; "iffy" service is softened by "usually small" checks.

### ☑ First Cabin  *American/Continental*  25 | 26 | 24 | $70

**Newport Beach** | Balboa Bay Club Resort & Spa | 1221 West Coast Hwy. (east of Newport Blvd.) | 949-645-5000 | www.balboabayclub.com

This "fabulous bayfront location" with an "enticing view" creates a "stunning setting" for "sumptuous" American-Continental repasts at Newport's Balboa Bay Club Resort & Spa where "starched white linens" and "unusually nice table settings" are "elegant" touches while service is "stellar" too; the "patio overlooking the bay" is "divine in spring and summer" but come Christmas, this is the "gold standard" "must" for the annual Boat Parade.

### Fish Market, The  *Seafood*  16 | 14 | 17 | $27

**Irvine** | Irvine Spectrum Ctr. | 85 Fortune Dr. (Pacifica St.) | 949-727-3474 | www.thefishmarket.com

Afishionados say this Irvine seafood chain can be a "good value" for "fresh", if "basic", fare, even if the "tired", "fish market-themed" decor strikes some as oddly "out of place" in Irvine's "mega" Spectrum Center; still, hurried diners note the oyster bar is "great for getting a fast meal" in this "bustling" venue.

### Fitness Pizza/Grill  *Mediterranean*  20 | 15 | 19 | $22

**Brea** | Gateway Plaza | 103 W. Imperial Hwy. (Brea Blvd.) | 714-672-0911
**Yorba Linda** | Yorba Linda Station | 18246 Imperial Hwy. (Yorba Linda Blvd.) | 714-993-5421
www.fitnessgrill.com

North County calorie counters "keep their diet on track" with "healthy" fare like "whole-wheat wraps", grilled fish and salads made from organic greens at these Mediterranean sibs where the nutritional info is listed right on the menu; service "varies", but boosters look beyond that and "nondescript" storefront digs for what they deem "hip" "neighborhood finds"; N.B. patio seating is available at both locations.

### Five Crowns *British*  | 24 | 24 | 24 | $48 |

**Corona del Mar** | 3801 E. PCH (Poppy Ave.) | 949-760-0331 |
www.lawrysonline.com

A touch of "merry olde England" awaits "loyal" customers who say this
"venerable" ivy-covered "landmark" in Corona del Mar is an "atmospheric" "no-brainer" for feasts of "wonderful Lawry's prime rib" and
"all the trimmings"; "cosseting" service from a staff that "seems proud
to work there" adds to the "charm" that's ratcheted up during the hol-
idays when "Dickens-esque" Christmas carolers rove the "dressed up"
quarters; P.S. those "silly" "serving wench" costumes are history
thanks to a recent wardrobe makeover.

### Five Feet *Chinese/French*  | 24 | 17 | 21 | VE |

**Laguna Beach** | 328 Glenneyre St. (bet. Forest Ave. & Mermaid St.) |
949-497-4955 | www.fivefeetrestaurants.com

"Michael Kang is a Laguna treasure" contend high-fivers of the chef-
owner's "super-hip" eatery serving "ridiculously inventive" Chinese-
New French "fusion" in "lively, arty" industrial surroundings; though
some say the new "prix fixe" format is "spectacular", the less-
enthused are "stressed" over the "limited" offerings (as well as
"cramped" quarters) and say it's since "lost some of its appeal."

### Fleming's Prime Steakhouse & Wine Bar *Steak*  | 25 | 23 | 23 | $55 |

**Newport Beach** | Fashion Island | 455 Newport Center Dr. (San Miguel Dr.) |
949-720-9633 | www.flemingssteakhouse.com
See review in Los Angeles Directory.

### Fox Sports Grill *Pub Food*  | 14 | 20 | 15 | $26 |

**Irvine** | Irvine Spectrum Ctr. | 31 Fortune Dr. (Pacifica St.) | 949-753-1369 |
www.foxsportsgrill.com

"On a big game day" you'll "get into the spirit of things" at this Irvine
Spectrum sports bar where baseball, football and soccer match-ups
are broadcast on "lots of TVs" (32 plasma and four giant screens,
which they "manage with a passion"); sure, the American chow is
"nothing special", but the glossy spectator arena is "cooler" than similar spots thanks to a "clubby" vibe and live DJs on weekends.

### French 75 *French*  | 21 | 23 | 20 | $45 |

**Laguna Beach** | 1464 S. PCH (bet. Calliope St. & Mountain Rd.) |
949-494-8444
**Newport Beach** | Fashion Island | 327 Newport Center Dr. (Atrium Ct.) |
949-640-2700
**French 75 Brasserie** *French*
**Irvine** | 13290 Jamboree Rd. (bet. Bryan Ave. & Irvine Blvd.) | 714-573-7600
www.culinaryadventures.com
See review in Los Angeles Directory.

### NEW Gabbi's Mexican Kitchen *Mexican*  ▽ | 26 | 23 | 22 | $28 |

**Orange** | 141 S. Glassell St. (Chapman Ave.) | 714-633-3038 |
www.gabbimex.com

This "new favorite" serving "delectable", "creative recipes from
Mexico" ("a chain it's not") is "just what the Orange circle needed" according to amigos; its low-lit, "sophisticated" atmosphere, "great service" and margs that are "sooo smooth" add to the reasons signage is

"not needed", though you may end up "circling the block numerous times" to find it.

### Gaucho Grill  *Argentinean/Steak*

| | | | |
|---|---|---|---|
| 18 | 14 | 17 | $25 |

**Brea** | 210 W. Birch St. (Brea Blvd.) | 714-990-9140 | www.gauchogrillrestaurant.com
See review in Los Angeles Directory.

### Gemmell's  *French/Continental*

| ▽ 23 | 18 | 21 | $47 |
|---|---|---|---|

**Dana Point** | 34471 Golden Lantern St. (Dana Point Harbor Dr.) | 949-234-0064 | www.gemmellsrestaurant.com
Dana Point's "very European" "little jewel" hides "in the corner of the harbor parking lot" serving "beautifully prepared" French-Continental dishes with "wonderful sauces" to a "following of regulars"; the "gracious hosts" "make you feel at home", and although there's "no view" of the water, a fireplace and other decor upgrades are in the works.

### ☑ Golden Truffle, The 🛢 Ⓜ  *Caribbean/French*

| 26 | 11 | 21 | $45 |
|---|---|---|---|

**Costa Mesa** | 1767 Newport Blvd. (bet. 17th & 18th Sts.) | 949-645-9858
"Ask what chef Greeley recommends" as "Alan always finds the high note" assure enthusiasts of the "inventive", "subtle" and seasonal Caribbean-French "concoctions" matched with a "superb wine list" at this Costa Mesa "strip-mall" scrapper; despite somewhat uneven service and a room that "needs refurbishing", what it "lacks in style" is compensated for by "one of OC's best chefs" (just be sure to go "when he's there").

### Gordon James Grill  *American*

| ▽ 20 | 22 | 20 | $41 |
|---|---|---|---|

**San Clemente** | 110 N. El Camino Real (Avenida Del Mar) | 949-498-9100 | www.gordonjamesgrill.com
Set in San Clemente pioneer Ole Hansen's "historic" well-preserved 1920s office, this "enjoyable", midrange-to-expensive New American serves hand-cut steaks, seafood and dishes "with a few twists" such as the "unique" fried string beans – a popular "treat" at the bar; surveyors say the staff is "attentive", adding it's both a "scene on the weekends" and a well-located "lunch spot" for "walking the shops of Del Mar."

### Green Parrot Café  *Californian*

| ▽ 24 | 19 | 20 | $27 |
|---|---|---|---|

**Santa Ana** | 2035 N. Main St. (bet. 17th St. & Santa Clara Ave.) | 714-550-6040 | www.greenparrotcafe.net
"Excellent" cooking lures Santa Ana eaters to this "tucked-away" Californian set in a mission-style Spanish courtyard and art gallery; it's a "friendly neighborhood bistro" that's not big on glitz, but the staff "tries hard to please."

### Gulfstream  *American/Seafood*

| 21 | 20 | 21 | $38 |
|---|---|---|---|

**Newport Beach** | 850 Avocado Ave. (PCH) | 949-718-0188 | www.hillstone.com
See review in Los Angeles Directory.

### Gulliver's  *British*

| 20 | 20 | 20 | $40 |
|---|---|---|---|

**Irvine** | 18482 MacArthur Blvd. (bet. I-405 & Michelson Dr.) | 949-833-8411 | www.gulliversrestaurant.com
Irvine's "old-line" "tavern" "close to the airport" remains an "Orange County institution" for "traditional" British fare in "big portions",

including "satisfying" prime rib and "creamed corn to die for" served by an "attentive staff"; many note the "hokey" "too-dark" digs are "showing their age" and suggest it "needs updating in every way", nevertheless, it's still a handy choice for "business lunches" and pre-flight meals.

### Gypsy Den *Californian*
17 | 17 | 14 | $18

**Costa Mesa** | The LAB | 2930 Bristol St. (bet. Baker St. & Randolph Ave.) | 714-549-7012
**Santa Ana** | 125 N. Broadway (2nd St.) | 714-835-8840
www.gypsyden.com

"Sit outside if you can" at these "groovy" "boho cafes" in Costa Mesa and Santa Ana serving "really affordable" Californian grub with a "variety of choices for vegetarians"; though some diners deem the "healthy" fare too "bland" and the service "slacker-paced", that still allows for "long talks" and "relaxing" to "live music" over coffee drinks and smoothies.

### Habana *Nuevo Latino*
21 | 20 | 19 | $31

**Costa Mesa** | The LAB | 2930 Bristol St. (bet. Baker St. & Randolph Ave.) | 714-556-0176

Costa Mesa feels "like a different country" at The LAB's "cool" "upscale" Nuevo Latino destination boasting "hearty, tasty" Caribbean-inspired cuisine; aside from the sometimes "slow" service, loyalists love the "romantic" heated patio glowing with candles and the "amazing mojitos", which enhance the atmosphere for a "date, party or night out" (even if you get "more bang for your buck at lunch").

### Heroes Bar & Grill ◑ *Pub Food*
16 | 16 | 16 | $20

**Fullerton** | 125 W. Santa Fe Ave. (N. Harbor Blvd.) | 714-738-4356 | www.heroesrestaurant.net
See review in Los Angeles Directory.

### ☒ Hobbit, The Ⓜ *Continental/French*
27 | 25 | 28 | $87

**Orange** | 2932 E. Chapman Ave. (Malena St.) | 714-997-1972 | www.hobbitrestaurant.com

"Prepare to spend hours" on this "unique" seven-course "adventure" in Orange where French-Continental feasts unfold "like posh private dinner parties" fit for "Gatsby", with chef Michael Philippi's "superb" "culinary delights" delivered by an "outstanding" staff that earns it the No. 1 score for Service in Orange County; the "warm" 1930s Spanish house, complete with a "theatrical" wine cellar, provides an "elegant" backdrop for "costly" meals that most find "unforgettable"; P.S. there's only one seating each night (Wednesday–Sunday), which must be "reserved well in advance."

### House of Blues ◑ *Southern*
15 | 20 | 16 | $33

**Anaheim** | Downtown Disney | 1530 S. Disneyland Dr. (off Harbor Blvd.) | 714-778-2583 | www.hob.com
See review in Los Angeles Directory.

### ☒ Houston's *American*
21 | 19 | 20 | $33

**Irvine** | Park Pl. | 2991 Michelson Dr. (Jamboree Rd.) | 949-833-0977 | www.hillstone.com
See review in Los Angeles Directory.

| | FOOD | DECOR | SERVICE | COST |
|---|---|---|---|---|

### hush *American*
21 | 23 | 19 | $57

**Laguna Beach** | 858 S. PCH (bet. Cleo & Thalia Sts.) | 949-497-3616 | www.hushrestaurant.com

Despite the "misleading" moniker, this "ultrasleek", "see-and-be-seen" boîte generates "sensory overload" from the "frenzied conversations" of "young, rich and beautiful" Laguna guests, who label its New American menu "comfort food with a nouveau twist"; while the "wine list never ends", wallet-watchers find that the food and service "fall short of the price" unless "you're on an expense account."

### Ichibiri *Japanese*
18 | 12 | 16 | $30

**Dana Point** | 16 Monarch Bay Plaza (Crown Valley Pkwy.) | 949-661-1544
**Laguna Niguel** | Rancho Niguel Shopping Ctr. | 27981 Greenfield Dr. (Crown Valley Pkwy.) | 949-362-8048
**San Clemente** | 1814 N. El Camino Real (Pico Ave.) | 949-361-0137

These South County's Japanese siblings are "local favorites" where "large and small parties" go for a "dinner show" around the teppanyaki grill featuring knife-acrobatics that "kids love"; maybe, the sushi doesn't wow and the dingy digs "need an upgrade", but daytime drop-ins call it a real "value for lunch"; the Laguna Niguel branch serves beer and wine only, while Dana Point and San Clemente have a full bar.

### ☑ Il Fornaio *Italian*
20 | 19 | 19 | $34

**Irvine** | Lakeshore Tower | 18051 Von Karman Ave. (bet. Main St. & Michelson Dr.) | 949-261-1444 | www.ilfornaio.com
See review in Los Angeles Directory.

### Infusion *American*
▽ 23 | 20 | 19 | $41

**Ladera Ranch** | Mercantile West Shopping Ctr. | 25612 Crown Valley Pkwy., Ste. L-1 (Antonio Pkwy.) | 949-364-1100 | www.infusionladera.com

Advocates call this "modern" bistro the "best entry" in "restaurant-starved" Ladera Ranch, praising its "different take" on "eclectic" New American dishes (such as maple-infused pork chops with mango-papaya salsa), which are presented with "visual flair" and accompanied by "fabulous drinks"; it's often "loud", but a wall of recessed candles makes the "small box" of a room extra "cozy", and "dining at the chef's counter" is a treat.

### Inka Grill *Peruvian*
19 | 11 | 18 | $18

**Costa Mesa** | 260 Bristol St. (Red Hill Ave.) | 714-444-4652
**Lake Forest** | 23600 Rockfield Blvd. (Lake Forest Dr.) | 949-587-9008
www.inkagrill.com

Offering a "welcome change from the ordinary", these "unusual" Peruvian grills serve a "tasty and varied" menu of "beef, chicken or seafood" dishes, as well as some veggie options, in "generous portions" with "lots of heat if you're looking for it"; since they're "reliable" and "cheap", few begrudge them the "lackluster" ambiance and "lunchtime waits."

### ☑ In-N-Out Burger ◑ *Hamburgers*
24 | 10 | 18 | $8

**Costa Mesa** | 594 W. 19th St. (bet. Anaheim & Maple Aves.)
**Huntington Beach** | 18062 Beach Blvd. (bet. Talbert Ave. & Taylor Dr.)
**Irvine** | 4115 Campus Dr. (bet. Bridge Rd. & Stanford Ct.)
**Laguna Niguel** | 27380 La Paz Rd. (Avenida Breve)

*(continued)*

**In-N-Out Burger**

**Tustin** | Tustin Mktpl. | 3020 El Camino Real (bet. East Dr. & Jamboree Rd.)
800-786-1000

www.in-n-out.com

Additional locations throughout Southern California

**See review in Los Angeles Directory.**

**Islands** *American*          16 | 16 | 17 | $16

**Brea** | 250 S. State College Blvd. (E. Birch St.) | 714-256-1666
**Fountain Valley** | 18621 Brookhurst St. (Ellis Ave.) | 714-962-0966
**Fullerton** | 2201 W. Malvern Ave. (N. Gilbert St.) | 714-992-6685
**Irvine** | 4020 Barranca Pkwy. (Culver Dr.) | 949-552-1888
**Newport Beach** | 1380 Bison Ave. (Macarthur Blvd.) | 949-219-0445

www.islandsrestaurants.com

Additional locations throughout Southern California

**See review in Los Angeles Directory.**

**Iva Lee's** *Cajun/Creole*          ▽ 23 | 20 | 20 | $39

**San Clemente** | DeNaults Plaza | 555 N. El Camino Real (Avenida Palizada) |
949-361-2855 | www.ivalees.com

Hungry customers with a hankering for Creole and "Cajun cooking at
its finest" hightail it down to this San Clemente "charmer" – a standout
in the area's "sparse dining scene"; its "attentive" owners, "quirky"
French Quarter–flavored digs (with a "special" patio for summer
nights) and "live blues and jazz" on the weekends make it a "pleasant
place to get together with friends."

**NEW Izakaya Zero** ◑ *Japanese*          – | – | – | M

**Huntington Beach** | 412 Walnut Ave. (Main St.) | 714-960-1278

Huntington Beach replaces its Asian lounge (Red Pearl Kitchen) with
this trendy Japanese tavern concept with a menu by Takashi Abe
(Bluefin); clean lines and natural surfaces lend hip polish to communal
digs suited to small plates of tobanyaki dishes and other pub grub
shared over sake or other drinks from the full bar.

**JACKshrimp** *Cajun*          17 | 12 | 15 | $25

**Aliso Viejo** | 26705 Aliso Creek Rd. (Pacific Park Dr.) | 949-448-0085
**Irvine** | Park Pl. | 3041 Michelson Dr. (Jamboree Rd.) | 949-252-1023
**Newport Beach** | 2400 W. PCH (Tustin Ave.) | 949-650-5577

www.jackshrimp.com

"Who knew something so simple" as "real", "spicy" Gulf shrimp and
bread "could be so heavenly"? ask acolytes of this casual Cajun trio
whose "scary good" "buttery secret sauce" is "certainly worth the an-
gioplasty"; though the Mardi Gras decorations do little to jazz it up,
and it's merely "average" to some, avid dippers say "c'est ci bon."

**Javier's Cantina & Grill** *Mexican*          22 | 18 | 19 | $29

**Irvine** | Irvine Spectrum Ctr. | 45 Fortune Dr. (Pacifica St.) | 949-872-2101
**Laguna Beach** | 480 S. PCH (Laguna Ave.) | 949-494-1239

www.javiers-cantina.com

"Muy bueno" approve amigos of this "very noisy" Mexican duo that's
"always mobbed" for "fresh, top-notch" "Baja fare" ("go for the crab
enchiladas") washed down with "killer 'ritas"; the original Laguna site,
which is set to relocate to Crystal Cove by late 2007, draws a "huge
bar crowd", while its "trendy counterpart" at the Irvine Spectrum is

"more upscale"; either way, they're a "no-brainer" for an "affordable" night out that's "a cut above the typical."

**Jerry's Wood-fired Dogs** *Hot Dogs*          20 | 10 | 15 | $9

**NEW Ladera Ranch** | 1701 Corporate Dr. (Antonio Pkwy.) | 949-364-7080
**La Habra** | Westridge Plaza | 1360 S. Beach Blvd. (Imperial Hwy.) | 562-697-4644
**Santa Ana** | Center on 17th St. | 226 E. 17th St. (Tustin Ave.) | 714-245-0200
www.jerrysdogs.com
Frank fans "woof!" it up at these three "small" counter-service joints known for their "delicious", mesquite-fired hot dogs and sausages loaded with "every fixin' imaginable", "so you feel like you're getting your money's worth"; since the "fantastic" burgers, "wonderful onion rings" and "housemade potato chips" also keep the cooks "busy at the grill", it might be "slow if you're trying to eat and run."

**Jody Maroni's Sausage Kingdom** *Hot Dogs*     19 | 7 | 14 | $10

**Orange** | The Block at Orange | 20 City Blvd. W. (City Dr.) | 714-769-3754 | www.jodymaroni.com
See review in Los Angeles Directory.

**Joe's Crab Shack** *Seafood*                   13 | 15 | 15 | $26

**Garden Grove** | 12011 Harbor Blvd. (Chapman Ave.) | 714-703-0505
**Newport Beach** | 2607 W. PCH (Tustin Ave.) | 949-650-1818
www.joescrabshack.com
See review in Los Angeles Directory.

**Johnny Rebs'** *BBQ*                           22 | 16 | 20 | $21

**Orange** | 2940 E. Chapman Ave. (bet. Malena Dr. & Prospect St.) | 714-633-3369 | www.johnnyrebs.com
See review in Los Angeles Directory.

**Johnny Rockets** *Hamburgers*                  15 | 15 | 16 | $13

**Irvine** | The Spectrum | 71 Fortune Dr. (Pacifica St.) | 949-753-8144
**Laguna Beach** | 188 PCH (Ocean Ave.) | 949-497-7252
**Orange** | 20 City Blvd. (Justice Ctr.) | 714-385-0086
www.johnnyrockets.com
Additional locations throughout Southern California
See review in Los Angeles Directory.

**Kantina** *Nuevo Latino*                     ▽ 18 | 22 | 16 | $39

**Newport Beach** | 2406 Newport Blvd. (26th St.) | 949-673-1400 | www.kantina.com
"Right on the bay", this crisp Newport Beacher offers prized "views of the marina" as well as the "beautiful servers" setting down Nuevo Latino eats, like filet mignon tacos, which are often "creative" but "take a back seat" to the "ripe" atmosphere; wise imbibers advise "heading straight upstairs" to the lounge and patio for "top-of-the-line margaritas" with a splash of mingling – you might just "get some digits"; P.S. there's a "dock available for boaters" too.

**NEW Kimera Restaurant Lounge** *Eclectic*    - | - | - | VE

**Irvine** | 19530 Jamboree Rd. (Macarthur Blvd.) | 949-261-1222 | www.kimerarestaurant.com
This natty newcomer from the Ghoukassian family (Bistango, Bayside) aims for Irvine's slick exec set and scene-savvy loungers with urbane

| | FOOD | DECOR | SERVICE | COST |
|---|---|---|---|---|

Eclectic cuisine (think chorizo-manchego pizza and hamachi with kimchi) and a vast wine and cocktail selection; wedged between office towers, the sharp-looking space also boasts a moody lounge done up in dark woods with live music nightly.

### King's Fish House  *Seafood*
**21 | 18 | 18 | $32**

**Laguna Hills** | 24001 Avenida de la Carlota (El Toro Rd.) | 949-586-1515
**Orange** | 1521 W. Katella Ave. (Main St.) | 714-771-6655
www.kingsfishhouse.com
See review in Los Angeles Directory.

### NEW K'ya  *Californian*
**– | – | – | E**

**Anaheim** | Hotel Ménage | 1221 S. Harbor Blvd. (W. Ball Rd.) | 714-758-0900
**Laguna Beach** | Hotel La Casa del Camino | 1287 S. PCH (Cress St.) | 949-376-9718
www.kyarestaurant.com
"Spectacular views" of Laguna's shoreline from the rooftop bar make "sunset cocktails a must" before tucking into "first-rate" large and small plates of Cal cuisine in the "cozy" downstairs at this boutique-hotel boîte (formerly Savoury's), staffed by "friendly" servers; its Anaheim sib is decorated in a similarly Mediterranean style, with the light-bite option of a pool bar with a pared-down menu.

### La Cave  ⑧ *Steak*
**21 | 17 | 21 | $43**

**Costa Mesa** | 1695 Irvine Ave., downstairs (17th St.) | 949-646-7944 | www.lacaverestaurant.com
"Sinatra would love" this 1962 Costa Mesa "throwback" "hidden" downstairs in a "funky" former wine cellar decked out with retro "red leather booths"; its "dynamite steaks" and "generous martinis" are enhanced by "solid service", "cool jazz" and tribute shows to Ol' Blue Eyes himself on Monday and Tuesdays, all of which entices both the "old-boy" crowd and the "younger set" into a "cozy cocoon made for romance" – or the "Rat Pack."

### NEW La Fondue  *Fondue*
**▽ 21 | 21 | 22 | $62**

**San Juan Capistrano** | 31761 Camino Capistrano (Ortega Hwy.) | 949-240-0300 | www.lafondue.com
"Intriguing", "eccentric" surroundings set the rococo scene at this San Juan Capistrano "change of pace" featuring "wild game for dipping" (think venison, alligator, boar) along with varied cheese fondues fit for "special-occasion" feasts or a "romantic dinner for two"; "impeccable" service pulls it all together, and if the "huge", four-course dinners seem "expensive", you can always "go late for a chocolate fondue nightcap."

### Landmark Steakhouse  Ⓜ *Steak*
**▽ 18 | 18 | 17 | $46**

**Corona del Mar** | 3520 East Coast Hwy. (Narcissus & Orchard Aves.) | 949-675-5556 | www.landmarknewport.com
Noted as "one of the only late-night" options in genteel CdM (they serve food until 11 PM or midnight), this steakhouse may have "melt-in-your-mouth" beef and "unique sides" that are "full of flavor", but locals know it "more for its bar scene", which some say is "probably the best part of the restaurant"; technically speaking, it "turns into a club" at 10 PM with DJs and dancing on weekends adding to the festive feel.

### Las Brisas  *Mexican/Seafood*

| 16 | 23 | 16 | $37 |

**Laguna Beach** | 361 Cliff Dr. (PCH) | 949-497-5434 |
www.lasbrisaslagunabeach.com

"Tourists and locals" swoon over the "incredible view of the Pacific" at this "popular" Laguna Beach venue that really "delivers" in terms of "outdoor dining" "California-style" (on a "clear day" there's "nowhere better"); however, "service is lacking" and critics find the "faux Mex" fare "overpriced" and only "half as memorable" as its "idyllic" location; still, "breakfasts" are a "happy surprise", as are the "margaritas."

### ☑ La Vie en Rose  ⑤ *French*

| 25 | 25 | 26 | $47 |

**Brea** | 240 S. State College Blvd. (Imperial Hwy.) | 714-529-8333 |
www.lavnrose.com

Francophiles fawn over this "charming" find in "unexpected" Brea where the "transporting" Normandy "farmhouse" decor sets the scene for "elegant" meals of "classic" French cooking enhanced by "unbeatable, attentive" service ("friendly" host Louis Laulhere "makes you feel welcome"); it's "a bit pricey", but wallet-watchers note the three-course prix fixe dinners are "a very good value."

### Lawry's Carvery  *American*

| 20 | 12 | 14 | $19 |

**Costa Mesa** | South Coast Plaza | 3333 Bristol St. (Sunflower Ave.) |
714-434-7788 | www.lawrysonline.com

"Lawry's quality" "without the pomp" "sure beats the usual food-court" offerings at this "pleasant" order-at-the-counter eatery in Costa Mesa's South Coast Plaza where "delicious" "prime rib" is carved to order for "gourmet sandwiches" that are "heaven on a bun for the weary shopper"; add in "hearty sides" and "fresh" salads, and you've got a "quick" "fix" "at a fraction of the price" of its swanky older sibs.

### Lazy Dog Cafe, The  *Eclectic*

| 19 | 17 | 21 | $21 |

**NEW** **Orange** | 1623 W. Katella Ave. (Main St.) | 714-769-7020
**Westminster** | Target Pavillions Shopping Ctr. | 16310 Beach Blvd. (MacDonald Ave.) | 714-500-1140
www.thelazydogcafe.com

See review in Los Angeles Directory.

### ☑ NEW Leatherby's
### Cafe Rouge  Ⓜ *Asian/Californian*

| 25 | 25 | 24 | $65 |

**Costa Mesa** | Orange County Performing Arts Ctr. | 615 Town Center Dr. (Ave. of the Arts) | 714-429-7640 | www.patinagroup.com

"It's a winner" enthuse admirers of this Costa Mesa newcomer that brings "definite sophistication" to the "über-modern" Segerstrom Concert Hall in which it's housed and is "worth an evening on its own merits" for "sensational" Cal-Asian cuisine that's "impeccably executed" – "exactly what you expect from the Patina Group"; the "quiet" room overlooks the "huge Richard Serra sculpture" outside through "curved glass walls" while "crisp", "attentive" service helps offset the "pricey" tabs.

### L'Hirondelle  Ⓜ *Belgian/French*

| ▽ 22 | 19 | 23 | $41 |

**San Juan Capistrano** | 31631 Camino Capistrano (Ortega Hwy.) |
949-661-0425 | www.lhirondellesjc.com

Named for the fabled swallows that return to San Juan Capistrano each spring, this "cozy" French-Belgian bistro with "nice owners" serves up "fantastic" "comfort" dishes (like roast duck) "done well"; the "cottagelike" setting is "perfect for lunch" or a "romantic date", especially "in the flower-filled garden on a pretty day."

### Ling & Louie's  *Pan-Asian*

∇ 17 | 22 | 16 | $27

**Irvine** | Irvine Spectrum Ctr. | 85 Fortune Dr. (bet. I-5 & I-405) | 949-585-0022 | www.lingandlouies.com

"Very nice" decor and a "beautiful patio" that's "great for people-watching" "do wonders to take your mind off" the "run-of-the-mill" "Westernized" Pan-Asian eats at this "upscale" chain link in the Irvine Spectrum; happy-hour "bargains" are a "big draw" and "reservations" are a plus for the pre-movie crowd.

### Loft, The  🖪🖾 *Hawaiian*

17 | 12 | 16 | $18

**Huntington Beach** | Huntington Plaza | 7862-B Warner Ave. (Beach Blvd.) | 714-842-2911 | www.thelofthawaii.com
See review in Los Angeles Directory.

### Lucca Cafe  *Mediterranean*

∇ 23 | 15 | 18 | $40

**Irvine** | Quail Hill Village Shopping Ctr. | 6507 Quail Hill Pkwy. (Sand Canyon Dr.) | 949-725-1773 | www.luccacafe.com

A "gem" in an Irvine shopping center, this "innovative" Mediterranean "neighborhood treasure" offers "casual bistro" fare at lunch while dinner is a showcase for an "excellent selection" of "small plates" (including "awesome" cheese and charcuterie platters) paired with "wines by the glass"; despite its "expensive" prices and "hot-and-cold" service, locals find it a "refreshing change" in this "chain-plagued" territory.

### Luciana's  *Italian*

22 | 21 | 22 | $39

**Dana Point** | 24312 Del Prado (bet. Blue Lantern & Ruby Lantern Sts.) | 949-661-6500 | www.lucianas.com

Dana Point's "established" "neighborhood favorite" charms the coastal set with "rustic" Northern Italian dishes and "sweet" service that's "kid-friendly" too; "cozy" digs are made more "romantic" by the fireplace while the "small bar" affords "locals" a "hangout" for "friendly meals."

### Lucille's Smokehouse Bar-B-Que  *BBQ*

22 | 19 | 19 | $25

**Brea** | 1639 E. Imperial Hwy. (Rte. 57) | 714-990-4944 | www.lucillesbbq.com
See review in Los Angeles Directory.

### Maggiano's Little Italy  *Italian*

19 | 19 | 18 | $28

**Costa Mesa** | South Coast Plaza | 3333 Bristol St. (Anton Blvd.) | 714-546-9550 | www.maggianos.com
See review in Los Angeles Directory.

### NEW Marché Moderne  *French*

- | - | - | E

**Costa Mesa** | South Coast Plaza | 3333 Bristol St. (Anton Blvd.) | 714-434-7900

Esteemed OC chef Florent Marneau (ex Pinot Provence) breaks out on his own at this luxe Costa Mesa mall site (last home to Troquet) that's been handsomely remade to suit his assured, market-inspired French cuisine; expect pricey seasonal fare informed by local and artisan producers plus graceful desserts by his pastry chef wife, Amelia.

FOOD | DECOR | SERVICE | COST

### Market City Caffe  *Californian/Italian*  | 18 | 17 | 17 | $23

**Brea** | 110 Birch St. (Imperial Hwy.) | 714-529-7005 |
www.marketcitycaffe.com
See review in Los Angeles Directory.

### Mascarpone's  Ⓜ *Italian*  ▽ 24 | 12 | 22 | $29

**Orange** | 1446 E. Katella Ave. (bet. California & Tustin Sts.) | 714-633-0101
Orange's "out-of-the-way" "little gem" has "minimal" frills yet sparkles for "superb" Northern Italian cooking and "terrific desserts" prepared by a "masterful chef" who adds "a Spanish flair" ("order ahead" for the "best paella"); oenophiles add that "lots of wines aren't on the list" so "ask for a recommendation" from the "friendly and efficient" staff that "knows your name after one visit"; N.B. closed in August.

### ⚡ Mastro's Ocean Club  *Seafood*  | 22 | 25 | 22 | $71

**Newport Beach** | Crystal Cove Promenade | 8112 E. Coast Hwy.
(Reef Point Dr.) | 949-376-6990 | www.mastrosoceanclub.com
"Stunning Pacific views", "swanky" nautical decor and "unbelievable steaks and seafood" draw "chic" Newport types to this "outrageously priced" offshoot of the Mastro's chainlet where entertainment comes in the form of live piano and "plastic surgery-watching"; sure, some say it's "glitz without substance", but party people and "sexy OC types" still select this "high-energy" spot as *the* place "to see and be seen."

### ⚡ Mastro's Steakhouse  *Steak*  | 25 | 22 | 23 | $70

**Costa Mesa** | 633 Anton Blvd. (Park Center Dr.) | 714-546-7405 |
www.mastrosoceanclub.com
See review in Los Angeles Directory.

### Mayur  *Indian*  | 21 | 15 | 19 | $37

**Corona del Mar** | 2931 E. PCH (bet. Heliotrope & Iris Aves.) | 949-675-6622 |
www.mayurindianrestaurant.com
Boosters of "authentic" Indian cuisine insist this Corona del Mar "jewel box" "hidden on PCH" uses "the freshest ingredients" around in creating "mouthwatering" fare that some dub among "the best" in the area; "portions are small" and the "à la carte" menu makes it feel "overpriced" to some, but in spite of both shortcomings, it remains a "local hangout."

### McCormick & Schmick's  *Seafood*  | 19 | 20 | 19 | $40

**Irvine** | 2000 Main St. (Gillette Ave.) | 949-756-0505 |
www.mccormickandschmicks.com
See review in Los Angeles Directory.

### Melting Pot, The  *Fondue*  | 19 | 19 | 20 | $45

**Irvine** | Jamboree Promenade | 2646 Dupont Dr. (Jamboree Rd.) |
949-955-3242 | www.meltingpot.com
See review in Los Angeles Directory.

### Memphis at the Santora  *Southern*  | 21 | 13 | 17 | $25

**Santa Ana** | Artists Vill. | 201 N. Broadway (2nd St.) | 714-564-1064
**Memphis Cafe**  *Southern*
**Costa Mesa** | 2920 Bristol St. (Randolph Ave.) | 714-432-7685
www.memphiscafe.com
You'll feel like "you're on your way to Graceland" swear supporters of these OC twins that attract "young and hip locals" for "tasty" Southern

specialties like pork chops and meatloaf that "fit the bill" in a "county lacking good soul food"; both locations ooze "retro coolness", especially when the "nightclub" action heats up on weekends when live DJs and "bartenders who pour a very good drink" are additional appeals.

### NEW Mesa Restaurant 🅢 🅜 *Italian*  — | — | — | E

**Costa Mesa** | 725 Baker St. (bet. Bristol St. & Randolph Ave.) | 714-557-6700

Smooth and self-aware, this hot newcomer in Costa Mesa is a SoBeCa district haven for scenesters lolling and smoking in the dramatic lounge that opens to the sky beneath a moving glass roof; its globally informed Italian cooking satisfies noshers in the adjacent alcove overlooking the trendy mise-en-scène.

### Mimi's Cafe *Diner*  17 | 17 | 16 | $19

**Anaheim** | 1240 N. Euclid St. (W. Romneya Dr.) | 714-535-1552
**Fountain Valley** | 18461 Brookhurst St. (Ellis Ave.) | 714-964-2533
**Laguna Niguel** | 27430 La Paz Rd. (Avila Rd.) | 949-643-0206
**Lake Forest** | 22651 Lake Forest Dr. (Muirlands Blvd.) | 949-457-1052
**Tustin** | 17231 E. 17th St. (I-55) | 714-544-5522
www.mimiscafe.com
Additional locations throughout Southern California
See review in Los Angeles Directory.

### Modo Mio Cucina Rustica *Italian*  22 | 19 | 20 | $37

**Newport Beach** | Crystal Cove Promenade | 7946 E. PCH (Crystal Heights Dr.) | 949-497-9770 | www.modomiocucinarustica.com
See review in Los Angeles Directory.

### Morton's The Steakhouse *Steak*  25 | 21 | 24 | $61

**NEW Anaheim** | 1895 S. Harbor Blvd. (W. Katella Ave.) | 714-621-0101
**Santa Ana** | South Coast Plaza Vill. | 1641 W. Sunflower Ave. (bet. Bear & Bristol Sts.) | 714-444-4834
www.mortons.com

"Quality steaks" "don't come any better" contend carnivores of these "sophisticated" chain links exalted for "amazing" beef and "excellent sides" served with "much fanfare" by an "impressive" staff; yes, they're "pricey", but pros proclaim they're "worth every penny"; still, if you're intent on keeping cost in check, take advantage of "lunch specials" or "happy hour" when the bar serves "half-price" apps that are "perfect with your martini."

### Motif *Eclectic*  23 | 25 | 24 | $65

**Monarch Beach** | St. Regis Resort, Monarch Bch. | 1 Monarch Beach Resort (PCH) | 949-234-3320 | www.stregismb.com

The "breathtaking view of the Pacific" is just one "reason to travel" to Monarch Beach's "spectacular" St. Regis resort where the "creative" Eclectic cuisine arrives in "presentations second to none", and "attentive" service makes guests feel like "royalty"; the $72 champagne brunch buffet may be "over the top" with a sense of excess that harkens back to the "'80s", but admirers assure it's "worth every penny."

### Mozambique *Eclectic*  19 | 21 | 18 | $46

**Laguna Beach** | 1740 S. PCH (Agate St.) | 949-715-7100 | www.mozambiqueoc.com

"Adventurous" eaters explore the "inventive" Eclectic offerings (with some "African-influenced" dishes seasoned with peri-peri pepper) at this "stylish" Laguna Beach compound alive with "squawking" "parrots in the entryway" and a choice of venues; the "hip" open-air Shebeen Lounge upstairs has a "good view", live music on weekends and a "singles"-heavy crowd while the dining room on the main level offers similarly "stunning" brightly colored rooms with a more "formal" feel.

## Mrs. Knott's Chicken Dinner. *American*   | 21 | 15 | 18 | $19 |

**Buena Park** | California MarketPlace | 8039 Beach Blvd. (La Palma Ave.) | 714-220-5080 | www.knotts.com

"Homestyle cooking" that "harkens back to a simpler time" keeps this American old-timer at Knott's Berry Farm "busy" with "families" who "line up" for "biscuits" and "fried chicken with all the fixing's" hustled by "motherly" waitresses in "cafeterialike" quarters; low prices equal big "bang for the buck", and if a few quibble that "nostalgia" trumps "quality", they're outvoted by those who deem this "sweet" spot "a classic"; N.B. entrance to the amusement park is not required.

## ☑ Mr. Stox *American*   | 24 | 23 | 25 | $52 |

**Anaheim** | 1105 E. Katella Ave. (bet. Lewis St. & State College Blvd.) | 714-634-2994 | www.mrstox.com

This "OC icon" in Anaheim "continues to shine" for "first-rate" "straight-forward" New American cuisine paired with "incredible wines", making it a "standby for any occasion"; it's "pricey", but "top-notch" treatment from the "attentive, knowledgeable staff" "defines class" and makes the "clubby", "old-fashioned" mahogany-and-hunter-green decor with "cozy booths" and a fireplace all the more "relaxing."

## Mulberry Street Ristorante *Pizza*   ▽ | 20 | 19 | 18 | $29 |

**Fullerton** | 114 W. Wilshire Ave. (Harbor Blvd.) | 714-525-1056

"Historic" Downtown Fullerton is home to this "little-known gem" that paesanis proclaim "feels like Little Italy" with "good, old-fashioned" Italian-American "red-sauce" fare plus "great New York pizza"; locals pack the small bar area, lending a "'*Cheers*'-like atmosphere" to the wood-paneled room.

## Muldoon's Dublin Pub & Celtic Bar ⓜ *Irish*   | 18 | 19 | 20 | $29 |

**Newport Beach** | 202 Newport Center Dr. (Anacapa Dr.) | 949-640-4110 | www.muldoonspub.com

Newport Center's "lively" "hangout" with "two bars" and a shaded patio is "great for a pint or four" say surveyors who favor it "after shopping at Fashion Island" or on weekends when "live music" adds to the festive atmosphere; a "very Irish" vibe comes via the "homestyle" "comfort food" like "fish 'n' chips" and some of the "best soda bread in town", which sets this "cozy" saloon apart from its "cookie-cutter corporate" competition nearby.

## ☑ Napa Rose *Californian*   | 27 | 26 | 27 | $62 |

**Anaheim** | Grand Californian Hotel | 1600 S. Disneyland Dr. (Katella Ave.) | 714-300-7170 | www.disneyland.com

"This is no Mickey Mouse operation" claim those captivated by this Anaheim "foodie mecca", voted OC's Most Popular restaurant, where "inspired" chef Andrew Sutton's "adventurous" and "masterfully executed" "wine-country" cuisine is bolstered by a "cellar that satisfies even the fussiest lush", and served by a "five-star" staff; the "elegant"

|  | FOOD | DECOR | SERVICE | COST |
|---|---|---|---|---|

dining room has a "rustic, Napa" feel, and while most appreciate the "family-friendly" vibe, a few quibble that "sweatshirts" and "kids on portable DVD players" have no place in such a "first-rate" establishment.

### Naples Ristorante e Pizzeria  *Pizza*
`17` `15` `15` `$23`

**Anaheim** | 1550 S. Disneyland Dr. (Ball Rd.) | 714-776-6200 | www.patinagroup.com

Downtown Disney's source for Southern Italian eats "satisfies" with "gooey pizzas" but the rest of the "limited menu" is deemed "nothing spectacular"; meanwhile, "crowded" conditions with "distracted" servers and "kids running around" encourage some park-goers to opt for "off-peak hours" or try "takeout."

### Native Foods  *Californian/Eclectic*
`22` `12` `17` `$16`

**Costa Mesa** | The Camp | 2937 Bristol St. (bet. Baker & Bear Sts.) | 714-751-2151 | www.nativefoods.com

See review in Los Angeles Directory.

### Natraj  *Indian*
`18` `12` `15` `$19`

**Foothill Ranch** | Food Festival Ct. | 26612 Towne Centre Dr. (bet. Alton & Bake Pkwys.) | 949-830-2015
**Irvine** | Irvine Market Pl. | 13246 Jamboree Rd. (Irvine Blvd.) | 714-665-0040
**Laguna Hills** | 24861 Alicia Pkwy. (Hon Ave.) | 949-581-4200
www.natrajusa.com

Of the "few decent Indian" options around OC, this "dependable", "locally owned" trio pleases with "plentiful" portions of "authentic" dishes including "many vegetarian options" all at "inexpensive" prices; "there's no decor to speak of" but service is "quick" enough, especially at the Foothill Ranch site, which is "counter service" only.

### Nello Cucina  *Italian*
`23` `17` `20` `$34`

**Costa Mesa** | South Coast Plaza | 3333 Bear St. (Sunflower Ave.) | 714-540-3365 | www.nellocucina.com

An "unexpected" "oasis" in Costa Mesa's South Coast Plaza, this little sib of upscale Antonello serves up "fabulous", "well-priced" Italian cuisine like "homemade pastas" and pizzas that have shoppers and matinee-goers "completely hooked"; "serene" environs include a "pleasant" pocket patio all the better to sidestep the "noisy" retail ambiance.

### Nesai  Ⓜ  *Californian/Italian*
`-` `-` `-` `E`

**Newport Beach** | 215-17 Riverside Ave. (off PCH) | 949-646-2333

Holed up on a side street off PCH, this Newport Beach bistro soothes its neighborhood clientele with modern Californian–Northern Italian cuisine that's soon to become more global; its slim wine list focuses on boutique labels, and the casual environs boast roomy booths, loads of greenery and even a bantam bar that invites solo dining.

### Nieuport 17  *Continental*
`22` `22` `21` `$44`

**Tustin** | Lafayette Ctr. | 13051 Newport Ave. (Irvine Blvd.) | 714-731-5130

"One of the great OC classics", this "attractive" Tustin Continental is a "haven" for "regulars" and "older crowds" "celebrating milestones" with "comforting" fare "from the '70s" like beef Wellington – all in "unique" quarters with "aviation memorabilia" lining the walls; a minority deems it "dated" and "overpriced" as well, but they're outnumbered by those who dub this "underappreciated" spot a "longtime favorite."

### NEW Nirvana Grille Ⓜ *Californian*

| - | - | - | E |

**Mission Viejo** | Marguerite Shopping Ctr. | 24031 Marguerite Pkwy., Ste. C (Trabuco Rd.) | 949-380-0027 | www.nirvanagrille.com

"Nirvana in the midst of culinary purgatory" proclaim proponents of this "noteworthy" addition to Mission Viejo's dining scene where the "simple", "strip-mall" digs don't detract from "terrific" Californian cooking by "highly pedigreed" chef Lindsay Rosales and "unusual" "wine pairings" by her husband Luis; the decor is "unpretentious" with terra-cotta tiling and fresh cut flowers on the tables, while tabs are equally humble, leading some locals to laud it as exactly the venue they've "been waiting for."

### Oceans 33° *Californian/Seafood*

| 19 | 19 | 18 | $37 |

**Mission Viejo** | The Shops at Mission Viejo | 799 The Shops at Mission Viejo (Crown Valley Pkwy.) | 949-365-0200 | www.oceans33.com

"Solid" seafood dishes plus some "interesting surprises" (like "amazing cocktails") make this "undiscovered" Mission Viejo mall eatery an "enjoyable" spot that's "a far cry" from the rest of the "food court" offerings (live jazz on weekends makes it especially "unique" for the area); a few find it "overpriced", but it's convenient "while shopping" and even better – "there's almost never a wait"; N.B. scores may not reflect a recent chef and owner change.

### Olde Ship, The *Pub Food*

| 18 | 19 | 17 | $23 |

**Fullerton** | 709 N. Harbor Blvd. (bet. Chapman & Union Aves.) | 714-871-7447
**Santa Ana** | 1120 W. 17th St. (bet. Bristol St. & Flower Ave.) | 714-550-6700
www.theoldeship.com

Expats and Anglophiles gather at these "bloody good" twins for "authentic" British pub grub washed down with a "large choice of U.K. ales and stouts" on tap; "welcoming", "old England" digs inspire "long talks over a pint" but beware, "weekend nights are packed") (especially when the Santa Ana branch hosts "great live bands") so "traditional breakfasts" on Saturday and Sunday mornings are "less crowded" options.

### NEW Old Vine Café *Eclectic*

| - | - | - | M |

**Costa Mesa** | The Camp | 2937 Bristol St., Ste. A-102 (Baker St.) | 714-545-1411 | www.oldvinecafe.com

The brothers McDonald helm this Eclectic Costa Mesa rookie located in neo-boho retail refuge The Camp, where chef Mark mans the kitchen and brother Brandon manages the front-of-house; an intriguing wine list blends globe-spanning dishes served morning to night (except on Mondays and Sundays, when it closes at 3 PM) with an emphasis on small plates, and there's a tasting menu option for dinner; a nook boutique offers wines and gourmet provisions to take away.

### O-Nami *Japanese*

| 16 | 10 | 11 | $26 |

**Laguna Hills** | Laguna Hills Mall | 24155 Laguna Hills Mall (El Toro Rd.) | 949-768-0500 | www.o-nami.com
See review in Los Angeles Directory.

| | FOOD | DECOR | SERVICE | COST |
|---|---|---|---|---|

### ☑ 162', Restaurant *Californian* — 24 | 27 | 24 | $64

**Dana Point** | Ritz-Carlton Laguna Niguel | 1 Ritz Carlton Dr. (PCH) | 949-240-2000 | www.ritzcarlton.com

"Heaven on earth" fawn fans of the Ritz-Carlton Laguna Niguel's "gorgeous" "cliff-top restaurant in Dana Point that sits 162 feet above the shoreline affording "breathtaking views" of the "shimmering Pacific"; "solid" Californian cuisine from an "imaginative" menu boasting "intriguing fusion elements" is "beautifully presented", while equally impressive service means it "generally lives up to its high price"; P.S. the "fantastic" brunch is especially popular with "wealthy" coastal locals.

### Onotria Wine Country Cuisine ☒ *Eclectic* — ▽ 24 | 19 | 20 | $47

**Costa Mesa** | 2831 Bristol St. (Bear St.) | 714-641-5952 | www.onotria.com

A "creative", "wine-friendly" menu distinguishes this midpriced Costa Mesa charmer where chef-owner Massimo Navarretta turns out "seasonal" Eclectic creations with an "emphasis on game meats" that pair with vintages from the 500-label cellar; the spacious, "rustic" digs with high beamed ceilings are deemed "too loud" by some, but the majority of reviewers raves this "gem" is "one of Orange County's best new additions."

### Opah *Californian/Seafood* — 23 | 21 | 20 | $38

**Aliso Viejo** | Aliso Viejo Town Ctr. | 26851 Aliso Creek Rd. (Enterprise St.) | 949-360-8822
**Irvine** | The Marketplace | 13122 Jamboree Rd. (Irvine Blvd.) | 714-508 8055
**Rancho Santa Margarita** | 22332 El Paseo (El Paseo) | 949-766-9988
www.opahrestaurant.com

"Desperate housewives" and "OC hipsters" "crowd" into this trio of "stylish" "suburban sanctuaries" where "great martinis", "fabulous appetizers" and "creative" Californian seafood dishes like coconut rice-crusted ahi tuna "never disappoint", even if service sometimes gets "bogged down"; after dark, the "singles scene" with "live music" can be a bit "deafening", so some "bring earplugs" while others retire to the "pleasant", "outdoor" seating areas.

### Original Fish Co. *Seafood* — 24 | 19 | 21 | $37

**Los Alamitos** | 11061 Los Alamitos Blvd. (Katella Ave.) | 562-594-4553 | www.originalfishcompany.com

For "fresher-than-fresh" fish and some of the "best clam chowder west of Maine", fin fiends head to land-locked Los Alamitos and "prepare to wait" (sorry, no reservations) at this "upscale" seafooder applauded for an "extensive selection" of dishes "prepared with a light touch"; though it "looks like a chain", alas, there's only one of this "local favorite" prompting a few out-of-towners to dub it a "worthy detour."

### ☑ Original Pancake House *Diner* — 23 | 10 | 17 | $14

**Aliso Viejo** | 26951 Moulton Pkwy. (Oso Pkwy.) | 949-643-8591
**Anaheim** | 1418 E. Lincoln Ave. (bet. East St. & State College Blvd.) | 714-535-9815 Ⓜ⇅
**Yorba Linda** | 18453 Yorba Linda Blvd. (bet. Imperial Hwy. & Lakeview Ave.) | 714-693-1390
www.originalpancakehouse.com
See review in Los Angeles Directory.

|  | FOOD | DECOR | SERVICE | COST |
|---|---|---|---|---|

## Outback Steakhouse  *Steak*  | 17 | 14 | 18 | $28 |

**Brea** | 402 Pointe Dr. (Lambert Rd.) | 714-990-8100
**Buena Park** | 7575 Beach Blvd. (Rte. 91) | 714-523-5788
**Costa Mesa** | 1670 Newport Blvd. (17th St.) | 949-631-8377
**Garden Grove** | 12001 Harbor Blvd. (Chapman Ave.) | 714-663-1107
www.outback.com
Additional locations throughout Southern California
See review in Los Angeles Directory.

## Oysters  *Asian/Californian*  | 23 | 18 | 21 | $46 |

**Corona del Mar** | 2515 E. PCH (MacArthur Blvd.) | 949-675-7411 |
www.oystersrestaurant.com
Supporters sup on "creative" Cal-Asian cuisine washed down with "superb specialty cocktails" ("ask for the deconstructed mojito!") at this "impressive" "local staple" located "just steps from the water" on PCH; the "well-trained staff", "live jazz" (Thursday–Saturday) and an "easygoing" vibe overcome digs that some find "tired" and a sometimes "noisy" atmosphere.

## NEW Palm Terrace  *American*  | – | – | – | E |
## (fka Pavilion)

**Newport Beach** | The Island Hotel | 690 Newport Ctr. Dr. (Santa Cruz Dr.) |
949-760-4920 | www.theislandhotel.com
With an open, tropical design that would made Tommy Bahama feel right at home (latticework doors, earth tones, retro lamps), the restaurant at The Island Hotel in Newport Beach returns after a multi-month renovation, with Bill Bracken (formerly at The Peninsula Beverly Hills) in the kitchen, turning out pricey New American dishes like truffled mac 'n' cheese, summer fish stew and 30-hour Kobe short ribs.

## Pane e Vino  *Italian*  | 21 | 20 | 19 | $38 |

**Brea** | 240 S. Brea Blvd. (Imperial Hwy.) | 714-256-7779 | www.panevino.biz
See review in Los Angeles Directory.

## Park Ave.  Ⓜ  *American*  | ▽ 25 | 26 | 23 | $34 |

**Stanton** | 11200 Beach Blvd. (Katella Ave.) | 714-901-4400 |
www.parkavedining.com
Restaurant-needy Stanton is the unexpected neighborhood for this "retro" "jewel" where chef-owner David Slay "elevates American dishes" with "fabulous", "reasonably priced" results; "delightful" details include "herbs from their garden" and "homemade" mixers for "yummy drinks."

## Pei Wei Asian Diner  *Pan-Asian*  | 16 | 13 | 14 | $16 |

**Irvine** | Oak Creek Vill. | 5781 Alton Pkwy. (bet. Jeffrey Rd. & Royal Oak) |
949-857-8700
**Newport Beach** | The Bluffs | 1302 Bison Ave. (MacArthur Blvd.) |
949-629-1000
www.peiwei.com
See review in Los Angeles Directory.

## Peppino's  *Italian*  | 18 | 12 | 16 | $22 |

**Aliso Viejo** | 26952 La Paz Rd. (Pacific Park Dr.) | 949-643-1355
**Foothill Ranch** | Foothill Ranch Towne Ctr. | 26612 Towne Centre Dr.
(bet. Alton & Bake Pkwys.) | 949-951-1210
**Lake Forest** | 23600 Rockfield Blvd. (Lake Forest Dr.) | 949-951-2611

|  | FOOD | DECOR | SERVICE | COST |
|---|---|---|---|---|

*(continued)*

## Peppino's

**Mission Viejo** | 27782 Vista del Lago (Marguerite Pkwy.) | 949-859-9556
www.peppinosonline.com

"NYC Italian" comes to the OC via this "casual", "red-sauce" mini-chain where "solid" pizzas and pastas are presented in "abundant", "family-style" portions; cons contend you shouldn't "expect much ambiance" (or service either), but it's "easy on the pocketbook" and "welcoming" to "families."

## Pescadou Bistro Ⓜ *French*     22 | 17 | 22 | $39

**Newport Beach** | 3325 Newport Blvd. (bet. Finley Ave. & 32nd St.) | 949-675-6990 | www.pescadoubistro.com

"Truly French!" exclaim enthusiasts of this "homey", "family-run" Newport Beach bistro offering "authentic" "country" fare via chef Jacques de Quillien's "outstanding", "authentic" menu and a rotating selection of "budget-oriented" "blackboard specials"; service is "welcoming", and "quaint" decor done up in sunny yellows is equally unpretentious and "charming."

## Ⓩ P.F. Chang's China Bistro *Chinese*    19 | 19 | 18 | $28

**Irvine** | Irvine Spectrum Ctr. | 61 Fortune Dr. (Pacifica St.) | 949-453-1211
**Mission Viejo** | The Shops at Mission Viejo | 800 The Shops at Mission Viejo (Crown Valley Pkwy.) | 949-364-6661
**Newport Beach** | Fashion Island | 1145 Newport Center Dr. (Santa Barbara Dr.) | 949-759-9007
www.pfchangs.com
See review in Los Angeles Directory.

## Pho 79 *Vietnamese*    21 | 8 | 13 | $11

**Garden Grove** | 9941 Hazard Ave. (Brookhurst St.) | 714-531-2490 ⌿
**Westminster** | Asian Garden Mall | 9200 Bolsa Ave. (bet. Bushard & Magnolia Sts.) | 714-893-1883
See review in Los Angeles Directory.

## Picante *Spanish*    ▽ 21 | 22 | 20 | $38

**Ladera Ranch** | Mercantile West Shopping Ctr. | 25606 Crown Valley Pkwy. (Sienna Pkwy.) | 949-364-7100

Suburbanites find themselves "transported to Spain" via this new Ladera Ranch "surprise" that's "worthwhile" for "delicious", "nicely presented" Iberian cuisine that diners deem "authentic" and well priced too; the "stunningly beautiful" room features wrought-iron details, high ceilings and chandeliers while the "charming" patio surrounded by orange trees is equally "pleasant."

## Picayo *French/Mediterranean*    22 | 18 | 21 | $49

**Laguna Beach** | 610 N. PCH (Boat Canyon Dr.) | 949-497-5051 | www.picayorestaurant.com

Enthusiasts overlook the "odd", "strip-mall" setting in favor of the "outstanding" "treasures" inside this "comfortable" Laguna Beach French-Med where the "enjoyable" fare is aided by "attentive" service; critics claim the cuisine is "inconsistent", noting a "decline in price-value ratio", though enthusiasts assert this "accommodating" spot is still a local "favorite."

| | FOOD | DECOR | SERVICE | COST |
|---|---|---|---|---|

**Pinot Provence** *French* — 25 | 24 | 23 | $57

**Costa Mesa** | Westin South Coast Plaza Hotel | 686 Anton Blvd. (Bristol St.) | 714-444-5900 | www.patinagroup.com

"Admirably French through and through" this "sophisticated" Patina Group effort set in the Westin South Coast Plaza is the place "to impress" with "divine", "delicately prepared" Gallic-Med cuisine that's "impeccably served" in a "romantic" space that evokes "the other Provence"; tabs can be "a little pricey", so those in-the-know suggest you take advantage of the "prix fixe lunch deals" and "free corkage policy" to keep the damage minimal; N.B. the Food score may not fully reflect a December 2006 chef change.

**Plums Café & Catering** *Pacific NW* — 24 | 15 | 19 | $21

**Costa Mesa** | Westport Square Shopping Ctr. | 369 E. 17th St. (Tustin Ave.) | 949-722-7586 | www.plumscafe.com

"A taste of the Pacific Northwest" comes to Costa Mesa via this "unassuming" "strip-mall" cafe that charms customers with its "Seattle vibe" and "wonderful" American regional breakfast and lunch dishes (like smoked salmon hash and berry waffles) prepared with the "freshest" "organic" ingredients; service can be "erratic" and the dining room may be a bit "lacking" in decor, but in spite of both, reviewers report it's "a hit" that "makes you feel better about yourself just by being there."

**Pomodoro Cucina Italiana** *Italian* — 17 | 14 | 17 | $22

**Aliso Viejo** | Aliso Viejo Town Ctr. | 26611 Aliso Creek Rd. (Enterprise St.) | 949-831-1400
**Irvine** | Oak Creek | 5789 Alton Pkwy. (Royal Oak) | 949-654-1100
**Laguna Beach** | 234 Forest Ave. (S. PCH) | 949-497-8222
**Newport Beach** | Newport Coast Shopping Ctr. | 21133 Newport Coast Dr. (N. PCH) | 949-759-1303
**Orange** | The Village | 2214 N. Tustin St., Ste. B (off E. Meats Ave.) | 714-998-3333
www.pastapomodoro.com
Additional locations throughout Southern California
See review in Los Angeles Directory.

**Portillo's Hot Dogs** *Hot Dogs* — 19 | 16 | 14 | $11

**Buena Park** | 8390 La Palma Ave. (bet. Dale St. & Stanton Ave.) | 714-220-6400 | www.portillos.com

"Chi-town transplants" are "ecstatic" over this "cheap", order-at-the-counter Buena Park chain link peddling Vienna dogs, Italian beef sandwiches and other "fatty", "flavorful" "delicacies" of the "Windy City" that "hit the spot"; "relocated" Midwesterners overlook "sticky tables", preferring to focus on the "nostalgic" decor "loaded with memorabilia" that's a constant reminder of "home, sweet home."

**NEW** **Port Restaurant/Bar** Ⓜ *American* — - | - | - | E

**Corona del Mar** | 440 Heliotrope Ave. (bet. PCH & 2nd Ave.) | 949-723-9685 | www.portcdm.com

This ocean-adjacent bungalow with Mediterranean decor (think lots of stone and polished concrete) boasts an outdoor patio, heated atrium and, perhaps most importantly, a veteran of the much-missed original Aubergine in the kitchen preparing its pricey New American fare; for those looking to make a night of it in Corona del Mar, there's a DJ Thursdays–Saturdays and live music on Sundays.

### Prego *Italian*

| 19 | 19 | 19 | $40 |

**Irvine** | 18420 Von Karman Ave. (Michelson Dr.) | 949-553-1333
This "steady performer" in Irvine is "still pleasing" for "business lunches" and family dinners, with "terrific" homemade pastas among other "reliable", "high-end" Italian fare; though it feels a bit "long in the tooth", the "inviting" surroundings and "beyond-friendly" staff ensure lots of loyal customers; N.B. the former Beverly Hills branch has reopened as Forte.

### Rainforest Cafe *American*

| 13 | 23 | 15 | $22 |

**Anaheim** | 1515 S. Disneyland Dr. (Katella Ave.) | 714-772-0413
**Costa Mesa** | South Coast Plaza | 3333 Bristol St. (Town Center Dr.) | 714-424-9200
www.rainforestcafe.com
See review in Los Angeles Directory.

### Ralph Brennan's Jazz Kitchen *Creole*

| 19 | 22 | 19 | $32 |

**Anaheim** | Downtown Disney | 1590 S. Disneyland Dr. (Magic Way) | 714-776-5200 | www.rbjazzkitchen.com
"Oh, what bliss to have Ralph on our side of the Mississippi" effuse N'Awlins lovers who appreciate the "hearty", "tasty but mild" Creole cooking that's "far better than you'd expect in the Disney location"; its "Big Easy-style" house boasts a "lovely upstairs terrace" and "live hot jazz" nightly, and if the dinner prices seem "too high", you can opt for the "more reasonable lunch" as well as "wonderful beignets" from the "walk-up window."

### ☑ Ramos House Café Ⓜ *American*

| 26 | 20 | 21 | $31 |

**San Juan Capistrano** | 31752 Los Rios St. (Ramos St.) | 949-443-1342 | www.ramoshouse.com
"Steps from the San Juan Capistrano mission", this "historic" abode (built in 1881) wows with chef-owner John Q. Humphreys' "phenomenal" Southern-accented New American dishes that bring out the "natural flavors of the ingredients"; a denim-donning staff ups the "character" of the "rustic", "garden-patio" setting where the somewhat "pricey" brunches kick off with a "famous" soju Bloody Mary and finish with "fighting over the last slice of buttermilk pie"; N.B. open until 3 PM, Tuesday–Sunday.

### Rendezvous *American*

| ∇ 24 | 22 | 26 | $49 |

**San Juan Capistrano** | San Juan Capistrano Train Station | 26701B Verdugo St. (Camino Capistrano) | 949-496-1006 | www.rendezvoussjc.com
A "vintage" setting in San Juan Capistrano's "old depot building", including some "intimate" tables inside 1927 Pullman train cars, is complemented by a "relaxed pace" at this New American "sleeper" co-owned by chef Peter Arachovitis; enthusiasts say "every dish is excellent" off the "inventive" seasonal menu, from the wood-fired game to the "creamy, tangy goat-cheese cheesecake", and the "romantic" evening "invites a stroll after dinner" in the Los Rios district.

### NEW Rick's Secret Spot ⊠ *BBQ*

| - | - | - | I |

**San Clemente** | 1030 Calle Sombra, Ste. G (Calle Amanecer) | 949-429-7768 | www.rickssecretspot.com
Disciples of "lip-smacking barbecue" "drool" over the "slow-cooked" "pork sandwich" and other smoked fare from this mostly take-out

mom-and-pop serving lunch in a San Clemente business park; regulars advise "get there early" since "they run out", and limited hours can make it challenge to "catch them when they're open."

**Ristorante Mamma Gina**  *Italian*  21 | 18 | 20 | $47

**Newport Beach** | 251 PCH (Bayside Dr.) | 949-673-9500 |
www.mammaginas.com

These twin trats in Newport Beach and Palm Desert are "still champion" for "old-school" Northern Italian fare served in an "upscale, reserved" atmosphere favored by "locals" who "want to impress"; despite a few complaints that it's "not worth the price", most deem it a "dependable" standby, complete with "good drinks" and nightly entertainment that make it a "pleasant" place for "after-dinner music."

**NEW** **Ristorante Max** ● *Italian*  ▽ 21 | 16 | 18 | $47

**Newport Beach** | 1617 Westcliff Dr. (Dover Dr.) | 949-515-8500
Inland Newport Beach feels "like Positano" – former home of chef-owner Massimo Carro – to admirers of this "Amalfi Coast–style" newcomer offering "real Italian" cookery that's "almost unheard of in SoCal"; critics cite "too-high prices and too-small portions", and while the whitewashed walls lighten the mood, some suggest it "needs a happier personality."

**Z** **Ritz Restaurant &**  24 | 24 | 25 | $59
**Garden, The**  *Continental*

**Newport Beach** | 880 Newport Center Dr. (Santa Barbara Dr.) |
949-720-1800 | www.ritzrestaurant.com

"Everything speaks class" at Fashion Island's "warm" and "welcoming" multiroom Continental where Newport's "upper crust" gathers over "old-world" "classics" (even "roast goose at Christmas") served by "top-notch" waiters in tuxes; the look is a "little decadent", enhanced by a "festive" bar and cigar patio, and while some gripe that it's "living on past glories", for many it's an "always-charming" "home-town club" that's "perfect for celebrating."

**Riviera at the Fireside** **Z** *Continental*  ▽ 24 | 22 | 26 | $48
**Westminster** | 13950 Springdale St. (I-405) | 714-897-0477 |
www.rivierarestaurant.net

"Skillful" "tuxedoed waiters bring memories of a bygone era" inside this "clubby" Westminster Continental specializing in "tableside preparations" of "flaming entrees" and desserts as well as other "traditional" indulgences; decked out with black booths and lots of wood, it has a "1950s look" that some call "overdue for refurbishment", but which generally suits the "leisurely, superb meal."

**Rosine's**  *Armenian/Mediterranean*  24 | 15 | 20 | $26
**Anaheim** | Ralph's Mkt. | 721 S. Weir Canyon Rd. (Serrano St.) |
714-283-5141 | www.rosines.com

"Awesome" Med-Armenian eats are the "gold in them thar Anaheim Hills" swear devotees of this "friendly" family-run cafe offering "delights" like "the best rotisserie chicken" with "secret garlic sauce" at "last century's prices"; add an "excellent" array of "affordable" wines and see why it's "crammed" at "peak times" – good thing "takeout is just as good as dining in"; P.S. a "larger" new sib in Corona offers more elbow room and a full bar.

### Rothschild's  *Continental/Italian*

22 | 22 | 24 | $46

**Corona del Mar** | 2407 E. PCH (MacArthur Blvd.) | 949-673-3750 | www.rothschildsrestaurant.com

A "well-deserved following" fawns over CdM's "cozy" Continental–Northern Italian "haunt" that's graced by 18th-century oil paintings, classical music and "impeccable" service; the ambiance is largely matched by "outstanding" pastas and other "exquisite" dishes, satisfying appetites for "old-fashioned romance."

### Royal Khyber  *Indian*

▽ 24 | 21 | 23 | $35

**Santa Ana** | South Coast Plaza Vill. | 1621 W. Sunflower Ave. (bet. Bear & Bristol Sts.) | 714-436-1010 | www.royalkhyber.com

Expect a "professional act" from South Coast Plaza's "high-end" Indian that offers "all the traditional foods" – many of them cooked in an imported tandoor oven – but adds a "gourmet twist and presentation" amid a richly toned room that enhances the "joy" of the meal; servers are "helpful with wine pairings", and the Sunday brunch buffet is "quick and excellent" for those who "like to drop in for some spice", especially before the theater.

### Royal Thai Cuisine  *Thai*

21 | 13 | 18 | $27

**Laguna Beach** | 1750 S. PCH (bet. Agate & Pearl Sts.) | 949-494-8424

**Newport Beach** | 4001 W. PCH (bet. Newport Blvd. & Superior Ave.) | 949-645-8424

www.royalthaicuisine.com

Offering "some of the better Thai around", these "quaint" "reasonably priced" coastal twins in Laguna and Newport with "not much competition" "consistently" deliver the "royal treatment" with an "entertaining" flaming chicken dish among other "winning" choices; most agree you go "for the food, not the atmosphere", but that's just fine with fans of one of the "best lunch deals in the OC."

### ☒ Roy's  *Hawaiian*

24 | 22 | 22 | $47

**Newport Beach** | Fashion Island | 453 Newport Center Dr. (San Miguel Dr.) | 949-640-7697 | www.roysrestaurant.com

See review in Los Angeles Directory.

### Ruby's  *Diner*

16 | 16 | 17 | $16

**Balboa** | 1 Balboa Pier (Palm Ave.) | 949-675-7829

**Irvine** | 4602 Barranca Pkwy. (Lake Rd.) | 949-552-7829

**Laguna Beach** | 30622 S. PCH (Wesley Dr.) | 949-497-7829

**Seal Beach** | Seal Beach Pier (Ocean Ave.) | 562-431-7829

**Tustin** | 13102 Newport Ave. (Irvine Blvd.) | 714-838-7829

www.rubys.com

Additional locations throughout Southern California

See review in Los Angeles Directory.

### Rusty Pelican  *Seafood*

19 | 20 | 20 | $39

**Newport Beach** | 2735 W. PCH (bet. Riverside & Tustin Aves.) | 949-642-3431 | www.rustypelican.com

Yes, "it's hard to find" "decent" dining with a "great view of the harbor", so fans swoop into this "casual" seafooder in Newport; despite the drawback of "long waits" for largely "ok" eats, it's "always packed" and locals know the bar menu offers the "best deal in town" for "watching sailboat races from the second floor" on "summer Thursdays."

**Rutabegorz** *Seafood/Vegetarian* — — — M

**Fullerton** | 211 N. Pomona Ave. (bet. Commonwealth & Wilshire Aves.) |
714-738-9339
**Orange** | 264 N. Glassell St. (bet. Maple & Palm Aves.) |
714-633-3260 Ⓢ
**Tustin** | 158 W. Main St. (El Camino Real) | 714-731-9807
www.rutabegorz.com

These "funky", enduring eateries housed in early-1900s buildings feel
retro with their newsprint menus of "healthy", "satisfying" soups and
giant salads among a roster of vegetarian, vegan, chicken and seafood
dishes, as well as homebaked desserts such as a "highly recommended"
cheesecake; both the food and the "quirky" style have attracted a
"regular" following since the Fullerton location opened in 1970.

**Ⓩ Ruth's Chris Steak House** *Steak* 25 21 23 $59

**Irvine** | 2961 Michaelson Dr. (Jamboree Rd.) | 949-252-8848 |
www.ruthschris.com
See review in Los Angeles Directory.

**Sabatino's Lido Shipyard** 22 12 18 $32
**Sausage Company** *Italian*

**Newport Beach** | 251 Shipyard Way (Lido Park Dr.) | 949-723-0621
This "special place" is "famous for unique" homemade sausage and
"boldly flavored" Sicilian feasts that inspire Newporters to dub it
"*Sopranos* on the bay"; just "ignore the decor" and the "so-so service"
but do "ask for the patio" especially when enjoying the champagne
brunch "on a sunny day"; P.S. you can also "take home three pounds"
of links to cook yourself.

**Sage** *American* 24 22 22 $47

**Newport Beach** | Eastbluff Shopping Ctr. | 2531 Eastbluff Dr. (Vista del Sol) |
949-718-9650 | www.sagerestaurant.com

**Sage on the Coast** *American*

**Newport Beach** | Crystal Cove Promenade | 7862 E. PCH
(Crystal Heights Dr.) | 949-715-7243 | www.sagerestaurant.com
"Creative" chef-owner Rich Mead "never ceases to amaze" report
advocates of his "fresh", "imaginative" New American fare offered
at dual Newport Beach locales that cater to a "well-heeled" "local
contingent" seeking a "relaxing" vibe that's "hip yet not snobbish";
the "chic" Crystal Cove site boasts a "covered patio with roaring
fireplace" while Eastbluff's "original charmer" has a heated "garden
setting" (and some say stronger service), but it's "hard to go wrong"
at either one.

**Salt Creek Grille** *Steak* 18 19 17 $34

**Dana Point** | 32802 PCH (Crown Valley Pkwy.) | 949-661-7799 |
www.saltcreekgrille.com
See review in Los Angeles Directory.

**Sam Woo** *Chinese* 20 10 12 $20

**Irvine** | 15333 Culver Dr. (Irvine Center Dr.) | 949-262-0688 |
www.samwooirvine.com
Irvine | Orange Tree Sq. | 54068 Walnut Ave. (Jeffrey Rd.) |
949-262-0128
See review in Los Angeles Directory.

| | FOOD | DECOR | SERVICE | COST |
|---|---|---|---|---|

### NEW Sapphire Laguna *Eclectic* ▽ 26 | 27 | 22 | $48

**Laguna Beach** | Old Pottery Pl. | 1200 S. Coast Hwy. (Brooks St.) |
949-715-9888 | www.sapphirellc.com

"Lucky" Laguna's "brand-new gem" (in the refurbished space of the former Pottery Shack) presents a "casual Craftsman environment" complete with a "lovely" "ocean-view patio" for year-round "alfresco dining" on "celebrity" chef-owner Azmin Ghahreman's Eclectic creations, which customers call "exciting" forays into "global cuisine" that "juxtapose flavors perfectly"; combined with "unobtrusive" service, the whole package is a "winner."

### Savannah Steak & Chop House *Seafood/Steak* 23 | 24 | 24 | $52

**Laguna Niguel** | Ocean Ranch Shopping Ctr. | 32441 Golden Lantern St. (Camino Del Avion) | 949-493-7107 | www.culinaryadventures.com

"Definitely on par with the big steak chains", Laguna Niguel's "special spot in the suburbs" (sib of French 75) provides "excellent" steak and seafood along with "calorie-packing" sides and "fine wines" recommended by a "superb" staff; its "old-style", "hunting-lodge" setting with fireplaces, big booths and ocean views feels like a "step back in time", aside from the "sky-high" prices, and live music Tuesday–Saturday makes the bar extra "attractive."

### Seafood Paradise *Chinese/Seafood* ▽ 21 | 11 | 14 | $21

**Westminster** | 8602 Westminster Blvd. (bet. Magnolia & Newland Sts.) | 714-893-6066

Head to Westminster for Chinese that's "better than in Chinatown" advise admirers of this specialist in "fresh seafood" and the "best damn dim sum" (served 10 AM–3 PM daily), which commands "long waits" unless you "get here early"; most anticipate expending "effort to get servers' attention" and barely blink at the mess-hall surroundings.

### NEW Sevens Steakhouse & Grille *Steak* – | – | – | E

**Tustin** | 17245 E. 17th St. (I-55) | 714-544-0021 |
www.sevenssteakhouse.com

Tustin's new indie player in the prime beef category is a former rib chain joint, now gussied up with vaulted wooden ceilings and a cushy lounge, and focused on upmarket chophouse fare like steaks, seafood and hearty sides; both the space and the breezy service have a casually tasteful air that suits this flush ZIP code, while the wine list is strong on Napa and Italian vintages.

### Shabu Shabu Ⓜ *Japanese* ▽ 25 | 13 | 23 | $23

**Mission Viejo** | 28715 Los Alisos Blvd. (off Rte. 241) | 949-588-3225
Swirling your own "fresh vegetables" and Angus beef in simmering broth means "you have to work before you eat", but you'll be rewarded by "surprisingly good" shabu-shabu at this Japanese "change of pace" in Mission Viejo; proprietress Kumi Hirokawa dubs herself "one hot mama" and fans say her bubbly presence "really makes the meal."

### Shades *American/Continental* – | – | – | E
### (fka Palm Court)

**Huntington Beach** | Hilton Waterfront Beach Resort | 21100 PCH (Huntington St.) | 714-845-8444 | www.waterfrontresort.com
Only the name has changed at Huntington's Beach's seaside-resort restaurant known for its courtyard with pool and ocean views that of-

fers a "great setting" for "artful", "consistent" meals of American-Continental cuisine; Sundays feature a buffet brunch of "nice quality", and there's live music on summer weekends.

### Sharky's Mexican Grill  *Mexican*

17 | 12 | 15 | $12

**Aliso Viejo** | 26811 Aliso Creek Rd. (Park Pl.) | 949-643-0900
**Irvine** | 6725 Quail Hill Pkwy. (Passage) | 949-856-1300
**Newport Beach** | 21119 Newport Coast Dr. (off N. PCH) | 949-729-1000
www.sharkys.com
Additional locations throughout Southern California
See review in Los Angeles Directory.

### Shenandoah at the Arbor  *Southern*

21 | 20 | 21 | $36

**Los Alamitos** | 10631 Los Alamitos Blvd. (Sausalito St.) | 562-431-1990 | www.shenandoahatthearbor.com
Los Alamitans "indulge" in Southern "home cooking" at this "quaint" cottage where "delicious" specialties like fried chicken and gumbo are served "without pretension"; reviewers especially recommend the "twinkle-lit outside patio" "surrounded by plants and a pond" for a "comfortable yet romantic repast."

### Side Street Cafe  *American*

∇ 18 | 9 | 17 | $15

**Costa Mesa** | 1799 Newport Blvd. (18th St.) | 949-650-1986
This daytime "favorite" draws a "diverse" Costa Mesa crowd for "tasty omelets" among other "simple" American eye-openers; the "homey decor" ain't much, but the service is "swift" and you can "sit outside with your dog"; P.S. weekend brunchers may want to "bring a mag" to make the wait go faster.

### NEW Silvera's Steakhouse  M *Steak*

- | - | - | VE

**Huntington Beach** | 126 Main St. (off PCH) | 714-969-9000 | www.silvera-steakhouse.com
Surf City's new haven for carnivores is a dark, debonair affair offering a menu of aged prime steaks with VIP prices plus martinis and wines to match; since the owner is Korn drummer David Silveria (whose name is shortened for the restaurant), and the bar menu is served until midnight, it's likely to lure a tuned-in entourage plus the odd rocker or two (though families will appreciate the kids' meals).

### Z 6ix Park Grill  *Californian*

∇ 21 | 19 | 19 | $40

**Irvine** | Hyatt Regency Irvine | 17900 Jamboree Rd. (I-405) | 949-225-6666 | www.hyatt.com
Itinerant execs and restless locals say they're "pleasantly surprised" that this slick dining room in the glossy Irvine Hyatt delivers "delightfully good" Californian fare like meat and fish grilled over specialty woods and give props to the "staff that's tops" too; also nice is the separate entrance that bypasses the hotel lobby hubbub and a newly snazzed up wine bar serving loads of West Coast vintages and tapas.

### Sorrento Grille  *Californian/Mediterranean*

22 | 21 | 21 | $47

**Laguna Beach** | 370 Glenneyre St. (Mermaid St.) | 949-494-8686 | www.culinaryadventures.com
Attracting a "hip and local" crowd, this "winning" Laguna cousin to French 75 and Chat Noir is "well known for martinis" and "enjoyable" Cal-Med fare that impresses with its "great cost-to-quality ratio"; the

high-ceilinged but "overcrowded" digs can grow "noisy as a leaf-blower testing lab" on "busy nights", but the upstairs tables offer a "more private experience."

### Souplantation  *American*  16 | 10 | 12 | $12

**Costa Mesa** | 1555 Adams Ave. (Royal Palm Dr.) | 714-556-1903
**Foothill Ranch** | 26572 Towne Centre Dr. (Market Pl.) | 949-472-1044
**Fountain Valley** | 11179 Talbert Ave. (Newhope St.) | 714-434-1814
**Irvine** | 2825 Main St. (Jamboree Rd.) | 949-474-8682
www.souplantation.com
Additional locations throughout Southern California
See review in Los Angeles Directory.

### Spaghettini Italian Grill & Jazz Club  *Italian*  20 | 22 | 20 | $43

**Seal Beach** | 3005 Old Ranch Pkwy. (bet. I-405 & Seal Beach Blvd.) | 562-596-2199 | www.spaghettini.com
"Well-prepared" Northern Italian dishes and "captivating jazz" most nights are the "perfect combination" at Seal Beach's "lovely" Tuscan-style "hideaway" for a "terrific evening out with family or friends" as well as a "fantastic Sunday brunch" (which is broadcast on The Wave radio station); although some patrons call it "pricey" considering the sometimes "average" offerings, the weekday happy hour features discounted bites and drinks.

### Spark Woodfire Grill  *American*  17 | 17 | 17 | $34

**Huntington Beach** | 300 PCH, 2nd fl. (Main St.) | 714-960-0996 | www.sparkwoodfiregrill.com
See review in Los Angeles Directory.

### ⚡ Splashes  *Californian/Mediterranean*  21 | 25 | 21 | $50

**Laguna Beach** | Surf & Sand Resort | 1555 S. Coast Hwy. (bet. Blue Bird Canyon Dr. & Calliope St.) | 949-497-4477 | www.surfandsandresort.com
"You can't dine closer to the ocean" than at this "gorgeous", fireplace-warmed respite at the Surf & Sand Resort, where reviewers relish the "spectacular" vista and feeling the mist off the "Laguna Beach waves", while discovering the "well-done" Cal-Med cuisine is "better than the view implies"; it's popular for "open-air" lunches and "romantic dinners", though shore-betters recommend "make a reservation" and "go early to catch the sunset."

### Steelhead Brewing Co.  *Pub Food*  16 | 14 | 15 | $21

**Irvine** | University Ctr. | 4175 Campus Dr. (Bridge Rd.) | 949-856-2227 | www.steelheadbrewery.com
"Solid" burgers and other "above-average" American pub grub, as well as wood-fired pizzas that fans "love", support the selection of "high-quality" "site-made brews" at this "easy", "after-work" stop by UCI; while some sniff it's "frat-boy central", that's no surprise considering specials like '$1 Taco Mondays.'

### NEW Stella's  *Italian*  ▽ 19 | 22 | 21 | $41

**Monarch Beach** | Monarch Bay Plaza | 17 Monarch Bay Plaza (off Crown Valley Pkwy.) | 949-234-1679 | www.stellasitalian.com
Coast-close Monarch Beach's Italian arrival in the former space of Mirabeau "looks promising", from the pastas and brick-oven pizzas to the "hot" bar to the outdoor fire pit; if the "execution" in the kitchen

and front-of-house that "needs polishing", supporters don't mind since the concept is an "improvement" that "could be great if they get it together."

**Stonefire Grill** *BBQ*  20 | 13 | 14 | $17

**Fountain Valley** | 18727 Brookhurst St. (Ellis Ave.) | 714-968-8300
**Irvine** | 3966 Barranca Pkwy. (bet. Paseo Westpark & Santa Rosa) |
949-777-1177
www.stonefiregrill.com
See review in Los Angeles Directory.

**☑ Stonehill Tavern** Ⓜ *American*  28 | 27 | 26 | $79

**Dana Point** | St. Regis Resort, Monarch Bch. | 1 Monarch Beach Resort (Niguel Rd.) | 949-234-3318 | www.michaelmina.net
"Star" chef Michael Mina's "smash hit" at the luxe St. Regis Resort "embodies OC chic" with a "phenomenal" take on New American dishes, highlighted in "artfully presented tastings" that are even "more beautiful" than the "endless parade of pretty people"; along with a "swanky" design by Tony Chi, patrons are impressed by the "first-class service" – just expect a little "noise" and some "prohibitive" costs, especially on the wine list.

**☑ Studio** *Californian/French*  27 | 27 | 26 | $84

**Laguna Beach** | St. Regis Resort, Monarch Bch. | 30801 S. PCH (Montage Dr.) | 949-715-6420 | www.studiolagunabeach.com
Smitten surveyors say "you don't want to leave, ever" after "sublime" dining in this Laguna resort destination "on a bluff" that "may be the most beautiful spot on the entire SoCal coast", flaunting wraparound vistas of "breaking Pacific waves" that buoy it to No. 1 for Decor in Orange County; the "top-notch" Cal–New French fare from chef James Boyce is equally "stunning", and "impeccable" service adds to an experience that feels like "no expense has been spared", so "forget what it costs" and "don't miss the sunset" (as there's less to see "after dark").

**☑ Summit House** *Continental*  25 | 26 | 24 | $45

**Fullerton** | 2000 E. Bastanchury Rd. (State College Blvd.) | 714-671-4111 | www.summithouse.net
"Ask for a window table" with "exquisite nighttime views" at this "celebratory" destination "atop Fullerton's hills" advise inlanders of this "legendary", "homey" mock mansion known for "traditional" Continental feasts ("excellent prime rib, steaks and John Dory") "plated with pride" and served by an "experienced, warm" staff; the "relaxing tavern" is also an appealing option, since "reservations aren't necessary and the live piano is wonderful."

**Sundried Tomato Café** *Californian*  22 | 17 | 20 | $33

**Laguna Beach** | 361 Forest Ave. (bet. Beach & Glenneyre Sts.) | 949-494-3312
**San Juan Capistrano** | Franciscan Plaza | 31781 Camino Capistrano (Ortega Hwy.) | 949-661-1167
www.thesundriedtomatocafe.com
These "easygoing" coastal cafes lure a "loyal clientele" for "nicely executed" Californian eats like "unusual salads, sandwiches" and the "savory" namesake soup; with their "gracious" service, "well-chosen" wine list and "attractive" patio seating, guests rely on them for "enjoyable", moderately priced meals.

| | FOOD | DECOR | SERVICE | COST |
|---|---|---|---|---|

### Sutra Lounge ☒ *Eclectic*
| | - | - | - | |

**Costa Mesa** | Triangle Sq. | 1870 Harbor Blvd. (bet. Newport Blvd. & 19th St.) | 949-722-7103 | www.sutrabar.com

A "clubbing crowd" heads to this multiroom Costa Mesa spot "to be seen" while grazing on Eclectic small plates like sashimi and steak Sutra, served with blueberry sauce; while the weekend DJs and "chic" Eastern stylings go a long way for some loungers, others say the fare needs to be "kicked up", adding "short skirts don't equal great service."

### S Vietnamese Fine Dining *Vietnamese*
| | ▽ 24 | 24 | 22 | $32 |

**Westminster** | 545 Westminster Mall Dr. (bet. Bolsa Ave. & Goldenwest St.) | 714-898-5092 | www.sfinedining.com

"High-end" "Vietnamese fusion" "was bound to happen sooner or later" and, "fortunately, it works" at this Westminster locale with "modern" decor that "probably warrants the higher prices" for this edge of Little Saigon; a "competent" staff and weekend piano music add to the "upmarket" appeal, making for a "charming" "date place."

### Table Ten *American*
| | ▽ 19 | 15 | 18 | $31 |

**Fullerton** | 124 W. Commonwealth Ave. (N. Harbor Blvd.) | 714-526-3210 | www.tableten.net

Downtown Fullerton's "intimate" "gem" is "one of the few" in the area offering "fresh, experimental" New American cuisine according to fans who also appreciate the "hard-to-resist" live jazz Wednesday-Sunday nights; meanwhile, dissenters point to inconsistent service, a menu and wine list that "need some improvement" and decor that's "not up to par with the price."

### ☒ Tabu Grill *Seafood/Steak*
| | 26 | 21 | 24 | $55 |

**Laguna Beach** | 2892 S. PCH (Nyes Pl.) | 949-494-7743 | www.tabugrill.com

"Utterly amazing" "big flavors" of surf 'n' turf cooking with a Pacific Rim touch distinguish Nancy Wilhelm's "shining star" where the "closely packed" "Lilliputian tables" benefit from "beautiful" Polynesian-inspired surroundings; the servers are "courteous" and "know their wines", so once guests get past the Laguna site's "limited parking" and "PCH traffic roaring outside the front door" ("where you sit can make a difference") to the "palate-pleasing meal", "everything else is forgotten"; P.S. "make reservations."

### Taco Loco ➊ *Eclectic*
| | 24 | 10 | 14 | $14 |

**Laguna Beach** | 640 S. PCH (bet. Cleo & Legion Sts.) | 949-497-1635

Lagunatics are loco for this "hippie" taco stand offering "unique" chow like "blackened mushroom tofu burgers" and the "best fish tacos" around for "crazy low prices"; surfers and tourists share tables right on PCH ("a short walk from the beach"), and if the "stoner's paradise" style of service is lacking, remember they're "open late" when most have closed in these parts.

### Taco Mesa *Californian/Mexican*
| | 24 | 8 | 15 | $12 |

**Costa Mesa** | 647 W. 19th St. (bet. Harbor Blvd. & Placentia Ave.) | 949-642-0629

*(continued)*

*(continued)*

### Taco Mesa

**Ladera Ranch** | Bridgepark Plaza | 27702 Crown Valley Pkwy.
(Marguerite Pkwy.) | 949-364-1957
**Mission Viejo** | Los Alisos Vill. | 22922 Los Alisos Blvd. (Trabuco Rd.) |
949-472-3144
**Orange** | Saddleback Shopping Ctr. | 3533 E. Chapman Ave. (Prospect St.) |
714-633-3922
www.tacomesa.net

South-of-the-border fare gets a "healthy" "twist" at this "innovative"
home-grown chainlet for "fresh", "zingy" Cal-Mex eats deemed "not
your typical" "rice and beans" fare; expect "unpretentious" digs, a
"friendly" counter staff and some of the "best taco bang for the buck
around"; N.B. they now take credit cards.

### Taco Rosa *Mexican*                    22 | 16 | 18 | $24

**Newport Beach** | Newport Hills Shopping Ctr. | 2632 San Miguel Dr.
(Bonita Canyon Dr.) | 949-720-0980
**NEW Tustin** | Marketplace, The | 13122 Jamboree Rd. (El Camino Real) |
714-505-6080
www.tacorosa.com

These "attractive", "upscale" sibs of Taco Mesa "don't believe in
bland" and offer a "great variety" of "flavorful", "nouveau" Mexican
specialties; "nice touches" like "homemade churros" and "the
best margaritas" made from "fresh-squeezed juices" compensate
for somewhat "inattentive" service; P.S. "don't miss" the "fab"
$13.95 champagne brunch.

### Taiko *Japanese*                    21 | 14 | 18 | $28

**Irvine** | Arbor Vill. | 14775 Jeffrey Rd. (Walnut Ave.) |
949-559-7190

"Prepare to wait" at Irvine's "tiny", "popular" Japanese "gem"
where acolytes appreciate the "mouthwatering" "sashimi cut in
humongous slices" and "creative" combo dinners; jaded types
"don't understand the popularity" and warn that "sushi connoisseurs might be disappointed" by the "inauthentic" fare in spite
of "reasonable prices."

### Taléo Mexican Grill *Mexican*                    23 | 20 | 20 | $31

**Irvine** | Park Pl. | 3309 Michelson Dr. (Jamboree Rd.) | 949-553-9002 |
www.taleomexicangrill.com

"A bit pricey for the genre, but worth the splurge", this Irvine Mexican
"kicks it up a notch" with "jazzed-up versions" of "classic dishes" like
"superb carnitas" and "sinfully indulgent mole"; service is "knowledgeable", while the open, airy setting includes a shaded patio that's
especially "enjoyable" on a warm evening.

### Tangata 🎫Ⓜ️ *Californian*                    ▽ 23 | 22 | 21 | $30

**Santa Ana** | Bowers Museum of Cultural Art | 2002 N. Main St. (20th St.) |
714-550-0906 | www.patinagroup.com

"Every bite excites" at this midpriced Patina Group cafe tucked into
Santa Ana's "remote" and "tranquil" Spanish courtyard within the
Bowers Museum; "patio seating" sets the scene "on nice days" for
"delightful lunches" of Californian cuisine that can include a "rather
good artisanal cheese plate" or the crème brûlée of the day.

| | FOOD | DECOR | SERVICE | COST |
|---|---|---|---|---|

### Tannins *Italian* ▽ 18 | 16 | 19 | $31

**San Juan Capistrano** | Rancho Ortega Plaza | 27211 Ortega Hwy.
(Rancho Viejo Rd.) | 949-218-3560 | www.tanninsrestaurant.com
Even if it's a "strip-mall" "wine bar" with "gourmet pretensions", this
San Juan Capistrano Italian is a "nice, cozy" choice for above "average" pizzas, pastas and entrees, plus "fairly priced" vino "flights" "selected with care"; some surveyors seek out the "more intimate" "new
lounge upstairs" (Ibiza at Tannins) that's "hopping" with a "late-night
menu" and "great live jazz" on weekends.

### TAPS Fish 23 | 21 | 21 | $34
### House & Brewery *American/Seafood*

**Brea** | 101 E. Imperial Hwy. (Brea Blvd.) | 714-257-0101 |
www.tapsbrea.com
"It has it all" attest enthusiasts of this "dependable" Brea seafooder
they say fits many "moods", choosing it for a "quick", "housebrewed
beer", a "cigar" on the "patio" or a "celebratory" meal of "top-of-the-
mark" American fare; service is "lovely", though "crowds" are an issue
especially during Sunday's "fab" brunch where live jazz is an additional draw; N.B. the Food score may not reflect a recent chef change.

### Ten Asian Bistro *Japanese/Pacific Rim* 22 | 25 | 19 | $41
**Newport Beach** | 4647 MacArthur Blvd. (bet. Birch St. & Campus Dr.) |
949-660-1010 | www.tenrestaurantgroup.com
A "deceptively boring" exterior yields to a "marvelously decorated",
"oh-so-chic" interior with waterfalls and a 16-ft. Buddha at Newport
Beach's "stylish", "upscale" "lounge" that lures a "hipster" crowd for
"amazing drinks", "specialty sushi" and other "fantastic" Pacific Rim
dishes; those who find it a bit too "rocking" inside may want to retire
to one of the two patio areas complete with fire pits; N.B. the Food
score may not reflect a January 2007 chef change.

### Thai Dishes *Thai* 18 | 11 | 17 | $18
**Fountain Valley** | 10065 Garfield Ave. (Brookhurst St.) | 714-962-1312
Additional locations throughout Southern California
See review in Los Angeles Directory.

### Thai This *Thai* 22 | 14 | 19 | $26
**Dana Point** | 24501 Del Prado (Amber Lantern St.) | 949-240-7944 |
www.thaithis.com
Dana Pointers delight in the "vividly flavored" fare at this "creative"
Thai eatery where "classic" dishes are reimagined in "original" ways,
prepared with the "freshest ingredients" and dubbed with "funny
names"; most ignore somewhat "sleepy" service and "nondescript"
digs considering there's "not much choice" for ethnic options
in the area.

### Thanh My ● *Vietnamese* ▽ 20 | 8 | 13 | $16
**Westminster** | 9553 Bolsa Ave. (bet. Brookhurst & Bushard Sts.) |
714-531-9540
This Westminster haunt in "Little Saigon" "epitomizes the common
man's restaurant" with "massive portions" of "authentic", "flavorful"
Vietnamese fare served up "fast" in bare-bones quarters; tabs are
"cheap" and it's also "open late" (till 1 AM), so folks freely overlook
"borderline rude service."

| | FOOD | DECOR | SERVICE | COST |
|---|---|---|---|---|

### 3Thirty3 Waterfront ⏺ *American* | 18 | 20 | 15 | $37

**Newport Beach** | 333 Bayside Dr. (PCH) | 949-673-8464 |
www.3thirty3nb.com

"Dark" and "modern", this Newport boîte "overflows with the beautiful crowd" lolling on "couches with a terrific view" of the harbor; while its New American sliders and small plates are "dependable" for lunch or a late-night bite (until 1:30 AM), most deem the dining "not for serious eaters" or anyone who minds "average" service and "limited high-table seating", since it's more about the "wine pours" and the "pick-up" scene.

### Ti Amo *Italian/Mediterranean* | 22 | 23 | 23 | $41

**South Laguna Beach** | 31727 S. PCH (3rd St.) | 949-499-5350 |
www.tiamolagunabeach.com

"Romance is in the air" at Laguna's "superb date spot" that's "lovely" for "intimate" dinners of "pricey" Italian-Mediterranean cuisine served in a converted 1928 home done up to resemble a Tuscan villa with candles, gauzy drapes and a working fireplace; service is appropriately "attentive", and though the less starry-eyed find the food "average tasting" and the scene "somewhat cheesy", for smitten surveyors, this is a "wonderful place" to "win over" someone special.

### Tommy Bahama Tropical Café *Caribbean* | 19 | 23 | 19 | $38

**Newport Beach** | Corona del Mar Plaza | 854 Avocado Ave.
(bet. Macarthur Blvd. & PCH) | 949-760-8686 | www.tommybahama.com

"Tropical" digs with lots of "florals" and "plenty of umbrella drinks" "transport diners to Nassau" at these Caribbean twins in Newport Beach and Palm Desert that fans favor for "creatively cooked" cuisine and "pleasant" patio seating made even more "relaxing" with a soundtrack of steel drums; cynics say the "fabulous environment" makes the "overpriced" "food taste better than it really is", though plenty disagree and elect to "continue the experience" by perusing the clothing and home furnishings at the "attached store."

### Tortilla Flats *Mexican* | 16 | 19 | 16 | $25

**Mission Viejo** | 27792 Vista del Lago (Marguerite Pkwy.) | 949-830-9980 |
www.tortillaflatsrestaurant.com

"Beautiful views" from a sprawling terrace overlooking manufactured Lake Mission Viejo are the main draw at this waterside eatery where it's "a shame" the "very ordinary" Mexican cookery "doesn't live up to" the "atmosphere"; prices are "high" too, but even critics concede it works "when you need a margarita" especially during "happy hour."

### Tortilla Jo's *Mexican* | 17 | 19 | 16 | $23

**Anaheim** | Downtown Disney | 1510 S. Disneyland Dr. (bet. Katella Ave. & Magic Way) | 714-535-5000 | www.patinagroup.com

The Patina Group's "busy", "family-friendly" yet "sophisticated" Mexican may strike some as a "little overpriced" (like "everything in Downtown Disney") but the "festive" atmosphere makes it a prime place for "boisterous parties, with or without kids"; food draws mixed reviews ("tasty" vs "dumbed down for tourists"), and critics warn that service is only "fair."

| | FOOD | DECOR | SERVICE | COST |
|---|---|---|---|---|

## Trabuco Oaks Steakhouse  *Steak*   ▽ 21 | 15 | 17 | $32

**Trabuco Canyon** | 20782 Trabuco Oaks Dr. (Trabuco Canyon Rd.) |
949-586-0722 | www.trabucooakssteakhouse.com

"Don't expect gourmet and don't wear a tie" warn regulars of this
decidedly "relaxed", "rustic" Trabuco Canyon steakhouse, an affordable "old standby" where cravats are "cut off" by the staff and
displayed on the wall; fans praise the "aged", "nicely marbled"
beef that's "cooked to perfection", though to some the "homey"
surroundings (there's a "tree growing through the center") come
off as "gimmicky."

## ☑ Tradition by Pascal  *French*   27 | 21 | 25 | $59
**(aka Pascal)**

**Newport Beach** | 1000 N. Bristol St. (Jamboree Rd.) | 949-263-9400 |
www.pascalnewportbeach.com

Chef-owner Pascal Olhats "continues to dazzle" "Newport foodies" with "classical", "unpretentious" French cookery (he "excels
with fish dishes") that's "still the best" for "wooing someone special"; loyalists "overlook" the "strip-mall location" because the
interior "oozes understated elegance" and the service is "first-
class", making a trip to this "high altar" of Gallic gastronomy
a "worthwhile treat."

## Turner New Zealand ☒ *Steak*   24 | 20 | 23 | $57

**Costa Mesa** | 650 Anton Blvd. (Park Center Dr.) | 714-668-0880

Costa Mesa's "very classy", very "pricey" Kiwi steakhouse caters to
carnivores with "melt-in-your-mouth lamb" and "high-quality",
"organic and hormone-free" beef imported from New Zealand and
offered up by hands-on owner Noel Turner; a few excitement seekers
deem the preparations too "simple" and the service "too scripted",
but most insist that this "terrifically located" (adjacent to South Coast
Plaza) spot "has the goods."

## 21 Oceanfront  *Seafood*   22 | 21 | 22 | $56

**Newport Beach** | 2100 W. Oceanfront (Balboa Blvd.) | 949-673-2100 |
www.21oceanfront.com

"They don't make them like this anymore" say supporters of this
"iconic" surf 'n' turfer off the Newport Beach pier where the
"fresh" fin fare is buoyed by "courteous" service and "worth every
penny" of the "pricey" tab; if a few find the "old-school" setting "a
little long in the tooth", their best bet is to have "a drink at the bar"
and gaze outward at the "lovely" sunset views.

## 230 Forest Avenue  *Californian*   25 | 19 | 21 | $43

**Laguna Beach** | 230 Forest Ave. (PCH) | 949-494-2545 |
www.230forestavenue.com

"Tourists at the tables and locals at the bar" stir up a "loud and
lively" atmosphere at this "upscale" Laguna Beach bistro and martini joint that feels like "New York by the beach"; its "delectable",
"innovative" Californian cuisine "surprises consistently", and despite "long waits" and service that can be "hampered" by the "tight
quarters", it's among the "best places to eat before one of the
summer festivals" – especially when you "snag a table outside" for
prime "people-watching."

| | FOOD | DECOR | SERVICE | COST |
|---|---|---|---|---|

### NEW Veggie Grill, The *Vegetarian* ▽ 20 | 15 | 23 | $13

**Irvine** | University Ctr. | 4213 Campus Dr. (bet. Culver & University Drs.) |
949-509-0003 | www.veggiegrill.com

"Who needs meat with food this good?" ask acolytes of this sunny
newcomer next to UCI featuring vegan and organic soups, salads and
"to-die-for sweet potato fries"; casual, order-at-the-counter service
and colorful, modern environs make it a "healthy change of pace."

### Vessia Ristorante *Italian* 22 | 18 | 24 | $36

**Irvine** | Crossroads Shopping Ctr. | 3966 Barranca Pkwy. (Culver Dr.) |
949-654-1155 | www.vessia.com

"Highly unusual" for "chain-heavy Irvine", this "family-run gem" of a
trattoria lures locals with "huge portions" of "much better than average",
"authentic" fare that is so Italian "you can sense that grandma's in the
kitchen"; in the bright front of the house, "sincerely warm" owner
Franco Vessia "assiduously works the tables" for a "nice personal touch."

### Villa Nova ⏺ *Italian* 19 | 20 | 21 | $45

**Newport Beach** | 3131 W. PCH (Newport Blvd.) | 949-642-7880 |
www.villanovarestaurant.com

Newport Beach's "over-50 crowd" gathers at this "classic" ersatz har-
borside villa for plates of "old-school Italian-American food" and
"views" of the waterfront "if you can get a window table"; though detractors find the eats "nothing to rave about", the "charming" service
and "warm atmosphere" make it a "great date spot"; P.S. the "laid-
back piano bar" is good for "relaxing after supper."

### Vine 🅂🅼 *Californian/Mediterranean* ▽ 25 | 19 | 23 | $50

**San Clemente** | 211 N. El Camino Real (Avenida Cabrillo) | 949-361-2079 |
www.vinesanclemente.com

This Cal-Med may be in "surf town" San Clemente but it has a "nice
Napa bistro feel" thanks to "surprising wines" and a "fabulous range"
of "excellent" dishes, including "nightly specials that make choosing
difficult"; the "small" space is "awkward but charming" and the service is "intelligent", causing some enthusiasts to label this "the best
place to eat in South county outside of Laguna."

### Vue *Californian* - | - | - | VE

**Dana Point** | Laguna Cliffs Marriott Resort | 25135 Park Lantern
(Dana Point Harbor Dr.) | 949-487-7555 | www.lagunacliffs.com

Perched atop a coastal bluff, the year-old restaurant at the Laguna
Cliff's Marriott (formerly the Regatta Grill) is "surprisingly good" and
even "exciting", offering midpriced "contemporary" Californian cuisine both indoors (in room decorated in relaxing earth tones) and
alfresco – with sweeping 180-degree vistas of Dana Point's harbor
and, if you time it right, colorful sunsets.

### Walt's Wharf *Seafood* 25 | 17 | 22 | $35

**Seal Beach** | 201 Main St. (Central St.) | 562-598-4433 | www.waltswharf.com

This "perpetually crowded" "little corner" fish house "across from the
pier" in Seal Beach "never disappoints" with its "fresh", "creative" seafood and "delectable pastas and salads"; "excellent" service and a "superb wine list" help offset the "long waits" – though locals know to go
for lunch when it takes reservations (it doesn't for dinner) and when
prices are a "value" to boot.

| | FOOD | DECOR | SERVICE | COST |
|---|---|---|---|---|

**Wasa** *Japanese* | 24 | 17 | 19 | $39

**Irvine** | Market Pl. | 13124 Jamboree Rd. (Irvine Blvd.) | 714-665-3338

**Newport Beach** | Bluffs Shopping Ctr. | 1346 Bison Ave. (MacArthur Blvd.) | 949-760-1511

www.wasasushi.com

"Innovative" Japanese "treasures" are arrayed in "knock-your-socks-off presentations" and topped with "signature sauces and garnishes" at this "slowly expanding" chainlet that draws loyal, local" sushi bar buffs; even "inconsistent" service and "long waits" on "weekend evenings" don't deter surveyors who say that these "small" and "trendy" slices of "heaven" are "worth the challenge."

**NEW Wicked Garden** *Californian/Mediterranean* | - | - | - | VE

**Dana Point** | Blue Lantern Plaza | 34085 PCH, Ste. 201 (Blue Lantern St.) | 949-493-7379

At this "sexy", bordellolike Dana Point newcomer, a "hip" crowd pays "New York prices" for Cal-Med food (and "generously poured" premium cocktails) that earns generally good reviews; some feel that the Gothic, "garish decor" (including heavy draperies and red, flickering candles) "detracts from the experience" but laud the "very friendly owners" who "work the room" at this "tucked away" haunt.

**Wild Artichoke, The** Ⓢ Ⓜ *Californian/Eclectic* | ▽ 24 | 16 | 22 | $36

**Yorba Linda** | Yorba Ranch Vill. | 4973A Yorba Ranch Rd. (Yorba Linda Blvd.) | 714-777-9646 | www.thewildartichoke.com

"Small is mighty" at sleepy Yorba Linda's "intimate", "strip-mall treasure" where "fresh", "gourmet" Cal-Eclectic "delights" are "well prepared" thanks to chef-owner James d'Aquila's "personal touch"; the sparsely decorated digs can feel "cramped" and "boring", but "friendly" service makes this a "wonderful" "neighborhood place."

**Wildfish Seafood Grille** *American/Seafood* | 23 | 22 | 21 | $48

**Newport Beach** | The Bluffs | 1370 Bison Ave. (MacArthur Blvd.) | 949-720-9925 | www.wildfishseafoodgrille.com

This "lively" Newport seafooder is the "place to be seen" for "hip" locals seeking "excellent" plates of steak and "super fresh fish" supported by a "great wine list" and "efficient, unassuming" hospitality; the "happening" scene is "upbeat" and "hectic", especially during the Sunday–Monday happy hour when the "half-price apps" and "$5 martinis" "can't be beat."

**Wingnuts** *BBQ* | 16 | 13 | 17 | $17

**Aliso Viejo** | 26711 Aliso Creek Rd. (Rte. 73) | 949-305-7700

**Costa Mesa** | Target Great Lands | 3030 Harbor Blvd. (Baker St.) | 714-434-7700

www.wingnuts.biz

"Messy" wings so big they're "apparently from mutantly large fowl" are the draw at this American where the chicken is "prepared a million ways" and there are "plenty of napkins" for dealing with the carnage; the "sports-bar" vibe comes complete with TVs but remains tame enough to be "good for families and gatherings", though detractors deem the eats "sorta boring" and "not the best or the cheapest."

|  | FOOD | DECOR | SERVICE | COST |
|---|---|---|---|---|

### Wolfgang Puck Cafe  *Californian*  | 18 | 16 | 17 | $27 |

**Costa Mesa** | South Coast Plaza | 3333 Bristol St. (Flower Blvd.) |
714-546-9653 | www.wolfgangpuck.com
See review in Los Angeles Directory.

### Wood Ranch BBQ & Grill  *BBQ*  | 20 | 17 | 18 | $26 |

**Anaheim Hills** | Anaheim Hills Festival | 8022 E. Santa Ana Canyon Rd.
(S. Festival Dr.) | 714-974-6660
**Rancho Santa Margarita** | El Paseo Plaza | 22352 El Paseo (bet. Alma Aldea &
el Portal) | 949-888-1100
www.woodranch.com
See review in Los Angeles Directory.

### Yard House  *American*  | 19 | 18 | 17 | $26 |

**Brea** | 160 S. Brea Blvd. (Birch St.) | 714-529-9273 ◗
**Costa Mesa** | Triangle Square Shopping Mall | 1875 Newport Blvd.
(bet. Harbor Blvd. & 19th St.) | 949-642-0090
**Irvine** | Irvine Spectrum Ctr. | 71 Fortune Dr. (Pacifica St.) | 949-753-9373
www.yardhouse.com
See review in Los Angeles Directory.

### Yi Dynasty  ☒ *Korean*  | – | – | – | M |

**Newport Beach** | 1701 Corinthian Way (Martingale Way) | 949-797-9292
"Grill-it-yourself" Korean BBQ meals are "well worth the lingering
odor" that diners take away from this spare, "upscale" eatery in
Newport Beach near John Wayne Airport; in addition to "prime
meats", "oh-so-filling" "tofu soups and tasty noodles", the menu also
offers "more exotic dishes" like tongue and tripe, though be warned
that at lunch, service can be "slow."

### Yves' Bistro  *French/Italian*  | 23 | 16 | 20 | $31 |

**Anaheim Hills** | Canyon Plaza | 5753 E. Santa Ana Canyon Rd.
(bet. Imperial Hwy. & Via Cortez) | 714-637-3733 | www.yvesbistro.com
This Anaheim Hills "cozy little bistro" is a "strip-mall" "surprise",
serving French-Italian fare that's "ambitious" for "vanilla north OC" –
especially the "excellent dessert soufflés", so "save room"; "accommodating and gracious owner" Yves Masquefa presides over the
"informal" space where solo diners can "sit at the bar and watch the
chefs work" in the open kitchen.

### Zankou Chicken  *Mediterranean*  | 22 | 6 | 12 | $11 |

**Anaheim** | 2424 W. Ball Rd., Ste. S & T (bet. Brookhurst & Magnolia Aves.) |
714-229-2060 | www.zankouchicken.com
See review in Los Angeles Directory.

### Zinc Cafe & Market  *Californian*  | 22 | 16 | 15 | $17 |

**Corona del Mar** | 3222 E. PCH (Marguerite Ave.) | 949-719-9462
**Laguna Beach** | 350 Ocean Ave. (Beach St.) | 949-494-6302
www.zinccafe.com
These "tiny but full-of-character" coast-hugging Californians lure locals
for "amazing lattes", "creative" vegetarian and vegan sandwiches and
"tasty sweets" in a "new-agey" atmosphere; the "dog-friendly" outdoor seating lends a "Euro feel", though some say the "self-serve
setup" is "awkward", and the newer Corona del Mar outpost "lacks the
soul" of the original Laguna location, which also offers a "great cheese
selection" and "avant-garde gifts" at its retail shop.

|  | FOOD | DECOR | SERVICE | COST |
|---|---|---|---|---|

### Zipangu ◑ Japanese
▽ 23 | 21 | 20 | $51

**Costa Mesa** | The LAB | 2930 Bristol St. (Randolph Ave.) | 714-545-2800 |
www.zipanguoc.com

"Small plates done well", including both "traditional" and "fusion" dishes, are the draw for "sushi and non-sushi eaters" alike at this trendy Costa Mesa Japanese tucked behind the "youth-inspired" LAB "anti-mall"; "happy-hour specials", "surprisingly reasonable prices" and "attentive service" by a "superb staff" cause devotees to swoon that it "compares to the cool Asian places in LA."

### NEW Zmario Italian
- | - | - | E

**Irvine** | 18912 MacArthur Blvd. (bet. Campus Dr. & Douglas) | 949-833-1900 |
www.myzmario.com

Revived and relocated to the landmark Chantelair edifice (facing John Wayne Airport) in early 2007, this new incarnation has a grander scale than its Tustin predecessor but still favors pricey, upmarket Northern Italian cookery geared toward the Irvine office set; a serpentine layout offers nooks suitable for everything from a romantic fireside chat to a garden lunch, plus a wine room perfect for business deal meals.

### Zov's Bistro 图 Mediterranean
25 | 19 | 21 | $38

**Tustin** | Enderle Ctr. | 17440 E. 17th St. (Yorba St.) | 714-838-8855
### Zov's Newport Coast Mediterranean
**NEW Newport Coast** | 21123 Newport Coast Dr. (San Joaquin Hills Rd.) |
949-760-9687
www.zovs.com

Chef-owner Zov Karamardian lovingly lays out "phenomenal" Mediterranean fare at her "hip" Tustin bistro where the food may be "haute" but the service is "down-home friendly"; those who flinch at the bistro's "pricey" menu opt for the "more casual", "always packed" adjoining bakery/cafe for "delectable" sandwiches, salads and "picture-perfect" pastries that "taste as good as they look"; N.B. a second bakery/cafe has opened in Newport Coast and a third is set for Irvine.

### Z'tejas Southwestern
18 | 16 | 16 | $26

**Costa Mesa** | South Coast Plaza | 3333 Bristol St. (Anton Blvd.) |
714-979-7469 | www.ztejas.com

South Coast Plaza's "happening" Southwestern "hangout" is "worth a visit on your next mall spree" thanks to "half-price appetizers" during happy hour, "outstanding margaritas" and cornbread that's "worth the trip"; the rest of the spicy meal "rates highly as bar food, somewhat lower for serious dining" say detractors, partly due to "spotty" service.

# PALM SPRINGS/ SANTA BARBARA RESTAURANT DIRECTORY

# Palm Springs & Environs

## TOP FOOD

27 Le Vallauris
26 Cuistot
25 Jillian's
Johannes
Sirocco

## TOP SERVICE

28 Le Vallauris
26 Wally's Desert
24 Le St. Germain
Sirocco
Cuistot

## TOP DECOR

28 Le Vallauris
26 Cuistot
Jillian's
25 Wally's Desert
24 Sirocco

## BEST BUYS

1. In-N-Out Burger
2. Original Pancake
3. Johnny Rockets
4. Ruby's
5. Native Foods

---

**Arnold Palmer's** Steak — | — | — | E

**La Quinta** | 78-164 Ave. 52 (Washington St.) | 760-771-4653 | www.arnoldpalmers.net

Tournament photos, trophies and other memorabilia decorate the walls at the famous golfer's La Quinta steakhouse, a "mecca" for duffers that also boasts fireplaces, a mountain view and a nine-hole putting green (for guests to enjoy); its "classic American" menu features pan-seared sea scallops, cowboy bone-in rib-eye and a banana split named for Palmer's hometown.

**AZUR** 🅂🅼 Californian/French — 22 | 21 | 22 | $68

**La Quinta** | La Quinta Resort & Club | 49-499 Eisenhower Dr. (Washington St.) | 760-564-7600 | www.laquintaresort.com

It's blue skies for devotees of this "high-quality" seasonal Cal-French located inside the "idyllic" La Quinta Resort & Club; nightly live jazz in the lounge adds to the "lovely ambiance", though detractors deem the caliber of both the cooking and service "not worthy of the prices", saying it's "living on its past" association with New York's Le Bernardin.

**Bellini** 🅂 Italian — ▽ 21 | 18 | 21 | $51

**Palm Desert** | 73-111 El Paseo (bet. Ocotillo Dr. & Sage Ln.) | 760-341-2626

"Affable" "husband-and-wife duo" Carlo and Marylena Pisano "treat all like family" at their "above-average" and "pretty" but "tiny" Palm Desert Italian; some are peeved by the "tourist" prices and even admirers admit the "space can feel cramped", but they "ignore it for the cannelloni"; N.B. closed from July to September.

**Billy Reed's** American — 16 | 13 | 19 | $23

**Palm Springs** | 1800 N. Palm Canyon Dr. (Vista Chino) | 760-325-1946

"Sweet" waiters and waitresses "who've been there forever" bring "mountainous portions" of "better-than-coffee-shop", "old-fashioned" American food, such as "mile-high" Boston cream pie, to the "retired crowd" in this "regular Palm Springs haunt"; as its "overblown Victorian" style reminds some of an "1890s whorehouse", young 'uns may find it "sorta stodgy" and "dowdy", but it's hard to argue with the "reasonable prices."

### BJ's *Pub Food*

**17 | 16 | 16 | $19**

**Corona** | The Crossings Shopping Ctr. | 2520 Tuscany Rd. (bet. Cajalco Rd. & Grand Oaks) | 951-271-3610

**Rancho Cucamonga** | 11520 Fourth St. (Buffalo Ave.) | 909-581-6750

**San Bernardino** | 1045 E. Harriman Pl. (Tippecanoe Ave.) | 909-380-7100

**NEW Temecula** | 26500 Ynez Rd. (Overland Dr.) | 951-252-8370

www.bjsbrewhouse.com

Additional locations throughout Southern California

See review in Los Angeles Directory.

### Blend *American*

**- | - | - | E**

**La Quinta** | 78-073 Calle Barcelona (bet. Avenida Bermudas & Desert Club Dr.) | 760-564-4771 | www.blendrestaurant.com

Chef-owner Kevin Kathman (ex French Laundry, Pinot Blanc) prepares pricey, market-driven New American fare, such as wild salmon tartare and pan-seared venison, matched by an extensive California-focused wine list at this spacious La Quinta destination that's well suited for small group dinners with five- and seven-course tasting menus available; it's best to call ahead since restaurant hours vary according to season.

### Café des Beaux-Arts *French*

**18 | 15 | 18 | $34**

**Palm Desert** | 73-640 El Paseo (Larkspur Ln.) | 760-346-0669 | www.cafedesbeauxarts.com

El Paseo pop-ins says the "French food and French style" "flash you back to those days in Paris" at this "casual" bistro "in the heart of the shopping area" of Palm Desert, where the cooking is "dependable", the staff is "welcoming" and the wraparound patio affords plenty of "people-watching"; N.B. closes every summer from July 5th through Labor Day Weekend.

### California Pizza Kitchen *Pizza*

**18 | 14 | 16 | $20**

**Rancho Cucamonga** | Victoria Gardens Mall | 12517 N. Mainstreet (bet. Kew & Monet Aves.) | 909-899-8611

**Riverside** | Riverside Plaza | 3540 Riverside Plaza Dr., Ste. 308 (Riverside Ave.) | 951-680-9362

**Temecula** | Promenade in Temecula | 40820 Winchester Rd. (bet. Margarita & Ynez Rds.) | 951-296-0575

**Palm Desert** | El Paseo Collection | 73-080 El Paseo, Ste. 8 (bet. Hwy. 74 & Ocotillo Dr.) | 760-776-5036

**Palm Springs** | Desert Fashion Plaza | 123 N. Palm Canyon Dr. (bet. Amado Rd. & Tahquitz Canyon Way) | 760-322-6075

www.cpk.com

Additional locations throughout Southern California

See review in Los Angeles Directory.

### Castelli's *Italian*

**23 | 17 | 21 | $50**

**Palm Desert** | 73-098 Hwy. 111 (Monterey Ave.) | 760-773-3365 | www.castellis.cc

"You expect Frank to walk in the door" at this "old-school to the max" Palm Desert Italian serving "traditional" dishes that earn generally good marks (e.g. "excellent" fettuccine Alfredo), and if some report "average" meals, the "nice touch" of nightly piano music helps compensate; the "bustling" room is staffed by "servers who are fiercely loyal to the regulars", among them the "golf crowd" going in for a "pricey" evening; N.B. closed from July to September.

FOOD | DECOR | SERVICE | COST

### Cedar Creek Inn *American*
19 | 20 | 19 | $33

**Palm Springs** | 1555 S. Palm Canyon Dr. (Sonora Rd.) | 760-325-7300 |
www.cedarcreekinn.com
See review in Orange County Directory.

### ☑ Cheesecake Factory *American*
20 | 18 | 18 | $26

**Rancho Cucamonga** | Victoria Gardens Mall | 12379 N. Mainstreet
(bet. Monet & Monticello Aves.) | 909-463-3011
**Rancho Mirage** | The River | 71-800 Rte. 111 (bet. Rancho Las Palmas Dr. &
Rancho Mirage Ln.) | 760-404-1400
www.thecheesecakefactory.com
Additional locations throughout Southern California
See review in Los Angeles Directory.

### Chop House *Steak*
21 | 20 | 20 | $54

**Palm Desert** | 74-040 Rte. 111 (Portola Ave.) | 760-779-9888 |
www.restaurantsofpalmsprings.com
**Palm Springs** | 262 S. Palm Canyon Dr. (bet. Arenas & Baristo Rds.) |
760-320-4500

"The red-meat revival continues" at this duo of "elegant" steakhouses in Palm Springs and Palm Desert that turn out some "very
good" meals, even if they're "not as dazzling" as some; although it
costs "big bucks", one bonus is that "entrees come with sides
rather than being à la carte", and the selection of 300-400 wines
further appeases appetites.

### Citrus City Grille *Californian*
20 | 18 | 18 | $32

**Riverside** | Riverside Plaza | 3555 Riverside Plaza Dr. (bet. Central &
Merrill Aves.) | 951-274-9099 | www.citruscitygrille.com
See review in Orange County Directory.

### Claim Jumper *American*
19 | 17 | 18 | $25

**Corona** | 380 McKinley St. (Promenade Ave.) | 951-735-6567
**Rancho Cucamonga** | 12499 Foothill Blvd. (I-15) | 909-899-8022
**San Bernardino** | 1905 S. Commercenter E. (Hospitality Ln.) | 909-383-1818
www.claimjumper.com
Additional locations throughout Southern California
See review in Los Angeles Directory.

### ☑ Cuistot Ⓜ *Californian/French*
26 | 26 | 24 | $68

**Palm Desert** | 72-595 El Paseo (Rte. 111) | 760-340-1000 |
www.cuistotrestaurant.com

"Panhandle on El Paseo if you have to" declare those delighted with chef-
owner Bernard Dervieux's "uniformly outstanding" (and "pricey")
Cal-French in Palm Desert that "keeps its standards high" with "beautifully presented" cuisine, an "impressive" 750-bottle selection of
wine and a "well-trained staff"; the "lovely" "château"-like setting provides an appropriately "charming" backdrop for what some say is "undoubtedly one of the best in the area" for "special-occasion" dining.

### Daily Grill *American*
18 | 17 | 18 | $30

**Palm Desert** | 73-061 El Paseo (Monterey Ave.) | 760-779-9911 |
www.dailygrill.com
See review in Los Angeles Directory.

### Falls Prime Steakhouse *Steak*
22 | 22 | 22 | $57

**La Quinta** | 78-430 Rte. 111 (Washington St.) | 760-777-9999

*(continued)*

## Falls Prime Steakhouse

**Palm Springs** | Mercado Plaza | 155 S. Palm Canyon Dr., 2nd fl.
(Arenas Rd.) | 760-416-8664
www.thefallsprimesteakhouse.com

"Exciting cocktails" (like the 'smokin' martini') poured by "friendly" bartenders plus "people-watching" pull patrons into this "busy" pair of steakhouses in La Quinta (with two waterfalls) and Palm Springs (where you can "grab a balcony seat on a warm night"); the "high-priced" meat satisfies most, with just a few contending that it "falls short."

## Gyu-Kaku ⑤ Ⓜ *Japanese*

| 20 | 18 | 18 | $31 |

**NEW** **Rancho Cucamonga** | Victoria Gardens Shopping Ctr. |
7893 Monet Ave. (Foothill Blvd.) | 650-270-4995 | www.gyu-kaku.com
See review in Los Angeles Directory.

## Hog's Breath Inn *American*

| 14 | 15 | 15 | $37 |

**La Quinta** | Old Town La Quinta | 78-065 Main St. (Calle Tampico) |
760-564-5556 | www.hogsbreathinnlaquinta.com

Western-themed decor and "movie memorabilia" from part-owner Clint Eastwood are the draws at this "gimmicky" American in Old Town La Quinta that plays host to a "noisy" "bar scene" appealing to "tourists"; yet with fare that's "only average" and service that can be "nonresponsive", skeptics sigh "it didn't make my day."

## Inka Grill *Peruvian*

| 19 | 11 | 18 | $18 |

**Temecula** | 26690 Ynez Rd. (Overland Dr.) | 951-699-2171 |
www.inkagrill.com
See review in Orange County Directory.

## ☑ In-N-Out Burger ● *Hamburgers*

| 24 | 10 | 18 | $8 |

**Corona** | 2305 Compton Ave. (bet. E. Ontario Ave. & Taber St.)
**Corona** | 450 Auto Center Dr. (bet. Rte. 91 & Wardlow Rd.)
**Riverside** | 6634 Clay St. (bet. General Rd. & Van Buren Blvd.)
**Riverside** | 72265 Varner Rd. (bet. Manufacturing & Ramon Rds.)
**Riverside** | 7467 Indiana Ave. (bet. Madison & Washington Sts.)
800-786-1000
www.in-n-out.com
Additional locations throughout Southern California
See review in Los Angeles Directory.

## Islands *American*

| 16 | 16 | 17 | $16 |

**Palm Desert** | 72-353 Rte. 111 (Desert Crossing) | 760-346-4007 |
www.islandsrestaurants.com
Additional locations throughout Southern California
See review in Los Angeles Directory.

## ☑ Jillian's ☒ *Continental*

| 25 | 26 | 23 | $60 |

**Palm Desert** | 74-155 El Paseo (Rte. 111) | 760-776-8242 |
www.jilliansfinedining.com

A "mainstay" on the "local top tier" and a "favorite special-occasion place" of many, this Palm Desert Continental practically "oozes class", with a "quaint, but formal" "private homelike setting", "romantic" courtyard, "superb" cuisine and "accommodating" service; it's "expensive" and reservations, which are required, "are not easy to come by", but most agree it's "worth the price" and "effort"; N.B. no shorts allowed.

| | FOOD | DECOR | SERVICE | COST |
|---|---|---|---|---|

## ☑ Johannes Ⓜ *Austrian* — 25 | 18 | 23 | $57

**Palm Springs** | 196 S. Indian Canyon Dr. (E. Arenas Rd.) | 760-778-0017 | www.johannesrestaurants.com

This "real find in Old Palm Springs" is a "pricey" "desert original" "known only to residents" that offers "outstanding", "adventurous" Austrian cuisine, including some of the "best Wiener schnitzel" around, paired with a "wonderful" wine list and enhanced by "astute" service; a mid-Survey redo of the "minimalist" space may not be reflected in the Decor score.

## John Henry's Ⓩ *Eclectic/French* — 22 | 13 | 22 | $31

**Palm Springs** | 1785 E. Tahquitz Canyon Way (Sunrise Way) | 760-327-7667

"Solid, inexpensive dinners" make this "homey" French-Eclectic a "pleasant place" in Palm Springs for "regular folks" who appreciate its "reliable" quality and "immense" portions; most commend the "efficient" staff, while suggesting "sitting outside if you can to avoid the boring interior"; N.B. closed June to October.

## Johnny Rebs' *BBQ* — 22 | 16 | 20 | $21

**Victorville** | 15051 Seventh St. (Victor Dr.) | 760-955-3700 | www.johnnyrebs.com

See review in Los Angeles Directory.

## Johnny Rockets *Hamburgers* — 15 | 15 | 16 | $13

**Rancho Mirage** | 71-800 Rte. 111 (Rancho Mirage Ln.) | 760-674-2064 | www.johnnyrockets.com

Additional locations throughout Southern California

See review in Los Angeles Directory.

## Kaiser Grille *American* — 16 | 16 | 16 | $32

**Palm Springs** | 205 S. Palm Canyon Dr. (Arenas Rd.) | 760-323-1003

"Early birds" "watch the interesting people walking by" on Palm Canyon Drive as they dig into "average" American dinners from this "standby" with outdoor seating; most deem it "ok for a quick bite, but not a lot more", since it "needs a tune-up on product, preparation and service."

## La Quinta Cliffhouse *American* — 18 | 21 | 18 | $42

**La Quinta** | 78-250 Rte. 111 (Washington St.) | 760-360-5991 | www.laquintacliffhouse.com

A "beautiful" historic ranch house is the setting for this "popular" La Quinta establishment where the "pleasant" atmosphere is bested only by its "dramatic cliffside location" and open-air patio affording "sunset views"; the New American fare is "reliable", if "not outstanding", and though some find it "pricey", tipplers tout the "happy-hour specials."

## Las Casuelas *Mexican* — 18 | 19 | 18 | $27

**Rancho Mirage** | 70-050 Rte. 111 (Via Florencio) | 760-328-8844 | www.lascasuelasnuevas.com

**La Quinta** | 78-480 Rte. 111 (Washington St.) | 760-777-7715 | www.lascasuelas.com

**Palm Springs** | 222 S. Palm Canyon Dr. (W. Arenas Rd.) | 760-325-2794 | www.lascasuelas.com

**Palm Springs** | 368 N. Palm Canyon Dr. (bet. Alejo & Amado Rds.) | 760-325-3213 | www.lascasuelas.com

"Popular with the over-tanned crowd", this "better-than-average local chain" dishes out "inexpensive" Mexican fare in "festive" environs; en-

*emigos* take aim at "mediocre" food "for the masses", but they still say they're "fun" for the "monster margaritas" and "chips" best enjoyed on the "patios under the stars."

### Le St. Germain  *French/Mediterranean*

24 | 23 | 24 | $59

**Indian Wells** | 74-985 Hwy. 111 (Cook St.) | 760-773-6511 | www.lestgermain.com

"Expertly" prepared and "elegantly served" French-Med cuisine "shines" at this "dressy" Indian Wells "favorite" for celebrating in a "pretty and peaceful" space; both its monthly wine dinners, which draw from the 500-label cellar, and seating on the enclosed patio make it a "dining oasis" for many.

### ⚡ Le Vallauris  *French/Mediterranean*

27 | 28 | 28 | $67

**Palm Springs** | 385 W. Tahquitz Canyon Way (N. Museum Dr.) | 760-325-5059 | www.levallauris.com

"Still the gold standard in the desert", this French-Mediterranean "gem" hits the trifecta as Palm Springs' No. 1 for Food, Decor and Service, thanks to an "outstanding" staff, a "romantic" "old-style French" dining room opening to "beautiful", "tree-shaded" patio and "superb", "classic" cuisine paired with an "excellent wine list"; it's "worth every dollar from your children's college fund" to experience what most agree is the "best restaurant in the Coachella Valley."

### LG's Prime Steakhouse  *Steak*

23 | 20 | 21 | $59

**La Quinta** | 78-525 Hwy. 111 (Washington St.) | 760-771-9911
**Palm Desert** | 74-225 Hwy. 111 (El Paseo) | 760-779-9799
**Palm Springs** | 255 S. Palm Canyon Dr. (bet. Arenas & Baristo Rds.) | 760-416-1779
www.lgsprimesteakhouse.com

"Wealthy" "golfer guys" drop "scads of green" on "high-quality steaks", "exceptional" Caesar salads made tableside and "birdbath-size" martinis at these "solid" restaurants voted Most Popular in the Palm Springs area, where "charming" owner Leon Greenberg adds a "personal touch"; the "awesome" La Quinta location, with its retractable roof, makes its siblings seem "dreary" by comparison, but all are equally "expensive."

### Lord Fletcher's ⓈⓂ  *Pub Food*

▽ 23 | 19 | 22 | $43

**Rancho Mirage** | 70385 Hwy. 111 (Country Club Rd.) | 760-328-1161 | www.lordfletcher.com

A "favorite of the country club set" for its "olde English" style, this Rancho Mirage British pub is a "good value" and a "dependable" option for "outstanding" grub and "generous" pours; even admirers agree, however, that after four decades it's starting to look a bit "antiquated" and in need of a "face-lift."

### Lucille's Smokehouse Bar-B-Que  *BBQ*

22 | 19 | 19 | $25

**Rancho Cucamonga** | 12624 N. Main St. (Foothill Blvd.) | 909-463-7427 | www.lucillesbbq.com
See review in Los Angeles Directory.

### Morton's The Steakhouse  *Steak*

25 | 21 | 24 | $61

**Palm Desert** | Desert Springs | 74-880 Country Club Dr. (Cook St.) | 760-340-6865 | www.mortons.com
See review in Orange County Directory.

| | FOOD | DECOR | SERVICE | COST |
|---|---|---|---|---|

### Native Foods ⑤ *Californian/Eclectic* — 22 | 12 | 17 | $16

**Palm Desert** | 73890 El Paseo (Portola Ave.) | 760-836-9396
**Palm Springs** | 1775 E. Palm Canyon Dr. (S. Sunrise Way) | 760-416-0070
www.nativefoods.com
See review in Los Angeles Directory.

### ☑ Original Pancake House *Diner* — 23 | 10 | 17 | $14

**Temecula** | 41377 Margarita Rd., Ste. F101 (Winchester Rd.) |
951-296-9016 | www.originalpancakehouse.com
See review in Los Angeles Directory.

### Outback Steakhouse *Steak* — 17 | 14 | 18 | $28

**San Bernardino** | 620 E. Hospitality Ln. (Waterman Ave.) | 909-890-0061
**Upland** | 530 N. Mountain Ave. (Arrow Hwy.) | 909-931-1050
**Palm Desert** | Waring Plaza | 72-220 Rte. 111 (Fred Waring Dr.) |
760-779-9068
www.outback.com
Additional locations throughout Southern California
See review in Los Angeles Directory.

### Picanha Churrascaria *Brazilian* — 19 | 15 | 19 | $39

**Palm Desert** | 73-399 El Paseo (San Pablo Ave.) | 760-674-3434 |
www.picanharestaurant.com
See review in Los Angeles Directory.

### Pomodoro Cucina Italiana *Italian* — 17 | 14 | 17 | $22

**Corona** | Hidden Valley Plaza | 510 Hidden Valley Pkwy. (off Rte. 15) |
951-808-1700 | www.pastapomodoro.com
Additional locations throughout Southern California
See review in Los Angeles Directory.

### Ristorante Mamma Gina *Italian* — 21 | 18 | 20 | $47

**Palm Desert** | 73-705 El Paseo (bet. Larkspur Ln. & San Luis Rey Ave.) |
760-568-9898 | www.mammagina.com
See review in Orange County Directory.

### Ristorante Tuscany *Italian* — ▽ 23 | 23 | 23 | $53

**Palm Desert** | JW Marriott Desert Springs Resort & Spa |
74855 Country Club Dr. (Cook St.) | 760-341-1839
"For a hotel restaurant" ("and a Marriott at that"), this "under-the-radar"
Palm Desert Italian wins raves for "surprisingly innovative" Tuscan
cuisine and "wonderful wines" served with "a touch of sophistication" in
a "beautiful" dining room "surrounded by water"; in all it makes for a
"memorable" evening that's worth experiencing "even as a local."

### Romano's Macaroni Grill *Italian* — 17 | 16 | 17 | $23

**Rancho Cucamonga** | Terra Vista Town Ctr. | 10742 Foothill Blvd.
(Aspen St.) | 909-484-3200
**Palm Desert** | 72920 Hwy. 111 (bet. Monterey Ave. & Town Center Way) |
760-837-1333
www.macaronigrill.com
See review in Los Angeles Directory.

### Rosine's *Armenian/Mediterranean* — 24 | 15 | 20 | $26

**NEW** **Corona** | The Crossings Shopping Ctr. | 2670 Tuscany Rd.,
Ste. 101 (Cahalco Rd.) | 951-372-9484 | www.rosines.com
See review in Orange County Directory.

| | FOOD | DECOR | SERVICE | COST |
|---|---|---|---|---|

## ⏻ Roy's *Hawaiian*

| 24 | 22 | 22 | $47 |

**Rancho Mirage** | 71-959 Rte. 111 (Magnesia Falls Dr.) | 760-340-9044 | www.roysrestaurant.com
See review in Los Angeles Directory.

## Ruby's *Diner*

| 16 | 16 | 17 | $16 |

**Riverside** | Tyler Galleria | 1298 Tyler St. (Magnolia Ave.) | 909-359-7829 | www.rubys.com
Additional locations throughout Southern California
See review in Los Angeles Directory.

## ⏻ Ruth's Chris Steak House *Steak*

| 25 | 21 | 23 | $59 |

**Palm Desert** | 74-740 Rte. 111 (Portola Ave.) | 760-779-1998 | www.ruthschris.com
See review in Los Angeles Directory.

## Shame on the Moon *American*

| - | - | - | M |

**Rancho Mirage** | 69950 Frank Sinatra Dr. (Golden State Ln.) | 760-324-5515 | www.shameonthemoon.com
A "welcoming" supper club with a "spectacular ambiance" thanks to cushy booths and a "hip" vibe, this gay-friendly Rancho Mirage "secret" offers a "broad" menu of "wonderful" American dishes like seared ahi steak and signature sautéed calf's liver all at moderate prices; service is "warm and "attentive", so the only downside is that it's so popular that reservations far in advance are often required; N.B. closed the last two weeks in August.

## ⏻ Sirocco *Italian*

| 25 | 24 | 24 | $57 |

**Indian Wells** | Renaissance Esmeralda Resort & Spa | 44-400 Indian Wells Ln. (Rte. 111) | 760-773-4444 | www.renaissanceesmeralda.com
"Genuine Italian chef" Livio Massignani turns out "marvelous" dishes that are "nothing short of heavenly" at this "expensive", "fine-dining" restaurant in Indian Wells' Renaissance Esmeralda Resort that some consider among "the best in the desert"; service is appropriately "solicitous" while the view of the Santa Rosa mountains helps make the "elegant" surroundings even more "spectacular."

## Sisley Italian Kitchen *Italian*

| 18 | 16 | 17 | $27 |

**Rancho Cucamonga** | Victoria Gardens Mall | 12594 N. Mainstreet (Eden Ave.) | 909-899-2554
See review in Los Angeles Directory.

## Souplantation *American*

| 16 | 10 | 12 | $12 |

**Rancho Cucamonga** | 8966 Foothill Blvd. (Vineyard Ave.) | 909-980-9690
**San Bernardino** | 228 W. Hospitality Ln. (Hunts Ln.) | 909-381-4772
**Temecula** | 26420 Ynez Rd. (Winchester Rd.) | 951-296-3922
www.souplantation.com
Additional locations throughout Southern California
See review in Los Angeles Directory.

## Tommy Bahama Tropical Café *Caribbean*

| 19 | 23 | 19 | $38 |

**Palm Desert** | The Gardens | 73-595 El Paseo (bet. Larkspur Ln. & San Pablo Ave.) | 760-836-0188 | www.tommybahama.com
See review in Orange County Directory.

FOOD | DECOR | SERVICE | COST

**Z Wally's Desert Turtle** *Continental*  25 | 25 | 26 | $72

**Rancho Mirage** | 71-775 Hwy. 111 (Rancho Las Palmas Dr.) | 760-568-9321 | www.wallys-desert-turtle.com

"Bring your manners and your gold card" to this "glamorous" Rancho Mirage standby catering to a "dressed-up" "old-money crowd" with "impeccably served" "traditional" Continental dishes like Dover sole and baked Alaska; some find the "opulent" interior with mirrored ceilings and crystal light fixtures a little too "Reagan '80s" and the vibe "geriatric", but loyalists insist that "special-occasion" dining "doesn't get any better" than at this longtime "favorite"; N.B. closed from July to mid-August.

**Yard House** ● *American*  19 | 18 | 17 | $26

**Rancho Cucamonga** | Victoria Gardens Mall | 12473 N. Mainstreet (Day Creek Blvd.) | 909-646-7116 | www.yardhouse.com
See review in Los Angeles Directory.

**Zip Fusion** *Japanese*  18 | 16 | 17 | $29

**Corona** | Crossings at Corona Mall | 2560 Tuscany St. (Grand Oaks) | 951-272-2177 | www.zipfusion.com
See review in Los Angeles Directory.

# Santa Barbara & Environs

| TOP FOOD | | TOP SERVICE | |
|---|---|---|---|
| 28 | Downey's | 27 | Downey's |
| 27 | Olio e Limone | 25 | Ballard Inn |
| 26 | Arigato Sushi | | Stella Mare's |
| | Bouchon | 24 | Louie's |
| | Ballard Inn | | Palace Grill |

| TOP DECOR | | BEST BUYS | |
|---|---|---|---|
| 25 | Stella Mare's | 1. | In-N-Out Burger |
| | Sevilla | 2. | Noah's NY Bagels |
| 24 | Ranch House | 3. | Baja Fresh Mex. |
| | Cafe Buenos Aires | 4. | Sharky's Mexican |
| | Cold Spring | 5. | La Super-Rica |

### Alcazar ⑤ Spanish            ▽ 19 | 18 | 22 | $32

**Santa Barbara** | 1812 Cliff Dr. (Lighthouse Rd.) | 805-962-0337 | www.alcazartapasbar.com

Santa Barbara imbibers head to this "hip" boîte in a "sleepy mesa neighborhood" for a little sangria (as well as "wonderful" cocktails) to go with their "socializing" and "consistent" Spanish dishes overseen by "owners who care"; though some sticklers say the food's more "random small plates" than tapas, hardly anyone minds after "a few mojitos."

### ☑ Arigato Sushi Japanese            26 | 18 | 20 | $40

**Santa Barbara** | 1225 State St. (bet. Anapamu & Victoria Sts.) | 805-965-6074

"One bite and you know why everyone" – "from rock stars to your fifth-grade teacher" – is chowing down on "masterful", "novel" preparations of the "freshest" sushi ("yellowtail that melts in your mouth") and cooked Japanese "delicacies" from "sensei" Wataru Kaneko in this "vibrant", "crowded" Downtown Santa Barbara "hot spot"; just remember, it "can get expensive" since "you can't help but overeat"; N.B. no reservations taken.

### Auberge at Ojai Ⓜ Californian/French            21 | 22 | 21 | $49

**Ojai** | 314 El Paseo Rd. (Ojai Ave.) | 805-646-2288 | www.aubergeatojai.com

Inside this "charming and warm converted house" (with a perpetual flame in the stone fireplace), chef-owner Christian Shaffer (Avenue) turns out "inventive" seasonal Cal-French fare for Ojai locals and travelers alike; both the "enchanting" view from the patio and "attentive" service suit "special occasions", though some naysayers complain about "Los Angeles attitude and prices"; N.B. no longer open for Sunday brunch.

### Austen's at the Pierpont Inn Californian            ▽ 19 | 19 | 21 | $40

**Ventura** | Pierpont Inn | 550 Sanjon Rd. (Harbor Blvd.) | 805-643-6144 | www.pierpontinn.com

"The view, the view" of the Channel Islands makes Ventura visitors want to "linger" in this dining room of the 1910 Craftsman-style Pierpont Inn perched on a rise above the Pacific; live music on the weekends, "excellent" service and "good" Californian fare, including Châteaubriand for two, keep the majority satisfied, though some call the cooking quality "variable from night to night."

| | FOOD | DECOR | SERVICE | COST |
|---|---|---|---|---|

**Baja Fresh Mexican Grill** *Mexican*  — 18 | 10 | 14 | $10

**Ventura** | Telephone Plaza | 4726-2 Telephone Rd. (Westinghouse St.) | 805-650-3535 | www.bajafresh.com
Additional locations throughout Southern California
See review in Los Angeles Directory.

**Z Ballard Inn & Restaurant, The M** *French*  — 26 | 23 | 25 | $52

**Ballard** | Ballard Inn | 2436 Baseline Ave. (bet. Alamo Pintado & Refugio Rds.) | 805-688-7770 | www.ballardinn.com
Chef-owner Budi Kazali turns out "sophisticated" New French dishes with "adventuresome" Asian touches that are "a treat for the palate" at this "elegant" eatery in the Ballard Inn where the "impressive" vino selection befits its location in the heart of Santa Barbara wine country; "enthusiastic" service shines while the "secluded" setting has some suggesting "do yourself a favor and book a room" at this "romantic" retreat and "make a weekend of it."

**NEW Bella Vista** *Californian*  — ▽ 26 | 28 | 28 | $67

**Montecito** | Four Seasons Resort, The Biltmore | 1260 Channel Dr. (off Hill Rd.) | 805-565-8237 | www.fourseasons.com
Following a renovation at Montecito's Biltmore Four Seasons, this "eclectic" Californian emerged with a retractable roof and "fantastic ocean view" through floor-to-ceiling windows and from a patio with a fire pit; its "extremely comfortable" seating and quality service add to the "total experience", and while diners describe the meals, including a caviar and champagne brunch, as "delicious", they conclude that "in the end you're paying more for the location than anything else."

**BJ's** *Pub Food*  — 17 | 16 | 16 | $19

**Oxnard** | Esplanade Plaza | 461 W. Esplanade Dr. (bet. Oxnard Blvd. & Vineyard Rd.) | 805-485-1124 | www.bjsbrewhouse.com
Additional locations throughout Southern California
See review in Los Angeles Directory.

**Blue Agave ●** *Eclectic*  — 19 | 20 | 21 | $34

**Santa Barbara** | 20 E. Cota St. (State St.) | www.blueagavesb.com
"An interesting cross-section of age ranges and menu choices" creates a truly Eclectic dining experience at this "lovely" Santa Barbara boîte where the staff contributes to the "warm" atmosphere, which includes a vibrant "bar scene"; "tasty" signatures like the duck carnita relleno and the buffalo burger are enhanced by what tequila tipplers tout as the "best margarita in town", and capped off with cigars for sale to smoke on the balcony.

**Z Bouchon** *Californian/French*  — 26 | 20 | 24 | $56

**Santa Barbara** | 9 W. Victoria St. (bet. Chapala & State Sts.) | 805-730-1160 | www.bouchonsantabarbara.com
"Wow!" rave reviewers of this Santa Barbara "delight" whose open kitchen offers "fantastic" Cal-French "wine-country" cuisine that "tempts all the senses", paired with an "in-depth" list of Central Coast labels well-suited to "celebrations"; its "intimate", candlelit setting features hardwood floors and a terrace that's enclosed in the winter, and the staff is "more than helpful", though a few are peeved about how "pricey" it is.

| | FOOD | DECOR | SERVICE | COST |
|---|---|---|---|---|

### NEW Brooks M *American*

| | - | - | - | E |

**Ventura** | 545 E. Thompson Blvd. (S. California St.) | 805-652-7070 | www.restaurantbrooks.com

Chef Andy Brooks has cooked with some of the best, including NAHA in Chicago, Lark Creek Cafe in NoCal and DC Coast in DC, and now he's making his debut as a chef-owner with this pricey New American in Ventura; although it's situated right in the middle of the lively antiques district, it sports a contemporary design of browns and blues.

### Brophy Bros. *Seafood*

| | 21 | 17 | 19 | $28 |

**Santa Barbara** | 119 Harbor Way (Shoreline Dr.) | 805-966-4418 | www.brophybros.com

One of "the best spots in town to catch the Santa Barbara coastal vibe", this marina mainstay boasts "terrific views", "pelicans practically on the windowsill" and the feel of a "fishermen's hangout" laud locals and LA "pilgrims" looking for "fresh-as-it-gets" seafood; just be ready for an "often rambunctious crowd" fueled by "stiff drinks" during the frequent "long waits for a table"; N.B. a new branch is opening in Ventura.

### Brothers Restaurant at Mattei's Tavern *American*

| | 24 | 20 | 22 | $47 |

**Los Olivos** | 2350 Railway Ave. (Foxen Canyon Rd.) | 805-688-4820 | www.matteistavern.com

Oenophiles pull up to this circa-1890 "stagecoach stop" in Los Olivos "after a day of wine tasting" to "enjoy a leisurely meal" of seasonal, "refreshingly flavored" American fare matched by "outstanding" vintages; although some find the menu a bit "limited", most admire the "informal" atmosphere and agree the service is "way above average."

### Brown Pelican, The *Californian*

| | 16 | 22 | 16 | $29 |

**Santa Barbara** | 2981½ Cliff Dr. (Las Positas Rd.) | 805-563-4960

"You can't beat the waterside location" or "relaxing views" of Hendry's Beach at this Santa Barbara spot that remains a "local hangout" in spite of service that "needs improvement" and "inconsistent" Californian fare; it's "best for breakfast" or "a laid-back brunch" on the open-air patio where the combination of "strong coffee" and "the sounds of the waves" deliver the ultimate "mind-clearing experience."

### Bucatini *Italian*

| | 22 | 15 | 20 | $34 |

**Santa Barbara** | 436 State St. (bet. E. Gutierrez & Haley Sts.) | 805-957-4177 | www.bucatini.com

"Sophisticated" Northern Italian dishes and wood-fired pizzas are a "good value for the quality and portion size" at this "very kid-friendly" trattoria on Santa Barbara's State Street that's a "local favorite"; a "heated patio" shaded by palm trees makes it a fine spot to "sit and people-watch" even if the passing traffic "can be noisy."

### Ca' Dario *Italian*

| | 25 | 19 | 22 | $42 |

**Santa Barbara** | 37 E. Victoria St. (Anacapa St.) | 805-884-9419 | www.cadario.net

"Everyone seems to know everyone" at this "popular" Santa Barbara trattoria where chef Dario Furlati "knows how to cook" "consistently excellent" "genuine" Northern Italian fare that "pleases even the most jaded" patrons; "friendly" servers work the "cozy", "rustic" room that some say is marred by "terrible acoustics" and too "tight" seating.

| | FOOD | DECOR | SERVICE | COST |
|---|---|---|---|---|

### Cafe Buenos Aires  *Argentinean*  | 16 | 24 | 19 | $38 |

**Santa Barbara** | 1316 State St. (bet. Arlington Ave. & E. Victoria St.) | 805-963-0242 | www.cafebuenosaires.com

A "lovely" "place to tango on Wednesday evenings" and visit before or after the Arlington Theatre, this Argentinean offers "decent" steaks, empanadas and tapas in a "cozy", Spanish-tiled interior and on "one of the most beautiful patios in Santa Barbara"; both the mojitos and the "friendly" service enhance the "romantic" atmosphere, which may be why some feel it "survives more on ambiance than food."

### Cafe del Sol  *Californian*  | 18 | 19 | 21 | $29 |

**Montecito** | 30 Los Patos Way (Cabrillo Blvd.) | 805-969-0448

"Easy, breezy" patio lunches lead into a "local bar scene" "driven by the margaritas" at this Californian (with a few Mexican choices) "tucked out of the way behind the bird refuge" in Montecito; while reviewers rate the food as rather "average" it's a "decent value for the money", and the quality service helps keep it "popular."

### Cafe Fiore  *Italian*  | 21 | 21 | 18 | $37 |

**Ventura** | 66 S. California St. (bet. Main St. & Santa Clara St.) | 805-653-1266 | www.fiorerestaurant.net

This "lively" Southern Italian "standout" in Ventura serves rustic pizzas and pastas along with "innovative" specials and "great" martinis; its pillow-backed booths, patio tables and "seats overlooking the kitchen" fan the flames for "date night", though the "service leaves much to be desired if you're not a regular" and the live music can get "too loud" – so it's no surprise the crowd "becomes much younger after 9 PM."

### California Pizza Kitchen  *Pizza*  | 18 | 14 | 16 | $20 |

**Ventura** | Pacific View Mall | 3301 E. Main St. (Mills Rd.) | 805-639-5060
**Santa Barbara** | Paseo Nuevo Mall | 719 Paseo Nuevo, on Chapala St. (De La Guerra St.) | 805-962-4648
www.cpk.com
Additional locations throughout Southern California
See review in Los Angeles Directory.

### Carlitos Cafe Y Cantina  *Mexican*  | 19 | 17 | 19 | $29 |

**Santa Barbara** | 1324 State St. (bet. Sola & Victoria Sts.) | 805-962-7117 | www.carlitos.com

The patio is "the place to be" at this "popular" Santa Barbara cousin to Cava, which plates up "consistent" Mexican dishes that are "easily shareable" – allowing groups to bring the per-person price "within reason"; although some disappointed diners judge the cuisine "generic", many are appeased by the "interesting live music" (Wednesday–Sunday) and "love the margaritas" to boot.

### Cava  *Pan-Latin*  | 21 | 21 | 21 | $37 |

**Montecito** | 1212 Coast Village Rd. (Olive Mill Rd.) | 805-969-8500 | www.cavarestaurant.com

Paella proponents appreciate the "innovative" Pan-Latin and "well-done" Spanish dishes at this "smart", tile-floored Montecito cafe (sister to Carlitos in Santa Barbara), where "friendly" servers, a "lovely" patio and live music Wednesday–Sunday buoy the "festive" atmosphere; although critics claim the fare is "not a good value", even they concede the "mean margaritas" "save the day."

| | FOOD | DECOR | SERVICE | COST |
|---|---|---|---|---|

### Chad's 🗷 *American*

**22 | 22 | 23 | $42**

**Santa Barbara** | 625 Chapala St. (bet. Cota & Ortega Sts.) | 805-568-1876 | www.chadsonline.com

A "young", "'in' spot" that's "not overly chic", this Santa Barbara "hangout" housed in a "charming" 19th-century Victorian house also serves "serious" New American fare with a few "Southern" touches; "improved" service is a boon for the "happy-hour" scene, though a few wonder "what's up with the psychedelic cow mural on the back bar?"

### China Pavilion *Chinese*

**▽ 23 | 17 | 20 | $24**

**Montecito** | 1070 Coast Village Rd. (bet. Hermosillo Dr. & Hot Springs Rd.) | 805-565-9380

**Santa Barbara** | 1202 Chapala St. (Anapamu St.) | 805-560-6028 www.china-pavilion.com

"You get more than you pay for" at this Santa Barbara and Montecito pair offering "excellent" Chinese food, such as "outstanding" walnut prawns and distinctive selections off the "special menu"; a largely "attentive" staff and "attractive" red-hued rooms enhance the "lovely ambiance."

### Cholada *Thai*

**▽ 26 | 9 | 22 | $20**

**Ventura** | 387 E. Main St. (bet. Oak & Palm Sts.) | 805-641-3573 | www.choladathaicuisine.com

See review in Los Angeles Directory.

### Cold Spring Tavern *American*

**19 | 24 | 18 | $32**

**Santa Barbara** | 5995 Stagecoach Rd. (Rte. 154) | 805-967-0066 | www.coldspringtavern.com

It's an "adventure" just traveling to this "unique" "stagecoach tavern" "tucked away on the mountainside" in Santa Barbara, whose well-preserved 1860s digs still "ooze character"; providing an American menu of "hearty" game items and "lumberjack breakfasts" accompanied by live country and blues on the weekends, it draws "bikers, cyclists, families and dogs", and even those who find the cooking "not quite destination-caliber" salute it as a "special place"; P.S. "ask to sit by the fireplace on a cold winter day."

### NEW C-Street *Californian*

**- | - | - | M**

**Ventura** | Crowne Plaza Ventura Beach Hotel | 450 E. Harbor Blvd. (S. California St.) | 805-648-2100 | www.cpventura.com

The name of this newly opened Californian in the Crowne Plaza Ventura Beach Hotel comes from the fabled destination for local surfers at the end of California Street, the waves of which are visible from its floor-to-ceiling windows; its wines are all locally produced, as are most of the ingredients on its midpriced menu.

### ☑ Downey's 🅼 *Californian/French*

**28 | 22 | 27 | $63**

**Santa Barbara** | 1305 State St. (Victoria St.) | 805-966-5006 | www.downeyssb.com

"Local produce and local charm" come together at this "classic", voted No. 1 for Food and Service in Santa Barbara, where "serious food lovers" sup on "luscious" Cal-French cuisine proffered by "perfectionist" chef-owner John Downey; wife Liz oversees the "pleasantly attentive" staff that gives the "small, elegant" space a "warm" feel, all the better to appreciate a "first-class" experience that sets the "benchmark" for "special-occasion dining" in the area.

| | FOOD | DECOR | SERVICE | COST |
|---|---|---|---|---|

### Eladio's *American*

▽ 19 | 18 | 20 | $37

**Santa Barbara** | Harbor View Inn | 1 State St. (Cabrillo Blvd.) | 805-963-4466 | www.harborviewinnsb.com

"Fresh, local ingredients" build the backbone of the menu, which recently changed from Italian to American, at this on-site eatery at the Harbor View Inn that offers "wonderful views" of the ocean as well as courtyard seating; only a few have found it so far, but those who have praise the service and "great breakfasts" that make it well-suited to the tourist-heavy clientele.

### Elements *Californian*

22 | 22 | 21 | $45

**Santa Barbara** | 129 E. Anapamu St. (bet. Anacapa & Santa Barbara Sts.) | 805-884-9218 | www.elementsrestaurantandbar.com

"Innovative", "well-executed" Californian fare served "without attitude" "impresses" "locals and tourists alike" at this "upscale" Santa Barbara boîte that takes a cue from the four elements in its "ever-changing" menu and "elegant" interior design affording "amazing views"; air, most notably, is represented by the "lovely patio" overlooking the city's "majestic" courthouse sunken gardens.

### El Paseo Ⓜ *Mexican*

15 | 23 | 18 | $24

**Santa Barbara** | 10 El Paseo (Anacapa St.) | 805-962-6050

"Beautiful Spanish decor" and a "pitcher of margaritas" make the "so-so" Mexican fare taste better say supporters of this Santa Barbara "standby" housed in a "stunning" 19th-century courtyard and gardens; despite a "fiesta" feel (enhanced by mariachi players on weekends), detractors feel it's "expensive for what it is" and suggest you "go for a drink" and "just enjoy the setting and its history."

### El Torito *Mexican*

15 | 15 | 16 | $21

**Santa Barbara** | 29 E. Cabrillo Blvd. (State St.) | 805-963-1968 | www.eltorito.com
Additional locations throughout Southern California
See review in Los Angeles Directory.

### Emilio's *Italian/Mediterranean*

24 | 20 | 22 | $45

**Santa Barbara** | 324 W. Cabrillo Blvd. (Bath St.) | 805-966-4426 | www.emiliosrestaurant.com

"A serious little restaurant", this Santa Barbara "foodie" "favorite" turns out "memorable" Med and Northern Italian dishes (paired with "well-chosen" wines) at tabs that are only "moderately expensive"; add in a staff that "makes an effort to attend to your every need" plus "views of the Pacific" and this "can't-miss" spot has more than a few customers kicking themselves, avowing "we should think of going more often."

### Enterprise Fish Co. *Seafood*

18 | 17 | 18 | $33

**Santa Barbara** | 225 State St. (bet. Montecido & State Sts.) | 805-962-3313 | www.enterprisefishco.com
See review in Los Angeles Directory.

### Epiphany *American*

17 | 18 | 18 | $52

**Santa Barbara** | 21 W. Victoria St. (State St.) | 805-564-7100 | www.epiphanysb.com

The low-lighting and red velvet drapes create a "sensual atmosphere", all the better to "cozy up with your honey" at this Santa Barbara New

|  | FOOD | DECOR | SERVICE | COST |
|--|------|-------|---------|------|

American; surveyors split on the food ("usually good" vs. "a bit over-priced", but it's hard to go wrong with "a drink at the bar."

**NEW Fresco at the Beach** *Californian* | 20 | 23 | 20 | $38 |

**Santa Barbara** | Santa Barbara Inn | 901 E. Cabrillo Blvd. (S. Milpas St.) | 805-963-0111 | www.frescosb.com

A "pleasant surprise" at the Santa Barbara Inn, this "comfortable" new Californian leads off with "fabulous ocean views" and follows with "skillfully made" signatures like rack of lamb and bouilla-baisse; though "a bit more casual" than its predecessor, Citronelle, it's also more "reasonably priced", and once the kitchen gets "up to speed" a few pros predict it'll be "top-notch"; P.S. several surveyors suggest it for "lunch."

**Hitching Post** *BBQ* | 23 | 14 | 19 | $42 |

**Buellton** | 406 E. Rte. 246 (½ mi. east of Rte. 101) | 805-688-0676 | www.hitchingpost2.com
**Casmalia** | 3325 Point Sal Rd. (Santo Rd.) | 805-937-6151 | www.hitchingpost1.com

"Barbecued mushrooms, filet mignon and a glass of red" make "a winning trifecta" proclaim proponents of these Central Coast–style BBQs in Buellton and Casmalia where the "fantastic" fare is further enhanced by "sensational wines" (including the Highliner Pinot Noir made by owners Frank and Bill Ostini); "all-inclusive" meals make both branches a "fantastic value", though longtime loyalists lament the onslaught of "tourists" since the Buellton location was featured in the film *Sideways*.

**Hungry Cat, The** ● *Seafood* | 24 | 15 | 20 | $41 |

**NEW Santa Barbara** | 1134 Chapala St. (bet. Anapamu & Figueroa Sts.) | 805-844-4701 | www.thehungrycat.com
See review in Los Angeles Directory.

**Ichiban Sushi** *Japanese* | ▽ 21 | 16 | 20 | $29 |

**Santa Barbara** | 1812 Cliff Dr. (Meigs Rd.) | 805-564-7653

Devotees dub this "low-key" Santa Barbara Japanese their "go-to" sushi spot, loving the "great camaraderie" of the knife-wielding chefs and the "neighborhood feel" of the communal tables; the "traditional" cuisine is "high-quality", but even so a disappointed few find them "reliable, but not exciting."

**In-N-Out Burger** ● *Hamburgers* | 24 | 10 | 18 | $8 |

**Goleta** | 4865 Calle Real (bet. N. Turnpike Rd. & Pebble Hill Pl.)
**Santa Barbara** | 1330 S. Bradley Rd. (bet. Columbia Dr. & E. Stowell Rd.)
800-786-1000
www.in-n-out.com
Additional locations throughout Southern California
See review in Los Angeles Directory.

**Intermezzo** *Californian* | ▽ 21 | 18 | 20 | $34 |

**Santa Barbara** | 813 Anacapa St. (bet. Canon Perdido & De La Guerra Sts.) | 805-966-9463 | www.winecask.com

Oenophiles appreciate this Santa Barbara small-plates spot for "light meals" of "wonderful" Californian wine-friendly eats paired with "excellent" vino by the glass, best enjoyed in "comfy chairs" near the fireplace; the less-enthused dub it "pretentious" and say it's "overpriced" for what's basically a "snack."

| | FOOD | DECOR | SERVICE | COST |
|---|---|---|---|---|

### Jade 🖼️Ⓜ️ Hawaiian

▽ 23 | 15 | 23 | $31

**Santa Barbara** | 3132 State St. (Las Positas Rd.) | 805-563-2007
Although it's "not on the radar of most" Santa Barbarans, cognoscenti tout Dustin and Jeannine Green's Hawaiian as a "delightful neighborhood" destination for "imaginative", "lovingly prepared" cuisine with an "Asian touch"; "everyone feels at home" in the "warm, cozy" setting, and service is "generally quick"; N.B. dinner only.

### Joe's Crab Shack  Seafood

13 | 15 | 15 | $26

**Ventura** | 567 San Jon Rd. (Vista Del Mar Pl.) | 805-643-3725 | www.joescrabshack.com
See review in Los Angeles Directory.

### Jonathan's at Peirano's  Californian/Mediterranean

22 | 19 | 22 | $38

**Ventura** | Peirano | 204 E. Main St. (bet. N. Ventura Ave. & Palm St.) | 805-648-4853 | www.jonathansatpeiranos.com
Housed in the historic Peirano's Grocery building across from the San Buenaventura Mission in Downtown Ventura, this Cal-Med "favorite" delivers "wonderful" dishes like cioppino and paella from "a chef who is serious about his food"; a "pleasant staff", recent renovations and new wine room seating are pluses; N.B. chef-owner Jason Collis also runs the adjoining J's Tapas & Martini Lounge.

### La Super-Rica ⊅ Mexican

26 | 6 | 13 | $14

**Santa Barbara** | 622 N. Milpas St. (Alphonse St.) | 805-963-4940
"Chat up your line-mates and enjoy" the wait advise fans of this "ramshackle roadside" restaurant, voted Most Popular in Santa Barbara, slapping "peerless" Mexican specialties like marinated pork onto "tortillas less than two minutes old"; impatient types hate the "slow, slow" counter service and moan "the cult following makes tables hard to nab."

### Los Arroyos  Mexican

22 | 15 | 17 | $22

**Montecito** | 1280 Coast Village Rd. (Olive Mill Rd.) | 805-969-9059
**Santa Barbara** | 14 W. Figueroa St. (bet. Chapala & State Sts.) | 805-962-5541
www.losarroyos.net
"Honest", "well-executed" Mexican fare makes this family-run duo "popular with locals" and "yuppies" who are drawn to selections like "don't-miss" seafood tacos with "homemade tortillas" and "authentic" salsas; Thursdays–Saturdays a live harp player graces the Montecito location, which is "somewhat grander" than its "quick" Santa Barbara sib, but both offer "value for the money."

### Los Olivos Cafe  Californian/Mediterranean

– | – | – | M

**Los Olivos** | 2879 Grand Ave. (Alamo Pintado Ave.) | 805-688-7265 | www.losolivoscafe.com
Over 500 vintages are cellared at this "bit of local history" in Los Olivos (featured in the movie Sideways) that's "not be missed when doing the tasting circuit" thanks to "fantastic" Cal-Med bites from chef Nat Ely; if you hit it between lunch and dinner, a lighter afternoon menu is available as are seats at the wine bar, where diners can take advantage of the tasting deal before 5 PM ($10 for five tastes).

### Louie's  *Californian*　　　　25 | 20 | 24 | $42

**Santa Barbara** | Upham Hotel | 1404 De La Vina St. (W. Sola St.) |
805-963-7003 | www.louiessb.com

Housed in Santa Barbara's "upscale" Upham Hotel, a "quiet" Victorian
with "lots of history", this "hidden gem" offers "creative", "up-to-
date" Californian cuisine and "spot-on" service in a "bistro"-like space
with "wooden floors" and a "nice porch"; a few find the menu "limited", but "excellent specials", a "choice" selection of wines and "romantic" ambiance contribute to a "wonderful dining experience."

### Lucky's  *Steak*　　　　24 | 22 | 22 | $65

**Montecito** | 1279 Coast Village Rd. (Olive Mill Rd.) | 805-565-7540 |
www.luckysmontecito.com

"The Rolls-Royces, Bentleys" and "Maseratis" parked out front signal
the presence of the local "who's who" at this high-end, "high-energy"
Montecito steakhouse serving "smashing" chops, a "deep wine list"
and "stiff drinks"; "service can be erratic", but with so "many celebrities to ogle" there's a "positive electricity in the air", and the "lively bar
crowd" "always makes for an interesting evening."

### Maravilla  Ⓜ *Californian*　　　　- | - | - | VE

**Ojai** | Ojai Valley Inn & Spa | 705 Country Club Dr. (Old Coast Hwy.) |
805-646-5511 | www.ojairesort.com

"No need" to get a body wrap for an epicurean "adventure" agree admirers of this "expensive but impressive" Californian in the Ojai Valley Inn &
Spa, whose staff treats diners "with care"; its "lovely surroundings" with
fireplaces, nightly piano music and mountain views enhance the "imaginative", Spanish-influenced meal; N.B. no children under 16 allowed.

### Mimosa  *French*　　　　21 | 17 | 20 | $33

**Santa Barbara** | 2700 De La Vina St. (Alamar Ave.) | 805-682-2272

"Charming chow on the cheap" attracts patrons who are "a bit older" to
this "steady" Santa Barbara French bistro that offers "fine" service, especially when chef/co-owner Derrick Melton tends bar for Friday happy
hour; still, some contend "there is no ambiance", so it's better suited for
prix fixe dinners with a "family member or friend, not a date."

### Miró  🅢Ⓜ *Spanish*　　　　▽ 26 | 26 | 27 | $86

**Santa Barbara** | Bacara Resort | 8301 Hollister Ave. (Rte. 101) |
805-968-0100 | www.bacararesort.com

"Tops for fine dining on the coast", this "movie-star hangout" in Santa
Barbara's Bacara Resort displays original sculptures by Joan Miró in a
"wonderful setting overlooking the Pacific"; the organic Basque-
Catalan cuisine is "delightful", the service "exceptional" and Spanish
guitarists grace the room on weekends, just expect "steep prices" and
"make sure to request an ocean view"; N.B. jacket suggested.

### Montecito Cafe  *Californian*　　　　24 | 20 | 22 | $37

**Montecito** | Montecito Inn | 1295 Coast Village Rd. (Olive Mill Ln.) |
805-969-3392 | www.montecitocafe.com

This "cheerful", "airy" Californian in the Montecito Inn provides "light,
bright, impeccably fresh" food that's "served with style"; it offers a
"tremendous value" that's rare for the "tony" town, though cognoscenti warn it's "always crowded" and "without reservations there's
usually a long wait."

### Noah's New York Bagels  *Sandwiches*

18 | 11 | 14 | $9

**Ventura** | Victoria Vill. | 1413 S. Victoria Ave. (bet. Ralston & Telephone Sts.) | 805-650-1413 | www.noahs.com
See review in Los Angeles Directory.

### ☑ Olio e Limone  *Italian*

27 | 19 | 23 | $53

**Santa Barbara** | 11 W. Victoria St. (bet. Chapala & State Sts.) | 805-899-2699 | www.olioelimone.com
Husband-and-wife-team Alberto and Elaine Morello pay "exquisite attention to detail" at this Santa Barbara "escape" offering "fresh pastas", "lightly" prepared fish and "rustic" meats among other Italian dishes; most call the service "tops" and the dining room (with a visible wine cellar) "polished", though it is "small and fills up quickly", and strikes some as "overpriced" even if "that's the nature of the town."

### Opal  *Californian/Eclectic*

21 | 18 | 21 | $37

**Santa Barbara** | 1325 State St. (Arlington Ave.) | 805-966-9676 | www.opalrestaurantandbar.com
For a bite before a show at the "historic Arlington Theatre", this "convivial" bistro in Santa Barbara offers "steady", "crowd-pleasing" Cal-Eclectic eats; owners Tina Takaya and Richard Yates helm "a well-run ship" of "knowledgeable" staffers who "get you into your seats on time", though the entertainment-hungry hordes can be rather "noisy", clamoring for "innovative cocktails" that "sure pack a punch."

### Outback Steakhouse  *Steak*

17 | 14 | 18 | $28

**Goleta** | 5690 Calle Real (bet. Fairview & Patterson Aves.) | 805-964-0599
**Oxnard** | 2341 Lockwood St. (Gonzales Rd.) | 805-988-4329
www.outback.com
Additional locations throughout Southern California
See review in Los Angeles Directory.

### Palace Grill  *Cajun/Creole*

22 | 18 | 24 | $35

**Santa Barbara** | 8 E. Cota St. (State St.) | 805-963-5000 | www.palacegrill.com
"If you like N'Awlins, you'll love" this "ragin' Cajun"-Creole "celebration" in Santa Barbara, where "exceptional" servers convey "rich" meals that begin with "a mélange of muffins" ("yum!") and "end with bread pudding (super yum!)", all washed down with the "signature" "hot martini"; just "get here early" on weekends (when reservations are only taken for the 5:30 PM seatings), or you'll be "standing in line" outside.

### Palazzio  *Italian*

18 | 18 | 18 | $26

**Santa Barbara** | 1026 State St. (bet. Carillo & Figueroa Sts.) | 805-564-1985 | www.palazzio.com
Whether you're saddled with the "grandkids", a carb-loading "college athlete" or just "starving and cheap", you're sure to "leave stuffed" at this family-style Santa Barbara Italian where "value"-priced pastas are served virtually by the "bucket"; also "attracting the crowds" are "addictive garlic rolls", "alfresco dining" and an "amazing honor-system wine setup."

### Pane e Vino  ☒ *Italian*

21 | 20 | 19 | $38

**Santa Barbara** | Upper Montecito Vill. | 1482 E. Valley Rd. (bet. Santa Angela Ln. & San Ysidro Rd.) | 805-969-9274
See review in Los Angeles Directory.

| | FOOD | DECOR | SERVICE | COST |
|---|---|---|---|---|

**Piatti** _Italian_ — 20 | 20 | 20 | $34

**Montecito** | 516 San Ysidro Rd. (E. Balley Rd.) | 805-969-7520 |
www.piatti.com

See review in Los Angeles Directory.

**Piranha Restaurant & Sushi** ⓜ _Japanese_ — ▽ 24 | 18 | 23 | $43

**Santa Barbara** | 714 State St. (W. Ortega St.) | 805-965-2980

"Ask the chefs to fix whatever they want" advise visitors to this
Downtown Santa Barbara Japanese from Koji Nomura, serving a "wide
variety" of items including lobster gyoza and crunchy banana spring
rolls; the "trendy" vibe makes it "fun to people-watch", though sometimes the fish bite back as the "price adds up" quickly.

**Ⓩ Ranch House** ⓜ _Californian_ — 25 | 24 | 24 | $54

**Ojai** | 500 S. Lomita Ave. (Tico Rd.) | 805-646-2360 |
www.theranchhouse.com

Its "remote location" in the "backwoods of Ojai" makes this "local
classic" absolutely "serene" according to day-trippers who say "Sunday
brunch on a sunny day is paradise"; the surrounding "fragrant" gardens
provide fresh herbs for the kitchen's "delightful" seasonal Californian
fare, which includes goods from the house bakery, while "fine wines"
and a "knowledgeable" staff finish the "spectacular combination."

**Rodney's Steakhouse** Ⓢⓜ _Steak_ — ▽ 25 | 19 | 21 | $52

**Santa Barbara** | Fess Parker Doubletree Resort | 633 E. Cabrillo Blvd.
(S. Salispuedes St.) | 805-884-8554 | www.rodneyssteakhouse.com

"Quality" steaks are the main event at this "pricey" chop house in the
Fess Parker Doubletree Resort in Santa Barbara; a few quibble that the
art deco decor has an "institutional" feel, but most proclaim it "unusually good for a hotel restaurant" and say that "attentive" service and
the "beautiful" view "of the beach" make up for any shortcomings.

**Sage & Onion** _American/European_ — 26 | 21 | 22 | $50

**Santa Barbara** | 34 E. Ortega St. (Anacapa St.) | 805-963-1012 |
www.sageandonion.com

"Excellent all around" claim those captivated by chef-owner Steven
Giles' "gem" in Santa Barbara where a "creative", "seasonal" Euro-
American menu is served in an "elegant" dining room by a staff that
"tends to your every need"; while it's "expensive", many recommend it
for "special occasions."

**Savoy Truffles** _American_ — ▽ 21 | 14 | 17 | $20

**Santa Barbara** | 24 W. Figueroa St. (State St.) | 805-966-2139 |
www.savoytruffles.com

"Attention to quality and flavor" plus a "scrumptious" "ever-changing"
menu of salads, sandwiches and other "comfort foods" make this Santa
Barbara "deli on steroids" a lunchtime "hot spot"; what it lacks in "atmosphere", it makes up for with "fast" service and "great value";
N.B. they also offer over 20 varieties of locally handcrafted truffles.

**71 Palm** Ⓢ _American/French_ — 20 | 20 | 20 | $44

**Ventura** | 71 N. Palm St. (bet. Main & Poli Sts.) | 805-653-7222 |
www.71palm.com

Francophiles find "European elegance in the heart of Ventura" at this
"delightful" French-American "surprise" that's "well-carried-out" by

chef-owner Didier Poirier; you can enhance the "romance" by "sitting near the fireplace" in the landmark Craftsman house, and while some say "puhlease" to the pricing and "pretentiousness", most appreciate its "pleasant" offerings; N.B. the Food score may not reflect a recent menu overhaul.

### ☑ Sevilla ⑤ *Pan-Latin* | 22 | 25 | 21 | $55 |

**Santa Barbara** | 428 Chapala St. (State St.) | 805-564-8446 | www.restaurantsevilla.com

"Big on sex appeal", this "dimly lit", "loungelike" Santa Barbara boîte lures "young singles" for "unusual", "excellently prepared" Pan-Latin dishes, fresh-fruit cocktails and a 300+ -bottle collection of wines; skeptics say it's "overpriced" and "inconsistent" adding that it feels a bit "short on substance."

### Sharky's Mexican Grill *Mexican* | 17 | 12 | 15 | $12 |

**Ventura** | Gateway Ctr. | 4960 Telephone Rd. (bet. Portola Rd. & Saratoga Ave.) | 805-339-9600 | www.sharkys.com
Additional locations throughout Southern California
**See review in Los Angeles Directory.**

### Sidecar Restaurant Ⓜ *American* | ▽ 22 | 18 | 23 | $39 |

**Ventura** | 3029 E. Main St. (bet. Mills & Telegraph Rds.) | 805-653-7433 | www.thesidecarrestaurant.com

Chef-owner Tim Kilcoyne's "inventive" American menu "highlights the freshest produce from the local farmer's market" at this "elegant" Ventura American set inside a refurbished 1910 Pullman train car; "outstanding service" and moderate tabs add to what loyalists laud as a "local" treat.

### Spice Avenue *Indian* | ▽ 19 | 13 | 16 | $25 |

**Santa Barbara** | 1027 State St. (Figueroa St.) | 805-965-6004 | www.spiceavenuesb.com

"Exotic teas" and imported beers and wines accompany the "hearty" Indian dishes at this family-run State Street Indian "staple" that some call "the best in town"; service is "quick" and the tabs "inexpensive" – the $7.95 lunch buffet is an especially "great deal."

### Square One Ⓜ *American* | ▽ 22 | 19 | 21 | $48 |

**Santa Barbara** | 14 E. Cota St. (State St.) | 805-965-4565

"Local ingredients" come into play in chef Jason Tuley's "beautifully prepared", "cutting-edge" New American creations at this Santa Barbara spot that "still feels like it hasn't been discovered yet"; digs are "stylish", if a bit on the "spartan" side, while a "personable" staff makes the whole experience "a pleasure" in spite of "high" prices.

### ☑ Stella Mare's Ⓜ *Californian* | 22 | 25 | 25 | $42 |

**Santa Barbara** | 50 Los Patos Way (Cabrio Blvd.) | 805-969-6705 | www.stellamares.com

"Lovely!" laud loyalists of this "charmer" (voted No. 1 for Decor in Santa Barbara) set in a former "Victorian home" and done up in "French country farmhouse" style with an "airy", "candlelit greenhouse room" as an added attraction; the "well-informed" staff ferries "creative" Californian cuisine including a "fantastic brunch" that's especially "popular."

| | FOOD | DECOR | SERVICE | COST |
|---|---|---|---|---|

### Sushi Ozekii ⬛ *Japanese* — — — M

**Ventura** | 1437 S. Victoria Ave., Ste. E (Ralston St.) | 805-477-9897 | www.ozekii.com

See review in Los Angeles Directory.

### Suzanne's Cuisine *French/Italian* 25 | 22 | 23 | $49

**Ojai** | 502 W. Ojai Ave. (Bristol Ave.) | 805-640-1961 | www.suzannescuisine.com

This "fantastic foodie place" from mother-daughter-team Suzanne Roll and Sandra Moore uses "fresh, local" ingredients from area farmers in its "superb", seasonal French-Italian fare; an "unassuming", "California casual" cafe "on the main drag in Ojai", it has a "peaceful garden area" out back making it "a delightful escape" that's worth it for a "special occasion" or a "trip" in itself.

### Tee-Off *Seafood/Steak* 21 | 15 | 20 | $38

**Santa Barbara** | Ontare Plaza | 3627 State St. (Ontare Rd.) | 805-687-1616

"A 19th hole for golfers who like a stiff one", this "dark", "classic 1950s lounge" in Santa Barbara's Ontare Plaza plays host to a "crusty local crowd" with "generous drinks" and "tender, flavorful" steaks; a few find it a bit "overpriced", but it's still a congenial "hang" that's a "favorite" in the area.

### 31 West *Californian* 18 | 18 | 18 | $44

**Santa Barbara** | Andalucía Hotel | 31 W. Carrillo St. (bet. Carrillo & Chipala Sts.) | 805-884-0300 | www.andaluciasb.com

The "simple", "eclectic" Californian cuisine garners mixed reviews at this bistro inside Santa Barbara's "lovely" Hotel Andalucía: some call it "tasty" while others leave "disappointed" by "inconsistency" in both the cooking and service, especially in light of the "high prices"; those who find the lobby setting "sterile" might opt instead for "happy hour with appetizers on the rooftop."

### Trattoria Grappolo *Italian* 25 | 18 | 23 | $37

**Santa Ynez** | 3687 Sagunto St. (Meadowvale Rd.) | 805-688-6899 | www.trattoriagrappolo.com

It's a "home away from home" claim those captivated by this "charming farmhouse" in Santa Ynez offering "amazing" "thin-crust" pizza fresh out of the wood-burning oven and other "outstanding", "authentic" Italian fare complemented by an "impressive" selection of wines; the "cozy" setting with "well-spaced tables" set with white tablecloths, reminds some of "Tuscany", while "friendly" service is another "homey" touch that adds up to a "joyful evening" for all.

### Trattoria Mollie ⬛ *Italian* 21 | 19 | 18 | $54

**Montecito** | 1250 Coast Village Rd. (Elizabeth Ln.) | 805-565-9381 | www.tmollie.com

"Personable" chef-owner Mollie Ahlstrand "works the room" of her "very 'in'" Montecito boîte serving "simple", "authentic" Tuscan fare like pizzas, pastas and her Oprah-endorsed turkey meatballs; the "sleek, modern space" has turned into a "come-to spot for stars" although a few gripe that "Joe citizen gets ignored" among the otherwise "rich and famous clientele."

|  | FOOD | DECOR | SERVICE | COST |
|---|---|---|---|---|

### Tre Lune *Italian*  21 | 20 | 18 | $47

**Montecito** | 1151 Coast Village Rd. (bet. Butterfly Ln. & Middle Rd.) |
805-969-2646

"Great thin-crust pizza" and other "red-sauce" classics please
Montecito denizens at this "local" Italian "hangout" that a few find
"overpriced"; still, a "friendly" staff and "hip" environs draw a steady
stream of customers, hence the room can be a little "noisy."

### Tupelo Junction *Southern*  23 | 18 | 21 | $32

**Santa Barbara** | 1218 State St. (bet. Anapamu & Victoria Sts.) |
805-899-3100 | www.tupelojunction.com

Adding a "high-end twist to Southern" "comfort food", this slice of
Mississippi in Santa Barbara is "nice for a complete change" – "if you
aren't on a diet"; the "fun menu" runs the gamut from "first-class
breakfasts", lunches and dinners to "awesome desserts" and, of
course, a "family"-friendly brunch, all delivered with down-home
"hospitality" – though some numbers-crunchers calculate "it
doesn't come cheap."

### Via Vai *Italian*  21 | 15 | 19 | $35

**Montecito** | Upper Vill. | 1483 E. Valley Rd. (San Ysidro Rd.) | 805-565-9393

"Crisp and yummy pizzas" from a wood-burning oven and "fresh-
tasting" pastas are why Montecitans come to this "informal, bustling",
"fairly priced" Italian trattoria; the "homey" "exposed-brick" interior is
often "noisy", being that "they're very nice to kids", but if you're looking for a little "romance", "sit on the patio facing the mountains for
a memorable experience."

### Westside Cellar
### Cafe & Wine Store *Eclectic*  22 | 21 | 22 | $41

**Ventura** | 222 E. Main St. (bet. Palm St. & Ventura Ave.) | 805-652-7013 |
www.westsidecellar.com

"Come for the wine, stay for the food" say fans of this Ventura boîte with
a "vast selection" of vintages (also sold in the adjoining shop) that are
poured for daily tastings between 3 and 5 PM; its "adventurous" Eclectic
menu offers "unusual combinations" as well as "gourmet cheeses"
served with impressive "attention to detail" in a "cozy" setting complete with a fireplace and local art on the exposed-brick walls.

### Wine Cask *Californian*  24 | 23 | 22 | $57

**Santa Barbara** | 813 Anacapa St. (bet. Canon Perdido & De La Guerra Sts.) |
805-966-9463 | www.winecask.com

The "astounding" 2,000-bottle wine list dazzles the most "discerning
oenophile" at this "gorgeous" longtime Santa Barbara eatery where
the "candlelit" setting with beamed ceilings and a fireplace is still the
site of "marriage proposals galore"; in spite of a recent chef and owner
change, the spirit of the "high-quality" Californian menu remains the
same with "well-executed" seasonal fare; N.B. the Los Olivos branch
closed in April 2007.

# ORANGE COUNTY/ PALM SPRINGS/ SANTA BARBARA INDEXES

Restaurant locations are indicated by the following abbreviations: Orange County=OC; Palm Springs & Environs=PS; and Santa Barbara & Environs=SB.

# Cuisines

Includes restaurant names, locations and Food ratings. ☑ indicates places with the highest ratings, popularity and importance.

## AMERICAN (NEW)

| | |
|---|---|
| Bayside \| **Newport Bch/OC** | 25 |
| Bistango \| **Irvine/OC** | 24 |
| Blend \| **La Quinta/PS** | - |
| **NEW** Brooks \| **Ventura/SB** | - |
| Cat/Custard Cup \| **La Habra/OC** | 23 |
| Chad's \| **SB** | 22 |
| Epiphany \| **SB** | 17 |
| Gordon James \| **San Clemente/OC** | 20 |
| hush \| **Laguna Bch/OC** | 21 |
| Infusion \| **Ladera Ranch/OC** | 23 |
| La Quinta Cliffhse. \| **La Quinta/PS** | 18 |
| ☑ Mr. Stox \| **Anaheim/OC** | 24 |
| **NEW** Palm Terrace \| **Newport Bch/OC** | - |
| Park Ave. \| **Stanton/OC** | 25 |
| **NEW** Port Rest. \| **Corona del Mar/OC** | - |
| ☑ Ramos House \| **San Juan Cap/OC** | 26 |
| Rendezvous \| **San Juan Cap/OC** | 24 |
| Sage \| **Newport Bch/OC** | 24 |
| Square One \| **SB** | 22 |
| ☑ Stonehill Tav. \| **Dana Pt/OC** | 28 |
| Table Ten \| **Fullerton/OC** | 19 |
| 3Thirty3 \| **Newport Bch/OC** | 18 |
| Wildfish/Grille \| **Newport Bch/OC** | 23 |
| Yard House \| **multi. loc.** | 19 |

## AMERICAN (TRADITIONAL)

| | |
|---|---|
| Arnold Palmer's \| **La Quinta/PS** | - |
| Bandera \| **Corona del Mar/OC** | 22 |
| Billy Reed's \| **PS** | 16 |
| BJ's \| **multi. loc.** | 17 |
| Bluewater Grill \| **Newport Bch/OC** | 20 |
| Britta's Café \| **Irvine/OC** | 20 |
| Brothers Rest. \| **Los Olivos/SB** | 24 |
| Café R&D \| **Newport Bch/OC** | 21 |
| Cedar Creek \| **multi. loc.** | 19 |
| ☑ Cheesecake Fact. \| **multi. loc.** | 20 |
| Claim Jumper \| **multi. loc.** | 19 |

| | |
|---|---|
| Cold Spring \| **SB** | 19 |
| **NEW** Commonwealth \| **Fullerton/OC** | - |
| Cottage \| **Laguna Bch/OC** | 17 |
| Daily Grill \| **multi. loc.** | 18 |
| Eladio's \| **SB** | 19 |
| Filling Station \| **Orange/OC** | 17 |
| ☑ First Cabin \| **Newport Bch/OC** | 25 |
| Five Crowns \| **Corona del Mar/OC** | 24 |
| Fox Sports \| **Irvine/OC** | 14 |
| Gulfstream \| **Newport Bch/OC** | 21 |
| Heroes B&G \| **Fullerton/OC** | 16 |
| Hog's Breath Inn \| **La Quinta/PS** | 14 |
| ☑ Houston's \| **Irvine/OC** | 21 |
| Islands \| **multi. loc.** | 16 |
| Johnny Rockets \| **multi. loc.** | 15 |
| Kaiser Grille \| **PS** | 16 |
| Lawry's Carvery \| **Costa Mesa/OC** | 20 |
| Mimi's Cafe \| **multi. loc.** | 17 |
| Mrs. Knott's \| **Buena Pk/OC** | 21 |
| ☑ Original Pancake \| **multi. loc.** | 23 |
| Park Ave. \| **Stanton/OC** | 25 |
| Rainforest Cafe \| **multi. loc.** | 13 |
| Ruby's \| **multi. loc.** | 16 |
| Sage & Onion \| **SB** | 26 |
| Savoy Truffles \| **SB** | 21 |
| Shades \| **Huntington Bch/OC** | - |
| Shame on Moon \| **Rancho Mirage/PS** | - |
| Sidecar Rest. \| **Ventura/SB** | 22 |
| Side Street Cafe \| **Costa Mesa/OC** | 18 |
| Souplantation \| **multi. loc.** | 16 |
| Spark Woodfire \| **Huntington Bch/OC** | 17 |
| Steelhead Brew. \| **Irvine/OC** | 16 |
| TAPS Fish \| **Brea/OC** | 23 |
| Wood Ranch BBQ \| **multi. loc.** | 20 |
| Yard House \| **multi. loc.** | 19 |

## ARGENTINEAN

| | |
|---|---|
| Cafe Buenos Aires \| **SB** | 16 |
| Gaucho Grill \| **Brea/OC** | 18 |

230 Forest Ave. | **Laguna Bch/OC** — 25

Vine | **San Clemente/OC** — 25

Vue | **Dana Pt/OC** — _

**NEW** Wicked Gdn. | **Dana Pt/OC** — _

Wild Artichoke | **Yorba Linda/OC** — 24

Wine Cask | **SB** — 24

Wolfgang Puck | **Costa Mesa/OC** — 18

Zinc Cafe | **multi. loc.** — 22

## CARIBBEAN

**Z** Golden Truffle | — 26
  **Costa Mesa/OC**

Tommy Bahama | **multi. loc.** — 19

## CHINESE

(* dim sum specialist)

Cali. Wok | **Costa Mesa/OC** — 18

China Pavilion | **multi. loc.** — 23

Five Feet | **Laguna Bch/OC** — 24

**Z** P.F. Chang's | **multi. loc.** — 19

Sam Woo* | **Irvine/OC** — 20

Seafood Paradise* | — 21
  **Westminster/OC**

## COFFEE SHOPS/DINERS

Duke's | **Huntington Bch/OC** — 17

Filling Station | **Orange/OC** — 17

Mimi's Cafe | **multi. loc.** — 17

**Z** Original Pancake | **multi. loc.** — 23

Ruby's | **multi. loc.** — 16

## CONTINENTAL

**Z** First Cabin | **Newport Bch/OC** — 25

Gemmell's | **Dana Pt/OC** — 23

**Z** Hobbit, The | **Orange/OC** — 27

**Z** Jillian's | **Palm Desert/PS** — 25

Nieuport 17 | **Tustin/OC** — 22

**Z** Ritz Rest./Gdn. | — 24
  **Newport Bch/OC**

Riviera at Fireside | — 24
  **Westminster/OC**

Rothschild's | **Corona del Mar/OC** — 22

Shades | **Huntington Bch/OC** — _

**Z** Summit Hse. | **Fullerton/OC** — 25

**Z** Wally's Desert | — 25
  **Rancho Mirage/PS**

## CREOLE

Iva Lee's | **San Clemente/OC** — 23

Palace Grill | **SB** — 22

Ralph Brennan's | **Anaheim/OC** — 19

## DESSERT

**Z** Cheesecake Fact. | **multi. loc.** — 20

Melting Pot | **Irvine/OC** — 19

## ECLECTIC

Aire | **Costa Mesa/OC** — 23

Blue Agave | **SB** — 19

Café/Tango | **Orange/OC** — 20

Dizz's As Is | **Laguna Bch/OC** — 23

**NEW** Eno | **Laguna Niguel/OC** — _

Infusion | **Ladera Ranch/OC** — 23

John Henry's | **PS** — 22

**NEW** Kimera | **Irvine/OC** — _

Lazy Dog | **multi. loc.** — 19

Motif | **Monarch Bch/OC** — 23

Mozambique | **Laguna Bch/OC** — 19

Native Foods | **multi. loc.** — 22

**NEW** Old Vine Café | — _
  **Costa Mesa/OC**

Onotria | **Costa Mesa/OC** — 24

Opal | **SB** — 21

**NEW** Sapphire Laguna | — 26
  **Laguna Bch/OC**

Sutra Lounge | **Costa Mesa/OC** — _

Taco Loco | **Laguna Bch/OC** — 24

Westside Cellar | **Ventura/SB** — 22

Wild Artichoke | **Yorba Linda/OC** — 24

## EUROPEAN

**NEW** Fresco/Beach | **SB** — 20

Sage & Onion | **SB** — 26

## FONDUE

**NEW** La Fondue | — 21
  **San Juan Cap/OC**

Melting Pot | **Irvine/OC** — 19

## FRENCH

Auberge at Ojai | **Ojai/SB** — 21

AZUR | **La Quinta/PS** — 22

**Z** Basilic | **Newport Bch/OC** — 28

**Z** Bouchon | **SB** — 26

Cellar | **Fullerton/OC** — 23

**Z** Cuistot | **Palm Desert/PS** — 26

**Z** Downey's | **SB** — 28

Gemmell's | **Dana Pt/OC** — 23

**Z** Golden Truffle | — 26
  **Costa Mesa/OC**

**Z** Hobbit, The | **Orange/OC** — 27

John Henry's | **PS** — 22

**Z** La Vie en Rose | **Brea/OC** — 25

| | |
|---|---|
| Le St. Germain \| **Indian Wells/PS** | 24 |
| 🗷 Le Vallauris \| **PS** | 27 |
| L'Hirondelle \| **San Juan Cap/OC** | 22 |
| **NEW** Marché Moderne \| **Costa Mesa/OC** | – |
| Mimosa \| **SB** | 21 |
| Picayo \| **Laguna Bch/OC** | 22 |
| Pinot Provence \| **Costa Mesa/OC** | 25 |
| 71 Palm \| **Ventura/SB** | 20 |
| Suzanne's \| **Ojai/SB** | 25 |
| 🗷 Tradition/Pascal \| **Newport Bch/OC** | 27 |
| Yves' Bistro \| **Anaheim Hills/OC** | 23 |

### FRENCH (BISTRO)

| | |
|---|---|
| Black Sheep \| **Tustin/OC** | 24 |
| Café/Beaux-Arts \| **Palm Desert/PS** | 18 |
| 🗷 Chat Noir \| **Costa Mesa/OC** | 21 |
| French 75 \| **multi. loc.** | 21 |
| Pescadou \| **Newport Bch/OC** | 22 |

### FRENCH (NEW)

| | |
|---|---|
| Ambrosia \| **Santa Ana/OC** | 24 |
| 🗷 Ballard Inn \| **Ballard/SB** | 26 |
| Five Feet \| **Laguna Bch/OC** | 24 |
| 🗷 Studio \| **Laguna Bch/OC** | 27 |

### HAMBURGERS

| | |
|---|---|
| 🗷 In-N-Out Burger \| **multi. loc.** | 24 |
| Islands \| **multi. loc.** | 16 |
| Johnny Rockets \| **multi. loc.** | 15 |
| Ruby's \| **multi. loc.** | 16 |

### HAWAIIAN

| | |
|---|---|
| Jade \| **SB** | 23 |
| Loft, The \| **Huntington Bch/OC** | 17 |
| 🗷 Roy's \| **multi. loc.** | 24 |

### HOT DOGS

| | |
|---|---|
| Jerry's/Dogs \| **multi. loc.** | 20 |
| Jody Maroni's \| **Orange/OC** | 19 |
| Portillo's Hot Dogs \| **Buena Pk/OC** | 19 |

### INDIAN

| | |
|---|---|
| Bukhara \| **Huntington Bch/OC** | – |
| Chakra \| **Irvine/OC** | 21 |
| Mayur \| **Corona del Mar/OC** | 21 |
| Natraj \| **multi. loc.** | 18 |
| Royal Khyber \| **Santa Ana/OC** | 24 |
| Spice Ave. \| **SB** | 19 |

### IRISH

| | |
|---|---|
| Muldoon's Dublin \| **Newport Bch/OC** | 18 |

### ITALIAN

(N=Northern; S=Southern)

| | |
|---|---|
| Anaheim White Hse. \| N \| **Anaheim/OC** | 24 |
| 🗷 Antonello \| **Santa Ana/OC** | 24 |
| Bellini \| **Palm Desert/PS** | 21 |
| Buca di Beppo \| S \| **multi. loc.** | 15 |
| Bucatini \| N \| **SB** | 22 |
| Ca' Dario \| **SB** | 25 |
| Cafe Fiore \| S \| **Ventura/SB** | 21 |
| Capriccio \| **Mission Viejo/OC** | 22 |
| Castelli's \| **Palm Desert/PS** | 23 |
| Dolce Rist. \| N \| **Newport Bch/OC** | 18 |
| Emilio's \| N \| **SB** | 24 |
| 🗷 Il Fornaio \| **Irvine/OC** | 20 |
| Luciana's \| N \| **Dana Pt/OC** | 22 |
| Maggiano's \| **Costa Mesa/OC** | 19 |
| Market City \| **Brea/OC** | 18 |
| Mascarpone's \| N \| **Orange/OC** | 24 |
| **NEW** Mesa Rest. \| **Costa Mesa/OC** | – |
| Modo Mio \| **Newport Bch/OC** | 22 |
| Mulberry St. Rist. \| **Fullerton/OC** | 20 |
| Naples \| S \| **Anaheim/OC** | 17 |
| Nello Cucina \| **Costa Mesa/OC** | 23 |
| Nesai \| N \| **Newport Bch/OC** | – |
| 🗷 Olio e Limone \| **SB** | 27 |
| Palazzio \| **SB** | 18 |
| Pane e Vino \| N \| **multi. loc.** | 21 |
| Peppino's \| **multi. loc.** | 18 |
| Piatti \| **Montecito/SB** | 20 |
| Pomodoro \| **multi. loc.** | 17 |
| Prego \| **Irvine/OC** | 19 |
| Rist. Mamma Gina \| N \| **multi. loc.** | 21 |
| **NEW** Rist. Max \| **Newport Bch/OC** | 21 |
| Rist. Tuscany \| N \| **Palm Desert/PS** | 23 |
| Romano's Macaroni \| **multi. loc.** | 17 |
| Rothschild's \| N \| **Corona del Mar/OC** | 22 |
| Sabatino's Sausage \| S \| **Newport Bch/OC** | 22 |
| 🗷 Sirocco \| **Indian Wells/PS** | 25 |
| Sisley Italian \| **Rancho Cuca/PS** | 18 |
| Spaghettini \| N \| **Seal Bch/OC** | 20 |

| | |
|---|---|
| NEW Stella's \| **Monarch Bch/OC** | 19 |
| Suzanne's \| **Ojai/SB** | 25 |
| Tannins \| **San Juan Cap/OC** | 18 |
| Ti Amo \| **S Laguna Bch/OC** | 22 |
| Tratt. Grappolo \| **Santa Ynez/SB** | 25 |
| Tratt. Mollie \| N \| **Montecito/SB** | 21 |
| Tre Lune \| **Montecito/SB** | 21 |
| Valentina Rist. \| **Mission Viejo/OC** | 12 |
| Vessia \| S \| **Irvine/OC** | 22 |
| Via Vai \| **Montecito/SB** | 21 |
| Villa Nova \| **Newport Bch/OC** | 19 |
| Yves' Bistro \| **Anaheim Hills/OC** | 23 |
| NEW Zmario \| **Irvine/OC** | - |

## JAPANESE

(* sushi specialist)

| | |
|---|---|
| Abe* \| **Newport Bch/OC** | 25 |
| Z Arigato Sushi* \| **SB** | 26 |
| Benihana* \| **multi. loc.** | 18 |
| Bluefin* \| **Newport Coast/OC** | 25 |
| Gyu-Kaku \| **Rancho Cuca/PS** | 20 |
| Ichiban Sushi* \| **SB** | 21 |
| Ichibiri* \| **multi. loc.** | 18 |
| NEW Izakaya Zero \| **Huntington Bch/OC** | - |
| O-Nami* \| **Laguna Hills/OC** | 16 |
| Piranha* \| **SB** | 24 |
| Shabu Shabu \| **Mission Viejo/OC** | 25 |
| Sushi Ozekii* \| **Ventura/SB** | - |
| Taiko* \| **Irvine/OC** | 21 |
| Ten* \| **Newport Bch/OC** | 22 |
| Wasa* \| **multi. loc.** | 24 |
| Zipangu \| **Costa Mesa/OC** | 23 |
| Zip Fusion* \| **Corona/PS** | 18 |

## KOREAN

(* barbecue specialist)

| | |
|---|---|
| BCD Tofu* \| **Garden Grove/OC** | 20 |
| Yi Dynasty* \| **Newport Bch/OC** | - |

## MEDITERRANEAN

| | |
|---|---|
| Catal/Uva Bar \| **Anaheim/OC** | 22 |
| Emilio's \| **SB** | 24 |
| Fitness Pizza \| **multi. loc.** | 20 |
| Jonathan's/Peirano \| **Ventura/SB** | 22 |
| Le St. Germain \| **Indian Wells/PS** | 24 |
| Z Le Vallauris \| **PS** | 27 |
| Los Olivos Cafe \| **Los Olivos/SB** | - |
| Lucca Cafe \| **Irvine/OC** | 23 |

| | |
|---|---|
| Picayo \| **Laguna Bch/OC** | 22 |
| Rosine's \| **Anaheim/OC** | 24 |
| Sorrento Grille \| **Laguna Bch/OC** | 22 |
| Z Splashes \| **Laguna Bch/OC** | 21 |
| Ti Amo \| **S Laguna Bch/OC** | 22 |
| Vine \| **San Clemente/OC** | 25 |
| NEW Wicked Gdn. \| **Dana Pt/OC** | - |
| Zankou Chicken \| **Anaheim/OC** | 22 |
| Zov's \| **multi. loc.** | 25 |

## MEXICAN

| | |
|---|---|
| Baja Fresh Mex. \| **multi. loc.** | 18 |
| Carlitos Cafe \| **SB** | 19 |
| Coyote Grill \| **Laguna Bch/OC** | 19 |
| El Cholo \| **multi. loc.** | 18 |
| El Paseo \| **SB** | 15 |
| El Torito \| **multi. loc.** | 15 |
| El Torito Grill \| **multi. loc.** | 18 |
| NEW Gabbi's Mex. \| **Orange/OC** | 26 |
| Javier's Cantina \| **multi. loc.** | 22 |
| Las Brisas \| **Laguna Bch/OC** | 16 |
| Las Casuelas \| **multi. loc.** | 18 |
| La Super-Rica \| **SB** | 26 |
| Los Arroyos \| **multi. loc.** | 22 |
| Sharky's Mex. \| **multi. loc.** | 17 |
| Taco Loco \| **Laguna Bch/OC** | 24 |
| Taco Mesa \| **multi. loc.** | 24 |
| Taco Rosa \| **multi. loc.** | 22 |
| Taléo Mexican \| **Irvine/OC** | 23 |
| Tortilla Flats \| **Mission Viejo/OC** | 16 |
| Tortilla Jo's \| **Anaheim/OC** | 17 |

## NEW ZEALAND

| | |
|---|---|
| Turner New Zealand \| **Costa Mesa/OC** | 24 |

## NUEVO LATINO

| | |
|---|---|
| Habana \| **Costa Mesa/OC** | 21 |
| Kantina \| **Newport Bch/OC** | 18 |

## PACIFIC NORTHWEST

| | |
|---|---|
| Plums Café \| **Costa Mesa/OC** | 24 |

## PACIFIC RIM

| | |
|---|---|
| Chimayo/Beach \| **Huntington Bch/OC** | 18 |
| Duke's \| **Huntington Bch/OC** | 17 |
| Ten \| **Newport Bch/OC** | 22 |

## PAN-ASIAN

| | |
|---|---|
| Ling & Louie's \| **Irvine/OC** | 17 |
| Pei Wei Diner \| **multi. loc.** | 16 |

OC/PS/SB

CUISINES

## SPANISH

(* tapas specialist)

| | |
|---|---|
| Alcazar* | **SB** | 19 |
| Black Sheep | **Tustin/OC** | 24 |
| Maravilla | **Ojai/SB** | - |
| Miró | **SB** | 26 |
| Picante | **Ladera Ranch/OC** | 21 |

## STEAKHOUSES

| | |
|---|---|
| Agora Churr. | **Irvine/OC** | 24 |
| Arnold Palmer's | **La Quinta/PS** | - |
| Benihana | **multi. loc.** | 18 |
| Bungalow | **Corona del Mar/OC** | 21 |
| Chart House | **multi. loc.** | 19 |
| Chop House | **multi. loc.** | 21 |
| Falls Prime Steak | **multi. loc.** | 22 |
| 55 Steak | **Anaheim/OC** | 23 |
| Fleming Prime | **Newport Bch/OC** | 25 |
| Gaucho Grill | **Brea/OC** | 18 |
| La Cave | **Costa Mesa/OC** | 21 |
| Landmark Steak | **Corona del Mar/OC** | 18 |
| LG's Prime Steak | **multi. loc.** | 23 |
| Lucky's | **Montecito/SB** | 24 |
| Z Mastro's Steak | **Costa Mesa/OC** | 25 |
| Morton's Steak | **multi. loc.** | 25 |
| Outback Steak | **multi. loc.** | 17 |
| Rodney's Steak | **SB** | 25 |
| Z Ruth's Chris | **multi. loc.** | 25 |
| Salt Creek | **Dana Pt/OC** | 18 |
| Savannah Steak | **Laguna Niguel/OC** | 23 |
| NEW Sevens Steak | **Tustin/OC** | - |
| NEW Silvera's Steak | **Huntington Bch/OC** | - |
| Z Tabu Grill | **Laguna Bch/OC** | 26 |
| Tee-Off | **SB** | 21 |
| Trabuco Oaks Steak | **Trabuco Canyon/OC** | 21 |
| Turner New Zealand | **Costa Mesa/OC** | 24 |

## SWISS

| | |
|---|---|
| Z Basilic | **Newport Bch/OC** | 28 |

## THAI

| | |
|---|---|
| Cholada | **Ventura/SB** | 26 |
| Royal Thai | **multi. loc.** | 21 |
| Thai Dishes | **Fountain Vly/OC** | 18 |
| Thai This | **Dana Pt/OC** | 22 |

## VEGETARIAN

(* vegan)

| | |
|---|---|
| Native Foods* | **multi. loc.** | 22 |
| Rutabegorz* | **multi. loc.** | - |
| NEW Veggie Grill* | **Irvine/OC** | 20 |
| Zinc Cafe | **multi. loc.** | 22 |

## VIETNAMESE

| | |
|---|---|
| NEW Brodard Chateau | **Garden Grove/OC** | 24 |
| Pho 79 | **multi. loc.** | 21 |
| S Vietnamese | **Westminster/OC** | 24 |
| Thanh My | **Westminster/OC** | 20 |

# Locations

Includes restaurant names, cuisines and Food ratings. ☒ indicates places with the highest ratings, popularity and importance.

## Orange County

### ALISO VIEJO

JACKshrimp | *Cajun* __17__
Opah | *Calif./Seafood* __23__
☒ Original Pancake | *Diner* __23__
Peppino's | *Italian* __18__
Pomodoro | *Italian* __17__
Sharky's Mex. | *Mex.* __17__
Wingnuts | *BBQ* __16__

### ANAHEIM/ANAHEIM HILLS

Alvarado's | *Calif.* __22__
Anaheim White Hse. | *Italian* __24__
Benihana | *Jap.* __18__
Catal/Uva Bar | *Med.* __22__
El Torito | *Mex.* __15__
55 Steak | *Steak* __23__
House of Blues | *Southern* __15__
NEW K'ya | *Calif.* __–__
Mimi's Cafe | *Diner* __17__
Morton's Steak | *Steak* __25__
☒ Mr. Stox | *Amer.* __24__
☒ Napa Rose | *Calif.* __27__
Naples | *Pizza* __17__
☒ Original Pancake | *Diner* __23__
Rainforest Cafe | *Amer.* __13__
Ralph Brennan's | *Creole* __19__
Rosine's | *Armenian/Med.* __24__
Tortilla Jo's | *Mex.* __17__
Wood Ranch BBQ | *BBQ* __20__
Yves' Bistro | *French/Italian* __23__
Zankou Chicken | *Med.* __22__

### BALBOA

Ruby's | *Diner* __16__

### BREA

Baja Fresh Mex. | *Mex.* __18__
BJ's | *Pub* __17__
Buca di Beppo | *Italian* __15__
Cali. Pizza Kitchen | *Pizza* __18__
Cedar Creek | *Amer.* __19__
☒ Cheesecake Fact. | *Amer.* __20__
Claim Jumper | *Amer.* __19__

El Torito Grill | *Mex.* __18__
Fitness Pizza | *Med.* __20__
Gaucho Grill | *Argent./Steak* __18__
Islands | *Amer.* __16__
☒ La Vie en Rose | *French* __25__
Lucille's BBQ | *BBQ* __22__
Market City | *Calif./Italian* __18__
Outback Steak | *Steak* __17__
Pane e Vino | *Italian* __21__
TAPS Fish | *Amer./Seafood* __23__
Yard House | *Amer.* __19__

### BUENA PARK

Mrs. Knott's | *Amer.* __21__
Outback Steak | *Steak* __17__
Portillo's Hot Dogs | *Hot Dogs* __19__

### CORONA DEL MAR

Bandera | *Amer./SW* __22__
Bungalow | *Seafood/Steak* __21__
Five Crowns | *British* __24__
Landmark Steak | *Steak* __18__
Mayur | *Indian* __21__
Oysters | *Asian/Calif.* __23__
NEW Port Rest. | *Amer.* __–__
Rothschild's | *Continental/Italian* __22__
Zinc Cafe | *Calif.* __22__

### COSTA MESA

Aire | *Eclectic* __23__
Baja Fresh Mex. | *Mex.* __18__
Cali. Wok | *Chinese* __18__
☒ Chat Noir | *French* __21__
Claim Jumper | *Amer.* __19__
☒ Golden Truffle | *Carib./French* __26__
Gypsy Den | *Calif.* __17__
Habana | *Nuevo Latino* __21__
Inka Grill | *Peruvian* __19__
☒ In-N-Out Burger | *Hamburgers* __24__
La Cave | *Steak* __21__
Lawry's Carvery | *Amer.* __20__
NEW ☒ Leatherby's | *Asian/Calif.* __25__
Maggiano's | *Italian* __19__

| | |
|---|---|
| NEW Marché Moderne | *French* | — |
| Z Mastro's Steak | *Steak* | 25 |
| Memphis | *Southern* | 21 |
| NEW Mesa Rest. | *Italian* | — |
| Native Foods | *Calif./Eclectic* | 22 |
| Nello Cucina | *Italian* | 23 |
| NEW Old Vine Café | *Eclectic* | — |
| Onotria | *Eclectic* | 24 |
| Outback Steak | *Steak* | 17 |
| Pinot Provence | *French* | 25 |
| Plums Café | *Pac. NW* | 24 |
| Rainforest Cafe | *Amer.* | 13 |
| Side Street Cafe | *Amer.* | 18 |
| Souplantation | *Amer.* | 16 |
| Sutra Lounge | *Eclectic* | — |
| Taco Mesa | *Calif./Mex.* | 24 |
| Turner New Zealand | *Steak* | 24 |
| Wingnuts | *BBQ* | 16 |
| Wolfgang Puck | *Calif.* | 18 |
| Yard House | *Amer.* | 19 |
| Zipangu | *Jap.* | 23 |
| Z'tejas | *SW* | 18 |

### CYPRESS

| | |
|---|---|
| Café Hiro | *Asian* | 24 |

### DANA POINT

| | |
|---|---|
| Chart House | *Seafood/Steak* | 19 |
| Gemmell's | *French/Continental* | 23 |
| Ichibiri | *Jap.* | 18 |
| Luciana's | *Italian* | 22 |
| Z 162' | *Calif.* | 24 |
| Salt Creek | *Steak* | 18 |
| Z Stonehill Tav. | *Amer.* | 28 |
| Thai This | *Thai* | 22 |
| Vue | *Calif.* | — |
| NEW Wicked Gdn. | *Calif./Med.* | — |

### FOOTHILL RANCH

| | |
|---|---|
| Natraj | *Indian* | 18 |
| Peppino's | *Italian* | 18 |
| Souplantation | *Amer.* | 16 |

### FOUNTAIN VALLEY

| | |
|---|---|
| Islands | *Amer.* | 16 |
| Mimi's Cafe | *Diner* | 17 |
| Souplantation | *Amer.* | 16 |
| Stonefire Grill | *BBQ* | 20 |
| Thai Dishes | *Thai* | 18 |

### FULLERTON

| | |
|---|---|
| Amazon Churr. | *Brazilian* | 16 |
| Café Hidalgo | *SW* | 19 |
| Cellar | *French* | 23 |
| NEW Commonwealth | *Amer.* | — |
| Heroes B&G | *Pub* | 16 |
| Islands | *Amer.* | 16 |
| Mulberry St. Rist. | *Pizza* | 20 |
| Olde Ship | *Pub* | 18 |
| Rutabegorz | *Seafood/Veg.* | — |
| Z Summit Hse. | *Continental* | 25 |
| Table Ten | *Amer.* | 19 |

### GARDEN GROVE

| | |
|---|---|
| BCD Tofu | *Korean* | 20 |
| NEW Brodard Chateau | *Viet.* | 24 |
| Buca di Beppo | *Italian* | 15 |
| Joe's Crab | *Seafood* | 13 |
| Outback Steak | *Steak* | 17 |
| Pho 79 | *Viet.* | 21 |

### HUNTINGTON BEACH

| | |
|---|---|
| BJ's | *Pub* | 17 |
| Buca di Beppo | *Italian* | 15 |
| Bukhara | *Indian* | — |
| Californian | *Calif.* | 23 |
| Chimayo/Beach | *Pac. Rim* | 18 |
| Duke's | *Pac. Rim* | 17 |
| Z In-N-Out Burger | *Hamburgers* | 24 |
| NEW Izakaya Zero | *Jap.* | — |
| Loft, The | *Hawaiian* | 17 |
| Shades | *Amer./Continental* | — |
| NEW Silvera's Steak | *Steak* | — |
| Spark Woodfire | *Amer.* | 17 |

### IRVINE

| | |
|---|---|
| Agora Churr. | *Brazilian* | 24 |
| Baja Fresh Mex. | *Mex.* | 18 |
| Bistango | *Amer.* | 24 |
| Britta's Café | *Amer.* | 20 |
| Buca di Beppo | *Italian* | 15 |
| Cali. Pizza Kitchen | *Pizza* | 18 |
| Chakra | *Indian* | 21 |
| Z Cheesecake Fact. | *Amer.* | 20 |
| Claim Jumper | *Amer.* | 19 |
| NEW Crystal Jade | *Asian* | 20 |
| Daily Grill | *Amer.* | 18 |
| El Cholo | *Mex.* | 18 |
| El Torito Grill | *Mex.* | 18 |

| Fish Market | *Seafood* | 16 |
| Fox Sports | *Pub* | 14 |
| French 75 | *French* | 21 |
| Gulliver's | *British* | 20 |
| ☑ Houston's | *Amer.* | 21 |
| ☑ Il Fornaio | *Italian* | 20 |
| ☑ In-N-Out Burger | *Hamburgers* | 24 |
| Islands | *Amer.* | 16 |
| JACKshrimp | *Cajun* | 17 |
| Javier's Cantina | *Mex.* | 22 |
| Johnny Rockets | *Hamburgers* | 15 |
| NEW Kimera | *Eclectic* | – |
| Ling & Louie's | *Pan-Asian* | 17 |
| Lucca Cafe | *Med.* | 23 |
| McCormick/Schmick | *Seafood* | 19 |
| Melting Pot | *Fondue* | 19 |
| Natraj | *Indian* | 18 |
| Opah | *Calif./Seafood* | 23 |
| Pei Wei Diner | *Pan-Asian* | 16 |
| ☑ P.F. Chang's | *Chinese* | 19 |
| Pomodoro | *Italian* | 17 |
| Prego | *Italian* | 19 |
| Ruby's | *Diner* | 16 |
| ☑ Ruth's Chris | *Steak* | 25 |
| Sam Woo | *Chinese* | 20 |
| Sharky's Mex. | *Mex.* | 17 |
| ☑ 6ix Park Grill | *Calif.* | 21 |
| Souplantation | *Amer.* | 16 |
| Steelhead Brew. | *Pub* | 16 |
| Stonefire Grill | *BBQ* | 20 |
| Taiko | *Jap.* | 21 |
| Taléo Mexican | *Mex.* | 23 |
| NEW Veggie Grill | *Veg.* | 20 |
| Vessia | *Italian* | 22 |
| Wasa | *Jap.* | 24 |
| Yard House | *Amer.* | 19 |
| NEW Zmario | *Italian* | – |

## LADERA RANCH

| Infusion | *Amer.* | 23 |
| Jerry's/Dogs | *Hot Dogs* | 20 |
| Picante | *Spanish* | 21 |
| Taco Mesa | *Calif./Mex.* | 24 |

## LAGUNA BEACH/ S. LAGUNA BEACH

| BJ's | *Pub* | 17 |
| Brussels Bistro | *Belgian* | 17 |
| ☑ Cafe Zoolu | *Calif.* | 26 |

| Cedar Creek | *Amer.* | 19 |
| Claes | *Seafood* | 23 |
| Cottage | *Amer.* | 17 |
| Coyote Grill | *Mex.* | 19 |
| Dizz's As Is | *Eclectic* | 23 |
| Five Feet | *Chinese/French* | 24 |
| French 75 | *French* | 21 |
| hush | *Amer.* | 21 |
| Javier's Cantina | *Mex.* | 22 |
| Johnny Rockets | *Hamburgers* | 15 |
| NEW K'ya | *Calif.* | – |
| Las Brisas | *Mex./Seafood* | 16 |
| Mozambique | *Eclectic* | 19 |
| Picayo | *French/Med.* | 22 |
| Pomodoro | *Italian* | 17 |
| Royal Thai | *Thai* | 21 |
| Ruby's | *Diner* | 16 |
| NEW Sapphire Laguna | *Eclectic* | 26 |
| Sorrento Grille | *Calif./Med.* | 22 |
| ☑ Splashes | *Calif./Med.* | 21 |
| ☑ Studio | *Calif./French* | 27 |
| Sundried Tomato | *Calif.* | 22 |
| ☑ Tabu Grill | *Seafood/Steak* | 26 |
| Taco Loco | *Eclectic* | 24 |
| Ti Amo | *Italian/Med.* | 22 |
| 230 Forest Ave. | *Calif.* | 25 |
| Zinc Cafe | *Calif.* | 22 |

## LAGUNA HILLS

| Baja Fresh Mex. | *Mex.* | 18 |
| BJ's | *Pub* | 17 |
| Claim Jumper | *Amer.* | 19 |
| King's Fish Hse. | *Seafood* | 21 |
| Natraj | *Indian* | 18 |
| O-Nami | *Jap.* | 16 |

## LAGUNA NIGUEL

| Cedar Creek | *Amer.* | 19 |
| NEW Eno | *Eclectic* | – |
| Ichibiri | *Jap.* | 18 |
| ☑ In-N-Out Burger | *Hamburgers* | 24 |
| Mimi's Cafe | *Diner* | 17 |
| Savannah Steak | *Seafood/Steak* | 23 |

## LA HABRA

| Cat/Custard Cup | *Amer./Calif.* | 23 |
| El Cholo | *Mex.* | 18 |
| Jerry's/Dogs | *Hot Dogs* | 20 |

## LAKE FOREST

Inka Grill | *Peruvian* — 19
Mimi's Cafe | *Diner* — 17
Peppino's | *Italian* — 18

## LOS ALAMITOS

Original Fish Co. | *Seafood* — 24
Shenandoah/Arbor | *Southern* — 21

## MISSION VIEJO

Cali. Pizza Kitchen | *Pizza* — 18
Capriccio | *Italian* — 22
Ⓩ Cheesecake Fact. | *Amer.* — 20
El Torito Grill | *Mex.* — 18
NEW Nirvana Grille | *Calif.* — –
Oceans 33° | *Calif./Seafood* — 19
Peppino's | *Italian* — 18
Ⓩ P.F. Chang's | *Chinese* — 19
Shabu Shabu | *Jap.* — 25
Taco Mesa | *Calif./Mex.* — 24
Tortilla Flats | *Mex.* — 16
Valentina Rist. | *Italian* — 12

## MONARCH BEACH

Crab Cove | *Seafood* — 19
Motif | *Eclectic* — 23
NEW Stella's | *Italian* — 19

## NEWPORT BEACH

Abe | *Jap.* — 25
bambu | *Calif.* — –
Ⓩ Basilic | *French/Swiss* — 28
Bayside | *Amer.* — 25
Benihana | *Jap.* — 18
BJ's | *Pub* — 17
Blue Coral | *Seafood* — 22
Bluewater Grill | *Amer./Seafood* — 20
Café R&D | *Amer.* — 21
Cannery Seafood | *Seafood* — 22
Chart House | *Seafood/Steak* — 19
Ⓩ Cheesecake Fact. | *Amer.* — 20
Crab Cooker | *Seafood* — 22
Daily Grill | *Amer.* — 18
Dolce Rist. | *Italian* — 18
El Torito Grill | *Mex.* — 18
Ⓩ First Cabin | — 25
    *Amer./Continental*
Fleming Prime | *Steak* — 25
French 75 | *French* — 21
Gulfstream | *Amer./Seafood* — 21
Islands | *Amer.* — 16

JACKshrimp | *Cajun* — 17
Joe's Crab | *Seafood* — 13
Kantina | *Nuevo Latino* — 18
Ⓩ Mastro's Ocean | *Seafood* — 22
Modo Mio | *Italian* — 22
Muldoon's Dublin | *Irish* — 18
Nesai | *Calif./Italian* — –
NEW Palm Terrace | *Amer.* — –
Pei Wei Diner | *Pan-Asian* — 16
Pescadou | *French* — 22
Ⓩ P.F. Chang's | *Chinese* — 19
Pomodoro | *Italian* — 17
Rist. Mamma Gina | *Italian* — 21
NEW Rist. Max | *Italian* — 21
Ⓩ Ritz Rest./Gdn. | *Continental* — 24
Royal Thai | *Thai* — 21
Ⓩ Roy's | *Hawaiian* — 24
Rusty Pelican | *Seafood* — 19
Sabatino's Sausage | *Italian* — 22
Sage | *Amer.* — 24
Sharky's Mex. | *Mex.* — 17
Taco Rosa | *Mex.* — 22
Ten | *Jap./Pac. Rim* — 22
3Thirty3 | *Amer.* — 18
Tommy Bahama | *Carib.* — 19
Ⓩ Tradition/Pascal | *French* — 27
21 Oceanfront | *Seafood* — 22
Villa Nova | *Italian* — 19
Wasa | *Jap.* — 24
Wildfish/Grille | *Amer./Seafood* — 23
Yi Dynasty | *Korean* — –

## NEWPORT COAST

Beachcomber | *Calif.* — 17
Bluefin | *Jap.* — 25
Zov's | *Med.* — 25

## ORANGE

Café/Tango | *Eclectic* — 20
Citrus | *Calif.* — 20
El Torito | *Mex.* — 15
Filling Station | *Diner* — 17
NEW Gabbi's Mex. | *Mex.* — 26
Ⓩ Hobbit, The | — 27
    *Continental/French*
Jody Maroni's | *Hot Dogs* — 19
Johnny Rebs' | *BBQ* — 22
Johnny Rockets | *Hamburgers* — 15
King's Fish Hse. | *Seafood* — 21
Lazy Dog | *Eclectic* — 19

Mascarpone's | *Italian*    24
Pomodoro | *Italian*    17
Rutabegorz | *Seafood/Veg.*    –
Taco Mesa | *Calif./Mex.*    24

## RANCHO SANTA MARGARITA

Opah | *Calif./Seafood*    23
Wood Ranch BBQ | *BBQ*    20

## SAN CLEMENTE

BeachFire | *Calif.*    18
Gordon James | *Amer.*    20
Ichibiri | *Jap.*    18
Iva Lee's | *Cajun/Creole*    23
NEW Rick's Secret Spot | *BBQ*    –
Vine | *Calif./Med.*    25

## SAN JUAN CAPISTRANO

Cedar Creek | *Amer.*    19
NEW La Fondue | *Fondue*    21
L'Hirondelle | *Belgian/French*    22
☑ Ramos House | *Amer.*    26
Rendezvous | *Amer.*    24
Sundried Tomato | *Calif.*    22
Tannins | *Italian*    18

## SANTA ANA

Ambrosia | *French*    24
☑ Antonello | *Italian*    24
Baja Fresh Mex. | *Mex.*    18
Cali. Pizza Kitchen | *Pizza*    18
Claim Jumper | *Amer.*    19
Darya | *Persian*    23
Green Parrot | *Calif.*    24
Gypsy Den | *Calif.*    17
Jerry's/Dogs | *Hot Dogs*    20
Memphis | *Southern*    21
Morton's Steak | *Steak*    25
Olde Ship | *Pub*    18
Royal Khyber | *Indian*    24
Tangata | *Calif.*    23

## SEAL BEACH

Ruby's | *Diner*    16
Spaghettini | *Italian*    20
Walt's Wharf | *Seafood*    25

## STANTON

Park Ave. | *Amer.*    25

## TRABUCO CANYON

Trabuco Oaks Steak | *Steak*    21

## TUSTIN

Black Sheep | *French/Spanish*    24
Cali. Pizza Kitchen | *Pizza*    18
Citrus | *Calif.*    20
Crab Cooker | *Seafood*    22
El Torito | *Mex.*    15
☑ In-N-Out Burger | *Hamburgers*    24
Mimi's Cafe | *Diner*    17
Nieuport 17 | *Continental*    22
Ruby's | *Diner*    16
Rutabegorz | *Seafood/Veg.*    –
NEW Sevens Steak | *Steak*    –
Taco Rosa | *Mex.*    22
Zov's | *Med.*    25

## WESTMINSTER

Lazy Dog | *Eclectic*    19
Pho 79 | *Viet.*    21
Riviera at Fireside | *Continental*    24
Seafood Paradise | *Chinese/Seafood*    21
S Vietnamese | *Viet.*    24
Thanh My | *Viet.*    20

## YORBA LINDA

El Torito | *Mex.*    15
Fitness Pizza | *Med.*    20
☑ Original Pancake | *Diner*    23
Wild Artichoke | *Calif./Eclectic*    24

# Palm Springs & Environs

## CORONA

BJ's | *Pub*    17
Claim Jumper | *Amer.*    19
☑ In-N-Out Burger | *Hamburgers*    24
Pomodoro | *Italian*    17
Rosine's | *Armenian/Med.*    24
Zip Fusion | *Jap.*    18

## INDIAN WELLS

Le St. Germain | *French/Med.*    24
☑ Sirocco | *Italian*    25

## LA QUINTA

Arnold Palmer's | *Steak*    –
AZUR | *Calif./French*    22
Blend | *Amer.*    –
Falls Prime Steak | *Steak*    22
Hog's Breath Inn | *Amer.*    14

La Quinta Cliffhse. | *Amer.* 18
Las Casuelas | *Mex.* 18
LG's Prime Steak | *Steak* 23

## PALM DESERT

Bellini | *Italian* 21
Café/Beaux-Arts | *French* 18
Cali. Pizza Kitchen | *Pizza* 18
Castelli's | *Italian* 23
Chop House | *Steak* 21
☑ Cuistot | *Calif./French* 26
Daily Grill | *Amer.* 18
Islands | *Amer.* 16
☑ Jillian's | *Continental* 25
LG's Prime Steak | *Steak* 23
Morton's Steak | *Steak* 25
Native Foods | *Calif./Eclectic* 22
Outback Steak | *Steak* 17
Picanha Churr. | *Brazilian* 19
Rist. Mamma Gina | *Italian* 21
Rist. Tuscany | *Italian* 23
Romano's Macaroni | *Italian* 17
☑ Ruth's Chris | *Steak* 25
Tommy Bahama | *Carib.* 19

## PALM SPRINGS

Billy Reed's | *Amer.* 16
Cali. Pizza Kitchen | *Pizza* 18
Cedar Creek | *Amer.* 19
Chop House | *Steak* 21
Falls Prime Steak | *Steak* 22
☑ Johannes | *Austrian* 25
John Henry's | *Eclectic/French* 22
Kaiser Grille | *Amer.* 16
Las Casuelas | *Mex.* 18
☑ Le Vallauris | *French/Med.* 27
LG's Prime Steak | *Steak* 23
Native Foods | *Calif./Eclectic* 22

## RANCHO CUCAMONGA

BJ's | *Pub* 17
Cali. Pizza Kitchen | *Pizza* 18
☑ Cheesecake Fact. | *Amer.* 20
Claim Jumper | *Amer.* 19
Gyu-Kaku | *Jap.* 20
Lucille's BBQ | *BBQ* 22
Romano's Macaroni | *Italian* 17
Sisley Italian | *Italian* 18
Souplantation | *Amer.* 16
Yard House | *Amer.* 19

## RANCHO MIRAGE

☑ Cheesecake Fact. | *Amer.* 20
Johnny Rockets | *Hamburgers* 15
Las Casuelas | *Mex.* 18
Lord Fletcher's | *Pub* 23
☑ Roy's | *Hawaiian* 24
Shame on Moon | *Amer.* –
☑ Wally's Desert | *Continental* 25

## RIVERSIDE

Cali. Pizza Kitchen | *Pizza* 18
Citrus | *Calif.* 20
☑ In-N-Out Burger | *Hamburgers* 24
Ruby's | *Diner* 16

## SAN BERNARDINO

BJ's | *Pub* 17
Claim Jumper | *Amer.* 19
Outback Steak | *Steak* 17
Souplantation | *Amer.* 16

## TEMECULA

BJ's | *Pub* 17
Cali. Pizza Kitchen | *Pizza* 18
Inka Grill | *Peruvian* 19
☑ Original Pancake | *Diner* 23
Souplantation | *Amer.* 16

## UPLAND

Outback Steak | *Steak* 17

## VICTORVILLE

Johnny Rebs' | *BBQ* 22

# Santa Barbara & Environs

## BALLARD

☑ Ballard Inn | *French* 26

## BUELLTON

Hitching Post | *BBQ* 23

## CASMALIA

Hitching Post | *BBQ* 23

## GOLETA

☑ In-N-Out Burger | *Hamburgers* 24
Outback Steak | *Steak* 17

## LOS OLIVOS

Brothers Rest. | *Amer.* 24
Los Olivos Cafe | *Calif./Med.* –

OC/PS/SB

LOCATIONS

# Special Features

Listings cover the best in each category and include restaurant names, locations and Food ratings. Multi-location restaurants' features may vary by branch. ☑ indicates places with the highest ratings, popularity and importance.

## BREAKFAST

(See also Hotel Dining)

| | |
|---|---|
| Beachcomber \| **Newport Coast/OC** | 17 |
| Britta's Café \| **Irvine/OC** | 20 |
| Cottage \| **Laguna Bch/OC** | 17 |
| Filling Station \| **Orange/OC** | 17 |
| NEW Old Vine Café \| **Costa Mesa/OC** | – |
| ☑ Original Pancake \| **multi. loc.** | 23 |
| Plums Café \| **Costa Mesa/OC** | 24 |
| ☑ Ramos House \| **San Juan Cap/OC** | 26 |
| Ruby's \| **multi. loc.** | 16 |
| Side Street Cafe \| **Costa Mesa/OC** | 18 |
| Zinc Cafe \| **multi. loc.** | 22 |

## BRUNCH

| | |
|---|---|
| Bayside \| **Newport Bch/OC** | 25 |
| Californian \| **Huntington Bch/OC** | 23 |
| Cannery Seafood \| **Newport Bch/OC** | 22 |
| Claes \| **Laguna Bch/OC** | 23 |
| Cold Spring \| **SB** | 19 |
| French 75 \| **Newport Bch/OC** | 21 |
| L'Hirondelle \| **San Juan Cap/OC** | 22 |
| ☑ 162' \| **Dana Pt/OC** | 24 |
| Pinot Provence \| **Costa Mesa/OC** | 25 |
| Plums Café \| **Costa Mesa/OC** | 24 |
| Ralph Brennan's \| **Anaheim/OC** | 19 |
| ☑ Ramos House \| **San Juan Cap/OC** | 26 |
| ☑ Ranch House \| **Ojai/SB** | 25 |
| Rist. Mamma Gina \| **Newport Bch/OC** | 21 |
| Sabatino's Sausage \| **Newport Bch/OC** | 22 |
| Spaghettini \| **Seal Bch/OC** | 20 |
| Taco Rosa \| **Newport Bch/OC** | 22 |
| TAPS Fish \| **Brea/OC** | 23 |

## BUFFET

(Check availability)

| | |
|---|---|
| Agora Churr. \| **Irvine/OC** | 24 |
| Amazon Churr. \| **Fullerton/OC** | 16 |
| NEW Bella Vista \| **Montecito/SB** | 26 |
| Bukhara \| **Huntington Bch/OC** | – |
| Duke's \| **Huntington Bch/OC** | 17 |
| El Paseo \| **SB** | 15 |
| El Torito Grill \| **multi. loc.** | 18 |
| Las Casuelas \| **Rancho Mirage/PS** | 18 |
| Mayur \| **Corona del Mar/OC** | 21 |
| Motif \| **Monarch Bch/OC** | 23 |
| Mrs. Knott's \| **Buena Pk/OC** | 21 |
| Natraj \| **Laguna Hills/OC** | 18 |
| O-Nami \| **Laguna Hills/OC** | 16 |
| Royal Khyber \| **Santa Ana/OC** | 24 |
| Savoy Truffles \| **SB** | 21 |
| Shades \| **Huntington Bch/OC** | – |
| Souplantation \| **multi. loc.** | 16 |
| Spice Ave. \| **SB** | 19 |

## BUSINESS DINING

| | |
|---|---|
| Anaheim White Hse. \| **Anaheim/OC** | 24 |
| ☑ Antonello \| **Santa Ana/OC** | 24 |
| Arnold Palmer's \| **La Quinta/PS** | 24 |
| Auberge at Ojai \| **Ojai/SB** | 21 |
| Bayside \| **Newport Bch/OC** | 25 |
| Bistango \| **Irvine/OC** | 24 |
| Blend \| **La Quinta/PS** | – |
| Blue Coral \| **Newport Bch/OC** | 22 |
| NEW Brooks \| **Ventura/SB** | – |
| Bucatini \| **SB** | 22 |
| Californian \| **Huntington Bch/OC** | 23 |
| Cat/Custard Cup \| **La Habra/OC** | 23 |
| Cellar \| **Fullerton/OC** | 23 |
| China Pavilion \| **SB** | 23 |
| NEW Crystal Jade \| **Irvine/OC** | 20 |
| NEW C-Street \| **Ventura/SB** | – |
| Daily Grill \| **Irvine/OC** | 18 |
| ☑ First Cabin \| **Newport Bch/OC** | 25 |
| Fleming Prime \| **Newport Bch/OC** | 25 |
| Gulliver's \| **Irvine/OC** | 20 |
| ☑ Houston's \| **Irvine/OC** | 21 |
| ☑ Il Fornaio \| **Irvine/OC** | 20 |

OC/PS/SB

SPECIAL FEATURES

| | | |
|---|---|---|
| ☑ Wally's Desert \| **Rancho Mirage/PS** | 25 | |
| Westside Cellar \| **Ventura/SB** | 22 | |

## CHEF'S TABLE

| | |
|---|---|
| Blend \| **La Quinta/PS** | – |
| ☑ Cuistot \| **Palm Desert/PS** | 26 |
| ☑ Mastro's Steak \| **Costa Mesa/OC** | 25 |
| ☑ Napa Rose \| **Anaheim/OC** | 27 |
| Rist. Tuscany \| **Palm Desert/PS** | 23 |
| ☑ Studio \| **Laguna Bch/OC** | 27 |
| NEW Wicked Gdn. \| **Dana Pt/OC** | – |

## COOL LOOS

| | |
|---|---|
| NEW La Fondue \| **San Juan Cap/OC** | 21 |
| NEW Mesa Rest. \| **Costa Mesa/OC** | – |
| Park Ave. \| **Stanton/OC** | 25 |
| Ralph Brennan's \| **Anaheim/OC** | 19 |
| NEW Wicked Gdn. \| **Dana Pt/OC** | – |
| Zov's \| **Tustin/OC** | 25 |

## CRITIC-PROOF

(Gets lots of business despite so-so food)

| | |
|---|---|
| Joe's Crab \| **multi. loc.** | 13 |
| Rainforest Cafe \| **multi. loc.** | 13 |

## DANCING

| | |
|---|---|
| Arnold Palmer's \| **La Quinta/PS** | – |
| Bistango \| **Irvine/OC** | 24 |
| Cafe Buenos Aires \| **SB** | 16 |
| Cafe Fiore \| **Ventura/SB** | 21 |
| ☑ First Cabin \| **Newport Bch/OC** | 25 |
| Landmark Steak \| **Corona del Mar/OC** | 18 |
| Las Casuelas \| **multi. loc.** | 18 |
| Sutra Lounge \| **Costa Mesa/OC** | – |
| Valentina Rist. \| **Mission Viejo/OC** | 12 |

## DESSERT

| | |
|---|---|
| ☑ Cheesecake Fact. \| **multi. loc.** | 20 |
| Filling Station \| **Orange/OC** | 17 |
| Intermezzo \| **SB** | 21 |
| NEW La Fondue \| **San Juan Cap/OC** | 21 |
| Lucca Cafe \| **Irvine/OC** | 23 |
| NEW Marché Moderne \| **Costa Mesa/OC** | – |

| | |
|---|---|
| Melting Pot \| **Irvine/OC** | 19 |
| Plums Café \| **Costa Mesa/OC** | 24 |
| NEW Sapphire Laguna \| **Laguna Bch/OC** | 26 |
| Zov's \| **Tustin/OC** | 25 |

## ENTERTAINMENT

(Call for days and times of performances)

| | |
|---|---|
| Bayside \| piano \| **Newport Bch/OC** | 25 |
| Bistango \| varies \| **Irvine/OC** | 24 |
| Cat/Custard Cup \| piano \| **La Habra/OC** | 23 |
| Cedar Creek \| varies \| **multi. loc.** | 19 |
| ☑ Chat Noir \| jazz \| **Costa Mesa/OC** | 21 |
| House of Blues \| varies \| **Anaheim/OC** | 15 |
| La Cave \| jazz \| **Costa Mesa/OC** | 21 |
| Lucille's BBQ \| blues \| **multi. loc.** | 22 |
| Market City \| strings \| **Brea/OC** | 18 |
| Mulberry St. Rist. \| karaoke \| **Fullerton/OC** | 20 |
| Nieuport 17 \| piano \| **Tustin/OC** | 22 |
| Oysters \| jazz \| **Corona del Mar/OC** | 23 |
| Ralph Brennan's \| jazz \| **Anaheim/OC** | 19 |
| Rist. Mamma Gina \| varies \| **Newport Bch/OC** | 21 |
| Romano's Macaroni \| opera \| **Rancho Cuca/PS** | 17 |
| Salt Creek \| varies \| **Dana Pt/OC** | 18 |
| Spaghettini \| jazz \| **Seal Bch/OC** | 20 |
| Sutra Lounge \| DJ \| **Costa Mesa/OC** | – |
| Villa Nova \| varies \| **Newport Bch/OC** | 19 |

## FAMILY-STYLE

| | |
|---|---|
| Benihana \| **Newport Bch/OC** | 18 |
| Buca di Beppo \| **multi. loc.** | 15 |
| Emilio's \| **SB** | 24 |
| Lucille's BBQ \| **multi. loc.** | 22 |
| Maggiano's \| **Costa Mesa/OC** | 19 |
| Naples \| **Anaheim/OC** | 17 |
| Palazzio \| **SB** | 18 |
| ☑ P.F. Chang's \| **multi. loc.** | 19 |
| Romano's Macaroni \| **multi. loc.** | 17 |
| Stonefire Grill \| **multi. loc.** | 20 |
| Tre Lune \| **Montecito/SB** | 21 |

## FIREPLACES

Anaheim White Hse. | **Anaheim/OC** — 24

Arnold Palmer's | **La Quinta/PS** — -

Auberge at Ojai | **Ojai/SB** — 21

Austen's/Pierpont | **Ventura/SB** — 19

☑ Ballard Inn | **Ballard/SB** — 26

BeachFire | **San Clemente/OC** — 18

NEW Bella Vista | **Montecito/SB** — 26

Blue Agave | **SB** — 19

Bluewater Grill | **Newport Bch/OC** — 20

Brothers Rest. | **Los Olivos/SB** — 24

Brussels Bistro | **Laguna Bch/OC** — 17

Cafe del Sol | **Montecito/SB** — 18

Cafe Fiore | **Ventura/SB** — 21

Californian | **Huntington Bch/OC** — 23

Catal/Uva Bar | **Anaheim/OC** — 22

Cat/Custard Cup | **La Habra/OC** — 23

Cava | **Montecito/SB** — 21

Cedar Creek | **multi. loc.** — 19

Chad's | **SB** — 22

Claim Jumper | **multi. loc.** — 19

Cold Spring | **SB** — 19

☑ Cuistot | **Palm Desert/PS** — 26

Dolce Rist. | **Newport Bch/OC** — 18

El Cholo | **multi. loc.** — 18

Epiphany | **SB** — 17

Falls Prime Steak | **multi. loc.** — 22

Five Crowns | **Corona del Mar/OC** — 24

Gulliver's | **Irvine/OC** — 20

Hitching Post | **Buellton/SB** — 23

Hog's Breath Inn | **La Quinta/PS** — 14

Intermezzo | **SB** — 21

NEW K'ya | **Laguna Bch/OC** — -

Landmark Steak | **Corona del Mar/OC** — 18

☑ La Vie en Rose | **Brea/OC** — 25

Lazy Dog | **Westminster/OC** — 19

Le St. Germain | **Indian Wells/PS** — 24

☑ Le Vallauris | **PS** — 27

LG's Prime Steak | **La Quinta/PS** — 23

Lord Fletcher's | **Rancho Mirage/PS** — 23

Los Olivos Cafe | **Los Olivos/SB** — -

Lucca Cafe | **Irvine/OC** — 23

Luciana's | **Dana Pt/OC** — 22

Maravilla | **Ojai/SB** — -

Miró | **SB** — 26

Mozambique | **Laguna Bch/OC** — 19

☑ Mr. Stox | **Anaheim/OC** — 24

Muldoon's Dublin | **Newport Bch/OC** — 18

☑ Napa Rose | **Anaheim/OC** — 27

Nieuport 17 | **Tustin/OC** — 22

☑ 162' | **Dana Pt/OC** — 24

Park Ave. | **Stanton/OC** — 25

Piatti | **Montecito/SB** — 20

Pinot Provence | **Costa Mesa/OC** — 25

NEW Port Rest. | **Corona del Mar/OC** — -

Rist. Mamma Gina | **Newport Bch/OC** — 21

Rodney's Steak | **SB** — 25

Sage | **Newport Bch/OC** — 24

Savannah Steak | **Laguna Niguel/OC** — 23

71 Palm | **Ventura/SB** — 20

Sorrento Grille | **Laguna Bch/OC** — 22

Spaghettini | **Seal Bch/OC** — 20

☑ Splashes | **Laguna Bch/OC** — 21

☑ Stella Mare's | **SB** — 22

☑ Stonehill Tav. | **Dana Pt/OC** — 28

☑ Studio | **Laguna Bch/OC** — 27

☑ Summit Hse. | **Fullerton/OC** — 25

Suzanne's | **Ojai/SB** — 25

Ti Amo | **S Laguna Bch/OC** — 22

Vine | **San Clemente/OC** — 25

Westside Cellar | **Ventura/SB** — 22

Wine Cask | **SB** — 24

NEW Zmario | **Irvine/OC** — -

## HISTORIC PLACES

(Year opened; * building)

1800 | Tupelo Junction* | **SB** — 23

1881 | Ramos House* | **San Juan Cap/OC** — 26

1886 | Cold Spring* | **SB** — 19

1887 | Jonathan's/Peirano* | **Ventura/SB** — 22

1890 | Brothers Rest.* | **Los Olivos/SB** — 24

1890 | Wine Cask* | **SB** — 24

1905 | Auberge at Ojai* | **Ojai/SB** — 21

1910 | Austen's/Pierpont | **Ventura/SB** — 19

Ritz-Carlton
  NEW Eno | Laguna Niguel/OC — | -

Ritz-Carlton Laguna Niguel
  162' | Dana Pt/OC | 24

Santa Barbara Inn
  NEW Fresco/Beach | SB | 20

St. Regis Monarch Bch.
  Motif | Monarch Bch/OC | 23
  Stonehill Tav. | Dana Pt/OC | 28
  Studio | Laguna Bch/OC | 27

Surf & Sand Resort
  Splashes | Laguna Bch/OC | 21

Upham Hotel
  Louie's | SB | 25

Westin South Coast Plaza Hotel
  Pinot Provence | Costa Mesa/OC | 25

## LATE DINING

(Weekday closing hour)

BCD Tofu | varies | Garden Grove/OC | 20

NEW Eno | 12 AM | Laguna Niguel/OC | -

Heroes B&G | varies | Fullerton/OC | 16

Hungry Cat | 12 AM | SB | 24

In-N-Out Burger | 1 AM | multi. loc. | 24

Taco Loco | 12 AM | Laguna Bch/OC | 24

Thanh My | 1 AM | Westminster/OC | 20

3Thirty3 | 2 AM | Newport Bch/OC | 18

Valentina Rist. | 12 AM | Mission Viejo/OC | 12

Villa Nova | 12 AM | Newport Bch/OC | 19

## LOCAL FAVORITES

BeachFire | San Clemente/OC | 18

Bungalow | Corona del Mar/OC | 21

Café Hiro | Cypress/OC | 24

Carlitos Cafe | SB | 19

Dizz's As Is | Laguna Bch/OC | 23

Filling Station | Orange/OC | 17

Golden Truffle | Costa Mesa/OC | 26

Ichiban Sushi | SB | 21

Iva Lee's | San Clemente/OC | 23

Jade | SB | 23

Javier's Cantina | Laguna Bch/OC | 22

Jerry's/Dogs | multi. loc. | 20

Jillian's | Palm Desert/PS | 25

La Cave | Costa Mesa/OC | 21

L'Hirondelle | San Juan Cap/OC | 22

Lucky's | Montecito/SB | 24

Mascarpone's | Orange/OC | 24

Miró | SB | 26

Pescadou | Newport Bch/OC | 22

Plums Café | Costa Mesa/OC | 24

Rosine's | Anaheim/OC | 24

Sabatino's Sausage | Newport Bch/OC | 22

Salt Creek | Dana Pt/OC | 18

Sorrento Grille | Laguna Bch/OC | 22

Table Ten | Fullerton/OC | 19

TAPS Fish | Brea/OC | 23

Tee-Off | SB | 21

21 Oceanfront | Newport Bch/OC | 22

Vessia | Irvine/OC | 22

Wild Artichoke | Yorba Linda/OC | 24

Wildfish/Grille | Newport Bch/OC | 23

## MICROBREWERIES

BJ's | multi. loc. | 17

Bouchon | SB | 26

Heroes B&G | Fullerton/OC | 16

McCormick/Schmick | Irvine/OC | 19

Steelhead Brew. | Irvine/OC | 16

TAPS Fish | Brea/OC | 23

Yard House | multi. loc. | 19

## NATURAL/ORGANIC

(These restaurants often or always use organic, local ingredients)

Auberge at Ojai | Ojai/SB | 21

Austen's/Pierpont | Ventura/SB | 19

AZUR | La Quinta/PS | 22

Baja Fresh Mex. | multi. loc. | 18

Ballard Inn | Ballard/SB | 26

BCD Tofu | Garden Grove/OC | 20

Bellini | Palm Desert/PS | 21

OC/PS/SB

SPECIAL FEATURES

Cellar | Fullerton/OC — 23

NEW C-Street | Ventura/SB — -

☒ First Cabin | Newport Bch/OC — 25

Fleming Prime | Newport Bch/OC — 25

NEW Marché Moderne | Costa Mesa/OC — -

☒ Mastro's Ocean | Newport Bch/OC — 22

☒ Mastro's Steak | Costa Mesa/OC — 25

Morton's Steak | multi. loc. — 25

☒ Mr. Stox | Anaheim/OC — 24

☒ 162' | Dana Pt/OC — 24

Pinot Provence | Costa Mesa/OC — 25

☒ Ritz Rest./Gdn. | Newport Bch/OC — 24

☒ Roy's | Newport Bch/OC — 24

☒ Stonehill Tav. | Dana Pt/OC — 28

☒ Studio | Laguna Bch/OC — 27

☒ Tradition/Pascal | Newport Bch/OC — 27

21 Oceanfront | Newport Bch/OC — 22

## PRIVATE ROOMS

(Restaurants charge less at off times; call for capacity)

Anaheim White Hse. | Anaheim/OC — 24

☒ Antonello | Santa Ana/OC — 24

Bayside | Newport Bch/OC — 25

Bistango | Irvine/OC — 24

NEW Brooks | Ventura/SB — -

Cat/Custard Cup | La Habra/OC — 23

Five Crowns | Corona del Mar/OC — 24

Fleming Prime | Newport Bch/OC — 25

Green Parrot | Santa Ana/OC — 24

☒ Hobbit, The | Orange/OC — 27

Jonathan's/Peirano | Ventura/SB — 22

☒ La Vie en Rose | Brea/OC — 25

Maggiano's | Costa Mesa/OC — 19

Melting Pot | Irvine/OC — 19

Motif | Monarch Bch/OC — 23

☒ Mr. Stox | Anaheim/OC — 24

☒ Napa Rose | Anaheim/OC — 27

Nieuport 17 | Tustin/OC — 22

Pinot Provence | Costa Mesa/OC — 25

Prego | Irvine/OC — 19

☒ Ritz Rest./Gdn. | Newport Bch/OC — 24

☒ Roy's | Newport Bch/OC — 24

Salt Creek | Dana Pt/OC — 18

☒ 6ix Park Grill | Irvine/OC — 21

☒ Studio | Laguna Bch/OC — 27

☒ Summit Hse. | Fullerton/OC — 25

Sutra Lounge | Costa Mesa/OC — -

TAPS Fish | Brea/OC — 23

21 Oceanfront | Newport Bch/OC — 22

Zov's | Tustin/OC — 25

## QUIET CONVERSATION

Alcazar | SB — 19

Ambrosia | Santa Ana/OC — 24

Anaheim White Hse. | Anaheim/OC — 24

☒ Antonello | Santa Ana/OC — 24

Arnold Palmer's | La Quinta/PS — -

Auberge at Ojai | Ojai/SB — 21

☒ Ballard Inn | Ballard/SB — 26

bambu | Newport Bch/OC — -

☒ Basilic | Newport Bch/OC — 28

Black Sheep | Tustin/OC — 24

Blend | La Quinta/PS — -

Bluefin | Newport Coast/OC — 25

NEW Brooks | Ventura/SB — -

Bucatini | SB — 22

Cafe Fiore | Ventura/SB — 21

Californian | Huntington Bch/OC — 23

Cellar | Fullerton/OC — 23

Claes | Laguna Bch/OC — 23

NEW C-Street | Ventura/SB — -

Dizz's As Is | Laguna Bch/OC — 23

Dolce Rist. | Newport Bch/OC — 18

NEW Eno | Laguna Niguel/OC — -

55 Steak | Anaheim/OC — 23

☒ First Cabin | Newport Bch/OC — 25

Five Crowns | Corona del Mar/OC — 24

Green Parrot | Santa Ana/OC — 24

Gulliver's | Irvine/OC — 20

Intermezzo | SB — 21

Jade | SB — 23

## RAW BARS

## ROMANTIC PLACES

NEW Marché Moderne | **Costa Mesa/OC** — ⏌

Mastro's Steak | **Costa Mesa/OC** — 25

Mr. Stox | **Anaheim/OC** — 24

Nieuport 17 | **Tustin/OC** — 22

162' | **Dana Pt/OC** — 24

Picante | **Ladera Ranch/OC** — 21

Pinot Provence | **Costa Mesa/OC** — 25

NEW Port Rest. | **Corona del Mar/OC** — ⏌

Ranch House | **Ojai/SB** — 25

Rendezvous | **San Juan Cap/OC** — 24

Ritz Rest./Gdn. | **Newport Bch/OC** — 24

Rothschild's | **Corona del Mar/OC** — 22

71 Palm | **Ventura/SB** — 20

Sevilla | **SB** — 22

Splashes | **Laguna Bch/OC** — 21

Stonehill Tav. | **Dana Pt/OC** — 28

Studio | **Laguna Bch/OC** — 27

31 West | **SB** — 18

Ti Amo | **S Laguna Bch/OC** — 22

Tradition/Pascal | **Newport Bch/OC** — 27

21 Oceanfront | **Newport Bch/OC** — 22

Villa Nova | **Newport Bch/OC** — 19

NEW Wicked Gdn. | **Dana Pt/OC** — ⏌

## SINGLES SCENES

Aire | **Costa Mesa/OC** — 23

Alcazar | **SB** — 19

Bayside | **Newport Bch/OC** — 25

BeachFire | **San Clemente/OC** — 18

Bistango | **Irvine/OC** — 24

NEW Brooks | **Ventura/SB** — ⏌

Bungalow | **Corona del Mar/OC** — 21

Chat Noir | **Costa Mesa/OC** — 21

NEW C-Street | **Ventura/SB** — ⏌

Elements | **SB** — 22

El Paseo | **SB** — 15

Gulfstream | **Newport Bch/OC** — 21

Javier's Cantina | **Laguna Bch/OC** — 22

Kantina | **Newport Bch/OC** — 18

Las Brisas | **Laguna Bch/OC** — 16

Mastro's Ocean | **Newport Bch/OC** — 22

Mastro's Steak | **Costa Mesa/OC** — 25

Memphis | **Costa Mesa/OC** — 21

Opah | **Aliso Viejo/OC** — 23

Oysters | **Corona del Mar/OC** — 23

Salt Creek | **Dana Pt/OC** — 18

Shame on Moon | **Rancho Mirage/PS** — ⏌

Sorrento Grille | **Laguna Bch/OC** — 22

Spaghettini | **Seal Bch/OC** — 20

Sutra Lounge | **Costa Mesa/OC** — ⏌

3Thirty3 | **Newport Bch/OC** — 18

Yard House | **multi. loc.** — 19

## SLEEPERS

(Good to excellent food, but little known)

Alvarado's | **Anaheim Hills/OC** — 22

Ambrosia | **Santa Ana/OC** — 24

NEW Bella Vista | **Montecito/SB** — 26

NEW Brodard Chateau | **Garden Grove/OC** — 24

Bucatini | **SB** — 22

Café Hiro | **Cypress/OC** — 24

Californian | **Huntington Bch/OC** — 23

Capriccio | **Mission Viejo/OC** — 22

Chad's | **SB** — 22

China Pavilion | **multi. loc.** — 23

55 Steak | **Anaheim/OC** — 23

NEW Gabbi's Mex. | **Orange/OC** — 26

Gemmell's | **Dana Pt/OC** — 23

Green Parrot | **Santa Ana/OC** — 24

Infusion | **Ladera Ranch/OC** — 23

Iva Lee's | **San Clemente/OC** — 23

Jade | **SB** — 23

Jonathan's/Peirano | **Ventura/SB** — 22

L'Hirondelle | **San Juan Cap/OC** — 22

Lord Fletcher's | **Rancho Mirage/PS** — 23

Lucca Cafe | **Irvine/OC** — 23

Mascarpone's | **Orange/OC** — 24

Miró | **SB** — 26

Onotria | **Costa Mesa/OC** — 24

Park Ave. | **Stanton/OC** — 25

Piranha | **SB** 24
Rendezvous | **San Juan Cap/OC** 24
Rist. Tuscany | **Palm Desert/PS** 23
Riviera at Fireside |
**Westminster/OC** 24
Rodney's Steak | **SB** 25
Royal Khyber | **Santa Ana/OC** 24
Shabu Shabu |
**Mission Viejo/OC** 25
Sidecar Rest. | **Ventura/SB** 22
Square One | **SB** 22
S Vietnamese |
**Westminster/OC** 24
Tangata | **Santa Ana/OC** 23
Vine | **San Clemente/OC** 25
Westside Cellar | **Ventura/SB** 22
Wild Artichoke |
**Yorba Linda/OC** 24
Zipangu | **Costa Mesa/OC** 23

## SPECIAL OCCASIONS

Ambrosia | **Santa Ana/OC** 24
Anaheim White Hse. |
**Anaheim/OC** 24
🛮 Antonello | **Santa Ana/OC** 24
Arnold Palmer's | **La Quinta/PS** ⌐
Auberge at Ojai | **Ojai/SB** 21
Bayside | **Newport Bch/OC** 25
Bistango | **Irvine/OC** 24
Blend | **La Quinta/PS** ⌐
Blue Coral | **Newport Bch/OC** 22
NEW Brooks | **Ventura/SB** ⌐
Bungalow | **Corona del Mar/OC** 21
Californian |
**Huntington Bch/OC** 23
Cellar | **Fullerton/OC** 23
NEW C-Street | **Ventura/SB** ⌐
🛮 Cuistot | **Palm Desert/PS** 26
Dizz's As Is | **Laguna Bch/OC** 23
🛮 Downey's | **SB** 28
Elements | **SB** 22
Five Crowns |
**Corona del Mar/OC** 24
Fleming Prime |
**Newport Bch/OC** 25
French 75 | **Laguna Bch/OC** 21
🛮 Hobbit, The | **Orange/OC** 27
🛮 Johannes | **PS** 25
NEW La Fondue |
**San Juan Cap/OC** 21
🛮 La Vie en Rose | **Brea/OC** 25

NEW 🛮 Leatherby's |
**Costa Mesa/OC** 25
Le St. Germain |
**Indian Wells/PS** 24
🛮 Le Vallauris | **PS** 27
NEW Marché Moderne |
**Costa Mesa/OC** ⌐
🛮 Mastro's Ocean |
**Newport Bch/OC** 22
🛮 Mastro's Steak |
**Costa Mesa/OC** 25
Melting Pot | **Irvine/OC** 19
Miró | **SB** 26
Morton's Steak | **multi. loc.** 25
🛮 Napa Rose | **Anaheim/OC** 27
Nieuport 17 | **Tustin/OC** 22
🛮 162' | **Dana Pt/OC** 24
Pinot Provence |
**Costa Mesa/OC** 25
🛮 Ranch House | **Ojai/SB** 25
Rendezvous | **San Juan Cap/OC** 24
Riviera at Fireside |
**Westminster/OC** 24
🛮 Roy's | **multi. loc.** 24
NEW Sapphire Laguna |
**Laguna Bch/OC** 26
71 Palm | **Ventura/SB** 20
🛮 Splashes | **Laguna Bch/OC** 21
Square One | **SB** 22
🛮 Stonehill Tav. | **Dana Pt/OC** 28
🛮 Studio | **Laguna Bch/OC** 27
31 West | **SB** 18
Ti Amo | **S Laguna Bch/OC** 22
🛮 Tradition/Pascal |
**Newport Bch/OC** 27
21 Oceanfront |
**Newport Bch/OC** 22
🛮 Wally's Desert |
**Rancho Mirage/PS** 25
Zip Fusion | **Corona/PS** 18

## TASTING MENUS

Abe | **Newport Bch/OC** 25
🛮 Ballard Inn | **Ballard/SB** 26
🛮 Basilic | **Newport Bch/OC** 28
Blend | **La Quinta/PS** ⌐
Bluefin | **Newport Coast/OC** 25
🛮 Bouchon | **SB** 26
NEW Brooks | **Ventura/SB** ⌐
Epiphany | **SB** 17
Five Feet | **Laguna Bch/OC** 24

| | |
|---|---|
| Green Parrot | **Santa Ana/OC** | 24 |
| **NEW ☑** Leatherby's | **Costa Mesa/OC** | 25 |
| Miró | **SB** | 26 |
| ☑ Napa Rose | **Anaheim/OC** | 27 |
| **NEW** Old Vine Café | **Costa Mesa/OC** | – |
| Rist. Tuscany | **Palm Desert/PS** | 23 |
| Sage & Onion | **SB** | 26 |
| Square One | **SB** | 22 |
| ☑ Stella Mare's | **SB** | 22 |
| ☑ Stonehill Tav. | **Dana Pt/OC** | 28 |
| ☑ Studio | **Laguna Bch/OC** | 27 |

## TRENDY

| | |
|---|---|
| Aire | **Costa Mesa/OC** | 23 |
| Alcazar | **SB** | 19 |
| Beachcomber | **Newport Coast/OC** | 17 |
| Bistango | **Irvine/OC** | 24 |
| Blue Coral | **Newport Bch/OC** | 22 |
| Bluefin | **Newport Coast/OC** | 25 |
| **NEW** Brooks | **Ventura/SB** | – |
| Café R&D | **Newport Bch/OC** | 21 |
| **NEW** Eno | **Laguna Niguel/OC** | – |
| Epiphany | **SB** | 17 |
| Fleming Prime | **Newport Bch/OC** | 25 |
| Fox Sports | **Irvine/OC** | 14 |
| Gulfstream | **Newport Bch/OC** | 21 |
| Hungry Cat | **SB** | 24 |
| hush | **Laguna Bch/OC** | 21 |
| **NEW** Izakaya Zero | **Huntington Bch/OC** | – |
| Kantina | **Newport Bch/OC** | 18 |
| **NEW** Kimera | **Irvine/OC** | – |
| La Cave | **Costa Mesa/OC** | 21 |
| **NEW** La Fondue | **San Juan Cap/OC** | 21 |
| **NEW** Marché Moderne | **Costa Mesa/OC** | – |
| ☑ Mastro's Ocean | **Newport Bch/OC** | 22 |
| ☑ Mastro's Steak | **Costa Mesa/OC** | 25 |
| **NEW** Mesa Rest. | **Costa Mesa/OC** | – |
| Mozambique | **Laguna Bch/OC** | 19 |
| **NEW** Sapphire Laguna | **Laguna Bch/OC** | 26 |
| Shame on Moon | **Rancho Mirage/PS** | – |

| | |
|---|---|
| ☑ Stonehill Tav. | **Dana Pt/OC** | 28 |
| Sutra Lounge | **Costa Mesa/OC** | – |
| Taléo Mexican | **Irvine/OC** | 23 |
| Ten | **Newport Bch/OC** | 22 |
| 3Thirty3 | **Newport Bch/OC** | 18 |
| **NEW** Veggie Grill | **Irvine/OC** | 20 |
| **NEW** Wicked Gdn. | **Dana Pt/OC** | – |
| Zipangu | **Costa Mesa/OC** | 23 |

## VIEWS

| | |
|---|---|
| Arnold Palmer's | **La Quinta/PS** | – |
| Auberge at Ojai | **Ojai/SB** | 21 |
| Austen's/Pierpont | **Ventura/SB** | 19 |
| AZUR | **La Quinta/PS** | 22 |
| ☑ Ballard Inn | **Ballard/SB** | 26 |
| **NEW** Bella Vista | **Montecito/SB** | 26 |
| Bellini | **Palm Desert/PS** | 21 |
| ☑ Bouchon | **SB** | 26 |
| Brown Pelican | **SB** | 16 |
| Ca' Dario | **SB** | 25 |
| Cafe Buenos Aires | **SB** | 16 |
| Cafe del Sol | **Montecito/SB** | 18 |
| Café/Beaux-Arts | **Palm Desert/PS** | 18 |
| Californian | **Huntington Bch/OC** | 23 |
| Cannery Seafood | **Newport Bch/OC** | 22 |
| Carlitos Cafe | **SB** | 19 |
| Cava | **Montecito/SB** | 21 |
| Chart House | **multi. loc.** | 19 |
| Chimayo/Beach | **Huntington Bch/OC** | 18 |
| China Pavilion | **SB** | 23 |
| Claes | **Laguna Bch/OC** | 23 |
| ☑ Cuistot | **Palm Desert/PS** | 26 |
| Duke's | **Huntington Bch/OC** | 17 |
| Eladio's | **SB** | 19 |
| Elements | **SB** | 22 |
| Emilio's | **SB** | 24 |
| Falls Prime Steak | **PS** | 22 |
| ☑ First Cabin | **Newport Bch/OC** | 25 |
| **NEW** Fresco/Beach | **SB** | 20 |
| ☑ Johannes | **PS** | 25 |
| Jonathan's/Peirano | **Ventura/SB** | 22 |
| Kantina | **Newport Bch/OC** | 18 |

NEW K'ya | Laguna Bch/OC  —

Las Brisas | Laguna Bch/OC  16

☑ Mastro's Ocean |  22
Newport Bch/OC

Miró | SB  26

Motif | Monarch Bch/OC  23

☑ 162' | Dana Pt/OC  24

Peppino's | Mission Viejo/OC  18

☑ Ranch House | Ojai/SB  25

Rist. Mamma Gina | Palm  21
Desert/PS

Rist. Tuscany | Palm Desert/PS  23

Ruby's | multi. loc.  16

Rusty Pelican |  19
Newport Bch/OC

Shades | Huntington Bch/OC  —

☑ Sirocco | Indian Wells/PS  25

☑ Splashes | Laguna Bch/OC  21

☑ Stella Mare's | SB  22

NEW Stella's | Monarch Bch/OC  19

☑ Studio | Laguna Bch/OC  27

☑ Summit Hse. | Fullerton/OC  25

Tortilla Flats | Mission Viejo/OC  16

21 Oceanfront |  22
Newport Bch/OC

Villa Nova | Newport Bch/OC  19

Vue | Dana Pt/OC  —

## VISITORS ON EXPENSE ACCOUNT

Ambrosia | Santa Ana/OC  24

Anaheim White Hse. |  24
Anaheim/OC

☑ Antonello | Santa Ana/OC  24

Arnold Palmer's | La Quinta/PS  —

Auberge at Ojai | Ojai/SB  21

Bayside | Newport Bch/OC  25

Bistango | Irvine/OC  24

Blue Coral | Newport Bch/OC  22

Bluefin | Newport Coast/OC  25

NEW Brooks | Ventura/SB  —

Cellar | Fullerton/OC  23

NEW C-Street | Ventura/SB  —

☑ Cuistot | Palm Desert/PS  26

☑ Downey's | SB  28

NEW Eno | Laguna Niguel/OC  —

Five Crowns |  24
Corona del Mar/OC

Five Feet | Laguna Bch/OC  24

Fleming Prime |  25
Newport Bch/OC

☑ Hobbit, The | Orange/OC  27

☑ Johannes | PS  25

NEW La Fondue |  21
San Juan Cap/OC

☑ La Vie en Rose | Brea/OC  25

NEW ☑ Leatherby's |  25
Costa Mesa/OC

Le St. Germain |  24
Indian Wells/PS

☑ Le Vallauris | PS  27

NEW Marché Moderne |  —
Costa Mesa/OC

☑ Mastro's Ocean |  22
Newport Bch/OC

☑ Mastro's Steak |  25
Costa Mesa/OC

Miró | SB  26

Morton's Steak | multi. loc.  25

Motif | Monarch Bch/OC  23

☑ Mr. Stox | Anaheim/OC  24

☑ Napa Rose | Anaheim/OC  27

☑ 162' | Dana Pt/OC  24

Onotria | Costa Mesa/OC  24

Pinot Provence |  25
Costa Mesa/OC

☑ Ranch House | Ojai/SB  25

Rendezvous | San Juan Cap/OC  24

☑ Ritz Rest./Gdn. |  24
Newport Bch/OC

Riviera at Fireside |  24
Westminster/OC

☑ Roy's | multi. loc.  24

☑ Ruth's Chris | Irvine/OC  25

NEW Sapphire Laguna |  26
Laguna Bch/OC

☑ Splashes | Laguna Bch/OC  21

Square One | SB  22

☑ Stonehill Tav. | Dana Pt/OC  28

☑ Studio | Laguna Bch/OC  27

☑ Summit Hse. | Fullerton/OC  25

31 West | SB  18

☑ Tradition/Pascal |  27
Newport Bch/OC

Turner New Zealand |  24
Costa Mesa/OC

21 Oceanfront |  22
Newport Bch/OC

☑ Wally's Desert |  25
Rancho Mirage/PS

Zov's | Tustin/OC  25

OC/PS/SB

SPECIAL FEATURES

## WATERSIDE

| | |
|---|---|
| Beachcomber \| **Newport Coast/OC** | 17 |
| NEW Bella Vista \| **Montecito/SB** | 26 |
| Bluewater Grill \| **Newport Bch/OC** | 20 |
| Brown Pelican \| **SB** | 16 |
| Cannery Seafood \| **Newport Bch/OC** | 22 |
| Cava \| **Montecito/SB** | 21 |
| Chart House \| **Newport Bch/OC** | 19 |
| ☑ Cheesecake Fact. \| **Rancho Mirage/PS** | 20 |
| Chimayo/Beach \| **Huntington Bch/OC** | 18 |
| Claes \| **Laguna Bch/OC** | 23 |
| Coyote Grill \| **Laguna Bch/OC** | 19 |
| Duke's \| **Huntington Bch/OC** | 17 |
| Eladio's \| **SB** | 19 |
| Emilio's \| **SB** | 24 |
| ☑ First Cabin \| **Newport Bch/OC** | 25 |
| Joe's Crab \| **Newport Bch/OC** | 13 |
| Kantina \| **Newport Bch/OC** | 18 |
| NEW K'ya \| **Laguna Bch/OC** | – |
| Las Brisas \| **Laguna Bch/OC** | 16 |
| Miró \| **SB** | 26 |
| Rist. Mamma Gina \| **Newport Bch/OC** | 21 |
| Ruby's \| **multi. loc.** | 16 |
| Rusty Pelican \| **Newport Bch/OC** | 19 |
| Shades \| **Huntington Bch/OC** | – |
| ☑ Splashes \| **Laguna Bch/OC** | 21 |
| ☑ Stella Mare's \| **SB** | 22 |
| ☑ Studio \| **Laguna Bch/OC** | 27 |
| 3Thirty3 \| **Newport Bch/OC** | 18 |
| Tortilla Flats \| **Mission Viejo/OC** | 16 |
| 21 Oceanfront \| **Newport Bch/OC** | 22 |
| Villa Nova \| **Newport Bch/OC** | 19 |
| Vue \| **Dana Pt/OC** | – |

## WINE BARS

| | |
|---|---|
| Ca' Dario \| **SB** | 25 |
| Citrus \| **Riverside/PS** | 20 |
| NEW Eno \| **Laguna Niguel/OC** | – |
| Fleming Prime \| **Newport Bch/OC** | 25 |
| Hungry Cat \| **SB** | 24 |
| Intermezzo \| **SB** | 21 |
| Jonathan's/Peirano \| **Ventura/SB** | 22 |
| Los Olivos Cafe \| **Los Olivos/SB** | – |
| Rosine's \| **Anaheim/OC** | 24 |
| ☑ 6ix Park Grill \| **Irvine/OC** | 21 |
| Tannins \| **San Juan Cap/OC** | 18 |
| Westside Cellar \| **Ventura/SB** | 22 |

## WINNING WINE LISTS

| | |
|---|---|
| Alcazar \| **SB** | 19 |
| Anaheim White Hse. \| **Anaheim/OC** | 24 |
| ☑ Antonello \| **Santa Ana/OC** | 24 |
| Auberge at Ojai \| **Ojai/SB** | 21 |
| Bayside \| **Newport Bch/OC** | 25 |
| Bistango \| **Irvine/OC** | 24 |
| Black Sheep \| **Tustin/OC** | 24 |
| Blend \| **La Quinta/PS** | – |
| Blue Coral \| **Newport Bch/OC** | 22 |
| NEW Brooks \| **Ventura/SB** | – |
| Cellar \| **Fullerton/OC** | 23 |
| Claes \| **Laguna Bch/OC** | 23 |
| Cold Spring \| **SB** | 19 |
| NEW C-Street \| **Ventura/SB** | – |
| ☑ Cuistot \| **Palm Desert/PS** | 26 |
| Elements \| **SB** | 22 |
| NEW Eno \| **Laguna Niguel/OC** | – |
| Five Crowns \| **Corona del Mar/OC** | 24 |
| Fleming Prime \| **Newport Bch/OC** | 25 |
| ☑ Golden Truffle \| **Costa Mesa/OC** | 26 |
| ☑ Hobbit, The \| **Orange/OC** | 27 |
| Intermezzo \| **SB** | 21 |
| Le St. Germain \| **Indian Wells/PS** | 24 |
| ☑ Le Vallauris \| **PS** | 27 |
| Lucca Cafe \| **Irvine/OC** | 23 |
| NEW Marché Moderne \| **Costa Mesa/OC** | – |
| ☑ Mastro's Steak \| **Costa Mesa/OC** | 25 |
| Miró \| **SB** | 26 |
| ☑ Mr. Stox \| **Anaheim/OC** | 24 |
| ☑ Napa Rose \| **Anaheim/OC** | 27 |
| NEW Old Vine Café \| **Costa Mesa/OC** | – |
| Onotria \| **Costa Mesa/OC** | 24 |

OC/PS/SB

SPECIAL FEATURES

# Wine Vintage Chart

This chart, based on our 0 to 30 scale, is designed to help you select wine. The ratings (by **Howard Stravitz**, a law professor at the University of South Carolina) reflect the vintage quality and the wine's readiness to drink. We exclude the 1987, 1991–1993 vintages because they are not that good. A dash indicates the wine is either past its peak or too young to rate.

| Whites | 86 | 88 | 89 | 90 | 94 | 95 | 96 | 97 | 98 | 99 | 00 | 01 | 02 | 03 | 04 | 05 |
|---|---|---|---|---|---|---|---|---|---|---|---|---|---|---|---|---|
| **French:** | | | | | | | | | | | | | | | | |
| Alsace | - | - | 26 | 26 | 25 | 24 | 24 | 23 | 26 | 24 | 26 | 27 | 25 | 22 | 24 | 25 |
| Burgundy | 25 | - | 23 | 22 | - | 28 | 27 | 24 | 23 | 26 | 25 | 24 | 27 | 23 | 25 | 26 |
| Loire Valley | - | - | - | - | - | - | - | - | - | 24 | 25 | 26 | 23 | 24 | 25 | |
| Champagne | 25 | 24 | 26 | 29 | - | 26 | 27 | 24 | 23 | 24 | 24 | 22 | 26 | - | - | - |
| Sauternes | 28 | 29 | 25 | 28 | - | 21 | 23 | 25 | 23 | 24 | 24 | 28 | 25 | 26 | 21 | 26 |
| **California:** | | | | | | | | | | | | | | | | |
| Chardonnay | - | - | - | - | - | - | - | - | 24 | 23 | 26 | 26 | 27 | 28 | 28 | 2 |
| Sauvignon Blanc | - | - | - | - | - | - | - | - | - | - | 27 | 28 | 26 | 27 | 2 | |
| **Austrian:** | | | | | | | | | | | | | | | | |
| Grüner Velt./ Riesling | - | - | - | - | - | 25 | 21 | 28 | 28 | 27 | 22 | 23 | 24 | 26 | 26 | 2 |
| **German:** | - | 25 | 26 | 27 | 24 | 23 | 26 | 25 | 26 | 23 | 21 | 29 | 27 | 25 | 26 | 26 |

| Reds | 86 | 88 | 89 | 90 | 94 | 95 | 96 | 97 | 98 | 99 | 00 | 01 | 02 | 03 | 04 | 05 |
|---|---|---|---|---|---|---|---|---|---|---|---|---|---|---|---|---|
| **French:** | | | | | | | | | | | | | | | | |
| Bordeaux | 25 | 23 | 25 | 29 | 22 | 26 | 25 | 23 | 25 | 24 | 29 | 26 | 24 | 25 | 23 | 2 |
| Burgundy | - | - | 24 | 26 | - | 26 | 27 | 26 | 22 | 27 | 22 | 24 | 27 | 24 | 24 | 25 |
| Rhône | - | 26 | 28 | 28 | 24 | 26 | 22 | 24 | 27 | 26 | 27 | 26 | - | 25 | 24 | - |
| Beaujolais | - | - | - | - | - | - | - | - | - | - | 24 | - | 23 | 27 | 23 | 28 |
| **California:** | | | | | | | | | | | | | | | | |
| Cab./Merlot | - | - | - | 28 | 29 | 27 | 25 | 28 | 23 | 26 | 22 | 27 | 26 | 25 | 24 | 2 |
| Pinot Noir | - | - | - | - | - | - | - | 24 | 23 | 24 | 23 | 27 | 28 | 26 | 23 | - |
| Zinfandel | - | - | - | - | - | - | - | - | - | - | 25 | 23 | 27 | 22 | - | |
| **Oregon:** | | | | | | | | | | | | | | | | |
| Pinot Noir | - | - | - | - | - | - | - | - | - | - | 26 | 27 | 24 | 25 | - | |
| **Italian:** | | | | | | | | | | | | | | | | |
| Tuscany | - | - | - | 25 | 22 | 24 | 20 | 29 | 24 | 27 | 24 | 26 | 20 | - | - | - |
| Piedmont | - | - | - | 27 | 27 | - | 23 | 26 | 27 | 26 | 25 | 28 | 27 | 20 | - | - |
| **Spanish:** | | | | | | | | | | | | | | | | |
| Rioja | - | - | - | - | 26 | 26 | 24 | 25 | 22 | 25 | 24 | 27 | 20 | 24 | 25 | - |
| Ribera del Duero/Priorat | - | - | - | - | 26 | 26 | 27 | 25 | 24 | 25 | 24 | 27 | 20 | 24 | 26 | - |
| **Australian:** | | | | | | | | | | | | | | | | |
| Shiraz/Cab. | - | - | - | - | 24 | 26 | 23 | 26 | 28 | 24 | 24 | 27 | 27 | 25 | 26 | - |

# Zagat Products

## RESTAURANTS & MAPS

America's Top Restaurants
Atlanta
Boston
Brooklyn
California Wine Country
Cape Cod & The Islands
Chicago (guide & map)
Connecticut
Downtown NYC
Europe's Top Restaurants
Hamptons (incl. wineries)
Las Vegas (incl. nightlife)
London
Long Island (incl. wineries)
Los Angeles I So. California
(guide & map)
Miami Beach
Miami I So. Florida
Montréal (best of)
New Jersey
New Jersey Shore
New Orleans (best of)
New York City (guide & map)
Palm Beach
Paris
Philadelphia
San Francisco (guide & map)
Seattle
St. Louis
Texas
Tokyo
Toronto (best of)
Vancouver (best of)
Washington, DC I Baltimore
Westchester I Hudson Valley

## LIFESTYLE GUIDES

America's Top Golf Courses
Movie Guide
Music Guide
NYC Marketplace
NYC Shopping

## NIGHTLIFE GUIDES

Las Vegas (incl. restaurants)
London
Los Angeles
New Orleans (best of)
New York City
San Francisco

## HOTEL & TRAVEL GUIDES

Top U.S. Hotels, Resorts & Spas
U.S. Family Travel
Walt Disney World Insider's Guide
World's Top Hotels, Resorts & Spa

## WEB & WIRELESS SERVICES

ZAGAT TO GO℠ for handhelds
Subscribe to ZAGAT.com

**Available wherever books are sold or at ZAGAT.com. To customize Zagat guides as gifts or marketing tools, call 800-540-9609.**

ISBN-13: 978-1-57006-908-6
ISBN-10: 1-57006-908-5